MW01000779

# Handbook of
# COUNSELOR
# PREPARATION

# Handbook of
# COUNSELOR
# PREPARATION

## Constructivist, Developmental, and Experiential Approaches

Edited by

## Garrett McAuliffe
*Old Dominion University*

## Karen Eriksen
*Eriksen Institute for Ethics*

**A·C·E·S**

ASSOCIATION FOR COUNSELOR
EDUCATION AND SUPERVISION

**Published in cooperation with the *Association for Counselor Education and Supervision (ACES)***

Los Angeles | London | New Delhi
Singapore | Washington DC

Copyright © 2011 by the Association for Counselor Education and Supervision

All rights reserved. No part of this book may be reproduced or utilized in any form or by any means, electronic or mechanical, including photocopying, recording, or by any information storage and retrieval system, without permission in writing from the publisher.

*For information:*

SAGE Publications, Inc.
2455 Teller Road
Thousand Oaks, California 91320
E-mail: order@sagepub.com

SAGE Publications Ltd.
1 Oliver's Yard
55 City Road
London EC1Y 1SP
United Kingdom

SAGE Publications India Pvt. Ltd.
B 1/I 1 Mohan Cooperative Industrial Area
Mathura Road, New Delhi 110 044
India

SAGE Publications Asia-Pacific Pte. Ltd.
33 Pekin Street #02-01
Far East Square
Singapore 048763

Printed in the United States of America

*Library of Congress Cataloging-in-Publication Data*

Handbook of counselor preparation: constructivist, developmental, and experiental approaches / [compiled by] Garrett McAuliffe, Karen Eriksen.
    p. cm.
Includes bibliographical references and index.
ISBN 978-1-4129-9177-3 (cloth)
    1. Counselors—Training of. 2. Counseling—Study and teaching. 3. Constructivism (Psychology) I. McAuliffe, Garrett. II. Eriksen, Karen.

BF636.65.H36 2011
158′30711—dc22          2010029316

This book is printed on acid-free paper.

10  11  12  13  14   10  9  8  7  6  5  4  3  2  1

| | |
|---|---|
| *Acquisitions Editor:* | Kassie Graves |
| *Editorial Assistant:* | Veronica K. Novak |
| *Managing Editor:* | Claudia A. Hoffman |
| *Production Editor:* | Libby Larson |
| *Permissions Editor:* | Adele Hutchinson |
| *Copy Editor:* | Sarah J. Duffy |
| *Typesetter:* | C&M Digitals (P) Ltd. |
| *Proofreader:* | Sally Jaskold |
| *Indexer:* | Kathy Paparchontis |
| *Cover Designer:* | Candice Harman |
| *Marketing Manager:* | Stephanie Adams |

# Contents

# Preface

Garrett J. McAuliffe

*True teachers defend their pupils against the teacher's own influence. Such teachers inspire self-trust. They guide their pupils' eyes from the teacher himself or herself to their own spirit that quickens them. The true teacher will have no disciple.*

Adapted from Bronson Alcott (1840)

*Through dialogue, the teacher-of-the-students and the students-of-the-teacher cease to exist and a new term emerges: teacher-student with students-teachers.*

Paolo Freire (1994, p. 80)

This is a book for those who would prepare counselors for their work. It is aimed at both graduate students who are training to be counselor educators and those who are already preparers of counselors. This book was inspired by three earlier volumes that we edited. Now, with new writing and up-to-date research, we present a text that brings together most of what can be done to educate future counselors in powerful ways.

The authors of this book believe that this work is sorely needed, as students mostly know us through our teaching. That is where future counselors are made. What can be more important? However, despite their position in "higher" education, of all educators, college instructors are the least prepared to teach. Preparers of counselors are no exception. Yet their light preparation in how to educate stands in ironic contrast with their weighty responsibility to protect future clients by producing ethical and intelligent counselors.

The litany of professors' lack of formal teaching training is well known: They study no methods; they are never, or rarely, observed; and their knowledge of educational psychology is minimal or nonexistent. And yet, each year thousands of professors in the counseling field enter classrooms to propound, pronounce, plead, cajole, demonstrate, evoke, stimulate, and generally act in ways that supposedly produce intellectually and emotionally sophisticated counselors and therapists.

Despite this short shrift given to teacher training, many counselor educators nevertheless struggle mightily to teach in energetic and innovative ways, hoping for felicitous results. Some go so far as to stretch inherited pedagogical boundaries, challenging the cult of expertise that has made professors into high knowledge priests and students into lay supplicants in so much of college teaching. These pedagogical boundary-stretchers attempt to create egalitarian atmospheres, participatory activities, opportunities for reflection, and experiential exercises in order to trigger development in future counselors. It is those efforts that we wish to extend in this volume.

We should note at this point that much has already been crafted well in counselor education. The curriculum is under constant revision, with more comprehensive and relevant content being added. In some courses, a high art for training has been developed. For example, instruction in basic helping skills has been sequential, layered, and experiential. Similarly, training in group counseling is, at its best, intensely experiential and self-reflective.

Despite these successes, the expert talking head seems still to be alive and well, as a walk down a college corridor will testify. For whatever reasons, the expert who delivers "finished" knowledge to the audience of students continues to dominate college teaching. Whether behind or in front of the lectern, or sitting on the desk, professors make pronouncements such as "Here is an especially effective counseling approach," or "Listen to my insightful diagnosis," or "Here's how to run a community agency." Perhaps it is easier for teachers to tell than to evoke. Lecturing and pronouncing feels safer to the instructor than does case analysis, demonstration, or discussion. At its worst, this banking deposit model of teaching, to use Freire's (1994) metaphor for instructor-centered teaching, communicates to students that knowledge is the domain of the few, who pass it on to the many. And such teaching replicates itself by communicating to future counselors that clients also can change through passive reception.

This teacher-as-expert and student-as-receiver model has been increasingly challenged as ineffective, particularly in this field, which aims to produce self-authorizing professionals. Some educators, such as bell hooks (1994) and Henry Giroux (2006), have opened up the conversation about who learns from whom and how power and privilege are used, toward what ends, in the classroom. They invite teachers to "not know," to deconstruct cherished notions of how knowledge is created, and to encourage tolerance for ambiguity and self-disclosure in the classroom. Such notions are enough to make most college teachers tremble.

I believe that, among the academic disciplines, counselor education is well poised for this type of conversation. Counselor training has always been touched by an experiential, participatory teaching brush. Counselor educators have traditionally incorporated both head and heart into the learning environment. Equality, genuineness, and respect have been watchwords for the profession. Awareness of people as socially constructed cultural beings is slowly infusing our curricula. This book attempts to build on these practices and to transform others so that an impactful, progressive mental health education can be implemented.

Thus we join the national conversation about the purposes and methods of higher education. In so doing, we hope, perhaps with hubris, to trigger a broad self-examination by current and future counselor educators—a dialogue on the nature of knowing, the political implications of teaching, and the content of mental health training.

In addition to being a response to the swirling discussions about higher education, this book is also a product of its authors' personal struggles to teach well. All of the contributors have experienced the palpable tension of entering a classroom filled with expectant and diverse adults. In that setting our consciences prick us—we all know well the time, money, and, yes, the spirit that most students pour into their educations. We ask ourselves, "Are we up to the task of meeting our students' hopes and expectations, aspirations that are so well voiced at orientations and in beginning classes?"

A final incentive for producing this book is the very pragmatic concern that the authors share about accountability for teaching, which is being increasingly demanded of college faculty. Student evaluations and peer reviews of instruction are becoming more important for the maintenance and progress of educators' careers; the citizenry views their primary job to be teaching. Teaching is the major arena in which educators meet the public, no matter how much writing, research, and professional presentations are part of the broad educational charge.

We ask you, the reader of this volume, to embrace the challenge of reflexively examining, or deconstructing, your common assumptions and methods in all areas of counselor education. Ask yourself, "What are the intended and unintended educational outcomes of students' experiences in the classroom, the library, the lab, and the advising office?" In that learner-centered, or constructivist vein, we eschew the notion that teachers can ever "provide" knowledge to another or "instill" understanding. Certainly the works of Piaget (1971), Dewey (1963), Freire (1994), and many other so-called progressive educators offer a severe challenge to the common banking deposit model of teaching. Instead, teaching can be considered to be the setting up of conditions for the learner to know, through a cycling and recycling of experience, reflection, and abstract conceptualization.

Our biases are these: We favor the constructivist and developmental educational theories. These theories ask us to pay attention to the learner's experience and to let the learner make sense for herself by struggling with ambiguities that are just beyond the level she can tolerate. We also favor the notion of the social construction of knowledge, as we might practice it through classroom discourse. We think that a fine metaphor for teaching is Robert Kegan's (1998) notion of over-the-shoulder inquiry, in which students puzzle together over problems that emerge during the many discourses of their education, discourses that are often instigated by the educator. We also favor an inclusive, dialogical program practice, from admissions through portfolio evaluation, in which we as faculty are learners-among-learners.

We offer this socially constructed project with humility, recognizing the boundedness of our vision by the historical, political, and cultural contexts of our times. It is up to the reader to try out these ideas, to expand them, and possibly to reject them in favor of more effective, complex ones.

Whom, specifically, is this book for? We expect it to be useful to all those who do, or will, prepare counselors. We hope that it might be a text in counselor education courses and a companion for practicing counselor educators.

This book is freshly written. Authors have been recruited, vetted, and edited to produce deep and accessible work. The book is divided into three segments, as follows.

Part I opens the discussion of constructivist and developmental teaching with principles and research, presenting the constructivist and developmental foundations of this work in Chapter 1, the pedagogies of three of the classic thinkers in the field in Chapter 2, explicit guidelines for teaching practice in Chapter 3, an overview of the phases of counselor development in Chapter 4, and a primer on six common teaching strategies in Chapter 5.

Part II meets the teacher's need for the practical with carefully crafted guides for teaching 17 content areas, or courses, in the counselor education curriculum.

Part III consists of innovative ideas for counselor education in general, from evaluating the outcomes of counselor education in Chapter 23, to a guide to the expansion of technology in the field in Chapter 24, to the bold proposal for narrative-based counselor education in Chapter 25.

This effort to trigger an examination of how we know and how we teach in the helping professions offers some ideas that are surprising and "border-crossing," to use Henry Giroux's (2006) phrase for a postmodern education. But these ideas also build on much that counselor educators already do well. We all stand on the shoulders of the giants who have taught us. But this book takes us a step beyond. It asks educators to empower and involve. It asks them to risk "losing control" over subject matter, to hear student voices, to pose dilemmas, to challenge their own assumptions in the presence of their students. In that regard, many counselor educators are already among the minority of educators who attempt to be "midwife" teachers, to use Belenky, Clinchy, Goldberger, and Tarule's (1986) vivid metaphor; that is, teachers who assist students in giving birth to their own ideas. We believe that this midwife role is one that the practicing counselor can also apply to himself, that of coaching clients to bring forth more adaptive stories in their lives and relationships.

No preface that purports to promote a constructivist frame for teaching should paradoxically end on so certain a note. Doubt and humility are central themes in constructivist thinking. Thus, these words are offered in the spirit of dialogue. We hope the conversation continues through your writing to us and your joining (or starting) the next teaching discussion at your local or national conference. We hope that this is but one foray in an evolving, ongoing engagement of the construction of the counselor in a postmodern environment. Let this volume be a warning, nevertheless, that we, as educators and as therapists, must live within the ambiguity of emergent understanding, of partial truths that must be rolled around on the tongues of dialogue. And let us be consistently reflective in our practices and on our most cherished notions.

We hope that more than a few ideas from this book will encourage risk taking and trigger experiments in teaching. Good. That is what we set out to do. Let us now begin.

## REFERENCES

Belenky, M. F., Clinchy, B. M., Goldberger, N. R., & Tarule, J. M. (1986). *Women's ways of knowing*. New York: Basic Books.

Dewey, J. (1963). *Experience and education*. New York: Collier. (Original work published 1938)

Freire, P. (1994). *Pedagogy of the oppressed*. New York: Continuum.

Giroux, H. A. (2006). *America on the edge: Henry Giroux on politics, culture, and education*. New York: Palgrave Macmillan.

hooks, b. (1994). *Teaching to transgress*. New York: Routledge.

Kegan, R. (1998). *In over our heads*. Cambridge, MA: Harvard.

Piaget, J. (1971). *Psychology and epistemology*. Harmondsworth, England: Penguin.

# Acknowledgments

The authors and SAGE thank the following reviewers for their helpful comments on earlier drafts of this manuscript.

Don Bubenzer, Kent State University

Catherine Y. Chang, Georgia State University

Stephen E. Craig, Western Michigan University

Gerard Lawson, Virginia Tech

Larry C. Loesch, University of Florida

Sylvia C. Nassar-McMillan, North Carolina State University

Terrell Awe Agahe Portman, The University of Iowa

John E. Queener, The University of Akron

# PART I

## Foundations: Constructivism, Development, Culture, and Teaching

CHAPTER

1

# Constructing Counselor Education

Garrett J. McAuliffe

*You probably teach very well without recognizing that, often, the more teaching, the less learning. Our job in adult education is not to cover a set of course materials, but to engage adults in effective and significant learning.*

Jane Vella, Adult Educator

With that declaration, Jane Vella (1994) challenges teachers to instigate something called *significant learning*. This certainly sounds like a desirable goal for all counselor educators. But what is significant learning? Is it the achievement of a set of specific counseling competencies? For sure. Is it a set of positive attitudes toward the work of helping? Yes, in the sense that attitude precedes much behavior. But, most of all, significant learning lies in the ability to perform what Schön (1991) defines as professional work—the use of judgment and considered action in ambiguous situations. Professional work is characterized by unclear problems with multiple dimensions. Such work is commonly fraught with ethical and value implications. The counselor often makes decisions in such situations in the moment. Counseling requires the ability to make commitments knowing that there are other choices that might be equally valid. From these conditions, it might be clear that the act of counseling does not lend itself to rote practice (Harris, 1993).

If counselors are to be prepared for the complexity of the work—in the form of multiple societal values, ethnicities, moral centers, gender expectations, and the like—then the designers of counselor education must prepare students (and themselves) to have a corresponding complexity. That complexity might take two forms: (1) a way of knowing that is reflexive and includes a tolerance for ambiguity and (2) the ability to be culturally relativistic.

In the first case, counselors must embrace uncertainty as an expected condition of the work. The counselor must consistently entertain the possibility "I might be wrong." Counselors must remind themselves, when they are tempted to make a glib assessment, or automatically adhere to a favored technique, "I must catch myself trying to be too complete," to use developmental theorist Robert Kegan's (1998) phrase. Counselors must be reflexive and tolerant of ambiguity.

The second requirement is cultural relativism. In order to work with all clients, counselors must be able to

3

de-center from their cultural assumptions. Those emerge from their gender, social class, ethnicity, sexual orientation, and religion. Walt Whitman framed this challenge in *Leaves of Grass:* "Re-examine all you have been told at school or church, or in any books, and dismiss whatever insults your soul." Whitman's words ask individuals to self-authorize (Kegan, 1998) their values. Similarly, philosopher Richard Rorty (1989) challenges individuals to be culturally de-centered, when they are taking a position, to think they might have "been initiated into the wrong tribe" (p. 75) on that value or issue. In this fluid, constructed social world, teachers and learners must regularly question their certainties, examining the limits of their knowing.

In sum, it is the position of this chapter, indeed of this entire book, that such a flexible, reflexive mindset, or way of knowing, is required for the work of professional counseling. The counselor's own mental complexity must match the requirements of the professional work. Of course, specific knowledge and skill competencies are also required for becoming a good group leader, career counselor, crisis intervener, and child advocate, to name a few professional counseling roles. But those skills must be applied provisionally, with situation, culture, and individual in mind. Given the fluidity of any knowledge base (just think about the single-minded adherence to psychoanalysis in the first half of the 20th century and the humanistic contagion of the second half), no professional can rely on a permanent set of understandings and expect to continue to do ethical and competent counseling. She or he must have the capacity of mind to fully engage and critically evaluate a fluid knowledge base, meet multiple professional roles, and recognize perspectives from diverse cultures.

## CONSTRUCTIVISM: AN OVERVIEW

Constructivism is the guiding metaphor for this book. The Latin origin of the word itself (*con* = with; *struere* = to build) refers to the communal act of making something, of putting together. From the constructivist perspective (also called *constructionist*, which will be explained later), humans do not "find" or "discover" knowledge, nor do they receive it from infallible authorities. Knowledge is continually created through conversations. These conversations occur through the sciences, the arts, religion, the media (e.g., blogs, talk shows), professional journals, and classroom discussion, to name some examples.

Constructivism is not a method. It is instead a way of understanding human meaning-making. It invites the individual into a world in which subjectivity is ultimate (but, lest we descend into total relativism, not all positions are equally helpful or defensible, as determined by a community's standards). Constructivism's central premise is that individuals actively create the world as they experience it. Individuals do not learn by copying some outside reality. Nor do they find knowledge as if it were a gem waiting to be uncovered in a mine (Gergen, 2009). They are actively involved in a joint enterprise with others in creating (constructing) new and preferably more helpful meanings. Some constructivist thinkers (which I will here call *developmental constructivists*) also emphasize the pre-understandings, or cognitive capacities, that individuals bring to experience. These two versions of constructivism are discussed next.

## Social Constructionism

Humans are always in a social surround, whether that consists of their internalized conceptions of the good and the beautiful (the social-in-the-individual) or the ongoing public conversations in media, religion, literature, and culture in general (the individual-in-the social), to name some examples. Social constructionism (note that the *tion* in the word is a mere convention from its usage by Berger and Luckmann [1966] in their classic *The Social Construction of Reality*) emphasizes the inevitably social, or communal, context of human meaning-making. All meaning is saturated in culture, history, place, and time. Humans are ineluctably shaped by the social forces of language and interaction. There is no "pure" thought that is not socially mediated.

Obvious examples of the social construction of meaning lie in the words humans use to describe their experience of the world, such as *sinful, gay, moral, mannerly,* and *beautiful.* Each of those words is heavily saturated with meanings that are created in human communities (e.g., ethnic cultures). Other obvious examples of socially constructed meanings are the norms that guide humans' thinking and behaving, such as cultural rules for interpersonal relations (e.g., greetings, politeness, honesty) and those for gender behavior (e.g., nurturing, aggressiveness). Less subtle are the implicit assumptions that guide thinking about what is good, true, and beautiful (e.g., a work ethic, salvation, conceptions of beauty).

Social constructionists propose that there is no pure knowledge, that is, there are no ideas that are outside of time and place, or chronology and geography, in Gergen's (2009) words. The very language that humans use is, of course, socially constructed. For example, the English word *love* cannot be directly translated into many languages. In Japanese, there is *suki,* which generally means *like* (e.g., food, movies), *koi* for passionate love, and *ai* for parental love. These terms are not directly translatable into the English word *love.*

In addition, it is not just the specific meaning of words, but the way in which they are used, that affects the construction of meaning in cultures. In Japanese culture, *koi* and *ai* are not often spoken directly to another—it is not common to say, "I love you" to a person. Humans are always more or less embedded in their language. Individual meaning-making is socially constructed.

Two terms, *discourse* and *deconstruction,* are associated with social construction. They will be discussed next.

## Discourse

The term *discourse* represents any particular socialized meaning system that informs a person's constructions. Therefore one can refer to, for example, a gender (e.g., male) discourse, a religious (e.g., Christian) discourse, a class (e.g., middle-class) discourse, an ethnic (e.g., Anglo American) discourse, a scientific (e.g., positivist) discourse, and a theoretical (e.g., humanistic) discourse.

Any thread of ideas might be called a discourse. In fact, the very concept of social construction is itself a discourse. The discourse of social construction is guided by the notion that humans are always constructing knowledge. Such a view contrasts with the spectator discourse about knowledge. Referring to the spectator view, Ahuja and colleagues (2008) say, "In such a view, the thinker pushes ideas and concepts around in his mental space like pieces of furniture—frozen concepts without a life of their own—making the assumption that the concepts

completely render the world they are meant to model" (Part One, para. 10). This notion is nonconstructivist in that it treats knowledge as found, rather than constructed by a community. By contrast, social constructionist thinking assumes the changeable, fluid nature of knowledge, that is always contingent on place and time, or discourse.

## Deconstruction

Any discourse can be analyzed for its foundations. Deconstruction is the act of examining the origins and implications of an idea, that is, seeking its roots in a particular discourse, such as in the zeitgeist of an era or in a thinker's biography (Gergen, 2009). Deconstruction challenges the idea that there are noncontextual, unquestionable verities or givens that can be known. All ideas can be subjected to deconstruction. There is no room for "that's just the way it is."

## Implications of Social Construction for Education

It follows, from the social constructionist perspective, that there are no realities that can be purely known beyond culture. The filters of such social identities as gender, age, race, religion, ethnicity, ability, class, and sexual orientation are pervasive lenses through which individuals create meanings. Teachers and counselors should be aware of the social constructions that inform their own assumptions, lest they treat their current understanding as "real" and therefore unassailable.

There are at least three dimensions of social constructionist thinking that have implications for counselor education. Burbules and Rice (1991) lay them out thus:

1.  **A rejection of absolutes**. Any declaration of objectively knowable universals results in the restriction of human possibilities. So-called metanarratives, such as grand counseling theories, are viewed as expressions of particular points of view. Therefore, meaning-makers must be humble and reflexive, exquisitely attuned to the limits of their conclusions. They are asked to be consistently aware of their standpoints, whether they be based in culture, situation, temperament, or other characteristics of the time, place, and person. This *standpoint awareness* has implications for teaching: Since knowledge is

something that is developed in community rather than an objectively determined verity, the teacher must be persistently self-reflective, be open to the limits of her or his current positions and methods, and be willing to seek feedback about teaching content and process from fellow learners, including students. Social constructionist educators are aware of the context that affects any perspectives that they may take on phenomena.

2. **The saturation of all social discourse with power or dominance**. Power pervades all human encounters, including the power of hierarchy, physical size, sexual appeal, money, and persuasion. In the classroom, teachers can unthinkingly perpetuate broader patterns of dominance, especially in their use of authority. Teachers can subtly reinforce or challenge existing power relationships through how or whether they encourage students' voices in the classroom, through how they use titles and names, through their openness to being questioned on their own teaching practices, and by being respectful or dismissive in responding to students. With this awareness of power, teachers can give assignments, grade tests, and lead discussions in ways in which the fundamental equality and value of all persons are respected. Counselor educators are thereby challenged to lift the veil of power to make sure that they are not perpetuating inequities. Methods for sharing power will be discussed throughout this book. They include teachers encouraging student feedback on course content and process, sharing their reasons for assignments, and revealing their own doubts.

3. **The celebration of difference.** Social constructionism assumes that the constitutive quality of existence is plurality. In contrast, the objectivist or essentialist stance proclaims that a diversity of ideas is a temporary state on the way to perfect knowing. From the social constructionist framework, any singular, unified discourse is to be treated skeptically, since it is likely that such discourse comes from the framework of the dominant group. For counselor educators, this assumption is a call to attend to the perspectives and experiences of so-called marginalized groups. Participation, it follows, is a correlate of social constructionism. Social constructionist educators therefore actively extend invitations to voices that might otherwise be excluded, in admissions, assignments, and topics for discussion, to name some examples.

Finally, there are at least two implications of the social constructionist impulse: humility and egalitarianism. In the first case, the knower should not take his positions too permanently, or seriously, since they are built on the shifting foundations of culture, era, and selected evidence (Gergen, 2009). Social constructionist counselors are therefore attuned to the discourses from which they speak, whether they be gender, ethnic, social class, or historical contexts, among others. Such counselors recognize the fluidity of all sense-making and the ongoing evolution of ideas. They will consistently ask, "What is another possibility?" and "From what discourse am I speaking?" That is a form of humility about truth claims.

In addition, social constructionism carries with it an inherent egalitarian impulse. Since knowledge is socially constructed, it is the province of all. There are no unassailable authorities. All are engaged in particular discourses, some of which are often valued more than others. Of course, this notion does not rule out expertise; it allows for deconstruction of such expertise and helps individuals avoid offering unthinking allegiance to experts.

The social constructionist curriculum thus sets a demanding agenda for the traditional teacher in all counselor educators. Social constructionism challenges that part of the educator that either believes in the sanctity of her own authority or believes that she has perfected the best methods for knowing and subsequently for counseling. It asks educators instead to embrace Paolo Freire's (1994) concept of learner as teacher and teacher as learner.

# CONSTRUCTIVE DEVELOPMENT

A second version of constructivism that is emphasized in this book is developmental. From this perspective, overall approaches to knowing can evolve from more rigid, authoritarian ways of knowing to more flexible, open, and reflective ones. Constructivist-developmental theory therefore has a hopeful premise. The constructivist-developmental formulation allows counselor educators to assess students' ways of knowing and to aim their teaching at increasing learners' relativism and self-authorship of ideas.

The origins of constructivist-developmental theory lie in the work of Jean Piaget (e.g., 1954). Piaget demonstrated that his children's minds were not empty, but that they instead actively processed the material with which they were presented in more and more complex ways as they developed. Kegan (1998) refers to this increasing complexity as expanded mental capacity.

Constructive development is related to how people come to know something, that is, what process they use to decide what is important. *How* can be distinguished from *what* a person thinks or believes. Thus, two students might hold similar political positions, but have arrived at them in different ways. Another word for the study of how people come to know is *epistemology.*

Many readers will be familiar with the concept of *stages* in the Piagetian and Kohlbergian traditions. The idea of stages is central to constructivist-developmental theory. However, it is a contested notion in that it implies a rigid way of knowing across situations.

A number of other terms are used to describe an overall epistemological tendency. In this chapter, the terms used interchangeably are *order of consciousness* (Kegan, 1998), *way of knowing* (Belenky, Clinchy, Goldberger, & Tarule, 1986), and the aforementioned *epistemology.* Each of these terms refers to an individual's overall approach to, or central tendency for, meaning-making. As mentioned earlier, an individual's way of knowing can range from a relatively closed, rigid, and simple way of processing to a more open, flexible, and complex one. Another way of describing such development is movement from a relatively external reliance on authority toward a more internal search for understandings.

For the purposes of this chapter, simplification of constructive development is required. Readers are referred to Belenky et al. (1986), Kegan (1998), Kohlberg (1981), and Perry (1998) for more expanded descriptions of constructive development.

Critics of constructivist-developmental theory offer at least two challenges, each of which needs to be qualified here. One is that the theory is hierarchical, in that later ways of knowing are valued more highly, and that therefore it is elitist, or "rankist." While developmental theory could conceivably be used that way, theorists have emphasized the achievement, or triumph over a more limited way of knowing, that each order of consciousness represents. Each is valuable.

The critique of rankism should be taken seriously, as individuals should not use developmental theory as a way of degrading other people. In fact, later stages of knowing are characterized by greater tolerance and openness. Developmental theorists discourage permanent labeling of individuals, instead recognizing the triumph and value that each stage represents. Again, developmental thinking is a hopeful enterprise. It encourages educators to stretch students' epistemologies toward openness and flexibility.

The second qualification about constructivist-developmental theory is that the stages of knowing are not "hard," that is, not absolute all of the time, in every situation. While there is evidence that individuals do tend to use a dominant way of knowing (Kegan, 1998), which might metaphorically be called their center of constructive gravity, they do not rely on only one way of knowing at all times. More relativistic, or self-authorizing, thinkers may rely on external authority and simple answers in situations in which they are naïve. Conversely, generally authority-reliant thinkers may "think for themselves" at times. Therefore, instead of using only one way of thinking at all times, it might instead be said that a person *tends* to operate out of certain frameworks. And those frameworks consist of shades, rather than rigid boundaries. Therefore, individuals tend to construct knowledge in a certain way, with elements of other ways of knowing always possible. And there are not only three or four hard stages for knowing. In fact, Kegan's constructive development theory uses 26 gradations of meaning-making tendencies that can be assessed in individuals (Lahey, Souvaine, Kegan, Goodman, & Felix, 1988).

# Three Epistemologies of Interest for Counselor Education

Three overall ways of knowing are of particular import for counselor education, as they represent the range of epistemologies that students of counseling utilize. These stages are called by various names in different theories. I will use the following terms, which are taken from a number of the parallel adult development theories: *received/conventional knowing, self-authorized knowing,* and *dialectical knowing.*

**Received/Conventional Knowing (Third Order of Consciousness).** The first position here will be variously called received (Belenky et al., 1986) or conventional (Kohlberg, 1981). The person operating from this way of knowing tends to be reliant on external norms or authorities for what to think and how to behave. Those authorities might be, for example, parents, teachers, religious texts, or clergy.

As noted before, it is important to remember that use of this epistemology is not total across situations (Moore, 1987). For example, a person who generally uses received knowing might show some self-authorization of ideas at times, if asked, "How did you come to know this was good or right?" In the case of counselor education, a student might experience doubt about the correctness of his received/conventional view of homosexuality because of his family or religion's strong negative feelings about gays. Nevertheless, he might also wonder, "How can I both have compassion, as my religion teaches me, and still condemn the physical expression of love in a same-sex relationship? Plus, I have heard that sexual orientation has a major biological component." That thought reflects a glimmer of self-authorization. It might be short-lived, with a quick retreat to the conventional views of the person's culture. It might, however, also blossom if his dilemma is nurtured by an environment that challenges him to think for himself. If those challenges, which Kegan calls (1998) the *culture of contradiction*, help the person think in a more complex way, they can lead to a revolution (or evolution) in his whole way of knowing toward self-authorization.

In general, students who operate largely out of received/conventional knowing assume that their culture is fixed and true, that the rules that they have inherited from family and church and community must be adhered to rigidly and completely. In the counseling workplace, they would ultimately rely on authorities, such as school principals or supervisors, rather than committing to a reasoning process about how to act.

Individuals who largely use received/conventional knowing cannot easily step outside of their inherited systems (e.g., culture, social norms) to question rules. They see the received systems as the way things are and must be. Those systems might be gender roles, social manners, received hierarchies of all kinds, or racial views. Thus, counselors who operate largely from received/conventional knowing are unlikely to challenge a system that is unresponsive to nondominant groups, such as gay students or migrant workers, if it differs from the system under which they were raised. The received system (e.g., culture, social norms) reigns for them. This author and his colleague (McAuliffe & Lovell, 2006) found students who largely used received knowing to be characterized by externality, surface thinking, concreteness, and solution-drivenness. Those qualities are problematic for professional work.

Most students of counseling operate from an order of consciousness that is either received/conventional knowing (Stage 3, also called the third order) or a mixture of Stage 3 and self-authorized knowing (Stage 4, or fourth order) (Eriksen & McAuliffe, 2003, 2006). The transitional way of knowing (3–4) has been called *subjective knowing* (Belenky et al., 1986) in that the individual relies on implicit subjective rationales for deciding on what is good or right, without reference to larger reasoning, scientific evidence, or other self-chosen procedures for deciding. Readers should note, nevertheless, that students of counseling commonly operate from that mixture of received and self-authorized epistemologies.

**Self-Authorized Knowing (Fourth Order of Consciousness).** If a person experiences received knowing as an unworkable means of deciding on what is right or good, she may open up to the fourth order of consciousness, or self-authorized knowing (Kegan, 1998). Somewhat corresponding terms for this way of knowing include *procedural knowing* (Belenky et al., 1986), *relativism* (Perry, 1998), and *postconventional thinking* (Kohlberg, 1981). At this stage, the individual can consistently use her own judgment and self-chosen procedures as sources of decision making. No pat answers based on tradition or authorities are acceptable. The self-authorizing knower no longer takes social conventions, such as family norms or peer models, as the ultimate guides for deciding, but rather weighs evidence about what is important in a situation. Perry calls this way of thinking relativism, as the individual now recognizes that knowledge varies according to the context, whether that is culture or the unique circumstances of a relationship.

Individuals who are self-authorizing approach complex situations realizing that they must use a self-defined procedure for deciding on what to believe or how to act. It follows that, using self-authorized knowing, individuals are not ultimately reliant on an external authority for how and what to think. Instead, people who are guided by this epistemology decide on what is right or good by looking each time at complex sources of evidence. For example, self-authorizing allows them to generate a relatively autonomous view on sexual orientation or gender roles, rather than relying on received religious or family rules.

The benefits of self-authorized thinking for counselors are at least twofold. First, and overall, self-authorized thinking enables counselors to make more nuanced counseling decisions in the midst of what is inherently ambiguous and complex work. More specifically, self-authorizing thinkers are likely to have the following characteristics: empathy, self-reflectiveness, insight, and tolerance for ambiguity (McAuliffe & Lovell, 2006). They are also more likely to challenge an oppressive status quo and engage in activism for oppressed groups (McAuliffe, Grothaus, Jensen, & Michel, 2010).

It should be noted again that there is no pure self-authorizing order of consciousness, or stage. Instead, each individual has a general tendency, or center of gravity (Laske, 2009), that will predispose him to certain ways of knowing. For example, all individuals will rely on authority occasionally, in specific situations. Beginning counselors might take a suggestion from a supervisor about how to work with a client. Supervisors will also dictate procedures for handling emergencies, for keeping records, and for evaluating progress. However, if self-authorized knowing is well consolidated, students will know that supervisors have also constructed their views. Students will take in the information for the moment, recognizing the supervisor's (or the text's) relative expertise. External authority can be important, but not ultimate, for the self-authorizing thinker.

As mentioned previously, students of counseling generally use aspects of both received (Stage 3) and self-authorized (Stage 4) knowing. Thus, it is not uncommon for students to be caught between hearing the authority of the teacher or supervisor and deciding for themselves. Students might experience ambivalence about authority as they waver between Stages 3 and 4. For example, the practicum student might express some adolescent-like rebellion about a supervisor's guidance,

due to the circumstance of teetering between using her own hunches and needing the input of a more expert practitioner. In Chapter 4, counselor ambivalence toward authority at certain career phases is described more fully. Overall, more self-authorizing knowers have greater ability to find their source of judgment amid the cacophony of supervisor, textbook, instructor, and peer voices on what to do as a counselor.

There are limits to self-authorized thinking. Individuals can become too enamored of their own procedures for deciding what is good or important. They can fall into the trap of certainty-by-method, that is, ultimate adherence to their own logic. For example, a counselor can hold too firmly to his self-defined version of multiculturalism, humanism, feminism, quantitative (or qualitative) research methods, diagnosis, and other hard-won points of view. Therefore, self-authorized thinkers face a new challenge: to question their self-defined certainties, to consider alternate formulations, to find greater understandings in seeming contradictions (Hanna & Ottens, 1995). That is the task of the next stage.

### Dialectical Knowing (Fifth Order of Consciousness).
The last of the adult stages will here be called the dialectical, or the fifth order of consciousness, following Basseches (1984) and Kegan (1998). Research indicates that people under 40 years of age do not consistently exhibit such a way of knowing. In general, fewer than 5 percent of adults have been found to use dialectical thinking as a dominant mode (Kegan, 1998). Thus, it is unlikely that counselor educators will encounter students (or faculty, for that matter) who demonstrate dialectical knowing. But it is useful to discuss this way of knowing because it reminds educators to attempt to take multiple perspectives and question their certainties, and to help some students who are ready to do so.

The term *dialectical* has a number of meanings, but, stated most simply, it refers to taking multiple perspectives and questioning assumptions. In this way of knowing, the thinker is especially attuned to the fact that she is constructing knowledge in a social manner in which ideas and values are created over time in communities, through shared discourse.

When individuals use dialectical thinking, they question the certainty of their own positions. In particular, they consistently look for the discourses from which they speak, such as those of gender, social class, or any other framework. They then consider alternate, even opposite views, seeing them as valuable contributions to emerging understanding of an issue. Kegan (1998) considers this order of consciousness to be, in fact, fully actualized social constructionist thinking, as described in a previous section of this chapter. With dialectical knowing, individuals seek contradiction, input, and dialogue. They look for the limits of their way of thinking. But the thinker need not be awash in a sea of relativism. In the process, the individual can make tentative commitments to positions (e.g. diagnoses, counseling theories), or what Perry (1998) calls *commitments in relativism*.

Counselors who think dialectically can question the foundations of any system, going back and forth between two or more perspectives. For example, the dialectical counselor would seek the limits of the humanistic principle of being "in the moment" with clients, perhaps by considering a diagnostic impression. In the process of doing so, the counselor would see the diagnostic scheme as a socially constructed system, coming from a particular set of psychiatric, theoretical, cultural, and research discourses, with their flaws and limitations. And the counselor would know that all of these formulations are tentative and temporary. He would seek the limitations in his thinking, thus embracing the playful expression that "contradiction is my friend."

Another iteration of consistent dialectical knowing is called *constructivist knowing* (Belenky et al., 1986). I will use the characteristics of constructivist knowing to explain this stage. Readers might list these characteristics and aspire to them.

The first characteristic of constructivist knowing lies in a person recognizing that she is *engaged in the construction of knowledge*. Such a perspective-sensitive stance is characterized by humility about the finality of one's beliefs. Consistent with the recognition of subjectivity is a second, related quality, namely, *accepting responsibility for continually evaluating one's assumptions about knowledge*. The constructivist counselor could live in the "permanent whitewater" of consistently checking on her position and being open to new information. A related, and third, characteristic lies in being intensely self-conscious, that is, *aware of one's own thoughts, judgments, moods, and desires*. Here the

individual can stand outside of her momentary perspective and examine its usefulness.

Beyond awareness of one's standpoints is, of course, the ability to understand the perspectives of others. In that vein, Belenky et al. (1986) found that constructivist counselors *can take positions outside of a particular frame of reference,* whether that frame be science, logic, culture, family, religion, a political perspective, or any other context. This extending of oneself beyond any one personal and cultural discourse is related to a fifth characteristic: a deepened ability to *attend to others and to feel related to them* in spite of what may be great differences. This connectedness would allow the counselor to attend to differences in cultures, personalities, and lifestyles, letting the universal and the different sit side by side.

A sixth characteristic of constructed knowing consists of a behavior: The constructivist thinker usually engages in *real talk,* as opposed to what the philosopher Jurgen Habermas (1984) called *concealed strategic* talk. Real talk means sharing ideas, listening carefully, and, in the process, encouraging emergent ideas to grow. The opposite of real talk would be having hidden agendas, masked metamessages that involve manipulation. Such talk requires the seventh characteristic of the constructivist counselor: the ability to *recognize the inevitability of conflict* and learning to engage it in a useful way. Internal conflict would be entertained as an opportunity to learn. External conflict would be similarly approached with a receptive posture.

The last two characteristics of constructivist knowing represent an activist impulse: Eighth, such knowers would consistently *notice what is going on with others and care about the lives of people around them* and, ninth, they would *want their voices and actions to make a difference in the world.* This author and his colleagues (McAuliffe et al., 2010) found such an activist stance to be particularly present in postconventional (Kohlberg, 1981) thinkers.

Despite the allure of dialectical thinking, it would not be a central goal of a constructivist counselor education, as students are not necessarily ready to question positions that they are still trying to self-authorize. However, knowing the characteristics of such thinking can point educators and future counselors in a direction that would make the counselors more humane, systems-challenging, and able to manage conflict. Indeed, these are qualities that counselor educators themselves, including the reader, might strive for.

As mentioned earlier, students of counseling generally think from a mix of received and self-authorized frameworks. Therefore, counselor education should focus on the movement toward a self-authorizing, relativistic order of consciousness. Kegan (1998) argues that that is the mental capacity required for beginning professionals.

## Implications of Constructive Development for Education

Constructivist-developmental theory can serve as a guide for counselor educators to assess student thinking and to stretch students toward self-authorized knowing. Teachers can trigger dilemmas that call into question students' received views about what is good and right. As students encounter topics such as invisible privilege, religious diversity, minority sexual orientation, authenticity in human relations, and theoretical integration, they are called to puzzle their own assumptions and come up with a way of knowing what is most useful for solving dilemmas. Those dilemmas can be intentionally presented by counselor educators.

As students encounter a diversity of ideas, educators can challenge them to generate their own answers to complex problems from real-life situations (e.g., by asking them to respond to cases, to engage in role-playing, to ponder ethical dilemmas). After such inductive learning opportunities are provided, students can be asked to reflect on the basis for their solutions and listen to others' ideas. Such a participatory environment contrasts with one in which an authority delivers truths. By contrast, the developmental educator sets up problematic situations, invites students to ponder the issues and choices involved, and, when students propose possibilities, asks the students, "How did you come to know that?" and "What is another perspective?" and "What might be various consequences of this decision?"

Authors in later chapters of this book will share teaching methods that instigate self-authorized knowing. They will suggest methods for challenging learners to generate their own ideas, to recognize the limits of external authorities, and to seek evidence for positions that they take. In that way, significant learning (Vella, 1994; see Chapter 3) might occur in the form of empowering future counselors to think for themselves.

## CONSTRUCTIVIST TEACHING AND COUNSELING IN GENERAL: THE PARALLEL

It might be seen from the preceding discussion that constructivist-oriented teaching prepares students for the complex work of counseling itself. Jean Peterson (personal communication, 2000), a counselor educator from Purdue University, lays out the implications of constructivist teaching for school counseling in this way:

> Students who have difficulty embracing [constructivist teaching] also often have difficulty going into a counseling session open to the experience of it, to the client's way of seeing the world, and to new ways of conceptualizing and strategizing. By contrast, students who begin to embrace [constructivist thinking] begin to leave "over-preparation" behind.
>
> It is certainly not just for typical counselor-client "sessions" that a constructivist approach models something important; it is also in helping our students to enter a school [or agency], be open to learning about the unique and idiosyncratic culture there, and have confidence that their "theory-building" will serve them well as they move into autonomous (and collaborative) professional behavior. Former school teachers who aspire to become school counselors often have difficulty with this "low-control" approach. However, once they can integrate their great strengths, they can be great school counselors. Students without a teaching background (the majority of my current students) are sometimes initially intimidated by the school culture. However, they, too, can be nudged into openness, acceptance of multiple perspectives (certainly including those of the teachers in their buildings), and tolerance for ambiguity (which all counselors must have, certainly no less so those in schools).

With this example, Peterson has described a hoped-for result of counselor education: the creation of the relativistic, self-authorizing counselor who can help clients become empowered, who can reflectively select among many interventions without being captive to one theoretical discourse, who is alert to the cultural context of the work, and who can examine any system of thinking or institution for its implications.

# CONCLUSION

Counselor education can share the goals of liberal arts education, that is, to free students from the narrow prejudices of their cultural and historical context. It is therefore a goal of counselor education to create skeptics, practitioners who accept no truth on hearsay, thinkers who can question their own foundations for knowing. Liberally educated counselors are those who are inclined to listen and hear, to pause and reflect on new phenomena, to look for evidence and counterevidence for their views, to practice humility and self-criticism, to nurture and empower the people around them, and to make and see connections among people and ideas that seem distant in time and space.

This introductory chapter is a request for counselor educators to pay attention to students' current ways of knowing, to help them be reflective and consider the limits of their knowing, all the while passionately committing themselves to the enhancement of human welfare and equity in human affairs.

# REFERENCES

Ahuja, S., Ebersole, J., Laske, O., Neiwert, P., Perez, M., & Stewart, R. (2008). Business leadership for an evolving planet: The need for transformational thinking in intercultural and international environments. *Integral Leadership Review, 8*. Retrieved July 12, 2010, from http://www.integralleadershipreview.com/archives-2008/2008-10/2008-10-article-ahuja.php

Basseches, M. (1984). *Dialectical thinking and adult development.* Norwood, NJ: Ablex.

Belenky, M. F., Clinchy, B. M., Goldberger, N. R., & Tarule, J. M. (1986). *Women's ways of knowing.* New York: Basic Books.

Berger, P. L., & Luckmann, T. (1966). *The social construction of reality: A treatise in the sociology of knowledge.* Garden City, NY: Doubleday.

Burbules, N. C., & Rice, S. (1991). Dialogue across differences. *Harvard Educational Review, 61*, 393–416.

Eriksen, K. P., & McAuliffe, G. J. (2003). A measure of counselor competency. *Counselor Education and Supervision, 43*(2), 120–133.

Eriksen, K. P., & McAuliffe, G. J. (2006). Constructive development and counselor competence. *Counselor Education and Supervision, 45*, 180–192.

Freire, P., & Freire, A. M. (1994). *Pedagogy of hope: Reliving pedagogy of the oppressed.* New York: Continuum.

Gergen, K. (2009). *An invitation to social construction.* Thousand Oaks, CA: Sage.

Habermas, J. (1984). *The theory of communicative action. Volume 1: Reason and the rationalization of society.* London: Heinemann.

Hanna, F. J., & Ottens, A. J. (1995). The role of wisdom in psychotherapy. *Journal of Psychotherapy Integration, 5*, 195–219.

Harris, I. B. (1993). New expectations for professional competence. In L. Curry, J. F. Wergin, & Associates (Eds.), *Educating professionals: Responding to new expectations for competence and accountability* (pp. 17–52). San Francisco: Jossey-Bass.

Kegan, R. (1998). *In over our heads: The mental demands of modern life.* Cambridge, MA: Harvard University Press.

Kohlberg, L. (1981). *The philosophy of moral development: Moral stages and the idea of justice.* San Francisco: Harper & Row.

Lahey, L., Souvaine, E., Kegan, R., Goodman, R., & Felix, S. (1988). *A guide to the subject-object interview: Its administration and interpretation.* Cambridge, MA: Harvard Graduate School of Education, Subject-Object Research Group.

Laske, O. E. (2009). *Measuring hidden dimensions of human systems: Foundations of requisite organization.* Medford, MA: Interdevelopmental Institute Press.

McAuliffe, G. J., Grothaus, T., Jensen, M., & Michel, R. (2010, March). *Ethnocentrism challenged: A study of intentional cultural de-centering.* Paper presented at the Annual Symposium of the Society for Research in Adult Development, Philadelphia.

McAuliffe, G. J., & Lovell, C. W. (2006). The influence of counselor epistemology on the helping interview: A qualitative study. *Journal of Counseling and Development, 8*, 308–317.

Moore, W. S. (1987). *Learning environment preferences.* Olympia, WA: Center for the Study of Intellectual Development.

Perry, W. G., Jr. (1998). *Forms of intellectual and ethical development in the college years: A scheme.* San Francisco: Jossey-Bass. (Original work published 1970)

Piaget, J. (1954). *The construction of reality in the child.* New York: Basic Books.

Rorty, R. (1989). *Contingency, irony, and solidarity.* New York: Cambridge University Press.

Schön, D. A. (1991). *The reflective practitioner: How professionals think in action.* Aldershot, UK: Avebury.

Vella, J. (1994). *Learning to listen, learning to teach: The power of dialogue in educating adults.* San Francisco: Jossey-Bass.

# 2

# Deep Learning

## The Work of Dewey, Kohlberg, and Kolb

Garrett J. McAuliffe

An introduction to the broad constructivist impulse and some of its implications for counselor education is now in place. This second chapter presents three influential theories that translate constructivist thinking into teaching practices. In this chapter, readers will be exposed to the experiential and developmental ideas of John Dewey, Lawrence Kohlberg, and David Kolb.

More educational theorists than these three exist, but these particular thinkers have made defining contributions to experiential and developmental education.

In anticipation of the ideas in this chapter, Activity 2.1 on the next page invites readers to recall powerful learning experiences from their own counselor education.

## ACTIVITY 2.1

Take a few minutes to recall your own counselor education. Try to recollect two experiences that were particularly important, in that they triggered a new way of thinking, introduced a significant worldview, or were emotionally stimulating. Such experiences can consist of discrete activities or discussions or more pervasive teaching-learning experiences. Name and explore two below.

**Learning Experience 1**

Description in a few sentences:

What made it powerful? Why was it impactful?

How would/do you carry it into your own counselor education work?

**Learning Experience 2**

Description in a few sentences:

What made it powerful? Why was it particularly impactful?

How would/do you carry it into your own counselor education work?

# DEEP PROCESSING

The notion of powerful learning has so far been kept vague. A more grounded and researched notion is the concept of deep processing, which will also be called *deep learning* here. The work of the three theorists that will be described later in this chapter aims at instigating deep processing in learners. For the sake of providing the reader with a foundation for the teaching methods described in the rest of this book, deep processing will be discussed next.

Cognitive psychologists distinguish between deep learning and surface learning (Craik & Tulving, 1975). This is an important distinction, given that this book promotes teaching strategies that encourage deep processing. A founding premise of the book is that such deep learning is required by counselors because their work requires them to use knowledge for important decisions under conditions of uncertainty.

Surface learning is defined as tacit acceptance of information and memorization of isolated and unlinked facts. In surface processing, the learner merely accumulates data, often through rote learning, with little attention to meaning. Individuals who are extrinsically motivated—for example, those who are focused primarily on obtaining a credential or a grade—are more likely to commit only to surface learning.

Deep processing, sometimes also called *semantic processing*, requires engaging meanings, not memorizing mere facts or disconnected information. It involves critical analysis of new ideas, linking them to already-known concepts and principles. Deep processing leads to both (1) understanding and (2) long-term retention of ideas so that they can be used for problem solving in unfamiliar contexts. The work of counseling requires such problem solving.

Deep learning is especially needed in disciplines in which the knowledge base and the methods for effective practice are less defined. Such is the field of counseling, in which practitioners must regularly work in unclear situations. As a result, counselors must consistently generate inferences, use reasoning, and transfer their general theoretical knowledge to the particular conditions that clients and students bring in to them.

Deep processing requires certain conditions in the actions of both the teacher and the learner. In general, instructors can instigate deep processing by using active approaches to teaching. But learners need sufficient motivation and a level of cognitive complexity to take full advantage of such teaching methods. Both teachers and students can participate in five activities that lead to deep learning. The work of Dewey, Kohlberg, and Kolb is consistent with these activities:

- making connections between concepts taught and personal experiences
- reflecting on how concrete specifics might indicate abstract patterns
- applying ideas taught in class to real-world situations
- connecting what one is learning to what one has learned previously
- discussing ideas with others while keeping oneself open to enlarging one's ideas based on encountering others' ideas

Although students can engage in most of these activities on their own, many will not do so without instructor challenge and support. Counselor educators can provide such encouragement through experience-rich teaching strategies.

# DEWEY: EXPERIENCE AND EDUCATION

The work of John Dewey stands as perhaps the most influential account of learner-engaged, experience-based education. The basics of Dewey's educational methods and purposes that are relevant to counselor education are presented here.

## Dewey's Critique of the Transmission Model

Dewey presented an alternative to the dominant transmission model of education that held sway in the first half of the 20th century. The transmission approach has continued to predominate in university classrooms (Magner, 1999). In that model, also called the *banking deposit* style of teaching by Paolo Freire (2000), an authority passes on information to passive learner-receivers, who are supposed to somehow absorb knowledge.

The transmission method implies that a "known" exists and that students are supplicants at the altar of conveyed knowledge. Dewey considered such an approach to have an elitist dimension. In his words, transmission resulted in "less competitive students yielding to boredom, losing interest, and deciding they had nothing to contribute which the teacher did not already know" (quoted in Fishman & McCarthy, 1998, p. 23). Dewey challenged this teacher- and content-centered approach to pedagogy.

It should be noted that Dewey was not a single-minded promoter of exclusively experiential education. He said that teachers must still transmit the conserved knowledge wealth of the past. Thus, in the counseling field, educators still need to convey the current canon of scientific methods and counseling theories, ones that have historically guided human communities. Everything need not be discovered anew by the learner. Of course, challenges to any canon, past or present, should also be discussed and tested in experience.

In the next sections of this chapter, I present five central Dewey annotations about education:

- the difference between reception and activity
- the need for learner interest and effort as conditions for powerful learning
- a description of two levels of experience, one relatively superficial and one deeper
- a five-step process for experiential teaching and learning
- Dewey's ideas on the ultimate purposes of education

## Reception Versus Activity in Learning

Dewey (1933) anticipated constructivism when he conceptualized the human mind as a meaning-making instrument, relentlessly driven to make sense of its world. He therefore utilized activity in his pedagogy: Dewey considered the most powerful learning experiences to be those that engaged learners in confronting problems, posing hypotheses, and taking action based on reasoning. He translated this overall conceptualization into five processes that were important for experiential learning. These will be described later in this section.

From Dewey's perspective, the common metaphors of teaching as transmitting, instilling, and covering, accompanied by the learning metaphor of absorbing, do not stimulate the mental activity required for powerful learning. In his view, the more passive the learning is, the less is retained and, worse, the less the learner can use knowledge in complex, real-world situations.

The work of counseling is very complex. Counselors, like all professionals, must make important decisions under conditions of uncertainty, a task that requires critical thinking capacities. They must be able to thoughtfully and purposefully use what they have learned. Therefore, transmission-oriented teaching strategies cannot produce learning that is sufficient for the knotty work of counseling.

To counter passive transmission in teaching, Dewey proposed that experience was required for powerful learning. The word can be traced to the Latin noun *experientia* (knowledge gained by repeated trials) and the verb *experiri* (to try, test). Experience implies action. This notion, I will show, is key for a counselor education that matches the demands of the job.

## Interest and Effort

According to Dewey (1933), powerful learning requires more than experience; the learner must possess interest and effort. Interest means that the learner's curiosity is triggered. Effort, as Dewey (1897) described it, lies in the tension between means and ends in action. The concepts are intertwined, as one begets the other. For example, a counselor who is concerned about a troubling case will make an effort to gather information by consulting with others and reflecting on options. In turn, her interest might be further sparked by the unraveling of possibilities.

**Interest.** Dewey proposed that educators instigate students' interest by helping them identify "for-whats," or goals for learning, ones that engage their interest. Students' interest is triggered when they can plainly see how they will benefit from what is being presented. At a minimum, they need to understand how what they are learning may be relevant to their lives. In Dewey's words, students would become "intent" when something was "urgent" to them (Fishman & McCarthy, 1998, p. 19).

**Effort.** Once students' interest has been triggered, their motivation for mental effort increases. Interest in a problem usually leads to the individual investing effort to solve it. In turn, this investment often begets further interest. Dewey proposed that students only learn when they become mentally engaged in solving problems. He was adamant: "There can be no effective school learning . . . without the learner's active participation" (quoted in Fishman & McCarthy, 1998, p. 20).

Students sometimes bring interest, a priori, to a topic. Such interest might lie in the awareness that they will need such knowledge to become successful in a professional role. However, learners are not automatically engaged by every topic. It is the teacher's task to stimulate interest in the content and to create situations in which students understand their need for the curriculum. They can then be prompted to engage in effort (Fishman & McCarthy, 1998).

Educators therefore need to know how to create conditions that generate both interest and effort. To instigate interest, for example, instructors might provide intriguing situations at the beginning of a lesson. Such interest-getting situations can include sharing anecdotes, assigning students to journal about daily life, providing video illustrations, creating experiments, doing demonstrations of counseling, and presenting cases. At times, instructors can even ask students to try out a concept or skill before it is taught in order to arouse their interest and questions. For instance, a novice might be asked to act out good listening in a role play as a prelude to teaching about listening. The next two sections outline both general and specific conditions for active, experiential learning.

## Two Levels of Experience

Students merely having experience of some kind is not sufficient for significant learning to occur, as will be seen in Kolb's experiential learning model later in this chapter. All individuals experience the world moment to moment, but they are not necessarily active in processing it.

For Dewey, experience operates on two levels. The initial encounter with a problem, that is, the original sensory input, is primary experience. However, such primary experience is not sufficient for learning. Instead, for powerful learning to occur, the individual must engage in secondary experience, which includes reflection on the meaning of the experience and testing of hypotheses about the utility of the experience for real-life situations. Educators can create the conditions for students to have such secondary experiences through student journaling, classroom discussion, role play, case study, and observation.

The order of such experiences is not rigid. As will be seen in Kolb's experiential learning model, learners can enter the process of experience, reflection, conceptualization, and testing at any point. For example, they can begin with (1) reading about concepts, follow with (2) reflection, and then (3) try out the ideas in action, which might lead to (4) further reflection, and so on. The process can be flipped, starting with (1) raw experience, followed by (2) reflection on it, and then (3) consideration of concepts that might capture the meanings of the experience.

If the encounter with a new idea, such as a counseling theory, comes first via reading and lecture, Dewey would propose that teachers instigate situations in which learners try to apply what they have heard or read to so-called problems, such as a case or a role play. Teachers would then ask students to raise questions and make hypotheses as to the utility of that counseling theory in the given situation.

Whatever the order, students need the secondary experiences of reflection, hypothesis testing, and trying out in order to do deep processing, or meaning-making. Thereby they can develop the capacity to generate thoughtful responses to complex situations, similar to those that they will eventually face as professionals (McAuliffe & Lovell, 2006).

## Five Steps in Experiential Learning

Dewey outlined five conditions that characterize the aforementioned secondary experience (Miettinen, 2000), and educators can implement them in teaching activities. These conditions are (1) indeterminate situations, (2) intellectualization, (3) working hypothesis, (4) reasoning, and (5) action. It should be noted that the twin conditions of learner interest and effort (or activity) pervade all five conditions.

**Indeterminate Situation.** First, learners encounter an indeterminate situation, one in which routine responses are not adequate. Because the needed action is not immediately apparent, learners have to pause in order to reflect before acting. During that pause, they examine the conditions, the resources available, obstacles to action, and ways to overcome these obstacles. For example, beginning students of counseling might be presented with a video that illustrates the case of a suicidal middle-aged man, Brendan, who has lost his job and his primary relationship. They might be asked what they would do, or even better, be invited to role play a short counseling session based on the case. Most beginning students would find themselves unable to generate any habitual responses because of the indeterminacy of the situation.

**Intellectualization.** Next comes intellectualization. Here students are encouraged to move from the initial pause caused by the unavailability of a habitual response to constructing a mental representation of the problem (e.g., "I must think about this situation and possible options and reasons for those options"). Students intellectualize the problem at this point, which does not mean for Dewey that they disregard emotion, but that they recognize the need to think about the problem in front of them (e.g., "I can't just do what my first impulse tells me in this situation"). Thus, in the case of Brendan, the suicidal man, after the initial case presentation or role play, the instructor might ask students to identify what the problem seems to be and why it seems to exist. Unlike automatic reactions to an event, the process of intellectualization consists of pondering the situation in a thoughtful way, rather than responding from habit (e.g., "I'll tell this man about my own difficulties and then advise him to relax").

**Working Hypothesis.** Third, the learners pause further to study the conditions of the situation (e.g., "Brendan seems depressed. Hmmm. I realize that he has been violent in the past.") and form a working hypothesis. Students might think, "This person's potential action is dangerous to himself and others, urgently so. I think I see it in his facial expression. I hear it in his statements. I note that he has lost his job and has no close social relations. If I act incorrectly, he might take his life. I need to know about special interventions useful for crisis situations. Perhaps I need to do some kind of assessment of the danger. Then I might have to be more active somehow. But how? Maybe I should alert some authorities? I think so."

**Reasoning.** Next, learners begin reasoning, which Dewey described as *thought experiments*. The learners can test their working hypotheses in light of the knowledge available. To encourage that process, an instructor might lead a class discussion on (1) how to assess the level of danger and (2) what options are available. Perhaps class members might propose doing a risk assessment by asking specific questions of the client. Then classmates and the instructor might generate counselor actions in light of findings from the risk assessment. Prior reading or lecture about crisis intervention may generate additional options to be considered. It should again be noted that students can hear and read about practices and ideas that are in the existing repertoire (i.e., conserved knowledge). Experiential education does not require that all learning be purely discovery, or done *sui generis*.

In the case of Brendan, after reasoning about possible responses to the crisis, the learners might say, "OK. I see. All crises are not the same, but they share some similarities. We can never completely predict suicide or violence. But we must check off some criteria in our minds and use our judgment. After we do that, we have a series of actions that we might take, actions that are more proactive than empathic responding."

**Action.** Finally, if powerful learning is to occur, learners must test the working hypotheses (i.e., the guidelines for crisis assessment and intervention) by taking action. Dewey here meant overt actions, not armchair speculation. The brain is activated by the attempt to try out hypotheses, even if the try-out is a simulation, like a role play. Thus, the instructor might have students go back to the original role play to try out the ideas learned during the class discussion, lecture, or reading.

This particular problem will not necessarily be resolved by taking the planned action, as students may discover circumstances that require modifying the working hypothesis. For example, the counselor-students may find that the role-played client does not have a plan to kill himself, that instead he is intellectualizing about the nature of suicide and a meaningful life. In that case, the students would need to revise their hypothesis to include these new cues. The central notion around Dewey's five experiential learning steps is that, in taking action after discussion and reflection, the students actively test a hypothesis, sometimes confirming and sometimes disconfirming it. Further learning is now possible as learners, rather than acting in a trial-and-error fashion, systematically and thoughtfully compare their findings with the original hypotheses.

## Purposes of Education

In Dewey's view, the aims of education are profoundly related to large social and individual purposes. Dewey described these purposes as being on two levels: proximate, or relatively immediate, and ultimate. The proximate ends lie in the learner's ability to apply thinking and skills to real-world problems. These ends can be seen in such tasks as students' counseling performance, test interpretation, and application of ethics to cases. The ultimate ends of education are to promote the social good.

Dewey was particularly concerned about two ultimate purposes for education: (1) preparing citizens to be critical thinkers in a democracy and (2) encouraging learners to promote good for all citizens. In the first case, Dewey (1916) held that experiential education was necessary for democracy to flourish. He proposed that citizens must be critical, reflective thinkers. They must not be beholden to received traditions that are automatically applied to the emerging problems related to how to live well in human communities. He believed that citizens in a democracy must learn to think for themselves, not passively receive dictates from authorities. Paolo Freire (2000), the Brazilian literacy educator, similarly proposes that education must empower all citizens to think for themselves, rather than being awed by elites and so-called experts. Such citizens should be able to make decisions by pausing and weighing evidence before acting, abilities that are enhanced by the previously mentioned five steps for experiential learning.

By contrast, authority-based teaching communicates that the experts know what and how to learn. In this context the learner's role is merely to listen and absorb. Dewey warned about such "fundamentalisms." Students must have opportunities to make choices, not merely to accept beliefs blindly on the basis of authority, fancy, or superstition. In that vein, Dewey urged educators to help students develop the inclination to scrutinize accepted language, practice, and belief.

In the sphere of enhancing social good, which today might be called *social justice*, Dewey proposed that the educational enterprise is ultimately moral. At the end of the day, education must be dedicated to the end of ensuring the welfare of the human community. He proposed that the ultimate purposes of education are to (1) promote cooperative living, (2) advance community welfare, and (3) improve the condition of others.

Such was not commonly the case, in Dewey's view. Jane Addams (quoted in Lagemann, 1985), the social reformer and friend of Dewey's, could have been speaking for him in the following words:

> We recall that the first colleges . . . were established to educate religious teachers. . . . As the college changed from teaching theology to teaching secular knowledge, the test of its success should have shifted from the power to save [people's] souls to the power to adjust them in healthful relations to nature and their fellow men. But the college failed to do this, and made the test of its success the mere collecting and disseminating of knowledge, elevating the means into an end and falling in love with its own achievements. (p. 35)

Toward these ends, Dewey urged educators to aim relentlessly at developing *traits of character* in students, which he believed supersede mere cognitive intelligence or the ability to think logically.

# APPLYING DEWEY'S CONCEPTS TO COUNSELOR EDUCATION

Counselor educators might ask themselves how their teaching and mentoring promotes the purposes that Dewey advanced for education. Are they preparing counselors who are critical thinkers? Are they encouraging learners to promote social good?

Dewey would propose an experiential counselor education. Counselor educators would therefore be seen as instigators, rather than instillers, of learning. They should, as much as possible, raise questions, encourage discussion, assign reflective writing, create classroom simulations, and plan out-of-class experiences, knowing that these activities trigger interest and effort in the learner. Students of counseling would be asked to construct understandings through encountering indeterminate situations from which they must create and test hypotheses. The future counselor would, as a result, be prepared to encounter the complex situations of professional life, in addition to the equally complex problems more broadly facing society.

Such experiential education is not boundary-less, nor willy-nilly. Dewey believed that instructors must provide structure and order, do careful planning, and have intentionality in their teaching. In fact, experiential learning takes a great deal more effort and planning than pulling notes or slides out of a file and delivering content to a class filled with passive students.

# KOHLBERG: DEVELOPMENT AS THE AIM OF EDUCATION

This next theorist was similarly concerned about educating citizens for critical thinking and a broad societal perspective. However, he added a developmental dimension. Lawrence Kohlberg was an heir to Dewey in that both he and Dewey were concerned with creating a genuinely liberal education, in the sense of the Latin meaning of *educare*, that is, "leading out." Kohlberg saw education as a way of leading students out of familiar, limited ways of knowing to more open, flexible, and reflexive ones.

Kohlberg plotted these evolving ways of knowing in a developmental stage scheme. Developmental thinking was described in general in Chapter 1. [For a detailed description of Kohlberg's moral development theory, the reader is referred to his writing (1969, 1985, 1987)]. Kohlberg proposed three broad stages, which are described in Table 2.1.

These stages share characteristics with other cognitive developmental theories (e.g., Belenky, Clinchy, Goldberger, & Tarule, 1986; Kegan, 1982, 1998; Perry, 1998). Kohlberg's theory focuses on the moral domain, but is broadly applicable to education in general (Power, Higgins, & Kohlberg, 1989). In fact, Kohlberg and Mayer (1972) called this approach *cognitive developmental*

*education*. Like Dewey's approach, it too is concerned with actively engaging learners in order to help them become self-authorized, principled thinkers. In a classic statement on the matter, Kohlberg and Mayer declared that cognitive development was the aim of education. It is this pedagogical dimension of his work that will be explored in this chapter.

Kohlberg proposed that educators could instigate changes in cognitive development under certain conditions. Following Piaget (Piaget, Gruber, & Vonèche, 1995), Kohlberg proposed that individuals expand their overall ways of knowing, or personal epistemologies, when they are presented with conditions that they can't assimilate into their current frameworks.

Kohlberg described methods for enhancing such epistemological development. He proposed that developmental education required *optimally mismatching* the learner's current way of knowing. In mismatching, the teacher stretches the learner by posing dilemmas that can't be resolved by the current way of knowing. Such dilemmas might include, for example, ethical conundrums that can't be resolved by reliance on conventional rules of a religion or a community. They might include multicultural challenges to ethnocentrism, such as issues around homosexuality or gender roles (Endicott, Bock, & Narvaez, 2003).

Kohlberg, like Dewey, challenged the transmission model of education. Transmission, he noted, merely reinforced the notion that authorities (e.g., texts, religious rules, ethnic customs) should be the purveyors of knowledge: "Traditional educators believe that their primary task is the transmission to the present generation of bodies of information and of rules . . . collected in the past [through] direct instruction of such information and rules" (Kohlberg & Mayer, 1972, p. 453).

Activity 2.2 asks readers to note their own encounters with the transmission model of teaching.

| TABLE 2.1 | Kohlberg's Moral Development Stages |
|---|---|
| Preconventional | Characterized by self-interest; empathy not present |
| Conventional | Characterized by unquestioned conformity to the conventions of the community; presence of a conscience and empathy |
| Postconventional | Characterized by commitment to care and justice, beyond the norms of a community |

Name at least one example of the transmission approach to education from your own life as it relates to moral rules or values in at least three of the following settings. Be specific by naming the teaching method and at least one moral rule or value.

Elementary School:

High School:

Religious Education:

How useful has this method of instilling been as a guide to living and as a means of helping you and others make moral or value decisions?

What are its limitations as a method of preparing students to live in contemporary society?

Name examples of how the transmission model has affected individuals and societies in at least one of these areas: race, religion, ethnicity, sexual orientation.

Kohlberg and Mayer (1972) were concerned about the conformist thinking that resulted from the transmission approach to teaching: "[The transmission model] emphasize[s] definition of educational goals in terms of fixed knowledge . . . assessed by standards of cultural correctness [and] internalization of basic moral rules of the culture" (pp. 453–454). As a result, transmission education is often a convention-maintaining method.

This convention-upholding model troubled Kohlberg, who had had direct experience with the horrors of Nazism. He wondered how people could unquestioningly adhere to norms that excluded and oppressed whole groups of people. His hope, like Dewey's, was that individuals could be educated to think beyond social conventions. He feared that automatic allegiance to authorities, either in person or in the form of texts, resulted in cruelty to others who did not or could not conform. As might be seen from the previous section, both Kohlberg and Dewey found there to be a seamless link between the cognitive and the moral. In both of their views, principled morality requires the capacity for flexible, complex thinking. Such thinking is characterized by a restless search for what constitutes care and justice. In Kohlberg and Mayer's (1972) words, education should promote "an active change in patterns of response to problematic social situations rather than the learning of culturally accepted rules" (p. 455).

This way of knowing can be a developmental goal of counselor education. Activity 2.3 challenges readers to apply Kohlberg's ideas to counselor education.

## ACTIVITY 2.3

From your knowledge of the work of the counselor, or from your personal experience as a counselor, name a situation in which counselors must be able to think for themselves, that is, be able to challenge conventions of a society or an organization in order to practice ethically. It might be an actual situation that you have experienced or one that you have heard about.

# Kohlberg's Developmental Alternative to the Transmission Model

Kohlberg, like Dewey, advocated for engaging students in active learning. He called for "an educational environment that actively stimulates development through the presentation of resolvable but genuine problems" (Power et al., 1989, p. 454). To this he added the developmental dimension. Following is an overview of Kohlberg's educational method. Readers will see parallels to teaching methods described in Chapter 1 and in Dewey's work.

According to Kohlberg, the developmental educator engages in two overall tasks: (1) assessing developmental readiness and (2) mismatching (challenging) that way of knowing with challenges that stretch the person's current approach.

As applied to counselor education, assessing readiness in a simple way can be done by assuming that most students of counseling tend to use a combination of conventional and postconventional knowing (McAuliffe & Lovell, 2006). Educators might therefore challenge students of counseling to consistently think in a postconventional way. Instructors can instigate relativistic thinking about the norms of an organization, a reference group (such as a religion), or a society. These institutions can be seen as constructions that are products of a group in a place and time. In Chapter 1, I labeled these two overall stances, using Belenky and colleagues' (1986) and Kegan's (1998) terms, *received* and *self-authorized* knowing.

For mismatching, Kohlberg proposed that instructors instigate *dilemma discussions,* that is, situations that require thoughtful consideration of multiple perspectives in order to make a decision on how to act. Following are examples of developmental instruction.

**Developmental Instruction Strategies: Topics That Mismatch**. Certain topics will trigger disequilibrium in many students' thinking. Such topics might include working with rebellious adolescents, considering the benefit of varying religious perspectives or worldviews, or having empathy for sexual offenders. Other disequilibrium-enhancing topics include experiencing the value of unconventional gender roles, sexual practices, or family structures, and dealing with issues of confidentiality with adolescent clients in relation to their parents. Each of these topics calls into question a conventional way of knowing and asks most students to stretch their reasoning, to step outside of convention and take it as "object" (Kegan, 1998).

The movement from a primarily conventional way of knowing to a more postconventional one can be begun simply by encouraging students to take other persons' perspectives. At least two ways to do that are to teach empathy and to teach cultural diversity.

For some students, the very notion of empathy itself is a mismatch, as it requires a suspension of their external locus. By contrast, conventional thinkers might be inclined to judge others only by the standards of their reference groups. In order to stretch their thinking, students who have inhabited a world of judgment, even condemnation, of beliefs and behaviors that are outside of their family or religious norms may be asked to play the role or take on the perspective of diverse clients. Instead of shaming, reprimanding, or advising such clients, the counselor-to-be is asked to imagine himself as if he were the client, putting aside judgment. Being empathic requires the student to "bracket" (mentally hold aside) his convention-derived point of view so as not to impose it on clients.

Another example from counselor education of challenging students to move beyond conventional thinking is to encourage cultural relativism. By learning the legitimacy of alternate cultural expressions, students can call into question the ultimacy of their received norms. When learning empathy or cultural relativism, students gain opportunities to de-center from their current perspectives. Again, these notions might be obvious to counselors and counselor educators, but they can be tremendous discoveries for more convention-reliant knowers.

The mismatching process (Step 2, above) requires the following conditions. The learner must be exposed to the next higher level of thought (e.g., in an advanced theory course or in internship, asking the student such questions as, "How did you decide that _____ counseling theory is useful? What are its limits? In what situations is it helpful? When is it unethical to use a single approach?"). In the process, the learner must experience conflict over the usefulness of her current way of thinking (Instructor: "You are working on ameliorating post-traumatic stress. So how does change occur at a primary, sensory level?" Student: "I used to take the professor's word that cognitive-behavioral counseling is necessary and sufficient for all situations. But for PTSD situations it seems to be inadequate alone."). Finally, the student is encouraged to rethink a problem using a new set of assumptions about how knowing is approached (Student: "My experience and the research evidence show that sensory experience is important for changing posttraumatic phobia responses. Classic cognitive-behavioral counseling doesn't tap into the senses directly. What about EMDR or exposure therapy? I must investigate and test them out. I thought I could rely on the single approach that my supervisor had taught me. I guess I will have to use my own experience and other evidence to decide on the most useful approach to working with trauma. Gee, I can't just rely on the experts for my decisions."). What has occurred in this simple example is the move from what Gilligan (1988) calls *face value* thinking to *multiple lens* thinking. Face value thinking is a default to concrete, conventional rules. Multiple lens thinking relies on the person having a center for judgment that takes received knowledge as one among many possibilities.

The overall process of mismatching is sometimes called *plus-one reasoning*, in that it asks students to think in terms of one stage beyond their current stage. In simple terms, a developmental pedagogy asks instructors to engage in three processes: (1) assessing the learner's current way of knowing (for beginning students of counseling, that is generally a mixture of conventional and postconventional thinking); (2) mismatching the learner's current way of thinking by presenting problem situations, or dilemmas, that call the current way of thinking into question, thereby arousing epistemological conflict in the learner about how to respond to the problematic situation; and (3) helping the learner consider alternate ways of resolving the problem. What is introduced in the process is a deliberative, reflective way of thinking, one that can be applied to other challenging or dilemma-ridden situations. In the process, the window to a self-authorized, postconventional way of knowing might be opened. There are indications that such a way of knowing enhances counselor advocacy and activism (McAuliffe, 2008).

## KOLB: THE EXPERIENTIAL LEARNING CYCLE

The next thinker, David Kolb, also made experience the centerpiece of his aptly named Experiential Learning Theory (ELT; Kolb & Kolb, 2008). Kolb added to the work of Dewey and Kohlberg by creating a learning cycle model for teaching and learning, which offers a visual representation of the power of triggering deep learning through a process of experience, reflection, conceptualization, and experimentation. Kolb's model is applicable to many learning environments, from classrooms to counseling sessions. Readers might note parallels between ELT and the social cognitive/cognitive behavioral traditions (e.g., Bandura, 1986; Beck, 1986; Goldfried & Davison, 1994). Those traditions emphasize the power of experience (e.g., Bandura's performance accomplishments) and reflection (e.g., Beck's having clients note errors in their thinking) in learning.

Kolb's learning cycle is depicted in Figure 2.1. It is a useful, clear device for reminding counselor educators to incorporate all four elements in teaching, when possible.

## Four Conditions for Significant Learning

The learning cycle outlines four conditions, or modes, that facilitate significant learning. Educators can use this cycle to plan units in courses, in workshops, and even in the whole curriculum. It reminds teachers that no one part of the cycle is sufficient alone.

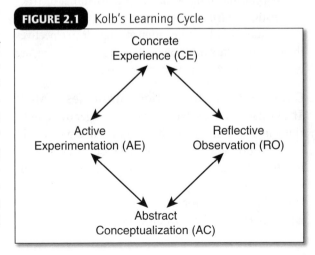

**FIGURE 2.1**  Kolb's Learning Cycle

Concrete Experience (CE)

Active Experimentation (AE)

Reflective Observation (RO)

Abstract Conceptualization (AC)

A student can enter the cycle at any point, that is, learning can happen in any order. It might be, for example, that (1) abstractions (AC) are presented in a lecture or in readings (e.g., learning definitions of defense mechanisms), followed by (2) reflections (RO) on their meaning (e.g., pondering the consequences of rationalization, repression, denial), followed by (3) a role play or example (CE; e.g., the Greek fable of the fox and the grapes, which depicts the fox's rationalization about not really wanting the grapes that were too high to reach), and succeeded by (4) noticing one's use of defense mechanisms in daily life (AE). Therefore, the following steps, which begin with concrete experience, present only one version of the order of these four modes.

**Concrete Experience.** Much learning begins with raw, concrete experience, which is parallel to what Dewey called *primary experience*. Such experience excites the senses and alerts the human organism. Instructors can plan concrete experiences to introduce new concepts. For instance, in the beginning counseling skills course, the instructor might have new students pair up and try to be "helpful" in whatever ways they can imagine to do so. During that time, students must be able to, in Kolb's (1984) words, "involve themselves fully, openly, and without bias" (p. 236) for it to be of most value. Thus, the role players must take risks and try to let their perceptions focus on the present moment. Concrete experience can also be vicarious, as in students observing a group or viewing a recorded counseling session. It can also consist of recollections from the past, such as "Think of a time in which you were helped" or "Think of concrete instances of how your family practiced gender roles."

**Reflective Observation.** As was seen earlier, Dewey made the point that the secondary experiences of reflecting and considering the implications of the experience are required for complex learning. Kolb (1984) also proposed this next step after primary experience, which he called *reflective observation*. In this step, the learner "must be able to observe and reflect on these [concrete] experiences from many perspectives" (p. 236). Students of counseling who have just tried out their "raw" helping skills might, for instance, ask (or be asked), "What did this experience mean?" "What would be another way of understanding it?" "How does it fit in with your prior understandings?" "What are the implications of what you observed or experienced?" The instructor might also ask the "clients," "What was it like to be listened to?" "What was helpful?" "What was not helpful?" "What does your experience imply for this course's intention to create an effective helping interview?"

A number of additional strategies for encouraging reflective observation exist for counselor educators. Instructors can ask students to write about concrete experiences such as the role plays or cultural immersion activities described previously. Instructors can also promote reflective observation by leading class discussions on the meanings of experiences. Such reflection can take the form of small-group discussion, journals, or reflection papers. In each case, students are encouraged to step back from the concrete experience in order to make sense of it from multiple angles. Later chapters will present specific ideas for such reflective observation in particular courses.

**Abstract Conceptualization.** At some point, learners must create guidelines for action across situations. In the example of role-playing helping skills, the student might think, "There is a pattern to what is helpful. What I noticed fits in with what I read about core conditions for helping." Both Kolb and Dewey emphasized that abstract conceptualization is best tested in the fire of experience, rather than studied in the abstract. As the ELT process has been described here, such concrete experience precedes conceptualization. That particular sequencing is therefore *inductive,* in that learners infer a generalized conclusion from particular instances. Such a concrete-to-abstract approach is powerful. It triggers Dewey's ideas of interest and effort on the part of learners, who are actively making meaning of their experience.

It should be noted that learning can occur from *deduction* as well, that is, noting the particular case as a demonstration of the general. Of course, learning is not always so linear, nor is it so neat. A teacher can introduce abstract notions and then provide examples, or do the opposite. Kolb would propose that counselor educators mix their methods, starting with experience sometimes and presenting abstract concepts at other times.

**Active Experimentation.** Further testing of the abstract conceptualizations that have been discovered through experience and reflection can occur through students trying out these generalizations in further experience. That is the mode of science labs. It is also the model for the counselor education practicum. Practicum students conduct experiments by trying to apply theory in actual counseling sessions. Practicum students thus have new, interest-generating experiences (CE/AE), reflect on them (RO; often with the help of a supervisor and/or a group), and figure out more complex conceptualizations (AC) about how to help. In parallel fashion, students in the beginning counseling skills course try out empathic responding (AE) after reading about it and perhaps seeing it. They then discover—with feedback, examples, and discussion—how they might mix such responses with other skills in a session (AC). That cycle can persist for professionals who are continually reflecting on their work. Those reflective practitioners can evolve into master counselors (Ronnestad & Skovholt, 2003) by regularly reflecting about (RO) alternate approaches (AC) and therefore leading themselves out of familiar, rote responses into experiments in actual sessions (AE). This is a lifelong cycle.

Educators can set the tone for lifelong learning by incorporating as many of Kolb's four elements as possible into their teaching. Counselor educators can vary instruction, layering in the different modes depending on the type of learning desired.

**Integrating the ETL Model Into Instruction.** Kolb and Kolb (2008) describe how the four modes can be integrated into a course or curriculum to create three increasingly complex levels of learning—registrative, interpretive, and integrative—each one deeper than the previous one:

1. *Registrative learning.* The traditional lecture course, for example, emphasizes registrative [or performance-oriented] learning. Here the information merely "registers" with the learner, so that she or he can "perform" it if needed, outside of a real-life context, such as on a multiple choice test. Lecture may result in registrative learning. It only uses the two learning modes of *reflection* and *abstraction*. There is little action. There also is little relation to personal experience. Similarly, mere raw experience, unaccompanied by reflection or conceptualization, results in registrative learning.

2. *Interpretive learning.* A second level of learning allows the learner to interpret abstractions into applications. It can occur if the instructor or curriculum requires practical application of concepts, through role plays, workbook exercises, or simulations. Here the modes of *abstraction* and *reflection* are supplemented by *action,* which together serve to further deepen conceptual understanding. Case studies and examples help learners connect abstractions to concrete experience.

3. *Integrative learning.* An even deeper level of learning, called "integrative," occurs when further personal *experience* is added. Internships or field projects encourage integrative learning. Deeper integrative learning can be enhanced by requiring students to *reflect.* Instructors can encourage such reflection through peer group discussions or journaling, through which students process their internship experiences. Linking these *activities* and reflections to the *conceptual* material, that is, adding abstract conceptualization, further enhances this level of learning. Clinical supervisors can promote such integrative learning by asking students to describe the principles (e.g., theories) that are being exhibited in their counseling internship work.

These three levels alert the counselor educator to potential choices for encouraging deeper learning, from promoting mere registrative learning to furthering integrative learning.

# The Four ELT Modes as Learning Styles

Kolb found that different learners prefer particular combinations of the four modes. For example, a philosophy professor might be inclined toward some combination of abstract conceptualization and reflective observation, whereas a practicing counselor might be drawn to concrete experience and reflective observation as dominant modes. Therefore, Kolb's model is both a description of conditions for all significant learning and a guide to individuals' preferred learning styles.

Kolb (1984) created a model in which people can be located in terms of their preferences on two axes: Abstract-Concrete and Active-Reflective (see Figure 2.2). The two poles are set up to portray opposite tendencies. Each learning style has strengths. Different individuals are inclined toward some combination of each, and all are valuable as conditions for learning. That is, instructors should mix the modes, as described above, when teaching groups of students.

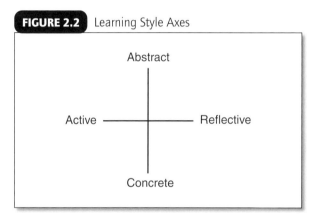

**FIGURE 2.2** Learning Style Axes

**Abstract–Concrete.** Both individuals and occupations may be oriented toward the abstract or the concrete mode. For example, the abstract mode is favored by academics and the university itself. The carpenter prefers the concrete. Abstraction is valuable, as knowing general patterns allows learners to apply theory across situations. Counselor educators, as academics, might be inclined toward abstraction. However, practicing counselors must also work in the concrete world of the interpersonal encounter, the emotions, and specific behaviors. And many students of counseling are not necessarily abstraction oriented. Therefore, counselor educators should be wary of overabstraction, ensuring that there is enough experiential activity and reflection to match learner styles. Readers might consider at this point which pole they favor in general. Both educators and students must come to appreciate the value of each, allowing an interplay between the two modes.

**Active–Reflective.** Action and reflection also exist in tension. Learners vary in their preferences for these polar modes, as do the requirements of occupations. For example, the physical therapist would be inclined toward action, whereas the teacher is likely to be inclined toward reflection. Readers might note which end of the active-reflective pole they prefer. As with the abstract-concrete axis, too much of one mode can be problematic. An over-inclination toward action could be impulsive; total reliance on reflection could be paralyzing and avoidant. Again, counselor educators should account for both modes in their teaching.

The four modes have career implications as well as teaching implications. In Kolb's (1984) words, "A mathematician may emphasize abstract concepts, while a poet may value concrete experience more highly. A manager may be primarily concerned with the active application of ideas, while a naturalist may concentrate on observing" (p. 237). The variations have counseling career implications. For example, the more abstract reflectors may favor psychodynamic approaches, whereas those who are inclined toward the concrete mode may be attracted to the experiential and arts-oriented therapies.

Kolb identified four types of learning styles, which are combinations of the four learning modes. Readers are encouraged to identify the type(s) toward which they are inclined.

- *Convergers (Abstract Experimenters).* Those with this learning style prefer to use reasoning (abstraction) to act on specific problems (experimentation). Abstract experimenters have focused interests (thus "converging") and are relatively unemotional in their approach to learning and problem solving. Engineers and those in the biological and physical sciences are likely to prefer this style.

- *Divergers (Concrete Reflectors).* This group is inclined toward reflecting on concrete experience. They are not inclined toward abstract, philosophical speculation that is not grounded in concrete situations. They like to imagine the meanings of personal situations, interpersonal relationships, and other human phenomena, using emotions as a guide (thus "diverging" as they reflect). Most counselors are oriented toward this learning style, as might be expected, as are those in the humanities fields.

- *Assimilators (Abstract Reflectors).* Individuals who prefer abstract reflection like to reason about phenomena. They are "idea people" who are less concerned about practice than are those with the other learning styles. Abstract reflectors are less oriented toward people and sensory experience than are those in the first two groups. They are commonly professors and researchers. Readers might recognize themselves or other counselor education professors as belonging to this group. Counseling theorists are also likely to be abstract reflectors. Those in this group, like all of the others, have much to offer in the way of research and speculations, but they must also manage their style. They should learn to be concrete and experiential when those modes are needed.

- *Accommodators (Concrete Experimenters).* Members of this group prefer to *do.* They like to carry out plans. They are also more inclined to take risks. They are likely to "just want the facts." They are liable to prefer intuition and to use trial-and-error to solve problems. They tend to be at ease with other people, but sometimes abrupt. They are not inclined to philosophize or to ask, "Why?" Occupations that utilize this learning style include massage therapy, nursing, carpentry, and computer technician work.

It is very important to note that (1) there are situations in which each of these styles is useful and occasions in which each is not and (2) individuals can utilize all of the styles when needed. Readers are invited to speculate on the application of learning styles for counselor education in Activity 2.4.

---

### ACTIVITY 2.4    APPLYING LEARNING STYLES TO COUNSELOR EDUCATION

Respond to the following two questions:

What are the implications of these learning styles for teaching in counselor education?

What combinations among the four (CE, RO, AC, AE) were most used in your experience in the counseling theories class? In the counseling skills class? In practicum or internship supervision?

## Assessing Learning Styles

Instructors can give Kolb's (1999) Learning Style Inventory (LSI) to assess their students' learning style inclinations at the beginning of a semester. Administering the inventory can serve two purposes. It can teach students about such styles, and it can help the teacher tailor the course to the varying styles. The LSI is available at www.haygroup.com/tl/Questionnaires_ Workbooks/Kolb_Learning_ Style_Inventory.aspx

## CONCLUSION

The work of John Dewey, Lawrence Kohlberg, and David Kolb that is described in this chapter is foundational for planning counseling courses and curricula. Each thinker's work reminds the educator that student engagement in experience is the basis for significant learning. However, experience alone is not enough. Educators must also provide opportunities for reflection inside and outside of class. Most of all, these theorists remind teachers to engage students' interest and to create conditions for active thinking and experiencing.

## REFERENCES

Bandura, A. (1986). *Social foundations of thought and action: A social cognitive theory.* Englewood Cliffs, NJ: Prentice Hall.

Beck, A. T. (1986). *Cognitive therapy and the emotional disorders.* New York: Meridian.

Belenky, M. F., Clinchy, B. M., Goldberger, N. R., & Tarule, J. M. (1986). *Women's ways of knowing.* New York: Basic Books.

Craik, F. I. M., & Tulving, E. (1975). Depth of processing and the retention of words in episodic memory. *Journal of Experimental Psychology: General, 104,* 268–294.

Dewey, J. (1897). The psychology of effort. *Philosophical Review, 6,* 43–56.

Dewey, J. (1916). *Democracy and education: An introduction to the philosophy of education.* New York: Macmillan.

Dewey, J. (1933). *How we think: A restatement of the relation of reflective thinking to the educative process.* Boston: D. C. Heath.

Endicott, L., Bock, T., & Narvaez, D. (2003). Moral reasoning, intercultural development, and multicultural experiences: Relations and cognitive underpinnings. *International Journal of Intercultural Relations, 27,* 403–419.

Fishman, S. M., & McCarthy, L. P. (1998). *John Dewey and the challenge of classroom practice.* New York: Teachers College Press.

Freire, P. (2000). *Pedagogy of the oppressed.* New York: Continuum.

Gilligan, C. (1988). *Mapping the moral domain: A contribution of women's thinking to psychological theory and education.* Cambridge, MA: Harvard University Press.

Goldfried, M. R., & Davison, G. C. (1994). *Clinical behavior therapy: Expanded edition.* New York: John Wiley & Sons.

Kegan, R. (1982). *The evolving self: Problem and process in human development.* Cambridge, MA: Harvard University Press.

Kegan, R. (1998). *In over our heads: The mental demands of modern life.* Cambridge, MA: Harvard University Press.

Kohlberg, L. (1969). Stage and sequence: The cognitive-developmental approach to socialization. In D. A. Goslin (Ed.), *The handbook of socialization theory and research* (pp. 347–480). Chicago: Rand McNally.

Kohlberg, L. (1985). The just community approach to moral education in theory and practice. In M. Berkowitz & F. Oser (Eds.), *Moral education: Theory and application* (pp. 27–88). Hillsdale, NJ: Lawrence Erlbaum.

Kohlberg, L. (1987). *Child psychology and childhood education: A cognitive developmental view.* New York: Longman.

Kohlberg, L., & Mayer, R. (1972). Development as the aim of education. *Harvard Educational Review, 42,* 449–496.

Kolb, A. Y., & Kolb, D. A. (2008). *Experiential learning theory: A dynamic, holistic approach to management learning, education and development* (Case Western Reserve Working Paper). Retrieved July 13, 2010, from http://www.learningfromexperience.com/images/uploads/ELT-Hbk-MLE&D-LFE-website-2-10-08.pdf

Kolb, D. A. (1984). *Experiential learning: Experience as the source of learning and development.* Englewood Cliffs, NJ: Prentice Hall.

Kolb, D. A. (1999). *Learning style inventory.* Boston: Hay/McBer Training Resources Group.

Lagemann, E. C. (1985). *Jane Addams on education.* New York: Teachers College Press.

Magner, D. K. (1999, September 8). The graying professoriate. *Chronicle of Higher Education*, pp. A18–19.

McAuliffe, G. J. (2008, March). Constructive development and cultural de-centering: A study of an intentional development-instigating intervention. Paper presented at the Annual Symposium of the Society for Research in Adult Development, New York.

McAuliffe, G. J., & Lovell, C. W. (2006). The influence of counselor epistemology on the helping interview: A qualitative study. *Journal of Counseling and Development, 8,* 308–317.

Miettinen, R. (2000). The concept of experiential learning and John Dewey' s theory of reflective thought and action. *International Journal of Lifelong Education, 19,* 54–72.

Perry, W. G., Jr. (1998). *Forms of intellectual and ethical development in the college years: A scheme.* San Francisco: Jossey-Bass. (Original work published 1970)

Piaget, J., Gruber, H. E., & Vonèche, J. J. (1995). *The essential Piaget.* Northvale, NJ: Aronson.

Power, F. C., Higgins, A., & Kohlberg, L. (1989). *Lawrence Kohlberg's approach to moral education.* New York: Columbia University Press.

Ronnestad, M. H., & Skovholt, T. M. (2003). The journey of the counselor and therapist: Research findings and perspectives on professional development. *Journal of Career Development, 30,* 5–44.

# Guidelines for Constructivist-Developmental Counselor Education

Garrett J. McAuliffe

afety. Relationship. Respect. Engagement. Application. Experience. Personalization. These are a few of the watchwords for a constructivist and developmental counselor education. These and other guidelines will be presented in this chapter. They are not unique. These guidelines are expressions of the traditions that were discussed in the previous two chapters and elsewhere—experiential learning, developmental instruction, adult education, social learning theory, feminist pedagogy, and educational psychology. They are here enumerated and summarized so that the educator might be reminded to consider them in the process of enacting a constructivist-developmental counselor education.

There are two major sections to this chapter. First, nine principles for adult education are presented, based on the work of Jane Vella (2002). Then, with that groundwork laid, ten constructivist-developmental guidelines for teaching are described. These two frameworks complement each other. By the end of this chapter, readers should have a solid grasp of some methods for an experientially based, student-centered pedagogy.

## Principles for Adult Education

I have condensed Jane Vella's (2002) principles for adult education into the following nine guidelines. Vella proposes that adults learn best when all of the learners share the responsibility for their educational experience. Therefore, the principles and specific suggestions that follow emphasize the notions of inclusion, participation, and equality among learners. They are particularly apt for counselor education.

**1. Create a feeling of safety**. Most students have known fear in the classroom. Individuals do not forget those moments. They often lead to negative self-attributions, even phobic reactions to certain subjects and situations. Excessive fear can beget avoidance. It can deter effort to learn a subject, as in, "I must be stupid at all math. I can't even begin to understand statistics. I give up." Learners instead need affirmation of their potential and their achievements. This does not mean flattery or empty praise, however. Students need to believe that this learning experience will work for them, that the conditions are set up for their success. How might teachers consistently create such an anticipation of success? Not by reducing the challenge to students and the effort expected. That would be the sugar-coated pedagogy that Dewey feared, as discussed in Chapter 2. Safety can be created in the company of demanding challenges. Vella suggests that instructors do the following to create safety:

- Help students gain confidence in the course design and in the teacher by (a) making the course design and the requirements clear and (b) sharing the teacher's background and passion for the subject.
- Help students become invested in the course by (a) asking learners about their expectations for the course and (b) asking them what norms they would propose for such conditions as breaks, respect, and monitoring air time.
- Be affirming. Acknowledge each student's contribution, whether verbal or written, in some way. Such affirmation will empower students to increase their spontaneous contributions.

**2. Ensure the existence of sound relationships.** The relationship between student and teacher stands out above all other factors as an influence on adult education (Vella, 2002), as it does with counseling. An adult-to-adult connection should characterize the counselor education classroom. For instance, instructors need to do the following:

- Address students by name.
- Be accessible (e.g., via email and phone).
- Explain their rationales for in-class activities and assignments.
- Challenge their initial or ongoing prejudices about particular students (e.g., those based on their personalities or appearance). Find a place in themselves to respect each learner, even when it is sometimes a struggle.

**3. Show respect for learners as agents.** Students need to be invested in their learning. They need to be active participants *with* the instructor, not passive recipients of the authority figure's pronouncements. When instructors ask adult students what and how they would like to learn, those students subsequently become engaged and intentional (Dewey's learning "for-what" is promoted, as described in Chapter 2). Here are some specific "respect-full" reminders:

- Treat adult students as capable of making decisions during the course, just as they do in the other parts

of their lives. Make the course content and process an open system—subject to student affirmations, additions, and critiques.
- Clarify when students are to be consultants who are making suggestions and when they are deliberators who are making decisions; allow the latter as much as possible.

**4. Engage learners.** Educators can get learners to be involved by setting up tasks that invite them to "get into it deeply," often in small groups. This principle incorporates Dewey's (1938/1963) and Kolb's (1984) emphasis on promoting experience, as discussed in Chapter 2. It also addresses Dewey's dual conditions for good teaching and learning: interest and effort. Instructors will know that they have engaged students when it becomes difficult to stop the "buzz" of discussion. Here are some reminders:

- Regularly engage learners in activity, making it difficult for them to extricate themselves. Such activities may include group processing of exercises from the text; role plays or simulations that apply concepts; and private, in-class writing on a question.
- Treat a learning task as an open question put to a small group, providing the materials and resources needed to respond. This inductive way of teaching poses concrete problem situations and asks students to generalize from them to other situations.
- Be wary of merely "covering" a set curriculum. An instructor may touch on all of the supposed content, but the learning may be insignificant and thin. Instead, use class time to explore a few topics more deeply and allow the reading to provide more detail. In fact, more is learned outside of class than during class, because reading, writing, experiencing, and thinking allow students to stop and make their own sense of ideas (McKeachie, Svinicki, & Hofer, 2006).

**5. Do regular needs assessments and practice accountability.** Students of counseling, like all learners, come to their education with a great deal of prior experience and with considerable knowledge. Teachers might therefore ask two questions of students, in varying forms: "What do you think you need to know?" and "What do you already know?" That baseline can guide the instructor in what to emphasize and de-emphasize. Of course, in general, syllabi curricula are already set, guided by the evolving, collective wisdom of a field (Dewey's *conserving* of knowledge). Nevertheless, an early assessment of existing student familiarity with, for example, helping skills, cultural diversity, or lifespan development can guide the emphases in a course and allow more experienced students to do advanced work or even mentoring of other students.

Instructors who do ongoing needs assessments are more accountable to their students. These formative evaluations allow adult learners to participate regularly in deciding what has been learned. They give the instructors a means of taking the classroom "temperature." For instance, at the end of class sessions, a teacher might take five minutes to ask, "What has been most useful for you today?" and "What might be changed for next time?" Instructors can ask students for periodic written commentaries on their experiences during the previous class, on the course in general, or on their learning so far. They might at times read such suggestions to the whole class in order to check out their relevance for other class members.

**6. Provide sequence and reinforcement.** Instructors, and the textbooks they choose, should start with simple ideas and then layer in complexity. Learners benefit from learning one idea, one theory, or one method before they are asked to compare, contrast, and integrate several ideas (or theories or methods). Instructors might use the following sequence: (1) start with simple, safe tasks; (2) take small steps toward building to the next tasks; (3) return to previously taught facts, skills, and attitudes in new and interesting ways during a course or throughout a curriculum (often called the *spiral curriculum* because of the way that instructors return to simple ideas in more complex ways as students move through a program of study); and (4) encourage students to experience and/or pay attention to the practical results of trying out ideas. If teachers flit from abstract concept to concept, failing to help students understand their foundations and applications, or if they bombard students with intricate explanations and exceptions, students will not only be confused but may also suffer from self-doubt about their capacities as learners and as future professionals.

**7. Provide opportunities for immediate application.** Good professional work requires a balance between understanding concepts and application. This principle is reminiscent of Kolb's proposal that abstract conceptualization be balanced with active experimentation. In this regard, for example, the instructor might ask students to engage in simulations or other applications of the concepts that they are learning. In the testing and assessment course, students should take tests and interpret them to each other. In the counseling theories course, students can role play each theory on a simple level. This idea of application can be extended to the whole counseling curriculum. Beyond class simulations, each course might be accompanied by a mini-practicum, a chance for theory to be tried out in practice. Students might then leave each class session with a skill to practice or an application to make.

**8. Practice equity.** Educators have often inherited, in Vella's (2002) words, "ancient hierarchical relationships" (p. 22) from their own schooling experiences. They remember teachers as masters, at whose feet they may have sat. In their own experience, teachers were "sages on the stage." Vella offers the alternative: "Adults need reinforcement of the human equity between teacher and student" (p. 17). Her ideas parallel the connected teaching notions of Belenky, Clinchy, Goldberger, and Tarule (1986) and other feminist pedagogy theorists. Counselor educators can therefore join learners in a circle of inquiry.

Possibilities for enacting equity are many. Teachers can ask students to call them by their first names. They can sit within the circle of learners as co-inquirers. They can show uncertainty and reveal the process of their thinking (Belenky et al., 1986; Freire, 2000; hooks, 1994; Schniedewind, 1987). They can self-disclose, laugh at themselves, bring students to conferences and present with them. As Vella says, "Time spent with learners . . . in a different role makes a big difference in their freedom to ask the disturbing question, to disagree with a point, or venture a novel opinion" (p. 21). Only with a fundamental equity in place can meaningful dialogue take place.

**9. Encourage teamwork.** Working in teams is a constant in most professional work and in much of the rest of life. When instructors ask students to participate on a team for a discussion or a project, they set up a parallel situation to professional teamwork in organizations. Teams in workplaces usually focus on producing a tangible product or solution. Such group work can be difficult, as working with others is "messier" than autonomously making one's own decisions. Members of groups have to negotiate, listen, agree, be empathic, disagree, and compromise. They need to propose and retreat, weigh and act, express and demur, as do participants in any project, whether they be the founders of a republic who are penning a constitution or colleagues who are drafting an individualized educational plan in a school. Vella thus offers some guidelines for teaching using teams of adults:

- Having students work in small group teams does not require that there be a small class. Teams can be formed within a group of over one hundred.
- Consider how to form teams. There are at least two ways: (1) let them form their own groups, which expresses respect for their capacities to find compatible partners, or (2) form teams for the class, which usually creates greater diversity and challenges students to move out of their personal and cultural comfort zones.
- Direct the teams toward a learning task, whether it be creating a list of ideas on poster paper or developing a simulated community agency.
- Have learners pay attention to the interpersonal *process* of working as a group, as well as the *product*. Specifically, invite learners to examine their roles on a team. Start with having them assess their usual roles (e.g., relationship maintenance, task achievement).
- Ask learners to assess formatively and summatively; that is, have them comment during and at the end of the project via journal entries, a structured questionnaire, or a commentary that is added to the final product on how they are working or have worked.

# CONSTRUCTIVIST-DEVELOPMENTAL TEACHING GUIDELINES

This section also offers guidelines for teaching adults. However, these guidelines are based in constructivist-developmental theory (see Chapter 1). They are conscious attempts to instigate procedural/self-authorized knowing, that is, students' capacities to think for themselves, take

multiple perspectives, use procedures for deciding on what to do, and be flexible in their thinking. These guidelines are adopted from many sources, including the classic work of Belenky et al. (1986), Knefelkamp (1984), Perry (1999), McKeachie et al. (2006), and Sprinthall and Sprinthall (1981).

These guidelines are not discrete; they overlap. Others could be added. Some echo Vella's (2002) principles. Readers should treat them as an attempt to translate constructivist-developmental thinking into action. They might serve as useful reminders for educators in constructing curricula, advising students, creating syllabi, and planning lessons. First I will list the 10 guidelines in three clusters. Then I will explain each more fully.

Lee Knefelkamp (1984) proposed the first three guidelines, which are broad and foundational, in her model of developmental instruction. The acronym ESP, for *experience, structure,* and *personalization,* might serve as an aid for remembering these essential guidelines.

1. Value and promote **experience.**

2. Vary the **structure.**

3. **Personalize** teaching.

The next five guidelines ask teachers to introduce students to the fluidity and ambiguity of knowing. They are ways to promote thoughtful reflection, as opposed to encouraging rote memorization. In the process, such methods can open a window to relativistic thinking, which is explained in Chapter 1 as the tendency to utilize reasoning to decide on a position (Perry, 1999). Using Jean Peterson's words that were quoted in Chapter 1, these teaching methods help the future counselor be "open to the experience of [a counseling session], to the client's way of seeing the world, and to new ways of conceptualizing and strategizing." One way to remember these next five guidelines is to use the acronym MACCC, for multiple, approximation, conflict, categorical, and commitment.

4. Emphasize **multiple** perspectives.

5. Value **approximation** over precision.

6. Recognize that **conflict** and dialectic are the norm. Encourage their expression.

7. Question **categorical** thinking.

8. Show **commitment** in the face of doubt.

The last two guidelines are particularly valuable for counselors, as they alert them to so-called "process" dimensions that are central to the work of counseling.

9. Encourage **intrapersonal** process awareness, or metacognition.

10. Accent **interpersonal** process commentary, or metalogue.

# Guideline 1—Value and promote experience

Experience is essential to learning, as was seen in Chapter 2. Experience is here defined as active participation in events or activities in a way that heightens attention and the senses. Sensory experience is a primary brain process. Individual learners vividly remember immediate sensory experience (Mesulam, 2000). Therefore, significant learning is related to having vivid sensory stimulation through active experiences. That is how Dewey's interest and effort are especially stimulated. Individuals usually more easily remember the frog dissection in high school biology lab than a specific history lecture. To illustrate the power of sensory experience, readers might recall a childhood experience in which they were scared, in pain, hot, cold, sad, or angry. Such a memory is easy to generate. It probably came back first in the form of an image, sound, smell, touch, or action. Then the meaning of the experience can be revived. Individuals do not remember words and abstractions as well as they do experiences.

Albert Bandura's (1986) findings on self-efficacy also underscore the power of experience. Bandura found that the most influential contribution to a sense of self-efficacy was performance accomplishment, that is, an occurrence in which an individual experiences success. Less powerful in influence was vicarious learning (e.g., watching a model be successful), and even less so was verbal persuasion (e.g., hearing about success). Thus

Bandura's social cognitive research reminds counselor educators to activate sensory experiences in order to help students learn and clients change.

Despite the evidence from cognitive psychology (e.g., Craik & Tulving, 1975), much college instruction continues to be dominated by teacher-centered, abstraction-oriented information giving (Chickering & Reisser, 1993; Magner, 1999). Teacher-centered instruction, often in the form of lectures, may be so common partly because it offers instructors more control. Role plays, simulations, and field experiences are "messier" in that instructors never know what will happen during and after them. That uncertainty includes teachers being unsure about what information demands will be placed on them and whether they will have the knowledge or skills to respond adequately.

Some disciplines have long used and valued experiential methods of teaching. As I alluded to earlier, science education engages students in laboratory experiments. During and after those experiments, students reflect on what they observed and make connections with scientific principles (following Kolb's experiential learning model). The parallels to such labs in counselor education are role plays, classroom simulations and exercises, team projects, interviewing and shadowing experts, case studies, out-of-class observations, and, of course, field work. Readers might, at this point, recall their own experiences of these types of activities in their counselor education programs and the impact these had on them as learners.

Counselor educators are especially well positioned to use these experiential methods to teach, as counseling practice itself often stimulates change by using metaphor, exploration of feelings, in-session experiences, gestalt exercises, client discovery, role play, and guided imagery. Therefore, educators need not lose their counselor creativity when they cross the teaching threshold.

However, experience alone is not the best teacher, as both Dewey and Kolb pointed out. Teachers must mix opportunities for experience with reflection so that sensing doesn't exclude sense-making. Perhaps Socrates' dictum "The unexamined life is not worth living" might be translated into "The unexamined experience does not create deep learning." In developmental terms, asking students to generate their own meanings from experiences, especially ones that conflict with their current understandings, can instigate greater self-direction and relativism.

In this emphasis on experience and reflection, the power of abstraction should not be dismissed. Helping students conceptualize phenomena as examples of abstract concepts allows students to generalize from situation to situation. Thus, for experience to move from specific, undifferentiated learning to generalizable knowledge, students must make sense through logical analysis, experiment, and dialogue. One way of combining these elements is to begin a class session with an experience (e.g., a group activity, a case) and then ask students to draw meanings out of the experience and discover the concepts behind it. In this inductive manner, experience leads to abstract conceptualization.

Different learners need different amounts of experience, depending on their developmental capacities. While all learners benefit from experience, more dualistic thinkers, that is, those characterized by the expectation that truth is known by authorities (Perry, 1999), require the heaviest dose of direct, concrete experience. By contrast, relativists are able to manage a greater amount of vicarious learning and abstraction (Knefelkamp, 1984). However, every learner can benefit from experience in the form of anecdotes, demonstrations, or activities.

# Guideline 2—Vary the structure

*Structure* refers to the degree to which instructors explicitly direct students and provide frameworks in assignments, lectures, and discussions. Higher degrees of structure might include the following:

- giving an outline for an assigned paper and a rubric of grading guidelines so that students have frameworks within which to work
- communicating an agenda at the beginning of each class that outlines the content and process of a class session, including the learning objectives
- explaining the context of a course, that is, how it fits into the curriculum in a major
- offering basic definitions of terms used
- providing study guides before exams, with an outline of key points to be tested, so that students might be guided to key topics

- reviewing previous material to cement learning
- providing examples of abstract concepts
- teaching students how to study effectively using a structured method

Each of these methods might be unnecessary or redundant for more relativistic thinkers. However, higher structure can support authority-reliant thinkers, giving them a framework for thinking within structured boundaries while keeping them from floundering.

**Structural Support.** Here is a simple guideline for structure in teaching: More concrete, dualistic thinkers find high levels of structure to be supportive of their current expectations and low levels of structure to be confusing, stressful, and over-challenging (Baxter Magolda, 2000; Knefelkamp, 1984). A high degree of structure matches the dualist's reliance on external authority for knowledge. By contrast, more relativistic thinkers often find high levels of structure to be constraining and low levels of structure to be freeing and enlivening.

Relativists' desire for lower degrees of structure makes sense, as relativists expect to create their own knowledge and make decisions after weighing evidence themselves. Structure does not necessarily impede relativists, as those students merely ignore the structures that don't fit with their conceptions of what ought to be. Students who show the multiplistic (Perry, 1999) or subjectivist (Belenky et al., 1986) epistemology that is typical of graduate counseling students may struggle with how much structure to attend to and how much of themselves to put into decisions.

**Structural Challenge.** The discussion of structure up to this point has focused on how the learning environment might support students' current developmental capacities. But developmental instruction also aims to challenge students to grow developmentally. It follows from the previous discussion that a challenge for more dualistic thinkers consists of providing lower levels of structure, that is, asking such students to decide what they think and how to structure a task.

Therefore, developmentally conscious instructors need to reduce structure at times so that more dualistic learners have the opportunity to create. For example, instead of a logically ordered lecture on a topic, the instructor might ask students to puzzle the solution to a problem and write their ideas on a board. Similarly, the instructor might provide only loose guidelines for a paper and allow students to choose a topic within a range of choices, thereby providing moderate structure so that dualistic students are required to make choices. Similarly, the instructor might provide some clear guidelines on skills to try (support) in a counseling practice session, understanding that the experience itself is ambiguous enough to be challenging.

By contrast, relativistic thinkers generally relish less structure. Their way of knowing is supported by open-ended tasks. For example, relativistic thinkers benefit from choosing their own topic of interest for a paper, analyzing a case from multiple perspectives, being asked questions about a case rather than being given directives, and co-constructing client assessments in groups with peers. Relativists thrive on creating knowledge by thinking through ideas—both within themselves and among colearners. For example, to support relativistic thinkers, an instructor might explain a counseling theory, but to challenge those thinkers, the instructor might ask them to critique that theory for its limitations. The lower structure of a discussion-oriented seminar is a support element for the readiness of the developmental needs of higher-order (relativistic, self-authorizing) thinkers. Thus, it is desirable, for relativists, for the instructor to assign a reading and simply ask for students' responses in class.

These notions can be confusing for instructors, however. Teachers might understandably ask, "How can I ever come up with lessons that adequately support and then challenge diverse learners?" Truly individualized instruction is not easy in most learning environments. Therefore, instructors can cycle through a variety of lower and higher structured methods. In Brookfield's (2006) words, "Given the bewildering complexity of teaching and learning, a good rule of thumb is to use a diversity of materials and methods in your practice" (p. 202).

All students benefit from a high level of structure when they encounter new material. Therefore, if learners are unfamiliar with a topic, a small number of ideas should be presented, accompanied by clear definitions and concrete illustrations. For example, counseling theories are commonly taught one at a time. Later, students can be asked to compare, contrast, and critique them. The common approach to teaching basic helping skills (e.g., Ivey, Ivey, & Zalaquett, 2010) is another illustration of the movement from high to low structure when presenting new material. In the microskills approach, the highly structured approach of teaching single skills provides support for all learners and then gives way to the less structured approach of asking students to perform those skills in unstructured interviews. At that point, more dualistic thinkers are initially over-challenged: They are being asked to apply new skills in the relatively amorphous environment of role-played counseling situations (McAuliffe & Lovell, 2006). These students benefit from more intense supervision of moment-to-moment practice. Some learners need their supervisor or instructor to offer directives, for example, "Try this" or "It seems that the client is scared. Where do you see fear?" More relativistic thinkers would instead need to be asked questions about a case or a session, for example, "What would you do?" or "What is your hunch?"

From the constructivist-developmental perspective, the overarching goal for all learners is that they be able to think for themselves based on reasoned consideration of evidence, so that, in practice, they can tolerate (and eventually thrive in) the ambiguity of the counseling enterprise. Such autonomous thinking can be nurtured in the developmental environment by varying the structure.

## Guideline 3—Personalize teaching

The quality of learning can be enhanced by personalizing the concepts, resulting in increased learner interest, ability to apply ideas, and empowerment. Personalized teaching can be defined as (1) promoting interactions among all participants in the learning environment and (2) making connections between the subject matter and individuals' personal lives and experiences.

In the first case, creating a participatory learning community demonstrates the co-construction of knowledge and empowers learners to see themselves as knowledge creators. Regarding making personal connections, ideas become more vital, alive, and relevant when they are connected to the familiar. Personalization engages students, therefore accounting for Dewey's first condition for learning: interest.

Personalization has a foundation in educational theorizing. For example, in one of his last writings, Carl Rogers (1983), commenting on the constructivist revolution, said that all knowledge is at the core a personal matter, not a disembodied entity that is somehow "found" by learners through purely abstract and objective procedures. In that perspective, he echoed Dewey. Brown, Collins, and Duguid (1989) showed that a classroom, program, or college culture that emphasizes authentic, personal relationships provides a superior ground for learning.

There are at least eight ways for the instructor to personalize the learning environment, all of which can be promoted by the instructor. Each will be discussed in detail.

- encouraging students to make personal connections with the subject matter
- being "present" in the classroom
- providing a challenging but nonpunitive environment
- instigating dialogue and interaction
- showing enthusiasm
- sharing the teaching methods
- offering individualized feedback and responses
- being accessible

The first is to encourage students to make *personal connections* with the subject matter. Teachers can link subject matter with students' personal experiences. For example, when teaching about ethnicity, the counselor educator can ask students to explore their own ethnicity by reading and interviewing family members. Similarly, students can plot their own experience at a developmental phase in the lifespan development course. Examples of such activities are given in the course-specific chapters that follow. In general, students can be asked to connect concepts in their reading with personal examples in their electronic commentaries or journals. In class, students might generate personal examples of situations in their lives that illustrate a concept, such as developmental tasks, or the experiences of empathy, assertiveness, career decision making, or various family dynamics.

The *instructor's personal presence in the classroom* is a second way of personalizing learning. The opposite is often the case: College teachers frequently take a dispassionate stance in presenting knowledge, guided by the search for objective truth. bell hooks (1994) calls this the "objectification of the teacher" (p. 16). In her view, objectivism requires that teachers' selves be emptied out so that the untidy personal contents of their lives and thinking don't intrude on their objectivity. Instructors often aim to present airtight objective-seeming arguments in the classroom, resulting in student intimidation. Belenky et al. (1986) describe the impersonal, expert teacher phenomenon in this way: "So long as teachers hide the imperfect processes of their thinking, allowing their students to glimpse only the polished products, students will remain convinced that only Einstein—or a professor—could think up a theory" (p. 215).

To show the emergent quality of knowing, instructors can instead be more transparent. hooks (1994) proposes that teachers occasionally share their uncertainties and personal life stories in the learning space. There are other ways to be more incomplete and human in the classroom. For example, instructors can explain how they came to make course decisions, so that the material or the learning process isn't reified as a canon in students' minds (Sinacore, Blaisure, Justin, Healy, & Brawer, 1999).

A third way to personalize learning is to allow class participants to struggle together to create knowledge in *a challenging but nonpunitive environment.* This sort of atmosphere enables all students to voice uncertainty without the fear of ridicule. Instructors contribute to this environment by their conversational presence in the classroom or elsewhere; during discussions, they can show their own uncertainties. In responding to student comments, instructors can verbally affirm, reflect, and extend student contributions. In that vein, Belenky et al. (1986) describe an instructor who responded to a student comment by saying, "What you're thinking is fine, but think more" (p. 218). Counselor educators can encourage students to ask, "Why?" and "How?" Further, instructors can invite uncertainty by asking students what they understand or don't understand about a topic.

Belenky and colleagues (1986) call this approach the *connected classroom*: It is a place in which everyone contributes and everyone's presence is valued. In the connected classroom, the instructor challenges everyone to take responsibility for the experience. The instructor encourages participants to listen to one another and to build on each other's ideas. The instructor helps create an atmosphere in which participants can, in Noddings's words, "nurture each other's thoughts to maturity" (cited in Belenky et al., 1986, p. 221). Noddings asks instructors to respond to student questions and offerings on the student's own terms, not in a point-counterpoint fashion of debate and competition. In a similar vein, Freire (2000) calls on teachers to help students *put their words on the world,* as opposed to treating knowledge as outside of themselves.

Such an encouraging environment does not require only affirmation. Dialogue and interaction do not have to be conspiracies of agreement. Differences among learners in assumptions, ideas, and cultures can be engaged and encouraged as necessary elements of building a learning community. Thus, personalized teaching is not sugar-coated pedagogy. It is not a case of "every idea is equally useful." Instead, the instructor and class members can work hard to puzzle meanings together, to reflect on the differences, to give evidence for their choices, and to evaluate the evidence further.

A fourth guideline for personalizing teaching and learning is to *instigate dialogue and interaction.* An interactive classroom can counter, or complement, the traditional model of college-teaching-as-lecturing. As mentioned in a previous chapter, Freire (2000) describes the traditional approach as the banking deposit method, in that the teacher's role is to fill students up with knowledge by making deposits of information. The students then store up the deposits, produce them at the required times (e.g., on tests), and come to envision knowledge as the exclusive province of experts like the teacher.

By contrast, Friere challenges instructors to shift to a midwife model of creating knowledge, in which the instructor helps students give birth to their own ideas by asking questions, encouraging free writing, and assigning reflection papers, to name a few examples. Such a model gives learners opportunities to gain confidence in their ideas and voices. In the dialogical classroom, instructors encourage students, during discussions, to participate in what Peter Elbow (2005) calls the *believing game.* There they consider, or temporarily believe in,

others' ideas seriously before challenging them. Elbow calls merely critiquing ideas to find their flaws the *doubting game.*

Methods for promoting interaction include discussions, buzz groups, and cooperative learning (McKeachie et al., 2006). When instructors ask a question, they might encourage participation by simply waiting at least five seconds for student responses. To promote student-to-student interaction, instructors can respond to a student statement by inquiring, "Who else has a view?" rather than commenting on each student's contribution. To further encourage learner contributions, instructors might occasionally invite every student to comment on a topic. Those comments might reflect uncertainty, or make a connection to other students' ideas, or take the form of a question. I present specific methods for leading discussions in Chapter 5.

*Enthusiasm* is a fifth dimension for creating a personalized environment. When instructors and students alike show excitement and emotion about ideas, learning becomes more potent. Such enthusiasm might extend beyond ideas to, in hooks's (1994) words, "interest in one another, in hearing one another's voices, in recognizing one another's presence" (p. 8). In many academic circles, showing excitement for ideas and for each other is considered to be a *transgression of boundaries* (hooks, 1994). In that vein, excitement in the traditional objectivist classroom may be viewed with suspicion or be seen as disruptive to the serious atmosphere that is assumed to be necessary for learning. However, in fact, learning becomes more potent in emotionally charged situations. Therefore, in the personalized constructivist classroom, instructors and students collectively aim to generate, show, and maintain enthusiasm.

Instructors might also extend their personal presence through being transparent at times, by *sharing the teaching methods* with the class along with the processes used to decide on those methods. Sinacore et al. (1999) describe how and why this might be done: "By reviewing not only the content of a syllabus but also the thinking behind the choices inherent in creating one, teachers make overt and public how and why they make the choices they do" (p. 268). "Giving away the method" of deciding takes away the aura of authority from teachers and allows students to be fellow deciders. In fact, instructors can give up further control by asking students to choose preferred methods and content from a menu of possibilities. The course itself can even be partly constructed by the students. For instance, students might suggest some of the course content areas, decide on the content of papers or group projects, or offer feedback on how the learning process is working for them and what could be added to make it more effective.

A seventh method of personalizing learning is to *offer individualized feedback and responses* on papers, recorded counseling session transcripts, and reflection journals, to name a few examples. Such feedback is a simple, although labor-intensive, way of helping students think critically about their ideas. In guided reflection (Sprinthall & Sprinthall, 1981), for example, instructors both affirm student ideas by being very specific about what works or is helpful (i.e., support) and challenge students to be self-authorizing (Kegan, 1998). To challenge, instructors can ask epistemology-evoking questions such as "What is another way to consider this idea?" and "How did you come to decide on this point of view?"

A final element in personalizing teaching is simply to *be accessible*. In Chickering and Reisser's (1993) words, "Frequent student-faculty contact in and out of classes is the most important factor in student motivation and involvement" (p. 374). Those authors share a few simple instructor strategies for increasing such contact: encourage students to drop by the office to ask questions or to discuss a topic; be willing to mentor students on career issues and personal concerns; share your own experiences, attitudes, and values; and know students by name within the first few weeks of the term.

Lest my enthusiasm for personalizing teaching appear overzealous, a proviso is needed. Sound learning can occur through lecture, and reason is a useful method for analysis. Personalizing instruction is not an invitation to reduce rigor. Instructors must challenge students to construct and give evidence for ideas. With that said, a personalized learning environment can engage learners who are often confident and enthusiastic in their desire and ability to construct knowledge.

# Guideline 4—Emphasize multiple perspectives

The work of counseling is characterized, like much professional work, by ambiguous situations in which important decisions must be made. To be effective, counselors must be able to reflect in action (Schön, 1983), that is, recognize their assumptions and weigh alternatives in the moment. In particular, they must account for the gender, ethnic, social class, and other cultural discourses that might influence their thinking. For example, a counselor may think, "This woman is gay and has been rejected by her family. I assume that she must be depressed and angry. But wait, she might have achieved some acceptance of that situation. Yet there is likely to be some hurt. I wonder what her gay identity status is. I must keep all of this in mind. I also have to watch my tendency to want to rescue her, as this kind of situation was an issue for me." While counselors can be guided by general theories of human change, each situation calls for unique formulations. Simplistic and rote answers are not helpful.

For this reason, counselors must learn to consider multiple perspectives on situations that they encounter. A notion that can help in this regard is dialectical thinking, that is, seeking out alternate formulations of a situation and attempting to incorporate those views into decisions on how to act (Basseches, 1984). Dialectical thinking helps preclude single-minded decision making. For instance, counselors might consider individual, cultural, situational, and personal factors that affect situations or cases at hand. A psychodynamically oriented counselor might, as a result of considering alternate perspectives, recognize the value of referring a client who is suffering from posttraumatic stress to behavioral exposure therapy. Indeed, taking multiple perspectives goes hand in hand with integrative thinking.

One way for instructors to encourage multiple perspective taking is to explore differing foundations of the curricular material. Instructors can ask, "What are the assumptions of this counseling theory?" "What are the limits of this helping method?" "What cultural worldview is this family counseling approach based on?" "How might this career theory have a gender bias?" "How might this diagnosis be fraught with potential class or gender bias?" In particular, an emphasis on cultural dimensions in counseling offers students a forum for serious consideration of the differing perspectives represented by gender, ability, race, religion, ethnicity, class, and sexual orientation as they relate to counseling. In response to cultural perspectives, a counselor educator can act as a "critical pedagogue," a teacher who helps students change their "stagnant or stereotypical views" about groups other than their own (Kanpol, 1994, p. 43).

The counseling theories course is a natural source of curricular material for examining multiple perspectives. At last count, over four hundred different counseling theories existed. For many students, the sheer abundance of solutions for helping presents a considerable epistemological challenge. Students sometimes complain, "If so many experts view this business of counseling in such radically different ways, surely some are at least posturing, if not dead wrong." If a teacher can support this confusion and challenge students to develop a means of wading through the theories, students can "tip over" to a relativistic understanding (Perry, 1999) that theories are only approximations. They can recognize that, in the business of becoming a counselor, selection of and commitment to a theoretical stance is helpful but not a final, unchangeable decision.

Other courses and topics, of course, offer additional possibilities for multiple perspective taking. Instructors can present the debates about the validity of assessment methods and diagnosis. They can explore controversies about legal matters and ethical dilemmas. In the counseling skills course and practicum, teachers can pose the perplexing quandary of giving directives to clients while also being person centered. Finally, the multicultural counseling course is rich with diversity of values and customs, all of which can be workable in their contexts. All of these topics and more present likely opportunities for exploring multiple perspectives.

A caution is in order. The multiple perspectives approach may be too easy a match for multiplistic thinkers, who are characterized by an "anything goes" understanding of knowledge (Perry, 1999). Those thinkers believe that everyone is simply entitled to her or his opinion. They will further drown in a sea of multiplicity if differing perspectives are merely offered side by side, without evidence or context for use. Students must learn that,

while multiple perspectives are explored and possibilities investigated, a counselor must make decisions based on one's current understanding of their usefulness.

# Guideline 5—Value approximation over precision

The work of counseling requires the counselor to maintain a tentative, emergent understanding of clients and the helping process. The work of counseling contrasts with that of fields such as computer technology, accounting, language instruction, and rocket science, each of which requires a higher level of precision in most situations.

First, and continually, counselors must allow their assessment of clients to surface. Approximation means hearing an emerging client story and formulating a response in the moment. Counselors must then launch tentatively into the waters of intervention, changing course with shifts in conditions. They must pause before intervening, lest they provide hasty nostrums for spurious concerns.

In fact, most social science constructions are actually approximations. For example, in the area of personality, a person is more or less extraverted or introverted (Quenk, 2000) or enterprising or investigative (Holland, 1997), to name a couple of examples. In the area of culture, approximation and tentativeness are especially important. Women are not categorically connected knowers (Belenky et al., 1986), Asians are not universally linked to extended families, and middle-class persons are not always achievement oriented, to name some common generalizations about groups. In the area of quantitative research, Type I errors (false positives) are often a result of the researcher prematurely declaring certainty. All concepts are themselves constructions, limited by the discourse from which they generate (Gergen, 1999).

To help students live with approximations, counselor educators can encourage students to *pause* and *speak in measured tones* (Belenky et al., 1986). Instructors can therefore encourage students to problematize what once seemed simple. For example, the teacher might ask, "Is the abstinence model of addiction treatment so effective? What about the harm reduction model instead?" Educators can model approximation in internship seminars by offering their own emerging case conceptualizations and offering counterevidence for their and others' conclusions. In fact, teaching basic helping skills, such as use of open questions and empathic responding, encourages students to stay with a partial and emergent understanding of the client's experience. In these ways, students learn that their constructs are always contingent—upon the lenses of their moods, cultures, procedures for deciding, personality styles, genders, and generation, among others.

There are a number of additional ways that counselor educators might encourage approximation. For example, they can introduce brainstorming, allowing all ideas to be aired, as part of staffing a case during fieldwork seminars (McAuliffe, 2004). Instructors' responses to students' contributions in class and to assignments can also demonstrate the value of approximation. During discussions, teachers can show respect for the partially formed ideas that students generate, by reflecting students' ideas and letting the class examine their viability. In these ways, educators encourage an ever-emerging and almost always revisable understanding, rather than premature closure on a seemingly known, static truth.

## Guideline 6—Recognize that conflict and dialectic are the norm. Encourage their expression

"Conflict is the norm?" readers might ask. "Why? Avoiding, or at least stifling, conflict is the norm for most people." Of course this is commonly the case, whether it consists of aversion to entertaining one's own doubt or encountering interpersonal conflict. However, this guideline asks counselor educators to help students embrace conflict. A previous section introduced the notion of dialectical thinking as a way of embracing and considering multiple perspectives. Dialectical thinking depends on seeking out contradiction to one's point of view or understanding. It is not easy to do. Most individuals prefer settlement rather than turbulence.

By contrast, Guideline 6 asks individuals to postpone the solace of harmony in favor of reaping the benefits of working through conflict. It asks counselors to, at least temporarily, live in the discomfort of conflict. This guideline asks counselor educators to help students face the conflict inherent in intra- and interpersonal learning. Perhaps the ancient Greeks captured the inevitability of conflict in their notion of *agon*, which refers to struggle or contest. One example of agon is the unstructured process group. Students squirm when the facilitator points out a tension in the room, but they manage to live through it. Similarly, in the counseling skills class, students learn to sit with the discomfort of clients' pain and doubt, learning that they cannot provide easy fixes for them. Studying difficult material well is itself an example of agon, as the learner must live with not knowing and struggle with more complex understandings through effortful dedication.

Counseling work itself is characterized by dynamic tensions. There are discrepancies between what the client seems to want and what the counselor perceives, between conflicting client impulses, between and among members of couples and families. Counselors must be able to engage conflict, from being with the rancor of disputing couples to handling the anger of a parent. In some cases, being able to live with agon might save a client's life, as when a counselor directly confronts a client's suicidal ideation by asking the client the bold, direct question, "Are you thinking of killing yourself?"

Learners might need help to see the advantage of working through conflict. Counselor educators, therefore, can encourage students to embrace conflict and dialectic as a norm. They can do so in a number of ways. First, they might ask students to assess their learned ways of dealing with, or avoiding, conflict. Second, they can model comfort with conflict. For example, they might verbalize a negative feeling in the classroom over an issue by saying, "I sense some tension in the room about this assignment. Would anyone like to bring it out in the open?" Another opportunity to model the embrace of conflict is to invite counterviews on any issue in a class. For example, in the social and cultural issues course, alternate views on affirmative action, privilege, and customs can be invited and then guided into respectful discourse.

# Guideline 7—Question categorical thinking

Making simple classifications in everyday life is convenient. Clients may make pejorative generalizations about themselves, such as "damaged," "stupid," or "hopeless." An adolescent is declared to be "bad." Peers call each other "nerds" or "jocks." A counselor labels a client "a narcissist." A family is called "dysfunctional." Such categorizing saves mental energy. But categorical thinking carries with it three dangers: reification, totalizing, and bifurcation.

**Reification.** The first hazard of categories is the reification of a mere label, that is, treating the words as if they represent a real thing. In this vein, the philosopher Richard Rorty (1989) warned about the ease of using thick, rigid vocabulary to describe phenomena. Individuals toss out such words as *professionalism, manners, decency,* or *superego* as if those labels represented objective, unquestionable entities. With those words, the individual often valorizes or demonizes a concept or a group of people. They are often seen as nonnegotiable. They are not seen as human constructions of a time and place. Instead, Rorty proposes that thin, flexible words be used, ones that can be applied to many concrete expressions. Therefore, "acting like a gentleman," which is a cultural norm, can be translated into the more flexible principle of "respect for others." A person can commit to a principle instead of a reified category.

Such a distinction can be made in counseling work. When diagnosing, counselors might use terms in an inflexible, rigid way, failing to recognize the elusive phenomenon that they are trying to describe. For them, the client *is* a "borderline," rather than "There are elements that I see in his lability and instability that seem to match some of the characteristics of the current construction called Borderline Personality Disorder." That second sentence takes more work, but is more nuanced.

**Totalizing.** The second danger of categorical thinking is totalizing, or seeing the whole person or behavior as fitting into a category. Thus, one person is called "intelligent" and another "stupid," as if those are total explanations of those two individuals in all arenas. A more nuanced sentiment might be "He shows the ability to solve certain problems, especially logical-mathematical ones. I wonder how he does with words. In what situations? What about his insight into people and social situations?" In the counseling field, such categories as "codependent," "enabling," "disorder," "addict," and "disabled" have been used rigidly, as if the labels fully represent the person.

**Bifurcation.** The final limiting dimension of categorical thinking is that it bifurcates phenomena, that is, treats them in either/or fashion. Thus someone who is "good" is the opposite of being "bad." In categorical thinking, there is no room for shades of gray and continua. Opposites abound: "enemy" or "friend," "believer" or "infidel," "good theory" or "bad theory," "behaviorist" or "nonbehaviorist." Rarely do such absolute dichotomies represent the complexity of phenomena.

To consistently question categorical thinking is to recognize one's own subjectivity, to be reflective about claims of "truth," to inhabit a socially constructed universe. In this universe, categories are to be treated as approximations, words that represent something that can never be known directly.

Some of the most sacred mental health categories can be presented as approximations, not as actual representations of phenomena. Yet students do not necessarily recognize that diagnostic categories are the product of a compromise decision made by a group of thinkers at one time in history and culture. Those individuals decided that a particular label would be applied to people who demonstrated a particular pattern of emotion, thinking, and behavior. The *Diagnostic and Statistical Manual* itself acknowledges the social construction of diagnostic categories, in a sense, by marking criteria for a diagnosis.

Therefore, it can't literally be said that a person "has" a mental disorder, such as dysthymia. Instead, counselors can treat the category as a shorthand. Dysthymia is a socially constructed category that represents an agreed-upon number of criteria, such as poor appetite, insomnia, fatigue, and consistent low mood for a long period of time. To counter this reification of socially constructed categories, counselors might use the phrase *diagnostic impression,* which acknowledges the subjectivity and approximation involved in the process.

Counselors can help themselves avoid categorical thinking by deconstructing their own reifications and generalizations. They can qualify their pronouncements with, "As it seems to me now . . ." or "The story I tell of this client . . . " or "From one perspective. . . ." Counselors can regularly ask themselves (e.g., in the context of a case conceptualization or a cultural characterization), "How is this view limited? How might others' experiences be different from the story that I have told?"

Such noncategorical thinking may be applied to each course in the counseling curriculum, not just the diagnosis course. For example, theories can be treated as approximations that the counselor selects tentatively to allow for the inclusion of interventions from other theoretical perspectives. Discussion of ethical dilemmas offers the chance for students to understand the influence of context and situation on interpreting guidelines. Individual and group counseling skills courses, practica, and internships offer real-world opportunities for challenging absolute categories. Students can be helped to see that phenomena are messy, even though categories allow humans to talk to each other in shorthand.

## Guideline 8—Show commitment in the face of doubt

The previous four guidelines ask students to be flexible and open-ended in their thinking. However, professional work is full of both big and small decisions that must be made. Counselors must take action in the world, often under uncertain conditions. They need a process for weighing evidence and a process for deciding.

This guideline gives the lie to the charges that counseling is value-free and that constructivism is an anything-goes multiplistic morass. Intellectual relativism does not necessarily imply moral equivocation. It is quite the opposite. A thoughtful relativism is associated with active moral concern, as the research of Kohlberg (1981), Rest (1995), and others attests.

Counselor educators can model the making of such commitments in a number of ways. For example, in counseling skills and internship courses, faculty can offer case conceptualizations, even diagnoses, however contingently. In the counseling skills course, instructors can help students act on their hunches when they are working with clients, while simultaneously challenging those students to find evidence for their inclinations. In another example, counselor educators can show commitment to equity in their daily words and actions. In addition, they can share their decision-making process for choosing readings and assignments in the face of multiple possibilities. All are examples of commitments in relativism (Perry, 1999).

## Guideline 9—Encourage intrapersonal process awareness, or metacognition

Metacognition consists of the "conscious monitoring of one's thought processes" (Henderson, 1996, p. 21). It might be seen as self-reflection. Metacognition requires the ability to reflect on one's immediate impressions and thoughts, evaluating one's internal experiences and searching for their causes. It is characteristic of relativistic-thinking counselors (McAuliffe & Lovell, 2006). This "thinking about their thinking" allows counselors to step back from experience and reflect on and evaluate it. As a result, metacognition enables intentional action or changes in behavior to occur when they are needed. Metacognition is what allows counselors to recognize countertransference and projections.

Students themselves need to learn to attend to their inner states as cues. For instance, one student reflected, "I felt so bored with this client. I could hardly stay awake. What was it she was doing that I reacted to? What *in me* drew such a performance? What can I do at moments like this while still being alert to my 'automatic' reactions?" Metacognition in this instance led to the student's awareness of countertransference. Counselor educators and supervisors often encourage counselor trainees to consistently go meta, that is, be self-reflective, in the actual course of an interaction. As a result, supervisors hope that trainees will be able to simultaneously consider their own personal history, immediate reactions, and client triggers for those reactions during a session.

Students' metacognitive abilities might increase in a number of ways. For instance, counselor supervisors might use the Interpersonal Process Recall (IPR) method. In IPR, the instructor asks trainees to identify their cognitions and feelings at any one point in a session (Kagan & Kagan, 1990). In addition, to increase metacognition, instructors might also regularly ask students during supervision to examine their own motivations, agendas, and countertransferences. Instructors might also ask students to write ongoing reflective commentaries on their session transcripts. Further, instructors might model their own inner processing, including internal debates, ambiguities, and uncertainties.

Of course, counselor educators can themselves also be metacognitive. They can reflect on their motivations, impulses, and automatic tendencies. For instance, an instructor might think, "I have a tendency to pronounce and entertain in front of the class. And I like playing the expert too. In fact, often I get threatened when my ideas are challenged." This educator might follow up such reflections with, "My playing the expert role does not empower learners, which is central to my job. I must challenge myself to give up the clever performance and take risks. I will open up discussion and questions more often, even take the risk of trying small-group activities and simulations in class."

# Guideline 10—Accent interpersonal process commentary, or metalogue

This last guideline also draws attention to process, that is, paying attention to the underlying issues and dynamics of an event. Process is the *how* of an event. It contrasts to content, or the *what*. Thus, in paying attention to interpersonal process, what a person says is of less interest than where in an interaction it occurs and what its intent is. A focus on the interpersonal process brings out the dynamics of the social system. Thus, in a relationship, a person might ask, "Did you give the children supper yet?" (the content). But based on intent, the context, and past dynamics, that request might represent an attempt at controlling the other person (the process). Metalogue represents the conscious monitoring of interpersonal dynamics and social processes at work among people.

The centrality of interpersonal process in the work of counseling is obvious to most, except perhaps for the most ardent behaviorist. This guideline charges counselor educators with directing students' attention, usually through questioning, to here-and-now interpersonal dynamics.

Metalogue is a natural focus in the group counseling course, in which instructors help students pay special attention to interpersonal dynamics. But instructors can ask students in any course to reflect on the interpersonal process—during small discussion groups or during the class in general. For instance, the instructor might ask, "Who played what role in the small-group discussion? Who played mediator, instigator, gatekeeper, leader?" The ensuing conversation itself becomes the metalogue, or the talk about the talk. In any class, the instructor might ask metalogue-evoking questions such as "What was the tone of our discussion?" "What was productive about it?" "What contributed to its being productive?" In this way, students learn to talk about the talk in ways that they can transfer to counseling work.

Group projects offer particular opportunities for interpersonal processing. Educators well know the struggle and frustration that students experience if their small group fails to function adequately and as a result falls behind in getting its project finished. To preclude such occurrences, instructors might prepare students for small-group work by alerting them to potential conflicts and by teaching them ways to ensure a functioning group (e.g., fair distribution of the workload, check-in opportunities regarding whether there are any concerns). Instructors might also mediate disputes in small groups, even choosing to process student group concerns during class. They might also, on any occasion, note and check in on "the feeling of the group." In any course, instructors can inquire about the here-and-now interpersonal relations and the overall social arrangements in class, with questions such as "What is going on in the room right now? What is important to pay attention to?" and "What are some group/interpersonal/social dynamics in this class?" (e.g., seating patterns by gender or ethnicity).

## ACTIVITY 3.1    GENERATING EXAMPLES OF THE 10 GUIDELINES

Review the preceding guidelines, and then do one of two things: (1) Observe a class with the intention of noting examples of any of the guidelines, or (2) generate an example from your own student or teaching learning experience that utilized each of the guidelines. The learning experience might be a conference session, a class session, a whole course, or another experience.

Value and promote **experience**.

Vary the **structure**.

**Personalize** teaching.

Emphasize **multiple** perspectives.

Value **approximation** over precision.

Recognize that **conflict** and **dialectic** are the norm. Encourage their expression.

Question **categorical** thinking.

Show **commitment** in the face of doubt.

Encourage **intrapersonal** process awareness, or metacognition.

Accent **interpersonal** process commentary, or metalogue.

## CONCLUSION

This chapter has presented two sets of guidelines for preparing counselors in an experiential, egalitarian fashion. Readers might use these ideas as instigations or inspirations to take risks. The results of those risks might be to create the next generation of counselors who can authorize their ideas, cooperate with others, and engage in reflective practice.

## REFERENCES

Bandura, A. (1986). *Social foundations of thought and action: A social cognitive theory.* Englewood Cliffs, NJ: Prentice Hall.

Basseches, M. (1984). *Dialectical thinking and adult development.* Norwood, NJ: Ablex.

Baxter Magolda, M. (2000). *Teaching to promote intellectual and personal maturity: Incorporating students' worldviews and identities into the learning process.* San Francisco: Jossey-Bass.

Belenky, M., Clinchy, B., Goldberger, N., & Tarule, J. (1986). *Women's ways of knowing.* New York: Basic Books.

Brookfield, S. (2006). *The skillful teacher: On technique, trust, and responsiveness in the classroom.* San Francisco: Jossey-Bass.

Brown, J. S., Collins, A., & Duguid, P. (1989). Situated cognition and the culture of learning. *Educational Researcher, 18,* 32–42.

Chickering, A., & Reisser, L. (1993). *Education and identity* (2nd ed.). San Francisco: Jossey Bass.

Craik, F. I. M., & Tulving, E. (1975). Depth of processing and the retention of words in episodic memory. *Journal of Experimental Psychology: General, 104,* 268–294.

Dewey, J. (1963). *Experience and education.* New York: Collier. (Original work published 1938)

Elbow, P. (2005). Bringing the rhetoric of assent and the believing game together—And into the classroom. *College English, 67,* 388–399.

Freire, P. (2000). *Pedagogy of the oppressed.* New York: Continuum.

Gergen, K. (1999). *An invitation to social construction.* Thousand Oaks, CA: Sage.

Henderson, J. G. (1996). *Reflective teaching: The study of your constructivist practices* (2nd ed.) Englewood Cliffs, NJ: Merrill.

Holland, J. (1997). *Making vocational choices: A theory of vocational personalities and work environments.* Odessa, FL: Psychological Assessment Resources.

hooks, b. (1994). *Teaching to transgress: Education as the practice of freedom.* New York: Routledge.

Ivey, A. E., Ivey, M. B., & Zalaquett, C. (2010). *Intentional interviewing and counseling* (7th ed.). Belmont, CA: Brooks-Cole.

Kagan, N., & Kagan, H. (1990). IPR: A validated model for the 1990s and beyond. *The Counseling Psychologist, 18,* 436–440.

Kanpol, B. (1994). *Critical pedagogy: An introduction.* Westport, CT: Bergin & Garvey.

Kegan, R. (1998). *In over our heads: The mental demands of modern life.* Cambridge, MA: Harvard University Press.

Knefelkamp, L. (1984). Developmental instruction. In L. L. Knefelkamp & R. R. Golec (Eds.), *A workbook for using the P-T-P Model* (pp. 29–35). Unpublished document developed for use in the University of Maryland Counseling and Personnel Services Department.

Kohlberg, L. (1981). *The philosophy of moral development: Moral stages and the idea of justice.* San Francisco: Harper & Row.

Kolb, D. (1984). *Experiential learning: Experience as the source of learning and development.* Englewood Cliffs, NJ: Prentice Hall.

Magner, D. K. (1999, September 8). The graying professoriate. *The Chronicle of Higher Education,* pp. A18–19.

McAuliffe, G. J. (2004). The constructive-developmental internship seminar: A hothouse for powerful student learning. *Human Service Education, 24,* 33–47.

McAuliffe, G. J., & Lovell, C. W. (2006). The influence of counselor epistemology on the helping interview: A qualitative study. *Journal of Counseling and Development, 8,* 308–317.

McKeachie, W. J., Svinicki, M. D., & Hofer, B. K. (2006). *Teaching tips.* Boston: Houghton Mifflin.

Mesulam, M. (2000). *Principles of behavioral and cognitive neurology.* New York: Oxford University Press.

Perry, W. G. (1999). *Forms of intellectual and ethical development in the college years.* New York: Holt, Rinehart & Winston.

Quenk, N. L. (2000). *Essentials of Myers-Briggs Type Indicator assessment.* Hoboken, NJ: John Wiley & Sons.

Rest, J. (1995). Notes for an aspiring researcher in moral development theory and practice. *Moral Education Forum, 20,* 11–14.

Rogers, C. R. (1983). *Freedom to learn for the 80's.* Columbus, OH: Merrill.

Rorty, R. (1989). *Contingency, irony, and solidarity.* New York: Cambridge University Press.

Schniedewind, N. (1987). Feminist values: Guidelines for teaching methodology in women's studies. In I. Shor (Ed.), *Freire for the classroom: A sourcebook for liberatory teaching* (pp. 170–179). Portsmouth, NH: Boynton/Cook.

Schön, D. (1983). *The reflective practitioner: How professionals think in action.* New York: Basic Books.

Sinacore, A. L., Blaisure, K. R., Justin, M., Healy, P., & Brawer, S. (1999). Promoting reflexivity in the classroom. *Teaching of Psychology, 26,* 267–270.

Sprinthall, R. C., & Sprinthall, N. A. (1981). *Educational psychology: A developmental approach.* Reading, MA: Addison-Wesley.

Vella, J. (2002). *Learning to listen, learning to teach: The power of dialogue in educating adults* (Rev. ed.). San Francisco: Jossey-Bass.

# 4

# Who Are the Learners?
# Phases of Counselor Development

Garrett J. McAuliffe

The beginning student in the counseling skills class is typically brimming with energy, somewhat anxious, and often confused by this seemingly exotic endeavor of helping. The intern is also excited and fearful, but about competence. The beginning practitioner is typically confident, perhaps too much so. The veteran counselor relies on stored knowledge to respond to clients, responding less self-consciously to client concerns. And so it goes through the counselor's career span. Each season of a counselor's life has characteristic emotions and attitudes, doubts and clarities. Or so Thomas Skovholt and Michael Rønnestad have proposed, based on their extensive study of counselors at all phases of development.

Since the learning needs of counselors and students of counseling change as they move through their careers, educators and supervisors must shift their strategies accordingly. The goal of this chapter is to describe the phases of counselor development, with an emphasis on the early phases, so that counselor educators can match their work to counselors' evolving learning needs.

## COUNSELOR DEVELOPMENT: PHASES

One of the great advances in understanding human behavior in the past 50 years has been in the area of adult development. In the past, the psychological action was seen as residing in childhood and adolescence. Adulthood was viewed as a long, uneventful playing-out of themes originating in early life. However, in the second half of the 20th century, interest in the phases and psychosocial tasks of adulthood emerged, particularly through the classic work of such thinkers as Erik Erikson (1978), Daniel Levinson (Levinson, 1978; Levinson & Levinson, 1996), and Donald Super (1963).

That work has been extended into the domain of counseling (Rønnestad & Skovholt, 2003; Skovholt, 2001; Skovholt & Rønnestad, 1995, 2003) in the form of the Phases of Therapist/Counselor Development (PTCD) model. (Note: the authors' names will be used in varying order, parallel to how they switch such order in their publications.) Skovholt and Rønnestad's work complements the other major phase theory of counselor development, the pioneering Integrated Developmental Model (IDM) of Stoltenberg, McNeill, and Delworth (1998). To provide a simple introduction to counselor phase development for the purposes of this volume, only Skovholt and Rønnestad's PCTD model will be described. Readers are invited to examine the IDM for a complementary view of counselor developmental tasks and domains of functioning throughout the career span.

Knowing the phases of a trainee's development can guide counselor educators and supervisors in selecting strategies that match the phase of a trainee's career life. Phases are related to characteristic emotions, thoughts, and behaviors. Knowing the tasks associated with each phase can also help counselor educators or supervisors in their efforts to coach counselors appropriately, so as to prevent stagnation and burnout. Such difficulties in professional life are reminders that positive counselor development is not inevitable, but is contingent on tasks and attitudes that must accompany each phase. The PTCD model can alert counselors to the developmental tasks needed to remain competent and energized.

In addition to identifying the phases that counselors go through during the course of their career, Rønnestad and Skovholt identified themes that pervade counselor development. I will begin by discussing the themes, then the phases. Four themes that are especially relevant for counselor education are discussed next; they can serve as a guide for counselor educators about the processes that they can influence in their teaching and supervision.

## IMPORTANT THEMES IN COUNSELOR DEVELOPMENT

Based on their qualitative study of over a hundred students and practitioners of counseling, Skovholt and Rønnestad (1995) proposed the following themes in counselor development.

First, Rønnestad and Skovholt indicate that, in their careers, counselors move from *greater externality* to *greater internality*. As will be seen in the upcoming description of the phases, in the early phases of counselor development, counselors-to-be are somewhat, and understandably, external and concrete. They generally rely on prescriptive rules and models for helping. Eventually, they internalize and integrate the many inputs of counseling models, assessment tools, and intervention techniques into their own style and show greater flexibility. This movement toward internality parallels a larger constructive developmental evolution that Belenky, Clinchy, Goldberger, and Tarule (1986) call *constructive knowing*, in which thinkers see approximation as the goal, not the precision of an absolute truth that applies in all situations. Guidelines 2 (varying structure) and 5 (valuing approximation) from Chapter 3 are particularly useful for increasing such internality.

High structure supports the learning needs of new students of counseling. Counselor educators can offer, for instance, step-by-step directions about how to implement skills and theories before asking students to use their judgment. Educators can also model counseling work themselves through demonstrations. Students will at first seem merely to imitate the models, and they will need to do so at first. However, they can soon be challenged to respond more creatively if they are put into ambiguous situations—for instance, role plays, cases that require critical thinking, and exercises that ask students to respond to ambiguous situations.

The second of the four themes to be discussed here is that, in order to develop, counselors need to be *reflective and committed to learning*. In Rønnestad and Skovholt's research, those counselors who developed did so by nondefensively questioning their practices and motivations as well as by asking others for feedback. By contrast, counselors who defended themselves against new learning stagnated. In light of this finding, counselor educators should help students recognize the value of remaining open to new experiences throughout their careers. Educators can model their own reflectiveness and subsequent evolution as professionals. They can also provide students with opportunities for reflection. For example, instructors can assign students to do personal journaling in response to readings and exercises.

A third theme of particular relevance to counselor education is *the presence and role of affect* in counselor development. The first noticeable emotion is anxiety. Students experience significant apprehension during the Beginning and Advanced Student phases as well the Novice Professional phase. The pressure of being evaluated, by themselves and others, the high stakes of working with distressed people, and the seeming amorphousness of the counseling situation all conspire to create anxiety. Counselor educators need to understand this anxiety and provide affirmation and structure early in counselors' careers.

A second type of affect in the early-phase are counselors' strong emotional responses to their professional elders, including their instructors. Early-phase counselors commonly have both pronounced positive and negative feelings, much like adolescents' responses to parents. This phenomenon seems to be related to counselor educators' roles as both models and evaluators. Rønnestad and Skovholt (2003) comment on the intensity of student responses:

> Strong admiration is expressed for those more advanced in the profession who possess behaviors or personal characteristics that are perceived as highly positive, such as intellectual brilliance, strong therapeutic skills, outstanding supervision ability, unusual emotional support for beginners, and the modeling of professional values in personal life. The interviewees informed us that negative reactions to professional elders were just as common and just as intense. Devaluation seems to occur at the same intensity level as idealization. Being in a dependent and relatively low power position is the fuel that propels the sometimes strong reaction. Professional elders are devalued if they possess behaviors perceived as highly negative. These include individuals such as a supervisor who is perceived as unfairly critical or a professor who teaches counseling but seems unable to practice it. (pp. 36–37)

Graduate students commonly experience some disenchantment with their education, especially in the area of learning concrete specifics for doing the work. Some of that criticism might be legitimate and a reminder of a missing-but-needed dimension of counselor education. The devaluation, however, is a reminder for educators to be developmentally supportive and to be transparent and nondefensive. In doing so, they become models for future counselors to avoid defensiveness. Overall, given these findings, counselor educators need to recognize the power students see in them. They should not overreact to either admiration or disparagement.

The fourth theme that is of particular interest for counselor education lies in the finding that *counselors'*

*personal lives are a major source of learning and support for professional work.* In particular, adversity in counselors' lives is valuable for becoming a better counselor. This finding led Rønnestad and Skovholt to suggest that suffering and wisdom may be interconnected. Fruitful outcomes of intense personal experiences included "increased ability to understand and relate to clients, increased tolerance and patience, heightened credibility as models, and greater awareness of what is effective helping" (Rønnestad & Skovholt, 2003, p. 35).

Positive personal life experiences also influence counselor development. Long-term caring relationships such as life partnerships and other sources of life satisfaction contribute to effective work with clients. In response to these findings, counselor educators might remind trainees to live deeply outside of the academic or work setting, as well as to get emotional support and to process life difficulties in ways that produce helpful insights.

Counselor educators can maximize the potential of students' personal experience for learning in a number of ways. Guideline 3 in Chapter 3 emphasizes the importance of personalization, as do notions of connected teaching in the work of Belenky et al. (1986), hooks (1994), and Vella (2002).

Reflection on personal experience can be asked for in a number of courses, such as the lifespan development and helping skills classes. Personal reflection is sometimes triggered by readings and text exercises. It can also be solicited after classroom sessions and small-group encounters, via "do-now" writing and message board commentaries, and other forms of journaling. Finally, counselor educators might also occasionally share dimensions of their own personal lives and struggles, when it might be helpful to the learning process. Students gain confidence in their ideas and in their personhoods from more transparent teachers (Belenky et al., 1986; hooks, 1994; Vella, 2002).

Rønnestad and Skovholt found that other individuals also assist students in reflecting on their negative and positive life experiences. For instance, educators can encourage students to learn from their own counseling, their colleagues, and their clients, not merely from readings, lectures, and conferences.

# THE PHASES OF THERAPIST/COUNSELOR DEVELOPMENT MODEL

The four themes previously discussed pervade all the phases of counselor development, which will now be presented in abridged form so that counselor educators might match their interventions with counselors' developmental needs.

As mentioned earlier, the PTCD model is based on a qualitative empirical study of one hundred counselors at different levels of experience. Rønnestad and Skovholt (2003) were curious, in their words, about "whether counselors/therapists develop as they gain more experience" (p. 7). The result was the model of six phases of counselor development that will be described shortly. But first, one overall finding must be mentioned.

Rønnestad and Skovholt (2003) concluded that positive development as a counselor is not automatic. Consistent with the second theme, described in the previous section, they said, "Continuous reflection is a prerequisite for optimal learning and professional development at all levels of experience" (p. 38). This "attitude of openness to new learning" (p. 39) distinguishes high-functioning students and counselors from stagnant and deteriorating counselors. This finding is noteworthy for counselor educators and supervisors, as they have a role in influencing students and supervisees to be contemplative and self-evaluative in their work.

As we explore the phases, certain ones will be of particular interest to counselor educators. These are the four early phases, which address the characteristics and tasks of new students and beginning counselors: Lay Helper, Beginning Student, Advanced Student, and Novice Professional.

## The Lay Helper Phase

Readers may remember their own attempts at helping before training. Such is the state for most students on the first day of the counseling skills class. The student in the Lay Helper phase is the untutored, pretraining "wannabe" counselor who arrives fresh to counselor education without any formal training in helping skills or theories. Lay Helpers may have, in the past, helped others as a friend, parent, or colleague. They may or may not have been a client at some point in the past. In either case, Lay Helpers rely at this point on whatever commonsense understandings they have about helping others.

Lay Helpers usually have four ways of helping: "to define the problem quickly, to provide strong emotional support, to provide sympathy, in contrast to empathy, and to give advice based on their own experience" (Rønnestad & Skovholt, 2003, pp. 28–29). Such is the haste to solve problems for Lay Helpers.

During this phase, the counselor-in-training defines the problem simply as the client's response to the counselor's first question, such as "What brings you to counseling?" Since Lay Helpers now know what the problem is, they feel quite confident that the time has arrived to offer advice. Thus, for example, a client concern about not getting a raise might be followed by "Have you asked your boss for a raise?" Or a child's concern about being bullied might be followed quickly by "You should stand up for yourself with that bully." In their offering of sympathetic support or simple advice, Lay Helpers can easily blur boundaries, becoming overly identified with clients and overly involved in fixing clients. They are soon disabused of the "immediate solution" fantasy that they may have held.

## The Beginning Student Phase

Now begins the conundrum as the learner in the Beginning Student phase asks, "How am I to be sufficiently helpful to another in such an ambiguous undertaking? I believe in this work, I am motivated to learn it, but this is really hard. I can't just memorize a formula for helping." Beginning Students demonstrate two seemingly contradictory impulses: enthusiasm for the new venture and intimidation about the complex tasks of professional counseling. So, in addition to passion, they often feel overwhelmed by the counseling ethos itself, particularly by its contrast to everyday discourse.

The tenuousness of new ventures takes its toll. For one, Beginning Students find themselves inundated by many novel ideas. Also, they often feel daunted by the challenges of balancing their personal lives with a heavy load of schoolwork and of establishing relationships with professors and new peers.

Most students in this phase wonder about what Rønnestad and Skovholt (2003) called their "suitability" for the field. The very idea of a counseling session often seems overwhelming. It may appear unbearably amorphous to them.

*Self-focus.* As a result, they are self-focused in the Beginning Student phase. They commonly ruminate on "What do I do or say?" "When do I say it?" and "How do I fill the time?" They have no stored repertoire for how to respond to clients in various circumstances. Skovholt and Rønnestad (1995) quote one student from their interviews: "At times I was so busy thinking about the instructions given in class and in the textbooks, that I barely heard the client" (p. 27). Beginning Students can hardly pay attention to clients, because they are so focused on their own concerns about responding "correctly" (Stoltenberg et al., 1998).

*Pleasing the client.* As part of this self-focus, beginning phase students want to please their clients with their work. They want clients to like them. These fantasies are not tenable in the long run for good, challenging counseling in which confronting client discrepancies is important.

*Teaching the Beginning Student.* What can counselor educators do to support and challenge learners in the Beginning Student phase? At least three themes need to be kept in mind: structure, modeling, and feedback.

In general, Beginning Students need high levels of structure in teaching and materials. Teaching and materials can first teach concepts in a linear and simple fashion. They can then layer in complexity. For example, counseling theories can be taught one at a time before they are compared and contrasted. In the helping relationships (skills) course, single counseling microskills can be introduced one by one before they are fully integrated (e.g., Ivey, Ivey, & Zalaquett, 2010). Clear guidelines for conducting a session, such as the use of a counseling skills scale to guide counseling behaviors (e.g., Eriksen & McAuliffe, 2003), offer Beginning Students the supportive structure that they need at this phase. Finally, in the case of teaching ethics, students in the introductory course can first learn the ethical guidelines and then later work on "fuzzy" cases, those in which ethical dilemmas present themselves. In sum, simple, straightforward introductions to ideas provide a foundation

for Beginning Students and improve confidence. Then complexity can be introduced.

Regarding the need for modeling, learners in the Beginning Student phase demonstrate a "true believer" dimension. They are eager to emulate and imitate models in the field, including the instructor, to attend to the message "This is the 'right' way to do things." Beginning Students may adopt a temporary counseling persona in response to watching an instructor or a renowned counselor whom they have read about or seen on video. Instructors can maximize this inclination to imitate by creating opportunities for vicarious learning through demonstrating, assigning field observations, and showing video-recorded sessions.

Beginning Students have other tasks at this phase as well. In order to develop, they must learn to take an open, self-reflective stance. They can be encouraged to avoid defensiveness or avoid acting in a way that is foreclosed. Skovholt and Rønnestad found that defensiveness leads to stagnation. However, Beginning Students may find openness to feedback to be difficult at times, as the competitive nature of academia may promote the tendency to "look good." Such impression management (Rønnestad & Skovholt, 2003) precludes the benefits that might otherwise be gained from constructive feedback, self-reflection, and risk taking. Instructors can counter the Beginning Student's inclinations to look good by modeling their own uncertainty and imperfection (Belenky et al., 1986), providing a nonhostile learning environment, and giving students multiple chances to succeed, with feedback offered between attempts.

## The Advanced Student Phase

Counselors-to-be continue to share the needs and characteristics of Beginning Students until they confront actual practice. That occurs in this next Advanced Student phase, which coincides with practicum and/or internship. Individuals find this phase to be another abrupt challenge. They are stretching their emotional and intellectual boundaries. They waver between vulnerability and confidence.

Eight of the themes that emerge at this phase will now be discussed in more detail: feelings of vulnerability versus emerging confidence, growing internality versus the need for external guidance, handling ambiguity, setting boundaries, having inadequate conceptual maps, disillusionment, orientation to a counseling theory, and need for intensive supervision and training. Skovholt and Rønnestad (2003) elaborated on their description of this phase in their article "Struggles of the Novice Counselor and Therapist." Some of these themes characterize both this phase and the next one, but they will be discussed here, as they are most vividly experienced in the Advanced Student phase.

*Vulnerability versus confidence.* A central theme of the Advanced Student phase is the experience of vulnerability. Students feel significant pressure to meet the graduate program requirements. There is a paradox here, when not-knowing meets need-to-know due to having to perform. A counselor's ability to feel vulnerable and to continue to learn while trying expertly to meet client needs requires the counselor to balance autonomy and dependence. Thus, Advanced Students need to, on the one hand, make relatively autonomous counseling decisions with clients while, on the other hand, relying on others for affirmation and instruction.

As an expression of insecurity, some students may hide their doubts, perhaps only revealing "good" counseling performances to supervisors. To counter this tendency, it is important for supervisors to provide a safe environment. The typically grade-free environment of many graduate internship seminars helps interns experience the freedom to "not know" and to reveal uncertainties while taking risks.

Students' emerging comfort with the basics of helping at this phase contrasts with the extreme reliance on instructor and supervisor direction of the previous phase. Therefore, individuals in the Advanced Student phase have greater trust in their ability to handle relatively straightforward cases, such as clients with decision-making, interpersonal conflict, and grief issues. Greater confidence in basic helping skills prevents Advanced Students from feeling completely daunted by the amorphousness of the counseling encounter. Thus, these counselors can usually "sit with" a client's struggles for as long as is needed.

*Growing internality versus the need for external guidance.* On one hand, individuals at the Advanced Student phase still need direct instruction, feedback, and modeling. However, they often complain that they don't get much opportunity to observe advanced practitioners during this time. To meet their needs, educators should provide opportunities for observation of other practitioners, encourage students to attend conference presentations, and offer students written guides for practice. The typical Advanced Student will devour these new ideas and suggestions for practice. In that vein, Rønnestad and Skovholt (2003) found that Advanced Students particularly desire opportunities to learn by watching advanced practitioners, attending conferences and other trainings, or receiving intensive supervision.

On the other hand, individuals in the Advanced Student phase also become increasingly internal. They now are beginning to exercise their own judgment about desirable counseling approaches. In fact, they are more willing to critique the instructor's feedback and instruction. Thus, the students' locus of control moves inward, at least in the counseling domain, during this phase.

Consistent with this increasing internality, the Advanced Student phase is a time of self-exploration. Students now more readily reflect on the influence of their own personalities on the work, their countertransferences and any defensiveness. Supervisors can facilitate this reflectiveness by asking students to monitor their internal responses to clients and to themselves. Such metacognition can be encouraged in a number of ways. Instructors might encourage students to openly share doubts. In observing student sessions, supervisors may probe for counselor affect and motivation. They can encourage reflective journaling. In isomorphic fashion, supervisors might model reflection, questioning, and interpretation in supervision sessions in order to challenge students to consider the impact of their emotional responses and learning histories on their work.

*Handling ambiguity.* Above all else, the ambiguity of the work of counseling can be overwhelming to Advanced Students, as well as to the new professional. For example, in internship, students might see all of the following early in their field experience: lonely transfer students, course change pleas, student conflict with teachers, sexuality dilemmas, student violence, and more. The work requires the almost simultaneous consideration of multiple frameworks (e.g., client, self, culture, in-room process, family, theories).

As a result of these factors, counselors cannot follow a rigid formula for practice, but must instead respond to clients' situations in the moment. As a result of these demands, counselors cannot use only their rational, intellectual faculties to work with clients. Counselors must trust hunches and other partially formed emotional promptings in order to act wisely. Those abilities contrast with the academic aptitudes that many students bring to the training program. In Skovholt and Rønnestad's (2003) words, "Many students are admitted to graduate school in the counseling and therapy professions because they excel at mastering the intellectual content in academic classes. However, this skill set does not translate directly to the complexity of practice" (p. 46).

To help new counselors, supervisors can model and teach the art of a counselor's handling ambiguity. New counselors can be helped to access their emotional responses, hunches, and other information within sessions. Instructors and supervisors can offer interns close, moment-to-moment supervision in order to teach them about the range of options available for any particular circumstance. Students might therefore learn to avoid formulaic and overly rigid responses. Subsequent chapters, especially Chapter 16, on teaching practicum and internship, offer counselor educators ideas about how to put these principles into action.

*Setting boundaries.* The emotional nature of counseling requires a delicate balancing act. Beginning helpers can teeter anywhere between the two extremes of (1) being overinvolved emotionally, in which case they might be consumed with clients' problems, feeling troubled outside of the session about the client's situation, and (2) being too emotionally detached, in which case they do not engage sufficiently with a client's emotions and are, as a result, less empathic than they need to be. Instead, counselors have to learn to engage optimally, which Skovholt (2001) refers to as the *cycle of caring*: at first empathically joining with clients, then challenging while supporting clients, and, finally, separating again and again from each client. Counselor educators need to help students to be alert to their own thoughts and feelings and to catch themselves when being too over- or underinvolved.

*Having inadequate conceptual maps.* Most beginning counselors approach their first encounters with clients, perhaps in practicum, armed with textbook knowledge and some role play experiences. Skovholt and Rønnestad compare this condition to the case of the novice canoeist who suddenly encounters whitewater rapids. The novice must somehow remain collected while wanting to panic. Similarly, each client tells a real, big-as-life story, and few formulaic answers exist. Much of the counselor's experience of being bewildered cannot be avoided. However, instructors and supervisors can help counselors anticipate some situations, as in cases when the client cries, or emotions need to be de-escalated, or concrete facts must be found. Many times, classic empathic responding has to suffice, along with some questions, until the counselor learns a better mental map of where to go.

There is no way for beginning counselors to evade these moments; they have to go through them. Otherwise, counselors may become stagnated or try to avoid difficult cases and uncomfortable moments. Some of the conceptual maps can be taught early in the program, such as a five-stage structure for an interview (Ivey et al., 2010). Others can be learned through self-reflection and supervision. Early learning can then be applied to future situations.

Despite the normative quality of this experience, beginning counselors will inevitably be somewhat dissatisfied with their training program for not preparing them sufficiently. In Skovholt and Rønnestad's (2003) words, "There is almost universal criticism by individuals at this point, with criticism directed to the courses, the professors, or the entire program. It is as if the novice is saying, 'If I was better trained, I wouldn't feel so lost and so incompetent'" (p. 54).

Counselor educators can heed this complaint and try to ensure that relevant learning experiences are available in the program, but they also can alert students to the inevitability of fluidity in the work. Counselor educators can also help by ensuring that interns receive less intense cases, are given some conceptual maps on how to manage sessions, and experience strong, close supervision. These supports assist the Advanced Student in persisting.

*Disillusionment (expecting too much).* Counselors enter the field because they want to positively affect lives.

But client change is slow. New counselors are surprised that clients remain stuck, resist changing, and fall back to old patterns. It was so much easier when they were counseling classmates in the skills class. They might ask, "Why am I doing this if no one seems to be changing?" This discovery can cause disillusionment in Advanced Students. Beginners must learn to give themselves credit for their good work, even when clients struggle or seemingly stagnate. Supervisors can help counselors see clients' momentary insights, exceptions to previous behavior, and long-term changes, even helping counselors think about the negative experiences clients avoided by participating in counseling. Supervisors can urge beginners to take the long-term view, perhaps by having counselors recall their own experiences as clients. Advanced students might note the support, risk-taking, and learning that resulted from being clients themselves, even if the learning was not always obvious at the time. Supervisors can also remind beginning counselors of the overall positive effects of counseling work, as evidenced by large-scale studies of counseling outcomes (Wampold, 2001).

*Orientation to a counseling theory.* Individuals at this phase must deal with the important question of a guiding theory. Rønnestad and Skovholt found that counselors take one of four orientations toward counseling theory at this phase. The first two are desirable, the last two problematic (Orlinsky & Rønnestad, 2005): (1) commitment to one theory but open to others, (2) making serial attachments to theories, (3) being laissez-faire with no commitment to theory, (4) being a "true believer" who fiercely defends one approach while rejecting others. Both the commitment to one theory with openness and serial attachment tendencies are associated with higher-quality counselor-client relationships than the laissez-faire and true believer orientations. In response to the laissez-faire student, supervisors could ask that the student adopt and commit to one theory for the course of the semester to allow full immersion in and understanding of the theory, before changing course to experience another. In the case of the foreclosed theoretical orientation, supervisors might challenge a counselor's rigid adherence to one method and offer alternate strategies. Group supervision that encourages peers to provide feedback and varied ideas can be especially helpful in this regard.

*Need for intensive supervision and training.* Students should not be left to drift during this crucial period, or they might not develop the needed competencies and self-awareness to become effective counselors. Without the give-and-take of intensive supervision, stagnation as a counselor looms as a possibility. Without the ongoing challenges and personal changes that result from intensive supervision, Advanced Students might leave training with a sense of "faking it." In addition to providing close critique of Advanced Students' work, supervisors also need to be affirming, noting how far students have come. In that way, the inevitable feelings of vulnerability and not knowing enough can be tempered by confidence and hope.

## The Novice Professional Phase

Although Rønnestad and Skovholt describe two phases of counselor development beyond the Novice Professional phase—Experienced Professional and Senior Professional—the Novice Professional phase will be the last phase presented here in detail, as this is the last phase of particular interest to counselor educators and the purpose of this book.

The Novice Professional phase occurs most commonly after students have completed the training program and are in the early part of their first job. This phase can be of interest to educators and supervisors because it sheds light on the preparation success of students' programs of study. It also tells counselor educators how their programs of study might need to be changed in order to better prepare counselors for their first jobs.

I will next present five themes that Skovholt and Rønnestad (2003) found in many counselors who were in the Novice Professional phase: need for further learning, finding one's own style, making a readjustment, learning to set boundaries, and desire for mentoring.

*Need for further learning.* Skovholt and Rønnestad found that Novice Professionals often assume that their educations have been complete and that they should be able to apply their training to most situations, without significant supervision. That expectation then meets the reality of the difficulty of the work. Instead, a sense of being underprepared to do the hard work of counseling often accompanies the first employment situation.

Counselors in the Novice Professional phase have to face the fact that their current skills do not work with all clients and issues. Beginning practitioners realize how much they have to learn in order to be effective with varied clients. Novice Professionals are then confronted with the limits of their existing approaches to helping. For example, Novice Professionals realize their lack of expertise in a number of areas, ranging from organizational protocols (e.g., procedures for emergencies in a particular setting) to specific psychological issues (e.g., how to respond to severe depression or psychoses). The new counselor may be heard to say, "I wasn't taught specifically how to work with [eating disorders, addictions, anger issues, anxiety disorders, etc.]." Clearly, learning must continue beyond graduate school.

*Finding one's own style.* These postgraduation surprises can be healthy alerts that urge counselors toward further self-reflection, personal counseling, and additional training. The surprises may also serve as opportunities to appreciate and optimize their own style. They can find their own combinations of informality, verbosity, calmness, liveliness, humor, seriousness, emotionality, or intellectuality, to name a few examples.

*Making a readjustment.* However, Skovholt and Rønnestad found that if there is a mismatch between the requirements of counseling work and the novice's personality, a major readjustment needs to occur. The adjustment might be as significant as changing actual occupations or as minor as specializing in certain types of clients and issues. It can also lead to taking on a management role in the organization.

Accordingly, supervisors can help counselors in the Novice Professional phase to use these early years to explore work environments that best match their capacities, personality, or interests, whether they be private practice, employment agencies, human relations departments, schools, agencies, or colleges.

*Learning to set boundaries.* Additional internal reflection is likely to be needed at this phase in the area of setting boundaries with clients. Although counselors may begin with the desire to help all clients and to do so with endless effort and energy, they increasingly recognize that they are not solely responsible for client improvement. This new awareness reduces the pressure on them. In particular, it helps Novice Professionals tighten their boundaries.

Tighter boundaries mean that sessions end in a timely fashion and home phone numbers stay private, rather than being given to clients. Novices, upon personal reflection, typically loosen up, allowing their sense of humor to infiltrate their work more often.

*Desire for mentoring.* Counselors in the Novice Professional phase typically report the desire for a mentor. Some licensure stipulations require intensive supervision; in other cases, counselors must obtain mentoring informally. Not all supervisors are successful at mentoring, however. Therefore, counselors should seek out such opportunities. Counselor educators and supervisors should promote strong mentoring early in the career of counselors in any way they can.

## CONCLUSION

The learning needs of counselors and students of counseling are not static; these needs change as they move through their careers. Therefore, counselor educators and supervisors must know the emerging and evolving needs of counselors-to-be at various phases in order to match and mismatch them for optimal learning.

## REFERENCES

Belenky, M. F., Clinchy, B. M., Goldberger, N. R., & Tarule, J. M. (1986). *Women's ways of knowing.* New York: Basic Books.

Eriksen, K. P., & McAuliffe, G. J. (2003). A measure of counselor competency. *Counselor Education and Supervision, 43,* 120–133.

Erikson, E. H. (1978). *Adulthood: Essays.* New York: Norton.

hooks, b. (1994). *Teaching to transgress: Education as the practice of freedom.* New York: Routledge.

Ivey, A. E., Ivey, M. B., & Zalaquett, C. (2010). *Intentional interviewing and counseling.* Belmont, CA: Brooks/Cole.

Levinson, D. J. (1978). *The seasons of a man's life.* New York: Knopf.

Levinson, D. J., & Levinson, J. D. (1996*). The seasons of a woman's life.* New York: Knopf.

Orlinsky, D. E., & Rønnestad, M. H. (2005). *How psychotherapists develop: A study of therapeutic work and professional growth.* Washington, DC: American Psychological Association.

Rønnestad, M. H., & Skovholt, T. M. (2003). The journey of the counselor and therapist: Research findings and perspectives on professional development. *Journal of Career Development, 30,* 5–44.

Skovholt, T. M. (2001). *The resilient practitioner: Burnout prevention and self-care strategies for counselors, therapists, teachers, and health professionals.* Boston: Allyn & Bacon.

Skovholt, T. M., & Rønnestad, M. H. (1995). *The evolving professional self: Stages and themes in therapist and counselor development.* New York: John Wiley & Sons.

Skovholt, T. M., & Rønnestad, M. H. (2003). Struggles of the novice counselor and therapist. *Journal of Career Development, 30,* 45–58.

Stoltenberg, C. D, McNeill. B., & Delworth, U. (1998). *IDM supervision: An integrated developmental model for supervising counselors and therapists.* San Francisco: Jossey-Bass.

Super, D. E. (1963). *Career development: Self-concept theory essays in vocational development.* New York: College Entrance Examination Board.

Vella, J. (2002). *Learning to listen, learning to teach: The power of dialogue in educating adults* (Rev. ed.). San Francisco: Jossey-Bass.

Wampold, B. E. (2001). *The great psychotherapy debate: Models, methods, and findings.* Mahwah, NJ: Lawrence Erlbaum.

# 5

# A Primer on Six Key Teaching Strategies

## Lecturing, Discussion, Questioning, Small Groups, Reading and Writing, and Improvisation

### Garrett J. McAuliffe

*What once appeared as the most effective and efficient way to teach and learn—the research university model of faculty who create knowledge and deliver it to students through lectures—falters under today's learning demands and with today's students. . . . [W]hat we know about human learning all argue[s] for using classroom strategies that actively involve students.*

Bette LaSere Erickson and Diane W. Strommer (2005, p. 249)

In the previous chapters, I made a case for an experientially based, socially constructed, and developmental counselor education. That case included some guidelines for teaching. But now it is time for specifics. When I was a schoolteacher, I would hear my colleagues say at conferences, "These reform ideas are all well and good. But what do I do on Monday?" It is a legitimate question. The moment-to-moment, day-to-day practice of teaching requires specific strategies. Educational philosophy is not enough. Instructors must make choices about content and process, they must create syllabi, and they must design assignments.

This chapter presents six sets of strategies for counselor education practice: lecturing, discussion, questioning, small groups, reading and writing, and improvisation. The strategies are presented within a constructivist and developmental framework.

## LECTURING

At this point readers might be thinking, "What? Lecture? What a way to kill enthusiasm and disempower students. Lecture tells students that the authority figure has all the knowledge, and that they must somehow receive it from her, only to spew back at a later time." Zealous humanistic and constructivist educators might mutter this disapproval. They might continue, "The lecture is dead. 'The sage on the stage' has been discredited in favor of 'the guide on the side.'" They might also challenge, "How can a teacher-centered method like lecturing ever fit in a book that is dedicated to constructivism and a field like counselor education, where the action must be in the learners so that they can make decisions in ambiguous situations?" These concerns may be good warnings. On the other hand, they may not acknowledge the value of the good lecture as a means of instigating curiosity and increasing understanding.

While it seems counterintuitive, lecture, thoughtfully designed and integrated into teaching, can be part of the construction. But educators must lecture well if they are to do it. First, I will remind readers of the reasons for not exclusively lecturing.

## Reasons for Not Lecturing

The major limit of lecturing is that there is less retention from lectures than from discussions and from more active means of learning (McKeachie, Svinicki, & Hofer, 2006). Lectures by themselves suffer from the lack of direct connection with experience. Therefore, students may find it more difficult to transfer lecture-based learning into practice.

Lectures are also inferior to reading in terms of retention. In reading, learners often work harder to fill in the blanks with their own understandings. In reading, students can pause, restate, write notes, and review at their own pace. All of these involve more active brain processes than are often used when hearing lectures.

Finally, lectures can be "deadly." The lecture may put students into a "velvet rut" in which the soporific drone in the background puts them to sleep. Dull presentation of otherwise powerful ideas can smother the fire of interest in students. Lecture provides little opportunity for high affect except on the part of the lecturer, who is usually having the most interesting time and who, ironically, is usually learning the most. It should be noted that students typically maintain high interest for no more than 10 minutes of a lecture. Lectures do not easily provide for the interest and effort that Dewey proposed as important for significant learning (see Chapter 2).

## Reasons for Lecturing

If educators eschew lecturing altogether in their commitment to more constructivist teaching, they are perhaps misunderstanding constructivism. Constructivism has broad shoulders. It is not a method; it is a guide.

The central notion of constructivism, as described in Chapter 1, is that the action is in the learner, and all are learners, including educators themselves. Let me reiterate two key points from Chapter 1: Social constructionism emphasizes the community creation of knowledge, not the "finding" of truth; and developmental constructivism asks educators to challenge *how* learners are thinking. Both approaches ask for teachers and students to be engaged in dialogue—with each other, with texts, with clients—which encourages equality among learners.

While it may seem counterintuitive, lecture *can* be part of the construction if it is thoughtfully designed and integrated into other methods. I will draw on the work of Wilbert McKeachie and colleagues (2006), Jerome Freiberg and Amy Driscoll (2005), and David Royse (2001) to describe the conditions for effective lecturing.

Lecture should be an intentionally chosen teaching method, decided upon from among options because it best achieves the learning goals. Like all teaching methods, it should not be chosen by default. And if done, it should not be a mere regurgitation of material that has already been read in a text.

If lecture is the method of choice, it offers at least seven advantages for learning: motivation, relevance, critical thinking, integration, modeling of thinking, common frame of reference, and efficiency. First, lecture can motivate, even inspire, listeners, as readers might remember from their own occasional experiences with engaging speakers. Second, it can provide up-to-date information that is not available in standard texts, which by necessity cannot be completely current. Third, lecture can stimulate critical thinking, especially if it is combined with questions that evoke student critique and ask students to give evidence for their ideas. (Such discussion-leading questions will be discussed in the next section.) Fourth, lecture can bring together material that is scattered across multiple sources, and it can link ideas to a particular domain (e.g., connecting research methods with counseling practice). Fifth, through lecture, students can observe models of thinking in action as the instructor works out his ideas and even shows uncertainty. Such modeling of incompleteness is encouraging to students, who often only see the finished product of a lecturer's well-prepared thoughts (Belenky, Clinchy, Goldberger, & Tarule, 1986). Sixth, lecture provides a common frame of reference to all students, from which discussion and follow-up projects can be launched. Finally, lecture is efficient, as a great deal of content can be covered in a short period of time.

## Guidelines for Lecturing

Lectures often fail because they are poorly organized, indifferently delivered, and seemingly irrelevant to students' interests. Instructors can minimize the negative aspects of lecture. If, after weighing the pros and cons above, instructors choose to lecture, or even to periodically present a mini-lecture, then they should note the following guidelines in order to keep lectures vibrant and help students make better sense of the material.

*Decide on the purpose of a lecture.* If the intention is to help students critically think about a topic, that is a good reason for a lecture. If it is to merely summarize knowledge presented in the reading, it is just as well that students only read the material.

*Prepare well.* Know the material. Read the original material, then find and/or review supplemental information, jotting down or highlighting key ideas. Find interesting background information on the topic, such as the origins of a counseling theory and the biography of its founder(s).

*Keep it simple.* Try to get no more than three or four major points across in one lecture.

*Start with a question, a problem, or a case,* and ask the class how they would deal with it. Then connect the problem, question, or case to the concepts on which you are lecturing. One example with which I am familiar lies in the case of the qualitative research instructor who brought in the contents of his trash baskets at home and asked students to decide what they could learn about the person from examining these articles. He then went on to lecture on how to analyze qualitative data.

*In the introduction, give an overview of the topic and the learning goals.* Include why it is important to do a lecture at this point.

*Provide a logical and hierarchical organization of concepts.* Present major points and then evidence supporting them. Do not digress. Do not report disconnected facts. Use previews (signposts) to tell students what is coming up. Indicate transitions from one topic to another.

*Connect the content* to previous and subsequent topics and classes and to applications that the students might engage in, such as projects, papers, and field experiences.

*Use examples.* Avoid too much abstraction. Ground concepts in concrete illustrations that connect to students' knowledge and experience, if possible. "Over-abstraction" is a major flaw of lecturing and a reason for poor retention, understanding, and application.

*Exhibit enthusiasm.* Don't lead with world-weariness, cynicism, or your own boredom with the topic. Enthusiasm and spontaneity arise from the bed of solid preparation.

*Vary nonverbals.* Make eye contact, move around, vary your voice, and use gestures. Do not read notes verbatim when lecturing.

*Keep an appropriate pace.* Match the students' level of understanding, as there is a danger of going too fast when you know a topic well. Don't overstimulate. Summarize periodically. Check in regularly with students about their level of understanding and whether they have any questions or comments.

*Vary the presentation.* Use humor. Pause at key points, punctuating an especially important concept with voice tone or gestures. Physically move to a different space to introduce another or an important topic. Go to the board to post ideas. That allows for more of a pause than does projected material. Do not merely read projected slides. Pause after a while for a few minutes to let pairs of students share notes and comments on what they understand up to that point.

*Use audiovisual media.* Access at least one sense besides hearing. Students report that they greatly appreciate projected visual material, such as slides and handouts. They also appreciate recordings of counseling sessions. However, keep slides simple. Busy slides are ineffective. Verbally expand on the slide content with definitions, explanations, and examples.

*Combine lecture with other methods,* such as demonstration (e.g., of empathic responding) or role play (e.g., of solution-focused counseling). Some other methods that can be combined with lecture include problem posting, that is, asking students what the problems are in a certain area (e.g., "What are some of the consequences of career indecision?" "What happened one time when you didn't feel listened to?"), the "minute paper" (midway through the lecture, ask students to write for one minute on a topic from the lecture), pairing students up to discuss what key points are striking them from a lecture, and discussion of a key set of questions in small groups.

## Mixing Lecture With Other Teaching Strategies

The following example demonstrates the idea of mixing a lecture with four other teaching strategies: beginning a class session by posing a problem, then using analogies as illustration, asking questions, and planning an activity. The topic of this example is John Holland's (1997) career theory of matching personality and environment. Many adult education principles from the previous chapters are embedded in this illustration, such as personalizing, stimulating reflection, requiring critique, incorporating affect, and instigating experience.

In this session on Holland's personality theory, I might begin by asking students to write down a job or activity that they disliked and the reasons for their displeasure (*problem posing*). I would post these reasons on the board. I would then share an analogy about colors or shapes and matching, for example, being a "blue" person in a "red" environment, or a "square peg" trying to fit into a "round hole" (*analogy illustration*).

After this concrete and personalized simple beginning, I would begin the lecture itself by linking to the previous activities, reminding them that matching is a central notion in Holland's theory. I would bring in the affective dimension by pointing out their distress in these previously named disliked jobs. I would then connect this distress to the mismatch between the job and their interests and abilities.

I would then provide an overview and/or an outline of the presentation. I would begin with simple notions—such as Holland's basic postulates—and end up with the complexities of congruence and differentiation in his hexagon of the six personality/environment stereotypes. I would also at some point share the origins of the theory in prior personality theory.

I would next illustrate Holland's six types by noting the probable Holland codes (i.e., dominant personality tendencies) of famous people or characters from popular media. I would share my enthusiasm for the explanatory power of the model (or the danger of its misuse). I would illustrate the theory further by telling of my own job dissatisfactions that emanated from the mismatch between my personality and my work environments; my discomfort in some Realistic-Conventional settings, such as auto repair garages; or my relative distaste for (and ineptitude in) Realistic and Conventional activities, such as house repair and financial record keeping.

In addition, I would extend the textbook material by showing students how the Holland codes can be used to assess career dissatisfaction. And I would ask them to think critically about the limits of the Self-Directed Search, which might underestimate some individuals' potentials, especially those from the nondominant gender or socioeconomic class, because past experience partially predicts test results. During the next class session, we would return to critiquing the theory and its uses.

I would next shift to a personalized activity, asking students to work in groups to discuss their own results on the previously taken Self Directed Search and to play with implied occupations in the Occupations Finder. Thus, they would engage in active experimentation (Kolb, 1984) in a number of ways. Finally, I would have students integrate Holland's model into their later class projects, such as doing a career self-assessment or an informational interview with a worker from a career that they might like to pursue.

By the end of this class session, the students would share a common foundation for further discussion and attempts to apply the theory. I would have no guarantee that they heard what I said, however. I would need to assess their understanding by direct inquiry, which might consist of having them write down the main points, as they conceive of them, at the end of the session or later through electronic submission.

## DISCUSSION

A second common method of teaching is leading discussions. Of course discussion can also be combined with lecture and other teaching methods.

# Advantages of Discussion

Discussion serves at least five purposes: building community, enhancing relativism, offering clarification, generating activity, and increasing affect.

First, discussion can create a community of learners. Belenky et al. (1986) called such a discussion-oriented space the *connected classroom*, a topic that is discussed in detail in Chapter 3.

Second, discussions have a development-enhancing power, as they put social construction into action. In that process, discussion promotes relativism (Perry, 1999), as students see knowledge emerging from a process of hypothesizing, weighing evidence, considering alternate perspectives, and reaching tentative conclusions as peers puzzle a problem. In contrast, if the instructor regularly "deposits" the content and gives students answers to problems, students can be left disempowered, dependent on experts for knowing. When they are recipients of such deposits, students have little experience with the hard work of dialogue, that is, the work of formulating questions, listening, tendering tentative solutions, and modifying their ideas based on hearing those of others. Discussion reveals to more dualistic thinkers the possibility of thinking for themselves, as they see peers demonstrate how to think and manage uncertainty. The capacity to use self-defined methods to "know" is the essence of relativistic, or self-authorized, knowing, as discussed in Chapter 1.

Discussion also allows learners to share their confusion and receive immediate feedback. That clarification doesn't happen as easily when students are reading alone or listening to a lecture. Discussion is also a classic means for promoting active learning, a way of encouraging the deep processing that was discussed in Chapter 2. Finally, discussion is also affectively engaging, therefore triggering student attention.

Despite these advantages, instructors are sometimes reluctant to lead discussions. Discussions are "untidy" and unpredictable; the teacher is not in control. Conflict might occur. While the following suggestions might allay some instructor discomfort, leading discussions does involve a risk. However, it is a risk worth taking for the sake of students' development.

# Guidelines for Leading Discussions

All discussions are not equal nor the same. The following guidelines for leading discussions are drawn from the works of Freiberg and Driscoll (2005), McKeachie et al. (2006), and Royse (2001) and are grouped into three categories: before, during, and after the discussion.

## Before the Discussion

**Preparing for Discussion.** Spontaneous exchange in the classroom is to be valued. It is often timely and riveting. But the road to spontaneity is paved with preparation. For students, preparation might consist of prior reading about a topic. Instructors must similarly be prepared. After also doing the assigned reading, if that is to be a beginning basis for the discussion, instructors can formulate and plan overall questions.

**Starting Discussion.** The ways of initiating discussion that will be described here are revealing the goals of the discussion, using an opening question, and providing a common experience.

*Revealing the goals.* First, instructors should make clear to students the goals for the discussion. More dualistic students are more likely to believe that they can learn from discussion if a clear goal is presented. For example, an instructor might say, "Today I would like us to decide when it is OK to break confidentiality. We will discuss some unclear situations. At the end of the discussion, perhaps we will better understand some of the choices involved in confidentiality."

*Using an opening question.* A discussion can be simply started with a question. That question can be based on previous reading. For example, in the area of school counseling, the instructor might begin with the question, "What are the reasons that the new model of school counseling was created?" After hearing some responses, the instructor might be prepared with follow-up questions such as "What are the new model's possible advantages? Disadvantages?"

"Problem posting" offers a related way for opening the discussion with a question, one that begins with a conundrum. The reasons for a problem are explored and posted for all to see. For example, the instructor might ask, "What are some of the reasons that people have difficulty in their careers?" or "Why might people of color be mistrustful of counseling?" The instructor then would write the students' ideas on the board for all to see. Following the posting, the class can engage in a discussion of the ideas and suggest solutions to the problem. A mini-lecture on the topic might also follow.

It is recommended that the instructor start with a question that invites divergent responses rather than one simple answer. (See the upcoming section in this chapter on types of questions.) Examples of divergent questions in a school counseling class could include "How can the school counselor balance the multiple roles of counseling and advocacy? When is it important to choose one or the other? Listen to this case. Let's discuss how the counselor might perform these multiple roles." Or in a counseling skills class: "What is helpful or not helpful when you are telling someone a concern of yours? What does that indicate about what counselors might do to be helpful?" Each of these questions invites multiple possibilities.

*Providing a common experience.* A shared experience can serve as the foundation for class discussions. Examples of shared experiences might include prior student reading, a short lecture, evocation of related past experiences, issues left over from the previous class, a vignette (e.g., a segment of a video), a role play, a short reading (e.g., a poem), previously submitted student-written commentaries on the reading or issues brought up in the previous class, or transcripts of a counseling session.

Each of these common experiences can be followed by a thought-provoking question such as "What place do you think religion has in counseling?"(after showing a video in which the client brings up religion-related issues) or "How does Robert Frost's poem 'The Road Not Taken' capture the consequences of career decisions?" (after reading that poem about life decisions and their consequences) or "How would an Adlerian work with the case of an adolescent, versus a solution-focused counselor?" (after reading a case to the class).

## During the Discussion

**Encouraging Student-to-Student Talk.** First, it should be noted that discussions do not have to be teacher dominated. Teachers commonly think that they

have to respond to each student comment. However, not all discussion must occur between student and teacher in a back-and-forth pattern. In a constructivism-informed discussion, student contributions are central. In that vein, Freiberg and Driscoll (2005) warn educators: "Because most teachers see their role as being the gatekeeper during questioning, it is difficult to change roles for discussion. The discussion may become too teacher dominated, which, in fact, foils discussion" (p. 223). Discussion leaders might instead practice moderation instead of taking turns with the students. In that way, they move from the role of giver of information to facilitator of information exchange or idea exchange. Most educators have seen too few models of the latter in their own schooling. University classes are usually teacher dominated, despite the fact that adults do not need that type of authority in order to learn (Vella, 2002). In fact, teacher-dominated classrooms can hurt students' development toward self-authorized thinking (Kegan, 1998).

Discussion can instead occur between student and student, in a "star" pattern. Such a model contrasts with the teacher-as-center prototype, in which comments go from instructor to student and back to the instructor, who comments on each student contribution. Instead, teachers can encourage student-to-student talk in groups by being silent, asking "Who else has a comment?" and calling on a student with an invitation such as, "What do you think?" To illustrate: A discussion might start with an initial inquiry, problem, or case. Then the instructor waits. A student responds, either voluntarily or by being asked. Then the instructor nods, thanks the student, and waits again. The instructor does not have to comment on the student's response. The instructor doesn't always have to be an active gatekeeper.

Here are two actual examples of stunted teacher-student discussion from my experience.

### Hiring a person with a disability, take 1

Student 1: If I were a business owner, I wouldn't hire a disabled person if it required the expense of putting in a ramp.

| | |
|---|---|
| **Teacher**: | So you really think that the disabled person would have to limit her jobs to accessible facilities and that's OK? |
| **Student**: | I guess so. . . . |
| **Teacher**: | Well, that's not OK. It's not inclusive and here's why. . . . |

## Working with a gay client, take 1

| | |
|---|---|
| **Student**: | I won't work with a gay person. It's against my religion. |
| **Teacher**: | You can't say that. It's against the ethical code. |
| **Student**: | [Silence] |

Here, by contrast, are examples of student-to-student exchange for each situation:

## Hiring a person with a disability, take 2

| | |
|---|---|
| **Student 1**: | If I were a coffee shop owner, I wouldn't hire a disabled person if it required the expense of putting in a ramp. |
| **Student 2**: | But that would be discriminatory. It's everyone's responsibility to try to create a level playing field. . . . |
| **Student 1**: | That's not the business owner's job. She has to make a living. |
| **Student 2**: | I don't think it would put the owner out of business. But it would create goodwill for the community. Maybe the owner would attract more persons with disabilities if she showed such inclusiveness. |
| **Student 1**: | But it shouldn't be required of private businesses. |
| **Student 2**: | Maybe the government can create incentives without requiring it. |
| | OR |

| | |
|---|---|
| **Student 3**: | I guess it depends on whether it costs too much. |
| **Student 1**: | Maybe large businesses can do it, but small ones can't always. |
| **Student 2**: | That doesn't get rid of the moral question. They can get a loan. Find a way to make it profitable—rent it to kids as a skateboard ramp after hours! |
| | (Laughter from class) |
| **Student 1**: | That's unrealistic, but maybe the disabled employee could help the owner find an agency that would help with the cost. . . . |
| | (The students go on parrying about the dual issues of moral responsibility and business profit.) |

## Working with a gay client, take 2

| | |
|---|---|
| **Student 3**: | I won't work with a gay person. It's against my religion. |
| **Teacher**: | What do class members think? |
| **Student 4**: | We have to work with all clients. We have to work on our biases in order to do so. |
| **Student 5**: | Besides, being gay isn't a choice. So discrimination against persons who are gay is like racial discrimination. |
| **Student 3**: | But my religion forbids homosexuality. |
| **Student 4**: | I wonder if the basic principles of your religion are, in fact, more inclusive than you realize. You know, your religion might consider charity, compassion, and a just society might be more important than worries about a client's sexual orientation. |

In each of the second set of scenarios, the instructor lets students struggle, nodding occasionally, and points to students with their hands up, instead of jumping in and delivering a summary of the issues. Most of the students stay attentive. The student-speakers feel particularly engaged. They have to struggle with a fuzzy situation. They gain confidence. They might now be better able to weigh evidence in future professional problem-solving situations.

More structured ways of encouraging student-to-student exchange include creating small breakout groups for discussion of the same questions one might ask the large group and setting up online discussions. In each of these settings, students generally feel freer to speak.

### Instructor Choices in Responding to Student Comments.

Readers might now see that, after a student speaks, the instructor has a number of options for encouraging continued student involvement in the discussion. They include nonverbal acknowledgment, silence, asking for others' responses, paraphrasing the comment, asking a question of the speaker, and posing a question to the other class members.

The first options are nondirective. They are simply to acknowledge ("Thank you") and/or be quiet, or ask, "Anyone else?" These less directive responses encourage student-to-student exchange, which can be enlivening and empowering for learners.

The instructor can also continue to respond in a relatively nondirective way by paraphrasing the student's response ("So you're saying that cognitive behavioral counseling may not get to a person's core issues"). A more directive option is to probe further. The instructor might, for instance, ask the student to elaborate, expand, or give an example ("Can you think of a situation in which you would notify a parent about an adolescent whom you are seeing?").

A teacher can instigate higher-level discussion by asking questions that trigger analysis (see the next section in this chapter), as in this example: "Yes, we have heard that family loyalty is central to this culture. But suppose the client is trying to break away from family rules. How might you respond? Why?" Here is another example of an analysis prompt, this time in a counseling skills class: "So empathic responding is usually said to be helpful. Can you think of an instance when it might not be so?" It should be noted that any of these prompts can be addressed to other class members, as in "Can anyone add another or a contrary example?"

### Encouraging Involvement.

Typically, 80% of instructor prompts are responded to by 20% of the students. There are a number of ways to mitigate this effect, including norm setting, wait time, private writing time, circular seating, name cards, and inviting all students to comment.

To establish a respectful, safe environment for discussion, norms can be established early in the course and reinforced. At the forming stage for the class, the instructor can ask students for input on desired norms for discussion and post their suggestions on the board. Students often ask for respect as a norm. Instructors can also suggest norms, such as the following:

- Respect others' ideas and personhood. Use a neutral, inquiring, or affirmative tone of voice, not a hostile or disparaging one.
- Actively listen; no shuffling papers or cross-talking.
- Monitor your "air time," that is, how long and how often you talk. Such attention to group communication is also an important skill for future counselors.

The remaining strategies for encouraging involvement are more mechanical. First of all, wait time is critical. Ten seconds of silence is a recommended minimum for allowing students to formulate their ideas. Such expanded wait times result in increased length of student responses, more evidence offered in student responses, and increased participation by reportedly less "able" students (Rowe, 1976). The typical instructor wait time of only one second after asking a question often instead increases passivity in students and decreases their confidence in their intellectual abilities.

Another strategy is for the instructor to raise a question and then give students 30 seconds or so to write down their thoughts on a topic. The instructor can simply call on a particular student and ask, "What did you write?" In this way, each student is likely to be ready with a potential contribution. (More on the topic of writing to learn will be discussed later in this chapter.)

Additional ways to encourage student involvement in discussions are logistical: The instructor can arrange seats in a circular, seminar style and use name cards.

Finally, an activity that can engage more students in discussions is asking each student, in turn, to respond to a prompt on a relatively safe question. Students might be prompted to express one idea learned from the text, the last class, or the current session. Or they might be asked their opinion on a topic. This "go around" activity increases alertness with less pressure than is true for more pointed types of questioning.

### After the Discussion

At some point, the teacher can summarize the key issues throughout and toward the end of the discussion, connecting points or making a generalization about what has been discussed. The same can be done for online discussions.

To reiterate: Discussion encourages students to generate their own reasoning and ultimately to self-authorize their thinking. Professional counseling requires these capacities.

# QUESTIONING

Questioning is the classic way of actively engaging students. It was Socrates' fundamental method of teaching. While questioning was mentioned in the previous sections on lecture and discussion, it is given its own section here because it can be applied to all of the teaching methods described in this chapter. And asking good questions requires skill and intentionality. It is learned.

Asking questions does not guarantee deep thinking, however. Questions vary in their level. This topic will be presented next, followed by specific strategies for questioning.

## Levels of Questions

Some questions check simple information retention; others engage students in critical thinking. Teachers often ask only lower-order questions. Kerry (1987) found that the overwhelming majority (96.4%) of questions asked by faculty are requests for facts.

In the most common model for classroom questioning, the instructor or a text provides information and the teacher asks for a recall of facts. In this way, the instructor checks for minimal understanding, a useful strategy during "facts and skills instruction." Instructors might also probe students' memory of slightly more complex content. For example, counselor educators might ask students about the origins of the counseling field, the characteristics of Gestalt therapy, the stages of racial identity, or the sequence to be used in reflecting feelings.

By contrast, a second major value of using questions in teaching is quite different: Questions can be employed to deepen student thinking and cognitive complexity. Such deep-thinking questioning is valuable, as students who can solve complex problems and make decisions under conditions of uncertainty (see Chapter 1) will become more self-sufficient as professionals. They must be able to make choices, particularly choices in the midst of dilemmas, based on evidence. Responding to deep-level questions can prepare them for those ways of thinking.

There are six levels of questions (adapted from Bloom, 1956). Some simply ask for *information* (e.g., "Who is considered to be the founder of the counseling field?"). Others inquire about *comprehension* (e.g., "What was the original intent of the vocational guidance movement?"). Still others ask students to *apply* knowledge (e.g., "What are some examples of defense mechanisms that people might use in everyday life?" "How might you respond if a client asks you for advice on whether to seek a divorce?"). To increase complexity, a question can ask for *analysis* (e.g., "How might a counselor's empathic responding lead to greater congruence in a client's life?" "Why do you think more students of color are in special education classes?"), *synthesis* (e.g., "How are solution-focused counseling and narrative therapy similar in their basic assumptions?"), and *evaluation* (e.g., "What might the counselor be doing in this session that is unhelpful, and why?").

The higher-order questions, such as those asking for analysis, synthesis, and evaluation, are often *divergent* in their effect, in that there is more than one possible response and the responses commonly lead to discussion. After a student responds to a divergence-inviting question, the instructor can follow up by asking the student to give a rationale or evidence for her response. For example, the instructor might first ask, "What are some possible assessments of this client's situation?" and, after students respond, follow with, "Why do you think so?" After asking the divergent question, the instructor should wait at least 10 seconds for a response, because students have to analyze the question, search their memories to find relevant facts, synthesize the facts and draw a conclusion, and then speak. As mentioned earlier, the instructor can also ask students to first write down their thoughts for a few seconds, thereby engaging all students.

Other types of divergent questions include those that ask for an opinion (e.g., "What is your view on women staying at home with children while a male partner works outside of the home?"), valuing (e.g., "How do you like this type of counseling? Why?"), response to a problem (even one the instructor doesn't know the answer to, e.g., "What should a counselor do if he knows his adolescent client is selling marijuana?"), connections (e.g., "What is both a cognitive and a humanistic explanation for this client's behavior? How might they both be useful?"), and critique (e.g., "Some say that counselors should not intervene in clients' decisions to end their life. What are your views, and what evidence do you have?"). Instructors can plan various types of questions in advance, using notes to themselves as cues.

In contrast to higher-order questions, lower-order questions are often *convergent*, that is, there is one correct answer. These include fact questions, which are the most common and the easiest to answer. Fact questions can serve the function of helping students learn basic notions (e.g., "What is one defense mechanism?" "What are the stages in Perry's cognitive development theory?" "What is one thing that a career inventory can measure?"). Another type of lower-order question is personalized, in that it relates to students' feeling responses, as in "What were you feeling when you saw that client in the video speak of the abuse?" Lower-order questions are useful for involving all of the students in the discussion, as learners experience them as easier and/or safer. However, because they are convergent, they do not lead to rich discussion.

## Basic Logistics for Asking Questions

Teachers face the following choices when they use questions as a teaching tool: How to ask? Whom to ask? When to ask? Some of these issues were addressed in

the earlier section on Discussion. To add to those suggestions, below are some tips derived from Freiberg and Driscoll's (2005) review of the teaching literature:

- *Before the asking,* write your questions down. You won't always think of them spontaneously, especially higher-order questions.
- *During the asking,* ask students to explain how they arrived at answers (e.g., "Why do you think that?").
- *Have students write* their responses to questions for a few seconds before responding. This strategy ensures that all students, especially the more introverted, will generate some thoughts.
- *To evaluate the effectiveness of students' understanding,* do not rely solely on asking, "Does everyone understand?" and then depend on the responses of a few students. Many students will be reluctant to admit that they do not understand. Instead, ask students to anonymously write down an uncertainty or a question about the topic. Then you can collect them and respond.
- *Watch your voice tone.* The classic "Why?" question is often seen as a veiled criticism. Similarly, instructors might be relaying sarcasm and frustration in their voice in asking, "How did you decide that?" The teacher's voice tone in asking for evidence can be inquiring without being critical.
- *In the case of deep reasoning questions* (application, analysis, synthesis, and evaluation), wait for responses by being silent so that students have a chance to formulate their ideas.

## The Limits of Questions

For all of their potential to increase student involvement, questions generally are a teacher-centered classroom activity. They inhibit discussion when they are overused. Questions also can exclude many learners when only a few students respond, leaving the rest to drift away or feel inadequate. Many questions fail to move students toward more procedural or self-authorized knowing (see Chapter 1) when they are of the low-level recall type.

Even when questioning is challenging and inclusive, students who tend to use more dualistic (Perry, 1999) or received knowing (Belenky et al., 1986) will be frustrated by questions that call for divergent responses. Those students will expect that there is "an" answer and that the answer will be delivered eventually. Instructors need to explain the place of "facts" and the importance of pondering temporary, contextually based solutions to problems.

## Students Asking Questions

Students can be invited to *ask* probing questions as well, in addition to answering them. Instructors can merely ask, "What are your questions?" and wait. If no response is forthcoming, students can be asked to write down one question or concern they have on the topic. Or teachers might direct students to a particular issue, for example, "Write down three questions that you have about gay and lesbian issues that haven't been addressed" or "What are your questions about the possible limitations of person-centered counseling?"

This sort of invitation encourages problem finding, which contrasts with a sole focus on problem solving. Problem finding has been associated with higher levels of cognitive complexity, particularly with post-formal reasoning (Yan & Arlin, 1995). The emerging constructivist counselor (Lovell & McAuliffe, 1997), for example, would be able to examine the conventions of counseling for their limits and power and would be inclined to regularly reinvent the work.

Most students do not ask questions, however. Mars (1984) found only 60 questions being asked by students across 30 class sessions, 28 of which were fact oriented or logistical. Only two questions were "deep." Perhaps educators discourage student questioning because they fear that they won't be able to answer the inquiries. I propose that instructors take the risk and welcome student inquiry, even disagreement, for the sake of students' cognitive development.

## SMALL GROUPS

Counselor educators are familiar with small-group work in courses that are experience based, especially in the helping skills classes, group counseling courses, and internship seminars. However, counselor educators may not realize the potential of small groups for increasing engagement and retention in other courses.

**The Problem.** As described in Chapter 2, passive reception of stimuli is anathema to deep learning. In Dewey's terms, students need to have interest and engage in effort for important learning to occur. With instructor-centered teaching methods, students remain in a relatively passive mode. Students remain relatively inactive during lectures, and most are nonparticipants in large-group discussions. These differences are understandable because students vary in their verbal skills and in their ways of processing information. The quieter students often make meaning of information internally and take more time to make sense and verbalize. Some quieter students are more introverted. Other nonparticipants may doubt the validity of their own ideas. Perhaps they use a received, or dualistic, way of knowing and thus do not value thinking for themselves. In contrast to the limited-participation norm in a large group, the small-group discussion engages all students in the connected classroom (Belenky et al., 1986).

**The Benefits of Small-Group Discussions.** Small-group work has the following advantages over large group discussion and lectures: (1) Students hear multiple views rather than only those in the text or those of the instructor; (2) students learn about group process, leadership, and communication, which are "meta"-goals of counselor education; (3) students achieve understandings that the instructor doesn't have time for; and (4) students recognize the power of peers' ideas, thus enhancing their own cognitive development toward relativism. In addition, small groups (5) reduce student isolation, (6) increase deep processing, and (7) encourage all learners to take responsibility for participating in a course.

**Formats.** Small-group discussions can vary in the level of structure provided, the timing of when they occur, their duration, and in their composition.

*Structure.* Less- and more-structured formats can be designed for group work. On the low-structure level, instructors can ask ad hoc groups of two to six students to discuss a central idea from the lesson (e.g., "What constitutes a good career decision?" "What is helpful for another person to do when you have a concern?" "How is trust an issue in cross-cultural counseling situations?").

Students in the small groups can generate their own ideas based on previous reading, experience, or both. They can then report to the larger group the main ideas that they have generated. By contrast, in more structured small-group discussions, the instructor usually provides a series of questions to which students respond and/or presents a dilemma or case. Further, in this case, the instructor might ask the group to reach a consensus or to comment on its interpersonal process. The teacher directs the students to report their responses or consensus to the larger group, perhaps on poster paper for all to see.

*Timing.* The timing of small-group work can also vary. Small groups can form early in, during, or after a class session. In the first case, a class session can begin with a small-group discussion, followed by a lecture on the topic. The prelecture small-group discussion might consist of students sharing their perceptions of the most important ideas in the assigned reading. Each group can then report back to the large group after about five minutes, and the instructor can post the ideas. This activity increases student attention and motivation to attend to the lecture by establishing an anticipatory mental set for the main points of the lecture. It also encourages all of the students to voice their thoughts when the class is large. In either case, all students in a prelecture small-group discussion become engaged in the topic of the day right away.

Small-group discussions can also occur during or after a lecture or large-group discussion. The instructor can stop the lecture and direct students to discuss the relevant topic in small groups. Guided by Bloom's (1956) taxonomy, the instructor can ask students to apply concepts, generate examples, connect new ideas to prior learning, and/or synthesize theories (e.g., in the latter case, group members might be asked, "How does narrative therapy share some elements with cognitive therapy?").

*Duration.* The duration of a small group's life cycle may vary as well. Simple ad hoc groups may meet only once to discuss a topic. Ongoing groups may last for part or all of a term. Such continuing groups are common in counseling skills practice sessions and in the group counseling course. In those cases, it serves the aims of the course to maintain group member continuity. Project groups, in which members do some of the work outside of class and some during class to prepare a presentation, may also last for part or all of the semester.

I recommend that project groups have occasional time to meet in class, especially as they are first forming. With that opportunity, the instructor can help the groups clarify guidelines and work out logistics. Further, such in-class project meetings help graduate students, who may live far from each other and have many other life commitments, with meeting logistics. In general, however, project groups commonly do most of their work outside of class.

*Composition.* The makeup of groups may vary. At least three strategies can be used for composing groups. They can be random, self-selected, or arranged by common interests. Random assignment is often desirable, as it enhances the possibility of ethnic, gender, and other diversity. One method of composing random groups is to ask students to count off up to the number of groups desired. Thus, if there are 24 students in class, and the instructor wishes to create groups of four, students would count off by sixes. Then, all of the students with the same number would meet together. The random method can be superior to asking students to form their own groups, which can result in groups with little to no ethnic or gender diversity, as students generally sit near others from their own cultural groups.

Another useful way of forming groups is by common interest in a topic. Whenever possible, project groups can be formed in this way, using a signup sheet. Students can put their first, second, and third choices, with the instructor making the final assignments so that the groups are relatively even in numbers. For example, in the diversity course, students might choose projects or presentations from among the topics of sexual orientation, social class, religion, and various ethnic groups, based on their prior background or interest.

Instructors can use small groups in every class of the counseling curriculum. Students find the time spent "buzzing" with peers about the course material to be stimulating and memorable. When combined with prior reading, subsequent lecture, and/or large-group discussion, learning is maximized.

# READING AND WRITING

Reading and writing are relatively private activities. Both, however, also instigate significant learning if they actively trigger deep processing.

# Reading to Learn

Reading, or better, studying, whether it is done on a computer screen or in a book, can be an active learning process. In fact, reading has been shown to be superior to lecture for learning (McKeachie et al., 2006). When reading, learners engage in a number of self-directed processing activities: pausing, thinking, recalling, translating the writer's words into their own words, going back to a concept that is poorly understood, and creating personal examples. Auditory and visual stimuli, such as lectures and videos, often move too fast for such processing.

Reading does not, however, automatically result in deep learning. Merely scanning one's eyes over a page does not result in retention. Instead, the word *studying* is better used to conceptualize the active learning processes needed for deep processing while reading. One classic formulation for studying is the PQ3R method of Preview, Question, Read, Recite, Review. (It should be noted that *read* is only one step in this technique.) In this method, learners preview upcoming material by scanning the chapter, and noting headings and figures. Next, they ask themselves questions about the upcoming reading, for example, "I wonder what Axis I of the *DSM* is?" In this way learners actively search for understanding. Third, learners read while pausing to comprehend. Then they recite, that is, look away after sections of text and speak or write the main ideas in their own words. Finally, learners review their notes and/or the chapter at the end of the study period. This method can be taught to students of counseling, perhaps in the introductory class.

Even if learners do not strictly follow the PQ3R approach, reading can still be superior to listening to a lecture or watching a video. Texts provide an organized structure for understanding what otherwise might seem like random information in a talk or in a recording. Therefore, reading is here considered a key teaching and learning method. Classroom activities, online and in-person discussions, and experiential activities might, in fact, be considered complementary to reading, rather than as substitutes for it.

*Encouraging reading.* In order to learn, students must first actually do the reading. Even graduate students may need external incentives for doing required reading. After all, students' lives are busy, and they will inevitably have to make choices about priorities, which at times may not include reading. Following are a number of strategies that encourage students to read.

To promote reading, instructors should make explicit references to the assigned reading in the subsequent class so that students know it is necessary to be prepared. Instructors can also be more active in how they encourage students to do assigned reading. Instructors can break students into small groups at the beginning of class, groups that are responsible for recalling the major points from the reading, and deciding on why they are important, and reporting their thoughts to the larger class. Alternatively, students can be asked to write a minute paper at the start of the class session, in which they name the key ideas that they got from the reading. In some cases, this minute paper serves as a pop quiz and is graded. In another method (one that I use), students submit electronic discussion board entries and responses based on the reading by the morning before the class session. In these postings, they pull out at least one idea from the reading and make a critical comment on it. The instructor then reads the commentaries before class, makes brief written comments, and refers back to the students' discussion board comments during class.

It should be clear now that reading to learn is an intentional, focused activity that can result in deep processing if it is done well.

# Writing to Learn

Writing, by its very nature, requires activity. As readers know, writing is more difficult to do than reading because it is a production task as opposed to a response task. Writing requires the construction and articulation of ideas in the learner's own words. Some examples of writing to learn have already been suggested in this chapter (e.g., the minute paper). Others will be included in subsequent chapters.

Writing serves multiple purposes. First, students can communicate with others by writing. Unfortunately, sometimes only the instructor reads student writing. It is desirable for students to share their writing at times. Writing also helps the writers themselves learn because it forces them to understand the material well enough to articulate ideas. Further, writing makes all students active in relation to the material, as compared with the passivity that is common for most students in listening to lectures and even discussions. Writing to learn can vary in its structure. Three types of writing have been distinguished: low-, middle-, and high-stakes writing.

Low-stakes writing is a particularly useful and underutilized way to enhance student engagement and processing. Students put down their ideas without editing and without being graded on correctness. Such writing can be done in or out of class. The previously mentioned out-of-class electronic discussion board commentaries on readings exemplify low-stakes writing.

In class, instructors can use low-stakes writing by asking students to express their responses to a question. In this way, instructors engage all students and give them time to think before they respond vocally. This on-the-spot writing provides time for thinking for slower verbal responders or those who are more hesitant to speak in class, which increases the likelihood that more perspectives will be heard. When the instructor subsequently calls on particular students, they can then respond more easily.

In-class low-stakes writing can be done at the beginning of the class and can be prompted in a number of ways, for example, by the instructor presenting a problem, asking students for their views on an issue, or simply inquiring about what struck students as interesting or important in the reading (e.g., "How might you engage a reluctant adolescent who has been sent to you?" "What are you thinking right now about diagnosis?" "What main points about social inequality struck you from the reading?"). Low-stakes writing can also be used in the middle of a class session, when attention seems to be flagging, and at the end of class (e.g., "What struck you in today's session?"). In case of the latter, I ask for written responses about what struck students in class each week in the electronic commentary.

Middle-stakes writing offers another relatively informal method for allowing students to reflect on ideas. A common example is the reflection paper, in which students describe and analyze personal experiences related to the topic. For example, in the family counseling course, students might write a few pages on their family-of-origin's structure and functions, perhaps adding their feelings as well. Reflection can be grade free, only being marked "yes" or "no" based on its being completed.

High-stakes writing is the familiar planned and edited paper. It too is a method for students to learn deeply. Since it is commonly discussed in the field, it will not be further explored here.

# IMPROVISATION

Instructor creativity and willingness to take risks can transform dry, abstract ideas in any subject into memorable, engaging experiences. This section introduces the notion of using improvisational activities in counseling classes. Subsequent chapters describe specific improvisational activities as they relate to particular courses in the counselor education curriculum.

The counseling curriculum, by nature of its being oriented to future practice, is fertile ground for experiential learning opportunities. In fact, at least four courses in the counseling curriculum (counseling skills, group counseling, practicum, and internship) often utilize improvisation as a matter of course. But the other courses as well, from theories through family counseling to testing and on and on, can be infused with improvisation.

Improvisation mimics actual professional work, in contrast with students reading about the work or even seeing or hearing illustrations of counseling. Improvisation is consistent with Bandura's (1986) research indicating that performance accomplishments are superior in their learning power to modeling and verbal persuasion (e.g., hearing a lecture, reading). Improvisation includes such activities as role play, simulation, and drama experiences.

Five qualities make improvisation a powerful learning tool: collaboration, inductive learning, activity, access to primary brain processes, and dialogue. First, it is collaborative in that students engage in negotiating, interacting, and offering feedback to one another. It is also commonly (but not always) induction oriented, that is, students generalize from concrete experience to generalizations. In terms of Kolb's experiential learning model (see Chapter 2), improvisation is a concrete experience that can and should lead to reflective observation, which, in turn, results in abstract conceptualization. A third quality of improvisation is that it is active; students must do something with the material beyond merely reading and writing. Fourth, improvisation engages primary processes in the brain; it triggers emotions and the five senses as students make meanings. Finally, improvisation is usually dialogical in that students exchange perceptions with each other during and after the activity.

Before reading guidelines on how to do improvisational learning activities, readers should note the illustrations of improvisation in counselor education in Box 5.1.

## BOX 5.1    EXAMPLES OF IMPROVISATIONAL ACTIVITIES FOR COUNSELOR EDUCATION

| |
|---|
| Having students counsel the instructor or another student during the first class meeting of a counseling techniques course, in order to discover the possibilities in helping and where they are beginning as novices |
| Doing triad training (Pedersen, 1999), in which students take on the roles of a counselor and a culturally different client while other students stand behind each of them and voice the possible thoughts of the counselor and client about cultural issues in the session |
| Having a counselor work with a simulated family to illustrate family dynamics or to try out family counseling skills |
| Creating a mock community counseling agency or staff meeting during the mental health counseling course |
| Having small groups plan and then act out various counseling theories in order to bring some of the concepts alive |
| Constructing a debate on the benefits of nondirective versus directive aspects of counseling |
| Having students plan and act out a problematic session on a religion-related issue with a client in order to stimulate discussion on the dynamics of counseling and religion |
| Having students counsel one another after they receive test results in the assessment class or the career class |
| Asking students to practice being assertive after generating situations in which they have difficulty |

## Instructor Hesitation About Improvisation

Most college instructors hesitate to include improvisation in their teaching strategies, usually defaulting to the common lecture-and-discussion means of teaching. Their hesitation generally arises from five concerns: unpredictability, student discomfort, planning, class time, and lack of information on improvisation.

First, improvisation is unpredictable and a bit messy. Once conditions have been set, improvisation may generate surprises, including questions that the instructor doesn't feel competent answering. This is one price that is paid for the vitality and spontaneity that is inherent in improvisation. But instructors' perfect knowledge is not a good model for students anyway. Instructors might respond to unpredictable turns by asking class members what they think or would do and by acknowledging the choices under ambiguous conditions that characterize much counseling work.

A second reason why instructors might hesitate to use improvisation is that such public spontaneity can become uncomfortable for some students. Improvisation requires performance of some kind, which is beyond many individuals' comfort zone. On the other hand, discomfort commonly accompanies important learning. If the atmosphere is sufficiently respectful, students will overcome this discomfort and take risks to discover aspects of themselves and ideas about counseling in action.

The third instructor hesitation about improvisation lies in the planning required to make it successful. To incorporate improvisation, instructors must know the content well and move beyond the default of lecturing on content to plan a learning activity.

A fourth reason why teachers may hesitate to incorporate improvisation is that they may believe that improvisational activities take too much class time. In fact, improvisation does take more time than lecture and discussion, because students "live out" the class content and then reflect on and discuss their experiences and learning. But the time can be worth it. While content can be covered in reading, deep learning requires learner activity. And improvisation can create learning that lasts and that is generally more relevant to future practice.

Finally, instructors may be uncertain about using improvisation because they simply don't know specific improvisations to try. Many of the upcoming chapters of this book are replete with concrete suggestions for improvisation.

## Methods for Implementing Improvisation

1. *Have a warm-up/introduction.* Precede the improvisation by presenting a case for students to play out, or have students read a scenario. You might ask, "What would you do in this case?" (to be followed by their tryout).

2. *Plan the physical setting and materials.* If it is a fishbowl demonstration, clear space in the room. If students will post ideas or pictures, bring in the needed paper, markers, and tape (or other necessary materials).

3. *Pick participants.* Asking for volunteers usually results in only participants who are already adept at performing. Instead, you can intentionally select students, particularly those with certain qualities. For example, in triad training on cross-gender counseling (see Chapter 12), a male counselor and a female client might be chosen, with a female "voice of the client" picked to stand behind the client and voice her possible thoughts. On the other hand, arbitrary assignment of roles, either random or by counting off, may also be useful (see description of how to construct groups in the previous section on small groups).

4. *Prepare observers for their tasks.* Give the observers of the simulation guidelines, either slight, such as "Note how realistic this session is," or more structured, such as a checklist of behaviors to watch for.

5. *Enact the improvisation.* The improvisation can be completely spontaneous or planned. In the latter case, if you want different groups to plan a dramatic scene or a role play, send them to private spaces with clear directions for the task and a clear and sufficient time frame for the simulation.

6. *Process the improvisation.* After the improvisation, let the actors talk first in order to reinforce the importance of their using their own judgments about their performance and choices. After actors talk, other participants and observers present their responses. Discussion may start with a question as simple as "What did you notice?" Other questions may include "What would you do that is similar or different?" "How did this improvisation illustrate _____?" You might post responses and ideas on the board.

7. *Optional: Try the improvisation again,* based on the feedback and reflections.

8. *Discuss again.* Generalize about the concepts that were illustrated.

In sum, counselor educators energize their classrooms by creating improvisational activities throughout the semester—to instigate interest in an upcoming topic, to illustrate previously read abstract concepts, to help students try out new, previously studied behaviors, and to trigger lively discussions.

## CONCLUSION

There are various strategies for teaching practice in seven overall domains: lecturing, discussion, questioning, small groups, reading and writing, and improvisation. All can be consistent with constructivist and developmental learning principles. Each can be done so that learners participate in creating their own knowledge. For that to occur, instructors need to plan both the content of a class and the process for delivering it. They also need to be willing to take the risks of encouraging inquiry, contradiction, and spontaneity in the learning space.

# REFERENCES

Bandura, A. (1986). *Social foundations of thought and action: A social cognitive theory.* Englewood Cliffs, NJ: Prentice Hall.

Belenky, M., Clinchy, B., Goldberger, N., & Tarule, J. (1986). *Women's ways of knowing.* New York: Basic Books.

Bloom, B. S. (1956). *A taxonomy of educational objectives.* New York: Longmans.

Erickson, B. L., & Strommer, D. W. (2005). Inside the first-year classroom: Challenges and constraints. In M. L. Upcraft, J. N. Gardner, & B. O. Barefoot (Eds.), *Challenging and supporting the first-year student: A handbook for improving the first year of college* (pp. 241–256). San Francisco: Jossey-Bass.

Freiberg, H. J., & Driscoll, A. (2005). *Universal teaching strategies.* Boston: Allyn & Bacon.

Holland, J. L. (1997). *Making vocational choices: A theory of vocational personalities and work environments.* Odessa, FL: Psychological Assessment Resources.

Kegan, R. (1998). *In over our heads: The mental demands of modern life.* Cambridge, MA: Harvard University Press.

Kerry, T. (1987). Classroom questions in England. *Questioning Exchange, 1,* 33.

Kolb, D. (1984). *Experiential learning: Experience as the source of learning and development.* Englewood Cliffs, NJ: Prentice Hall.

Lovell, C. W., & McAuliffe, G. J. (1997). Principles of constructivist training and education. In T. Sexton & B. Griffin (Eds.), *Constructivist thinking in counseling practice, research, and training* (pp. 134–156). New York: Teachers College Press.

Mars, J. (1984). Questioning in Czechoslovakia. *Questioning Exchange, 5,* 8–11.

McKeachie, W. J., Svinicki, M. D., & Hofer, B. K. (2006). *Teaching tips.* Boston: Houghton Mifflin.

Pedersen, P. (1999). *Hidden messages in culture-centered counseling: A triad training model.* Thousand Oaks, CA: Sage.

Perry, W. G., Jr. (1999). *Forms of intellectual and ethical development in the college years.* New York: Holt, Rinehart & Winston.

Rowe, M. B. (1976). The pausing principle: Two invitations to inquiry. *Journal of College Science Teaching, 5,* 258–260.

Royse, D. (2001). *Teaching tips for college and university instructors: A practical guide.* Boston: Allyn & Bacon.

Vella, J. (2002). *Learning to listen, learning to teach: The power of dialogue in educating adults* (Rev. ed.). San Francisco: Jossey-Bass.

Yan, B., & Arlin, P. K. (1995). Nonabsolute/relativistic thinking: A common factor underlying models of postformal reasoning? *Journal of Adult Development, 2,* 223–240.

# PART II

## A Guide to Individual Courses and Topics in the Counselor Education Curriculum

# 6

# Teaching Introduction to Counseling

Yvonne L. Callaway and Sue A. Stickel

The introductory course, as indicated by its name, orients students to the awareness, knowledge, and skills needed for professional counseling in school, agency, and college settings. It is commonly the first opportunity to socialize students into the culture of counseling. New students begin to know themselves in the context of professional performance parameters. They begin to understand the knowledge base and skill sets that they will develop through subsequent courses and clinical experiences. Our hope is that the Introduction to Counseling course will provide students with a tool kit that enables them to critically examine the multiple approaches to counseling that they will encounter in their future coursework and to construct the field with us, their educators.

During the introductory course, faculty serve as models for counselors-in-training (CITs), identifying both what to know and how to know. Faculty strive to promote the recognition of diverse perspectives by presenting multiple paradigms for negotiating their own life experiences, changes in society and the workplace, and the delivery of counseling services. During the exploration of multiple paradigms, faculty can also challenge students to alter the ways in which they develop understanding. For instance, students can be challenged to take positions outside their personal frames of reference and to develop a tolerance for cognitive dissonance.

During this course, faculty offer both a comprehensive introduction to the counseling profession and information about how counseling interfaces with other helping professions. This course sets the stage for the core and specialization courses to follow. For instance, students build their understandings of professional practice, including ethical guidelines, program standards, licensing requirements, and multicultural and advocacy competencies. From these foundations, a beginning professional identity emerges, as well as expectations and guidelines for personal and professional growth.

This chapter presents an instructional design for the introductory course in counseling based on the constructivist approaches presented throughout this book. We explore methodologies aimed at helping faculty challenge students and themselves to participate experientially, particularly through feedback, egalitarianism, and dialogue. We present sample assignments for enhancing students' understanding of self and others in the context of practice counseling sessions.

Four experiential learning and constructivist elements, as described in early chapters in this book, particularly guide this course design. They are, along with examples of particular methods,

- *encouraging learner engagement in the learning processes* (e.g., through using multiple experiential instructional modalities),

- *emphasizing personalization and ownership* (e.g., facilitated by interactive discussions, guided by opportunities for students to work with faculty as co-constructors of the learning experience),
- *valuing intrapersonal process* (e.g., through writing assignments and self-assessments),
- *promoting interpersonal learning* (e.g., through dyad and small-group activities).

A primary assumption underlying the introductory course is that the training experience will *change* the trainee. As described in earlier chapters, CITs need to achieve a basic level of personal cognitive development to successfully negotiate current training challenges and future professional responsibilities. Such personal mastery is growth oriented rather than remedial. Accordingly, we challenge students in three ways during this course, under the rubric of awareness, knowledge, and skill. We challenge them

a. to enhance their cognitive development by examining their willingness to question assumptions (awareness),
b. to become informed about the parameters of professional counseling (knowledge),
c. to use empathy, group skills, and other counseling competencies (skill).

The course also highlights the necessity of students struggling with biases and learning the strengths and limitations of their current worldviews. The goals of the introductory course, and of the overall curriculum that follows, aim to help students become what is referred to in Chapter 1 as more *culturally de-centered*.

# COURSE STRUCTURE AND INSTRUCTIONAL PROCESSES

In addition to gaining understanding of the origins, purposes, and diverse approaches in the counseling field, in a constructivist counselor education model, students are asked to become self-authorizing and socially critical professionals. Toward that end, counselor educators vary instructional strategies, emphasizing experience, active learning, and reflective practice, as discussed in Chapter 2. Counselor educators also create a classroom climate and culture consistent with constructivist-developmental guidelines. In this chapter, we include five dimensions of a participatory, co-constructive learning environment: classroom structure, ground rules, feedback norms, guided practice, and individual reflection assignments. Table 6.1 connects the learning objectives, content, processes, and learning activities with the relevant constructivist principles from earlier chapters that undergird our teaching of this course.

**TABLE 6.1** Course Content, Processes, Learning Activities, and Constructivist Principles

| Learning Objectives | Content | Processes | Learning Activities | Constructivist Principles |
|---|---|---|---|---|
| Demonstrate awareness of differing views of human nature and examine multiple counseling perspectives and models. | Counseling theories<br><br>Identity development models<br><br>Multicultural and advocacy competencies | Individual reflection<br><br>Personal sharing in dyads<br><br>Small- and large-group discussions<br><br>Simulations<br><br>Case study evaluation | Individual Reflection 1<br><br>Team Teach-Back<br><br>Personal Wellness Assets<br><br>Social Justice Advocacy Initiative<br><br>Individual Experience Option B | People construct their worldview from a context-based perspective.<br><br>Knowledge is derived through a social, inductive, and qualitative process.<br><br>Development is contextual. |

| Learning Objectives | Content | Processes | Learning Activities | Constructivist Principles |
|---|---|---|---|---|
| Demonstrate the ability to conceptualize the interaction among culture, diversity, and social context on the one hand, and counseling relationships and the applicability of counseling theories and interventions on the other. | Basic counseling process and helping relationship<br><br>Etic and emic cultural references<br><br>History of counseling<br><br>Dimensions of personal identity from multicultural counseling competencies | Individual reflection<br><br>Discussions in dyads<br><br>Small and large groups<br><br>Role plays<br><br>Guided practice in developing cultural conceptualizations<br><br>Analysis/reaction to counseling videos | Individual Reflection 1<br><br>Team Teach-Back<br><br>Social Justice Advocacy Initiative | Reality is multiform.<br><br>Individuals serve as their own historians in confronting the past as an organizing framework of thought and feeling that must be assimilated into present structures. |
| Be knowledgeable about professional communities, roles, services, and credentials, and demonstrate commitment to involvement in professional and client advocacy. | American Counseling Association, divisions, and state associations<br><br>Ethical standards<br><br>Technology applications<br><br>Settings and specializations | Journal article evaluation and review<br><br>Classroom lecture<br><br>Small- and large-group discussion<br><br>Development of ethical scenarios<br><br>Individual projects | Individual Reflections 2 and 3<br><br>Individual Experience Options A, B, and C<br><br>Social Justice Advocacy Initiative | Meaning-making is self evolution. |
| Be aware of current issues and trends in the helping professions. | Counseling theories and models<br><br>Multicultural and advocacy competencies<br><br>Professional history<br><br>Counseling settings and specializations<br><br>Ethical standards<br><br>Crisis and trauma as special needs | Individual reflection and assessment<br><br>Small- and large-group presentations<br><br>Individual projects using online resources | Individual Reflections 1 and 3<br><br>Literature Review<br><br>Team Teach-Back | Individuals are producers of their own development.<br><br>Language constitutes reality. |
| Effectively use opportunities for enhancing self-awareness and personal growth. | Basic counseling process and relationship<br><br>Identity development models<br><br>Dimensions of personal identity from multicultural and advocacy competencies | Individual reflection and assessment<br><br>Personal sharing in dyads | Individual Reflections 1 and 4<br><br>Individual Experience Options A, B, and C | Cognition is an active relating of events.<br><br>Human development is a process of attributing meaning to experience in a personal context. |

# Course Structure

Conceptually, we divide the Introduction to Counseling course into three stages: the context of professional helping, development of a professional knowledge base, and integration of awareness and knowledge. The content is not exclusive to a given stage; however, the emphasis is somewhat different for each stage. For example, learning objectives for the introductory stage emphasize professional counseling roles and ethics. Students also learn about the core values of social justice and cultural competency. The American Counseling Association's (ACA) Code of Ethics, identity development models, and social justice and multicultural counseling competencies are introduced. In the beginning sessions, individual reflection and experience options may be used to help students enhance their awareness of self and others in the context of helping relationships. Individual Reflections 1 and 2, the Personal Wellness Assessment, or Individual Experience Options A and B are assigned during this stage of the course (see descriptions of activities below). In a 15-week term, about five weeks are devoted to Stage 1.

Stage 2, development of a professional knowledge base, introduces professional history, counseling theories, basic counseling process and helping relationships, professional organizations, technology applications, and counseling settings and specializations. Students review and evaluate professional journal articles, create individual projects such as the Literature Review using both online and library resources, practice case analysis in small groups, and develop counseling scenarios and role plays for large-group discussions. Other assignments that support students' development include Individual Reflections 3 and 4 and Individual Experience Option C. About seven weeks of the term focus on Stage 2.

Stage 3, integration of awareness and knowledge, is the focus of the final three weeks. The Team Teach-Back and Social Justice Advocacy Initiative assignments provide a framework within which students demonstrate mastery of the course learning objectives (see Table 6.1). Because the content of the course's three stages is not mutually exclusive, assignments may be interchangeable during different stages depending on student needs.

Establishing a climate that facilitates co-constructed learning and interaction depends on attention to group structure. This structure includes both physical arrangements and the interactions of individual members in the group (Gladding, 2008). We recommend a circular seating arrangement, one that promotes student-to-student interactions. A circle can also reinforce the equalization of voices. The power of this configuration as an instructional intervention is exponential. A circle (a) more effectively engages the group dynamics associated with the formation stage of productive groups, (b) reinforces a norm of participation in the learning process, (c) supports risk taking by group members, and (d) increases the expression of multiple perspectives (Gladding, 2008). In addition to using a circle configuration, instructors can use dyads and small groups for discussions and activities. Dyadic and small-group processing allows members of the learning group to better get to know one another and communicates the need for all members to participate in creating knowledge. The interpersonal process that accompanies such discussions can enhance students' abilities to accommodate one another's differences.

# Ground Rules

The ground rules for the learning environment in the introductory course can be co-constructed with students during the initial meeting. In this process, students work first in dyads, then in small groups, and finally in the large group to discuss, modify, and/or offer support for behavior norms. Their own norms may be supplemented by suggestions from the instructor. Instructors might ensure that particular ground rules are considered, such as the desirability of active involvement, respect, confidentiality, freedom from judgment, and sharing personally, rather than posing as an expert. In the initial discussion about ground rules, students assess their readiness for adopting these rules and offer clarifying examples of related behavioral expectations for themselves, other students, and the instructor. During the semester, the instructor can periodically stop the classroom activities to check on how successfully these ground rules are being carried out or how well they are working for students.

# Establishing Feedback Norms

To determine student readiness for new content and learning activities, the instructor solicits regular feedback about the *what* and the *how*, that is, the content learned and the group processes by which it is learned. For instance, it may be helpful to periodically review the course purpose, goals, and ground rules in order to allow students to progressively define professional counseling competency based on their emerging experience with the class and the course knowledge base. Through such engagement and expression, students become co-constructors of the learning environment, and traditional classroom power relationships can be deconstructed. Dialogue among students and faculty creates clarity concerning the course content and collaboration. Such dialogue also provides a gauge for instructors to check (and modify, as required) the appropriateness of the level and quantity of didactic content.

The Team Teach-Back activity illustrates co-construction of the course content and generation of concurrent feedback to let faculty know students' level of understanding of principles. In this assignment, students use specific information from the counseling knowledge base (e.g., ethics, multicultural concerns, social justice) to develop their conceptualizations about professional counseling roles and responsibilities. They then tie these abstractions into actions and engagement in the classroom and the learning process.

The Team Teach-Back is a collaborative effort that follows the format of a professional counseling conference. Teams of about three to four students each prepare and present 45- to 60-minute conference presentations about an evidence-based counseling practice that has been introduced thus far in class. These groups of students become, in effect, specialists in some type of counseling. For example, past student groups created presentations on classroom guidance for middle school students, short-term counseling groups in residence halls, and counseling groups for adolescents in residential and foster care.

Presentations should cover the history of this type of counseling strategy; foundational theories or models related to the topic; major, distinguishing features of this method of help-giving; expected benefits for clients; types of clients who would be served; counseling techniques likely to be employed; an example of what counseling strategies would look like from this perspective (for instance, doing a role play, simulation, or case presentation); current or expected need for this type of counseling strategy (e.g., economic and sociopolitical issues, current news reports); sources of professional development on this topic outside of graduate training programs; and representative places in the local geographic area where this type of counseling takes place (places to refer to) or could take place (should the counselors want to practice this way in the future).

The presentation groups thus simulate active participation in professional conferences. Presentations demonstrate students' abilities to advocate for particular evidence-based counseling applications in a variety of counseling settings. As a result of the presentations, all of the students become more familiar with the settings where counseling takes place and are better able to decide which setting (e.g., school, community, college) fits best for them.

The Team Teach-Back allows students to maximize their involvement in the learning process by constructing a lesson for their peers. Thus, students take responsibility for getting what they need and want. Also, a sense of classroom community often blossoms from these team projects. Students' newfound sense of connection then encourages them to share their views in future large-group discussions.

# Guided Practice

The field of counseling seems to be moving toward what Ivey, Ivey, and Zalaquett (2010) identify as skill integration. In this effort, novice helpers appreciate frameworks that assist them in learning and applying multiple theoretical models. Guided practice involves using inquiry focused on familiar examples to help students enhance their understanding of new material (Rosenshine, 1979). Guided practice offers one way for students to match the abstract conceptualizations presented in textbooks with specific counseling situations and clients. During guided practice in this course, students reflect on (a) information and insight gained from the readings, (b) how the new information and insight may be related to professional competency and personal style, and (c) how they would apply learning to real-world situations.

In a typical sequence of guided practice, students initially complete individual experiential assignments, such as the Personal Wellness Assessment. For example, students may reflect on the importance of their wellness as CITs. They then discuss their responses in small groups during class time or in online threaded discussions.

Guided practice, as here described, offers a number of benefits. For one, individual and small-group assignments guide students in the process of sharing self-observations in a group setting. Giving and receiving feedback also helps them learn to monitor self-talk. That monitoring encourages awareness of bias, which in turn helps to preclude the unconscious imposition of biases on clients and others. Further, when students share their individually generated reflections during classroom exchanges and hear others' reflections, they make more powerful connections between the content and themselves and build communities of learning with their future colleagues (interpersonal learning). Most important, after interpersonal learning and discussions of multiple perspectives, students report an increased capacity "to attend to others and to feel related to them in spite of what may be great differences" (McAuliffe & Lovell, 2000, p. 20).

## Individual Reflection Assignments

To make guided practice effective, we offer CITs both challenge and support. For instance, preparation rubrics for each learning assignment guide and support students in reflecting on personal awareness, content knowledge, and skill practice. A strong and continuous emphasis on careful self-observation and assessment challenges students to carefully reflect on major issues related to professional counseling and their career development. The Individual Reflection assignments are an example of such preparation rubrics.

In the course of requiring students to reflect on the information presented in the course, the Individual Reflection assignments enhance intra- and interpersonal process awareness by helping students examine their personal values and how they make meaning of their experiences. Content for these assignments follows the topical calendar for course readings, lectures, and activities. The questions used in these assignments may be adjusted to make them relevant for other courses. Four Individual Reflection assignment examples follow.

**Individual Reflection 1—Multicultural Counseling Competencies.** This assignment encourages students to create and resolve their own cognitive dissonance relative to sociocultural diversity. Students respond to the following items, supporting their comments with information from the readings.

1. Identify something learned about members of diverse cultural identification groups (e.g., ethnic, racial, LGBT) that were discussed in the text. Discuss how new learning refutes previous stereotypes and/or assumptions that you may have held about members of these groups.

2. Using an individual identity development model, identify two examples of social and cultural influences on your development, and contrast them with two differences you might expect to find with a client from a culturally different group.

**Individual Reflection 2—ACA Ethical Guidelines.** Students begin to identify the relationship between ethical codes and professional responsibility. For each scenario that follows, students must (a) identify the nature of the scenario and (b) defend the counselor's decision or describe what the counselor might have done instead.

Scenario 1: A Licensed Professional Counselor (LPC) on staff at a community agency recently began seeing a 16-year-old client who presented with symptoms of depression. The LPC tells the client's parents that she would like to speak to the client's school counselor and teachers. The parents indicate that they are uncomfortable with the LPC contacting their child's school because they don't want the counselor to get a "bad impression" of their child based on what may be in his school record.

Scenario 2: A Licensed Professional Counselor (LPC) on staff at an agency that specializes in substance abuse treatment has been working with a young woman client for two months when the client indicates that she has been abusing amphetamines for over a year as a way to reduce her weight. The LPC determines that the client meets the *DSM* diagnostic criteria 304.40 Amphetamine Dependence. The LPC has never worked with a client presenting with substance dependence, nor has the LPC been trained in the treatment of substance dependence.

### Individual Reflection 3—Technology and Counseling (Present and Future).

This assignment encourages students to identify how counseling is influenced by contemporary social patterns and technology. These are the instructions for this assignment:

1. Access the website of a professional association related to your specialty area (www.counseling .org provides access to a variety of specialties). Select information relevant to your future work. Summarize the information, and describe how it would be useful.

2. Identify an ethical scenario that could emerge from use of the Internet in counseling. Develop a discussion guide for this scenario using the ethical guidelines.

### Individual Reflection 4—Professional Development.

The purpose of this assignment is to engage students in planning for ongoing professional development, during and beyond the master's degree program. Students respond to the following items, supporting their comments with information from the readings.

1. Identify your areas of strength and needed improvement as a CIT.

2. Based on the above, identify three professional development goals, one short-term, one intermediate, and one long-term.

3. Develop a plan to achieve these goals.

## Literature Review Assignment

In the introductory course, students are responsible for being diligent and for challenging their ways of knowing. Therefore, they take responsibility not only for reading materials and completing assignments in a timely manner, but also for synthesizing information in order to make informed decisions about their own academic development. They are encouraged to develop their own professional paradigm, a paradigm that is not to be built on following any particular faculty member's manner of thinking or on maintaining the status quo, but is instead self-authorized (Kegan, 1998).

In the Literature Review assignment, students begin to construct their own professional paradigm by selecting a topic that builds their specialized knowledge base and increases their knowledge of current issues in counseling. Faculty use this assignment to clarify academic expectations for reading and analyzing research literature and to support students in successfully meeting those expectations. Students are guided in their struggle to conceptualize knowledge about evidence-based practice and specific issues faced by clients and counselors (e.g., relapse prevention strategies for adolescents, the first-year college experience for female students). Additions or alternatives to Steps 4 and 5 below are (a) inviting a panel of practicing counselors from specialized settings and fields to speak in class (high school and college counselors, addictions counselors, counselors working in the justice system) or (b) contacting, visiting, and interviewing practicing counselors at their workplaces. For the alternative options, students develop an interview protocol and write up the interview responses in narrative form. The instructions for the Literature Review assignment are as follows:

1. Students individualize learning by selecting a topic about which to expand their knowledge base.

2. Students select at least five recent research articles.

3. Students review and familiarize themselves with the research questions, hypotheses, and methodology in the selected articles.

4. Students write a research paper that demonstrates their ability to synthesize, compare, and contrast current research on the selected topic.

5. Students become competent in using the American Psychological Association's (APA) publication manual and professional counseling journals. They demonstrate competency by preparing their research papers in accordance with APA formatting and writing guidelines.

## Personal Wellness Assessment

In the Personal Wellness Assessment, counselor educators provide specific direction to the general proposition "Counselor, know thyself." CITs apply models of wellness and identity development to themselves in the attempt to become more familiar with the knowledge base of counseling and with helpful tools for their continued professional development. Wellness models focus on the identification of strengths and resources and, therefore, encourage counselors to conceptualize mental health on a continuum, to focus on multiple dimensions and elements, and to assess and increase well-being and functioning. During this assignment, CITs use structured assignments to self-assess and to identify personal and professional development goals. The overarching goal is to induct students into the strenuous, ongoing work of becoming a professional counselor.

The course text and required supplements provide the primary knowledge base and models of development and intervention to be used in this assignment. Many texts designed for the introductory course provide individual chapters relevant to needs of this assignment (e.g., Capuzzi & Gross, 2008; Gibson & Mitchell, 2007; Gladding, 2008; Nugent & Jones, 2008). The instructions to students are as follows:

Part I: Most of the issues and problems that individuals experience are developmental, transitional, or situational, and therefore are natural and normal. In order to understand these normal processes and to serve a diverse group of clients, counselors need to understand and incorporate into their work knowledge of lifespan development, sociopolitical histories, and current conditions (e.g., world events, policies and laws, local safety issues). Using a wellness model from your readings (e.g., Myers, Sweeney, & Witmer, 2010) as a guide, apply these concepts in constructing your own personal wellness assessment.

Part II: Consider the following topics as you describe your own development thus far. Identify where you have come from, where you are heading, and your current "condition" in these areas of development:

1. Family relationships
2. Other relationships (e.g., work, community, religion)
3. Career/job
4. Living environment

## Social Justice Advocacy Initiative

Students continue to build their own professional paradigm with the Social Justice Advocacy Initiative. In this assignment, the instructor guides students in learning to identify social justice disparities and in developing individual plans for expanding counseling roles through advocacy for clients and the profession. CITs will then be better prepared to use the technical knowledge of the field selectively and artfully to instigate changes in themselves and for individual clients and systems. Toward these ends, instructors support students in seeking new cultural learning experiences, both inside and outside of the classroom, that match and mismatch their current developmental level and identified needs. Students' reflective thinking and self-assessment skills become enhanced as an initial dimension of such experiential learning.

Most texts incorporate chapters outlining the multicultural nature of counseling and how to work with culturally diverse clients. We use one of the introductory books (e.g., Capuzzi & Gross, 2008; Gibson & Mitchell, 2007; Gladding, 2008; Nugent & Jones, 2008) along with supplements that specifically address professional guidelines and best practices for the operationalization of multicultural and advocacy competencies. For instance, we use the Multicultural Counseling Competencies (Arredondo et al., 1996) and the Advocacy Competency Domains (Ratts, Toporek, & Lewis, 2010), respectively. The Multicultural Counseling Competencies include the Dimensions of Personal Identity Model, which provides a framework for understanding that everyone possesses a personal, political, and historical culture. The Advocacy Competency Domains identify pivotal steps for both systems change interventions and empowerment strategies in direct counseling. Cultural identity development models such as those of Helms (1990) and Sue and Sue (2008) provide support for seeing a client's worldview from an *emic* perspective.

After students participate in lectures, small-group case study presentations, and large-group follow-up discussions to encourage their self-expression and to teach them how to question their thinking, they set goals for empowering themselves and personalizing their learning experiences. For example, students clarify professional expectations and become familiar with the Advocacy Competency Domains (Ratts et al., 2010) and specific steps in the advocacy process (Eriksen, 1996). Using current events and research, students develop an advocacy project that demonstrates their ability to identify and articulate social justice issues for an oppressed group (of which they are not members). During this assignment, CITs demonstrate the ability to synthesize theory and practice, as well as to identify goals for professional engagement beyond the classroom. They then develop a 7- to 10-minute presentation and one-page handout that incorporate the following:

1. identification of a social justice issue and a scenario that presents a challenging human story

2. two intervention ideas for public systems intervention (macro level), one reactive and one proactive

3. two intervention ideas for the community/organization intervention level, one reactive and one proactive

4. two intervention ideas for working with individual clients (micro level), one reactive and one proactive

Students next identify a possible negative consequence that could result from these initiatives. They explain what they would do to avoid negative outcomes and what they would do if negative consequences occurred.

## Individual Experience Options Assignments

Following the principles discussed in Chapters 1, 2, and 3, faculty personalize their teaching by guiding students in continued reflective thinking about how their own development and experiences influence their training. Instructors coach students as they apply counseling approaches to themselves and others. They also challenge students to intentionally create cognitive dissonance. This combination assists students in focusing on how the introductory course content and learning experiences can be integrated into their cognitive, affective, and behavioral understandings, both personally and professionally. The Individual Experience Options, described below, serve as guided practice for students as they develop reflective thinking skills and construct paradigms for practicing professional counseling.

Individual Experience Option assignments provide a framework for students to assume responsibility for connecting *what* to know with *how* to know by personalizing the learning experience to their readiness and need. Three possible activity options are offered: (a) counseling series, (b) cultural immersion, and (c) professional development.

*Option A: Counseling Series*

I. Students arrange to participate in a minimum of five counseling sessions (individual or group).

II. Students write a self-reflective paper covering the following guiding questions.
  A. What is the most potentially difficult aspect of counseling?
  B. What is the most potentially rewarding aspect of counseling?
  C. What personal and professional benefits did you gain from your counseling experience?

*Option B: Cultural Immersion*

I. Students attend a minimum of three activities that are centered in a cultural experience different from their own.

*(Continued)*

(Continued)

    II. Students write a self-reflective paper covering the following guiding questions.
        A. How have these experiences influenced your views about cultural diversity?
        B. How have these experiences enhanced your personal and professional development?
        C. Use A and B above to identify a professional development goal and a plan of action to achieve this goal.

*Option C: Professional Activity*

Option C focuses on extended learning outside the classroom. This option is designed by the student. It must include a clear rationale and specific learning objectives. The design requires instructor agreement and usually a learning contract that specifies the criteria and timeline of achieving the learning objectives.

Students may, alternatively, elect to interview a professional counselor at her or his work site or to attend a professional conference in order to gain knowledge of how theory translates to practice in a specific area of interest. If they choose this option, they receive the following instructions:

Complete the interview or attend the conference and write a paper covering the following guiding questions.

A. How have these experiences influenced your views about professional counseling?
B. How have these experiences enhanced your personal and professional development?
C. Use A and B above to identify a professional development goal and a plan of action to achieve this goal.

# CONCLUDING REFLECTIONS ON TEACHING THE INTRODUCTORY COURSE

The responsibility of creating a climate for constructive developmental education and guiding students in optimizing the learning process is daunting, to say the least. Modeling openness to diverse perspectives and resistance to confirmatory bias often feels like a yeoman's task. Yet the introductory course holds the possibility of generating excitement and positive synergy for faculty and students alike. The excitement of having students embark on a journey toward becoming professional counselors and the synergy of being part of the learning community are highlights of teaching the introductory course.

Counselor educators cannot necessarily anticipate the eventual professional reality that students may experience as they progress in their careers. However, beginning students are usually ready to try new skills and behaviors and to explore the personal and social dimensions of their identity. Lively, student-centered class sessions invoke cognitive and affective challenges when students engage in complex reflective practices. During the introductory course, our students have demonstrated the ability to tolerate the disequilibrium that results from engagement in the learning experience. They have also been capable of generating questions and methods of inquiry. We see in students' writings their intentional application of reflective thinking in negotiating interpersonal relationships. Observing these "ah-ha" moments of discovery makes teaching the introductory course inspirational. However, during the introductory course, faculty may also be challenged. They are likely to experience a tension between structure and freedom, between what they want students to know (the content) and how students best go about understanding and deconstructing that knowledge (the process).

The model for teaching the introductory course that is presented here has evolved from our collective experiences, from our evaluations of guided practice assignments, and from our observations of student performance in subsequent classes. By the end of this introductory course, we hope that students will not only have achieved its five learning objectives, but also developed a commitment to personal and professional growth that will last throughout their training and careers.

# REFERENCES

Arredondo, P., Toporek, R., Brown, S. P., Jones, J., Locke, D. C., Sanchez, J., et al. (1996). *Operationalization of the multicultural counseling competencies.* Alexandria, VA: American Counseling Association.

Capuzzi, D., & Gross, D. R. (2008). *Introduction to the counseling profession* (5th ed.).Upper Saddle River, NJ: Pearson Education.

Eriksen, K. (1996). *Making an impact: A handbook on counselor advocacy.* Minneapolis, MN: Accelerated Development.

Gibson, R. L., & Mitchell, M. (2007). *Introduction to counseling and guidance* (7th ed.). Upper Saddle River, NJ: Pearson Education.

Gladding, S. T. (2008). *Counseling: A comprehensive profession* (6th ed.). Upper Saddle River, NJ: Pearson Education.

Helms, J. E. (1990). *Black and white racial identity: Theory, research and practice.* New York: Greenwood Press.

Ivey, A. E., Ivey, M. B., & Zalaquett, C. P. (2010). *Intentional interviewing and counseling* (7th ed.). Belmont, CA: Brooks/Cole.

Kegan, R. (1998). *In over our heads: The mental demands of modern life.* Cambridge, MA: Harvard University Press.

McAuliffe, G. J., & Lovell, C. (2000). Encouraging transformation: Guidelines for constructivist and developmental instruction. In G. McAuliffe & K. Eriksen (Eds.), *Preparing counselors and therapists: Creating constructivist and developmental programs* (pp. 14–41). Alexandria, VA: Association of Counselor Educators and Supervisors.

Myers, J. E., Sweeney, T. J., & Witmer, M. (2010). *Wellness Evaluation of Lifestyles: A holistic model of wellness.* Retrieved July 27, 2010, from http://www.mindgarden.com/products/wells.htm

Nugent, F. A., & Jones, K. D. (2008). *Introduction to the profession of counseling* (5th ed.). Upper Saddle River, NJ: Pearson Education.

Ratts, M. J., Toporek, R. L., & Lewis, J. A. (2010). *ACA advocacy competencies: A social justice framework.* Alexandria, VA: American Counseling Association.

Rosenshine, B. (1979). Content, time and direct instruction. In P. L. Peterson & H. J. Walberg (Eds.), *Research on teaching* (pp. 335–351). Berkley, CA: McCutchan.

Sue, D. W., & Sue, D. (2008). *Counseling the culturally diverse: Theory and practice* (4th ed.). New York: John Wiley & Sons.

# Constructing the Counseling Skills Course

Karen P. Eriksen and Garrett J. McAuliffe

*"This is a whole new way of being," said a student. "In other parts of my life, I am a mother and a teacher and a boss. I am supposed to be in charge and tell everyone else what to do. To just sit and listen, follow the client, and reflect back to them what I hear is very strange and new. And I find it very difficult."*

Indeed, the Counseling Skills course—taught under the rubric of Interviewing Skills, the Helping Interview, or Techniques of Individual Counseling— is designed to introduce graduate or undergraduate students to ways of working and interacting with others that differ from what they have previously known. Beginning students' experiences with interviewing and helping have usually been restricted to parental admonition, religious prescription, and secondary school college advising. Or "helping" for them, at its most concrete, might bring up visions of changing a flat tire for someone on the road, bandaging a wound, or washing the dishes. It usually surprises students that what we aim to teach them is not, at least initially, directive or advice oriented, despite its goal of influencing others toward behavior change and good decision making. We must not underestimate the pervasiveness of such a directive vision of helping on the part of neophyte counselors.

## Inviting Personal Evolution

In contrast to their initial perspectives on helping, students discover that counseling is largely about two or more people discovering a new story, one that works better than the story that was previously held or known. The initial counseling course asks students, as interviewers, to let interviewees hold the power, to evoke the client's agenda, and to encourage counselees' willingness to question all advisors. This sort of helping requires an epistemological leap for most beginning counseling students—it is difficult for counselors-in-training to conceive of a client as self-authoring when they have yet to embrace their own authority, when they have yet to become self-defining (Kegan, 1994; Lovell & McAuliffe, 1996; Neukrug & McAuliffe, 1993). It is even more difficult for beginning counselors to dwell in the murky waters of a helping interview that is co-constructed.

The counseling skills course, then, as we propose it, is more than learning mere skills. We propose a way of helping that hinges on a worldview in which meanings are made in the context of a relationship, a relationship that reflects a respect for human beings' abilities to help themselves. As a result, the tasks we propose for the counseling skills course have the potential to challenge students in personally important ways, despite what appears to be mechanically teaching one microskill at a time. Developing active listening skills has changed our students' lives rather dramatically in both epistemological capacity and day-to-day relationships.

## Moving From Other- to Self-Authorizing Thinking

The counseling skills course can instigate an evolution in students' ways of knowing by inviting them to view human norms, values, and views of reality as socially created constructions. It has the potential to move students from being defined by others to defining themselves, a shift Belenky, Clinchy, Goldberger, and Tarule (1996) would call moving from a *received* or *subjective* way of knowing to a *procedural*, even *constructivist* way of knowing. Evidence exists that fewer than 30% of adults are able to consistently think reflectively and procedurally (Kegan, 1998). And our research indicates that our students are no exception. They enter our programs fully capable of listening to authorities and delivering directives, but not yet fully capable of living in a socially constructed universe. Very few reach procedural, self-authoring, or post-conventional ways of being by the time they graduate. Some will fluctuate from an authority-reliant tendency to an occasional self-authorizing capacity. Therefore, students will most likely be authority dependent (Lovell & McAuliffe, 1996); that is, they will be

- embedded in or subject to their relationships and to rules (e.g., saying to the instructor, "How long does the paper need to be?" "What do you want us to do this week?" "I didn't do what I wanted to on this paper because I didn't think that was what you would want."),
- able to meet their own needs, but more likely to sacrifice these to meet another's needs (e.g., letting practice counseling sessions go on long beyond the

required time and long beyond their comfort zone because the client is still distressed and seems to need to talk),
- able to hold an inner dialogue, but likely to merely experience feelings rather than to be able to name them or think about them (e.g., when asked to name feelings during class or during counseling sessions, they can only identify "bad" or "good" or "frustrated," which represents a limited awareness of or ability to identify their own feelings and a limited range of possible feelings; difficulty stepping back and examining these feelings in journals),
- determined and defined by others (e.g., difficulty saying no in work or personal situations; difficulty questioning the instructor's or program's authority),
- needing to maintain relationships, be approved of, and not challenge conventions,
- more likely to experience undifferentiated fusion in relationships (intimacy requires knowing where you end and the other begins; students' difficulties expressing or being aware of their own inner experiences in the presence of another's pain indicates a problem with this and thus with meeting the client with her or his whole self),
- intuitive in their approach to helping, following unexamined inner urges, sometimes reactively (difficulty standing back from a counseling session and explaining why they did what they did, and analyzing or evaluating their own or the client's behavior, or the counseling relationship; reactively jumping in with inappropriate responses, seeming to get pulled in by some clients' ways of talking or behaving).

While each of these characteristics can be seen as a strength of its own, in that each contributes to a student's ability to care for other people and their pain, they limit counselors' abilities to live within the ambiguity of counseling work, to set reasonable boundaries between themselves and the client (and the client's problem), to work independently and reflectively, and to plunge into the very personal depths that they are trying to help clients to explore.

## Development-Enhancing Instruction

Instructors need to optimally support and challenge (Sanford, 1966) students in order to help them move toward a more evidence-based way of making meaning. *Support* might mean celebrating their kindness and ability to tune in carefully to clients. It also means offering the structure, direction, and authority needed by people who are more concrete and authority reliant. *Challenge* means urging students to think about why they are doing what they are doing, to examine their multiple and even contradictory inner urges, to decide whether preserving conventions and relationships at all costs is helpful to them, to establish a separateness from others' definitions, and to be self-reflective. Such challenges have the potential to stretch students to a place of greater autonomy, to self-authoring, and to taking responsibility for their own behavior. They may, as a result, exhibit a more consistent identity across contexts and a greater ability to give evidence for their current beliefs and positions.

For instance, immediate personal benefits emerge for students through discovering and voicing their personal views: For the first time, they may say no to unhealthy relationships and work settings, express feelings in relationships, and expect deeper levels of intimacy with significant others. Complementarily, students discover the legitimacy of others' views and, in the process, move from an authoritarian toward a dialogical epistemology, or from dualism to greater relativism (Benack, 1988; Neukrug & McAuliffe, 1993). Not only are these changes revolutionary for the students, but they may catch those who are in the students' lives unaware, requiring changes that those significant others had not anticipated and may not be happy about. Thus, the shock waves that can emanate from a course such as this may resound further than either the students or their significant others would have expected.

In a much more concrete sense, the counseling skills course may—in fact, should—improve students' interpersonal relationships. Counseling skills include the basic communication skills that are fundamental to effective family and organizational life. As a result, students rather immediately apply these newfound skills to both professional and personal relationships (Ivey, 1994).

## Practicing What We Preach

Responsible and developmentally aware instructors understand the anxiety that can be produced in these challenging circumstances, and as a result they engage students in a manner that is parallel, or isomorphic, to the counselor-client relationship. For instance, just as the counselor-client relationship is usually grounded in the core conditions of empathy, respect, and unconditional positive regard (Carkhuff & Berenson, 1977) and, in most traditions, in an egalitarian—as opposed to an authoritarian—relationship, so too the instructor develops relationships with students based on respect, genuineness, and positive regard. Just as helpers can never change clients, but can expect them to construct new meanings and try on new behaviors, the instructor, in an effort to foster progression through developmental stages, similarly encourages and challenges students to envision and try on new ways of being. Just as counselors do not expect clients to change in significant ways merely by being *told* "the right answer," instructors understand that merely lecturing on material seldom produces the desired student change. Just as many counselors believe that clients' lives will be enhanced and problems will be reduced if clients advance developmentally, many counselor educators believe that epistemological progress in students should improve their work as counselors (Lovell & McAuliffe, 1996). And finally, just as counselors use the assets that clients bring into counseling sessions in creating solutions with clients, instructors value the expertise that students bring into the classroom as a result of life experiences. Thus, instructors refuse to serve as the sole knowledge bearers.

For each of the desired counseling skills, the learning objectives, activities, and constructivist principles in Table 7.1 apply. Specific skills would be determined by the instructor and perhaps by the text used. However, the skills typically include those cited in the Counseling Skills Scale in Appendix C on page 107, such as Developing a Therapeutic Relationship, Managing the Session, Paraphrasing, Summarizing, Reflecting Feeling, Using Immediacy, Observing Themes and Patterns, Reflecting Meaning and Values, Pointing Out Discrepancies, Questioning, Requesting Concrete Examples, and the various strategies for Creating Change.

**TABLE 7.1**   Course Objectives, Activities, and Constructivist Principles

| Learning Objectives | Content | Learning Processes and Activities | Constructivist Principles |
|---|---|---|---|
| Know textbook material on basic counseling skills | Attending<br>Primary empathy<br>Advanced empathy<br>Goals and objectives | • Read text<br>• Answer study questions<br>• Take quizzes<br>• Classroom discussions | Providing structure to support interpersonal knowers |
| Apply textbook principles, identifying skills and their purposes, to counseling demonstrations, videos, and own counseling | How to perform counseling skills | • Instructor skills demonstrations<br>• Expert video demonstrations<br>• Seatwork<br>• Targeted observations<br>• Classroom discussions | Applying principles, breaking down ambiguous stimuli into manageable parts, asking for evidence of position, including diversity of perspectives = challenge toward procedural knowing |
| Demonstrate increasing proficiency in basic counseling skills | More complex applications of counseling skills to real-world, ambiguous situations | • In-class practice with peer and instructor feedback<br>• Between-class video- or audio-recorded practice with peer feedback<br>• Midterm and final videos with instructor feedback | Applying skills in action, creating real-world ambiguity, and deciding for oneself all = challenge toward procedural knowing<br><br>Using structured grading rubrics and feedback sheets = support |
| Demonstrate ability to reflect on work, evaluate own skills, make plans for improvement | How to evaluate and analyze own and others' counseling skills | • Reflection papers<br>• Transcripts<br>• Individual goal setting<br>• All with instructor feedback | Standing back from own work and from self to evaluate = challenge toward procedural knowing<br><br>Using exemplars, grading rubrics, and feedback sheets = support |
| Develop awareness of personal issues that may interfere with skills delivery | Personal issues and their impact on counseling skills | • Reflection papers with instructor feedback | Standing back from self to evaluate = challenge toward procedural knowing<br><br>Using exemplars, grading rubrics, and clear instructions = support |

# THE LEARNING SEQUENCE: A BIAS TOWARD ACTIVITY

In the counseling skills course, we consider activity necessary to retention, and we structure the activity very specifically in order to support conventional learners. The sequence of activities in the course might proceed as follows: Read, reflect, discuss in class; observe, critique, apply in action during class, critique, practice outside of class, reflect, critique. Initially, students read about the topic or skill, using a book that breaks counseling into subskills. Then, prior to class, students try out the chapter's suggestions as a way of interacting with and reflecting upon the chapter's material. During the following class, instructors and students briefly discuss the key points of the reading, watch an instructor or video-recorded model demonstrate the skills, and critically evaluate the demonstration. They then try out the new skills during class in practice counseling sessions, with observers looking on. After the brief counseling sessions, students evaluate their own and their peers' performance. Class discussion of the experience also helps to cement learning, identify needed areas for further guidance, and prepare students for between-class practice. Between class sessions, students conduct a counseling interview with either classmates or undergraduate volunteers, specifically focusing on a skill-of-the-week. Finally, following Schön (1983) and others' emphasis on reflection, students write in a journal about the feelings and thoughts that emerged during the experience, evaluate their success in performing the skills, and consider reasons for failures or difficulties and ways to improve.

# Independent Learning: Reading, Writing, and Quizzing

We use a book that breaks the actions of the helping interview into manageable, learnable subskills. Students progress from performing concrete and discrete tasks to combining these into more complex behaviors. Study questions for each reading assignment (e.g., "What are the goals of attending behavior?" "What are the best uses for questioning?") and pop quizzes may be used to support (Sanford, 1966) students who cannot consistently utilize a relatively autonomous way of knowing, who are more concrete or convention dependent (Loevinger, 1976), and who, as a result, need the structure and external motivation that study questions and perhaps quizzes provide (Widick, Knefelkamp, & Parker, 1975). Students may dislike the quizzes, and instructors may be reluctant to generate such negative responses, but without externally imposed structure, students may lack the internal intention to prepare adequately for class. (After the quizzes have done their work—that is, getting students to read and think about the reading in preparation for class—I [Eriksen] generally throw out the grades, which makes everyone very happy.) We are sure that most faculty are familiar with these learning strategies.

# Social Learning: In-Class Discussions, Observations, and Experimentation

Group experiences may create different knowledge than what has developed independently. The activities in this section are "social" events. As such, they offer experiences of the power of interacting with peers to develop insights and the power of constructing knowledge together.

## Seatwork and Discussion: Asking for Evidence

Instructors challenge students by posing questions that require students to think for themselves, to consider different perspectives, and to offer evidence for assertions. For example, in initial discussions about video or live demonstrations of paraphrasing, the instructor may challenge students to stand back from the immediate skill and think for themselves by asking at a more macro level, "What is the point of paraphrasing? Why do we do it?" Students might respond by saying that they really feel heard when someone listening to them uses paraphrasing, that this seems to be the best way to let people know that you understand them. Students might further indicate that paraphrasing gives clients the space to explore and allows clients to construct their own answers and ideas. As a result, paraphrasing opens a window to constructivism, as students envision how merely reflecting a client's words more simply and clearly can open new meanings for the client. The steps for teaching paraphrasing might include the following:

a. presenting a *vignette*, such as this interviewee quote: "I am really upset about the grade I got in my ethics course. I worked really hard, harder than the others in my group worked, and some of them got better grades than I did. I just don't know what that teacher expects."

b. asking students to do *seatwork,* that is, to privately write various formulaic responses ("You feel . . . because . . .), such as "You are feeling really concerned about your grade and the teacher's expectations" or "You seem to feel angry that you worked so hard and it didn't pay off."

c. asking students to consider how to put these formulaic responses into *more natural feeling words* such as "You are saying . . ." and "It seems. . . ."

d. asking them to
   - *reflect* on how it would feel to use such responses,
   - *share* with one another their *ideas* about responses, and
   - *give evidence* for their answers.

## Video Observation

Another layer of activity is added when students critique one another's practice counseling sessions. Rather than merely receiving knowledge through viewing a video (or live demonstration), students again participate in creating knowledge. The constructivist instructor might engage students in actively watching demonstration videos by directing different students to focus on specific client characteristics and responses. Instructors might also direct different students to watch for various microskills and counselor characteristics. For instance, particular students would note eye contact, body language, and vocal tone; paraphrasing; or questioning. Students might be urged to note situational choices in interviewing as they track both when skills were used and how skillfully they were used. The instructor may also ask students how they would feel if they had been the client, a question that recognizes both the value of student input and the fact that "real" clients would have very similar perspectives to, at this point, "naïve" students.

The instructor might then switch from a micro focus toward a macro level of understanding by asking students to continually think about whether the goals of the microskill are being accomplished. For example, when attending is the skill-of-the-week, students might be asked, "Is the counselor demonstrating care, interest, and positive regard while performing the skills?" or "Are these attitudes encouraging trust and promoting client verbalization?" These strategies challenge students to generate answers from within, to build on what they already know, to contribute information from their own experiences, experiences that even the instructor may not share. The strategies promote an egalitarian atmosphere and challenge students to be active in their own learning experience.

The constructivist instructor uses video observation as more than passive reception; instead, instructors actively engage students in creating possibilities and stimulate the community of students to work together in creating possibilities. The instructor also challenges students to give effective feedback to one another. Reflecting on and specifically analyzing peers' counseling in preparation for offering feedback helps students know how to improve and think independently about their own counseling. Helpful feedback might be defined as "tentatively and specifically giving voice to one's own experience of another's behavior, usually using an 'I' statement" (Eriksen & Bruck, this volume). Global negative or positive evaluations are discouraged in favor of specific observations. For instance, if a student says, "I think the counselor was very caring," the instructor asks, "What did you see specifically that led you to that conclusion? And how did you feel when the counselor did what she did?" The manner of questioning is always such that it indicates, "Your view is important. Whatever your view is, we will listen. And also, if you are going to state a view, you need to give reasons for it." Again, in this manner, co-construction of knowledge is demonstrated and an environment conducive to students' expression of their own voices is created.

During the feedback process, the instructor gives the student counselor whose video was viewed the responsibility for soliciting feedback and doing some self-critique. The initial questions from the instructor to the student counselor are "How did you feel during this segment of the video?" "What were you trying to accomplish?" "What did you feel successful at?" "What would you have changed if you had it to do over again?" "What help would you like from the class?" This line of questioning communicates that students have choices about what kind of and how much feedback they receive and that they determine what would be most helpful to them and when they have received as much as they find helpful.

In addition to facilitating the feedback process while viewing student videos, the instructor asks students to tune in to their own experiences of the counseling session. The instructor asks the student counselors whose videos were viewed how they felt during the session and asks them to trust their own internal indicators about what worked or did not work. The instructor asks a similar question of the other class members. This line of questioning communicates the importance of students' internal processes, their own voices, and their subjective experience.

During such discussions and demonstrations, the teacher poses questions to the class, challenges rigid positions, urges students to challenge each other and the teacher, and takes positions opposing those stated by students in order to get them to think about other possibilities. Again, because constructing knowledge together and constructing the best possible products are the goals of any course, the instructor poses questions that encourage expressions of multiple perspectives. In doing so, the instructor communicates that without each student finding her or his voice, the answers generated might be less than the optimal, which only a diverse group can create.

Watching videos of student interviews brings concrete examples of both problems and counseling skills into the classroom and is thus invaluable to skill development. However, viewing videos may also create obstacles to student epistemological development if supervision is viewed traditionally. Traditionally, the expert instructor supervising the videos watches and evaluates the learner's performance of counseling and then offers "expert" advice about what to do next with the client. The learner is expected to be in a receptive mode in order to be considered open to supervision. Such traditional supervision poses obstacles to student development because it supports only a received way of knowing (Belenky et al., 1986) and fails to challenge students to generate their own ideas. Clearly, we are presenting a very different approach to viewing videos here.

## Live Demonstration

Students benefit from observing expertise-in-action, so instructors who are counseling experts offer their students a gift by demonstrating their expertise. Instructors who are less expert might bring in videos of expert counselors-in-action. However, instructors may also give up the expert role or challenge the supposed "experts." When, in a live demonstration, the supposed expert instructor makes "mistakes," he may acknowledge

publicly how his efforts didn't work well and what he might have done differently if given another chance. The instructor might expose his own thinking process as it occurred during the session. In this way the threat level of learning counseling skills is reduced and the emerging, situation-driven use of them is demonstrated.

## Role Play

Instructors might also challenge students by asking them to spontaneously role-play fictitious cases in small groups. The cases might be accompanied by questions that ask students to do such things as "give three effective paraphrases a counselor might use in response to the client's concerns."

## Simulation

Alternatively, students might generate planned simulations, or scripts, for demonstrating the skills. Groups of students might discuss, decide on, and then act out effective use of paraphrases. During these activities, students must reach beyond what they have been told by the book or the instructor and generate knowledge. They also begin thinking ahead to real-world situations and thus preparing themselves to face professional challenges. They access many avenues and styles of learning, tapping into all three of the learning domains—cognition, behavior, and affect—in the process.

# In-Class and Out-of-Class Practice

In some helping fields, little or no practice of counseling skills occurs before the first practicum. Thankfully, that has not been the case in counseling for the past generation. However, for those who teach the helping interview course with minimal opportunity for practice of skills, a reminder of theory and research related to education may be warranted here. For instance, Kolb's (1984) model indicates the need for regular and sequential experimentation in learning. Such application contributes to retention (Dale, 1969), as it requires the performance, not just the recognition, of a behavior. Bandura's (1997) work also has demonstrated the primacy of performance over vicarious learning.

Thus after students have read about the skills and observed and analyzed demonstrations of skills, they need to try out the skills during and after the class period. Most students find such practice to be anxiety producing. They are asked to dwell in the netherworld of not quite knowing enough yet being asked to perform. They thus discover that practice, rather than perfection, generates many questions and concerns.

Therefore, to balance the inherent challenge of this task, supports need to be provided. In the safety of the classroom, for instance, students can immediately be coached, their questions can be answered during teachable moments, they can get relatively nonthreatening feedback (because no grade is involved) from a variety of peers, and they can prepare for the longer between-class practice sessions.

Other support may be gleaned from providing a very clear structure for practice. For instance, the instructor may divide the class into triads and issue the following instructions: "For five minutes, one person is the counselor, another the client, and another the observer. Then, for two minutes the counselor self-evaluates using the previous discussion of the subskills components to guide the self-evaluation. For two minutes, the client talks about how she or he felt while participating in the counseling, also using the previous discussion as a guide. And for two minutes, the observer offers feedback, using the Feedback Sheets to structure the process." The Feedback Sheets that I (Eriksen) use ask clients or observers to answer the following questions: What is your gut reaction to the interviewer's style and way of being? How would (did) you feel if you were (as) the client? Identify the specific (assigned) skills that the interviewer did. Which of these did the interviewer do particularly well? Identify the skills done that were not specifically assigned. Did these interfere with time to do the assigned skills? Did they seem natural? Necessary?

Requiring students to offer their own observations communicates clearly that the views of each member are to be valued. I (Eriksen) have often had students indicate that they only wanted feedback from me because they somehow believed that my knowledge would be more helpful or accurate. While I believe that I have much to offer and do share my impressions with students, I also share with them that, semester after semester, when I read and listen to the peer feedback, I find it to be congruent with my own impressions of students' performance. They are usually surprised at this. In response to their surprise, I ask them to consider that in the "real" world, clients are people just like *them*. And counselors-in-training ought to be very interested in their clients' opinions about how helpful they are. After all, the clients are the ones who will choose whether or not to return for more counseling on the basis of whether they evaluate the work to be helpful and the counselor to be caring.

Students continue the benefits of classroom practice by practicing outside of class with a peer or an undergraduate volunteer what they have learned in class each week. During the early part of the course, these counseling sessions are short and highly structured, designed to help them practice one microskill at a time. As the semester progresses, sessions increase in time and complexity; students add subskills, building toward a coherent session. Out-of-class counseling sessions provide a fairly safe environment for counseling, free from direct evaluation or observation. The aspiring counselors try on new behaviors, make mistakes, recover from their missteps, and explore the boundaries of what counseling means.

The between-class requirement that students practice interviewing skills sends them out on their own into the realm of ambiguity. Active encounters with real-life challenges stimulate students to question how and when to apply certain skills and the reasons for choosing them. These encounters may also create doubt about the usefulness of specific skills.

Such try-outs, while fluid and relatively spontaneous, are not amorphous, however. Instructors provide developmentally appropriate structure for these between-class practice sessions. For instance, instructors tell students that the sessions are to be a specific length of time, they are to include certain subskills, and they are to be audio- or video-recorded. I (Eriksen) also provide students with Feedback Sheets (as outlined above) to structure the feedback that they offer to one another.

## Self-Assessment and Reflection

Theorists (e.g., Kegan, 1982) consider the ability to reflect on one's life to be a developmental achievement.

Self-reflection requires the capacity to take oneself as "object," something that many students are not consistently able to do at the time that they begin graduate school (Kegan, 1998; Neukrug & McAuliffe, 1993). The reflection on action (Schön & Argyris, 1995) involved in trying out what is read and then reflecting during structured journaling communicates the value of pausing and speaking in measured tones, which are characteristic of evidence-based, procedural knowing (Belenky et al., 1996), or institutional (Kegan, 1982) or modernist knowing (Kegan, 1998). Many of the course activities discussed thus far have incorporated self-critique and reflection. However, here we discuss these more explicitly.

Following in-class and between-class practice sessions, we ask students to carefully consider, through self-assessment papers, what they have done, how well they have done it, and what they would do differently next time. Students must thus stand back from what is or has been, from their own behavior, and from their relationship with the client and think carefully about all of it. They write journal entries about how they felt and what they thought while practicing counseling. They also reflect on what personal, family, and cultural history might have contributed to the feelings they had while counseling. For example, because of personal history and defenses, some students have a difficult time with confrontation, others with simple listening.

For most students, reflection is a significant challenge; as a result, instructors need to offer substantial levels of support. I (Eriksen) have found that offering specific guidelines and exemplars contributes to that support. Exemplars illustrate what I think reflection or self-assessment might look like. These serve to "hold" students who have never reflected before while they try on a new way of knowing (see Appendix A on page 102 for instructions and exemplars that are offered to students).

Since self-reflection can't be "wrong," we do not recommend giving grades for journal entries or self-assessment papers. However, instructors might, when students periodically hand in their reflections, offer ongoing feedback and pose questions about what students have written. This feedback creates a kind of dialogue, which gives instructors a chance to support and challenge students toward new developmental levels. For instance, in response to a student who reports events or facts, I (Eriksen) write such supportive statements as "You seem to have assessed *what* happened quite descriptively" along with writing challenging questions such as "How did you feel when this happened?" "What did you think when she said that?" "What meaning do you make of this behavior?" If students offer absolutist statements or opinions without evidence, instructors might support them by responding, "You seem very clear about what you think in this situation," while challenging them with "What other possible ways of evaluating the situation might there be?" If instructors are able to offer the appropriate balance of support and challenge, students ought to feel safe enough to reach more deeply into themselves in future reflections.

The benefits of this cycle of active reading, demonstration, discussion, and activity are numerous. *Better retention is assured* when students must generate knowledge or produce an idea or action (McNamara, Scott, & Bess, 2000). *Procedural knowing emerges* through the challenge to analyze both macro and micro dimensions of counseling skills, through stimulating students to think beyond their subjective impressions and to give evidence for their evaluations, and through posing questions that generate conflicting views. *Better solutions are constructed* in the context of a community of learners from diverse cultures and with varied experiences through challenging students to fully voice their diverse opinions and urging them to decide together what to do about disagreements. Such dialogically generated knowledge can be more useful than independently generated ideas.

In addition, the *emergent nature of knowledge is demonstrated* when the instructor becomes a question poser rather than only an answer giver. Continually asking, "What do you think?" "Who agrees?" "Why or why not?" "Who feels differently?" "What if . . . ?" challenges students to take risks, to put themselves on the line, to offer tentative ideas rather than waiting until they discover the "right" answers. During such unfinished discussions, out of the space between human beings in community, new ideas and thoughts emerge. Many are the times that I (Eriksen) have entered the classroom armed with questions and a list of the particular answers I think the class should "discover," only to find that during the discussion the class generates more and sometimes better answers than I constructed on my own. While it seems right that I, as the instructor, initially take responsibility for posing questions, and refereeing among different positions, I also need to make space for and respect the questions and answers that students generate from their own life experiences and thinking processes.

# EVALUATION

## Formative Evaluation

I (Eriksen) conceive of evaluation in this course as an ongoing dialogue, a co-constructed process in which the entire class community participates. Most of the evaluation is based on observable behavior and the ability to make sense of two factors: one's own and the client's behavior. Students regularly offer feedback to challenge each other to reach the height of their ability. Peers watch for signals about whether feedback is being perceived as helpful. They own their own reactions and try to be very specific about what worked and how they determined that it worked. The instructor makes every effort to offer both support and challenge in the feedback given.

Evaluation or feedback takes several forms. Students first self-evaluate, in order to evoke their own voices about their performance after in-class role plays, after reviewing their practice session videos and throughout the semester in journals and reflective papers.

Peer evaluation is also central. Following their self-evaluation of in-class role plays, students solicit input from their peers. After between-class practice sessions, counselors solicit input from their "clients." The instructor then asks students to include what they hear from peers in their written self-assessments. Emphasizing the importance of self- and peer evaluation communicates the importance of students developing their own voice and trusting their intuition.

Instructor evaluation is, of course, also part of the ongoing dialogue. Our input as veteran helper-educators is critical to student learning and to our gatekeeping role for the protection of future clients. When evaluating, the constructivist instructor intentionally balances support and challenge. In that vein, when reviewing class role plays and videos of student sessions, the instructor points out and evokes strengths and competencies. The instructor also assertively and clearly critiques what isn't working, makes suggestions about alternate interventions, and offers comments on what she or he perceives to be most or least helpful.

This ongoing dialogue, or formative evaluation, offers students the opportunity to respond to and challenge the instructor throughout the semester. However, the process can still be quite threatening or challenging for some students. Yet it is difficult to conceive of helping students improve without offering them feedback on what does and doesn't work. If students become over-challenged, instructors will need to increase support (for instance, provide greater structure and direction or express appreciation for a student's interpersonal [Kegan, 1998] capacities). Once students feel safely supported, instructors may experience greater success in offering suggestions for improvement.

## Summative Evaluation

At the middle and end of the semester, instructors typically offer summative evaluations analyzing and evaluating students' mastery of counseling skills and their ability to think about what clients most need from the counselor. Thus, I (Eriksen) use a process of evaluation that merely continues what students have been doing all semester. They turn in mid-semester and end-of-semester video demonstrations of an exemplary counseling session, accompanied by both a transcript that explains what skills they were using and why and a self-evaluation of their performance. As a support prior to completing the mid-semester and final videos, I make a grading sheet available to students that lists the specific skills required in the videos (whatever skills have been covered in class to date; see Appendix C) and how grades will be determined. I also provide specific instructions and exemplars for the transcript and the self-evaluation (see Appendices A and B).

In response to the students' submissions, the instructor offers feedback that includes her perceptions of what worked well; other possible interventions, to extend the counselor's range of possibilities; and interventions that might be better received by the client. For the midsemester videos, the instructor indicates specific improvements (e.g., examples of the words a counselor might actually say) that students might make in order to improve their grade on the final video. Such feedback offers students a sense that they have some control in the evaluation process, countering their feelings that evaluation is done "to" them. Students are rarely surprised at their end-of-semester grades. Finally, I (Eriksen) give students the opportunity to redo their final videos if they are unhappy with their grades or their performances. Students have repeatedly found this specific feedback and the opportunity for a redo to be some of the most helpful elements of this course.

## CONCLUSION

We believe that promoting development is fundamental to educating effective counselors. While many readers may find little new in this chapter's presentation of the counseling skills course, others may not have considered how to ground the course in a constructivist or developmental framework or how to use the coursework to promote development. As you review our ideas about how this course might be structured, we hope that you notice that we have attempted to make the learning experiences as active, experiential, and inductive as possible. We hope that you realize our attempt to offer opportunities and challenges for students to develop their own voices and to access their own inner stores of knowledge. We hope it is clear that we have valued each person's experiences and asked students to bring their experiences to the classroom discussions. We believe that only when each person's voice is heard are we likely to come up with the best ideas and that these ideas are continually emerging. Finally, we believe that learning communities are the best environments for creating knowledge. The Counseling Skills course can be such a gathering.

## REFERENCES

Bandura, A. (1997). *Self-efficacy: The exercise of control.* New York: W. H. Freeman.

Belenky, M., Clinchy, B., Goldberger, N., & Tarule, J. (1996). *Women's ways of knowing.* New York: Basic Books.

Benack, S. (1988). Relativistic thought: A cognitive basis for empathy in counseling. *Counselor Education and Supervision, 27*(3), 216–232.

Carkhuff, R. R., & Berenson, B. G. (1977). *Beyond counseling and therapy.* New York: Holt, Rinehart & Winston.

Dale, E. (1969). *Audio-visual methods in teaching.* New York: Holt, Rinehart & Winston.

Ivey, A. E. (1994). Intentional interviewing and counseling (3rd ed.). Pacific Grove, CA: Brooks/Cole.

Kegan, R. (1982). *The evolving self: Problem and process in human development.* Cambridge, MA: Harvard University Press.

Kegan, R. (1998). *In over our heads: The mental demands of modern life.* Cambridge, MA: Harvard University Press.

Kolb, D. (1984). *Experiential learning.* Englewood Cliffs, NJ: Prentice Hall.

Loevinger, J. (1976). *Ego development.* San Francisco: Jossey-Bass.

Lovell, C., & McAuliffe, G. (1996, October). *From nonconstructivist to constructivist counseling.* Paper presented at the quadrennial meeting of the Association for Counselor Education and Supervision, Portland, OR.

McNamara, D. S., Scott, J., & Bess, T. (2000). Building blocks of knowledge: Constructivism from a cognitive perspective. In G. McAuliffe & K. Eriksen (Eds.), *Preparing counselors and therapists: Creating constructivist and developmental programs* (pp. 62–76). Alexandria, VA: Association for Counselor Education and Supervision.

Neukrug, E. S., & McAuliffe, G. J. (1993). Cognitive development and human service education. *Human Service Education, 13,* 13–26.

Sanford, N. (1966). *Self and society.* New York: Atherton Press.

Schön, D. A. (1983). *The reflective practitioner.* New York: Basic Books.

Schön, D. A., & Argyris, C. (1995). *Organizational learning: Theory, method, and practice.* Boston: Addison-Wesley Longman.

Widick, C., Knefelkamp, L. L., & Parker, C. A. (1975). The counselor as a developmental instructor. *Counselor Education and Supervision, 14*(4), 286–296.

# Appendix A
## Self-Assessment/Reflection

The purpose of reflection is to think about or introspect about the material you are learning and the experiences you are having in class and outside of class. Reflection means many things to many people. However, in our rushed lifestyle we often do not stop to reflect, and thus live an unexamined life. For the purpose of this assignment, you will write an end-of-semester reflection paper that responds to and evaluates your experiences during Counseling I.

Write a five-page, double-spaced, 12-size-font, grammatically correct, well-organized paper evaluating yourself as a counselor. Address the specific skills you have read about, been directed to work on, discussed, and practiced during and between classes. Give evidence for your statements. Let me know that you are aware of your strengths, your growing edges, and the personal issues that may impact your work as a counselor. In addition to the examples stated below that reflect on specific skills, please evaluate yourself overall as a counselor.

Reflection should include the following:

1. Statement of the situation: This includes a sentence or two about "what happened." For instance, "When I was practicing reflective listening today with my best friend, I found it hard to keep listening and not make suggestions about what she should do to solve her problem." It may be tempting to include a lot more than a sentence or two. In fact, it may be tempting to journal only about events. Make every attempt to contain yourself.

2. Your thoughts about the situation: Beyond the actual facts of the situation is your interpretation or thoughts about it. Your interpretation impacts both your feelings about it and your decisions about how to respond. An example of thoughts about the situation above might be "I had thought previously that I was a good listener. And now I realize that while I care a lot about my friends, I am usually putting a lot of input into our conversations, rather than allowing space for them to talk fully about themselves."

3. Your feelings about these thoughts: Feelings are feelings, not thoughts. That is, feelings are angry, sad, hurt, happy, exuberant, discouraged, etc. If you find yourself saying, "I feel that . . ." or "I feel as though . . ." or "I feel like . . . ," you are expressing a thought or opinion, not a feeling. An example of a feeling reaction to the thought expressed above in #2 might be "I am disappointed when I look back on all the conversations I have had with friends, when I think I might not have been as caring as I wanted to be. I feel hopeful that now I can care more effectively. I also am excited about trying these skills out on friends and on real clients. I feel encouraged that something relatively simple might help people a lot."

4. Your related issues or reasons: This includes your ideas about how your experiences, and your thoughts and feelings about your experiences, might be related to your own issues or history. It is important to understand that experiences, feelings, and thoughts do not just happen, for you or for your "clients" and loved ones. They have some roots in a person's history, culture, gender, religion, or other previous experiences. Understanding yourself and why you respond in certain ways is the first step to making choices and having greater control in the future about how you respond. It is particularly important in the mental health field to understand yourself, because clients and mental health organizations will "push many buttons" if you don't (and perhaps even if you do) understand and have some conscious control over yourself. Further, if you find yourself in trouble, it will probably be necessary to understand your responses to the troubling situation in order to get yourself out of trouble. An example of issues or history related to the situation expressed above might be "I realize that in my family people didn't listen very much. In fact, people felt that the most loving thing to do was to provide a solution to the problem the other person was expressing. Many times we would end up arguing over why it was or wasn't a good solution. I often felt as though no one really cared about why I was bringing up the problem in the

first place. Now I know that it was because even though people cared, they were not expressing to me their understanding of what I was saying. So in those moments, I didn't think they cared very much."

Make sure to answer questions such as the following:

- What is my gut reaction about my style and way of being during counseling sessions? How would I have felt if I were the client?
- What specific (assigned) skills do I do? How well do I do them? How successful are they in accomplishing what the interventions should accomplish? Explain.
- Do the interventions that I deliver seem natural? Necessary?
- What two or three things will I work on next semester?
- What are my thoughts/opinions about the learning process and how I am doing with it?

## SAMPLE WEEKLY REFLECTION PAPER/SKILLS SECTION

*This week in class we were talking about reflective listening. I found it hard to keep listening and not make suggestions about what my partner should do to solve her problem. I spent some time watching people outside of class too, and found that many people don't really listen. I was also noticing that an awful lot of people don't make eye contact or maintain an open position. Sometimes they don't ask many questions before they respond either.*

*I also tried in my practice session and with my friends to do the reflective listening. While it was hard not to give solutions or suggestions, I found that the other person talked more if I listened. A couple of people actually expressed to me that they appreciated my listening instead of giving solutions. I think I was successful about half the time. I didn't realize it would be so hard. When I did listen and reflect effectively, my "client" did talk more, and did talk more openly. When I reflected, but didn't quite get it right, she corrected me, but didn't seem too upset by my not being right. It seemed that when I reflected feelings, the whole session changed into something deeper and more meaningful. She reported that she felt understood and cared for when we spoke afterward. I am finding that attending is easier after practicing it for a couple of weeks. I find myself leaning forward more*

*naturally, maintaining eye contact without staring, and using a tone of voice that seems less forced. It is hard to keep questions open. I asked both closed and open questions, and the open questions seemed to work better. But you can really see how questioning can interfere with attending and reflecting. Sometimes it seemed that when I questioned her, she was stymied and it seemed to interfere with her train of thought. Next time I plan to really focus on the client and worry less about my responses. I think that will help me know what to reflect, what is most important to reflect. I think it will help me ask only necessary and on-target questions. And I think that that kind of focus will naturally make me attend well.*

*I had thought previously that I was a good listener. And now I realize that while I care a lot about my friends, I am usually putting a lot of input into our conversations, rather than allowing space for them to talk fully about themselves. I am disappointed when I look back on all the conversations I have had with friends before, when I think I might not have been as caring as I wanted to be. I feel hopeful that now I can care more effectively. I also am excited about trying these skills out on friends and on real clients. I feel encouraged that something relatively simple might help people a lot.*

*I realize that in my family people didn't listen very much. In fact, people felt that the most loving thing to do was to provide a solution to the problem the other person was expressing. Many times we would end up arguing over why it was or wasn't a good solution. I often felt as though no one really cared about why I was bringing up the problem in the first place. Now I know that it was because even though people cared, they were not expressing to me their understanding of what I was saying. So in those moments, I didn't think they cared very much.*

*I have also been wondering about what the value of all this is. I mean, if most people don't do this attending and probing and listening, why should we? Is it normal? Is this what it means to be a counselor? Are we supposed to be different from other people? I mean, it isn't really just something you do at work, like some computer person would do computer skills. We are talking here about a way of being, a change in us personally. I can't imagine that we can just do it at work and not do it in the rest of our lives. So will people think we are weird? Will people think we are psychoanalyzing them? Are we asking questions and paying* attention to things that no one really wants us to? Might we be embarrassing them to focus in on such personal things? Somehow it seems OK to do this with clients or patients. But I don't know about doing it in my personal life.

And yet, when I think of the people who have made the most impact on my life, they seem to ask these kinds of questions and have paid attention to me and listened to me in the ways this class is teaching. I feel kind of confused about which way to go. But I am challenged to find out what seems right. I guess it is no surprise given the way my family is that I would wonder about this. And it certainly has not helped to be this new way in my family. They don't notice that I am listening. They just ask me why I am being so quiet, what's wrong with me. I guess I will have to practice on friends for now.

## SAMPLE FINAL SELF-EVALUATION PAPER

As I look back over the semester, I am surprised by what I was unable to do initially and what comes quite easily now. I suppose that is the way it is with new skills. They seem so foreign initially. But I am happy with what I have accomplished. I find that attending comes quite easily now. I am able to keep eye contact and to maintain an open body position. I find myself able to communicate clearly that I am with the person and to follow in a more relaxed way what they are saying. I do question sometimes whether I should do this with everyone. I mean, if I attend this way, won't it mean that even people I won't want to listen to will be hanging on me? I am not sure I want that. I may have to develop some nonattending skills—of course, not when I am working as a counselor—but for those times when I really don't have time or when it is someone I don't want to encourage.

Questioning is something I have never had a problem with. My mother used to tell me that I asked more questions than anyone she knew. I find that I never run out of questions because I am really interested in what people have to say. I am finding that I am better now at asking open questions. I also have learned a little better how to ask questions that will help the client explore, rather than questions that are just to satisfy my curiosity. I think I will probably have to remember to use fewer questions and to use the other skills more.

**[and so on, evaluating yourself on each of the skills, identifying strengths and areas to still work on, examining the progress you have made]**

This is an example of what your transcript might look like. Notice that all of the clients' words are included. Then the counselor's words are included, followed by naming the skill that has been used and including some explanation of why that skill seemed appropriate at that time. If it seems as though some other skill might have been appropriate, or as though you might have said it differently or more clearly, include that also. Then reflect on whether the intervention had the desired impact on the client.

| Verbatim Session | Skill Used and Reason | Evaluation of Intervention— Better Option? | Impact on Client |
|---|---|---|---|
| **Client**: I really want to talk about my roommate. She has been giving me all kinds of trouble lately. | | | |
| **Counselor:** Uh-huh. | Minimal encourage, to encourage client to continue talking without interrupting the flow of expression | | |
| **Client:** I come in at night and she is waiting for me at the door with complaints of some kind: I have eaten some of her food, or I have left some dishes in the sink, or I was making too much noise last night on the computer, or with my stereo, or talking on the phone. | | | This was effective and helpful in encouraging continued talk by client. |
| **Counselor:** You are upset that she has so many complaints. | Paraphrase, to communicate my understanding of what the client is saying and to let the client know that I am with her. | Could have been clearer on the feeling, as this feeling is rather ambiguous. | |
| **Client:** Right! I can't believe she is so constant about the complaints, and has so many, and about so many picky things. I find myself dreading coming home at night, wondering what she is going to be upset about next. I find myself wondering if | | | She really seems to indicate that she felt heard, that I was with her. And she is encouraged to keep talking about what is bothering her, about important issues. |

*(Continued)*

(Continued)

| Verbatim Session | Skill Used and Reason | Evaluation of Intervention—Better Option? | Impact on Client |
|---|---|---|---|
| I am going to get evicted and not have a place to live, because she will complain to the landlord. I'm not sure I would even care at this point because it is so awful living with her right now. | | | |
| **Counselor**: You are not just upset, but you also worry about a place to live and whether you will be in trouble with the landlord | Reflection of feeling and content, to take session to deeper level while letting the client know that I understand what she is experiencing, letting her know that I am right with her, empathizing with her. | Again, *upset* is a rather ambiguous feeling word. Could have used *distressed*, or *irritated*, or *annoyed*. I think I successfully capture a couple of different feelings here to help her feel understood. | |

# Appendix C
## Counseling Skills Scale-R (CSS)

University Name _____    Student Name _____

Review by Audio_____Video_____Transcript_____    Faculty  Name _____

Reviewed After Skills _____Practicum _____School Intern _____Comm/MH Intern _____

Grade faculty anticipates student will receive_____

This survey assesses the quality of student performance of counseling skills. It divides 19 specific microskills into six groupings (in caps following roman numerals). Please first rate the student's microskills as –2, –1, 0, +1, or +2 according to the scale below. Then summarize each grouping of skills by adding and averaging its individual microskills scores. Place that average in the blank following the grouping heading. NOTE: If a skill is not performed but does not seem necessary, then assign it an NN and average only those skills performed into mean grouping scores. If a skill is not performed but should have been, then give it a –1 score and average it with the rest of the skills performed under that super-heading.

+2   Highly developed: helpful, well timed, and consistently well performed

+1   Well developed: helpful and well timed when performed, but not consistently smooth

 0   Developing skills: somewhat helpful, too many missed opportunities

–1   Continue practice: not helpful or well timed, or no skill existent when it should be

–2   Major adjustment needed: not at all helpful or well timed, harmful

NN   Not performed, but not necessary; (an)other skill(s) within this grouping used to effectively meet this grouping's goals

### I.  SHOWS INTEREST AND APPRECIATION                                    Group Score _____

1.  **Body Language and Appearance**—Maintains open, relaxed, confident posture with appropriate eye contact. Forward lean, comfortable position shows interest. Uses head nods and body gestures to encourage client talk. Maintains professional dress.    –2 –1 0 +1 +2

2.  **Minimal Encouragers**—Repeats key words and phrases. Uses prompts (uh-huh, okay, right, yes) to let client know she or he is heard. Uses silence helpfully.    –2 –1 0 +1 +2

3.  **Vocal Tone**—Uses vocal tone that matches the sense of the session and session goals. Vocal tone communicates caring and connection with the client.    –2 –1 0 +1 +2

4.  **Evoking and Punctuating Client Strengths**—Session grounded in appreciation of and belief in client and in client strengths and accomplishments.    –2 –1 0 +1 +2 NN

## II. ENCOURAGES EXPLORATION (Primary Empathy)    Group Score _____

5. **Questioning**—Asks open-ended questions that encourage the client to continue talking and to provide information. Uses judiciously when needed and when theoretically consistent. Does not overuse questions.

−2 −1 0 +1 +2 NN

6. **Requesting Concrete and Specific Examples**—Asks for concrete and specific instances when client provides vague generalities. ("Could you give me an example of [or specifics about] how he might show you love?")

−2 −1 0 +1 +2 NN

7. **Paraphrasing (reflection of content)**—Engages in brief, accurate, and clear rephrasing of what the client has expressed.

−2 −1 0 +1 +2 NN

8. **Summarizing**—Makes statements at key (a few) moments in the session that capture the overall sense of what the client has been expressing.

−2 −1 0 +1 +2 NN

## III. DEEPENS THE SESSION (Advanced Empathy)    Group Score _____

9. **Reflecting Feeling**—States succinctly the feeling and the content of the problem faced by the client ("You feel _____ when _____.")

−2 −1 0 +1 +2 NN

10. **Using Immediacy**—Reflects here-and-now session experiences of the client or the counselor—how session is going, how relationship is going, nonverbals that client is not expressing verbally. ("As we talk about _____ problem, I sense you are feeling _____ about me. In turn, I'm feeling _____ about how you are viewing the problem right now.")

−2 −1 0 +1 +2 NN

11. **Observing Themes and Patterns**—Identifies more overarching patterns of client acting, thinking, or behaving that may be related to the problem ("In _____ situations, you regularly do _____ [or think _____ or feel _____], which seems to lead to _____, which causes you problems.")

−2 −1 0 +1 +2 NN

12. **Challenging/Pointing Out Discrepancies**—Expresses observations of discrepancies between plans and behaviors, between desires and actions, etc. ("You expect yourself to do _____ when facing the problem of _____, but you do _____ instead. What do you make of this?")

−2 −1 0 +1 +2 NN

13. **Reflecting Meaning and Values**—Reflects the unexpressed meaning or belief/value system that is behind the words the client is saying. ("You feel strongly about your choice to _____ because it reflects values you were raised with.")

−2 −1 0 +1 +2 NN

## IV. ENCOURAGES CHANGE    Group Score _____

14. **Determining Goals and Desired Outcomes**—Collaboratively determines outcomes toward which the counseling process will aim. Helps client set goals. Miracle question or alternative.

−2 −1 0 +1 +2 NN

15. **Using Strategies for Creating Change**—Uses theoretically consistent and intentional intervention strategies to help client move forward toward treatment goals (such as setting up reinforcement systems, using guided imagery, directives, self-disclosure, interpretation, information, instruction, search for exceptions or past successes).

–2 –1 0 +1 +2 NN

16. **Considering Alternatives and Their Consequences**—Helps client review and evaluate possible solutions. ("One option would be _____, and that would mean _____. Another option would be _____.")

–2 –1 0 +1 +2 NN

17. **Planning Action and Anticipating Possible Obstacles**—Reaches agreement about actions to take between sessions, who is responsible for them, and when they will be done. Helps client identify obstacles that might interfere and decide how to handle them. ("So, you will do _____ by _____ date. What could prevent you from accomplishing your plan?")

–2 –1 0 +1 +2 NN

## V. DEVELOPS THERAPEUTIC RELATIONSHIP

Score _____

18. **Consistently engaging in caring manner with client,** particularly by demonstrating such core conditions as genuineness and authenticity, warmth and acceptance, respect and positive regard, and empathy.

–2 –1 0 +1 +2

## VI. MANAGES THE SESSION

Score _____

19. **Opening session smoothly and warmly greeting client.** Begins work on counseling issues in a timely way. Structures session, directing client naturally through opening, exploration, deeper understanding, creating change, and closing; focuses client on essence of issues at a level deep enough to promote positive movement. Smoothly and warmly ends the session in a timely way, planning for future sessions or for termination.

–2 –1 0 +1 +2

**TOTAL CSS SCORE** (add grouping averages): _____

**Instructor Comments:**

© Karen Eriksen. Permission to copy after participating in rater training and contingent on sending results back to Karen Eriksen.

# 8

# Teaching Theories for the Constructivist Counselor

Donald A. Strano and Michael G. Ignelzi

What differentiates a technician from a professional? It *is* possible to train counselors to apply techniques that are derived from one or more models of counseling. However, counselors who are merely technically trained will not be likely to make informed choices when faced with the unique stories that clients present. Such technicians will not have the ability to organize new information in ways that will help them respond meaningfully. They will lack the spontaneity, such as the ability to construct useful metaphors in novel situations, that the work requires. Keeny (1990, 1991) compares the process of counseling to that of performance art; in his terms, the counselor is an improvisational performer. Minuchin and Fishman (1981) draw a parallel between training to be a Samurai swordsman and training to be a family counselor, emphasizing the development of a whole person who moves beyond the rote application of technique. Hoffman (1992) describes counseling as a conversational art. The communication approach of Watzlawick, Weakland, and Fisch (1974) underscores this view. Clearly, each of these conceptualizations moves the practice of counseling beyond mere application of techniques.

One difficulty in teaching counseling theories lies in the intersection between students' meaning-making capacities and their abilities to utilize theory. Students eventually internalize theory through an act of co-construction with a source (e.g., a written text, a professor's statements). But if, according to constructivist principles, all knowledge is constructed and cannot be separated from the knower, then there will be differences in how individuals learn about and incorporate theory.

For example, many beginning graduate students of counseling are largely reliant on external authority and conventional norms for direction (called the 3rd Order, or the socialized mind, in Robert Kegan's model of meaning-making development; Kegan, 1998; Kegan & Lahey, 2009). They are likely to adopt and use theory in a rote and mechanized way (Lovell & McAuliffe, 1997; McAuliffe & Lovell, 2006; Neukrug & McAuliffe, 1992) rather than critically thinking about and evaluating the material. This automatic adherence to externally derived concrete rules relates to 3rd-Order thinkers being "embedded in or subject to relationships, roles, and rules" (Eriksen, 2006, p. 294). Although 3rd-Order meaning-makers are capable of empathizing with another's experience, they are likely to subordinate their points of view in favor of the relationship (Eriksen, 2006). This is largely because the "self coheres by its alignment with, and loyalty to, that with which it identifies" (Kegan

& Lahey, 2009, p. 17). As a result, 3rd-Order meaning-makers are inclined to accept a theory wholly, without reflection or modification, solely because a person in authority or a source of authority (e.g., book, formal theory) presented it.

Contrast this inclination with how theory is constructed from a more self-authored position (Kegan's 4th Order, or the self-authoring mind), where external or formal theories are reflected upon, evaluated, and adapted into the individual's own self-authored theory, a theory that is consistent with the person's values and experiences. In Kegan and Lahey's (2009) words, the self-authoring "self coheres by its alignment with its own belief system/ideology/personal code; by its ability to self-direct, take stands, set limits, and create and regulate its boundaries on behalf of its own voice" (p. 17). This 4th-Order meaning-making structure allows one to "internalize multiple points of view, reflect on them, and construct one's own theory about oneself and one's experience" (Ignelzi, 2000, p. 8).

The comparison of these two ways of making meaning demonstrates that the use students make of existing theories will be affected by their level of cognitive complexity. Kegan (1998) suggests that the demands of modern life are beyond the cognitive ability of most individuals, and yet the 4th Order is required for professional decision making, that is, important choices made under conditions of uncertainty (McAuliffe, 2006). As a result, many counselors are in over their heads when we ask them to learn and integrate formal counseling theory into their own personal theory and practice. Therefore, teaching counseling theory must include not only informing students about specific theories, but providing the challenge and support necessary to promote counselors' meaning-making capacities.

## COURSE CONTEXT

The simplest purpose of a counseling theories course is to introduce the notion of counseling theory and its place in the conceptualization of human beings and their problems. Beyond this basic function, the theories course serves four broad purposes when placed early in an entry-level counseling program. First, it introduces the purpose of theories in counseling. Second, it presents a range of possible theories. Third, as mentioned in the introduction, it provides an opportunity to promote students' meaning-making capacities or cognitive complexity. And fourth, if it is taught in conjunction with the lifespan development course (ideally, with lifespan in the previous semester), it encourages students to integrate developmental and counseling models, in congruence with counseling's professional identity.

The overall focus of this course's content is understanding and utilizing theory as a framework for the construction of further knowledge and practice—whether this is in further coursework, skill development, professional reading, case conceptualization, or actual counseling. But the theories course can also enhance students' meaning-making capacities by using constructivist-developmental modes of teaching. This movement to a higher level of cognitive complexity can be crucial, as it affects students' abilities to use the course content in the real-life contexts of counseling. It is our position as authors that developmental and counseling theories cannot be separated into completely discrete categories. Instead, they must be integrated into a more complex model that utilizes both constructivist-developmental and social constructionist theories to describe the whole person in context, whether that person be the student or a client.

## SELECTION OF THEORIES

The selection of specific counseling theories to be included in an entry-level class—out of more than four hundred possible counseling theories (Corsini & Wedding, 2000)—can be difficult. From a constructivist perspective, there are no "true" theories. While, in practice, a counselor may make a commitment to one or more theories on the basis of some pragmatic evidence, an instructor should not privilege one theory over another in this course. Further, it is important to keep in mind that theories themselves are constructions that may be useful without being correct or true (Patterson & Watkins, 1996). There continue to be conflicting positions on the assertion that all approaches to counseling are essentially equivalent in effectiveness (Luborsky, Rosenthal, & Diguer, 2002). Further, a meta-analysis looking at factors that contribute to clients' reported change during the counseling process (Miller, Duncan, & Hubble, 1997) concluded that specific theory and technique account for the smallest portion of that change (Lambert, 1992).

Therefore, if theory is understood to be a "story," that is, a claim to understanding human change based on a set of propositions, rather than an essential truth, then pragmatism guides the instructor's selection of theories for inclusion in this course. This pragmatic choice is based on what will best contribute to the achievement of the course objectives (e.g., the students' development of cognitive complexity and the ability to use theory in a complex manner). The theories identified in the outline in the next section of this chapter are therefore based on our pragmatic view of what best meets this objective and the specific class activities. Different individuals may select different sets of theories to include in the course. Similarly, from a postmodern perspective, the counselor's choice of theory becomes a pragmatic choice, rather than one based on a knowable reality. Hansen (2006) describes the choice of counseling theory in these words: "According to the neopragmatic perspective, the criteria for theory selection should be based on whether a theoretical perspective is helpful in meeting the objectives of a particular counseling situation" (p. 294).

However, it seems that the factors that actually contribute to a counselor's choice of theoretical orientation are more often related to practitioners seeking a "true" theory. That inclination fits with the idea of final truth sought by more dualistic thinkers (McAuliffe & Lovell, 2006; Neukrug & McAuliffe, 1992). That is, some counselors show their dualism in choosing a theory based on received course content, readings assigned in courses, and attachment to supervisors (Freeman, Hayes, Kuch, & Taub, 2007).

## COURSE OVERVIEW: PROCESS AND CONTENT

So how do we influence the process by which future counselors choose a theory? It must occur through a set of coordinated learning materials and experiences that both challenge and support the knower. From a constructivist perspective, language (and thus narrative) is the filter through which individuals construct their world. In turn, individuals are bound by the limits of that language or

narrative (Bateson, 1972). For example, were one to choose Adlerian theory as the theory of choice, the Adlerian construct of a lifestyle would be a narrative that would limit one's ideas about the client's problem and how to address it.

For new meaning to be created, there would need to be sources of novel information—in cybernetic terms, *noise* (Bateson, 1979; Fruggeri, 1992). Noise consists of information that can't be handled by a person's current way of knowing. Instructors would selectively present noise, rather than presenting it randomly. As Becvar and Becvar (2006) state, noise "must be meaningful. It must be couched in the clients' [or students'] language and must fit their world view" (p. 300). The presence of this meaningful information is essential in promoting the construction of new meaning. In the same way that clients need a source of novel information to construct new meaning, so too do counseling students. Counselor educators present meaningful noise, in the form of counseling theories, to students who are unfamiliar with them.

However, novel information must be presented in such a way as to provide both stability (supporting the person's current frame of reference) and change (challenging the person's current frame of reference). Therefore, in addition to presenting the new content of these theories, the instructor needs to match the organization of this noise (that is, how simply or complexly to present the ideas) to the students' level of meaning-making. As students progress through a reflexive exploration of the nature and meaning of counseling theories, such matching contributes the support that is necessary for growth and change. This matching can be seen in the course outline included in this chapter, for example, where humanistic/existential theories are covered at the same time that students are challenged to explore their language of personal responsibility. Thus, theories should be selected and organized to mirror the process of change in cognitive complexity as students move toward higher orders of consciousness.

The primary goal of this course is to help students develop a flexible, relativistic methodology regarding theory usage. Such a methodology will allow them to intentionally reconstruct their theory throughout their professional lives. We divide the theories course into three phases. Following is an overview of the phases. A more detailed description of each will be presented below. We begin with the assumption that all humans use the theories that they construct themselves to make meaning out of the world, a theory that didn't require taking a counseling theories course. For our purposes here we will refer to this as *personal theory*.

Phase 1 (discovery and ownership of currently preferred personal theory) is characterized by an active, experiential process in which instructors facilitate students' awareness of their own use of personal theory in general. Students are challenged to become reflective about the purpose and function of theory. Instructors also challenge, or perturb, positivist assumptions regarding truth, reality, metanarratives, and the form of knowledge.

During Phase 2 (informing personal theory), instructors help students expand and develop their own personal theory into a personal counseling theory. During this phase, instructors "planfully" challenge students' meaning-making through instigating dyadic interaction and process. Parallel to students' personal exploration, instructors create the meaningful noise of learning existing counseling theories as one means of promoting students' constructive development.

Phase 3 (reconstructing personal theory) provides learners with the opportunity to work with their personal counseling theories. This phase involves the active deconstruction of a theory through a thematic analysis of students' counseling activities—making explicit the assumptions, values, and so on that underlie the theory. Students put their evolving personal counseling theory into action during a counseling role play. Other students observe the role play and generate descriptors from formal theories presented previously, reconstructing theory—a step toward integration.

## Course Outline

The specific topics that we include in the course follow the outline presented in Table 8.1. The table also provides an overview of course objectives, content, processes, learning activities, and relevant constructivist principles, as they relate to the three phases of the course.

**TABLE 8.1** Course Objectives, Content, Processes, Learning Activities, and Constructivist Principles

| I. Discovery and Ownership of Personal Theory | | | |
|---|---|---|---|
| *Learning Objectives* | *Content* | *Processes and Activities* | *Constructivist Principles* |
| Develop awareness of the use of theory in everyday life | What is theory?<br>– Origins<br>– Story<br>– Narrative | Individual and group reflections on personal views and assumptions that affect our internalized philosophy of counseling | Humans are active organizers of their experience. |
| Explore how current personal theory impacts choices and behaviors | What purpose does theory serve?<br>– Organizing structure<br>– Grammar for constructing meaning | Class discussions and written paper on how personal views and beliefs influence evolving personal theory of counseling | The discernment of the way things are is a function of our beliefs.<br>The process of perceiving an experience constructs reality. |
| Demonstrate an understanding of the function of theory in professional counseling | Personal theory construction<br>– About self<br>– About actions<br>– About future | Class discussions and written paper on how personal views and beliefs influence evolving personal theory of counseling | Reality is storied through language and narrative.<br>A change in language equals a change in the experience. |
| Challenge positivist assumptions regarding truth and reality | | The professor will use student writing to help demonstrate that theory generation is a personalized and constructive process. | The process of describing an experience constructs reality.<br>The rejection of absolutes—there are no metanarratives. |

| Learning Objectives | Content | Processes and Activities | Constructivist Principles |
|---|---|---|---|
| Enhance personal ability to construct meaning in more complex ways around an individual issue | Diagnosing one's own internalized immunity to change<br><br>Methods to transcend that immunity<br><br>Internal language steps:<br>1. Complaint to commitment<br>2. Blame to personal responsibility<br>3. Resolutions to competing commitments<br>4. Moving from assumptions that hold us to assumptions we hold | Reframing constructs through discussion<br><br>Individual reflection on each step<br><br>Dyadic (reflexive) processing of individual constructions<br><br>Reflective writing about the impact of the experience on students' development | Development in cognitive capacity requires support (matching current ways of knowing) and challenge (mismatching current level of complexity).<br>　– Disequilibration<br>　– Cognitive dissonance<br><br>Reflexivity is central in the construction of meaning.<br><br>Meaning is constructed through relationship (contrast).<br><br>Reality is storied through language and narrative. |
| Apply external theories to the process of personal exploration | Humanistic/existential approaches<br><br>Postmodern and systemic approaches<br><br>Cognitive approaches | Reflective notes on readings:<br>　– One thing I don't understand<br>　– One thing I have an opinion about<br>　– One thing I'd like to discuss more<br><br>Review of prior weeks' emerging themes from reflective notes<br><br>Student-led discussion related to session topic emerging from students' reading notes<br><br>In-class writing in response to stimulus question<br><br>Processing written response | The teacher is a mediator between the knower and the known.<br><br>It is the task of the educator to trigger transformations in how students construct knowledge.<br><br>Knowledge is actively constructed by the individual—you can't separate knowledge from the knower.<br><br>The process of describing an experience constructs reality. |

*III. Reconstructing Personal Theory*

| Learning Objectives | Content | Processes and Activities | Constructivist Principles |
|---|---|---|---|
| Identify common themes across multiple theories | Humanistic/existential approaches<br><br>Postmodern and systemic approaches<br><br>Cognitive approaches | Students work in triads, rotating between counselor, client, and observer<br><br>Student generation of descriptive words for each theory<br><br>Qualitative—thematic analysis of theories covered in class<br><br>Class discussion of meta theory—dimensions meta to the theories discussed | The process of perceiving an experience constructs reality.<br><br>The process of describing an experience constructs reality.<br><br>The rejection of absolutes—there are no metanarratives.<br><br>Social constructionism invites an analysis of how we construct and use our professional knowledge. |

*(Continued)*

| | | | |
|---|---|---|---|
| **TABLE 8.1** (Continued) | | | |
| Integrate multiple formal theories into personal counseling theory | | Guided reflection on the theory both from students' personal experience in the triadic learning activity and their assessment of the utility of the theory to their own developing personal theory of counseling<br><br>Final paper reflecting on student's own experiencing of each theory in relation to their developing personal theory of counseling | The process of describing an experience constructs reality.<br><br>Language is a defining framework rather than a reporting or representational device for our experience.<br><br>A change in language equals a change in the experience. |

# IN-CLASS STRUCTURE, ACTIVITIES, AND ASSIGNMENTS

A central focus of this counseling theories course is assisting students in their developmental transformations toward more complex forms of meaning-making while simultaneously introducing them to counseling theories, in clusters organized by type. The transformation toward greater developmental complexity instigates more complex thinking about both the self and professional practice. What follows are detailed examples of how this course would be organized in three sequential phases. Phase 1 would last three weeks, Phase 2, six weeks, and Phase 3, five weeks.

## Phase 1: Discovery and Ownership of Personal Theory

There are two hoped-for outcomes of this phase of the course. The first is to increase students' awareness of their own personal, implicit theories. The second is to help them recognize that those theories have value because they represent the internalized wisdom that the students have constructed through their life experiences and consideration of those experiences. The chief instructional methods for such change are instigating self-reflection through activities that engage the students in active theory construction about their own meaning-making. Such activities include reflective writing on assigned readings and structured discussion.

The first several meetings of the course focus on becoming aware of and articulating one's own personal theories as related to human behavior, more generally, and the counseling process, more specifically. Most beginning graduate students are likely to assume that theories about counseling/helping are objective truths handed down largely or entirely by external sources (i.e., formal counseling theories published in books and/or taught by the professor). Students are not fully aware that they each must actively construct internal, personal theories about what makes a good helper during the counseling process. If formal theories of counseling are introduced before students discover and articulate their own personal theories of helping, students will view learning these theories as an externalized and uncritical adoption of rote theoretical concepts and prescriptions.

In order to promote a reflective process, no formal theories are introduced during the first few classes. Instead, students engage in a collaborative and reflective process focused on several questions: What role does theory play in your day-to-day life? How do you use theory in addressing everyday issues? What are the types of problems that lend themselves to personal counseling, and why? How can the counselor best help clients with the problems that they present in counseling? Students discuss these questions with each other and with the instructor and then write about their answers. The professor uses this student-generated material to illustrate that theory generation, no matter who does it, is a personalized and constructive process and that students themselves already have their own understandings of how to be of assistance to others. As such, the presentation of formal theory later in the class is aimed at helping students reconstruct and revise their own evolving theories of counseling and to build more complex and coordinated personal theories of counseling.

We have found that another benefit of this "discovery and ownership of personal theory" approach is that students typically generate personal or informal theories based on their experiences and intuition that contain many assumptions and conceptualizations that are similar to formal theories of counseling. As such, when counseling theories are introduced later in the course, they tend to confirm to students that they have and should use their own developing understandings. Students also learn that formal theories have value in helping to "organize and articulate better what we intuitively know or already have observed" (Strange & King, 1990, p. 21). This process has the valuable developmental effect of illustrating to students that they may begin to "author" their own meaning-making about the practice of counseling.

## Phase 2: Informing Personal Theory

The second phase of the course utilizes an adaptation of Kegan and Lahey's (2001, 2009) Internal Languages for Transformation (ILT) process. We pair this process with the presentation of formal counseling theories and concepts. As such, we inform the counseling theories through directly linking a personalized, experiential process (i.e., ILT) with the relevant assumptions and concepts from the theories. Students better understand the formal theories and their relationship to the students' own developing personal theory when they *experience* components of the formal theories.

The aim of ILT is to help individuals understand how they actively construct their own resistance to change and how they can create the change that they seek in their lives and, ultimately, in themselves. Kegan and Lahey (2009) invite individuals to create their own "immunity X-ray or map" as a tool for reframing and transforming how they make meaning of their own immunity to change and for using strategies to transcend that immunity: "The purpose of these activities is simultaneously to promote your own personal learning and to introduce you to a new technology designed to create enough cognitive and emotional 'thrust' that you can at least temporarily win some distance from your own dynamic equilibrium" (p. 7). The ILT process is consistent with the developmental transformations that are reflective of 3rd-Order (the socialized self), 4th-Order (the self-authoring self), and 5th-Order (the transforming self) meaning-making in Kegan's developmental model (Kegan, 1998; Kegan & Lahey, 2009) as well as the parallel transformations of received knowing, self-authorized knowing, and dialectical knowing described by McAuliffe in Chapter 1 of this book.

The ILT process uses concepts that are parallel to those from a number of counseling theories. Therefore, we integrate this developmental transformation process into the content of much of the course. The ILT process involves four steps for diagnosing one's own internalized immunity to change. Steps 1 and 2 connect well with humanistic and existential counseling theories by addressing personal awareness, authenticity, acceptance of self, and openness to experience. Step 3 is related to postmodern and systemic counseling theories in its focus away from either/or thinking and toward pluralism, multiple truths, and social interchange. And Step 4 shares commonalities with cognitive counseling theories through exploration of belief systems, internal language, and dialogue as the construction of meaning. Thus, while not specifically designed by Kegan and Lahey as a vehicle for teaching counseling theories, the ILT process can perform dual duties: first, as a method of personally experiencing the types of reframing and change processes that are embedded in different counseling theories and approaches and, second, as a means of providing opportunities to promote students' thinking toward higher levels of cognitive development. Table 8.2 outlines the four steps of the ILT process and identifies conceptually related counseling theories and developmental transformations.

| TABLE 8.2 | Internal Languages for Transformation Process Steps and Related Counseling Theories | |
|---|---|---|
| *Steps* | *Counseling Theories Conceptually Related* | *Developmental Transitions Influenced* |
| 1. Commitment<br><br>Identify goals for personal and/or professional improvement (i.e., behaviors and/or attitudes that the individual is committed to changing). | Humanistic and existential | 3rd Order (received knowing)—4th Order (self-authorized knowing) |
| 2. Doing/Not Doing Instead<br><br>Identify specific behaviors engaged in that work against meeting particular goals or commitments from Step 1. | Humanistic and existential | 3rd Order (received knowing)—4th Order (self-authorized knowing) |
| 3. Competing Commitments<br><br>Uncover the competing and hidden commitments held (typically based on fears) that support the obstructive behaviors identified in Step 2. | Postmodern and systemic | 4th Order (self-authorized knowing)—5th Order (dialectical knowing) |
| 4. Big Assumptions<br><br>Uncover the untested assumptions being made that underlie and support the competing commitments of Step 3. These big assumptions are typically quite extreme, often containing perceived catastrophic consequences to the self. | Cognitive | 4th Order (self-authorized knowing)—5th Order (dialectical knowing) |

Students first individually work through each of the four ILT steps during this phase of the course. They then reflect further by sharing their experiences with an assigned classmate. Kegan and Lahey's (2001) book *How the Way We Talk Can Change the Way We Work* is required for the class and is used as a workbook in this process. After completion of each step, the professor presents the formal counseling theories and approaches most related to the particular step just experienced. As a result, students can connect their own developmentally transformative experiences with counseling theories and strategies that aim to facilitate similar transformations in clients. This process of transformative change gives counseling students a better understanding of the theories and how the related approaches might be experienced by a client.

After the class completes all four ILT steps and the counseling theory presentations during Phase 2 of the course, the instructor guides the students in exploring the relationships among the ILT process, the related counseling theories, and the goals of developmental transformations (e.g., Kegan's orders). Students write about the effects of this experience on their own development as well as on their perceptions about effective counseling through the application of the theories presented.

A brief description of how the ILT process (Kegan & Lahey, 2001, 2009) is specifically utilized in the counseling theories course is provided next.

## ILT Step 1: Identifying Improvement Goals/Commitments

During the first step in the ILT process, students identify a few goals for personal and/or professional improvement, that is, behaviors or attitudes that they are committed to changing. Kegan and Lahey (2001, 2009) posit that when individuals are asked to identify how their lives might be improved, they often identify others as the source of their complaints or whose attitudes and behaviors need to change in order for them to experience improvement. An example of a complaint that a beginning counseling student might identify is that clients often don't talk enough during counseling sessions, forcing the counselor to fill the silences with talk and advice giving.

The ILT process asks individuals to transform the language of what might be seen as complaints to the language of commitment by posing the question "What commitments or convictions that you hold are actually implied [in your complaints]?" (Kegan & Lahey, 2001, p. 21). An example of a commitment or improvement goal that a beginning counseling student might identify at this step is to become a better listener and become more comfortable with silence during counseling sessions. This shift in language or reframing from complaint to commitment mirrors what often occurs in humanistic counseling. In that tradition, the counselor attempts to help clients realize their personal role in and responsibility for their presenting issues. The humanistic counselor emphasizes how clients typically have more authority over changing their situations than they may understand. The reframing process also illustrates the logic that underlies the developmental transformation from the co-constructed meaning-making of 3rd-Order reasoning (e.g., that others are responsible for one's feelings, as one is responsible for theirs) to the more self-authored reasoning of the 4th Order (e.g., individuals, including oneself, have control over and can take responsibility for their own feelings).

## ILT Step 2: Understanding the Behavior(s) That Keep Us From Realizing Our Improvement Goals/Commitments

In this step of the ILT process, students identify specific behaviors in which they engage that work against meeting a particular goal or commitment of theirs. The focus here, as in Step 1, is on personal responsibility and action. This step asks, "What are you doing, or not doing, that is keeping your commitment from being more fully realized?" (Kegan & Lahey, 2001, p. 33).

Kegan and Lahey (2009) assert that it is important to view these obstructive behaviors respectfully. They contain useful information that helps individuals better understand the nature of the challenge faced in achieving the changes they desire. Elements of humanistic counseling theories and 4th Order (self-authoring) meaning-making are embedded in this step of the process as well. The beginning counseling student referenced in Step 1 above might identify that she often inserts her views during the counseling interaction instead of listening more intently to what her client says. In addition, she identifies her tendency to break moments of silence by asking questions or giving her opinion. Thus, at the end of Step 2, students have identified obstructive behaviors (those that keep them from realizing their improvement goals).

## ILT Step 3: Discovering Hidden Competing Commitments to Our Improvement Goals/Commitments

Kegan and Lahey (2001) contend that individuals hold *competing commitments* that undermine their improvement goals. These competing commitments underlie and support the obstructive behaviors identified in Step 2. These commitments are based on individuals' fears and are often hidden from their own awareness. This dynamic largely accounts for individuals' immunity to change. The work of Step 3 is to uncover these fears and to understand that individuals hold these fears, or competing commitments, just as strongly as they do their improvement goals. These fears amount to "an active commitment of [individuals] to keep the thing [they] are afraid of from happening" (p. 49).

To uncover these fears and commitments, Kegan and Lahey (2009) suggest, "Have a look at the [Step] 2 list and answer the following questions about each of those entries: If I imagine myself trying to do the *opposite* of this, what is the most uncomfortable or worrisome or outright scary feeling that comes up for me?" (pp. 238–239). Returning to our beginning counseling student illustration, the student might identify that, if she did more listening to her clients, allowed for more silence during sessions, and engaged in less advice giving, her clients would view her as not knowing how to help them with their problems, and, as such, she would be a poor counselor. The student's competing commitment is to not be seen by others as incompetent.

Another set of counseling theories can be taught parallel to ILT Step 3. The dialectic nature of moving between the competing and often contradictory commitments that individuals simultaneously hold (e.g., our goals right beside our fears related to actually achieving those goals), is a major focus of postmodern and systemic counseling models. Awareness and appreciation of the dialectical characteristics of the self's meaning-making (i.e., becoming comfortable with the multiple systems of belief within ourselves) is also a central characteristic of the 5th Order, or the self-transforming mind, in Kegan's developmental theory (Kegan, 1998; Kegan & Lahey, 2009). That mind can seek and hold contradictions to current positions. The self-transforming mind "coheres through its ability not to confuse internal consistency with wholeness or completeness, and through its alignment with the dialectic rather than either pole" (Kegan & Lahey, 2009, p. 17).

## ILT Step 4: Uncovering the Big Assumptions We Are Making

In this last step of the ILT process, students uncover the often hidden Big Assumptions they make that underlie their Step 3 commitments. These assumptions, according to Kegan and Lahey (2001), are beliefs that individuals have that they accept as truth. As such, "they are not so much the assumptions we have as they are the assumptions *that have us*" (p. 68). A person is captive to her or his Big Assumptions, not able to reflect on them as constructions.

Big Assumptions typically are quite extreme, often envisioning catastrophic consequences to the self. For example, the aforementioned beginning counseling student may assume that if her clients did, in fact, view her as a poor counselor—because she listened more instead of giving frequent advice on their problems—she would be a failure and have to find another occupation. She would find that to be an intolerable possibility. Treating such untested assumptions as true, when they might not be so and, in fact, probably are not true, strongly contributes to a person's immunity to change. It might be seen that this process of uncovering

an individual's internal assumptions and processing their influence on the individual's behavior is at the heart of many of the cognitive approaches to counseling. Therefore, cognitive approaches are presented along with Step 4 in the course.

## Reading and Assignments

During Phase 2 of the course (informing personal theory), class time is divided between having students process their ILT experience in dyads and the instructor leading class discussions on the ILT process and its relation to assigned readings on humanistic/existential, postmodern/systemic, and cognitive counseling theories. The experience of personally working through the ILT process gives students concrete illustrations of the related conceptual material contained in these theories. Teaching counseling theories in coordination with the ILT experience also highlights how central personal reflection and individual development are to the process of counseling. Students respond to readings on the formal theories in reflective notes and bring their notes to class. They write responses to three questions:

- What is one thing from the reading that I don't understand?
- What is one thing that I have an opinion about?
- What is one thing that I would like to discuss further?

These reflective notes serve at least three purposes. First, they encourage students to focus on their own ideas (i.e., their personal theories) while encountering the formal counseling theories in the reading. The notes invite students to self-author their responses to the theories. Second, the reflective notes place students in a collaborative learning posture whereby they actively assist the instructor in setting the agenda for class discussions. This posture further communicates to students that they are the authors of their own learning and development. Third, students' responses to these questions provide the instructor with a clear indication of how well the students understand the theories and where they might be struggling.

The instructor collects students' reflective notes at the end of each class, examining them for shared and/or important questions or themes that may need further clarification or discussion. The themes identified are then discussed at the beginning of the next class to connect the ongoing process of students' learning with formal theory and with students' evolving personal counseling theories.

During Phase 2 students also write weekly mini reflective papers on two matters: (1) how the formal theories presented are influencing their evolving personal theories of counseling and (2) how the ILT process that they are experiencing is affecting their understanding of themselves as developing individuals and counselors. The instructor provides written feedback on these papers, feedback that is aimed at providing individualized support to students in their process of building more complex, articulate conceptualizations of their theory and their development.

# Phase 3: Reconstructing Personal Theory (Espoused Theory Versus Theory in Use)

During the experiential learning of Phase 3, students reflect on the formal theories of counseling that they have studied along with their developing personal counseling theory. They do so concurrently with testing hypotheses as to the validity and value of these theoretical concepts during simulated counseling situations. As discussed in Chapter 2, Dewey (1964) refers to this type of experience as *secondary experience* in that students are actively engaged in trying out these concepts and ideas-in-action and reflecting on their application.

One challenge for students during this phase is to connect the formal counseling theories with their developing personal counseling theory as they try out the counseling *techniques* from the various theories that they studied in Phase 2. It should be noted that this part of the course is likely to be more effective if students have completed a basic techniques (e.g., basic microskills; Ivey & Ivey, 2003) course prior to (or at least simultaneously with) the theories class.

## Triadic Counseling Simulations and Reflection

Beginning with Phase 3, the first half of each class asks students to form triads and engage in brief (five- to ten-minute) intentional conversations. Students assume three roles: client, counselor, and observer. The client discusses either a real or assigned issue that might be commonly experienced by a client and that lends itself to the application of the theories studied in the course. Students practice responding to the client with what they believe would be a helpful counseling approach, as informed by the formal theory that the class is learning. The session is video-recorded. Afterward, all members of the triad write a brief reflection on the interaction, identifying elements of formal theory within the conversation. The members of the triad then switch roles and repeat the process.

During the second half of each class, video segments from the previously recorded triadic interactions are reviewed by the entire class. The instructor stops each video at random points and poses stimulus questions such as the following:

1. What is going on?

2. What formal theory or theories best explain what is happening?

3. How is theory, personal and/or formal, being utilized by the counselor?

4. What seems effective or not about the use of these theories in this interaction?

Student responses are discussed and processed. This set of activities offers students a hands-on, practical opportunity to, first, deconstruct the formal theories introduced in the course and, then, begin reconstructing and integrating these theories with their own evolving personal counseling theory.

## Thematic Analysis Activity

A valuable concluding activity, thematic analysis, used in this phase of the course also aims to promote the deconstruction and integration of formal theories. Students brainstorm and generate as many one-word descriptors for each theory as possible. The instructor then guides the class in a discussion to identify themes that cut across theories. The students construct alternative dimensions with which to integrate multiple formal theories with their personal counseling theory.

## Espoused Theories Versus Theories in Use

There is an additional important learning benefit of the triadic counseling simulations/reflections and thematic analysis activity. These experiences introduce students to the important distinction between espoused theories and theories in use (Argyris & Schön, 1974, 1996). Such a distinction has direct relevance for the effective application of theory to practice—it ultimately affects a counselor's authenticity.

Espoused theories are those that individuals articulate when they attempt to describe, explain, or predict behavior. Theories in use are the implicit rules that individuals actually use to guide their behavior. Argyris and Schön (1974, 1996) found that individuals often reveal significant incongruities between their espoused theories and their theories in use—how individuals describe their behavior is often different from how they actually behave and how their behavior is perceived by others. To be perceived as authentic and competent by their clients, it is critical that counselors actually use the theories and approaches that they espouse. The course activities described above provide counseling students with feedback that increases their awareness of their own theory-to-practice discrepancies. They may continue to reduce such inconsistencies as they move through their subsequent counselor education and training.

## Final Course Paper

Phase 3 concludes with the final course assignment, a reflective paper. This paper provides further opportunity for students to integrate aspects of the formal theories that they have learned during the course with their developing personal theories of how to effectively engage in the art of counseling and to reflect on their own continuing development. Students respond to two central questions in the final paper:

1. What is my current personal theory about how to effectively assist others as a counselor, how is that theory informed by formal counseling theories that have been studied in this course, and how will I continue working toward enhancing my personal theory as I progress through my counselor training program?

2. What is my assessment of my own personal and professional development based on my experiences in this course (e.g., the ILT process, the theory-to-practice counseling simulations), and how will I continue working toward more advanced developmental complexity as I gain further experience in my advanced counseling courses and fieldwork?

The final reflective paper intends to provide a working blueprint for students' ongoing learning and development as they continue their journey toward becoming a counseling professional.

# CONCLUDING REFLECTIONS

We end with a challenge. Kottler (2002) asks if the theories course has become obsolete. He cites, as origins for his question, the counseling profession's movement toward eclectic practice, toward a cookbook approach that pairs specific interventions with particular problems (consistent with the "evidence-based" movement), the limited application of theories in their pure form, and the influence of managed care. We are also concerned with those matters. However, it is our position that a basic course in counseling theory, if taught in a constructivist fashion, can serve multiple purposes.

We believe that the ability to use theory is an essential part of being a professional counselor, in contrast with being a mere technician. The question for counselors is not whether one uses theory, but how one uses theory. This course is guided by the notion that how counselors use theory reflects their level of cognitive complexity.

This aim focuses us on an educational challenge. Research indicates that the majority of adults in our society do not fully reach a 4th Order of meaning-making, that is, a self-authoring level of adult development (Kegan, 1998; Kegan & Lahey, 2009). Neukrug and McAuliffe (1992) found this to be true with counseling students as well. The prior stage of meaning-making, the socialized mind, is not adequate for the complex, dialectical, and improvisational task of counseling. In fact, it can be argued that some ability for 5th-Order, or transforming, meaning-making (Kegan 1998; Kegan & Lahey, 2009) may be necessary for advanced proficiency at such complex counseling tasks.

Kegan (1998) suggests that involvement in a counseling program, if it is developmentally challenging, may enhance cognitive development. Therefore, counselor educators need to consider promoting their students' cognitive complexity as a central aim of their teaching. A counseling theories class can be a rich environment in which to accomplish such a task.

# REFERENCES

Argyris, C., & Schön, D. A. (1974). *Theory in practice: Increasing professional effectiveness*. San Francisco: Jossey-Bass.

Argyris, C., & Schön, D. A. (1996). *Organizational learning II: Theory, method, and practice*. Reading, MA: Addison-Wesley.

Bateson, G. (1972). *Steps to an ecology of mind*. New York: Ballantine.

Bateson, G. (1979). *Mind and nature: A necessary unity*. New York: E. P. Dutton.

Becvar, D. S., & Becvar, R. J. (2006). *Family therapy: A systemic integration* (6th ed.). Boston: Allyn & Bacon.

Corsini, R. J., & Wedding, D. (2000). *Current psychotherapies* (6th ed.). Itaska, IL: Peacock.

Dewey, J. (1964). The need for a philosophy of education. In R. D. Archambault (Ed.), *John Dewey on education: Selected writings*. Chicago: University of Chicago Press.

Eriksen, K. (2006). The constructive developmental theory of Robert Kegan. *Family Journal: Counseling and Therapy for Couples and Families, 14*(3), 290–298.

Freeman, M. S., Hayes, B. G., Kuch, T. H., & Taub, G. (2007). Personality: A predictor of theoretical orientation of students enrolled in a counseling theories course. *Counselor Education and Supervision, 46,* 254–265.

Fruggeri, L. (1992). Therapeutic process as the social construction of change. In S. McNamee & K. J. Gergan (Eds.), *Therapy as social construction* (pp. 40–53). London: Sage.

Hansen, J. T. (2006). Counseling theories within a postmodernist epistemology: New roles for theories in counseling practice. *Journal of Counseling & Development, 84,* 291–297.

Hoffman, L. (1992). A reflective stance for family therapy. In S. McNamee & K. J. Gergan (Eds.), *Therapy as social construction* (pp. 7–24). London: Sage.

Ignelzi, M. (2000). Meaning-making in the learning and teaching process. In M. B. Baxter Magolda (Ed.), *Teaching to promote intellectual and personal maturity: Incorporating students' worldviews and identities into the learning process* (pp. 5–14). San Francisco: Jossey-Bass.

Ivey, A. E., & Ivey, M. B. (2003). *Intentional interviewing and counseling*. Pacific Grove, CA: Brooks/Cole.

Keeny, B. P. (1990). Improvisational therapy: Evolving one's own clinical style. *Contemporary Family Therapy, 12*(4), 271–277.

Keeny, B. P. (1991). *Improvisational therapy: A practical guide for creative clinical strategies*. New York: Guilford Press.

Kegan, R. (1998). *In over our heads: The mental demands of modern life*. Cambridge, MA: Harvard University Press.

Kegan, R., & Lahey, L. L. (2001). *How the way we talk can change the way we work*. San Francisco: Jossey-Bass.

Kegan, R., & Lahey, L. L. (2009). *Immunity to change: How to overcome it and unlock the potential in yourself and your organization*. Boston: Harvard Business School Press.

Kottler, J. A. (2002). *Theories in counseling and psychotherapy: An experiential approach*. Boston: Allyn & Bacon.

Lambert, M. J. (1992). Implications of outcome research of psychotherapy integration. In J. C. Norcross & M. R. Goldfried (Eds.), *Handbook of psychotherapy integration*. New York: Basic Books.

Lovell, C. W., & McAuliffe, G. J. (1997). Principles of constructivist training and education. In T. Sexton & B. Griffin (Eds.), *Constructivist thinking in counseling practice, research, and training* (pp. 134–156). New York: Teachers College Press.

Luborsky, L., Rosenthal, R., & Diguer, L. (2002). The Dodo bird verdict is alive and well—mostly. *Clinical Psychology: Science and Practice, 9,* 2–12.

McAuliffe, G. J. (2006). The evolution of professional competence. In C. H. Hoare (Ed.), *The intersection of adult development and learning: A handbook of theory, research and practice* (pp. 476–496). New York: Oxford University Press.

McAuliffe, G. J., & Lovell, C. W. (2006). The influence of counselor epistemology on the helping interview: A qualitative study. *Journal of Counseling and Development, 8,* 308–317.

Miller, S. D., Duncan, B. L., & Hubble, M. A. (1997). *Escape from Babel: Toward a unifying language for psychotherapy practice.* New York: W. W. Norton.

Minuchin, S., & Fishman, C. H. (1981). *Family therapy techniques.* Cambridge, MA: Harvard University Press.

Neukrug, E. S., & McAuliffe, G. J. (1992). Cognitive development and human service education. *Human Service Education, 13,* 13–26.

O'Hanlon, W. H., & Weiner-Davis, M. (1989). *In search of solutions: A new direction in psychotherapy.* New York: W. W. Norton.

Patterson, C. H., & Watkins, C. E. (1996). *Theories of psychotherapy* (5th ed.). New York: HarperCollins.

Strange, C. C., & King, P. M. (1990). The professional practice of student development. In D. G. Creamer and Associates (Eds.), *College student development: Theory and practice for the 1990's.* Alexandria, VA: American College Personnel Association.

Watzlawick, P., Weakland, J., & Fisch, R. (1974). *Change, principles of problem formation and problem resolution.* New York: W. W. Norton.

# Teaching Assessment and Testing

Yegan Pillay and Sheri Pickover

*That the world is made up of atoms and individuals who possess emotion is not for us a matter of cultural belief. Any reasonable person would reach the same conclusion. Yet, as we presume the reality and the truth of our own beliefs, so do we trample on the realities of others.*

Gergen (1999, p. 17)

Gergen's perspective on the inevitable social construction of reality bears great relevance to the teaching of assessment and testing. Objective test scores supposedly exist (the atoms, in Gergen's example). And yet, the foundations and interpretations of tests are always constructed. This chapter focuses on strategies for teaching assessment and testing that integrate both objective and subjective components, so that reality can be constructed in a manner that is beneficial to the client. In this chapter, the teaching of psychological assessment will be guided by an alertness to social construction. Therefore, we begin with a discussion of the history and social construction of testing.

## A HISTORY OF TESTING

Assessment and testing can be traced to the 18th century with Johann Casper Lavater's work on scientific physiognomy, and to the growth in the 1830s and beyond of phrenology, craniometry, and anthropometry (Sokal, 1984). Psychological assessment as it is known today can

credit its genesis to the confluence of several factors during the 1890s—namely, the founding of the American Psychological Association, the philanthropy of foundations such as the Commonwealth Fund and the Carnegie Corporation, and the legislative and executive action of the federal government in its search for societal order (Baruth & Robinson, 1987; Sokal, 1984).

Testing was thus impacted by the intersection of the *disciplinary regimes* of psychology, psychiatry, and philanthropy. From Michel Foucault's (1965) perspective, disciplinary regimes refer to the power that various disciplines, such as psychiatry, psychology, and medicine, exert on society in determining the level of functioning of consumers of services. Gergen (1999) expanded the concept to indicate that socially sanctioned disciplines develop language and classifications—for example, definitions of what is normal or abnormal—and, through research procedures, influence public policy. The consequences of the mental health disciplinary regime have been the labeling and ordering—and, sometimes, subjugation—of individuals through disciplinary language.

And that regime has expanded. The expansion of psychiatry and psychology has meant an exponential growth in the classifications of mental disorders. The number of such disorders has multiplied from approximately 40 in the late 1930s to over 300 at the turn of the 21st century (Gergen, 1999). The increase in classifications parallels the burgeoning use of hitherto unknown pharmaceutical drugs to treat previously unknown mental disorders. The increase in the number of mental disorders and the accompanying increase in prescription drugs to treat the disorders challenge counselors to question the role that mental health disciplines play in maintaining the status quo through classification and labeling. A common presumption of mental health professionals, following the medical model, has been that they are the knowers of the realities of others. The nomenclature used to describe clients—for example, as schizophrenic, histrionic, or borderline—presumes the existence of monolithic disordered identities that are defined by those labels. And yet, the presence and use of such nomenclature obfuscates the multiplicity of personal identities, that is, the fact that people are more than the labels that a discipline attributes to them.

## THE SOCIAL CONSTRUCTIONIST PERSPECTIVE

The social constructionist perspective instead recognizes and values *multiple* identities, with mental illness perhaps being only one component of identity. In so doing, this perspective deconstructs the objectivist's assumption of a universal truth in favor of the historical and cultural specificity of an individual's reality (Winslade & Geroski, 2008).

This discussion of the social construction of testing and the social power of test creators and users should not be interpreted as a rejection of testing. Psychological testing can have great value in providing a shorthand for counselors and a confirmatory tool that can be used in concert with other assessment measures, such as the intake interview. The counselor, for example, can make a decision about the next phase of treatment based on the results of assessments such as the Beck Depression Inventory (Beck, Steer, & Brown, 1996), the Wechsler Adult Intelligence Scale–Revised (Wechsler, 1997), and the Substance Abuse Subtle Screening Inventory (Miller, 1994). Similarly,

psychological assessment can be of value to clients who might find comfort in having a name for a condition and information about possible treatment options. For example, a parent may be relieved to know that her or his child's poor academic performance is due to an assessed learning disability and that accommodations exist that can compensate for the challenges that the child experiences in an academic setting. The course in assessment and testing can include all of these possibilities.

The sections that follow examine the context, aims, methods, and challenges related to teaching an assessment and testing course. This chapter also addresses the role that the social constructivist perspective can play as instructors create learning environments that trigger what Vygotsky (1962) refers to as the *internal development processes in students.*

## COURSE CONTEXT AND PHILOSOPHICAL APPLICATIONS

The testing and assessment course as described here is designed for master's-level counseling students, although many of these ideas may also be applied to an advanced assessment course. The content of the course is meant to meet the accreditation requirements of the Council for Accreditation of Counseling and Related Educational Programs (CACREP; 2009) and the licensure requirements for clinical mental health counselors, addictions counselors, and college and school counselors.

The testing and assessment course prepares future counselors to understand the role of psychological testing and clinical evaluation during the diagnostic process. Students also explore ethical issues in handling and administering psychological assessment instruments, including potential forms of bias in interpreting assessment results.

A social constructionist perspective provides a template for the course as we teach it and challenges objectivist positions on labeling and pathology. In particular, the guideline mentioned in Chapter 3 that "social science constructions are approximations" informs the course. In that vein, students encounter multiple sources of assessment, comprising a continuum. We urge students to move away from giving clients a diagnostic label based entirely on *DSM-IV-TR* criteria or on standardized psychometric testing and toward utilizing a variety of assessment measures, including the client's verbal narrative, psychological assessment scores, *DSM* criteria, and other relevant information in the collaborative construction of the client's reality.

Particular challenges exist in teaching the assessment and testing course. For instance, counselors-in-training commonly view testing and assessment with a mixture of dread and limited interest. Students particularly demonstrate anxiety when faced with learning such psychometric concepts as statistics.

The second challenge for the constructivist educator is helping students "get behind" the testing paradigm to deconstruct its foundations. Thus, a tension exists between teaching basic information about testing and examining its foundations and uses. Given these classroom dynamics, the pedagogical approach must be deliberate and intentional. Our approach is based on Vygotskian social constructivist principles.

Social constructivist thinking (not to be confused with social constructionism) describes learning as it exists in a social context. Vygotsky (1962) asserts that the relationship between thought and language is a continual back-and-forth process and that learning can be seen as both developmental and relational. A primary element of social constructivist education is recognizing learner readiness, in the form of the learner's zone of proximal development (ZPD; Vygotsky, 1978). The ZPD is the difference between a learner's actual current development capacity and her or his next potential level of development.

After identifying the learner's ZPD, instructors use the principles of social constructivist education to help students move to their next potential level of development. The procedure used to help students develop in this way is called *scaffolding* (Vygotsky, 1978). During scaffolding, learners are not just taught so-called content. Instead, they are helped to see how their thinking changes through interactions with a teacher or peer, and how their knowledge evolves. This process adds to students' existing knowledge base through the assimilation of new information. We achieve this process through varied experiential activities, including small-group discussions, journaling, presentations, review of the literature, test administration, and report writing.

## COURSE CONTENT AND PROCESS

We divide the course into four units: (1) Learning Historical Perspectives and Types of Assessments; (2) Understanding Statistical Concepts, Basic Assessment Concepts, and Reliability and Validity; (3) Conducting Unstructured Interviews and Mental Health Assessments; and (4) Conducting a Standardized Assessment Battery and Writing an Assessment Report. Table 9.1 outlines relevant CACREP (2009) learning objectives, the corresponding constructivist principles, and the content and processes for each learning objective. Following Table 9.1 is a detailed explanation of how we integrate each of the objectives into the corresponding unit. To assist readers, we have divided each unit into specific instructor interventions and student activities.

**TABLE 9.1**  Course Objectives, Constructivist Principles, Content, and Processes

| Learning Objective | Constructivist Principles | Content | Processes |
|---|---|---|---|
| Demonstrate an understanding of historical perspectives concerning assessment. CACREP Standards II 7(a) | Power relations in society intersect with language and have influenced the accompanying discourse of knowledge. The empiricist/dualist nature of truth—including psychological functioning—is supplanted by contextual, socially constructed rescripted narrative about psychological functioning. | History of assessment Cultural history Activity theory | Journaling Group presentation Critique research paper Small-group discussion |

*(Continued)*

**TABLE 9.1** (Continued)

| Learning Objective | Constructivist Principles | Content | Processes |
|---|---|---|---|
| Demonstrate an understanding of basic concepts of standardized and nonstandardized testing and other assessment techniques. CACREP Standards II 7(b)(c) | Knowledge is related to psychological functioning as a co-construction rather than the absolutist objective universals. Agents of the disciplinary regime (e.g. counselors, counselor educators) are humble and reflexive and are cognizant that there are limits of the determinations made relevant to psychological functioning that are contextualized in the community. | Developmental history Unstructured interview Mental Status Exam Neurological assessment Personality assessment Cognitive assessment Projective testing | Dyads Small-group discussion Psychological report writing Journaling Administration/scoring of assessment Interpretation of results |
| Demonstrate an understanding of statistical concepts. CACREP Standards II 7(c) | Knowledge must be built on developmental foundations. Counselors are only able to understand the limits of counseling assessment once they have developed a sound understanding of the psychometric properties used to create the assessments. | Psychometric properties of assessments Ordinal, nominal, interval, and ratio scales Normal distribution Mean, mode, median, and standard deviation Pearson Product-Moment correlation coefficient Test critiques | Critique research paper Small-group discussion |
| Demonstrate an understanding of reliability and validity and the relationship between reliability and validity. CACREP Standards II 7(d)(e) | The language of the unitary "disciplinary regime" as it relates to reliability and validity is replaced with socially constructed knowledge regarding what is valid and reliable from the vantage point of various cultures that find themselves at the margins. | Test-retest, split half reliability Construct, content, and criterion-referenced validity Predictive and concurrent validity Personality assessment Cognitive assessment Projective testing | Journaling Group discussion Group presentation Critique research paper |
| Demonstrate an understanding of how diversity and assessment intersect. CACREP Standards II 7(f) | Individuals and groups make meaning of self and construct, and deconstruct knowledge within the context of their phenomenological reality. | Multicultural counseling competency Cultural bias in testing Cultural historical activity theory | Journaling Group discussion Group presentation Psychological report |
| Demonstrate knowledge of ethical strategies for selecting, administering, and interpreting assessment instruments. CACREP Standards II 7(g) | Relativistic and reflexive thinking as to what constitutes the truth is explored. Knowledge emanates from communal relations. | American Counseling Association ethical standards Cultural bias in testing | Case conceptualization Group discussion Journaling |

# Unit 1: Historical Perspectives and Types of Assessments

This unit exposes students to the historical evolution of a variety of currently used assessment instruments and their sociocultural contexts. In addition, students examine the assessments through critical lenses, for example, reviewing the original sample that was used in the test development, cultural biases, and ethical considerations for using assessment measures in the contemporary cultural context.

## Objective 1: Understanding Historical Perspectives

We assign readings and journaling, and conduct large-group discussions. These assignments invite the master's counseling students to think about assessments from the perspectives of the counselor, the client, and society.

1. *Readings.* Students read textbook material and additional readings on the history of assessments.

2. *Journaling.* Students journal thoughts and emotions related to the readings. Specifically, we ask students to consider the following questions in their journals:

   - Please discuss how you believe that psychological assessments, including intelligence tests, have changed the world (based on your readings).
   - What are some ways that you see psychological/ counseling assessment being used to help individuals?
   - In what ways might counseling assessments be detrimental to individuals?

3. *Group discussion.* During a group discussion, we ask students to share their journals with one another. The discussion can be accomplished in either small groups or one large group, depending on the size of the class.

4. *Ongoing journaling.* In addition to the first journaling assignment, students journal twice weekly throughout the course. Throughout their journaling, students explore how their views regarding assessment and testing are evolving. We ask students to specifically address the following areas,

but we also encourage them to add their own thoughts, ideas, and concerns:

- the value of assessment and testing for the therapeutic alliance
- precautions that need to be exercised by counseling professionals
- cultural bias in psychometric measures

## Objective 2: Increasing Familiarity With Types of Assessment

To accomplish this objective, we direct students to participate in small task groups, and then each group presents what it has developed. Next, we lead the class in a large-group discussion.

We first ask students to divide into task groups of two or three students. The small groups identify the types of assessments used by counselors, psychologists, and social workers by reading the text, interviewing professionals in the field, and reading peer-reviewed scholarly research. With instructor support, each group presents a particular category of assessment instruments to the class (e.g., projective tests, personality tests, career tests, ability tests, achievement tests). Students explain the historical development of each measure. While this process consists largely of information gathering, working in groups offers students the opportunity to tune in to one another's perspectives about the tools that they present. Students then write their responses to each type of assessment in their journals and share their journal responses during class discussions.

# Unit 2: Understanding Statistical Concepts, Basic Assessment Concepts, and Reliability and Validity

The test-review task group project described above has two goals. The first is to move students beyond a perfunctory memorization of statistical concepts and to link the knowledge of psychometric concepts to cultural and ethical competency. The second is to demonstrate the relationships among knowledge of psychometric principles, advocacy, and social justice issues. When students become able to effectively examine the psychometric properties of a chosen assessment tool, they can begin to make ethical decisions about testing particular clients. For example, a reliable and valid assessment tool may nevertheless be culturally inappropriate for a particular client because use of the resulting score may cause harm rather than helping the client. The point here is to emphasize the imprecise nature of test construction and scoring, and to increase critical thinking about score interpretation.

## Objective 1: Understanding Statistical Concepts

We use traditional lecture and small- and large-group discussions to extend the task group learning to student mastery of the psychometric concepts needed for assessment interpretation.

1. *Lecture.* Lectures review types of scales, descriptive statistics, interpretation of standard scores, and evaluation of data based on sampling procedures. We discuss the normal curve and standard error of measurement, interpretation of correlation coefficients, types of reliability and validity, test bias, the testing environment, and ethical concepts related to informed consent, confidentiality, and competence.

2. *Small-group discussion.* We then break the class into small groups and ask them to apply lecture material to particular situations. The aim is to increase students' familiarity with these testing concepts. The small-group assignments include finding descriptive statistics for an array of numbers, creating a normal curve, and converting raw scores into standard scores.

## Objective 2: Understanding Basic Assessment Concepts and Concepts of Reliability and Validity

In meeting this objective, we again lecture and lead large-group discussions. Again, the purpose is to encourage students to gain mastery of testing concepts.

1. *Lecture.* We review basic assessment concepts such as test standardization, test bias, and appropriate test

environment. Students then brainstorm in a large group how these concepts might affect their future clients. Students share from their journals how learning about these concepts is affecting their thoughts about assessment.

2. *Journaling.* We review the American Counseling Association ethical code as it relates to assessment and again ask students to process their reactions in their journals and during class discussions.

3. *Review.* We review the mathematical properties of different types of correlations used in test construction and then review the types of validity and reliability.

## Objective 3: Mastering Concepts in Context of Client Need

We present cases and ask small groups to discuss the cases, form test-review task groups, and journal.

1. *Small-group discussion.* Students break into small groups, and we provide them with test manuals of assessments that are commonly used by counselors— for instance, the Beck Depression Inventory (Beck et al., 1996) or the Substance Abuse Subtle Screening Inventory (Miller, 1994). During class, students review the manuals and locate the information on sample size and type, reliability, validity, type of scale, and test construction. The manuals rotate through each group so that each student has the opportunity to review different kinds of manuals.

2. *Large-group discussion.* After each group has reviewed all of the manuals, we conduct a large-group discussion to examine the specific qualities of the assessment:
   - What are the age-range limitations for this test?
   - What are the reliability and validity statistics for the test?
   - Review the items for face validity and possible cultural bias.
   - What are the ramifications for the client and counselor if the manual does not provide an ethnic breakdown for the sample?
   - What are the ramifications for the client and counselor if the manual reports low reliability and/or validity data?

3. *Case study.* We present a case (see the Appendix on page 135) to the class and ask students to consider the following questions both in class and while journaling:

   - What issues of test bias and a problematic testing environment might have been/were present in the case study?
   - How did knowledge of psychometric concepts assist the counselor in advocating for this client?
   - How might cultural/gender/social class issues present in the client and/or in the assessment impact outcomes for the client?

4. *Small-task group assignment.* We break the class into task dyads and assign them the task of writing a 10-page test critique. Each dyad chooses two counseling assessments (e.g., two self-esteem assessments, two depression inventories) that purport to measure the same construct. They then write a test critique that involves reviewing the history, test construction, psychometric properties, ethical concerns, and cultural issues inherent in both assessments. The dyads also compare and contrast the two assessments based on these concepts. Specifically, students respond to the following questions:

   - Which assessment (if any) appears to best measure the purported construct? Why?
   - Which assessment (if any) best addresses cultural/gender/social class issues?
   - Which assessment (if any) provides the most detail to assist the counselor in providing treatment?
   - Which assessment (if any) best addresses potential ethical issues, such as counselor competency? In other words, is the test standardized with a specific protocol, and if not, how might administration by untrained counselors impact clients?

# Unit 3: Conducting Unstructured Interviews and Mental Health Assessments

The third unit of the course in testing and assessment consists of introducing students to the art of clinical assessment. Here students learn to conduct in-person interviews and do more comprehensive assessments. Master's students learn to administer and interpret assessments in several steps. During the first step, they begin to recognize themselves as an assessment tool. They become aware of the potential for subjective bias, especially when gathering and interpreting qualitative data. They also discuss potential impacts of bias on clients.

## Objective 1: Viewing Self as an Assessment Tool Through the Use of a Self-Narrative Assignment

Students write a comprehensive autobiographical self-narrative that documents early childhood recollections, developmental milestones, and various experiences throughout their lifespan. In a way, this self-narrative replicates the initial intake interview of a typical clinical assessment. Students share their self-narrative with peers.

This assignment achieves two main objectives. First, students increase their understanding of their narrative as a product of cultural influences, one that is influenced by factors that are external to themselves. As a result, students' awareness of the social context of their own life narrative increases, and as they share with peers, they more readily recognize the uniqueness of each person's life narrative.

Second, this self-assessment exercise lays the groundwork for students' understanding of a client's phenomenological reality. By seeing that their own narratives describe one of many possible scripts, students begin to understand how anyone's narrative will be bound by her or his own points of reference. When students have achieved an understanding of their own phenomenological reality, they are favorably positioned to fully hear the phenomenological world of their clients.

The self narrative has several steps:

1. *The write-up.* Students write a narrative that includes three elements.

   - significant personal historical antecedents in their lives, such as a family crisis, divorce, or personal illness (Students include all childhood recollections up to the point of their current view of self. This task is commonly viewed as a developmental history. We provide students with a structured developmental history template or offer them the opportunity to create an unstructured developmental history.)

- a self-administered mental status exam
- positive assets and areas for growth

2. *Peer analysis and profiling.* Students assign an arbitrary four-digit number to their narrative in order to maintain anonymity among their peers. We then randomly distribute the narratives or personal background information to students in the class. Students develop a clinical profile of their peer based on the "interview" or write-up.

3. *Class discussion and journaling.* After students have drafted a clinical profile of their peer, they share the clinical profile with the class without discussion. Then each student spends 15 minutes of class time journaling about the process. We ask students to journal on (a) their thoughts about the clinical profile of their peer, (b) their thoughts and feelings about how they hope to be perceived, and (c) their thoughts and feelings about the peer's actual perceptions. Students then share these processed thoughts and emotions in a class discussion.

# Unit 4: Conducting a Standardized Assessment Battery and Writing an Assessment Report

During the final segment of the course, we teach students how to administer, score, and interpret the standardized assessments most commonly used by master's-level school, college, addictions, and mental health counselors. The purpose of this assignment is not only to ensure that students have basic mastery of conducting assessments, but also to serve as a culmination of learning from previous units, encouraging students to find meaning beyond the rudimentary test score interpretations.

This process is guided by two social constructivist assumptions. First, instructors recognize that students inherently have the potential to assimilate new information and to move to the higher reaches of their ZPD. Second, students must be active agents in their learning. As students move forward in their ZPD, they evidence increased levels of competence and confidence. Students make comments such as "I was not aware that I could

administer, interpret, and write a psychological report," "This is not as difficult as I first thought," and "I am fascinated by the connection between the person's narrative (background history) and the similar themes that are evident in the various assessments." These comments indicate that the distance between the level of actual development and the level of potential development has been narrowed.

## Objective 1: Learning to Conduct a Standardized Assessment Battery

We demonstrate test administration to the large group, facilitate discussions about the process, and encourage small-group discussions.

1. *Large-group discussion.* We begin by demonstrating the administration of several tests typically used by counselors in a community or school setting. We lead discussions about the process and answer questions.

2. *Small-group activity with large-group discussion.* Students form dyads and either take the test or take turns administering the test to each other. They then score the tests in class with our support. We provide each dyad with step-by-step instructions on scoring the test. Then in a large-group lecture and discussion, we explain how to interpret the score. These steps are completed for each test. Typically, we train students in a battery of five tests: a career test, a brief achievement test, a brief intelligence test, a personality test, and a substance abuse assessment.

## Objective 2: Conducting a Standardized Assessment

We orchestrate and facilitate small task groups through several steps.

1. *Dyads.* First, we randomly place students into dyads. Students who have already worked with each other during instruction are reassigned.

2. *Assessment battery and interview.* Next, students conduct an assessment battery on the dyad partner both during and outside of class. Each student administers five assessments to a peer and conducts an unstructured interview with the peer.

3. *Scoring and synopsis.* Each student then scores the battery and provides a detailed synopsis of the unstructured interview.

4. *Data.* Each student turns in a packet of data to the instructor that includes the following:
   - each test administered
   - all scoring information
   - a detailed synopsis of the unstructured interview

We grade the data packets for scoring accuracy and correct administration, remove all identifying data from the packets, and redistribute the packets to different students in the class. We ask students to ensure that they do not receive their own data packet or the one that they administered.

Students journal about the experience of conducting an assessment and being the subject of the assessment and then discuss their responses in the next class session.

## Objective 3: Writing an Assessment Report

To meet this objective, we lecture and conduct individual supervision with students.

1. *Demonstration.* Using templates and examples from the textbook, we demonstrate how to write a counseling assessment report that covers behavioral observations, test limitations and bias, scores, and relevant recommendations.

2. *Report based on data packet.* Each student individually writes a report based on the data packet received from us. Students turn in each section as they complete it for feedback and recommendations.

3. *Individual feedback.* Once the report is complete, we meet individually with each student to provide detailed suggestions for improving the final report. The student then completes the report and submits it for grading.

4. *Assessment battery and interview.* Once this process is complete, students conduct the same assessment battery and unstructured interview with a peer outside of the course. We provide students with an informed consent form that explains to the peer that the student is in the process of learning to administer these assessments and cannot provide the peer with the results.

5. *Assessment report.* Students then draft an assessment report without instructor support based on this new assessment battery.

At the end of the course, we ask students to share their journals with one another and write a final journal entry that reflects on their intellectual and emotional development throughout the course.

## CONCLUDING REFLECTIONS

The graduated pedagogical method that we use in teaching the assessment and testing course epitomizes the notion that an optimum level of knowledge is attained through social interaction with the instructor and peers. It is also consistent with the position taken by Douthit (2008), who asserts that "the teacher/facilitator is not merely transmitting information; rather, she is modeling, through the use of meaningful activity, how to think about the information being transmitted" (p. 93). The step-by-step method of promoting incremental knowledge acquisition results in empowering students—allowing them to be active agents in their education rather than docile recipients of information.

## RESOURCES

Burr, V. (2003). *An introduction to social constructionism.* London: Routledge.

Kozulin, A., Gindis, B., Ageyev, V. S., & Miller, S. M. (2003). *Vygotsky's educational theory in cultural context.* Cambridge, UK: Cambridge University Press.

Roth, W., & Lee, Y. (2007). "Vygotsky's neglected legacy": Cultural–historical activity theory. *Review of Educational Research, 77*(2), 186–232.

## REFERENCES

Baruth, L. G., & Robinson, E. H. (1987). An *introduction to the counseling profession.* Englewood Cliffs, NJ: Prentice Hall.

Beck A. T., Steer R. A., & Brown G. K. (1996). *Beck Depression Inventory 2nd Ed. Manual.* San Antonio, TX: Psychological Corporation.

Council for Accreditation of Counseling and Related Educational Programs. (2009). *The 2009 standards.* Retrieved July 20, 2010, from http://www.cacrep.org/doc/2009%20Standards%20with%20cover.pdf

Douthit, K. Z. (2008). Cognition, culture and society: Understanding cognitive development in the tradition of Vygotsky. In K. Kraus (Ed.), *Lenses: Applying lifespan development theories in counseling* (pp. 83–118). Boston: Houghton Mifflin.

Foucault, M. (1965). *Madness and civilization: A history of insanity in the age of reason* (R. H., Trans.). New York: Pantheon Books.

Gergen, K. J. (1999). *An invitation to social construction.* Thousand Oaks, CA: Sage.

Miller, G. A. (1994). *The Substance Abuse Subtle Screening Inventory manual: Adult SASSI-2 Manual Supplement.* Spencer, IN: Spencer Evening World.

Sokal, M. M. (1984). Approaches to the history of psychological testing. *History of Education Quarterly, 24,* 419–430.

Wechsler, D. (1997). *WAIS-III administration and scoring manual.* San Antonio, TX: Psychological Corporation.

Winslade, J., & Geroski, A. (2008). A social constructionist view of development. In K. Kraus (Ed.), *Lenses: Applying lifespan development theories in counseling* (pp. 7–51). Boston: Houghton Mifflin.

Vygotsky, L. S. (1962). *Thought and language.* Cambridge, MA: MIT Press.

Vygotsky, L. S. (1978). *Mind in society: The development of higher psychological processes.* Cambridge, MA: Harvard University Press.

# Appendix A
## Case Study

As a supervisor for a juvenile delinquency program, I had the responsibility for determining placement for adjudicated youth. A 15-year-old who had been truant for several months was awaiting long-term residential placement. She had been charged as an incorrigible minor for truancy from home and for prostitution. The teen had been a victim of incest and had not coped well with being returned home. Psychological assessments are routinely administered to youth within four days of their arrest, and these scores are used for placement. This young woman had scored below 70 on the Wechsler Intelligence Scale for Children. She therefore became ineligible for a low-security placement based solely on her IQ score. I learned that the intake worker, as a result, planned to place her in a high-security placement (the only facility willing to provide for mentally impaired youth). I intervened on her behalf, based on my knowledge of standard deviation, the test bias inherent in the testing situation, and the cultural bias present in the assessment. I presented these issues to the administrators of the low-security facility, who then agreed to allow the client into the more appropriate program.

# 10

# Teaching Group Counseling: A Constructivist Approach

Karen P. Eriksen and Bill Bruck

In his small yet profound book *How People Change*, Alex Whelis (1973) suggests that identity consists of the integration of behavior and that we are more than just how we behave. He implies in the following quote that what we learn affects how we think, how we feel, and what we feel capable of in the world: "A young man who learns to drive a car thinks differently, thereby feels differently. When he meets a pretty girl who lives fifty miles away, the encounter carries implications he could not have felt as a bus rider. We may say, then, that he not only drives a car but has become a driver" (p. 79).

Similarly, in constructivist strategies for teaching group counseling, counselor educators do not merely teach discrete counseling skills, content, or attitudes. They communicate a mode of being-in-the-world—an identity for themselves and their students. They socialize their students into the counseling profession and into group counseling, and by doing so, help them *become* group counselors.

Robert Kegan (1982, 1998) might say that educators aim to promote students' development from the interpersonal way of knowing, in which rules and relationships are defined by others, to an institutional way of knowing, in which students are able to step back from rules and relationships, think critically about them, and make their own considered decisions about what directions seem best to pursue (thus seeing themselves as an "institution," with its own self-authored procedures for functioning). From this new developmental perspective, they have more fully achieved the identity of counselor.

This developmental potential is nowhere more true than in the teaching of group counseling, in which students experience "being in a group" while concurrently being challenged to "become aware of what is happening in the group" (i.e., the process) and to use their own feeling experiences to inform that awareness. In that spirit, we offer a course design in this chapter that incorporates constructivist thinking into the overall structure of the group counseling course and its individual assignments.

# COURSE OVERVIEW

**TABLE 10.1** Course Objectives, Activities, and Constructivist Principles

| Learning Objectives | Learning Activities | Constructivist Principles |
| --- | --- | --- |
| Know textbook material on group counseling. | <ul><li>Read text</li><li>Participate in class psychoeducational group discussions/activities related to text material</li><li>Apply text concepts to in-class group experience in reflection papers</li></ul> | Providing structure to support interpersonal knowers—clear assignments, reflection paper exemplars, clear feedback on reflection papers<br><br>Challenge by applying complex concepts to real-life "messy" scenarios |
| Develop task, psychoeducational, and process group skills—as group member, group leader, process observer. | <ul><li>Instructor-as-leader modeling skills, directing attention to specifics, coaching students-as-leaders, directing processing of group</li><li>Reflection papers to identify and evaluate own and others' skills and experiences</li><li>Practice skills of each role during participation in task, psychoeducational, and process groups</li></ul> | Applications of principles; breaking down ambiguous stimuli into manageable parts; asking students to stand outside experience, thinking about it; and evaluating effectiveness = challenge toward procedural knowing |
| Prepare a group, with all component parts. | <ul><li>Task group to develop psychoeducational group</li><li>Research, decide, develop, and write out all component parts for 10 weeks</li><li>Demonstrate one segment of group with class members serving as group</li></ul> | Applications in action creates real-world ambiguity, requires deciding for oneself = challenge toward procedural knowing<br><br>Specific point-by-point instructions, grading rubrics, and feedback sheets = support |
| Develop awareness of personal issues that may interfere with skills delivery. | <ul><li>Full participation as process group member</li><li>Self-evaluative reflection papers with instructor feedback</li></ul> | Standing back from self to evaluate = challenge toward procedural knowing<br><br>Exemplars, grading rubrics, and clear instructions = support |

# COURSE DESIGN

The Group Counseling course provides graduate counseling students with the knowledge and skills needed to lead, with supervision, a variety of counseling groups. Any group course design should be grounded in the core group worker competencies specified by the Association for Specialists in Group Work (ASGW; 2000). As we have designed the course, students develop knowledge competencies and skills competencies by participating in, leading, and developing a counseling and/or psychotherapy process group, a psychoeducational group, and a task group. In each of these groups, students have opportunities to be group members, group leaders, and process observers, all with the support and assistance of instructors. In each of these groups, students participate in an opening exercise, the work of the group, "processing" how the group went, and a closing exercise.

We assume that students take the Group Counseling class toward the end of the first year or beginning of the second year of their programs. The design we suggest here assumes that students have had the basic counseling skills course in which they mastered a range of helping skills. We also assume that they have had the theories course in which they both encountered different theories and had the opportunity to practice some of each theory's strategies, thus augmenting their basic skills.

The group class, then, in addition to specific group skills, can offer students the opportunity to apply previously learned skills in a group setting and to understand how different theories might be actualized in a group format.

The structure of the course consists of four elements: process groups, psychoeducational class groups, task groups, and the psychoeducational group project. These elements meet the ASGW requirements and give students experiences in the varieties of groups that they are likely to lead in their future practice. What follows are descriptions of how these elements might be incorporated into the group course.

Further, because of ethical needs to avoid dual roles, we have designed the course to have two instructors: the instructor of record, who teaches the content part of the course and gives students grades, and the counselor instructor, who leads the process group, behaves as a counselor in the field might behave with respect to the process group, and gives no grades. The counselor instructor lets the instructor of record know that students have attended the process group, but does not inform the instructor of record about anything that goes on in the process group. The counselor instructor discusses the need for confidentiality and the limits of confidentiality during the initial process group, and informs students that, similarly to group counseling out in the field, nothing that is discussed in the process group will be discussed outside of the group. Students can thus feel assured that their personal issues and struggles will not affect their grades.

## Process Group

Students participate in a once-a-week process group (ours have lasted 90 minutes, for 15 weeks, although some programs have such groups meet for two-hour sessions over 10 weeks) in which they experience a counseling group firsthand, guided by a skilled group counselor (the counselor instructor) who is not a full-time faculty member or the course's instructor of record. The counselor instructor may be a doctoral student or an adjunct faculty member. Students do not receive a grade on their participation in the process group, nor is anything about their participation discussed with anyone else, including the faculty member who is responsible for giving students grades for the course or evaluating their progress in the program.

Although ASGW distinguishes between counseling and psychotherapy groups, and recommends that leaders be clear from the outset about which they are leading, it seems that overlaps between counseling and psychotherapy are a bit unpredictable in a student group. Regardless, it is a personally charged experience. The group may begin as a means for students to invest in their own personal growth and development and to learn about group process while doing so. But experience has shown that when group members begin to feel safe, they often tearfully mention sexual abuse, substance abuse, and longstanding relationship difficulties, and the corresponding diagnoses that have resulted. Although the counselor instructor from the beginning needs to remain clear that resolving these difficulties is not the role of the group, and that additional professional help will most certainly be needed should such issues become apparent, group members frequently bring up serious issues and are given the opportunity during the process group to have others listen to them and care for them. Tearful, "deep" sessions are not unusual.

Initial process group meetings are led by the counselor instructor and begin similarly to any counseling group. The counselor instructor discusses rules and roles and boundaries, and then moves on to trust building and how to share process comments. Students may be asked to choose something to work on or something that they wish to get out of the group experience.

After a few weeks, students themselves lead group sessions with the coaching and assistance of the counselor instructor. Each student leads at least one group session, sometimes with the assistance of a coleader. Students also take turns as process observers who sit outside of the group, outside of the emotional "work," to carefully observe the way in which the group is functioning. They tune in to the emotional depth, the ways in which people interact together, whether something important is accomplished, and whether important issues or processes or emotions have been missed. At the end of the group, the process observer joins the group leader and members in processing how the group went.

Initially, the group leader may start the group with a "feeling round," in which members state a current feeling and briefly say anything they wish about why they are feeling that way. Sometimes the feeling round circles the group a number of times, and students are given instructions to move from vague, ambiguous feelings (e.g., bad, good) to more vulnerable feelings (e.g. angry, sad). This sort of start to a group can help everyone become centered and present to each other and the group.

After the feeling round or other group opening exercise, the leader may ask if group members have any brief unfinished business or if anyone wishes to have some time in the group that day. The remainder of the group is then divided among the people who have said they would like some group time. As group members speak about their issue, the counselor instructor or the student leader uses group leadership skills to respond and to urge group member interaction about the issue. If the student leader becomes stuck at some point, the counselor instructor may offer some ideas about how to proceed or may model some group leadership skills.

Group leaders may also have planned certain activities in case group members do not ask for time in the group on a particular day. For instance, I (Bruck) have used the following:

> It's been a really important learning experience for me to understand what some of my strengths and weaknesses are as a counselor, particularly how I initially come across to clients. For example, some people notice the fact that I always seem to take my shoes off. Some people are bothered by it, and some aren't. But it was good to get the feedback that everyone notices it, because frankly I forget that I do it. That may seem like a silly example, but I'm wondering, since we have time tonight, if there's anyone else here who might be interested in receiving feedback on how they come across to others when they are in counseling roles.

Anyone who volunteers to receive feedback is given control of asking for it and saying when she or he has heard enough. The group leader supports and guides group members in giving feedback in a helpful way and in helping the volunteer process what she or he has heard. The group leader also might lead experiential activities that increase students' awareness and encourage them to interact or receive feedback from others. For instance, the leader might guide a deep relaxation with guided imagery, have students visualize in response to music, or ask students to discuss a time when they were powerfully moved emotionally. This is the perfect time to try out activities that they are learning about in the content portion of the course.

At the end of the group, the group leader leads members in processing the group experience. The group leader may ask group members, "How was the group for you?" or "How did we do as a group?" or "What was it like being in group this evening?" She or he actively listens to the responses, punctuating key points, and invites the process observer to share observations. If the group leader, group members, or process observer seem to have missed key processes, the counselor instructor lets them know what she or he observed about the group process. The group leader may then close the group by asking students to express how they are feeling, to say one sentence about their experience in the group, or to state any unfinished business that might need to be addressed during the next group.

Counselor instructors have a number of roles in this model. When they are leading the group, of course they model helpful group leadership. But beyond modeling, they also explain what they are doing and why, linking their explanations to what the group members say they have experienced. Counselor instructors use the language of the text so that the written word comes alive in experience. When students lead the group, instructors continue to link the conceptual material from the text to the experience during the group processing time.

Within 12 hours of the group experience, students write a one-page journal entry about their experience in the group, an entry that uses no group members' names and is electronically submitted to the counselor instructor. Students focus on how the group dynamics evolved in light of the readings and class presentations. They describe their own experience as participants in the group, how their experience relates to the overall group process and to becoming a group facilitator, and their experiences as group facilitators and/or process observers. To offer structure for a rather ambiguous task, students are provided with the following questions as prompts:

1. How did I participate in the group? What did I gain from it? OR Why did I choose not to participate?

2. How can I apply class readings and content to what I observed in group today? (group stages, roles, factors, types)

3. What did I learn about myself? (thoughts, feelings, behaviors)

4. How successful was I in practicing appropriate interpersonal skills?

5. How effective was I in actualizing my intra- and interpersonal goals?

When counselor instructors review journal entries, they are able to better understand students' conceptual understandings about groups and their current experiences of the group. This information offers instructors material for future processing sessions, for encouraging students, and for clarifying any misconceptions.

A constructive developmental perspective requires that those who promote development offer both adequate challenges and supports in order to prevent students from finding themselves underchallenged and bored or, in contrast, in over their heads. Most counselor instructors will be largely self-authorizing knowers and so should be quite capable of facilitating student development. However, if instructors lack constructive development knowledge, they may not be aware that some group tasks may overchallenge some students. And counselor instructors may not—given that they may not be full-time academics—know how to offer adequate scaffolding to hold students in the anxiety of newness and the vulnerability of openness. It is hoped, therefore, that the suggestions that follow about support and challenge may offer assistance.

Most students entering counselor education programs show the epistemology of interpersonal/received ways of knowing (Eriksen & McAuliffe, 2003, 2006; Kegan, 1998; Neukrug & McAuliffe, 1993). Therefore, instructors need to match students' interpersonal characteristics *and* gently urge them toward institutional characteristics. The specifics of these ways of knowing were reviewed in Chapter 1. However, ideas about how to apply them to this course are offered here.

The process group and reflection papers/journals are perhaps the most epistemologically challenging part of the course for two reasons. First, they are inherently ambiguous. Second, the journaling requires students to step back from their experiences in order to reflect, critically think, apply theory to practice, and give (or perhaps it would be better to say "develop") their own perspectives. In the face of all of this challenge, therefore, strong supports are needed. Such support might include

(a) very clearly and specifically articulating the expectations of process group participants; (b) offering step-by-step instructions about how to write reflection papers or journal entries; (c) creating exemplars of reflection papers or journal entries, and offering specific feedback to students following initial entries; (d) taking the lead, modeling and explaining, when students experience initial anxieties; (e) allowing for and giving examples of structured activities for starting groups that students might use when they are leading; or (f) offering specific questions to guide processing. Directions for reflections or journaling are provided in the Appendix on page 150.

## Psychoeducational Class Group

Students also meet weekly with the instructor of record for the Group Counseling class. However, we choose not to conduct the class as a traditional lecture-and-discussion. Instead, for most topics, we conduct at least part of the class as a psychoeducational group, with a leader and a process observer, and time to process the in-class group experience. The topic for the group, rather than life skills or effective parenting, as might happen in a school or counseling center, is "how to lead a group," "how to handle difficult group members," "the stages of a group," or any of the topics of other chapters that are typically included in a group counseling text.

During class, the instructor serves as the leader of the psychoeducational group for the first few weeks of class. Group discussions are conducted in the usual ways about the topics included in the textbook chapters. The difference is that the instructor also carefully models the group leadership skills that have been discussed in the chapters. After the first few weeks, the instructor asks for volunteers to colead the class group, ensuring that all students have the experience of leadership. When leading, the instructor models opening the group, checks in with group members about key questions on the content for that week, and begins with a triggering question (e.g., "What was most important to you in this week's reading?"). The instructor models basic listening skills (e.g., eye contact, attentiveness, reflective comments) as well as basic group leadership skills, such as the following:

- creating a safe group environment
- facilitating interaction among group members

- intervening judiciously to help maintain the focus of conversation between participants
  - clarifying and summarizing participants' statements
  - eliciting members' participation in a supportive way
  - redirecting comments and observations to group members
  - reinforcing desired behaviors
  - modeling appropriate risk taking for group members
  - stimulating group affect
  - working with tension and conflict
- being sensitive to culturally diverse needs
- helping members set goals
- understanding and appropriately responding to the stage of the group

The instructor similarly urges group members to actively participate in making the group effective by doing the following:

- listening attentively and respectfully
- attending to other class members nonverbally (e.g., maintaining good eye contact)
- expressing him- or herself clearly and concisely
- giving appropriate feedback
- being responsible for his or her feelings and observations using "I" statements
- engaging in both support and challenge

The content of the class group parallels the content of the reading for that particular week. The group discussions serve to punctuate reading content, generate questions and answers about the content, and stimulate active thinking and reflection on the content. Such sessions are particularly alive because that same content is being acted out in the process of the group even as students speak about it. Students are thus asked to be "in" the group and to stand outside and think about it concurrently, or within a close time span. For example, after students have read the chapter on leading the first stage of a group, they participate in a group opening exercise, discuss leading the first stage, process how the leader did in leading the first stage, and reflect on how the leadership impacted them as group members.

The leader might say, for instance, "Close your eyes for a moment and imagine yourself as a leader beginning a group. What feelings does that generate? Now open your eyes and share one word to describe your feelings." The group members would then, one at a time, share their word. During the group, the leader would initiate a discussion on how to lead initial groups, would demonstrate appropriate boundary setting, and would model group leadership skills. After the group, the instructor might ask students how the leader actualized the content from the textbook, how well the leader led, and what impact the way in which she or he led had on the group members themselves. An added benefit of running the class in this way is that students are motivated to read the text actively, as they will be leading or participating in the group related to that content.

The content of the class group, which is common to most texts on group counseling, includes definitions, types of groups, group dynamics, effective group leadership, leadership skills, screening potential members, beginning and organizing a group, assessment and evaluation, goal setting, stages of groups, problem clients, termination issues, and groups for specific populations (e.g., different age groups, different types of problems).

The difference between a typical lecture-and-discussion class and the psychoeducational group conducted for didactic purposes during this class is that students and group leaders actually conduct a group, which provides a very active learning experience. Further, after the first few weeks, the instructor of record relinquishes group leadership to the students, so students learn to be leaders. First the instructor and then the student leaders aim to demonstrate and try out leader roles (some of which parallel typical class instructor roles, were instructors to actually use them well). Sometimes students take on assigned roles to help stimulate learning. For instance, during the week in which students read about problem clients, group members might adopt roles as people with those problems during the group experience so that instructors have the chance to demonstrate how to manage problematic behavior. Any topics that do not lend themselves to a psychoeducational group can be discussed in the more typical lecture-and-discussion format.

At the end of each class group, leaders (students and instructor), the process observer, and group members process the group. The process observer comments on how the group went, what affective dimensions and other processes she observed, and how well the group did at the task of covering and understanding that week's content. The instructor coaches the process observer and adds whatever process comments are necessary to ensure that students understand the group's process and content for the day. Group members also contribute their process observations in response to the instructor's questions about how the group went for them, how effective it was for them in mastering the content, what learning needs persist for them, and what ideas they have about functioning better as a group the next week.

The instructor leads the first few sessions alone, as mentioned above. However, after the initial weeks, the instructor partners with student leaders to conduct the group. Student leaders are usually very apprehensive about leading. So the instructor provides encouragement and reassurance that students are not being judged or graded on their performance and that this is an opportunity to try on a new role so that they won't have to try it on for the first time with actual clients.

Because of the inherent challenges in taking on this new role as group leader, I (Eriksen) have found it helpful to offer structure and emotional support prior to the class. I typically call or email student leaders during the week before class to check in on how they might want to begin the group, to offer specific ideas, and to assure them that I will be right beside them every step of the way. During class, while student leaders facilitate the group, the instructor can do a number of things to ensure that the class gets a reasonable group experience with a good deal of content. The instructor can sit beside leaders and whisper ideas into their ears when needed. The instructor may even coach student leaders with very specific directions. It is good to periodically take timeouts to process or model or instruct. During processing time, group members also offer that week's leader input on her or his strengths in leading that week and offer suggestions for future group leadership.

At times, the instructor takes over group leadership in order to model particular skills or to ensure that the class has covered the content, particularly when students have questions that require more expert explanations. For instance, when the instructor assigns various "problem client" roles to group members, members often play the roles so dramatically that the student leaders find themselves stumped as to how to keep the group going

and how to stop the problematic behavior. In such a situation, the instructor might take over and model various strategies for handling problem clients. In this way, the group fluctuates back and forth between the ambiguity of experience and newness and process, and the structure of specific guidance and modeling.

Because there are no exams in the course, the instructor can ask students to demonstrate their content knowledge in reflection papers. Within 12 hours of the classroom group experience, students write a one-page, double-spaced reflection paper in which they apply the week's content to their experience in the group. Reflection papers challenge students developmentally. As mentioned previously, most counseling students think partially from a more automatic or concrete frame (i.e., the interpersonal/received knowing stage), and to progress developmentally, they need to step back from their experience and relationships; think about them; and make decisions about how they feel, what they think, and what they will do with what they have discovered. Therefore, their reflection on the relationships between the textbook's content and concepts and the experiences within the group challenges students to use more complex thinking and reasoning. To support them, the instructor provides specific instructions on what is to be included in the reflection papers and how many points will be received for each requirement. Here are some suggested stimulus questions that might be given to students for the reflection papers:

1. How successful was the group leader in leading the group? Give examples as evidence.

2. What group processes did you observe?

3. How did you participate (or not) in these group processes? Why or why not?

4. Apply the most important concepts from your readings to what you observed about leadership and process.

The instructor might also provide an exemplar of a reflection paper, with side comments on which parts of it qualify as evaluation, examples, group process, self-reflection, and application of textbook content (or other requirements). Further, after students turn in the first two reflection papers, the instructor might offer specific feedback and pointers on meeting the requirements so that students will understand how to best learn from the reflection experience.

Of course, there are limits to the use of psychoeducational groups for processing the content of the Group Counseling course. Some course content cannot be fully experienced in the class psychoeducational group, such as learning about groups for children, teens, elderly people, addicts, or depressed people. And a psychoeducational group can feel a bit repetitive after 12 weeks. So the instructor can interrupt the weekly class group with videos and other demonstrations. For instance, students have brought children to class so that the instructor can demonstrate a children's group. For one class, a play therapist demonstrated and explained what she would do, while the students acted as children. We video-recorded the demonstration for use in future classes. In other situations, the Yalom group counseling videos might be used to instruct on process groups.

## Task Groups

Students also participate regularly together in task groups to develop a psychoeducational group and to plan their end-of-class presentations. Their specific task is to design a 10-week psychoeducational group experience that they might conduct later, in their practicum/internship experience or in the school or counseling center where they will eventually work. Four or five students who are interested in a similar topic (e.g., parenting, children with attention deficit hyperactivity disorder, children going through divorce) gather for short periods of time during class and regularly outside of class. The purpose is twofold: to experience and learn about the process of a task group and to learn about psychoeducational groups.

The process of operating as a task group is as follows. For each task group meeting, groups select a leader and a process observer. The group members pay attention to both content and process: They not only conduct the task of developing the psychoeducational program, but also take time to receive and respond to the process observer's comments. The group members rotate leader and process observer roles. They supplement their work together with phone calls and emails. Then, at each in-person meeting, the process observer also reports on observations of phone and email interactions.

To continue the developmental learning discussed above, group members comment on the process of the task group in their weekly reflection papers. Their reflections also help the instructor stay aware of any process difficulties that might develop in the group. To further ensure the overall success of the task groups, students are instructed to ask for help immediately should process difficulties impair their group functioning, so that the instructor can offer assistance. Given that many of the students use an interpersonal/received way of knowing much of the time, and that conflict is inherent in human interactions (particularly among people with many differences who are under time constraints and experiencing scarcity of resources), and that interpersonal knowers do not handle conflict in ways that will be helpful to task groups, the instructor can assume that task group members will experience developmental challenges that will require her or his assistance.

Therefore, during the semester the instructor periodically initiates discussions about the task group process to determine what is going well and what is not. The instructor can then offer any assistance, instruction, or support that may be needed. Without specific attention to task group processes, task groups can deteriorate to the lowest common denominator. As students often report, "I always do everything on group projects" or "Angela didn't do anything, but she got the same grade as the rest of us. How is that fair?" or "I hate group projects. There are always people who do nothing, people who are impossible to work with, and a couple of us who are scrambling at the last minute to make up the difference."

As a result of the risks, groups need to be reminded that sacrificing group principles and practices (in the interest of time, because they have forgotten the point of the task group, etc.) leads to less effective groups, and that if they have veered away from these principles and practices, they may be headed toward the dysfunctionalities that they have experienced in past small groups. Further, veering away from the assigned group processing tasks can mean sacrificing an important part of the learning experience. From a constructivist-developmental perspective, these authoritative reminders, deliberate discussions, and instructions offer support for experiences of ambiguity that will challenge students who operate from an interpersonal/received frame of knowing.

# Psychoeducational Group Project

The psychoeducational group that task group members develop familiarizes students with the nature of planning and leading groups related to particular client or student issues. As a result of this project, students will have a group ready for their internship or first job and the know-how to develop a psychoeducational group on a needed topic.

Students choose to create a group that is relevant to their interests. As the assignment says, "At the end of this process, it is hoped that you and your classmates will have a practical blueprint for an actual 10-week psychoeducational group that you will be able to use in the future." The assignment also aims to help students integrate in action many of the concepts presented in the reading and reviewed in class. Although this type of group project, in requiring research and writing, will be somewhat familiar to most students from other courses, the process of working as a task group, as described above, will substantially challenge them because working together on an assigned task is inherently messy and fraught with potential dangers. Therefore, students may be supported by the following specific instructions:

- Review at least two commercially developed psychoeducational groups so as to see the elements that are included as a guide for developing your own.
- Decide the specific topic for your group—something that is needed by a particular population of clients or students, but different from what you have located commercially. Describe the group that you are proposing to conduct. What are the goals and objectives? What are the potential benefits to participants? (Be sure to have some research to back up your claims.)
- From what theoretical orientation will you be operating? What attracted you to this theory, and why? How does your theoretical orientation affect the content and the process of the group? How does it affect your stance as the counselor? What is the effectiveness of this theory with this type of group participant? (Be sure to have some research to back up your claims.)
- Describe the content for each of the 10 weeks of the group—goals and objectives, activities, didactic materials, discussion questions. (Again, supported by the literature.) Keep in mind what we know

about the ways that people learn and change (i.e., theory). You may use a published book as the basis for the content.

- Who is your target audience? What will you have to do to get clients to sign up for the group?
- How will you market or present your concept to the public, facility, or constituency (funders, school administration, etc.)? Develop marketing materials.
- Describe the parameters of the group (size, frequency, length, ages of participants, gender).
- What will be your policy on attendance, contact outside of group, and confidentiality? How will you handle deviations from these policies?
- Develop and present any forms that will be given to the group to sign (re: informed consent, confidentiality, etc.).
- Explicitly state what you expect during each of the different stages of the evolving group process (forming, storming, norming, performing, terminating). What kinds of conflict do you expect from group members? (Be sure to have some research to back up your claims.)
- Discuss potential problems that could arise in your group and how you will handle them.
- Be prepared to discuss and defend your group proposal in class.

At the end of the semester, each group spends an hour of class time conducting one segment of their program. Each group member is to be actively involved in the presentation. The presentations are evaluated on criteria appropriate for the delivery of a professional proposal, on successful group leadership, and on effective group process. Groups prepare and distribute written materials on their program that will enable their class members to present the program. Students are thus prepared to lead several psychoeducational groups when they reach their internship or first job.

## THE CONSTRUCTIVIST PRINCIPLES

As is perhaps obvious, how the course is structured expresses a number of the constructivist elements outlined in Chapter 3. Following are some links between constructivist teaching and the course in group counseling as we have designed it.

## Personalize the Teaching

Instructors personalize their teaching by building authentic relationships with students and promoting a sense of community. They take risks in being transparent with students, creating a true mentor-student relationship. They engage in the process of teaching in a personal and authentic way, staying in constant contact with the group; modeling courage, honesty, and authenticity; and being willing to take risks and to self-disclose when appropriate. They emphasize dialogue and interaction, show enthusiasm, and offer individualized feedback and responses.

The nature of the Group Counseling course also demands that students bring themselves fully and personally into the classroom experience, which builds strong personal and emotional connections among class members. In the privacy of the process group, students share quite intimately, and so develop an intensity of emotion around the course material. In the large class session, students participate actively as group members and leaders, and they engage with the class content actively and personally. In the task group, the challenges of creating a psychoeducational group and weathering inevitable interpersonal, time, and scheduling conflicts either strengthen or weaken the sense of connection. The intensity of all of these interactions, the sense that "we're all in this together" builds a sense of connection similar to that experienced by client groups who have been together for a period of time.

## Vary the Structure

Professional speakers suggest that the instructional mode be varied every eight minutes. They remind counselor educators that they teach a TV generation, and, like it or not, on television there are no more than eight minutes between commercials. The implication of this principle is that instructors' teaching strategies must engage and hold the learners' attention and engage learners who have different learning styles. These principles are just as true for university education.

As we have designed the course, students experience a wide range of learning structures—different types of groups; regular interruptions for mini-instructions and processing; reflective writing; researching and creating a psychoeducational group; and presenting their work to others. There is truly never a dull moment.

## Value and Promote Experience

The Group Counseling class values and promotes experience as much as or more than many courses in the counseling curriculum. We aim to have students experience something of each of the types of groups and each of the roles in a group. Students bring all aspects of themselves to the group experience, including thoughts, feelings, and behaviors. This experiencing creates the intensity necessary for powerful learning. In particular, participating in realistic roles and experiences prepares students more relevantly for their professional experiences than does mere reading, taking a test, and writing a report.

## Encourage Intrapersonal Process Awareness, or Metacognition

Learning is more than mere experiencing, as described in Chapter 2. It also requires regular reflection on and abstraction from experience. It requires both "being fully in" and "standing outside, looking in on" experiences. For this reason, each week students process the groups and reflect on their own experience in the groups in journals and reflection papers.

Earlier, we stated that metacognition (the conscious monitoring of one's thought processes) is key for the practitioner who would become a constructivist. Group counselors need to be aware of the thoughts, feelings, and judgments they experience while leading groups. Then, metacognitively, they need to be able to recognize the source of any issues in their personal history, introjected values, or belief systems that may be triggered by the group's process. In Gestalt terms, group counselors need to understand their areas of blockage so that they don't live out their own agendas at their clients' expense.

## Recognize That Conflict and Dialectic Are the Norm

The meaning of this guideline is very different for an experiential Group Counseling course than for many other courses. In most courses, conflicts are limited to intellectual disagreements, although even intellectual conflicts often have emotional and interpersonal dimensions. The Group Counseling course, however, is explicitly designed for learning about conflict. In particular, one of the explicitly stated goals of training groups is to teach students how to work with interpersonal conflict.

The method for doing so is taught in this course and it involves several steps. The instructor assists each of the parties in conflict to (1) make a clear statement of their position, (2) identify and express their feelings in a clear manner, (3) identify values and beliefs that underlie their feelings, (4) clearly express these to the other person, and (5) state what they want from the other person. These steps continue until both parties believe that necessary feelings, thoughts, and desires have been expressed, that they have been heard, and that they have come to a reasonable solution. Thus, instructors communicate that conflict is expected and normal, they help students develop the capacity to approach conflict helpfully, and they reduce students' avoidance of talking about conflicts. As a result, the Group Counseling course becomes a laboratory for students to learn how to handle conflict at all levels and, in so doing, to build honest and open relationships with other students. Such relationships constitute the basis for a learning community.

## Show Commitment in the Face of Doubt

Counseling groups are characterized by often scary ambiguity. Members express anger, feelings are hurt, vulnerabilities are experienced, and secrets are revealed. Moreover, group members are often painfully frank and may not speak or behave in the ways that instructors would prefer. They may judge each other and say hurtful things. They may remain silent or stay aggressively intellectual.

Group leaders often experience an emotional quandary, asking themselves, "Will things work out?" "Should I stop this now?" "Hadn't I better take control of this session?" Beginning group leaders all too often opt for control. They structure the session, give members feedback directly, or say, "Enough is enough. It's time to change the subject." Their methods often reflect their own anxieties and doubts.

Experienced group leaders have a saying: "Trust in the process." Group leaders need to recognize that groups learn to police themselves: They get tired of the difficult, controlling member. They don't like it when one person is ganged up on. And they institute self-correcting mechanisms.

Instructors leading the process or class groups have the same doubts that counseling group leaders do. They ask themselves, "Will this be a positive learning experience for my students?" It is often hard for instructors to let go and trust in the process. Their experiences echo the experience of the parent whose child is riding a bicycle around the neighborhood for the first time without the parent's accompaniment. However, the commitment that instructors maintain to the group process in the face of personal and professional fears also teaches students. Their commitment models the type of trust in group process that instructors hope students will have in the counseling groups that they will eventually lead themselves.

## CHALLENGES IN USING THE CONSTRUCTIVIST APPROACH FOR TEACHING GROUP COUNSELING

Using a constructivist approach to teach the Group Counseling course presents both opportunities and challenges at professional and ethical levels. Counselor educators attempt to teach certain key attitudes throughout counselor preparation programs—these reflect what we see as best practices within the counseling profession.

The three types of group experiences in this course offer opportunities for such attitude development. First, the process group offers students a safe and structured environment for growth as people and as professionals. The class psychoeducational group similarly provides an opportunity for students to learn about both group process and key aspects (content) of group counseling. Instructors can observe and evaluate not only content mastery and skills, but underlying attitudes and even areas of psychological blockage that may impact the trainee's effectiveness or appropriateness for the field. Finally, the task group offers students the opportunity to take this knowledge "on the road," trying out what they have learned on a task that has personal and professional relevance.

A caveat is necessary here. It is sometimes difficult to maintain reasonable boundaries between the intellectual and the emotional, the personal and the academic. Although constructivist teaching advocates consideration of multiple dimensions of the person during the learning process and promotes engaging the student at a number of different levels, it doesn't advocate replacing an academic class with group therapy. However, the intensity of being in a process group and actively processing other group experiences may blur boundaries and overchallenge students and faculty. Faculty need at least self-authorizing/institutional capacities (Kegan, 1982, 1998) in order to navigate these complexities. Yet many faculty themselves are not consistently able to use that way of knowing (Granello, 2010).

In turn, students are challenged by the Group Counseling course to stretch themselves developmentally. For example, one particular attitude that is taught is taking responsibility for one's actions. Counselors know that this characteristically means not blaming others for their situations, but recognizing that we have choices that have led us to, and that continue to lead us on, the path we are taking. In our experience, a constructivist approach to group counseling can be a watershed opportunity for students to face such a responsibility, to "own their own stuff."

However, this stretching is a process that is fraught with emotional landmines that may explode if adequate supports are not provided. And it may be difficult for instructors who are teaching classes of 25 to 30 students to know when additional supports are needed until the explosions happen. Combine all of this with the emotional power and difficulty of some of the psychological issues that students bring into a program, some of which motivated them to become counselors, and it becomes clear that instructors need to be alert to student overchallenge at all times.

For instance, in one university, the 2.5-hour class was divided in half, with half of the students participating in the process group while the other half participated in the content class. As scheduling issues would have it, they all came in to the content part of the class right after their process group. They often looked shell shocked, bleary eyed, and tearful. They frequently reported that they had dealt with very difficult material during the process group. And they found it very hard to shift gears to get the most out of the content part of the class. I (Eriksen) found it necessary to do "closing off" exercises or visualizations so that they could try to put the lid on the tremendous emotional upheaval they were still experiencing.

Further, in one task group, one member created problems for the other members. Her hostility about the way the class was being conducted led to her refusal to process the task group or to involve the instructor when problems developed. She was most likely overchallenged by the unexpected experiential components of the course and needed clearer directions and supports. As a result of poor task group functioning, the final project did not conform with expectations, and the group was asked to redo the project to meet the requirements. This group member's hostility then exploded outward until the department chair became involved. In the resulting conversations and in reviewing task group members' reflection papers, it was clear that the group had been dysfunctional all along; that boundaries had been breached; that certain members had not fulfilled their responsibilities; and that, rather than asking for help immediately, the group had lost focus, control, and the ability to perform functionally. Early intervention and more regular checking in with group members might have forestalled the ongoing group dysfunction.

## CONCLUSION

Taught from a constructivist point of view, the course in group counseling aims at more than teaching group leadership skills. It aims at promoting students' development toward self-authorized knowing. Learning experiences are powerful and sometimes conflictual. However, the group experiences *can* teach students to build relationships characterized by openness, authenticity, and courage. These relationships then constitute the ground upon which other educational activities within the counselor education program may be built. This type of educational experience forms an essential link in the chain of socializing events that result in a student's evolution into a self-authorizing counselor.

# REFERENCES

Association for Specialists in Group Work. (2000). *Professional standards for the training of group workers.* Retrieved July 21, 2010, from http://www.asgw.org/PDF/training_standards.pdf

Eriksen, K. P., & McAuliffe, G. J. (2003). A measure of counselor competency. *Counselor Education and Supervision, 43,* 120–133.

Eriksen, K. P., & McAuliffe, G. J. (2006). Constructive development and counselor competence. *Counselor Education and Supervision, 45,* 180–192.

Granello, D. H. (2010). Cognitive complexity among practicing counselors: How thinking changes with experience. *Journal of Counseling & Development, 88,* 92–100.

Kegan, R. (1982). *The evolving self: Problem and process in human development.* Cambridge, MA: Harvard University Press.

Kegan, R. (1998). *In over our heads: The mental demands of modern life.* Cambridge, MA: Harvard University Press.

Neukrug, E. S., & McAuliffe, G. J. (1993). Cognitive development and human services education. *Human Services Education, 13,* 13–26.

Whelis, A. (1973). *How people change.* New York: HarperPerennial.

The purpose of journaling is to think or introspect about the material you are learning and the experiences you are having in class and outside of class. Reflection means many things to many people; however, in our rushed lifestyle we often do not stop to reflect, and thus live an unexamined life. For the purposes of this assignment, address the specific skills you have read about, been directed to work on, discussed, and practiced during and between classes. Give evidence for your statements. Let me know that you are aware of your strengths, your growing edges, and the personal issues that may impact your work as a counselor. In addition to the examples stated below that reflect on specific skills, please evaluate yourself overall as a counselor.

Journaling should include the following:

Statement of the purpose of the group and whether you felt the purpose was accomplished. Start with some overarching conclusions you would make about the group that day. Then ensure you support each conclusion you make with the following:

1. *Statement of the situation.* This includes a sentence or two about "what happened." For instance, "The leader began the group by asking what the most important learning was from the chapter" or "I noticed that three of the group members talked a good deal, while others were silent," or "When we began talking about leadership styles, the leader seemed to lose eye contact with group members." It may be tempting to include a lot more than a sentence or two. In fact, it may be tempting to journal only about events. Make every attempt to contain yourself.

2. *Your thoughts about the situation.* Beyond the actual facts of the situation are your interpretations or thoughts about it, including the concepts from the reading. Your interpretation impacts both your feelings about it and your decisions about how to respond. An example of thoughts about the situations above might be "This seemed an appropriate first question to get us started, and it left space for us in the conversation," "I wondered what need the

talkative group members had, or if they were trying to help the leader out. I also wondered if the more silent group members felt left out. We didn't seem to be fully functioning as a group as long as everyone wasn't fully participating," or "I wondered if the leader lost eye contact because she was thinking about how well she was doing as a leader while people talked about leadership, and whether she felt more like a participant than the leader." Were one to connect one's observations to the reading, one might indicate, "The leader took charge and laid out the group's purpose by asking this particular question, yet she remained a democratic leader in allowing and expecting all of us to contribute to understanding the chapter," or "I wondered if some of the members would monopolize the group and if the others would stay silent and uninvolved."

3. *Your feelings about these thoughts.* Feelings are feelings, not thoughts. That is, feelings are *angry, sad, hurt, happy, exuberant, discouraged,* and so on. If you find yourself saying, "I feel that . . ." or "I feel as though . . ." or "I feel like . . . ," you are expressing a thought or opinion, not a feeling. An example of a feeling reaction to the thoughts expressed above in #2 might be "I felt comfortable with the leader's style and initial questions; I felt welcomed to contribute," "I was nervous about whether I was talking too much, and worried that the silent people might be silent because I was dominating," or "When the leader lost eye contact, I felt nervous about whether she was abdicating her leader role, and felt pressured to help her out."

4. *Your goals for yourself as a leader or group member based on your observations.* In keeping with the previous examples, "I plan to let the leader know next time specifically how her leadership style encouraged my participation in the group," "I will invite the silent members to participate next time, whether I am a leader or a group member, and I will truly listen to them," and "When I am a leader, I will try to focus on the group members' processes rather than my own issues, even though that might be hard."

Make sure to include:

- specific process observations (anyone observing would notice these; not evaluations)
- applications of reading to what you observe
- your interpretation of or the meaning you ascribe to your observations
- how the group experience is affecting you individually, and the group process more generally
- what you will do with this information

The following are some good examples from student journals:

## Specific Process Observations

Some of the ways the leader provided structure were by explaining tasks, asking questions, and guiding the group in specific directions. The group leader did an excellent job in working with silence: She allowed appropriate silence to encourage members to speak up and to make sure that members had time to think about what had been and what was being said.

One noticeable process was the respect that all the members had for one another: Some of the ways that this took place were through members taking turns speaking, not speaking over others, and actively listening to one another.

The leader gave the members positive affirmation by using words like *good* and *exactly*.

Everyone seemed to participate in the group both by answering questions and by staying involved with the group, which was seen in their body language as they leaned forward in their seats or maintained eye contact with the leader and other group members.

## Interpretation of Observations

It seemed as though G. did not like silence and may have felt a responsibility to fill the space.

I felt as though L. was put on the spot. She was clearly trying her best, but had not been given all of the information ahead of time about expectations.

People appeared to be too involved emotionally with the theme and tried to elaborate, forgetting perhaps the didactics part of the discussion.

## Application of Reading Concepts

Some group members said they are typically quiet people, but due to the group process of contagion did decide to participate in the discussion.

This led to a sense of group cohesiveness.

This was an example of how we had established an element of universality.

What was evident was the social influence that comes about as the group members interact and attitudes and opinions are formed.

## Statements About One's Own Experience

I felt more relaxed in the group because I did not have to be a caregiver, and at this early stage of the experience that sometimes feels strange and uncomfortable.

I felt anxious because I would like to have input ideas into the discussion, yet I did not feel comfortable enough in my understanding of the text and did not want to look stupid in front of my peers.

I had a lot of anxiety because I was not exactly sure what was expected of me.

## What You Will Do With This Information

I hope that I will learn from each leader so as to have a better sense of the leader's role when it is my turn to lead the group.

When I am a leader, I will use eye contact to encourage quieter members to participate.

I also would like to paraphrase what people say during group so as to punctuate key points and clarify or reiterate information.

# Teaching Research Methods for Counselors

Varunee Faii Sangganjanavanich and Linda L. Black

H uman beings seem to be innately curious. They wonder, investigate, reflect, test, encounter errors and successes, and test again, often in that order. Sometimes they learn by coincidence or sheer luck. Counseling too is about curiosity and inquiry into the human condition, our existence, and our world. Yet many students of counseling experience feelings ranging from doubt to dread when they consider the process of research. In fact, Heppner, Kivlighan, and Wampold (1999) noted that a majority of counseling students in their study were anxious about the research class. And after taking it, students reported that it was their least favorite course.

But do and use research we must. The field of counseling has been moving toward evidence-based and data-driven practice (Sexton, Schofield, & Whiston, 1997; Sexton, Whiston, Bleuer, & Walz, 1997; Whiston & Coker, 2000). Both emphasize the importance of accountability. For that reason, counselors must be able to comprehend, critique, and utilize research-based knowledge. The research course plays a central and significant role in helping counselors-to-be understand the value, necessity, and utility of research beyond the concepts that they need in order to pass various exams or coursework.

We, the authors of this chapter, believe that student distaste for research occurs, in part, because the purpose and nature of inquiry have been ripped from their personal and contextual moorings. The terms *research*, *statistics*, and *empirical validation* seem to raise images of dry, abstract, and silencing procedures. A majority of ideas introduced in contemporary research appear absolute and procedural. The process of learning about research seems, traditionally, to have distanced counselors from their personal sense of curiosity and wonder. Counselors and helping professionals have become unnecessarily detached from the process of inquiry. Counselor educators, indeed all human beings, have a passion for knowing who, what, where, how, why, and under what conditions emotions, behaviors, and cognitions emerge, interact, diminish, and change. In the course described in this chapter, we wish to ignite that same passion for inquiry, investigation, and examination in our students.

## PERSONAL AND STUDENT MOTIVATION

We enjoy the process of learning. And learning depends on our willingness to inquire, explore, and investigate phenomena. These goals fit particularly well within a course on research and inquiry. However, for too long, counselor educators have seen students shrink at the idea of engaging in research because those students report that "it is irrelevant," "it is just math and I am not good at math," and (our favorite) "only professors read journals." Our students' perceptions make sense to us because we believe that much of the current counselor education curriculum related to research detaches the *knower* from the *known*. Instructors, textbooks, and curriculum standards typically focus on having learners recite the structure and tools of research (e.g., design, statistics, data analysis procedures, proposal writing) rather than encouraging learners to recognize the ubiquity of the research process in their everyday lives.

Instead, as *we* teach the research class, we aim to guide our students through a personally transformative process. We begin the course by asking students to identify their assumptions, beliefs, and expectations related to the process of research. As students uncover their assumptions, we concurrently inform them of the processes that they implicitly or explicitly utilize as they investigate phenomena.

The content, context, process, and timing of these discussions are central to the purpose of the research course. For instance, we initially ask students to read and reflect on a case study in which a substantial number of clients at a treatment agency report intensifying and increasingly severe depressive symptoms that seem to correspond with the onset of counseling (content). In the case situation, emergency calls have escalated and voluntary hospitalizations have increased.

In response to the case, students consider whether it would be relevant for their treatment team to investigate. Students then individually and collectively brainstorm the possible precursors, influences, impacts, and events (context) that may account for the clients' reports. As students generate hypotheses, they consider their rationale(s) for the nature, type, and extent of information that they wish to collect, a time line and plan to identify and secure key informants, and a reliable plan to secure the desired information (processes). Students engage in this activity during portions of three class meetings (timing) in order to facilitate deeper expression, allow for checking in with their peers and the instructor, and encourage exploration of the professional literature. The activity culminates in writing a plan (a research design and human subjects review application) to address questions that the class has generated. This case study process allows students to discuss and discover how research helps people address and investigate a mystery. Thus, students learn that research is something done by individuals like themselves (students) to answer vital questions.

# INTEGRATION OF CONSTRUCTIVIST PERSPECTIVES: A NEW PARADIGM IN TEACHING RESEARCH COURSES

Although some may view the instruction of a research or inquiry course as daunting, we see it as a welcome opportunity. The course in research methods is an opportunity to move learners from a relatively received way of knowing (receive and reproduce knowledge) to a procedural one (use objective procedures to obtain and communicate understanding). A developmental framework for the course thus provides an outline of a process in which the instructor can engage students where they are and invite them to develop along a trajectory, thus coming to understand the research process in a manner that makes better sense to them.

In addition, *constructivism* provides an avenue for individuals to learn through their experience. *Social constructionsim* emphasizes that individuals are influenced by social forces, such as families, cultures, and classes (Gergen, 2009). As researchers, it is inescapable that our perceptions and preconceived notions are colored by our societal surroundings. In addition, our judgments are clouded by self-definition and self-authorization as we develop personal meaning to suit who we are. Challenges are presented when the researchers perpetuate inequalities by confirming their assumptions about "how things should be" and fail to examine "how things are." These challenges force us, the counselor educators, to *deconstruct,* or explore possibilities to support equality in counseling research in order to fulfill the social justice mission of our profession.

Integrating constructivist perspectives into teaching research courses does present challenges for the learner as well as the instructor. However, success means that both learner and instructor experience an active and dynamic teaching-learning process. In this constructivist educational mode, ideas, beliefs, and truth are examined, personalized, and contextualized. Thus, a joint enterprise between learner and instructor needs to be present in the classroom (McAuliffe & Eriksen, 2002).

## COURSE CONTEXT

Like other so-called content-based classes, the research methods class is commonly taught as a single course in a master's program of study. It is typically delivered through classroom lecture and is generally assessed by exam questions that mainly focus on how well students can memorize theoretical concepts and terminology. Students are rarely assessed on the practical aspects of conducting research. In some institutions, the research methods class is taught by faculty external to the counseling program. As counselor educators, we believe that the research methods class is most effectively taught and assessed through constructivist, developmental, and experiential methods, which can best be conducted by those familiar with such perspectives.

Consistent with the tenets of constructivist teaching, we conceptualize the research methods class as one in which learners are first exposed to broad ideas or concepts (the whole) rather than small bits of information or data (fragments). Introducing learners to the context of research and inquiry (the whole) encourages them to think carefully about the relevance of fragmentary knowledge, when it is presented, in order to refine their understanding of the whole concept. A social constructivist approach to teaching is consistent with the expectations of counselor-as-advocate as classroom discussions increase the opportunity for learners' self-determination and self-regulation, as well as the synthesis, transfer, and application of co-constructed knowledge to clinical and educational settings. Further, in an era in which the field of counseling emphasizes the importance of social justice and advocacy for clients (Gibson, 2009), the integrity of our services is crucial. But how do we know that what we do is working? Researchers and scholars have focused on outcome research or evidence-based practice to answer this challenging question. In turn, we need to update counselor education curricula and pedagogy to answer this challenge, for instance, by increasing the use of action research and the transparency of research procedures. Integrating constructivist perspectives when teaching research courses not only adds accountability to outcome research, but also improves the process of knowing and research integrity.

# CONTENT AND LEARNING OBJECTIVES

Through active participation and critical thinking, learners have an opportunity to discover their learning capacities as well as to co-construct the knowledge of research methods with their peers and their instructors. Specifically, learners will question how, why, and through what methods research is initiated. The process of inquiry and the desire to know and understand are an innately human enterprise. The research methods course, in our opinion, should embolden the desire to know. The course learning objectives, content, processes, and constructivist principles are summarized in Table 11.1.

**TABLE 11.1**  Research Methods Course Learning Objectives, Content, Processes, and Constructivist Principles

| Learning Objectives | Content | Processes and Activities | Constructivist Principles |
|---|---|---|---|
| Verbalize personal understanding of research in the students' lives, expectations, fears, and hopes as they learn this process. | Ways of knowing (how we know what we know)<br><br>Common hopes and fears about research, individual capacities, utility of the course<br><br>Significance of research | Opening dialogue on learner-generated questions, perspectives generated through individual reflection<br><br>Weekly question to stimulate classroom discussion<br><br>Journal of my journey | People construct their worldview from a context-based perspective.<br><br>Co-construction is a result of an egalitarian relationship between learners and educators. |
| Demonstrate understanding of how one arrives at a hypothesis and how and why one may test that theory, idea, and belief. | Theories/theoretical constructs in research<br><br>Epistemology in research<br><br>Relevancy of research in counseling and helping professions | Opening dialogue on learner-generated questions, perspectives generated through individual reflection<br><br>Weekly question to stimulate classroom discussion | Each individual's story has a personal, subjective meaning attached to it.<br><br>Personal experience is ambiguous and may be understood and interpreted in multiple ways. |

(Continued)

**TABLE 11.1** (Continued)

| Learning Objectives | Content | Processes and Activities | Constructivist Principles |
|---|---|---|---|
| | | Counseling vs. research theoretical orientation<br><br>"What do I want to know?" dyads<br><br>"You will find out!" small groups<br><br>Lecture/discussion | |
| Demonstrate and share knowledge of quantitative and qualitative research methods in counseling and helping professions. | Research methods (how we reliably know what we know)<br><br>Quantitative methods<br><br>Qualitative methods<br><br>Research methods in counseling and helping professions<br><br>Current trends and special considerations in counseling and helping profession research | Opening dialogue on learner-generated questions, perspectives generated through individual reflection<br><br>Weekly question to stimulate classroom discussion<br><br>"What do I want to know?" dyads<br><br>"Multiple perspectives" small groups<br><br>"Is it the same story?" triads<br><br>"Bias is everywhere" small groups<br><br>Journal article evaluation and review | Reality is multiform.<br><br>There is no "absolute" truth.<br><br>Truth is seen as a union between the self-interpreted narrative and a social construction.<br><br>Exposure of multiple perspectives allows learners to examine their assumptions and preconceived notions. |
| Demonstrate the ability to conduct and evaluate quantitative and qualitative research in the counseling profession. | Research outcomes and evaluation<br><br>Application of research | Opening dialogue on learner-generated questions, perspectives generated through individual reflection<br><br>Weekly question to stimulate classroom discussion<br><br>Lecture/discussion | An integration of constructivist perspectives in teaching research courses adds not only accountability in outcome research, but also in a process of knowing and obtaining research integrity. |
| Demonstrate the ability to think critically about social factors (e.g., cultural issues, socioeconomic status, discourse) that influence research methods in counseling and helping professions. | Multicultural issues and considerations in conducting research<br><br>Confounding factors in counseling research<br><br>Advocacy and accountability of researchers in counseling profession | Opening dialogue on learner-generated questions, perspectives generated through individual reflection<br><br>Weekly question to stimulate classroom discussion<br><br>Lecture/discussion | Sociopolitical perspectives influence how individuals construct knowledge about themselves and others. |
| Become aware of ethical issues in conducting research in counseling and helping professions. | Ethical decision-making model<br><br>Philosophy of human subject research<br><br>Professional ethical standards in research<br><br>Multicultural issues in research | Opening dialogue on learner-generated questions, perspectives generated through individual reflection<br><br>Weekly question to stimulate classroom discussion<br><br>Lecture/discussion | Have students see the connectedness of knowledge and experience a holistic approach in examining research. |

A more detailed description of the learning objectives of this course follows:

*Participants will voice their beliefs, assumptions, concerns, and hopes for their learning and experience in a research course.* In the beginning of the course, participants have opportunities to share their thoughts and expectations regarding this course with their peers and their instructor. This objective aims to inform educators about learners' frames of reference in research as well as their expectations for the course.

*Participants will demonstrate understanding of the role of epistemology in research.* Learners need to understand how an approach to knowing influences what is known. Participants thus learn about and demonstrate their understanding of the epistemologies behind various research designs and methods.

*Participants will demonstrate understanding of the utility and relevance of quantitative and qualitative research design and methodology in counseling.* Participants identify and distinguish among characteristics of quantitative and qualitative research. They also become able to communicate their understanding of the utility and relevance of both methods and designs as applied to counseling-related questions.

*Participants will demonstrate the ability to conduct and evaluate quantitative and qualitative studies.* Learners gain a basic understanding of key concepts, design, statistics, procedure, validity and reliability, and findings through actively carrying out research and evaluating research from professional counseling journals.

*Participants will demonstrate the ability to think critically about social factors (e.g., cultural issues, socioeconomic status) that influence research methods in counseling and helping professions.* Since research findings are generally influenced by contextual factors such as culture, participants need to be able to identify the impact of these factors on researchers as well as on research inquiry.

*Participants will understand ethical issues in conducting research in counseling and know codes of conduct for researchers.* Ethical issues are crucial in conducting research. Participants learn and examine their roles and responsibilities as researchers in human subject research.

# CLASS STRUCTURE AND ACTIVITIES

Constructivist education philosophy considers experiential learning to be a means for learners to enhance their learning experience (D. Kolb, 1984; A. Y. Kolb & Kolb, 2005). Experiential activities help to create an active and ongoing involvement among learners and between learners and educators. In the research course, we believe that experiential activities are particularly crucial because they assist learners in translating abstract knowledge into practical applications. Suggested experiential activities are listed below:

*Opening dialogue:* Classes each week include learner-generated comments and questions to demonstrate the centrality of an ongoing dialogue for student and instructor learning. The open dialogue not only provides an opportunity for learners to voice their perspectives and to inquire about topics they are interested in knowing about, but it also allows the instructor to personalize the classroom environment to serve the individual needs of each learner. This activity occurs throughout the class course.

*Weekly questions:* Each week, the instructor initiates a series of questions to stimulate discussion among learners during class. Answers to these questions are processed as a group.

*"What do I want to know?" activity:* This activity prompts learners to consider and share with a partner their questions on three possible topics: (1) topics that they are particularly interested in, (2) processes that they do not understand, or (3) constructs that they would like to investigate further. Their answers to what they would like to know, understand, or investigate form their research question. Learners work with a different classmate each time this activity occurs, and it occurs every other week from the first week to the middle of the course, in order to help learners formulate their research ideas. By sharing their research ideas with others, learners refine their research idea (i.e., research question).

*"You will find out" activity:* This activity offers learners the opportunity to experience the differences between modernist and postmodernist approaches in research. After grouping learners into four groups, the instructor assigns a series of research questions to groups. Each

group generates a research question(s), design, and method from the perspective of one of the conceptual approaches. Then each group presents its ideas to the class. Learners benefit from hearing the different conceptual perspectives that are generated by other groups.

*Multiple perspectives:* The instructor also invites course participation outside of the classroom, in some location near the classroom, or elsewhere on campus where people are interacting. Learners privately observe the same situation at the same time. When they finish observing, they share their data from the observations. Students together consider such questions as "What did you observe?" "How did you make sense of what you observed?" "What was the primary focus of your attention?" and "How did your observations differ from those of others?" This activity aims to help learners understand potential biases that may be based on preconceived notions and, as a result, helps to illustrate the biases that can influence research.

*"Is it the same story?" activity:* The purpose of this activity is similar to the multiple perspectives activity. Learners work in triads. Two group members, independently of one another (one leaves the room so as not to be influenced by the other's interview), conduct an interview with a third person, asking about that person's perception of being a graduate student and her or his experience in graduate school. Then, after both students have independently completed their interviews, they meet to share what they have discovered. Similar to the multiple perspectives activity, this activity emphasizes the range of potential biases that may emerge from one's preconceived notions, biases that may interfere with the objectivity of the research.

*"Bias is everywhere" activity:* Learners participate in a brief "study" by taking a brief but reliable and valid assessment. The instructor selects one of many psychological assessments or standardized tests that can be administered and scored within 20–25 minutes (e.g., Career Thoughts Inventory, Myers-Briggs Type Indicator Form M, Stress Index for Parents of Adolescents). The instructor also states the purpose of the study to the class (the activity assumes that every group is conducting the same study). Each learner scores her or his own test, following the instructions on the scoring procedures. The scores for all class members are written on the board. After the assessment, learners separate into groups of four or five. Each group uses the results that are written on the

board to write a report on its findings. They also write up a discussion of the findings. In general, the students, as individuals and as a collective unit, impose their preconceived notions and assumptions onto the results or findings, and thus, to a certain degree, they report what they want to report, rather than what the results indicate. The purpose of this activity is to demonstrate that, although quantitative research claims to be objective, bias is hard to eliminate (the instructor might ask students, "Why did the researcher choose to report some parts of the results, and not others?"). This activity also improves learners' abilities to be thoughtful researchers and consumers of research products.

*"Dilemmas" activity:* The purpose of this activity is for students to demonstrate knowledge about ethical dilemmas in research. It also encourages students to co-construct this knowledge. In this activity, three to four learners form a group, and each group receives a different case study. Groups discuss any ethical dilemmas that are evident in their assigned case studies and generate ideas about how they would manage the dilemmas in order to meet ethical standards for research. (A sample case study is provided in the Appendix on page 161.)

*"Writing Institutional Review Board (IRB)" activity:* Students complete this activity during class. The purpose is to provide learners with a practical experience in writing an IRB proposal for human subjects research. The instructor presents a poorly written IRB proposal to learners. Together, learners critique the IRB proposal. Then the instructor asks them to develop a better IRB proposal based on knowledge that they have obtained from classroom lectures and discussions, as well as from prior readings about ethics and responsibilities of researchers who conduct studies with human subjects. Each learner has the opportunity to contribute to the IRB proposal while developing this document with other students.

As demonstrated in our activities, we believe that counselor educators can integrate constructivist teaching into their research courses. Counselor educators can implement these experiential activities to help counselors-in-training, as individual and collective units, generate research ideas, create and understand meanings of research paradigms and methods, and reflect on what they have read about research. Openness and self-reflection are encouraged as students learn not only to appreciate but also to celebrate differences derived from diverse ideas and interactions (Burbules & Rice, 1991).

# ASSIGNMENTS

The values held by constructivist educators that guide course assignments include believing in and utilizing the meaning-making capacity of students, openness to varied teaching methods and goals, flexibility, and reflexivity (McAuliffe & Eriksen, 2002). These values provide the basic operational structure within which to organize a constructivist approach to teaching. The following assignments, therefore, facilitate learners' reflections on research in counseling.

*Counseling vs. research theoretical framework:* Learners write a paper to identify their current theoretical orientation for counseling and their theoretical framework in research (e.g., descriptive, explanatory, predictive, prescriptive theories). Instructions to learners include the following:

- Identify and describe at least three basic principles of your theoretical frameworks in both counseling and research.
- Explain how your theoretical framework in counseling fits or does not fit with your theoretical framework in research.
- Describe how these conceptual frameworks may impact you when you are conducting research.

*Bias management:* Learners identify one of their own potential biases that may interfere with their conducting research. They then suggest at least three ways to manage biases during a research procedure (e.g., research questions, data collection, data analysis, presenting/reporting findings).

*Research consumer 1:* Learners find a quantitative research article of interest related to counseling. They critique its key concepts, design, statistics, procedures, and plans related to validity and reliability and findings. Students evaluate the following areas:

- research method (sample, data collection, and statistical analysis)
- threats to internal validity
- threats to external validity

*Research consumer 2:* Learners find a qualitative research article of interest related to counseling. They critique its key concepts, approach, procedure, credibility

and trustworthiness, and findings. Students evaluate the following areas:

- research method (participants, data collection, and data analysis)
- credibility
- trustworthiness

*Journal of my journey:* The journaling assignment gives learners the opportunity to critically examine and reflect on their perceptions and experiences throughout the course. In the journal, students respond to questions such as the following:

- How do you see yourself as a researcher?
- What are the biggest challenges that you face in this course?
- How does the experience in this course impact you as a person?

The recommended assignments are designed to focus learners' attention on their personal reflections and experiences related to the production and consumption of research and inquiry. We believe that identification and articulation of learners' voices as investigators of phenomena can create a sense of personal empowerment and competence related to research attitudes, knowledge, and skills.

# CONCLUDING REFLECTIONS

This course begins with the assumption that most counseling students experience some hesitancy related to the course on research methodologies. We believe that, within the context of the research methods course, students need the opportunity to voice and address their concerns, beliefs, assumptions, and strengths related to research and inquiry. In addition, faculty must be willing to engage in an ongoing dialogue in which learners and instructors transform what is unknown and irrelevant into what is known and relevant. Constructivist approaches to research pedagogy allow learners to translate abstract concepts into practical realities in research. A dialogical approach to understanding the purposes, processes, and content of research aids counselors-in-training in becoming critical consumers and producers of meaningful and relevant research. As a result, learners become responsible and accountable for utilizing and initiating outcome research. We believe that a more invitational and less hierarchical manner of instruction leads to less passive and more open, engaged, involved, and curious learners.

# REFERENCES

Burbules, N. C., & Rice, S. (1991). Dialogue across differences. *Harvard Educational Review, 61,* 393–416.

Gergen, K. (2009). *An invitation to social construction.* Thousand Oaks, CA: Sage.

Gibson, D. M. (2009). Advocacy counseling: Being an effective agent of change for clients. In B. T. Erford (Ed.), *Orientation to the counseling profession: Advocacy, ethics, and essential professional foundations* (pp. 340–358). Upper Saddle River, NJ: Pearson Education.

Heppner, P. P., Kivlighan, D. M., Jr., & Wampold, B. E. (1999). *Research design in counseling* (2nd ed.). Pacific Grove, CA: Brooks/Cole.

Kolb, A. Y., & Kolb, D. A. (2005). Learning styles and learning spaces: Enhancing experiential learning in higher education. *Academy of Management Learning and Education, 4,* 193–212.

Kolb, D. (1984). *Experiential learning: Experience as the source of learning and development.* Englewood Cliffs, NJ: Prentice Hall.

McAuliffe, G., & Eriksen, K. (2002). *Teaching strategies for constructivist and developmental counselor education.* Westport, CT: Bergin & Garvey.

Sexton, T. L., Schofield, T. L., & Whiston, S. C. (1997). Evidence-based practice: A pragmatic model to unify counseling. *Counseling and Human Development, 30*(3). Love Publishing: Denver, CO.

Sexton, T. L., Whiston, S. C., Bleuer, J. C., & Walz, G. R. (1997). *Integrating outcome research into counseling practice and training.* Alexandria, VA: American Counseling Association.

Whiston, S. C., & Coker, J. K. (2000). Reconstructing clinical training: Implications from research. *Counselor Education and Supervision. 39,* 218–227.

# Appendix
## The Right to Participate in Research

Anna and her colleagues decided to investigate the quality of services provided to clients at a local counseling agency in which they were employed. The research, funded entirely by the state, was a preliminary or pilot project. As a group, Anna and her colleagues started to provide, without screening, free counseling service to individuals who requested the service. Anna and her colleagues made it clear that this project would not benefit individuals in any way. This project was approved by the Institutional Review Board of the counseling agency.

Because the community surrounding the agency was largely Latino, many Latino clients showed up to receive this free counseling. However, many of the Latino clients spoke primarily Spanish. Anna and her colleagues knew very little Spanish, and their language capacities were not enough for even basic conversation. Anna, as a primary investigator, decided to hire a translator to help with the process. It seemed to work well for a while.

However, last week, Anna found herself in a difficult position. A translator failed to show up for an initial appointment for the new client, Gilda. Nevertheless, Gilda insisted in participating in the session. Gilda understood some English, but not enough to participate in a meaningful conversation. She stated in Spanish that she needed help and that it was an emergency. That was all Anna could understand. Anna decided to offer counseling to Gilda, even though they both had a hard time understanding the other. Anna thought Gilda would not return to counseling after experiencing such a language barrier, but she was wrong. Gilda came back, and Anna felt obligated to provide counseling to her. By session 4, Anna had not been able to obtain Gilda's consent to participate in the research because Gilda could not read or write in English. The translator never showed up. In order to comply with ethical guidelines for conducting research with human subjects, Anna wanted to find a way to translate the document into Spanish so that Gilda could understand, but Anna had no resources. As a result, Anna felt she had to stop providing counseling services to Gilda and other clients who were on a wait list to participate in this research because of her inability to obtain participants' consent.

Anna's colleagues were disturbed by this incident. One of the research team members, Charlie, mentioned that the fact that Anna denied services to Gilda and others was unethical and discriminating against Spanish-speaking populations who might benefit from these services and the research. Charlie also added that everybody had a right to participate in this research according to the proposal submitted to the IRB. Anna had no idea how to respond, and she kept asking herself, "Did I make a wrong decision?"

# 12

# Teaching Social and Cultural Issues in Counseling

Aretha Marbley, Janeé Steele, and Garrett J. McAuliffe

## THE CASE OF THE NOVICE MULTICULTURAL COUNSELOR EDUCATOR

*Dr. Rebel Moore is a newly hired assistant professor in counselor education at one of the most prestigious doctoral/research-intensive universities in the North Central region of the United States. She describes herself, without an apology or explanation, as an "army brat" of mixed ethnicity. People typically describe her physical features as ambiguous. It is difficult to place her within any ethnic or racial category based solely on her physical characteristics. White students are unsure of her ethnic group affiliation, but clearly see her as a female faculty member of color who is culturally diverse. African American students see her as being Black. Hispanic/Latino students believe that she is Latina. Asian students think she is Asian. Native American students think that she could be of Indian blood.*

*Dr. Moore was assigned to teach, to her surprise, a counseling and diversity course, even though her training, expertise, and interests are in educational measurement and career instrumentation. Despite her rich and diverse cultural background, world travels, and broad worldview, she felt that she was unprepared to teach a master's-level counseling course in diversity. With the exception of the one course in multicultural counseling that she had taken during her doctoral program, she had little formal experience or training in cultural competency or in teaching diversity counseling. As a result, in a panic she pulled out her old syllabus and the course book from the diversity counseling class that she had taken some eight years earlier. She began hungrily reading and thumbing through everything she could get her hands on for some ideas. She selected activities that she could use to teach this course, hoping to competently prepare her students to work with, and fight for, people from all backgrounds.*

Surprisingly, even in this era Dr. Moore is typical not only of many professors who are commonly asked or required to teach diversity courses because of their race or sexual orientation, or because of a lack of available faculty members who are qualified to teach multicultural classes. In fact, it represents the experience of the first author of this chapter. Similarly, even the more seasoned multicultural counselor educators feel inadequate to the task of teaching such a course. They are hungry for effective instructional strategies to help them teach this course more effectively. This chapter is therefore for all of the Rebel Moores, that is, counselor educators of any race, ethnicity, gender, sexual orientation, ability, or religion who expect to teach the course in multicultural counseling. It should be noted that such a course may go by various titles, such as Social and Cultural Issues in Counseling, Diversity and Counseling, or Culture and Counseling. We will use these terms interchangeably.

## THE CHARGE

This chapter is a crash course in teaching multicultural dimensions of counseling. In the following pages, we hope to help you teach potentially the most paradigm-upending course in the counseling curriculum. This is a paradoxical topic—very important since culture pervades all human life: We are always individuals in a social context, *but* we are not sure how to teach it. It is not a topic that is as clear about practice as are other topics in the counseling curriculum, such as theories, skills, and testing. So in this chapter, we offer an overview, with as many specifics as possible, on how to teach this extensive and seemingly amorphous topic.

In this chapter and in the class itself, we hope to transform what was once defined as *counseling*. Notions of social construction, epistemology, diversity, ethnicity, disparity, advocacy, and more will guide the discussion. You, the potential instructor, must be ready for the challenges of upending students' assumptions and established mores. Thus, teaching multicultural counseling is for those who are bold enough to face new social realities. The task will require self-challenge and a willingness to embrace conflict and uncertainty. Its difficulty will be matched only by its importance.

To paraphrase Robert Kegan (1998), students must decide whether they "have culture" or culture "has them."

In the process, they are asked to become cultural relativists (Bennett, 1998). They will depart on a journey to relativize all knowledge, that is, to see the socially constructed story that cultures tell about how to live well. Therefore, teaching social and cultural issues in counseling is, in effect, opening an epistemological door. How students come to know what is good, true, and beautiful becomes subject to the cultural story that they are embedded in at the moment. For that relativism to emerge, the course must be taught in ways that challenge students' culture-centrism.

The teaching of culturally alert counseling is a deceptive and difficult venture. Students are being asked to give up their old, familiar allegiances to the customary cultural practices, rituals, and rules for living. They are being asked to de-center from the world that they have inhabited until now and transform into a new persona. Of course, students must become minimally facile in all three areas of multicultural competency (awareness, knowledge, and skills). And they must be able to infuse culture into all of their work, without stereotyping or losing the ability to also recognize the individual. However, the de-centering agenda is hidden within such learning activities as explorations of cultural self-awareness, readings on ethnicity and race, excursions into the social construction of gender, and experiences of tension involved in learning about sexual orientation. There is more to the multicultural counseling course than learning about cultural customs.

## Guiding Notions

Six notions guide the teaching of culturally alert counseling. The first five are related to the content of the course: constructivism, comprehensiveness, diversity versus disparity, competencies, and the interplay of culture-universality and individuality. The sixth is about teaching process: experience, personalization, and reflection.

The first guiding notion speaks to grounding the course and future counseling in a constructivist conceptual foundation. Culture is treated as an expression of the overall idea of *social construction*, that is, the notion that all individuals are ultimately embedded in discourses or assumptions about what is good, true, and beautiful for them. And *constructive development* alerts us to our relationship to cultures—do they have us or do we have them? Like the fish in water, we, including counselors, are often unaware of the surround that envelops us. Awareness of our social construction, or discourse alertness, makes us reflective about our assumptions—including our privileges, oppressions, and hierarchies. This invitation to reflexivity asks us to give up our vain attempts at total objectivity. As we will see, this is a leap for many students of counseling. Social construction represents the ultimate subjectivity in human discourse, the fact that we are always making meaning in a social/cultural context.

The second guiding notion, *comprehensiveness*, represents two thrusts. One is a broad definition of culture. It includes everyone. All groups are "cultured"—including the dominant or majority groups. It is important that students learn about White European American culture as well as the cultures of people of color, about middle-class culture as well as the cultures of poor and working-class persons, about the culture of men as well as of women, about the culture of dominant religions as well as of minority religions. Comprehensiveness includes all of those social groups that humans belong to, ones that form a person's values and assumptions about the good life, what to strive for, and how to behave. Culture is also external: It may affect how others see and act toward us. Therefore, culture includes the traditional notion of ethnicity, but is extended to include social class, gender, disability, sexual orientation, and religion or spirituality.

The third guiding notion is *diversity versus disparity*. We will discuss this distinction later. Let it suffice to say at this point that both are important. We cannot discuss cultural diversity without adding a discussion of power and differential access to the things that matter in society.

The fourth guiding notion asks students to develop *multicultural competencies*. These are the well-known triumvirate of awareness, knowledge, and skills. We must teach to all three, especially the third, which is given short shrift in much of counselor preparation. The field of multicultural counseling has been long on cultural awareness and cultural knowledge, but short on actual applications. The counseling expression "Insight is not enough" applies to multicultural competencies as much as it applies to the practice of counseling and the experience of clients more broadly. Just as clients have to move beyond insight to action, counselors must move beyond comprehension to

culturally alert behaviors. Therefore, in this chapter we have paid much attention to actual skills for culturally alert practice. We therefore delineate for learners the range of culturally alert counseling skills. We have divided them into accessibility, assessment, and intervention.

The fifth guiding notion is that both *universality* and *individuality* are important. Culture is one of at least three explanations of human behavior (Speight, Myers, Cox, & Highlen, 1991). The others are individuality, which includes temperament and personality, and the universal human qualities that we all share.

Finally, the sixth guiding notion for teaching culturally alert counseling relates to the *teaching process*. Powerful learning incorporates experience, personalization, and reflection as learning modes. We now know well that students learn through a combination of experience and reflection. Therefore, in teaching the multicultural counseling course, instructors instigate student interaction with the ideas, including independent and group activities. Experience includes personalizing the learning, that is, asking for personal reflection and disclosures both in and out of the classroom, before getting buried in a sea of abstraction.

# TWO THEORETICAL FRAMEWORKS FOR TEACHING MULTICULTURAL COUNSELING

Two particular frameworks set multicultural counseling apart from traditional Western counseling: Multicultural Counseling and Therapy Theory (MCT) and Multicultural Social Justice Criticism (MSJC). Both upend the individualistic status quo of the dominant counseling paradigm by asking counselors to think about clients' contexts and to be critical about the social arrangements, not just the individual choices, that result in clients' self-doubt, lack of resources, and barriers to life success. The two themes that pervade these frameworks are the importance of *context* and the ability to be *critical*.

## Multicultural Counseling and Therapy Theory

MCT (Sue, Ivey, & Pedersen, 1996) contrasts with common counseling theories in that it emphasizes a collectivistic approach to counseling and counseling training. As such, it is foundational for the teaching of multicultural counseling. Following is a summary of key points from MCT.

MCT is actually a theory of theories (a metatheory) about counseling. A key dimension of MCT is its emphasis on context versus the individual. It stresses the notion that both counselor and client identities are embedded in individual, family, and cultural contexts. People do not live free of the contexts that affect and inform them. However, not all individuals have the same relationship with their contexts. That is where cultural identity theory comes in, reminding counselors that clients vary in their attitudes toward the self, others of the same group, others of a different group, and the dominant group. The counseling relationship is affected by these attitudes; for instance, these attitudes affect the trust and mutual understanding between client and counselor.

Another key MCT point lies in matching practice with culture—that is, the effectiveness of counseling is enhanced when the strategies are consistent with the cultural background of the client. MCT also reminds counselors that professional counselors are not the only ones helping people. Multiple helpers are used by culturally different groups and societies. These helpers include family, clergy, friends, and indigenous healers. Finally, MCT makes a strong case for counselors to move beyond "repair" or "correction," toward playing a role in the liberation of consciousness. The liberation of consciousness consists of helping clients see themselves not only in relationship to themselves and their choices, but also in terms of their cultural context—a context that includes the personal, family, groups, and organizations. Liberation of consciousness as a counseling goal contrasts with the individualistic self-actualization goal of some traditional counseling.

# Multicultural Social Justice Criticism

The multicultural counseling course, as we propose it, urges both students and faculty to become socially critical, even about their own attempts at advocacy. That is, it urges all course participants to become alert to discrimination, domination, and subordination of all types,

including in the writings and actions of teachers of multicultural counseling.

MCSJ particularly calls counselor educators to combine activism and scholarship. That call includes identifying the suppression of voices within the academy specifically, including the well-intentioned multicultural and social justice scholarship that, ironically, might negatively affect people from oppressed backgrounds. By placing the multiculturalism and social justice movements and scholarship themselves at the center of analysis, MSJC is a tool that may be used to guard against a nonreflective multiculturalism.

MSJC empowers marginalized persons. It encourages the participants in research and the students in counseling programs to speak from their lived experiences and to be understood within the context of their own culture stories rather than just through the scholarship of academicians. MSJC asks for open dialogue among all voices in the counseling and counselor education enterprises (i.e., scholars, teachers, students, and clients).

MSJC analyzes any theoretical tradition, worldview, ideological framework, or paradigm, including those in this chapter and throughout this book, that silences voices and reeks of elitism. MSJC is an internal tool that the instructor and students can use to challenge the multicultural-social justice research, theories, epistemologies, and ideology for evidence of bias, discrimination, and cultural encapsulation. In essence, MSJC is a teaching tool to raise critical awareness about the way the mainstream can afflict the marginalized—even when they mean well and are trying to help.

MSJC also opens social constructionism itself to critique. For example, the social constructionist skepticism about final truth claims in any area of human knowing might be considered a luxury afforded to affluent, dominant group members who are in the middle-class academy.

Both MCT and MSCJ use activism and multicultural scholarship in counselor education to increase understanding of the roles that marginality and social injustice play in classroom dynamics, training, curriculum bias, and academic assessment, evaluation, and achievement. These ideas guide the teaching of our proposed course in multicultural counseling.

# THE TOPICS

The course in multicultural counseling can be divided into four units: Introduction to Basic Notions (Culture, Social Justice), Ethnicity and Race, Nonethnic Cultural Groups, and Skills for Multicultural Counseling. This section enumerates the topics of the course, as we have conceived it. Table 12.1 outlines the objectives, content, activities, and constructivist principles that guide the course.

**TABLE 12.1** Course Objectives, Content, Activities, and Constructivist Principles

| Learning Objectives | Content | Activities and Processes | Constructivist Principles |
|---|---|---|---|
| Awareness:<br><br>Uncover hidden curricula<br><br>Develop a critical, political consciousness | Context and individual<br><br>Multicultural social justice criticism—discrimination, domination, subordination<br><br>Definitions of culture<br><br>Relationship between mental health and the overall social order | Social group membership activity<br><br>Attitudes toward diversity<br><br>Sample privilege inventory<br><br>Ethnic self-awareness assessment<br><br>Asking for feedback, encouraging student voices, and sharing the teaching methods and choices<br><br>Discussion board | Experiential; community building; reflective<br><br>Tell life story, an internal and subjective narrative<br><br>Evolve biographical narrative under continuous revision<br><br>Create own reality through continuous reflection on their unique life experiences<br><br>Help clients discern patterns, hence meaning, from previous life experiences and assist them with understanding and giving voice to their life stories |
| Knowledge:<br><br>Define key concepts such as *social justice, social diversity, culture, gender, oppression, privilege, hegemony, ideology,* and *politics*<br><br>describe the values associated with social justice advocacy | Liberation of consciousness<br><br>Social justice/disparity<br><br>Social stratification<br><br>Privilege and oppression<br><br>Attitudes<br><br>Ethnicity race/pan-ethnic groupings<br><br>Nonethnic cultural groupings (gender, sexual orientation, disability, religion) | Cultural de-centering activity<br><br>Cultural self-authorizing/de-centering activity<br><br>Lessons from the media<br><br>Stages of oppressive to anti-oppressive thinking<br><br>Immersion assignment<br><br>Discussion/presentations on cultural groups<br><br>Readings, video demonstrations, and cultural informants<br><br>Self-assessments | Promotes constructive development—name received values and norms, challenge them, develop more self-authorized perspectives<br><br>Coauthors of stories in progress<br><br>Value multiple realities<br><br>Value dialogue<br><br>Question the internal learning and meaning-making processes of the client<br><br>Create counseling environments that balance both the security and the challenge necessary for growth |
| Skills and Action:<br><br>Demonstrate competence in implementing specific social justice advocacy interventions, such as empowerment, prevention, or outreach activities in school, university, or community settings | Multicultural counseling and therapy theory<br><br>Culturally relevant strategies<br><br>Activism and empowerment<br><br>Dialogue that includes all voices<br><br>Social justice advocacy<br><br>Accessibility, assessment, intervention | Diversity/social justice action plan<br><br>Readings and video demonstration | Instigate experiences to encourage the development of mindfulness, receptive inquiry, and meaning-making facilitation in future counselors |

*(Continued)*

| TABLE 12.1 (Continued) | | | |
|---|---|---|---|
| *Learning Objectives* | *Content* | *Activities and Processes* | *Constructivist Principles* |
| Personal change toward greater sensitivity, critical thinking skills (de-centering) | Constructivism, comprehensiveness, competencies | Experience<br><br>Personalization<br><br>Reflection<br><br>Promote safety through clear guidelines, confidentiality, respect | Culture as an expression of the overall idea of social construction, i.e., the notion that all individuals are ultimately embedded in discourses, i.e., assumptions about what is good, true, and beautiful for them<br><br>De-centering, relativize what they know about living well<br><br>Constructive development alerts us to our relationship to cultures—do they have us or do we have them? |

# UNIT 1: INTRODUCTION TO CULTURE AND SOCIAL JUSTICE

Unit 1, the Introduction to Culture and Social Justice, includes activities to trigger thinking about culture.

## The *What, Why,* and *How* of Culture in Counseling

In the beginning of our teaching, we orient students to the *what, why,* and *how* of culture (McAuliffe, 2008). Regarding the *what,* we begin with an inclusive, defensible definition of culture, one that honors culture as a group's way of adapting to environments and to caring for each other. Culture includes internalized norms as well as external expressions, and may be illustrated in school cultures, work cultures, family cultures, neighborhood cultures, and so on. As mentioned earlier, we define culture broadly, beyond the usual categories of ethnicity and race.

We recommend three activities for introducing the major themes of such a course. First, we recommend an introductory activity that triggers students' thinking about their own multiple cultural identities (see Appendix A on page 179). Students simply name their cultural group memberships and, in each case, whether they are members of dominant or nondominant groups. This activity has value in a number of ways. It is experiential and engages students in the ways that are described in earlier chapters. It also raises issues to be covered in

the course, such as labels, categories, hierarchies, and statuses. Additionally, it engages students actively in group introductions and community building.

Two other introductory activities help to raise the themes for the entire course. One activity introduces students to the range of possible attitudes toward cultural diversity (see Appendix B on page 180). It awakens them to the continuum of such attitudes. Students privately name various cultural groups, such as poor persons, gay persons, persons from a different ethnic or religious group, and then place their own attitudes on the scale. This activity serves as a wake-up call for many students, who begin, as a result, to understand the growth that they might need in attitudes toward diversity. It also triggers rethinking their attitudes.

The third introductory activity, The Cultural De-Centering Activity (CDCA; McAuliffe & Milliken, 2009), promotes constructive development, in line with Robert Kegan's (1982, 1998) adult development theory (see Appendix C on page 181). This activity asks students to determine their relationship with their cultures, to decide whether "culture has them" or they "have culture." Through engaging in the CDCA, students might define, and then consider, their relationships to their received cultural norms.

Specifically, the CDCA asks students to name received, maybe taken-for-granted cultural values and norms and then to contradict them, with the goal of eventually claiming, or reclaiming, their values for themselves. The activity can move students from using largely received knowing to embracing a more self-authorized way of claiming their values and behaviors. Again, the question, "Do you have culture or does culture have you?" helps students walk through this process. This activity sometimes has a shock value, as students realize, for example, that they haven't considered their own views on religion, sexual orientation, and ethnic norms.

## Social Justice

After this broad introduction to culture, a more focused presentation of the central topic of social justice can follow. We have framed the topic in terms of the previously mentioned distinction between diversity and disparity. The simple and benign notion of cultural diversity masks the more sinister notion of social disparity. The tough issues of hierarchies, power, and differential access to social capital need to be presented. But they need to be accessible—and palatable—for a broad audience. They can't be overstated in an "oppression rant." On the other hand, counselor educators also can't pull any punches by minimizing the importance of the topic. These are tough ideas to grasp.

Counselor educators who teach this subject area encounter several specific pedagogical challenges. Learning environments that foster the sensitivity, awareness, and critical thinking skills necessary to be an effective social justice advocate can be especially difficult to create. Culture and social justice, as topics, are charged with controversial political issues that can elicit fear and other emotions or defensive reactions. Consequently, counselor educators need to structure the learning experiences in a way that promotes safety and allows students to share ideas without fear of retaliation. This includes establishing classroom guidelines that lay out expectations for confidentiality, providing students with time to process their feelings, and making sure that students express their thoughts and ideas in a respectful manner (Adams, 1997; Steele, 2008).

Some counselor educators and other writers object to promoting widespread social justice advocacy. Most of these objections reflect reservations about the extent to which political or other social values should influence counseling or be part of counselor education (see Canfield, 2008; Drapela, 1974; Lockhard & Stack, 2008). Hunsaker (2008), for example, suggested that social justice advocacy was a sort of values imposition that, according to traditional counseling practice, should be guarded against. His argument was that social justice advocacy requires both counselors and clients to promote ideologically biased values that may conflict with one's faith or personal beliefs.

Students of counseling often express similar concerns. In particular, students frequently assume that ethical counseling practice—that is, not imposing their values on their clients—requires a kind of objectivity and value-neutrality that is opposed to the basic tenets of social justice advocacy. However, current understandings of counseling point to it as an inherently values-laden process. Values are reflected in selection of assessment procedures, the issues to which counselors attend during sessions, treatment planning, the selection of interventions, and how counseling outcomes are evaluated (Corey, Corey, & Callanan, 2007). Students need assistance in navigating these often murky waters as they pursue ethical counseling practice. Helping students embrace social justice advocacy, which focuses on achieving specific social objectives, is therefore often particularly difficult. As a result, this challenge needs to be addressed explicitly.

The first premise for teaching social justice is that social injustice is related to the central work of counseling. It is often an antecedent to mental health disorder and an obstacle to human development (Lee & Hipolito-Delgado, 2007). For example, in the case of racism, racist incidents often result in posttrauma-like symptoms that parallel those experienced by survivors of rape and domestic violence (Bryant-Davis & Ocampo, 2005). Several studies have found that racist experiences are correlated with increased alcohol consumption, depressive symptoms, lower self-esteem, problems with memory and concentration, difficulty trusting people who are racially similar to the perpetrators, self-blame, hyperarousal, and anxiety. These are similar to posttraumatic symptoms.

The second premise regarding the need for teaching social justice is that counselors have a moral and ethical obligation to take action against oppression. Oppression, or the absence of social justice, is the result of both political and psychological processes. In his classic text on oppression and social intervention, Goldenberg (1978) defined oppression as "the existence of certain social imperatives which manifest themselves through the promulgation of practices aimed at containing or otherwise limiting the development of people" (p. 15). Obvious examples of oppression based on this definition are the Jim Crow and segregation laws that existed in the United States until the late 1960s. From a psychological perspective, however, Goldenberg understood oppression as any experience wherein an individual is "alienated, isolated, and insulated from the society of which he [sic] nominally remains a member" (p. 3). This oppressive experience is initiated and perpetuated in an individual's life through psychological processes that include learned helplessness, internalization of feelings of inferiority, identification with the oppressor, self-fulfilling prophesies, groupthink, and stereotypes (Prilleltensky, 1997).

In true constructivist fashion, the incorporation of social justice into a future counselor's schema of counseling practice requires that there be doubt about the sufficiency of traditional forms of counseling and support for a new and broader conceptualization of the meaning of counseling. The topic is so important, and contested, that it deserves two meta-objectives, which are discussed next.

## Social Justice–Oriented Objectives

For this course, and this unit, a distinction between so-called micro- and macro-objectives (Giroux, 1988) is especially important. Micro-objectives, according to Giroux, refer to traditional course objectives that describe the knowledge or skills learners should acquire. In the teaching of social justice advocacy, such micro-objectives include helping students (a) define key concepts such as *social justice, social diversity, culture, gender, oppression, privilege, hegemony, ideology,* and *politics;* (b) describe the values associated with social justice advocacy; and (c) identify or demonstrate competence in implementing specific social justice advocacy interventions—such as empowerment, prevention, or outreach activities in school, university, or community settings.

Macro-objectives, on the other hand, are broad. They speak to understanding the relationship between counseling and its larger sociopolitical context. Macro-objectives ask students to take a meta perspective on the field and its place in society. Giroux (1988) identified two macro-objectives that are particularly important for

social justice advocacy education: helping students (a) uncover hidden curricula and (b) develop a critical political consciousness.

**1. Helping students uncover hidden curricula.** The hidden curricula can be defined as any implicit social messages that are communicated through course content and structure (Giroux, 1988). In this course, instructors can help students examine power relationships, which can be done in two ways: (1) examining unspoken power differentials within the classroom setting and identifying the consequences of such differentials in both the classroom and society-at-large and (2) uncovering implicit values represented in counseling texts and standards of practice.

Regarding power differentials in the classroom, the teacher-student relationship itself is of particular relevance. Traditionally, the instructor's power and authority go unquestioned in classrooms. The instructor is viewed as the expert, and the student's primary task is to imitate or memorize information as it is presented. Examples of this in counselor education are behavior-based approaches to skills training wherein the instructor is conceptualized as a role model who seeks to train similar behaviors in students, using a combination of didactic instruction, imitative learning, and positive reinforcement techniques. According to Freire (1993), this approach, when exclusively used, furthers the aims of an oppressive society by teaching students to accept the roles imposed upon them and limiting the development of their creativity and critical thinking skills. Such authority-centered instruction affects society-at-large, because the same power differentials might be replicated with counselors and their clients once students become professionals. Some of the strategies discussed in the first three chapters of this book can create a more egalitarian atmosphere in the classroom. They include asking for feedback, encouraging student voices, and sharing the teaching methods and choices.

The second aspect of making any hidden curriculum explicit lies beyond the classroom. It involves uncovering implicit values represented through counseling texts and standards of practice. Some values, although unspoken, have an extremely important effect on social justice advocacy. One such value is individualism. Most major theories of counseling, including psychodynamic, existential-humanistic, cognitive, and behavioral theories, are characterized by individualism. According to Martín-Baró (1994), individualism in counseling reinforces oppressive societal structures by locating problems and problem solving only within the individual, rather than challenging the social issues that are often antecedent to the individual's mental health concerns. Goldenberg (1978) furthered this idea by adding that individualism perpetuates oppression by making it appear as if it is primarily individuals who are oppressive, as opposed to governmental or institutional bodies, thereby mitigating the need for widespread social change efforts in the profession. When such individualism plays out in the counseling field, counselors abandon systemic and institutional advocacy efforts in favor of "self-advocacy" interventions that have little impact beyond the individual.

## 2. Developing a critical, political consciousness.

The second social justice–oriented meta-objective involves helping students become aware of the relationship between mental health and the overall social order. According to Giroux (1988), "this objective does not mean stressing political content in the most literal sense of the term, but suggests providing students with a methodology that allows them to look beyond their private lives to an understanding of the political, social, and economic foundations of the larger society" (p. 52). In other words, the objective is not an attempt to force students to adopt specific political ideologies or stances on political issues. Instead, it can be defined as a group method of discussing and analyzing the nature and social origins of personal problems, with the ultimate goal of increasing self-awareness and developing specific strategies for social change (Parker & Fukuyama, 2007).

As part of the development of a critical political consciousness, instructors should help students identify issues that have an impact on human suffering in their communities. The issues critical to their community will have differing levels of importance to various individuals. Some may feel a calling to address issues related to immigration. Others may choose to be involved in advocating for anti–employment discrimination laws. Still others may fight for equity in college admissions.

A way of enacting this objective is to ask students to create socially critical action plans (see Appendix D on page 182). Such an activity is consistent with Freire's (1993) suggestion that developing a critical consciousness can be promoted by engaging students in identifying problems and their sociopolitical sources within real-world, as opposed to theoretical, contexts through personal narratives. Freire believed that students feel connected and challenged to respond to issues that have a basis in their lived realities. With this connection, or awareness, students can then identify avenues for social change in problems that have mental health ramifications. The following four topics should be addressed in teaching social justice in this course (McAuliffe, Danner, Grothaus, & Doyle, 2008).

*Social stratification.* In the beginning of this unit, students need an overall introduction to social stratification in society and to the differential access that various groups have to the things that matter, such as material goods, power, knowledge of how to negotiate systems, and wealth.

*Increasing awareness of privilege and oppression.* One possible activity to inform students about social stratification is a discussion of privilege. Members of nondominant and marginalized cultural groups often nod their heads when power disparity is discussed. Dominant group members often don't get it. Therefore, discovery, or inductive, methods may help students build their own hypotheses about social disparity. The Privilege Activity (see Appendix E on page 183) and ensuing discussions of what the results might mean offer possibilities for discovery. Lessons From the Media (see Appendix F on page 184) focuses students on implicit messages that we all hear in the media. These messages are pervasive and may lead to stereotyping.

Critical in such discovery is student recognition of multiple sources of privilege and oppression, rather than focusing on only one racial or ethnic group. Therefore, the text and instructor can present multiple privileges and oppressions by race, ethnicity, gender, social class, and sexual orientation. Some privileges and oppressions are more powerful than others, however, so it is important not to trivialize any of them, for example, by overemphasizing situational oppression of White males in particular contexts.

*Attitudes.* Another activity for triggering awareness of biased attitudes adapts a stage model of bias developed by Michael D'Andrea and Judy Daniels (1999; see Appendix G on page 185). Students plot their own past or present attitudes or speculate on the attitudes of figures from their families, the media, history, or literature. In the process, students are often shaken from their torpor into a more socially critical and activist stance.

*Social justice advocacy.* Students benefit from learning how to take action to address inequity. Social justice advocacy consists of the direct interventions counselors can take against oppression and discrimination, particularly within social and political contexts. The Diversity/Social Justice Action Plan encourages such actions and is outlined in Appendix D. Members of dominant groups might be introduced to the term *ally* so that they can participate in the corrective action of social justice advocacy and not wallow in unnecessary guilt or resentment.

Social justice advocacy may occur at the individual level; however, interventions aimed at creating change within social and political arenas are also important. Such interventions may include prevention, outreach, empowerment, and direct political intervention (Crethar, Torres Rivera, & Nash, 2008; Vera & Speight, 2007). Social justice advocacy may also include research or scholarship aimed at challenging laws, policies, or practices that are adverse to the mental health of marginalized individuals (Steele, 2008).

# UNIT 2: ETHNICITY AND RACE

To this point, we have established the overall foundations for the rest of a course in culturally alert counseling. Now it is time to introduce two contested and central topics: ethnicity and race. Race and ethnicity have dominated the social arrangements in the United States and many other countries, and, as a result, they need to be discussed and disaggregated early in the course. Discussions of race and ethnicity form the core of the next section of the course. As you will see, we treat race as a distinct and separate notion from ethnicity.

## Ethnicity

Ethnicity is not a simple concept, but we have found the following definition to be useful: Ethnicity is the recognition by both the members of a group and others of common social ties among people due to shared geographic origins, memories of an historical past, cultural heritage, religious affiliation, language or dialect, and/or tribal affiliation. Ethnicity is both self-defined and other-defined. It is a socially constructed and messy concept. There is no pure ethnicity. It is a story told by one's people and others.

From our perspective, everyone, not only so-called minority groups, is assumed to have ethnicity. Students need to learn that they have all been enculturated into ethnic norms and values, whether "American," "Southern," "Puerto Rican," "Italian American," "African American," or some other group. When teaching about ethnicity, four major concepts should be explored: enculturation, acculturation, salience, and optional ethnicity. These topics offer a nuanced understanding of ethnicity, as opposed to a simplistic stereotyped one.

We propose discussing ethnicity before race because it is a more benign concept. Introducing less threatening concepts early in a course assists students in developing the trust that will be necessary to handle more difficult and controversial conversations with openness and respect later in the course. Students should read about their own specific ethnic groups so that some discovery might occur. Another activity that assists students in personalizing concepts related to ethnicity and makes them useful is the Ethnic Self-Awareness activity (McAuliffe, Gomez, & Grothaus, 2008) in Appendix H (page 187). Ethnically naïve students may find the activity a bit baffling and, as a result, may struggle with it.

Students should leave this unit with an awareness of themselves as ethnically and socially constructed beings who have reflected on their ethnic assumptions and become more aware of the relativism of those assumptions. They will, as a result, become more knowledgeable about the part that ethnicity might play in clients' lives.

## Race

Now comes the topic that has been called the American Crucible, the test of the viability of the United States as a democratic community—that is, race. Race has been contested as a murky concept that must be addressed head-on as divisive and hierarchical. Challenges to the notion of race need to be highlighted in the course, particularly the work of anthropologist Franz Boas in the early 20th century. Its historical origins need to be deconstructed, especially in the eugenics theories of the past two centuries.

Students need to learn about the nature of race. People tend to categorize themselves into race categories based on physical and visible characteristics such as skin color, hair texture, shape of nose, and eye color. Research shows that race accounts for a small percentage of the differences that exist among ethnic/racial groups. That is to say, racial differences *between* these groups are small, a lot smaller than variations *within* the groups. The concept of race as defined by physical features or intellectual abilities is not valid from a biological perspective; therefore, physical traits reflect phenotype and do not provide information on genes.

Some notable scholars, including writers such as James Baldwin and W. E. B. Dubois, believed that the concept of race was created by opportunist White European and American elites and has been used to deny property, power, and status to non-White groups for more than four centuries. In other words, *race* is a psychological, socially constructed (and even federally legislated) but unneeded term that has been imported into mental health from a racist society.

Therefore, the use of the concept of race to separate peoples into better and lesser needs to be discussed during the course. Race and racism are recognized as universal phenomena, with a particularly American twist and legacy. The contemporary status of race and racism may be described through discussions of differences in wealth, housing, jobs, and criminal justice. Subtle color-blind racism and covert racism may be explored in concepts such as "good ole boy networks." Again, it is useful to personalize the concepts. Classroom discussion can help. But instructors should not put students on the spot, as if they represent a race.

Personalizing race and making it a discussable topic may be enhanced by asking students to engage in racial identity awareness activities, including plotting the stage theories of racial identity, one for people of color and one for White persons (see McAuliffe, Gomez, & Grothaus, 2008, for two models). Students might plot themselves or people they know, speculatively, in order to deepen their understanding of racial identity. In addition, the class might discuss the complex subject of biracial and multiracial identity and its potential importance in clients' lives.

## Individual Pan-ethnic Groupings

An overall discussion of ethnicity ends the conceptual phase of this unit. Now students learn some particulars about specific ethnic groups. They also explore common elements across groups, for instance, the degree to which cultures are collectivist and hierarchical cultures versus individualistic and egalitarian ones.

Teaching about specific ethnic groups presents certain perils, as students may overgeneralize about groups and stereotype individuals. We refer you back to the previously mentioned interplay among the cultural, individual, and universal elements in human life. We also risk superficiality when we discuss characteristics of particular ethnic groups because the time for covering specifics about ethnic groups is limited. A counselor educator might ask, "How am I to teach enough about particular ethnic groups in the time allotted? And how am I to know enough about each group? After all, I am not an anthropologist."

We have found one solution in lumping disparate but related groups of peoples into panethnic groupings based on the sociological literature and the U.S. Census listing of major ethnic groups. Such groupings of peoples are problematic. The approximations are awkward and only partially accurate. Examples of panethnic groupings for a U.S. setting might include the following:

- African Americans (including or not including Caribbean and African peoples)
- European Americans (often disaggregated into a number of subgroups such as Northern European Protestants, Eastern Europeans, Mediterranean peoples, Southern Whites, and Irish Catholics, depending on the region of the country)
- American Indians/Native Peoples
- Southeast and East Asians/Pacific Islanders
- South Asians
- Middle Easterners
- Latino/Latina Americans

Given the choice to lump, instructors must ensure that students have a working knowledge of the major characteristics of some members of these groups, as well as of their experiences in the United States. We propose that students need three types of knowledge about ethnic groups:

- the history of each group in the United States
- their major cultural values and characteristics
- guidelines for counseling members of these groups

Texts for the course should contain all three elements, but should be supplemented by video demonstrations of counseling sessions with members of different groups. As mentioned previously, students need to see actual multicultural counseling skills. The videos model in action the abstract concepts that students read about in their texts. Periodic video stops offer students opportunities for commenting on and critically thinking about what they are seeing

When discussing particular cultural groups, we recommend that small groups of students lead interactive discussions/presentations on their assigned group. Clear assignments for the segments of the presentation help to structure the presentations or discussions. For instance, students would open with an interest-generating "instigation" (such as a video clip) that illustrates some of the issues related to the particular group. Students might then lead a discussion based on student responses to the instigation, present some key issues about the group under consideration (see the three key topics mentioned previously), to build in opportunities for participation by everyone in the class.

I (McAuliffe) also find it very important to have outside discussants join the class session who know about each cultural group. These cultural informants can offer personalized illustrations of the ideas in the readings and offer a nuanced, nonstereotypical view of the cultures. I invite the guests and ask them to respond to the presentations and videos. At a university or in the larger community, there are usually individuals who are willing to serve in this capacity. These discussants do not make a presentation, but merely respond to the students' presentations.

# UNIT 3: NONETHNIC CULTURAL GROUPS

Unit 3 of the course takes the discussion of culture beyond ethnicity and race. Now come the fairly recent additions to the conversation on multicultural counseling: cultural groupings that are not based on ethnicity. For clarity's sake, we refer to these nonethnic cultural groupings as *social groups*.

Clients' and counselors' lives are socially constructed. Therefore all humans are part of the discourses surrounding social class, gender, sexual orientation, religion, and disability. Discourses form on both clients' self-perceptions and on how they are treated by others. This section, therefore, continues the social construction theme of the course by countering the counseling field's, and the general American, tendency to explain client behavior from a hyperindividualistic perspective. We discuss teaching strategies for each of five possible social groups and use the three multicultural competency areas of awareness, knowledge, and skills to guide the discussions.

## Social Class

Counselor educators might introduce social class self-awareness at the beginning of this discussion, as it is often dismissed in the American conversation and is often conflated with race and ethnicity in students' minds. For example, we have students begin building their awareness with a social class self-assessment such as the one in Box 12.1.

---

**BOX 12.1    SAMPLE OF SOCIAL CLASS-EVOKING QUESTIONS**

Respond to the following questions and discuss in groups.

1. What occupation(s) did your parents have?
2. What occupational roles are valued/devalued in your family?
3. At what age did children leave home?
4. Why did children leave home? What did that say about your social class?
5. At what age did your parents and persons in your extended family marry, in general?
6. What was the family idea of a vacation growing up? What were your experiences?

---

Through this activity and readings on social class and the specific values of each social class, students discover hidden class rules that guide their and others' aspirations, expectations, and opportunities. After inductive discovery, the instructor can present the overall notion of class, especially its internal and external dimensions—both how individuals see themselves and how others see them. Then, instructors can direct students to consider the all-important issue of counselor class bias. Finally, instructors can coach students in strategies for counseling members of various social classes.

## Gender

Next, the important and pervasive issue of gender can be discussed. Like the other social group topics, discussions of gender could comprise a whole course. Gender can be explored through discussion of both women's and men's socialization and biologies as well as the potential effects of various sex combinations for counseling. Gender-alert counseling, including feminist counseling approaches, should be part of the discussion. As with the sessions on particular ethnicities, cultural informants with expertise in gender issues may be invited to share their perspectives with the class.

## Sexual Orientation/Lesbian, Gay, Bisexual, Transgender Issues

The most contested social issue of our times is sexual orientation. The lesbian, gay, bisexual, or transgendered (LGBT) world may be relatively unknown to some students. Yet the dilemmas and struggles of LGBT individuals particularly call on counselor educators to develop their students' expertise in working with LGBT clients.

Such expertise begins with students' reflections on their attitudes and knowledge about LGBT issues, reflections that may be triggered by the activity in Box 12.2. Students can respond to assessment questions anonymously, and then the instructor can collect the assessments and share the trends. In discussions that follow, instructors can urge a frank exchange of views, with class members sharing their differing perspectives. The notion of a "formal assessment" is not meant to communicate that correct answers exist for each question. The assessment merely triggers important discussions about LGBT issues.

---

### BOX 12.2    SAMPLE OF LGBT AWARENESS AND KNOWLEDGE QUESTIONS

Place a T for True or F for False in the blank before each question.

1. I believe that homosexuality is a sin.
2. I would feel disappointed if I learned that my child was lesbian, gay, bisexual, or transgendered (LGBT).
3. Same-sex couples should be allowed to marry.
4. Children should be taught that being gay is a normal and healthy way for people to be.
5. If a member of my sex asked me out for a date, I would feel flattered.
6. Most lesbians hate men.
7. Lesbianism is the result of traumatic relationships with men.
8. Gay men are more likely than heterosexual men to be pedophiles.
9. Most men who display effeminate traits are gay.
10. Bisexual men and women are really "closeted" gay men and lesbians.

*(Continued)*

(Continued)

11. I have LGBT friends.

12. Someone has "come out" to me in the past two years.

13. I am familiar with religious groups that welcome and affirm LGBT persons.

14. I know someone who has been beaten up or murdered because of their sexual orientation.

15. I have attended LGBT establishments and events, such as a gay bar or a gay pride festival.

16. I understand the costs of "coming out" that LGBT persons face.

17. I am knowledgeable about a variety of reactions a parent might have after learning that her or his child is LGBT.

18. I am familiar with the community resources in my area for LGBT persons (e.g., bookstores, hotlines, support groups, bars).

19. I understand the significance of the Stonewall riots to the LGBT community.

20. I am knowledgeable about the conditions of "triple jeopardy" that affect lesbians and bisexual women of color.

*Source:* Adapted from Szymanski, 2008.

A related activity provides a safe way to get the most important, and hidden, topics out in the open. Students might write down any questions they have about homosexuality and then pass in the papers. Guest discussants could then respond to the students' questions.

At least four topics need to be discussed in this subunit: gay identity development, transgenderedness, bisexuality, and particular counseling issues that may arise with members of these groups. Video demonstration of counseling with LGBT clients may serve to evoke discussion and offer models for such work.

## Disability

Some counseling programs, especially rehabilitation counseling, discuss disability in distinct courses. However, all counselors need some awareness of disability, and so we include a subunit on disability in the multicultural counseling course. We begin discussions of disability with awareness-raising simulations and readings, making distinctions between visible and invisible disabilities and presenting the notion that all individuals are "temporarily abled." We teach counseling strategies that aim to empower clients and to recognize both the universal and unique issues for clients with disabilities. And finally, we discuss language, as in all cultural discussions, including the terms *handicapped, disabled, differently abled,* and *challenged.*

## Religion

Religion and spirituality in counseling, the last social grouping that we currently discuss, is still fairly unusual in counseling programs. Some students need to be convinced of the importance of including religion and spirituality in counseling. When we point out the power of religion in the United States, the power to affect valuing, guilt, sexual behavior, and family roles and hierarchies, its importance in the counseling room becomes more apparent. Discussions of religion's importance may require instructors to help students distinguish between the terms *religion* and *spirituality.*

Once doubtful students become persuaded of the importance of religion and spirituality in counseling, a number of specific topics might be discussed. For instance, instructors might engage students in conversations about both helpful and harmful dimensions of faith. We also like to return to the idea of received and self-authorized values that was mentioned in Chapter 1 by introducing the ideas of *religion of origin* and *religion of choice*. That distinction can be an important one for clients who are struggling with morals, values, and relationships. Relatedly, we consider the stages of faith development. As a self-awareness activity, I (McAuliffe) have students complete an Internet-based "Religion Finder," which matches their values with various religions.

The next challenge is how to ensure that students receive an introduction to the basic tenets of the world's religions. We opt for taking a light brush to many traditions, with little time in class spent on any one. The instructor can emphasize a particular religion that students are likely to encounter based on geographic location. For example, student presenters in some parts of the United States might research evangelical Christianity, while Catholicism becomes the focus in other locations, and Islam in still others. Students should also become familiar with nonreligious beliefs, such as agnosticism and humanism, as counselors also encounter clients who identify with these belief systems.

Finally, students need the opportunity to understand counseling that incorporates religion. As with each topic, students benefit from discussions and video or live demonstrations of actual counseling with clients whose faith intersects with their counseling needs.

# UNIT 4: SKILLS FOR MULTICULTURAL COUNSELING

Culturally alert counseling rarely is given the time it deserves in counselor education programs. Students have complained in the past that counselor education is long on cultural awareness and knowledge but short on the teaching of actual skills in this area. In response to this understandable need, Unit 4 of the course summarizes culturally alert counseling skills. However, we must also acknowledge that culturally alert counseling is not an explicit method; it is instead a sensibility that is put into action.

One literature review identified at least 26 separate culturally alert counseling practices (McAuliffe, Grothaus, Pare, & Wininger, 2008). They are divided into three groupings: (culturally alert) accessibility, assessment, and intervention. Readings and video demonstrations can reveal how to enact such skills as gaining trust, broaching culture as it might be relevant to counseling

issues, applying narrative theory, diagnosing in a culturally alert way, and applying common practices selectively to members of different ethnic groups. Students might be reminded that culturally alert counseling is an inexact art rather than a specific counseling theory.

## Other Activities

In this course, students engage in at least three major activities. In the immersion experience, they interact for at least one hour with members of another cultural group, preferably a nondominant group in society or a group with which they are unfamiliar (see Appendix I on page 188). They also interview a member of that group. Additionally, students make weekly comments on an electronic discussion board. As mentioned in Chapter 5, such an assignment allows all students—including those who might not feel confident enough to engage in discussions in class—to contribute to discussions and to interact with one another on new and sometimes difficult topics. Finally, as mentioned earlier, each student leads a discussion about a particular cultural group. Guidelines for that assignment are in Appendix J on page 190.

## CONCLUSION

We have tried to pour into this chapter and into our teaching of the multicultural counseling course our passion for culture and social justice. In particular, we emphasize three themes: a recognition that all individuals are cultural, a concern for the pain that oppression causes many clients, and a practical bent aimed at giving future counselors skills that they can use. This work is rewarding. A recent practicum student of one of the authors was heard to say, "I use the skills from the course and book every day in practicum." The teacher was honored.

## REFERENCES

Adams, M. (1997). Pedagogical frameworks for social justice education. In M. Adams, L. A. Bell, & P. Griffin (Eds.), *Teaching for diversity and social justice: A sourcebook* (pp. 30–43). New York: Routledge.

Bennett, M. J. (1998). *Basic concepts of intercultural communication: Selected readings.* Yarmouth, ME: Intercultural Press.

Bryant-Davis, T., & Ocampo, C. (2005). Racist incident-based trauma. *The Counseling Psychologist, 33*, 479–500.

Canfield, B. S. (2008, January). Valuing diversity of thought [From the President]. *Counseling Today*, p. 5.

Corey, G., Corey, M. S., & Callanan, P. (2007). *Issues and ethics in the helping profession* (7th ed.). Belmont, CA: Thomson Brooks/Cole.

Crethar, H. C., Torres Rivera, E., & Nash, S. (2008). In search of common threads: Linking multicultural, feminist, and social justice counseling paradigms. *Journal of Counseling & Development, 86*, 269–278.

D'Andrea, M., & Daniels, J. (1999). Assessing the different psychological dispositions of White racism: A comprehensive model for counselor educators. In M. Kiselica (Ed.), *Addressing the problem of racism and prejudice in counselor education* (pp. 59–88). Alexandria, VA: American Counseling Association.

Drapela, V. J. (1974). Counselors, not political agitators. *Personnel and Guidance Journal, 52*(7), 449–453.

Freire, P. (1993). *Pedagogy of the oppressed*. New York: Continuum.

Giroux, H. A. (1988). *Teachers as intellectuals: Toward a critical pedagogy of learning*. New York: Bergin & Garvey.

Goldenberg, I. I. (1978). *Oppression and social intervention*. Chicago: Nelson-Hall.

Hunsaker, R. (2008, April). Social justice: An inconvenient irony [Opinion]. *Counseling Today*, pp. 21, 43.

Kegan, R. (1982). *The evolving self: Problem and process in human development*. Cambridge, MA: Harvard University Press.

Kegan, R. (1998). *In over our heads: The mental demands of modern life*. Cambridge, MA: Harvard University Press.

Lee, C. C., & Hipolito-Delgado, C. P. (2007). Introduction: Counselors as agents of social justice. In C. C. Lee (Ed.), *Counseling for social justice* (2nd ed., pp. xiii–xxviii). Alexandria, VA: American Counseling Association.

Lockhard, F. W., & Stack, C. L. (2008, January). ACA's role doesn't include supporting personal political agendas [Letters]. *Counseling Today*, p. 4.

Martín-Baró, I. (1994). *Writings for a liberation psychology*. Cambridge, MA: Harvard University Press.

McAuliffe, G. J. (2008). *Culturally alert counseling: A comprehensive introduction*. Thousand Oaks, CA: Sage.

McAuliffe, G. J., Danner, M., Grothaus, T., & Doyle, L. (2008). Social diversity and social justice. In G. J. McAuliffe (Ed.) *Culturally alert counseling: A comprehensive introduction* (pp. 45–83). Thousand Oaks, CA: Sage.

McAuliffe, G. J., Gomez, E., & Grothaus, T. (2008). Race. In G. J. McAuliffe (Ed.) *Culturally alert counseling: A comprehensive introduction*. Thousand Oaks, CA: Sage.

McAuliffe, G. J., Grothaus, T., Pare, D., & Wininger, A. (2008). The practice of culturally alert counseling. In G. J. McAuliffe (Ed.), *Culturally alert counseling: A comprehensive introduction*. Thousand Oaks, CA: Sage.

McAuliffe, G. J., & Milliken, T. (2009). Promoting cultural relativism in counselors through the cultural de-centering model. *International Journal for the Advancement of Counselling, 31*, 118–129.

McIntosh, P. (1998). White privilege, color, and crime: A personal account. In C. R. Mann & M. S. Zatz (Eds.), *Images of color, images of crime* (pp. 207–216). Los Angeles: Roxbury.

Parker, W. M., & Fukuyama, M. A. (2007). *Consciousness-raising: A primer for multicultural counseling* (3rd ed.). Springfield, IL: Charles C. Thomas.

Prilleltensky, I. (1997). Values, assumptions and practices: Assessing the moral implications of psychological discourse and action. *American Psychologist, 52*, 517–535.

Speight, S. L., Myers, L., Cox, C. I., & Highlen, P. S. (1991). A redefinition of multicultural counseling. *Journal of Counseling and Development, 70*, 29–36.

Steele, J. M. (2008). Preparing counselors to advocate for social justice: A liberation model. *Counselor Education and Supervision, 48*(2), 74–85.

Sue, D. W., Ivey, M. B., & Pedersen, P. B. (1996). *A theory of multicultural counseling and therapy*. Pacific Grove, CA: Brooks/Cole.

Szymanski, D. M. (2008). Lesbian, gay, bisexual, and transgendered clients. In G. J. McAuliffe (Ed.), *Culturally alert counseling: A comprehensive introduction* (pp. 466–505). Thousand Oaks, CA: Sage.

Vera, E. M., & Speight, S. L. (2007). Advocacy, outreach, and prevention: Integrating social action roles in professional training. In E. Aldarondo (Ed.), *Advancing social justice through clinical practice* (pp. 373–389). Mahwah, NJ: Lawrence Erlbaum.

# Appendix A
## Social Group Membership Activity

This introductory activity triggers students' thinking about their own multiple cultural identities. Students simply name their cultural group memberships and whether they are members of dominant or nondominant groups in each case. Here is a template for the activity:

| Provide a name and status for your current group membership(s): | |
| --- | --- |
| **NAME OF YOUR CULTURAL GROUP(S):** | **GENERAL STATUS OF YOUR GROUP (DOMINANT/NONDOMINANT)** |
| Ethnicity: | |
| Race: | |
| Social class or socioeconomic status (e.g., upper middle class, poor, working class):<br><br>Of origin:<br><br>Current: | |
| Gender: | |
| Ability: | |
| [Sexual orientation]: (Do not share as part of the activity) | |
| Religion:<br><br>Of origin:<br><br>Current: | |

Students complete this activity privately, then share their results in groups of four or five. They note trends and questions in a small-group discussion, and then share those topics with the larger group. The instructor is responsible for posting the emerging issues from this activity, including labels and the idea of dominant and non-dominant status. This is a gentle opening that communicates to students that they all have culture and that most of them have some dominant and nondominant statuses. It brings up many of the issues in the course around labels, categories, hierarchies, and statuses. It introduces the key cultural categories. It also helps students get acquainted with each other and build a sense of community.

# Appendix B
## Attitudes Toward Diversity

This activity is based on a scale of attitudes developed by Dorothy Riddle (n.d.). It introduces students to the range of possible attitudes about cultural diversity. It alerts students to the growth that may be needed in their attitudes toward diversity, and it also triggers students to consider rethinking their attitudes.

The instructor asks students to privately read over and note groups for whom they have each of the corresponding attitudes. Then, class discussion explores the range of attitudes individuals might have toward differences.

| THE RIDDLE SCALE: ATTITUDES TOWARD DIFFERENCES |
|---|
| **Repulsion:** Views people who are different as strange, sick, crazy, and aversive. Views anything that will change them to be more "normal" or a part of the mainstream as justifiable. |
| **Pity:** Views people who are different as somehow born that way and feels that that is pitiful. Sees being different as definitely immature and less preferred, so to help those poor individuals one should reinforce normal behaviors. |
| **Tolerance:** Sees being different as just a phase of development that most people "grow out" of. Thus one should protect and tolerate those who are different as one does a child who is still learning. |
| **Acceptance:** Implies that one needs to make accommodations for another's differences; does not acknowledge that the other's identity may be of the same value as one's own. |
| **Support:** Works to safeguard the rights of those who are different. One may be uncomfortable oneself but is aware of the climate and the irrational unfairness in our society. |
| **Admiration:** Acknowledges that being different in our society takes strength. One is willing to truly look at oneself and work on one's own personal biases. |
| **Appreciation:** Values the diversity of people and is willing to confront insensitive attitudes. |
| **Nurturance:** Assumes the differences in people are indispensable in society. Views differences with genuine affection and delight and is willing to be an advocate of those differences. |

# Appendix C
## Cultural De-Centering Activity

This introductory activity can be conducted in the first or second class (McAuliffe, 2008; McAuliffe & Milliken, 2009). It is based on the constructive development theory of Robert Kegan (1982, 1998), and other developmental thinkers, in which epistemological change occurs through the experience of a challenge to one's way of knowing.

This activity asks students to determine their relationship to their cultures, that is, to decide whether "culture has them" or they "have culture." First, students name received, or maybe taken-for-granted, cultural values and norms (enculturated ones); then students contradict these values and norms. Next, they name their current positions, and finally they describe how they decided on these positions. The activity aims to move students from taking received cultural norms for granted to embracing a more self-authorized way of claiming their values and behaviors. Again, the phrase "Do you have culture or does culture have you?" is a helpful metaphor throughout the process. This activity sometimes has a shock value, as students realize that they have not decided for themselves about their views on religion, sexual orientation, and ethnic norms.

---

### CULTURAL SELF-AUTHORIZING/DE-CENTERING ACTIVITY

Re-examine all you have been told at school or church [or home] or in any book, dismiss what insults your own soul.

—Walt Whitman, *Leaves of Grass*

*Received:* Name values and norms you received (learned) from your cultures.


*Contradiction:* Name an alternative position to the received one.


*Current:* Name your current view on the topic.


*Epistemology:* Name the basis for your current view (how you decided on it).

---

After completing this activity privately, students comment on an electronic discussion board and then discuss their findings in small groups. Students become models for each other of a reflective, questioning stance toward received norms and values. Some are triggered to consider a more self-authorized way of knowing on important issues.

# Appendix D
## The Diversity/Social Justice Action Plan

This activity is grounded in the cultural competency domains (attitudes and beliefs, knowledge, and skills) put forth by Sue, Arredondo, and McDavis's (1992) cultural counseling competency guidelines and standards for counselors. It is inclusive of other frameworks (e.g., social constructionism, MCT, social advocacy); that is, the activity demonstrates the need for culturally competent counselors to have an awareness of their own cultural worldview and attitudes toward cultural differences; knowledge of different cultural practices and worldviews; culturally appropriate skills; and the ability to expand their awareness, knowledge, and understanding of the worldview of their culturally different clients in order to develop culturally appropriate intervention strategies. The activity is divided into four parts: proposal, action plans, journals, and written summary of each experience as it relates to the field of counseling.

In the activity, students identify personal, social, or educational growth goals relative to social justice or multiculturalism counseling. Students select and become involved in three multicultural experiences called *diversity* or *social justice action plans*. They choose an unfamiliar population and submit an action plan proposal with specific objectives and activities to meet these objectives. The action plans must enhance students' knowledge, attitude, and skills in the areas of diversity, multiculturalism, and social justice. The proposal must receive approval from the instructor.

Students begin with an activity within their comfort zone. Then, to meet the objectives of the action plan experience, they move from a distant to more active affiliation with their selected multicultural group. In other words, the first action plan experience should be observational (Level 1), the second should be information seeking (Level II), and the third should involve more direct participation (Level III).

In the proposal, students identify one overall goal and at least three objectives for each of the three action plans (beginning with observation and ending with direct participation). For example, the goal might be to achieve a higher level of comfort with African Americans. The first objective might be to gain knowledge about African Americans through reading about their history, seeing a movie, or driving through an African American neighborhood. The second objective might be to achieve a deeper level of comfort and understanding through involvement in more personal-social activities (e.g., attend a lecture about African Americans, talk to an African American community leader). The third objective would be to gain a deeper understanding of African American life through having dinner with an African American coworker. To assure that students feel safe, and to minimize harm, students write and submit journals weekly throughout this activity and semester.

In the final part of the activity, students submit a summary of each of their multicultural or social justice experiences. In the summary, they identify and briefly describe (a) the experiences, (b) personal objectives for each of the experiences (ways they hope to learn, change, or grow), (c) feelings about or reactions to the experiences, (d) how the experiences were supported or not supported by concepts found in the multicultural or social justice literature, and (e) implications of the experiences for diversity and social justice in mental health. Students debrief by sharing their reactions to their experiences in online groups as well as in class.

# Appendix E
## Sample Privilege Inventory

I. Following are some of the invisible privileges that members of various dominant groups carry, as delineated by McIntosh (1998). Compare your situation with those listed here. Check off those that are accurate for you.

- On the day that I move into the new housing I have chosen, I can be pretty sure that my new neighbors will be neutral or pleasant to me.
- When I am told about our national heritage or about "civilization," I am shown that people of my color (or gender) made it what it is.
- I can do well in a challenging situation without being called a credit to my race (or gender, or sexual orientation).
- I went to school with my friends and was not humiliated when I was labeled and placed in different settings than they were.
- I can easily buy posters, postcards, picture books, greeting cards, dolls, toys, and children's magazines featuring mostly people of my own race (or sexual orientation).
- I can go home from most meetings of organizations to which I belong feeling somewhat connected, rather than isolated, out of place, outnumbered, unheard, held at a distance, or feared.
- I can arrange to protect my children most of the time from people who might not like them.
- I did not need to teach my children about racism for their own daily protection.

- In my neighborhood, any police officer who might need to arrest people in my family is likely to be a person of my race.
- Lawbreaking by the U.S. government with regard to treaties with American Indian people was not taught to me as a criminal aspect of my racial heritage.
- The Constitution that I am subject to was created by people of my ethnic heritage and sex to apply to people of my ethnic heritage and to not apply to people of other races or sex.
- Those who have been able to afford the high costs of legal and/or medical training have been, for the most part, people of my race.
- If I stand in line at a bank teller's window, no one looks strangely at me, as though they have a problem with my being there.
- If I am laughing with friends on a street at night, or talking loudly in a parking lot, it is not assumed that I am dangerous or a member of a gang.
- A realtor has never discriminated against me to "protect property values."
- Bad race relations in the United States are not attributed to my race's criminal behavior, despite a history of race-related breaking of laws by Whites over the entire span of Anglo-European life on this continent.

II. Now comment on what you thought, felt, and noticed as a result of this inventory.

# Appendix F
## Lessons From the Media

**Purpose:** The purpose of this exercise is to help students become aware of how the media influences their perceptions of various cultural groups. This exercise extends Proposition 2 of MCT theory, that is, that both counselor and client identities are embedded in multiple levels of experience and varying contexts, such as individual, family, and culture. In this exercise, students examine the nearly universal cultural influence of pop culture, something that helps to shape both counselor and client identities. When experience with a cultural group outside of one's own is limited, what is learned through the media can form almost the entire basis of what one knows about that cultural group. Unfortunately, media portrayals of many cultural groups are often negatively (or sometimes positively) biased, which can lead to stereotypes that many times go unrecognized and decrease cultural competence.

**The Activity:** In this exercise, students select images and texts from different forms of media such as television, movies, newspapers, magazines, and artwork, looking for hidden or explicit messages that convey ideas about race, gender, or any of the other cultural groupings mentioned at the beginning of the chapter. After examining the media for the messages within, students then compare the messages they have discovered against their own perceptions of the cultural groups under study. Students should answer the following questions:

- How similar are my own perceptions to those depicted in the media?

- Are the depictions and my perceptions mostly positive or negative?
- What impact might these media influences have on my work with clients from this group?
- What impact might media influences have on clients' perceptions of themselves?

Students can also draw conclusions about themes such as beauty, intelligence, or work ethic.

**Illustration:** As an example of how this activity might be used in a classroom, instructors might lead a discussion about media influences on self-esteem and opinions about beauty among African American girls. Students can look at a variety of media artifacts and see how American beauty standards are characterized by Eurocentric hair, body types, and facial features, and then discuss and read firsthand accounts, like those depicted in the documentary *Good Hair* (Rock & O'Donnell, 2009), of the effect that a Eurocentric standard of beauty has on African American girls with kinky hair and African body types and facial features. Students can conclude the discussion about how they could use culturally alert counseling skills in order to address this problem in their work with African American girls dealing with low self-esteem or other related issues. Students could even discuss how they might use principles from critical multicultural social justice theory to develop social justice advocacy interventions as part of an effort to address this problem within a community context.

# Appendix G
## Stages of Oppressive to Anti-Oppressive Thinking

Note: The three categories of *cognitive*, *affective*, and *behavioral* are used as devices in the stages described here to distinguish thinking, feeling, and acting. The interaction of those three dimensions of human functioning is duly noted.

### STAGE 1: IMPULSIVE

*Cognitive dimensions:* Simplistic thinking (e.g., "Women just want a man's money," "The Irish are drunks").

*Affective dimensions:* Overt feelings of hostility and aggressiveness toward others from different cultural groups.

*Behavioral dimensions:* Marginal impulse control. Potential to create a "community of hatred" in which negative views of other cultural groups are condoned. Note: Alcohol/drug misuse often triggers regression to this stage in people who otherwise appear to be functioning at a later stage of prejudice/anti-prejudice.

### STAGE 2: DUALISTIC-RATIONAL

*Cognitive dimensions:* More logical than at the Impulsive Stage, but unable to consistently take the perspectives of "different others." Strong within-group identification and alliance. Rationalizes cultural separatism ("They are different from us, and lesser").

*Affective dimensions:* Superficial social politeness that masks negative feelings toward different others. Resentment of persons who promote social justice. Fear about persons from different cultural groups (e.g., "They are violence-prone").

*Behavioral dimensions:* Less overt aggression toward different others than at Stage 1, due to the impulse control of conventional thinking. A tenuous truce: In stressful situations, aggression and violence are expressed. The research on conflict in Northern Ireland confirms this tendency for groups who seem to function peacefully together to join into factions when a group-related incident occurs.

### STAGE 3: LIBERAL

#### (The modal position for counselors and counselor educators)

*Cognitive dimensions:* Abstract reasoning common. Recognizes universal human rights. Aware of legitimacy of different worldviews. Interested in knowing more about cultural differences.

*Affective dimensions:* "Passionless thoughtfulness": Apathetic disposition about racial/ethnic tensions and injustice in society. Isolated from cultural others, partly through economic stratification.

*Behavioral dimensions:* Voices liberal views about cultural diversity and social justice but does not take action (doesn't "walk the talk") in professional and personal lives. Minimal risk taking. Does not initiate discussions on social justice issues.

*(Continued)*

(Continued)

## STAGE 4: PRINCIPLED

*Cognitive dimensions:* Appreciates the relativism of human views and ideas, including the construction of one's own values and opinions. Aware of the importance of having an open mind to the inaccuracies in one's own thinking.

*Affective dimensions:* Has greater access to inner emotional lives. Shows variety of responses to oppression, from continuing apathy to passionate, complex, and more accurate expression of feelings about injustice.

*Behavioral dimensions:* Range from continuing inaction to sometimes addressing social ills in professional and personal lives. However, lacks ability to act in sustained, effective ways to change unjust or potentially unjust social arrangements.

## STAGE 5: PRINCIPLED ACTIVIST

### (Few counselors found at this stage)

*Cognitive dimensions:* Has expanded understanding of the multiple factors in social injustice, including educational, religious, political, and economic underpinnings. Has clearer ideas on ways to create change to reduce oppression.

*Affective dimensions:* Non-naïve hopefulness about the capacity of humans to improve conditions based on well-developed ideas for social reform. Passionate about reducing human cruelty, especially as it is extended through social arrangements. Seen by many at other stages as too confrontational.

*Behavioral dimensions:* Tenacious action in all areas (e.g., institutional, one-to-one, outreach, neighborhood, family domains). As counselor, is strengths vs. problem-oriented, empowerment vs. adjustment.

# Appendix H
## Ethnic Self-Awareness

Complete the following questions on your ethnicity. Note areas of uncertainty or confusion on your part. What do they say about your ethnic awareness? How influential is your ethnic socialization on you, even without your awareness? Where does your ethnicity "have you," as opposed to your "having it." The following activity will serve as an alert to work you might do on your ethnicity.

1.  What generation(s) in the United States do you represent? (Native American Indians can answer "about 11,000 years on the continent" if they wish.) Explain.

2.  What is your current relationship to and identification with your ethnic culture(s), including where you place yourself on the Cultural Group Orientation Model, including its salience for you?

3.  Describe one moment or time (specific or general) when you became aware of your culture (if you have had that opportunity), for example, when you went to college, a religious event, social event; traveled; stayed with other people; or read something.

4.  Identify some of the characteristics of your ethnic culture(s), including the following:

    a.  any cultural customs practiced by your immediate or extended family
    b.  foods
    c.  celebrations
    d.  rituals
    e.  traditions
    f.  social behaviors
    g.  manners
    h.  beliefs practiced in your family
    i.  customs you prize the most

5.  What is the influence of your ethnicity on how you think and act? Consider elements of your worldview, how that worldview has been shaped, and how your worldview influences your interactions with others.

6.  What culturally different groups and behaviors do members of your group commonly share a prejudice against or discriminate against? How are/were issues of race and ethnicity discussed/addressed in your family? What stereotypes, jokes, statements, were made of other groups (from your earliest recollection)? Do these sentiments persist today?

7.  Make a statement of something about the culture that you are:

    a.  proud of
    b.  ambivalent about/unsure of/not attracted to

8.  What other influences that might be related to your ethnicity impact your culturally influenced worldview, such as social class, race, and religion? What might a counselor need to know about your ethnic group in order to be helpful?

# Appendix I
## Guidelines for Immersion Assignment

**Purpose:** To have students empathically experience new-ness in the form of a different and nondominant culture so that they might relativize cultural norms and learn about a specific group. Emphasis on emotional responses and self-reflections.

First, students choose a nondominant cultural group in U.S. society of which they are NOT a member (or one of their choice, with instructor approval) from among the following examples. (Note: Amount of risk and newness is a factor in grading.)

- African Americans (including subgroups, e.g., Haitian, other Caribbean, African)
- Latino/as/Hispanics (including subgroups, e.g., Puerto Ricans, Mexicans)
- Asians (including subgroups, e.g., East Asians, South Asians, Pacific Islanders)
- Middle Easterners (including, e.g., Lebanese, Moroccans, Palestinians)
- American Indians (including, e.g., Cherokee, Mohawk, Lakota, Hopi)
- Individuals with disabilities (preferably visible)
- Lesbians and/or gay men
- Transgendered persons
- Persons who are in poverty
- Persons from Appalachia
- Religious minorities or unfamiliar (to you) religious groups
- Recent immigrants
- Other?

I. After choosing a cultural group, students do the following:

1. Make contact with someone from the group through referral from someone you know (including class members). Tell the person that you are interested in her or his culture because you want to work effectively with people from this culture in your future.

2. Conduct an interview with someone from the group, as guided by the questions below

3. Participate in an experience alone (not with a class-mate), as described below.

4. Write the report, as directed below.

5. (Possibly) Share your experiences in class, if time allows.

II. Individuals chosen for the interviews must not be your own family members or friends. Here is a recommended procedure:

1. First, *do some reading* about the culture from at least two sources besides the related chapter in the text (e.g., journal articles; book chapters in *Ethnicity and Family Therapy, A Different Mirror*).

2. *Conduct an interview* with one member of that group, especially someone for whom that group member-ship is important, about her or his experience as a member of that group in the areas raised by the read-ing. See guidelines below.

3. Join that person for a *one-hour "plunge" experience* within that cultural group, e.g., a social event, a reli-gious service, a meeting, a festival, a gathering, an extended family experience.

III. Write an approximately eight-page double-spaced report (excluding title page, abstract, and reference list) using the numbering system below. In general, use APA format. Give the report a title of your choice. The report should include the following:

A. A description of the plunge experience itself, including observations and subjective experience. (about one page)

B. A biographical sketch of the interviewee gathered through the interview. (about one paragraph)

C. The content of the interview, including the following (you can add more questions if you'd like):

1. How important is membership in that group to the person?

2. What in particular is important?

3. How does this membership affect her or his life?

4. What is a source of pride and/or a positive dimension of being in that group?

5. What is a less desirable or negative dimension of the group's culture and/or of her or his membership?

6. How does that group membership affect:

   a. Social life?
   b. Career?
   c. Housing/geographical location?
   d. Other issues, e.g., influence on movement in society, in the larger community, political activity, anything else?

7. What would that person like counselors to know about the group and its members?

8. A comparison/contrast of your interviewee with the generalizations and/or stereotypes of this group (e.g., referring to the sources you used in section "a")

9. A comment on any intersections of oppression that the person might have (e.g., being lesbian, poor, and Latina)

10. Factors to keep in mind if you were counseling this person or consulting with her or him (e.g., with her or him as a parent and you as a school counselor). Articulate why counselors must be aware of the cultural factors when they are counseling members of the targeted group and its potential impact on the counseling process.

11. Knowledge that you have gained about yourself through your interactions in this project, including a critical analysis of your own attitudes, beliefs, assumptions, and behaviors as related to this culturally different group.

All reports must be double spaced and use APA format. I recommend that you consult the *Publication Manual of the American Psychological Association.* Reports must be well organized, express concepts in a clear and fluid manner, and develop ideas with enough elaboration and detail to adequately cover the subject. The proper mechanics of writing (e.g., spelling, punctuation, verb tense) are required.

You may be asked to share key facts, thoughts, and feelings about the plunge experience at the last class session, i.e., describe your experience and its impact on you to the class.

**Time:** maximum one hour, including open discussion time at end. In groups, students will study one ethnic or social group, as assigned in class. They will do the following:

Study and research the chosen group or topic using both the related chapter in the text and at least one other source. Emphasize (1) key characteristics of members of the group (e.g., qualified generalizations about shared values, history), (2) education- or counseling-related issues (e.g., mental health, acculturation, oppression), and (3) possible strategies for working with members.

Note: All students in the class will have read the related chapter. As a result, they will be familiar with some of the cultural history and/or characteristics of the group before your workshop. Therefore, while you can choose to address cultural history and/or characteristics of the group through an opening discussion, activity, or review, the majority of time can be spent on mental health, counseling, or other issues affecting this group. Your group can decide on the balance needed. Just know that the class will have beginning familiarity with some basic material on the group. That doesn't mean you can't return to that material in an activity or in a new way. You decide on what you want to do, as all educators must, based on what you think is most important to do in the time allowed in order to achieve learning goals.

Remember that your workshop is only an introduction to issues and a chance for class members to discuss them. Your hope should be that, with this experience in class, students might remember some ideas and seek out more information when they are at work in the profession.

Each team member should utilize at least one resource in addition to the chapter and contribute it to the project. Those resources can include (1) in-person visits, observations, participation, and interviews with members and activities of this group; (2) journals and books (e.g., a relevant chapter from *Ethnicity and Family Therapy*); (3) popular and documentary-style films on the topic ; (4) autobiography, fiction, and creative non-fiction work that evokes the culture and issues of this group; and (5) manuals on interventions for members of this group.

## POSSIBLE STRUCTURE OF THE WORKSHOP:

A. Opening: Bring out the topic, and create interest with a beginning activity or question(s) for discussion that involves the audience (e.g., a discussion/processing of some or all of the activities that students have done in the related chapter, a video/film segment that illustrates some of the points, a self-assessment activity, a true/false activity about the group, a story that generates discussion, a role play or other demonstration of a teaching or counseling session or program idea that illustrates an issue or issues in working with that cultural group).

B. Middle: An interactive mini-presentation/discussion/sharing about the group or topic that includes room for discussion and questions from the class. Imagine that you are at a conference and you have one hour to introduce a naïve audience to your topic. Here are four possible dimensions you might include:

1. [Optional example] Some important major characteristics of the group (e.g., the group's most salient values, norms, behaviors, and worldview and their potential impact on the educational or counseling process). [Note: The class will have read the related chapter on this topic.]

2. [Optional example] The critical historical and current experiences (including social, economic, and political status/power in the United States and experiences of oppression/discrimination/disenfranchisement) that have significantly contributed to the group's identity, values, behaviors, worldview, and overall life experience. In this regard, also discuss their potential impact on the educational or counseling

process. [Note: The class will have read some material from the related chapter on this topic.]

3. Professional/mental health issues related to working with this group (e.g., communication styles, career issues, substance use patterns, sexuality values, family configuration, attitudes toward professional help).

4. Demonstration or discussion of some interventions in your professional interest area (e.g., counseling methods, psychoeducation, programming) that might result in more effective work with members of this group (i.e., interventions).

C. Discussion: Required minimum of 15 minutes of response and discussion time for the guest discussant and the class members. You can begin with "What struck you?" or "What comes up for you?" or "Any comments?" and let the discussion happen. You needn't have answers or be expert. Just let the class talk. Here the discussant(s) and the instructor will assist with the discussion. This part is required, or points will be lost.

D. Handing in of the outline and any materials and references used for the workshop to the instructor as well as to the class (as if giving the audience a handout at a conference). These can include such things as PowerPoint notes, a workshop outline, discussion questions, key facts to remember, or a short abstract of the three topics (information from a, b, c, and/or d above under section "B")

E. If there is a video available, leave time for the instructor to show it and facilitate a discussion.

# 13

# Teaching Lifespan Development

Jean Sunde Peterson and Karen P. Eriksen

Two years ago, a middle-aged student, in his evaluation of a largely experiential Human Growth and Development course, said, "Excellent integration of reading, discussion, interpersonal experiences, presentations, and writing assignments. I expected a dull, dry academic experience. The continual personalization of the material and the connection to the counseling experience made for a lively and interesting semester." That comment was gratifying because the course's learning process, as we teach it, often demands that students be willing to stretch themselves beyond what is familiar, preferred, and comfortable. That year, a somewhat younger student offered another positive perspective: "I grew personally. Every aspect of the course was valuable."

Not all reviews were unqualifiedly positive. A student in her late 20s said, "The self-study paper was beneficial, but I found it difficult due to my bottled-up personality. Some issues surfaced during writing that I realized I had not dealt with." Comments of the youngest students, just out of undergraduate studies, varied from "This course provides students with a real picture of what we will need to deal with" to "Would prefer more discussion of the text" and "I think class time could have been used in a more efficient way."

These varied comments represent a typical range of evaluative feedback for this experientially based course. In fact, it is here that the *content* of the human development course and its *process* meet. The comments may reflect differences in age, life experience, personality, and temperament. They may also, however, reflect differences in constructive capacity (Perry, 1981), as laid out in Chapter 1. We find Perry's positions of intellectual development through which adults progress and Belenky, Clinchy, Goldberger, and Tarule's (1986) parallel model to be guides for teaching. According to Perry, for instance, instructors could potentially encounter many ways of student knowing in a class. Counselor educators must be prepared to respect, and respond nonjudgmentally to, such individual differences (Komives & Woodard, 1996).

## APPLICATION OF DEVELOPMENTAL THEORY TO TEACHING THE COURSE

Development is neither simple nor linear. Individual students tend to operate within a range of developmental stages (Lamborn & Fischer, 1988). Helms (1995) therefore argues for a broader conception in the form of a "phasic" view of "stages," with stages representing "interactive themes rather than mutually exclusive categories" (p. 183). Given the complexities of developmental identification, it is nevertheless clear that, in any one course, there are many audiences, all varying in readiness and style. It therefore seems imperative that instructors recognize students' development and preferences before teaching them so that the instruction might match students' cognitive development and learning preferences.

There are voices that warn teachers to not be simplistic about matching development and instruction. For example, King (1996) suggests that educators should be wary of labeling students as though they "possess only one set of talents, skills, or sensitivities, [and focus on helping students] effectively adapt their methods of learning to the specific tasks and contexts at hand" (p. 231). Thus, the pure matching of development with instruction is probably not realistic. However, the use of multiple methods can encourage students to exert themselves and practice new strategies for learning (McMillan & Forsyth, 1991). And students may be motivated in part by activities that help them meet their developmental needs.

In this course, with these perspectives in mind, we attempt to address multiple learner needs, using personalized, experiential dimensions of constructivist teaching, not only to raise awareness about human development in general, but also to enhance motivation. Toward those ends, students are purposefully bombarded with ambiguity, incongruity, multiple perspectives, and incompleteness—four conditions that trigger all students' constructive development.

When I (Peterson) was first assigned the course, I knew I did not want to merely "cover the content," even though I felt responsible for preparing students for the human development portion of the comprehensive and licensure exams. I wanted the course to help students develop a framework for understanding themselves and their future clients. I wanted them to learn inductively, constructing their own knowledge, knowledge that would be meaningful because it would represent a "connection between what they [were] learning and their overall life experiences" (hooks, 1994, p. 19). With Kegan's (1994) self-authorizing way of knowing in mind, I considered that I wanted them to learn to read in an active, questioning way and to be self-directed. I wanted them to write "to parts of themselves, conducting an inner conversation" (Kegan, 1994, p. 284), not just to write to me for my approval. I hoped some might experience, as a prelude to working with future clients, a respectful discovery of others' worlds, while accepting their own vulnerability to discovering another world within themselves as a result.

Yet keeping Perry's and Kegan's theories in mind, I knew that there would be students who would be preoccupied with pursuing my approval, at the expense of transformation toward the kind of self-direction and self-authoring that I had in mind. I wanted to generate honest self-examination, which might be overchallenging to some. I therefore needed to respect each student, regardless of cognitive capacity. I needed to offer a bridge that was "well anchored on both sides, with as much respect for where it begins as for where it ends" (Kegan, 1994, p. 62). I needed to provide an appropriate mix of challenge and support to encourage continued intellectual growth (cf. Perry, 1981). I also wanted to create an environment in which students could embrace their relational ties (i.e., for confirmation and cooperation) while simultaneously adopting a new, more developmentally advanced, self-authorizing perspective on them (cf. Kegan, 1994, pp. 243, 294) in the interest of applying such new understanding in their future work.

My own preferred teaching and learning style is experiential. I do not learn well auditorially, and thus, possibly as a result of projective identification, I have never been comfortable lecturing at length to students. I am aware that an individual often teaches in a style that matches her or his own learning style (Delworth & Hanson, 1989) and that students who are taught in a style that is incompatible with their own often have difficulty succeeding (Kolb, 1984; Witkin, 1976). I therefore wondered how best to accommodate both my own and my students' needs as I attempted to move them toward reflective thinking (see King & Kitchener, 1994) and toward constructing their own knowledge, and moving away from relying on knowledge received from another source (cf. Komives & Woodard, 1996).

## A Course That Transforms Through Experience and Reflection

The methodology and format of what, as we teach it, has become a largely experiential course has evolved with transformation in mind. The course aims not only to nudge students toward new ways of thinking about the nature of knowing and about human life phases, but also to transform students through those learning experiences into a different kind of counselor. Students change in many ways during this course, according to their feedback at the end of this personalized learning experience.

The course is heavily oriented toward the experiential. The experiential dimensions are meant to move students away from expecting to passively receive "objective" knowledge and toward active engagement in integrating and applying diverse understandings, as well as toward increased tolerance for ambiguity and incompleteness. Examples of such experience- and reflection-oriented activities include students applying developmental concepts to themselves in writing, regularly interacting with and interviewing individuals who represent various developmental phases, and conducting a written dialogue with the instructor through "response paragraphs" after each experience.

Through direct contact with persons from the entire lifespan, most students appear to gain comfort with populations that they previously thought were "off limits," newly considering them in terms of counseling practice. Some who have taken the course late in their programs have called it one of their most vital experiences in becoming a counselor. By contrast, a few have been frustrated and stressed by the nearly weekly experiential activities, perhaps feeling overchallenged in terms of self-authorizing their learning (Kegan, 1994; Widick, Parker, & Knefelkamp, 1978). For example, needing certainty, students might find not having an outline to guide an interview to be threatening. Needing "truth," they might find it difficult to tolerate an interviewee's political or religious views if they differ from their own.

Despite these challenges, this experientially based course continues to receive strong support from the vast majority of students who take it. They no longer make quick and stereotyping pronouncements about either human development or particular age groups or populations. They recognize many more of their own "issues." They seem to be more comfortable with ambiguity and, consequently, with client surprises. In short, they have moved significantly forward in the process of becoming counselors.

## CONSTRUCTIVIST PRINCIPLES AT WORK

What follow are the constructivist principles that guide this human development course: personalizing teaching, valuing and promoting experience, hearing student voices, and encouraging multiple perspectives. Table 13.1 summarizes constructive developmental principles as they apply to the learning experiences described below.

**TABLE 13.1** Course Objectives, Activities, and Constructivist Principles

| Learning Objectives | Learning Activities | Constructivist Principles |
|---|---|---|
| Know textbook material on human development. | • Read text<br>• Develop questions/activities for children/adult visitors<br>• Develop lists of developmental concepts/theory to observe in visitors<br>• Classroom discussions of reading before visitors arrive<br>• Final exam | Providing structure to support dualistic knowers |
| Apply developmental theory and concepts to people throughout the lifespan. | • Conduct counseling activities/questioning with visitors<br>• Observe, discuss, and reflect in response papers on the developmental theory and concepts | Applications of principles in action (breaking down ambiguous stimuli into manageable parts, asking for evidence of position, including diversity of perspectives) creates real-world ambiguity, requires deciding for oneself, standing back from own work to evaluate = challenge toward procedural knowing.<br><br>Structured grading rubrics and feedback sheets = support. |

(Continued)

| TABLE 13.1 (Continued) | | |
|---|---|---|
| *Learning Objectives* | *Learning Activities* | *Constructivist Principles* |
| Apply developmental theory and concepts to themselves. | • Constructive development paper<br>• Final paper | Applications in action (personalizing the learning) creates real-world ambiguity, requires deciding for oneself, standing back from own work and from self to evaluate = challenge toward procedural knowing.<br><br>Structured grading rubrics and feedback sheets = support. |
| Demonstrate age- and content-appropriate counseling with children and adults. | • Instructor modeling of questions with guests<br>• Students conduct counseling activities/questioning with visitors | Applications of principles in action (breaking down ambiguous stimuli into manageable parts, asking for evidence of position, including diversity of perspectives) creates real-world ambiguity, requires deciding for oneself = challenge toward procedural knowing. |
| Advance developmentally | • Dialectical discourse<br>• Hearing student voices<br>• Entertaining multiple perspectives<br>• Applying theory/critical thinking<br>• Personalized learning<br>• Process questions<br>• Abdicating authority role<br>• Modeling incompleteness | |

# Personalizing Teaching

Learning is enhanced when the person of the teacher and the person of the student are brought into the classroom. This includes paying attention to individual personalities and learning styles as well as sharing personal stories and experiences. But we also require students to personalize their experiences in this course by asking them to apply developmental principles to themselves in two possible papers.

## The Teacher

A teacher's personality and self-presentation are among the social factors that contribute to classroom atmosphere and, ultimately, to student learning (cf. hooks, 1994, pp. 129–166). Above all, as teachers we are also learners. We see our students, as well as our clients, as our teachers, at the same time as they share their thoughts and experiences and make sense of their lives. We communicate our fascination with the complexity of human nature. We present real but anonymous clients from our own counseling practices, applying both systems and developmental perspectives.

These personal references help us demonstrate how we use the developmental template when forming hypotheses about clients. We rarely lecture in class. However, we do provide minilectures on findings from our own developmental research. The fact that these findings are from our own studies seems to invite challenge and discussion. Thereby, we hope to communicate that we are lifelong learners, excited about pursuing questions of interest to us and eager for continued learning through thoughtful feedback.

In order to further personalize learning, we self-disclose, choosing carefully what we share, in the interest of modeling appropriate professional discretion. That kind of risk taking on our part, a professor's "linking confessional narratives to academic discussions so as to show how experience can illuminate and enhance our understanding of academic material" (hooks, 1994, p. 21), may give students permission to engage in similar risk taking. We intend to communicate that we are complex and dynamic human beings.

Self-disclosure can take other and less obvious forms, of course. We frequently employ immediacy in responding to students' comments and nonverbal behaviors. In doing so, we try to model openness to learning and to multiple perspectives by communicating genuine interest in students' comments, whether they are consistent with or divergent from ours and others'.

On this personal level, we are continually self-reflective about the teacher-learner relationship (cf. hooks, 1994; Schön, 1987).

We often find ourselves hypersensitively replaying our interactions with students for several hours after each class meeting, wondering, for example, if the students and we interpreted each other's comments as they were meant.

## The Students

We also want our students to personalize their learning. We encourage them to do so by asking them to respond personally to the readings, ask for their feelings and self-evaluations in response to interactions with class visitors, and ask them to apply developmental understandings to their own lives in a final paper. We also process in-class relationships and ways of being in the class with others.

For instance, we encourage students to come to class each week with a written list of five things in the readings that they found interesting, confusing, doubtful, or incredible. We begin class by asking a different student each week to share the list, a process that invariably provokes discussion. Sometimes, we turn this into a quiz experience by directing them to write for 10 minutes about a specific item on their list. They begin such writing with "I" and then explain why they noticed a particular finding or conclusion among the many possibilities in each chapter. We ask them to offer evidence of their understanding of the concepts presented. We then discuss what various students have noted as their interests and needs for approximately one-third of every class meeting.

We also bring personalization into the in-class interactions with children, adolescents, and adults, which are a fundamental part of the course. For example, during debriefings following these in-class interactions, we insist on an honest self-assessment of what worked in interacting with differently aged people and what did not. We ask students how they felt and what they might have been reminded of in themselves.

We further personalize our teaching by attending to the construction of relationships in class. We wait until we feel confident that relationship changes have occurred and will be recognized before we process the changes. Then we call attention to these evolving relationships, noting not only that this phenomenon parallels the building of trust in the counselor-client relationship, but also that it probably contributes to tolerance for complexity in the learning environment. We laud students for this growing collective tolerance, as it is warranted, unabashedly and simultaneously communicating our bias in that direction.

## The Constructivist-Developmental Paper

Research indicates that when students learn constructivist-developmental theory and are encouraged to apply it to themselves, they progress developmentally. So at the beginning of the course, I (Eriksen) administer the Defining Issues Test (DIT; Rest & Narvaez, 1999), which assesses students' moral development, à la Kohlberg, and the Learning Environments Preferences Scale (LEP; Moore, 1989), which assesses students' cognitive complexity, à la Perry.

Then, during discussions of young adult development (where most of our students find themselves), we discuss different theories of this phase of development, not only to respect and gain from discoveries of various fields, but also to enhance students' awareness of their own evolutionary cognitive development. We refer, for example, to Perry's (1970) scheme regarding how students move from dualistic, truth-versus-falsehood thinking to conceptual relativism and then to self-chosen commitment; to Riegel's (1973) concept of dialectical adult thought; to Labouvie-Vief's (1984) advocacy of exposure to complexity as a way to escape dualistic thinking; and to Kegan's (1982) emphasis on the continued development of systems of meaning. Loevinger (1976) views developmental stages as somewhat related to chronological age, but not necessarily dependent on it, and the age panels across the lifespan underscore that reality during this course. Making sense of theories about nonphasic development (e.g., Kegan, 1982; Kohlberg, 1981; Loevinger, 1976; Piaget, 1932/1965) is not so difficult when real children, adolescents, and adults are regularly interacting with the students and representing wide variations within age groups.

After exposure to a variety of constructivist-developmental theories, we give students their DIT and LEP scores and ask them to assess themselves. They indicate characteristics relevant to their stage, the stage they have emerged from, and the stage they are aiming for, with supporting stories or examples. They also propose growth-enhancing activities to help them advance developmentally. If they don't agree with their scores, they identify the stage they believe themselves to primarily operate from, using the same sorts of evidence to justify their conclusions.

Students often find this paper very difficult, so I (Eriksen) offer as much structure (exemplars and grading rubrics) as possible and offer counseling-like support when needed. However, they also find the experience of thinking about themselves in this way to be development producing and very enlightening. I ask them to include what they discover in the final paper. The tasks of this assignment could just be included as part of the final paper assignment. However, it often feels like such a monumental challenge to students that it seems to require boundaries and support so as not to overchallenge them.

## The Final Paper

Throughout all of the interactive experiences, students remain aware of the self-study paper that they will eventually have to write. By midterm, they have begun the time-consuming process of organizing it. Their frequent identification with young interviewees has helped them focus on their own school years. During postinterview class discussions about various developmental stages, they have also been reminded to make notes for later reference. The assignment for the paper is as follows:

Write a paper about four to six developmental phases with yourself as the subject. (If you wish not to use yourself as the subject of your paper, you may write the paper with someone else as the subject. This person must be at least 30 years of age and will be named in the paper only by pseudonym. The content of your paper will be based on in-depth interviews with this person.) The paper should be no more than 20 pages in length and should use APA style. You may want to conduct some interviews of family members in order to gain insight about your own development, but that is not a requirement. Choose from the following phases: Infancy and Early Childhood, ages 0–5; Middle Childhood, ages 6–11; Adolescence, ages 12–19; Early Adulthood, ages 20–39; Middle Adulthood, ages 40–59; Over 60.

As you discuss each stage, consider *major influences* (e.g., individuals, family/sibling constellation, personal responsibilities and roles in family, institutions, circumstances), *role models* (e.g., at school, at home, in extended family, in neighborhood/community), and *"nodal" life events* (e.g., moves, injuries, trauma, illness, death of someone close, changes/losses, "successes," "failures"). Include *references to developmental theorists* (at least four times). Consider these questions (listed only to give you ideas):

1. Keeping in mind that "typical" is a social construction, what aspects of your life represent *typical or atypical development* in each phase?

2. In each phase, what evidence shows that you were moving forward, "on hold," or "stuck" in regard to *developmental tasks?*

3. What were the *easiest phases* for you?

4. What were the *most difficult phases* for you?

5. What were some questions, feelings, or concerns you had during each phase or during the most difficult phases?

6. What were some "problems in living" that were related to developmental issues and that, if you had had comfortable access to counseling, could have been alleviated or lessened by such services—at least by having an objective, knowledgeable listener?

7. What kinds of counseling interventions might have been helpful?

8. What developmental theoretical perspectives are reflected in these interventions?

9. What prevented (or might have prevented) your receiving some intervention? (Or, if you experienced some sort of intervention, what kind was it?)

10. Where are you now developmentally? (What phase[s] or stage? Are you "stuck"? Where are you *in* the phase[s] or stage?)

11. If you could go back and traverse a particular phase or stage again, which would it be, and what would you do differently?

As you write this paper, remember that you are in charge of the content. As your instructor, I promise confidentiality. No one will see your paper, no copy will be made, it will be returned to you in person at the end of the semester, and there will be absolutely no discussion of the content outside of any potential discussion between you and your instructor—unless you cite something from it in class yourself.

The rationale behind assigning this paper is that it is helpful for counselors-in-training to be aware of their own issues—"trigger areas," vulnerabilities, concerns, and history—as they work with clients, no matter what the clients' ages or phases. The more aware counselors are of themselves, and the more they can actively and accurately monitor their responses during sessions, the more effective they can be and the more they can allow exploration and growth in clients.

To date, all students taking this course have written the final paper with themselves as subject. Their feedback has indicated that the assignment is an invigorating, positive (even though perhaps difficult at times), growth-producing experience and is quite helpful in their training as counselors. When they have finished the final paper, they have expressed appreciation for the process. The final paper is a culminating activity, requiring linkages among theory, the earlier experiential dimensions of the course, personal insights gained throughout the course, and courage and discretion in self-presentation.

Routinely, during the weeks just preceding submission of the paper, there are phone calls from students requesting individual meetings to process complex emotions or "stuckness." When the papers are all submitted, we "process the process" as a group, and most describe a long and complex process. When the processing begins, some erupt with pent-up emotions as they share their experiences. Some report that interviews with family members rekindled or precipitated new family connections. The actual writing process seems to be a solitary, pensive, and sometimes lonely activity. Students appear collectively to be proud of their accomplishment, and they often interject references to theorists in their comments. During such end-of-semester processing, it becomes clear that developmental theory has been personalized—and sometimes challenged. The theories students used to analyze their own development for the paper are not likely to be forgotten. They have also become a community of learners, as advocated by

Belenky et al. (1986), and usually are overtly and warmly supportive of each other during this discussion.

# Valuing and Promoting Experience

Experiential learning is central in the human development course as we have designed it. Most central to the course are the students' experiences with people of various age groups. Students create activities to do with children of different ages and develop interview questions and interview panels of teens and adults of different ages.

## Interactive Interviews

Almost every week the students interact with real people who represent various life phases. In pursuit of such interactions, we may invite individuals from the community into class or take field trips to schools or other institutions. Each week's group represents a particular age range so that students become acquainted with individuals who can teach them about developmental experiences across the lifespan. There are several goals for these interactions:

- Students come to see clients, in the person of these informants, as potential teachers for themselves and see themselves as learners in the counseling relationship.
- Students become acquainted with and comfortable with people at various developmental levels.
- Students have the opportunity to corroborate or challenge what is presented in the textbook and handouts about development.
- Students gain experience in adapting communication to various developmental levels.
- Students anticipate ways in which developmental tasks and issues may intersect with diagnosable problems in clients.

Each week at least one student expresses anxiety about interacting with a particular age group. Such discomfort may stem simply from moving out of a personal comfort zone, away from familiarity. It may also reflect the potential for loss of control. Students who are not usually risk takers sometimes comment on their tense anticipation as they face new experiences. We normalize and

process this anxiety before the guests arrive, or before we leave campus, often reviewing basic listening skills and sometimes pairing students who are anxious with those who are more experienced with a particular age group.

Here are some illustrations of types of experiences students have had during the human development course:

> The second class meeting may begin with an hour-long visit to the neonatal unit at a local hospital, during which parent concerns are noted as potential counseling issues. A nurse comments on neonatal tasks and development and demonstrates neonatal reflexes.

> During the following weeks, the course moves through childhood and adolescence. Students may see a demonstration of and then apply play therapy with preschoolers at a Head Start facility. They may interact with various groups of children either in school classrooms, at the local Boys and Girls Club, or on campus (children from the Scouts often receive merit badges for their contribution to our class). Students may interact with at-risk adolescents at a local alternative school. If the class is held in the evening, these groups may come to our campus classroom.

> When the focus shifts to adulthood, class members or others who are in their 20s, 30s, 40s, 50s, and 60s participate in in-class panel discussions, again for approximately one hour during each meeting.

> As we approach the end of life, students may visit a retirement facility or we may invite Hospice representatives into class to share the experiences and needs of people at the end of life.

## General Format for Interactions With Children and Teens

The emphasis in students' interacting with school-age children and adolescents is on learning about development during the school years. The format for these interactions remains fairly constant across sessions. In order to engage a child or adolescent in comfortable conversation, each graduate student prepares an "instigating" activity for the visitors, such as asking for a drawing (e.g., their family, their classroom, their house), completion of sentence stems (e.g., "If I could live anywhere in the world . . . ," "My friends think I'm . . ."), responses to open-ended questions (e.g., "If you were king, what would you change about the world?"), interactions with toys or games (e.g., Battleship, doll house, action figures), or responses to a thematic activity (e.g., "If you could send each person in your family on a special vacation, where would you send them?" "Tell me about the nicest time you ever had with someone from your family.").

For these activities to be most productive as learning experiences, students consider the developmental needs of the children that they will interact with as they prepare activities for their class interactions with particular ages of children. The instructor places two books containing children's activities (Peterson, 1993, 1995) on reserve in the library for students to use as references for ages preschool through 18, but the instructor also encourages students to be creative and independent in their approach. We emphasize that the techniques are meant to generate conversation that includes more than just "favorite things." However, to value students' prior experiences and knowledge, and to value trying on new behavior, students are free to follow the interviewee in any direction. The goal is to engage efficiently with the client groups, given time constraints, and to allow clients to teach the students about the clients themselves, without students imposing meaning based only on their own experiences. Most students quickly find that some structure is advantageous and less threatening for all involved in this type of brief interaction.

During the actual classroom interactions, the children or teens are "distributed" among individual or paired counseling students. The counseling students interact with the children or teens using their prepared techniques. After 10 to 15 minutes, the students move to a second interviewee. Students also spend approximately 20 minutes doing a group interview with a panel of the children's parents, who are encouraged to interact with each other as well as with the counseling students. Students interview the parents about their own developmental and parenting issues and about issues related to the development of their children. Sometimes the children are even invited to interview their parents; in this case, guidelines are established in the interest of discretion and comfort for all participants.

## Reflection and Response Paragraphs

After the classroom interactions with children and their parents, students write a two-page response paper to turn in during the following class. In the paper, they describe the technique that they used to engage the children and any adaptations they made in order to make the technique appropriate to that person's development-related capabilities and interests. They explain how the child's or adolescent's behaviors fit into what had previously been learned about development. In the case of the class having conducted an interview of a group of parents or group of students at a school, the students also add comments about what they observed about development in the group as a whole. Reflecting on the interviews provides students with an opportunity to focus on the constructivist notion of how each child or teen was constructing meaning.

The students also write about their own comfort level in being with this age group, as well as the effectiveness of their techniques in engaging the interviewees. Such appraisal of effectiveness is based on students' own subjective judgment, reflecting the phenomenological world to which they are learning to pay attention. The students might also include in their reflection how their current view of development affected their questioning and interaction. We have found that the submitted paragraphs become increasingly process oriented and reflective of interpersonal nuance as the semester progresses.

We do not grade these responsive paragraphs, but we do give a plus mark if they represent thoughtful commentary about development. We write responses in the margins to recognize observations or comments about development. Such responses are meant to discourage students from writing only narratives about the facts (i.e., what happened during the interviews). Among many purposes these assignments serve, they give students guidance and practice in writing about human development in preparation for their final paper. That paper is also expected to be more than merely a factual recounting. If some students are still making few reflective comments about development when half of the responsive papers have been submitted, in spite of our written and oral admonitions, we mark their papers with a check, a certain number of which may ultimately lower their course grade.

At each class meeting, we set aside time for the students to share their observations, techniques, and comfort level with interacting with children of different ages and their parents. Their increasingly forthright comments and their vulnerability while sharing uncomfortable moments from the interviews contribute to a growing sense of classroom community, which emerges from an "engaged pedagogy" (hooks, 1994, p. 20) that values student expression. Again, we refer to meaning construction by asking, "How were you constructing meaning during the interview? How did that influence your questioning? How are you continuing to construct meaning during this discussion?"

## Panels of Adults

When the course shifts to the topic of adulthood, class members or others who are in their 20s, 30s, 40s, 50s, and 60s participate in in-class panel discussions, again for approximately one hour during each class meeting. Our participation in an appropriate age panel reminds them that we also are "developing people." Occasionally, representatives from every decade through near-retirement are members of the class. Usually, however, individuals from the community must be recruited to supplement the few in class who represent the older age decades. Eventually the class takes another field trip, spending time at a retirement center, again interviewing individuals and a panel, but with no requirement for pre-planned techniques for the individual interviews. Finally, a hospice representative might speak to us at our last class meeting.

For the in-class panel discussions, panels of four or five guest discussants representing each age group seem to work best, offering enough panelists for variety in perspective and experience, and yet giving panelists sufficient time to elaborate on their thoughts. Although the panels may not fully represent a developmental life stage, a small panel that shares life experiences, struggles, strengths, and wishes can generate a great deal of thought-provoking material about a particular stage.

We usually begin the interviews of guest panelists ourselves by asking open-ended, developmental questions about differences from the preceding age/decade's experiences, about changing roles and relationships with various members of the family of origin and the current family, and about new concerns and thoughts relative to direction, career, meaning, goals, and health. Students then take over the responsibility for interviewing the

panel. Later in the semester, students take over the now-familiar interviewing format almost entirely. On occasion, if a student's question or remark is indiscreet or discomfiting, we might interrupt to give a panelist permission not to respond. At other times, we might extend our own questioning as we become aware of the potential for hearing some particularly instructive information from a group of guests. Generally, however, the students' questions will be thoughtful and appropriate, and require few interruptions. Their comments and responses seem to become more supportive and facilitative as the semester progresses.

Unlike with the interviews with children and their parents, the students do not write responsive paragraphs concerning the adult panels. This is because they are occupied with other writing at that point in the course and because they have already developed the skills for interaction and an ability to self-monitor and reflect.

## Preparing Students for Interview Experiences

To enhance student learning, provide motivation for completing the reading, and provide structure for those students who need it, I (Eriksen) prepare students for their experiences with visitors of different ages. For instance, in addition to asking students to plan an age-appropriate activity for children, I ask them to develop questions that they would like to ask teen and adult panels. I suggest that, while they are reading the chapter assigned for that week, they make a list of developmental indicators or concepts about which they would like to know more. They then watch for these indicators in the children and create questions related to these indicators for the adult panelists.

I also assist students in processing the lists that they have created from their readings. Prior to the classroom interactions with the children, I review students' lists of developmental indicators and coach them to expand their lists if necessary. Prior to their interviews of adult panels, students share the questions they have generated for the panelists. Then, as a class, they decide which questions would elicit the best developmental information. These classroom discussions give the instructor the chance to highlight key developmental concepts, correct any misconceptions, and urge changes in unhelpful or inappropriate questions.

## Postinterview Discussions

After the interviews, activities, or panels, we discuss students' experiences with the process and with what they have discovered; again, we ask them to apply developmental theory or add to their own emerging theories of development. We ask what impressed them the most and what surprised them the most. We ask them to compare what they heard and observed to the previous age group. Students have often been amazed at some information, touched by some comment, reminded of someone, or helped to understand someone in their own lives.

In both the interviews and the postpanel discussions, students inductively gather "data" through the interaction with both the guests and each other. In the process of interviewing and in the discussions that follow, they may add their own theories of development to those about which they have been reading. Then, in one essay question on the final exam, students are asked to articulate their own inductively drawn theory of adult development, based on knowledge they gained from three of the adult panels. They thus demonstrate that they have constructed their own knowledge, reflecting what Kolb (1984) calls *deep learning*.

## Dialogue in the Face of Differences

Students rarely agree fully with one another during the postinterview discussions. They may differ on their conceptualization of the children and their parents or the members of the panels that they have interviewed. They argue most about the earlier developmental stages. By contrast, it seems to be more difficult for them to challenge a perception about panelists older than they are.

The textbook information provides the most material for such dialogues. Whether it is about parental discipline, relationship issues, gender differences and socialization, young adult developmental tasks, emotional expressiveness, moral development, or family roles, students engage each other readily, sometimes in a confrontational manner. We try to use such situations to point out communication patterns, to draw attention

to internal processes (students' metacognitions), and to affirm the idea of multiple perspectives. Given the tendency toward confrontation during discussions, we aim to follow Yalom's (1997) ideas about providing sufficient safety and support; with appropriate feedback and honesty of expression, the group tensions that emerge can be processed, leading to a therapeutic "corrective emotional experience" (p. 26). When these necessary conditions exist in the human development course, both bonding and intrapersonal awareness are enhanced.

Further, students' cognitive development also seems to progress as they gradually and "correctively" build tolerance for differences between themselves and others; they even learn to value such differences (cf. Loevinger, 1976). Giroux (1981) speaks of developing a pedagogy that, through dialogue and supportive interaction, helps students move beyond the "taken-for-grantedness" (p. 124) that shapes their view of the world. Students in this course seem to develop a "dialectical language" that enables them "to understand the meaning of frame of reference" (p. 124), a worthy goal in the development of counseling expertise.

Whatever cognitive conflict occurs for them as they struggle to integrate new information into existing structures, many students in this course qualitatively change by resolving disequilibrium through the process of accommodation (cf. Wadsworth, 1979). Students often report that they know themselves better than before and are more comfortable with the self they have explored, which perhaps reflects movement along a continuum of identity development (cf., e.g., Chickering, 1969; Erikson, 1980; Widick et al., 1978) and development as an "organization of increasing complexity" (Sanford, 1967, p. 47).

## Hearing Student Voices

The third constructivist theme that is integral to this human development course is that of hearing and honoring students' voices. The general focus on development, the open-endedness-within-structure of class activities, and the students' participation in the panels all encourage them to lend their unique voices to the discussions. The almost total absence of traditional teacher lectures and the general de-emphasis on fact and "truth" also help to keep the focus on student contribution.

The papers, too, offer an opportunity for students to give voice to themselves and to their experiences. Whether on the reflective paragraphs or on the final paper, we give them feedback through notes in the margins, establishing a written dialogue that continues throughout the course. They learn early that personalized comments evoke personal responses, even though our part of the dialogue is relatively brief. We believe that validating their thoughts and opinions nurtures the teacher-student relationship and students' personal growth. We are "noticing" them. Evaluations have included statements such as "I appreciated your personal involvement with me," "Insightful comments on my paper," "Sensitive responses to comments and ideas in my papers," and "Particularly nurturing and validating comments on papers."

## Encouraging Multiple Perspectives

The fourth constructivist theme of the course lies in evoking and offering multiple perspectives on ideas and situations. For example, during most of the interviews, at least two students (perhaps four, if they work in pairs) interview a single child or adolescent. This means that opportunities exist to observe multiple reactions to a single experience. The follow-up discussions routinely include divergent assessments of those who were interviewed. The "age panels" also underscore individual differences and perceptions. Even though each panel generally represents remarkable commonality regarding developmental concerns, panelists may articulate widely varying views on the aging process, on relationship issues, on what is "normal," on family-of-origin contributions to developmental concerns, and even on what it is like to be 10 (or 20, 40, or 65) years old. Considerable variation may be evident within each age group regarding development and life experience.

### Just One Perspective Among Many

Because we invest heavily in hearing student voices and valuing multiple perspectives, we hope that our own perspectives become just one among many. We try not to present ourselves as authorities, no matter how much we have studied a particular area. The theorists that we study also add their various perspectives. Based on his clinical experience, the author of our textbook one year (Rice, 1997) often included personal comments in addition to documented information. The students appeared to feel freer to argue with his opinions than with the cited research. Interestingly, even though the text served as an authoritative framework for the course, students' willingness to dispute it helped the textbook become just another perspective that semester, one with potential value like all perspectives in class, but one that could be challenged as students constructed meaning.

In order to help students see our perspective or the textbook's perspective as one among many, we try to laud students for insights and commend them for risk taking when they express divergent views in response to readings or panelists and when they are creative in their writing. We also emphasize the phenomenological nature of counseling—including that both counselor's and client's perspectives are affected by a multitude of factors, including cultural lenses (cf. Peterson, 1997, 1999).

### Process Questions

At times, we stop the adult panel discussions and ask process questions of the class: "What was your gut reaction to what she just said?" "What is going on for you right now (e.g., when '40-somethings' are reassessing their career choices)?" "What feelings were evoked (e.g., when a panelist reveals he has already had three heart attacks at age 43)?" "What is it like to witness this clever bantering (in a panel of individuals over age 60)?" "Give these folks some feedback about how you are responding to their sharing so much." Even during energetic discussions among class members, we sometimes stop and ask process questions, communicating that their thoughts and experiences are valuable and underscoring the wide variety of intrapersonal experiences in the class. We also mean to enhance their ability to monitor their own thoughts and feelings during future interactions with clients.

### Interpersonal Connections

Heightened intrapersonal awareness enhances the interpersonal connections in class, especially as students gain confidence in expressing themselves and can validate their own experiences and perspectives. We are interested in these connections at two levels: building community for the sake of comfortable communication and personal growth, and parallel learning about group interaction for the sake of professional development. Class discussion, especially during debriefings after hands-on experiences, regularly addresses the interpersonal dynamics of the groups we interact with and even of the graduate class itself. We inject systemic observations of a classroom we visited, a group of at-risk teens, or a group of retirees. We want them to become sensitive observers of group dynamics, of nonverbal behavior, and of communication sequences. We also hope that they can learn "how to listen, how to hear one another" (hooks, 1994, p. 150). Students frequently include comments in their final papers about their interpersonal styles and roles at various developmental stages, and about their struggles with differentiation issues (cf. Bowen, 1978). For this we give credit to their raised awareness of interpersonal dynamics and the social "embeddedness" that Kegan (1982) describes.

## Facing Incongruity

The experiential dimensions of the course provide many unsettling inconsistencies and incongruities for students, but incongruity may also suddenly appear among class members themselves. As we become better and better acquainted, and as each student serves as a self-disclosing panel member, we invariably discover complexity within the students themselves. Incongruities also appear when we interact with those we interview. Surprises emerge, especially when interacting with those in the later developmental stages—rejuvenation, resilience, activity, and insights, for example. At first glance, a panel may appear to be a relatively homogeneous, middle-class, educated group. However, they invariably present developmental diversity. Usually guests are articulate and quickly warm up to sharing their experiences and insights with counseling students. However, *because* they present themselves well, revelations concerning childhood poverty, trauma, deprivation, personal loss, or significant health concerns "don't fit" and teach prospective counselors about client surprises.

These interactive experiences, with their multiple perspectives, paradoxes, and incongruities, generate insights that are applied in the final paper. The students have been bombarded with contrasts and contradictions in this complex learning process, and their papers attest to their personal growth and ability to view themselves and others more complexly.

## Valuing Approximation Over Precision

It is comparatively easy to be precise and sure when examining abstract concepts, hypothetical clients, and imaginary (or real, but "digested") cases. It is less easy when sitting cross-legged on the floor with an unkempt and needy six-year-old; sitting across a narrow table from an angry, disenfranchised teenage survivor of abuse; interacting with a panel of 11-year-olds; hearing a middle-aged woman reveal childhood trauma; or interviewing an irascible 80-year-old military retiree in a wheelchair. Contact with real people challenges any belief that counseling is an exact science or that counseling programs will provide recipes for responding to clients.

In their responsive papers, students discuss directions they might explore in a second session, but they are well aware that their hypotheses are tentative and subject to change. The atmosphere of the class moves and shifts, as do the relationships that develop within the class, and these have an impact on the learning that takes place. Class discussion is also a dynamic, recursive process of constructing knowledge. Similarly, when a student wants a prescribed format for the papers, we encourage unique and personal expression to match the unique situations and developing lives that are represented. For essay questions on tests, hoping to encourage awareness of King and Kitchener's (1994) sixth and seventh stages, we try to de-emphasize the idea of "right answers," giving credit for well-reasoned arguments, even if they disagree with the textbook or other sources. Our clinical examples might include references to directions taken without suggesting that they were the only possibilities.

## Modeling Incompleteness

We chose counseling as a career because we wanted to immerse ourselves in a field in which we would never "arrive" or be bored. We have accumulated enough experience that we can approach a new client and each counseling session with some degree of confidence that we will be able to respond appropriately and help clients live more effectively. Every client teaches us, and we are fascinated by how we are continually informed about human nature and human development. But counselors have moments of great doubt, and there is not always someone available to ask for assistance. Like our clients, we are human; we are "becoming." We comment on our humanness now and then in order to help alleviate student anxiety. We model error, glaringly at times, as when we ask poor-quality questions of panelists or respond clumsily. Students see us accept our own ineptitude.

Our high tolerance for ambiguity is probably apparent in how we set up this course each year. We comment in class about the uncertainty that we experience, often reminding students that uncertainty also exists when a counselor anticipates a session with a client. But the complexity, and the fact that the content is always new, helps to generate energy in us, which we assume has a positive effect on the experience of students. We hope that we are modeling that not being sure can be both alright and energizing.

Near the end of the course, usually after the final papers are submitted, students seem to feel less burdened by the intensity of the course and begin to comment about its administrative complexity. We seize that opportunity to repeat the explanation of our teaching methodology. Those students with a high need for structure and order, who may never have quit wishing for lectures on the textbook, may be more relieved than the others that the course is nearly done. However, usually they now recognize the value of the experiential, open-ended nature of the course. We process their experience.

## REFLECTIONS ON OUR EXPERIENCES TEACHING HUMAN GROWTH AND DEVELOPMENT

Not everything we have tried in Human Growth and Development has been effective, and each semester we try new approaches in the interest of improvement. As varied as the format and methodology have been, not all learning styles and developmental levels have been accommodated with adequate balance, and strategies meant to foster accountability regarding textbook reading (quizzes, for instance) have not always been perceived as valuable. We continue to try to devise effective ways to encourage faithful reading, particularly through intrinsic means.

Because many opportunities exist in this course for written expression and personalized learning, and because we want to accommodate students whose learning preferences and cognitive development contribute to their comfort with an exam format, we continue to use multiple-choice and short-answer questions for about half of the midterm and final examinations. The other half of the exams consists of fairly open-ended essay questions. Most of the "objective" questions require more than simple recall. Nevertheless, we continue to try to devise more personalized ways of assessing familiarity with established literature in the field.

The responsive writing, according to most, has been valuable, but is "too much writing" for some students. The guest groups have always received high marks, but the field trips have been uncomfortable and stressful for a few students. No matter how much we present a rationale for the experiential dimension, there are some students, perhaps those representing Perry's (1970) first three positions or the received knowledge of Belenky et al. (1986), who do not agree that the interaction with "developing" people is important. However, these students' resistance, or their reticence, has not deterred us from approaching human development with this particular format. We do our best to nurture them toward greater tolerance for ambiguity, and we encourage them to process their frustrations both in and out of class.

Only once have I (Peterson) experienced a class that demonstrated, as I perceived it, considerable collective resistance to the field experiences. That year I had an unusually small class (eight students), all age 22 or 23 except one, who was 26. I still have many questions about what made the experience more difficult and less positive that year, although I suspect that the age homogeneity, developmental level, and personality structure of the students all played a part.

The format and methodology of this course demand intense personal involvement from everyone. An atmosphere of sustained interpersonal engagement exists, much like what hooks (1994) describes as fluid movement among the various parts of the experience. The substantial involvement, responsibility, and creativity required of the teacher and the students create a developmentally powerful system (cf. Astin, 1985). Perhaps as a result of the nature of the learning, student-to-student and student-to-teacher bonding develops more significantly in this course than in other courses that we teach. Students become something different from what they once were: They understand themselves, human development, and the counseling relationship better at the end than they did at the outset. They have been exposed to social complexity (cf. Labouvie-Vief, 1984) and have *made sense* of the experience, in Loevinger's (1976) terms. They have moved along the continuum of becoming a counselor.

One of the most profound comments made by a student at the end of the class was, "It feels as though this class is with me everywhere I go," and he then gave examples. It seemed that the class had expanded beyond its boundaries, becoming personally relevant in many different life circumstances and becoming ingrained in the student's way of knowing himself and the world. As a result of being part of this tremendously growth-producing and alive experience, we feel very much alive ourselves as counselor educators, continually prodded into growth.

# REFERENCES

Astin, A. W. (1985). *Achieving educational excellence: A critical assessment of priorities and practices in higher education.* San Francisco: Jossey-Bass.

Belenky, M. F., Clinchy, B. M., Goldberger, N. R., & Tarule, J. M. (1986). *Women's ways of knowing: The development of self, voice, and mind.* New York: Basic Books.

Bowen, M. (1978). *Family therapy in clinical practice.* New York: Jason Aronson.

Chickering, A. W. (1969). *Education and identity.* San Francisco: Jossey-Bass.

Delworth, U., & Hanson, G. R. (1989). *Student services: A handbook for the profession* (2nd ed.). San Francisco: Jossey-Bass.

Erikson, E. H. (1980). *Identity and the life cycle.* New York: Routledge.

Giroux, H. (1981). *Ideology, culture, and the process of schooling.* Philadelphia: Temple University Press.

Helms, J. E. (1995). An update of Helms's white and people of color racial identity models. In J. G. Ponterotto, J. M. Casas, L. A. Suzuki, & C. M. Alexander (Eds.), *Handbook of multicultural counseling* (pp. 181–191). Thousand Oaks, CA: Sage.

hooks, b. (1994). *Teaching to transgress: Education as the practice of freedom.* New York: Routledge.

Kegan, R. (1982). *The evolving self: Problem and process in human development.* Cambridge, MA: Harvard University Press.

Kegan, R. (1998). *In over our heads: The mental demands of modern life.* Cambridge, MA: Harvard University Press.

King, P. M. (1996). Student cognition and learning. In S. R. Komives & D. B. Woodard, Jr. (Eds.), *Student services: A handbook for the profession* (3rd ed., pp. 218–243). San Francisco: Jossey-Bass.

King, P. M., & Kitchener, K. S. (1994). *Developing reflective judgment: Understanding and promoting intellectual growth and critical thinking in adolescents and adults.* San Francisco: Jossey-Bass.

Kohlberg, L. (1981). *The philosophy of moral development.* New York: Harper & Row.

Kolb, D. (1984). *Experiential learning: Experience as the source of learning and development.* Englewood Cliffs, NJ: Prentice Hall.

Labouvie-Vief, G. (1984). Logic and self-regulation from youth to maturity: A model. In M. L. Commons, F. A. Richards, & C. Armon (Eds.), *Beyond formal operations: Late adolescence and adult cognitive development* (pp. 158–179). New York: Praeger.

Lamborn, S. D., & Fischer, K. W. (1988). Optimal and functional levels in cognitive development: The individual's developmental range. *Newsletter of the International Society for the Study of Behavioral Development, 14*(2), 1–4.

Loevinger, J. (1976). *Ego development: Conceptions and theories.* San Francisco: Jossey-Bass.

McMillan, J. H., & Forsyth, D. R. (1991). What theories of motivation say about why learners learn. In R. J. Menges & M. D. Svinicki (Eds.), *College teaching: From theory to practice* (New Directions for Teaching and Learning No. 45, pp. 39–52). San Francisco: Jossey-Bass.

Moore, W. S. (1989). The learning environment preferences: Exploring the construct validity of an objective measure of the Perry scheme of intellectual development. *Journal of College Student Development, 30,* 504–514.

Perry, W. G. (1970). *Forms of intellectual and ethical development in the college years: A scheme.* New York: Holt, Rinehart & Winston.

Perry, W. G. (1981). Cognitive and ethical growth: The making of meaning. In A. W. Chickering (Eds.), *The modern American college: Responding to the new realities of diverse students and a changing society* (pp. 76–116). San Francisco: Jossey-Bass.

Peterson, J. S. (1993). *Talk with teens about self and stress.* Minneapolis, MN: Free Spirit.

Peterson, J. S. (1995). *Talk with teens about feelings, family, relationships, and the future.* Minneapolis, MN: Free Spirit.

Peterson, J. S. (1997). Naming gifted children: An example of unintended "reproduction." *Journal for the Education of the Gifted, 21,* 82–100.

Peterson, J. S. (1999). Gifted—through whose cultural lens? An application of the postpositivistic mode of inquiry. *Journal for the Education of the Gifted, 22,* 354–383.

Piaget, J. (1965). The moral judgment of the child (Trans. M. Gabain). New York: Free Press. (Original work published 1932)

Rest, J., & Narvaez, D. (Eds.). (1999). *Moral development in the professions: Psychology and applied ethics.* Hillsdale, NJ: Lawrence Erlbaum.

Rice, F. P. (1997). *Human development: A lifespan approach.* Englewood Cliffs, NJ: Prentice Hall.

Riegel, K. (1973). Dialectic operations: The final period of cognitive development. *Human Development, 16,* 346–370.

Sanford, N. (1967). *Where colleges fail: A study of the student as a person.* San Francisco: Jossey-Bass.

Schön, D. (1987). *Educating the reflective practitioner.* San Francisco: Jossey-Bass.

Wadsworth, B. J. (1979). *Piaget's theory of cognitive development* (2nd ed.). New York: Longman.

Widick, C., Parker, C. A., & Knefelkamp, L. (1978). Erik Erikson and psychosocial development. In L. Knefelkamp, C. Widick, & C. A. Parker (Eds.), *Applying new developmental findings* (New Directions for Student Services No. 4, pp. 1–17). San Francisco: Jossey-Bass.

Witkin, H. A. (1976). Cognitive style in academic performance and in teacher-student relations. In S. Messick (Eds.), *Individuality in learning* (pp. 38–72). San Francisco: Jossey-Bass.

Yalom, I. D. (1997). *The theory and practice of group psychotherapy.* New York: Basic Books.

# 14

# Teaching Career Development

Judy Emmett and Garrett J. McAuliffe

In the constructivist paradigm, human beings are, by nature, self-organizing creatures (Peavy, 1992, 1994), as opposed to stimulus-response organisms, information processors, or sets of traits. Individuals make sense of their lives through continuous reflection upon their experiences. It is the task of the career counselor to help the client make sense of those experiences in relation to life role choices. And it is the task of the career counselor educator to evoke the counselor's role in the construction of career.

From the constructivist lens (Hansen, 1997; Peavy, 1992, 1995; Savickas, 1993), career is much more than a job or an objective chronology of one's job history. It can be described as the telling of a life story, an internal and subjective narrative (Bateson, 1990; Cochran, 1992; Peavy, 1993), rather than an objective chronology of a person's job history. This subjectivist emphasis is iterated, for instance, by Peavy (1995), who has described career as an "evolving biographical narrative under continuous revision" (p. 2). Similarly, Miller-Tiedeman (1987) suggests that everyone has a career—it is one's life.

But career has not always been viewed this way. For three quarters of a century, career counseling was presented as a process of "true reasoning" by which a person's traits were matched to the requirements of an occupation (Parsons, 1909). People coming to career counselors were viewed primarily as combinations of psychometric traits to be measured and matched to single best occupations;

the counselor served the role of expert technician. In this view, counselors alone had the knowledge, thus the power, to enable clients to identify the best occupational choices (Peavy, 1993; Savickas, 1993).

Constructivists, however, emphasize the role of individual meaning-makers in creating their own reality through continuous reflection upon their unique life experiences. Thus, constructivist career counseling assumes a more facilitative, collaborative, less directive focus. Instead of counselors having the power, they empower clients (Hoskins, 1995). Constructivist career counselors help clients discern patterns, hence meaning, from previous life experiences and assist them with understanding and giving voice to their emerging life stories. Clients become able to make decisions and to extend or modify their life stories because of new understandings about what has influenced their choices and about what meaning they have ascribed to past experiences. Cochran (1992) describes constructivist career counselors as coauthors of stories in progress.

According to Peavy (1992, 1993), constructivist career counselors value multiple realities, believing that there is no one right way to see the world and no one best way to go about constructing or interpreting one's life story. Constructivist counselors, therefore, value dialogue that enhances both their own understanding of the client's perspective and the client's understanding of her or his own world. During such dialogue, the counselor listens for and reflectively questions the internal learning and meaning-making processes of the client. Counselors help clients recognize the impact and the constraints of their individual contexts and cultures upon both their experiences and their interpretations of those experiences. During dialogue, constructivist career counselors remain authentically present to their clients and create counseling environments that balance both the security and the challenge necessary for growth. Such dialogue promotes the understanding that empowers and informs future choice making.

Peavy (1994) proposes that effective constructivist career counselors possess specific competencies. The first is *mindfulness:* the ability to observe oneself, to understand oneself as a constructed(ing) person, with a personal "life career" story composed of personally and socially constructed interpretations, assumptions, and biases. To the extent that counselors are mindful, they attend to a client without imposing their own meanings or direction onto the client's emerging life story. The second competency is *receptive inquiry:* creating a climate in which clients feel safe when being respectfully questioned about their assumptions and interpretations of past experiences. Counselors empower clients to critically examine their actions, their beliefs, and the contextual influences on their thinking, their choices, and their lives. The third competency is *meaning-making facilitation:* possessing a repertoire of strategies and skills necessary to assist clients in discovering themes, patterns, and meanings ascribed to their life stories.

Counselor education, then, needs to instigate experiences that are likely to encourage the development in future counselors of mindfulness, receptive inquiry, and meaning-making facilitation. In general, constructivist career counselor educators should provide safe and challenging learning environments in which students can reflect upon their own career stories and understand the experiences and influences that have shaped and will continue to shape them as counselors. In the process, they can themselves learn to be mindful and thus become able to encourage future clients to do the same.

In addition to such personal career reflection, students also need opportunities to engage in actual career counseling and reflect upon their interpretation of those experiences, in order to recognize the emerging meanings they are making as prospective career counselors. They learn through these experiences how to use career theories, career assessments, and career information resources. They thus experience and practice techniques that promote receptive inquiry and meaning-making (Peavy, 1994).

This chapter describes how the traditional elements of a career counseling course—such as the teaching of career theory, career assessment, career information resources, and the career counseling process—might be viewed through a constructivist lens. We offer selected learning activities and assignments that might be useful for the education of constructivist career counselors. The chapter concludes with reflections on the value of a constructivist approach for the training of career counselors. We therein propose that constructivist career counseling is, in fact, the most relevant approach to contemporary career counseling in the context of current socioeconomic and workplace realities. Table 14.1 summarizes the objectives, content, activities, and constructivist principles represented in the career course as we have developed it.

**TABLE 14.1** Course Objectives, Content, Activities, and Constructivist Principles

| Learning Objectives | Content | Activities and Processes | Constructivist Principles |
|---|---|---|---|
| Understand and stay open to diverse assumptions and experiences that influence people's construction of career. | Career as construction<br>Discovery/class process | Case exploration exercise<br>Instructor anecdote<br>StoryTech 1<br>Guidelines presented<br>Self-reflection | Career as the telling of a life story, an internal and subjective narrative<br>Evolving biographical narrative under continuous revision<br>Creating one's own reality through continuous reflection upon unique life experiences<br>Help clients discern patterns, hence meaning, from previous life experiences and assist them with understanding and giving voice to their life stories |

| Learning Objectives | Content | Activities and Processes | Constructivist Principles |
|---|---|---|---|
| Assess central themes, patterns, or contexts in personal/client history. | Constructivist vs. objectivist assessment<br><br>Assessment tools<br><br>Lifelong decision-making strategies | Take Self-Directed Search or other career assessments<br><br>Discussions about constructivist understandings and uses of assessments with clients<br><br>Collaborative exploration in dyads, with observers<br><br>Role plays of collaborations, feedback from class on metacognitions/metalogue<br><br>Laddering exercise<br><br>StoryTech 4<br><br>Audio- or video-record collaborative discussion of assessment with client<br><br>Critique of peer recording | Coauthors of stories in progress<br><br>Value multiple realities<br><br>Value dialogue<br><br>Question the internal learning and meaning-making processes of the client<br><br>Create counseling environments that balance both the security and the challenge necessary for growth |
| Develop skills and understanding of roles of career counselor. | | StoryTech 3 | Instigate experiences to encourage the development of mindfulness, receptive inquiry, and meaning-making facilitation in future counselors |
| Understand and effectively utilize/deconstruct usefulness of career theory in counseling and designing programs. | Career patterns<br><br>Decision making<br><br>Planning<br><br>Self-efficacy<br><br>Development | Career interview<br><br>Discussion/comparison of results<br><br>Application of career theory to interviewees and interviewers (classroom discussion)<br><br>Life story written about interviewee, with plan for counseling | Value approximation<br><br>See conflict (among theories) as a norm<br><br>Emphasize experience |
| Effectively use occupational information. | Career information sources<br><br>Assumptions about their uses | Grab bag exercise<br><br>Role play career counselors<br><br>Case study—proposal for information sources<br><br>Application to life story<br><br>Story Tech 5 and reflection | Deconstruct theories<br><br>Value experience |
| Develop identity of career counselor. | | Story Tech 6 and reflection | |

# INTRODUCTORY SESSION IN A CONSTRUCTIVIST CAREER COUNSELING COURSE

The introductory session, as we have structured it, sets the tone for the rest of the semester. In summary, the session begins with a case exploration exercise. The instructor then shares a personal and illustrative story from her or his experiences as a career counselor. Subsequently, the instructor reviews classroom guidelines and then introduces StoryTech, a narrative technique that students use throughout the course.

## Case Exploration Exercise

The career counseling course begins by immediately exploring a case instead of presenting an introductory lecture. This activity exposes students to multiple ways of viewing career issues and the career counseling process. It is an inductive strategy for helping students create knowledge as a group. They identify their "natural" approach to career counseling as only one of several possible approaches by working on one of the cases described in texts such as *Developmental Career Counseling and Assessment* (Seligman, 1994). In response to the case, they individually define what they believe to be the career issue(s) for the person described in the case, imagine what a desirable outcome would be for the client, and plan what they would do as counselors to facilitate that outcome. Students consider how differences and similarities between themselves and the client in race, ethnicity, gender, socioeconomic background, age, sexual orientation, or physical or mental ability might affect their thinking about or working with this client. Students then meet in small groups to discuss their thinking.

Finally, the instructor leads the whole class in a discussion of the approaches taken and the strategies chosen, and what these indicate about the meanings of career, career counseling, and the roles and strategies of the career counselor. During the discussion, the instructor highlights the multiplicity of approaches that were named and that are possible. The instructor guides the students to reflect on how their past experiences may have influenced them to construct their current ideas about career and career counseling (Peavy, 1995).

## Instructor Anecdote

Next in this first session, I (Emmett) further introduce the course with a personal story, allowing students to see me as a colearner along with them, a career counselor-in-process. This story illustrates the importance of career counselors knowing the meanings that they have ascribed to career and knowing, and that these meanings have been constructed out of their interpretations of events, events that have occurred within the personal and sociocultural contexts of their lives.

As I share in this case, I had originally constructed a definition of career that gave high priority to the values of independent choice and personal fulfillment. I attempted to assist a second-generation Asian male student choose a college major based on these same values. This student came from a family in which the eldest son was expected to choose an occupation that would begin the family legacy in the United States. Because of that cultural value, my approach to helping him make an independent choice based on what he found most fulfilling was disrespectful and counterproductive. At that time, I did not understand that the personal meanings that I had ascribed to career were not universal and that my role as a career counselor was to help clients clarify the meaning of their *own* life stories.

## Sharing the Constructivist Approach

I (Emmett) share with the class that, in hindsight, I see that I did not serve this student well. I tell students that I have structured their career counseling class with the hope that they will learn *not* to do what I did. However, I acknowledge that I can only present them with ideas and with the opportunities for experiences and for reflection upon those experiences. I cannot give them the knowledge or the skills that they will use as counselors. They must, and they will, construct that knowledge and those skills themselves, through experience, reflection, conceptualization, and experimentation (see discussion of Kolb in Chapter 2). The final entry on the class syllabus sums up this philosophy: "It is my belief that although I can introduce and present to you in this class potentially relevant information and techniques, it is only through your interaction with the ideas and the skills presented that you will be able to construct personally and professionally relevant knowledge and skills. I look forward to working with you in this process."

Because the personal exploration that is structured into this course requires a classroom atmosphere of both challenge and support, the instructor also offers students a list of classroom guidelines during the introductory class session. These guidelines, adapted from *Counselor Education for the Twenty-First Century* (Brotherton, 1996), encourage students to respect other people and their positions and to maintain an open mind in seriously considering perspectives different from their own. The guidelines acknowledge the courage needed to explore one's own beliefs as well as to consider those of other students, and the resistance and discomfort that they may expect to experience from time to time. Finally, the guidelines express the expectation that students will be active participants in the work of the group and that they will treat confidentially what is shared during that work. Such guidelines help to establish a climate for the honest reflection and authentic dialogue that is needed to create a learning community. Our modifications of Brotherton's guidelines are included in Appendix A to this chapter.

## Written Visualizations

The final activity of the first class session is the introductory experience with StoryTech. The title of the experience is the term created by professor and futurist Arthur Harkins of the University of Minnesota to describe a structured visioning process. Each StoryTech instrument consists of a series of open-ended lead statements. Students respond to these leads by creating visualized stories. Such stories feature the student writers telling their own life story, enjoying a perfect day, identifying troublesome career beliefs, confronting personal feelings about the career future and the overwhelming array of career information available, and functioning effectively as a career counselor with clients. This technique, and its use in a career counseling class, has been described in detail elsewhere (Emmett & Harkins, 1997).

Throughout this course, students complete written visualizations. They then respond to a series of reflective questions designed to illuminate themes or patterns in their stories and to project how their personal beliefs may both help and hinder their work with some clients. Students examine their stories for insights into their personal views on life, on work, and on career. They reflect on how their unique life experiences as persons of a particular race, gender, class, culture, sexual orientation, or age have influenced those views. In addition, they reflect on how their particular experiences and viewpoints influence how they view career counseling and how they imagine they will themselves do career counseling. Finally, students identify areas in which to seek feedback from their classmates.

In the initial StoryTech experience, students describe themselves as children, recalling how they dealt with significant life events, and then characterize their approach to life as the title of a book. In reflecting on their stories, students look for central themes and for indications of contexts in which they will likely be helpful (or not) to their future clients. Appendices B–F at the end of the chapter present several StoryTechs and their accompanying reflection questions.

Classmates meet every two to three weeks in the same reflection group of two to four students to share their StoryTechs. They both give and receive feedback about how they view the role of a career counselor and how they are likely to interact with clients in a career counseling setting. At the end of the semester, students write essays in which they synthesize their life (career) stories. They reflect how their own life stories will affect how they practice as career counselors, incorporating what they have learned about themselves as counselors throughout the semester.

## TEACHING CAREER THEORY

A central feature of a career counseling course is the teaching of career theory. Theories about career patterns, decision making, planning, self-efficacy, and development attempt to explain patterns that students might look for in counseling individuals and designing programs. There is also a more hidden reason for examining several prominent career theories. Deconstructing theories can illustrate the constructed nature of knowledge. When comparing career theorists' ideas and explanations about people's career lives, students become aware that no one "best" or "perfect" explanation exists for how people make career decisions or integrate their life roles. Further, when students examine the historical and individual contexts in which the career theorists developed their theories, they find out how the varied life experiences of theorists and the theorists' varied interpretations of those experiences resulted in the construction of different career theories. Each theory potentially offers some important understandings; no theory completely explains career choice or career development for all people. Each theory is both skewed and incomplete.

The recognition of how careers and career theories are constructed can ultimately affect how students go about actual counseling. First, students can extend this realization about the construction of career theory into their work with clients. They can also become aware of the career theory(ies) by which they themselves operate. Finally, they can become alert to the informal career theories that have already been constructed by their clients.

## Discovering Theory Through Career Interviews

The major vehicle for a personalized, experiential approach to teaching career theories is to have students engage in career interviews. Students are directed to ask a family member, friend, neighbor, or classmate simply how she or he thinks about career. They may further ask interviewees any questions that they wish to ask or may engage in any topic of discussion that seems relevant to career. Students then bring the results of these interviews back to class and share them with classmates. We discuss and reflect upon similarities and differences in responses to similar questions and what they might mean about both the questioner and the person questioned.

Students examine these interviews through the lenses of different career theories (e.g., typological, developmental, existential, decision making, behavioral, social cognitive, information processing, value-based) to determine the usefulness of their theories in their work with particular clients. Students discover that they almost always favor some theoretical views more than others. They also begin to understand that clients too operate from belief systems that more closely resemble those of one theorist over another.

Finally, when students examine the interview questions they chose or the topics of discussion they chose to pursue, they begin to see how their choice of focus reveals their implicit career theories. When they intentionally change focus in successive interviews, they begin to appreciate how they are, in fact, choosing different career theories with which to work. They are in the process of constructing working theories based on their current experiences.

The final assignment for the theory section of the course is for students to tell the life story of their interviewee. Then, from the points of view of several theorists, they explain the client's career development and how a counselor would use each particular theory to work with

the client. Finally, they choose elements of two theories to direct their work with that client, reflecting on how their own social identity (race, gender, age, class, etc.) might influence their choice of theories and their work with that client. Thus, they synthesize and evaluate the various career theories and integrate selected elements of the theories with strategies for using them in a constructivist manner with clients.

# TEACHING CAREER ASSESSMENT

Perhaps nowhere else is the distinction between an objectivist (logical positivist) and a constructivist (postmodern) approach to career counseling clearer than in the arena of career assessment. An objectivist view of assessment assumes that the counselor can evaluate or measure the client from the outside. In that frame, a client becomes a set of scores or psychometric traits that allow a counselor to tell the client where she or he "fits" into the world of work. In contrast, a constructivist career counselor considers assessment techniques or strategies to be only one source of information for heightening self-awareness and empowerment for clients, one strategy for helping clients clarify who they are as whole persons, where they find meaning in life, and where they belong (Savickas, 1993).

Further, an objectivist approach to career assessment tends to focus quantitatively on how much of a trait a client possesses or how strong that trait is relative to other traits. In contrast, the constructivist career counselor helps clients make choices based on the implications of their beliefs, values, interests, and abilities. Peavy (1996) describes constructivist career assessment as an intervention that is aimed at increasing clients' capacities to reconstruct their life stories. Clients thus use the results of their assessments to reflect upon and to explore future choices that make sense in terms of their whole lives. In essence, then, constructivist career counselors view career assessment as a collaborative counselor-client project that has the goal of clarifying clients' self-related constructs (what clients "know" about self and work) as those constructs relate to the plot of their whole life stories.

During the assessment segment of the course, students read the article "Reforming Career Appraisals to Meet the Needs of Clients in the 1990s" (Healy, 1990) to discover the contrasts between traditional (objectivist) and reformed (constructivist) approaches to career assessment. This article is still relevant today, 20 years later. In it, Healy contrasts both the goals and the roles of the counselor in these two approaches to career assessment. Healy's discussion of how the role of the counselor changes in reformed appraisal depending upon the needs of the client can be especially helpful to students. Further, he describes how, in traditional assessment, the counselor *explains to* a client the results of the assessment. By contrast, in reformed appraisal, counselor and client *collaborate on* (i.e., construct together) the meaning of the assessment for that particular client. Similarly, traditional counselors *report scores* (i.e., the traits measured by the assessment instrument), while constructivist counselors *help clients explore the contexts of their lives* that might explain these particular trends. They explore with clients how changes in life circumstances might result in different scores. In traditional assessment, counselors help clients *translate the scores into immediate occupational choices.* In reformed appraisal, counselors assist in that matchmaking and *empower clients to learn how to assess their own abilities, values, and interests, and how to use such self-assessment in a process of lifelong decision making.* In a variation on looking at test summary scores, counseling students are also taught to help clients examine individual test items in order to see how their responses influenced the results. This method challenges the objectivist authority of statistics-based test results, relativizing them as a product of the client's own subjective choices.

In addition to using traditional testing as a springboard for interpretation, constructivist career counselors often utilize assessment techniques that are, in themselves, constructivist by nature. For instance, Peavy (1996) suggests using such self-assessment activities as journaling, autobiography, and a technique called *conceptual mapping.* In conceptual mapping, clients indicate "self" in a circle in the center of a page. They proceed to fill in this page with the persons, events, and experiences that are significant in relation to their current career concerns. Finally, they draw "maps" indicating the relationships between and among these elements and the self. These maps become graphic representations of the meaning, hence the power, of these elements on the career decision-making process.

Other constructivist career assessment tools have been described by Forster (1992). They include portfolios and a tool he named Goals Review and Organizing Workbook (GROW). In GROW, clients identify several meaningful past activities or events. They then cluster these events into "like" groups. Clients proceed to write goals based on these personal constructs, to prioritize these goals, and finally to rate the activities in which they are currently engaged according to how well they match the goals derived from their most meaningful personal constructs. This process parallels the self-help approach to skills clustering that has been popularized by Bolles (2007).

Another constructivist assessment technique is Neimeyer's (1992) version of Kelly's (1955) Role Construct Repertory Test, which Neimeyer calls *career laddering.* In this activity, clients participate in a structured interview in which they reveal the relative importance of work-related constructs. Neimeyer gives the example of a client who identified three occupations of interest—teacher, paramedic, and musician. The client then located a way in which two of these were like each other but were different from the third. She identified teacher and musician as similar (in that they were, to her, "more creative") and different from paramedic (which she described as "more technical"). She then discovered that she preferred a creative rather than a technical occupation. And the interview continued.

Other clients selecting the same three occupations might choose teacher and paramedic as similar because they are service occupations, or musicians and paramedics because they have mathematical skills, or teaching as requiring less constant risk taking than the occupations of musician or paramedic. As clients reflect on which of the identified dimensions they prefer, they reveal personal constructs that are significant for their career decisions. Neimeyer (1993), in *Constructivist Assessment: A Casebook*, offers more specific details and examples of these constructivist techniques and describes additional constructivist assessments and techniques.

Whether the particular assessment technique consists of a test, a narrative, or another experience, the purpose of all constructivist assessment techniques can be characterized in three ways: to elicit (1) clients' personal constructs related to career, (2) the relationship of these constructs to one another, and (3) the relative importance of these constructs to a given client. Thus, counselors assist clients in recognizing ways in which they have organized their career schemas and the effects that such organization has had upon their thoughts, feelings, and dilemmas concerning career.

A constructivist counselor can also use the more conventional assessments in a constructivist manner. For example, a counselor may review the results of the Self-Directed Search (Holland, 1994) collaboratively with a client. The counselor can evoke the story behind these results by interviewing the client about the experiences and influences on the client's life that may explain this current summary of interests and inclinations. The counselor can also review the specific items to evoke the meanings behind them for the client. Together, counselor and client speculate on the future, asking what might happen if the client were to make alternate choices that would provide different experiences and influences. Counselors help clients make meaning of current scores and use them to make the proximate decisions that will influence the next chapter of their life stories.

In class, the instructor can lead the entire class in the constructivist approach described in the preceding paragraph to working with the Self-Directed Search. Initially, the instructor can contrast what a counselor would say to a client if the counselor were following the traditional model of assessment versus the reformed appraisal model (Healy, 1990). The entire class then might review sample Self-Directed Search results and identify possible areas for exploration with that client. As they suggest questions and topics for exploration, the instructor might periodically stop the discussion, asking students to reflect on how the suggested question or topic reveals some of their own assumptions about both career assessment and the role of a career counselor using assessments. Two simultaneous learning processes occur in this fashion. For one, students practice the constructivist use of assessments. At the same time, they also listen to themselves and to each other, thereby becoming sensitive to how their decisions about what to discuss with clients reveal their own beliefs about the role of the career counselor relative to assessment.

Students can also, as part of the course, take both standardized and nonstandardized career assessments themselves. They might complete, for example, the Self-Directed Search, the Strong Interest Inventory (Strong & Hansen, 1994), and the StoryTech in which they write their description of "My Perfect Day." They might then practice working with the results of the Self-Directed Search and the StoryTech in a constructivist manner. To do so, students would follow the writing, reflection, and group feedback procedures described earlier for the StoryTech. Then, in pairs, using the Self-Directed Search results of their StoryTech partner, along with that partner's "My Perfect Day" StoryTech, they would outline topics for collaborative exploration with their partners. They would next proceed to explore themes and discover the meaning that these themes have for that person.

For each student pair working with assessments in this fashion, another student would observe and offer feedback about the success of the student counselor in conducting a reformed (constructivist) career appraisal. When time permits, several student pairs might role play their collaborative assessments for the class, asking for feedback from all class members. The focus of the feedback would be on the metacognitions and the metalogue that occurred between role play partners.

Another way to both introduce a constructivist assessment technique and promote the constructivist education of counselors is to use Neimeyer's (1992) laddering technique in conjunction with the results of an inventory such as the Strong Interest Inventory. As described earlier, in a career laddering activity, a person selects any three career-related items (e.g., assessed occupations, interests) and identifies two of the three as being like each other but different from the third. The person then identifies a quality shared by the first two, but not by the third. Next she or he identifies which quality is preferred and examines this preference. The exercise continues in a similar fashion as students identify some key career constructs and a hierarchy of personal values that reveal how they construct personal meanings and make career choices.

For this activity, students can use the "ladder" with the 10 occupations identified as "most like them" by the Strong Interest Inventory. Although many counseling students commonly select the same occupational titles as one another, what soon becomes evident are the diverse ways in which individual students group these occupations and the multiplicity of perspectives that they use to think about them. Laddering, then, provides another opportunity for counselors-in-training to appreciate differences among people in both perspectives and in the contexts that affect their constructions of meaning. Engaging in this exercise reminds students that unless they are mindful, and unless they are careful to adopt an ongoing attitude of receptive and respectful inquiry toward clients, career assessment results may take on the meanings imposed on them by the counselor.

As a final requirement for the assessment section of the course, students audio- or video-record themselves discussing the results of an assessment with a "client." They critique their own recordings as to how well they have enacted the principles of reformed appraisal. They also listen for indications of the assumptions that they make regarding the nature of career assessments or the role of a career counselor working with assessments. Finally, they critique a peer's taped interview using the same criteria. Students receive grades on their ability to conduct a constructivist assessment (reformed appraisal) as well as on their ability to recognize how their assumptions affect their collaborative assessments with clients.

## TEACHING THE USE OF OCCUPATIONAL INFORMATION

Constructivists do not believe that neutral or objective information can be known. The essence of constructivism is, after all, that people create knowledge by making meaning through reflecting on their experiences, as discussed in the beginning chapters of this book. According to Spokane (1992), the content of occupational information, then, does not determine its power. As he states, "We can no longer reasonably insist that presenting simple information to a client will result in beneficial effects" (p. 230). Rather, it is the processing of the information by the counselor and the client that is most critical and that becomes the focus of constructivist career counseling. Constructivist career counselors concentrate on helping clients make career information personally usable, while not neglecting ongoing attention to the counselors' own career constructs or personal filters that may affect their use of information with clients.

According to Hoskins (1995), counselors disempower clients when they simply dispense information out of context or when they do not help clients learn to access information for themselves. Thus, for constructivist career counselors, the question is not "What information can I give the client?" but rather "How can I help the client acquire and use this information?" This distinction is critical in an era characterized by immense quantities of easily accessible occupational information. The lure of offering occupational information through electronic or computerized sources, in particular, should be modified by the awareness that merely giving clients access to career information is not enough. Clients may attribute authority to the information they receive, especially from computerized systems, that goes beyond the power that this resource should confer. In the case of computerized test results, clients often need a counselor's assistance to deconstruct their attributions, to clarify why they need occupational information, to name what purpose they expect that it will fulfill for them, and to learn how to make their *own* sense of the information accessed.

Deborah Bloch (1989) distinguishes career information from career knowledge. She defines career *information* as the facts or data that people need to know in order to make decisions for their lives. This information may be data about jobs (e.g., salary, preparation needed) or about themselves (e.g., personal abilities, values as they pertain to occupational choices). Data of these types are more or less constantly being presented to people as they go through life. Individuals selectively attend to and attribute value to career data, as they do to all other types of information. In order to process this data into personally relevant career *knowledge,* clients must be able to connect the data to cognitive frameworks, or schemata, that are already in place (i.e., they must assimilate these new bits of information into life stories that are already under construction). In other instances, clients may choose to revise cognitive schemata and rewrite their life stories in order to accommodate significant new information.

Three elements are central to a client's constructing a viable career story. First, to convert objective occupational *information* into personalized career *knowledge,* clients must be self-reflective and self-aware, that is, they need to become aware of the meanings of their life stories. Second, they need to receive sufficient bits of relevant career-related data in usable formats. Finally, clients need to actively integrate isolated bits of career-related data into their life stories. Counselors help clients with the three tasks of (1) clarifying their sense of self, (2) obtaining adequate and relevant career information, and (3) transforming this information into personal career knowledge.

Several instructional strategies help counseling students learn the process of converting occupational information into career knowledge. After students become familiar with multiple occupational information resources, as well as with the principles described by Bloch (1989), students can be led in an information request or "grab bag" exercise. In this activity, students draw out of an envelope requests for occupational information that are frequently heard by career counselors. Typical client requests may include the following: "What's the best school for engineering, and can I still apply to that school for next semester?" "Am I smart enough to go to the university?" "Which jobs are most secure?" "I see lots of job openings for engineering operations analyst. How long does the training for that job take?" "I know I need to go to a good school if I want to get a good job, right? So what's the best school in the state?"

Counseling students take turns reading the requests they have drawn. They then talk about how they might respond to those requests. Students not only identify the information source(s) that they might use to help the clients, but they reflect on what they were thinking about the client request as they made those decisions. Some students focus only on identifying an accurate source for the requested information and authoritatively answering the client with responses such as "The deadline for application to schools can be found in the red file" or "You will need a 26 or better on the ACT to apply to that school" or "You can find the occupational outlook for that field in the *Occupational Outlook Handbook* on the shelf." Other students focus more on the client's experience, seeking to understand the context in which the request for information was made. As each student responds, the instructor asks the other students to note assumptions about the roles of the career counselor that are implied by the focus of the student's response.

In a variation on this exercise, counseling students role play career counselors who have varying core values. The instructor asks, "If a career counselor has a core value of 'helping,' how might that affect her or his use of information with a client?" and "If a counselor has a core value of 'knowledge,' or of 'respect,' how might these values affect the decisions the counselor might make about which information sources to use and how to use those sources with a client?" This exercise helps students reflect on the constructed nature of their own career knowledge and behavior and the effects that their constructions may have on clients.

In another exercise on the use of occupational information, groups of students receive a career counseling case and put together a proposal for both the types of information that they would use with the client and how they would go about helping the client convert the information into usable career knowledge. As the different groups report on their proposals, the instructor attends to the meaning of the differences in both the information sources recommended and the counseling approaches taken.

As the final assignment for this section of the course, students identify examples of both occupational information and career knowledge for the "client" whose life story they told in their first essay (i.e., the assignment referred to in the Teaching Career Theory section). They then prepare a list of occupational information resources that they would use with that client, justifying their choice based on the individual life story and the unique needs of the client. Finally, students outline how they would use the information in such a way as to help clients convert the information into usable career knowledge.

## CONCLUSION

Teaching constructivist career counseling can be isomorphic with the work of career counseling itself. Career counseling has been characterized as essentially a process of instigating client discovery (Spokane, 1992). Career counselors assist clients in examining the beliefs and the constructs they have used to create meaning in their lives. Counselors additionally help clients hypothesize alternative constructs, test out those constructs, and develop action plans for implementing the constructs that promise to be useful in extending or rewriting their life stories. The constructivist teaching of career counseling follows the same process. Counseling students examine the beliefs and constructs that they have about themselves as career counselors. They experience the diversity of constructs about career counseling held by their peers. They have the opportunity during the class to hypothesize alternative constructs and to test the effects that those alternate constructs have upon their conduct of career counseling sessions. As they learn to examine their own career-related constructs, they learn the process of helping clients do likewise.

Throughout the course, students have the opportunity to observe career counseling being demonstrated by the instructor and by peers. They visualize themselves doing career counseling using the StoryTech method. They role play career counseling sessions, and they record themselves conducting actual career counseling interviews and reformed appraisal (constructivist assessment) sessions. In each of these activities, they have opportunities for self-reflection and chances to both give and receive feedback to and from both instructors and peers. The instructor encourages them to become mindful and to develop skills for receptive inquiry, which will in turn help them understand how people create meaning and purpose for themselves, that is, how people develop coherent life stories. Students learn constructivist career counseling skills, then, through constructivist learning experiences. They experience multiple perspectives with the resulting conflict and dialectic among perspectives. They learn through experience and reflection on those experiences. They focus on the metacognitions and metalogue within and among themselves. In the face of their changing constructs of themselves as career counselors, they commit to pictures of themselves as career counselors that are stable enough to be represented in their current career portfolios, yet flexible enough to allow for continued development throughout their professional careers as constructivist (career) counselors.

## SOME FINAL REFLECTIONS

Teaching career counseling in a constructivist fashion has many advantages. A major advantage lies in the personal relevance of the constructivist paradigm to career counseling students, as all counseling students have careers themselves. This personalized dimension brings the material alive and makes the constructivist mode easily understandable.

A further advantage lies in the ease of access that students have to clients: Most people, such as neighbors, friends, and classmates, are happy to talk to career counseling students about their lives and their work and how they have come to make the choices that they have made. Therefore, ample opportunity exists for multiple experiences and perspectives to be brought into the career class. The class then provides the opportunity and the structure for reflection upon those experiences and perspectives. Through experience, students learn to see themselves and others as unique individuals who are influenced by their cultural backgrounds and the contexts in which they construct their life stories.

Constructivist career counseling has a further advantage in its synchronicity with the demands of a 21st-century ethos, one in which intellectual and cultural diversity are pervasive. In that vein, constructivism encourages counselors to become competent with clientele who hold differing worldviews, a necessity in meeting today's mental health needs. Career clients' worldviews profoundly affect their lives and their career decisions; these worldviews may be very different from those of their counselors. To avoid inappropriately imposing their own worldviews on their clients, counselors need to recognize those worldviews as well as the implications that these have for how counselors do career counseling. A constructivist education that values multiple perspectives and that teaches the skills of mindfulness and receptive inquiry makes that more likely.

A final advantage lies in the applicability of a constructivist approach for social change. Some years ago, Peavy (1993) proposed that the constructivist approach to counseling, and especially to career counseling, was the most appropriate response in a postindustrial society characterized by rapid, unpredictable change. In other words, in a society in which all (objective) "truths" about life and career are being called into question, constructivism is a viable paradigm. He suggested that people would, by necessity, continually define and redefine who they are, where they fit, and what meaning they ascribe to their lives. Constructivism, with its emphasis on creating personal meaning, may be the approach most helpful to clients in a time of societal uncertainty.

As relevant as constructivist career counseling may be, however, potentially daunting challenges exist in teaching from a constructivist perspective. Young students, especially those who come into counseling programs directly from a typical undergraduate experience, have not always had enough experiences themselves or made enough life choices to be able to recognize patterns in their lives or their choices. It is also difficult for them to recognize all the contextual influences on those choices.

In addition to the challenges posed by chronological age, a constructivist approach to career can be confusing, and even upsetting, to students who think in more external, dualistic (Perry, 1970) ways. Chapters 1 and 3 of this volume highlight the support that such students will need. To support those students, a more structured approach to some of the activities and assignments and to the principles of constructivist career counseling in general may be needed. Instructors may model self-reflective constructivist attitudes, thereby letting students "get a peek at" their own internal dialogues. Developmentally attuned instructors will remember to be as specific and structured as possible with instructions. They should also be as generous as possible with examples when assigning activities that may challenge the comfort level of dualistic thinkers. Instructors must exhibit genuine understanding and acceptance of students at all developmental levels, affirming them for how they currently think and supporting their struggles with new and challenging ideas and behaviors.

In particular, many students find it difficult to translate constructivist perspectives on career into programs or into currently existing systems. Students preparing to be school counselors, for example, find it difficult to imagine ways to plan career development programs for heterogeneous groups of students, programs that are sensitive to the constructed nature of individual students' careers.

Constructivist career counseling education is best implemented in the context of counselor education programs in which constructivist principles are being implemented across the entire program. Perhaps the time will come when more and more counselor educators will see their role as that of organizing for learning rather than directly transmitting information about preferred practices.

# REFERENCES

Bateson, M. C. (1990). *Composing a life.* New York: Penguin.

Bloch, D. P. (1989). From career information to career knowledge: Self, search, and synthesis. *Journal of Career Development, 16,* 119–127.

Bolles, R. N. (2007). *The 2007 what color is your parachute? A practical manual for job-hunters and career-changers.* Berkeley, CA: Ten Speed Press.

Brotherton, S. J. (1996). *Counselor education for the twenty-first century.* Westport, CT: Bergin & Garvey.

Cochran, L. (1992). The career project. *Journal of Career Development, 18,* 187–198.

Emmett, J. D., & Harkins, A. M. (1997). Story tech: Exploring the use of a narrative technique for training career counselors. *Counselor Education and Supervision, 37,* 60–73.

Forster, J. R. (1992). Eliciting personal constructs and articulating goals. *Journal of Career Development, 18,* 175–185.

Hansen, L. S. (1997). *Integrative life planning: Critical tasks for career development and changing life patterns.* San Francisco: Jossey-Bass.

Healy, C. C. (1990). Reforming career appraisals to meet the needs of clients in the 1990s. *Counseling Psychologist, 18,* 213–225.

Holland, J. L. (1994). *Self-directed search (SDS).* Odessa, FL: Psychological Assessment Resources.

Hoskins, M. (1995). Constructivist approaches for career counselors. *ERIC Digest.* ERIC Document Reproduction Service No. ED401505

Kelly, G. (1955). *The psychology of personal constructs.* New York: Norton.

Miller-Tiedeman, A. (1987). *How to not make it . . . and succeed: The truth about your lifecareer.* Los Angeles: LIFE-CAREER Foundation.

Neimeyer, G. J. (1992). Personal constructs in career counseling and development. *Journal of Career Development, 18,* 163–173.

Neimeyer, G. (Ed.). (1993). *Constructivist assessment: A casebook.* Newbury Park, CA: Sage.

Parsons, F. (1909). *Choosing a vocation.* Boston: Houghton Mifflin.

Peavy, R. V. (1992). A constructivist model of training for career counselors. *Journal of Career Development, 18,* 215–228.

Peavy, R. V. (1993). Envisioning the future: Worklife and counselling. *Canadian Journal of Counselling, 27,* 123–139.

Peavy, R. V. (1994). Constructivist counselling: A prospectus. *Guidance and Counseling, 9,* 3–12.

Peavy, R. V. (1995). Constructivist career counseling. *ERIC Digest.* ERIC Document Reproduction Service No. ED401504

Peavy, R. V. (1996). Constructivist career counseling and assessment. *Guidance and Counseling, 11,* 8–14.

Perry, W. (1970). *Forms of intellectual and ethical development in the college years: A scheme.* New York: Holt, Rinehart & Winston.

Savickas, M. L. (1993). Career counseling in the postmodern era. *Journal of Cognitive Psychotherapy, 7,* 205–215.

Seligman, L. (1994). *Developmental career counseling and assessment* (2nd ed.). Thousand Oaks, CA: Sage.

Spokane, A. R. (1992). Personal constructs and careers: A reaction. *Journal of Career Development, 18,* 229–236.

Strong, E. K., Jr., Hansen, J. C. (1994). *Strong interest inventory.* Palo Alto, CA: Consulting Psychologists Press.

# Appendix A
## Career Classroom Guidelines

1. ***Maintain confidentiality.*** Confidentiality is one of the most important ethical principles governing the establishment of trusting relationships. People are more likely to share information if there is trust and a commitment to keep the information between/among those with whom it is shared. In a class, this guideline encourages the formation of a trusting, working bond between students and the instructor.

2. ***Actively participate*** in the activities, discussions, and exercises. Some students are more accustomed to the "banking" method of education, whereby the teacher "deposits" information and the student is a somewhat passive recipient. Learning in this course requires your active engagement with the material and with each other.

3. ***Exercise respect and positive regard*** for your colearners in this class. Stretch your tolerance and consideration of viewpoints and experiences other than your own, and be willing to share your own viewpoints and experiences, especially if they seem to contradict or extend those of the majority in the class.

4. ***Maintain an open mind*** and be willing to consider views, beliefs, lifestyles, and values that are different from your own. New ideas and shifts in life views can only begin when minds are open.

5. ***Acknowledge your resistance or discomfort*** to some concepts, and be willing to explore (for yourself in a safe space) its meaning for you and for your career as a counselor.

6. ***Exercise the courage*** needed to explore new ideas as well as your own thinking, feelings, and reactions.

7. ***Be honest.*** It takes honesty and courage to risk examining oneself and to consider change. This is what you will be asking of your own future clients and students.

It is about 10 years into the future. Today is a very special time to gather for my family/circle of special friends. It is time when I always gather with this group of people.

- What is the event that brings us all together?
- Who would be there?

Often at these gatherings, we spend time reflecting on the past and looking ahead to a positive future. It seems to be a time for telling each other the stories of our lives—where we have been, where we are going, what the meaning of our lives has been.

At the last couple of these gatherings, I have realized that I am held in great respect by these people. Many of them seek me out for the wisdom that I continue to gain in my productive and satisfying career as a counselor. Today, one of the younger members of the group sits down next to me and, with great respect and real eagerness to understand, asks me to tell a story—the story of my life. Who is this younger person?

_____

She or he wants to know what my life has been about, and so I begin:

- "I was the little boy/girl who . . ."
- "I always loved to . . ."
- "As I grew up, more than anything else, I always wanted to . . ."
- "And I always admired people who . . ."
- "My life was not always easy, though. Some of the difficulties I faced were . . ."
- "I dealt with these difficulties by . . ."
- "I experienced times when I was very happy and times when I was very sad. Sometimes I was excited and enthusiastic, at other times I became discouraged or frightened. As I look back now, I see my life as an attempt to . . ."
- "At the present, I am most satisfied with . . ."
- "and I'm struggling most with . . ."
- "Right now, I guess I see my life as an attempt to . . ."

- "Thank you so much for asking. Actually, I've often thought about creating something that would tell the story of my life. Most likely, I would make a . . ."
- "Currently, I am at peace with my past, energized by the present, and I can hardly wait to write the next chapter of my life. If I had to give my life story a title, I would call it '_____'"
- "and the very next chapter would be called _____."

# REFLECTION ON STORYTECH 1: LIFE STORY

General Directions: As you reflect on your own StoryTech 1: Life Story, focus on discovering insight into the following areas. Consider what feedback from peers might help.

1. What are my views on work, on career, on life?

2. How have my unique life experiences, as a person of a particular age, gender, class, culture, religious background, sexual orientation, etc., affected these views?

3. What role do my experiences and my point of view play in _how I view_ "career" and "career counseling"?

4. How will my experiences and my point of view affect _how I do_ career counseling and career development?

## Reflection Questions for StoryTech 1

- When I think about my life story, I see me describing myself as a person who . . .
- A central theme of the story seems to be . . .
- What I see in my own story that may help me function as a counselor who helps others tell their own stories is . . .
- What I notice in my story that might make it difficult for me to help others tell their own stories is . . .
- After reflecting on my own StoryTech 1, I would like to think more about or explore or get feedback from my peers or others on . . .

It is about 10 years from now. I am a competent, highly respected counselor working at my dream job.

- Where am I working?
- Who are my students/clients; what are they like?
- What is my office/work space like?
- A typical day in this job will find me . . .
- As I go through this typical day, I feel . . .

Coming back from lunch today, I find two messages. One is from a former student/client. When I return the call, I find that this person wants to tell me about the latest events in her or his career/life. This person is so happy, and thanks me profusely for helping her or him in the past.

- What is she or he so grateful to me for?

The second message is from a current student/client who wants to meet with me this afternoon to discuss a career issue.

- Who is this person?
- What does she or he want to discuss with me?

There is a knock on my door—this person has arrived.

- What do the two of us discuss?

All of my experience these last 10 years has taught me that I can help persons like this talk about their lives in ways that they find useful in dealing with career issues.

- How do I go about talking with (counseling) this person?

As this person leaves, she or he says, "Thanks so much. You really helped me. I sure feel better than when I first came to you. I'm really looking forward to the next meeting."

- What has happened that results in this mutual satisfaction and anticipation of our next time together?

# REFLECTION ON STORYTECH 2: MYSELF AS A CAREER COUNSELOR

General Directions: As you reflect on your own StoryTech 2: Myself as a Career Counselor, focus on discovering insight into the following areas. Consider what feedback from peers might help.

1. What are my views on work, on career, on life?

2. How have my unique life experiences, as a person of a particular age, gender, class, culture, religious background, sexual orientation, etc., affected these views?

3. What role do my experiences and my point of view play in how I view "career" and "career counseling"?

4. How will my experiences and my point of view affect how I do career counseling and career development?

## Reflection Questions for StoryTech 2

- From my responses to this story, I appear to view the *purpose* of career counseling/development to be . . .
- How does the purpose of career counseling as revealed by the StoryTech compare to my stated beliefs about the purpose of career counseling?
- From my responses to this story, I seem to believe that some of the most helpful/effective ways a counselor can go about the *process* of career counseling/career development are . . .
- From what I've observed about myself so far through reflecting on my responses to my stories, I believe that some of my greatest strengths in career counseling will be . . .
- Some of the areas in which I may have difficulty might be . . .

# Appendix D
## StoryTech 3: My Perfect Day

"Have a nice day." People say that to me all the time. Do they really mean it? Do they really know what a "nice day"—a perfect day—would be like for me? Well, let me tell you.

- What would make a perfect day for me would be to wake up, leisurely, in (location) . . .
- What makes this such a favorite spot for me is . . .
- Living with me is . . .
- I would be well rested and eager to start my day. I've planned it to be filled with my favorite activities—those things that bring me the most energy and fulfillment.
- In the morning, I will . . .
- In the afternoon, I have planned to . . .
- In the evening, I am looking forward to . . .
- What I most look forward to accomplishing today is . . .
- Not everyone understands why I like days like this, but when I have one, I always feel so . . .
- As I drift off to sleep, I smile with satisfaction and say to myself, "I *did* have a nice day—actually, a perfect day. Thanks."

## REFLECTION ON STORYTECH 3: MY PERFECT DAY

General Directions: As you reflect on your own StoryTech 3: My Perfect Day, focus on discovering insight into the following areas. Consider what feedback from peers might help.

1. What are my views on work, on career, on life?
2. How have my unique life experiences, as a person of a particular age, gender, class, culture, religious background, sexual orientation, etc., affected these views?
3. What role do my experiences and my point of view play in how I view "career" and "career counseling"?
4. How will my experiences and my point of view affect how I do career counseling and career development?

## Reflection Questions for StoryTech 3

- When I look at StoryTech 3 as a career assessment tool, it seems to suggest that my interests are . . .
- My values are . . .
- My personality is . . .
- The roles most salient to me are . . .
- What this suggests to me in terms of who I am, relative to the work aspects of my life, is . . .
- In terms of my overall career development, this suggests . . .

# Appendix E
## StoryTech 4: Using Career Information

It is about 10 years from now. I am about to begin my eighth year of employment at _____. I remember how thrilled I was to be hired here–having a chance to really make a difference in the lives of _____ (population I work with). These people are so eager for career information and so appreciative of my efforts. It seems that they can never get enough, and I am always on the alert for better ways to help them. Still, sometimes I feel myself getting overwhelmed. This is, after all, the Information Age. At times there seems to be no end to the information that comes to me daily via all of my sophisticated telecommunications career information delivery systems. How to get a handle on it all? As this new work year begins, I reflect on this concern.

- The information most of my counselees seem to be seeking is . . .
- The biggest concern they have with regard to career information is . . .
- Just lately, I have begun to really realize that my own view about what constitutes "good" career information and the role that it plays in career decision making greatly affects the services I provide. I jot down my personal response to the following: I believe "good" career information is . . .
- My role with regard to that "good" career information is . . .
- As I look at my own response, I realize that my students/clients have been affected by my personal beliefs both about *what* good career information is and *how* I use it with them. It has affected them in the following ways:
- This is a real eye-opener. In fact, I am not "doing it all." And yet, I *am* a very effective counselor dealing with career issues. I have the appreciation and respect of my counselees, both present and past. Perhaps I can attribute my success with these people to believing in and living the motto I have framed and hung in my career information center: "_____"

## REFLECTION ON STORYTECH 4: USING CAREER INFORMATION

General Directions: As you reflect on your own StoryTech 4: Using Career Information, focus on discovering insight into the following areas. Consider what feedback from peers might help.

1. What are my views on work, on career, on life?

2. How have my unique life experiences, as a person of a particular age, gender, class, culture, religious background, sexual orientation, etc., affected these views?

3. What role do my experiences and my point of view play in how I view "career" and "career counseling"?

4. How will my experiences and my point of view affect how I do career counseling and career development?

## Reflection Questions for StoryTech 4

- From my responses to StoryTech 4, I seem to believe that the kind of information that my students/clients need most is . . .
- I can best help them by . . .
- My beliefs about how I can be most helpful to others with their career informational needs are undoubtedly based on my own experiences. Personal experience(s) that may explain how I came to hold these beliefs might be . . .
- With my unique perspective(s) on career information, the type(s) of students/clients I would most likely serve very well is . . .
- Based on my unique perspective(s) on career information, there are some persons whose career information needs I might find it difficult to meet. These would be persons who . . .

In my work as a counselor, dealing with career issues has been especially difficult these past few months. More and more of my counselees seem to be expressing the attitude "Things are changing so fast. Why even bother engaging in a plan-full process of career exploration, career planning, career decision making, or career preparation?"

- This lack of predictability about the future has affected them so that they seem to feel . . .
- I am empathic, yet dealing with them day after day has become stressful. Sometimes I find it difficult to maintain a positive attitude. What makes it especially difficult for me is . . .
- I have given myself the time to go on a "working retreat" to a spot that has always been energizing and refreshing to me. Where do I go?
- My goal for myself in the next few hours is to clarify my own beliefs and feelings about the rapidity of change now and in the future. Not being able to help my counselees find definite "answers" makes me feel . . .
- I find myself handling it by . . .
- Actually, as I think about it more, my feelings are somewhat mixed. When I look at them negatively, I sometimes feel . . .
- My main concern for my counselees is . . .
- And yet, viewed from a more positive perspective, it also seems that . . .
- The hopeful possibilities I can see for my counselees are . . .
- Overall, mostly I feel . . .
- because I believe . . .
- It has been good to get away and take time to clarify my own thoughts and feelings. A path of action seems clearer to me now. As I return to my job, refreshed and recommitted to helping students/clients with career information issues, I plan to put my new insights and convictions into practice. The first thing(s) I will need to do is . . .

## REFLECTION ON STORYTECH 5: THE FUTURE

General Directions: As you reflect on your own StoryTech 5: The Future, focus on discovering insight into the following areas. Consider what feedback from peers might help.

1. What are my views on work, on career, on life?

2. How have my unique life experiences, as a person of a particular age, gender, class, culture, religious background, sexual orientation, etc., affected these views?

3. What role do my experiences and my point of view play in how I view "career" and "career counseling"?

4. How will my experiences and my point of view affect how I do career counseling and career development?

## Reflection Questions for StoryTech 5

- When I look at the future and the rapidity of change and the effects that change will have on career counseling/development, my overall feeling seems to be . . .
- One way that I might look at those feeling(s) in a little more depth would be . . .
- When I reflect back on all my previous StoryTechs (Life Story, Myself as a Career Counselor, Using Career Information, and My Perfect Day), as well as this StoryTech, one or two things that stand out are . . .
- From reflecting on my "stories," I see my greatest strength(s) as a counselor dealing with career to be . . .
- And the areas of potential difficulty might be . . .

# Creating Courses in Constructivist Supervision

Seth Olson, Brian Mistler, and James S. Korcuska

*The teacher, however great, can never give their knowledge to the pupil; the pupil must create his/her own knowledge.*

Hazrat Inayat Khan, Sufi teacher

Before we began writing about an experiential, constructivist-oriented model of teaching the supervision course, our first thought was this: Although we have each worked from an experiential orientation for some time, who are we to presume the authority to be spokespersons for this approach to teaching supervision? Our answer, both to ourselves and to you the reader, is that we do not in any way claim to speak for counselor educators, supervision, supervisors, constructivists, or any other interest group beyond ourselves. What we offer herein is but one model—*a* model of constructivist-experiential supervision training, and not *the* model.

We prefer not to "teach" supervision. Rather, we prefer to create learning environments and activities from which learners become supervisors and, perhaps, teachers of supervision. Our preference for this kind of education roots itself in the idea that there is little worth knowing that one can teach to others (Rogers, 1969). If we are not teachers, then what is our role? Scott Russell Sanders (1998)

answers simply: We are guides. As guides, we focus attention on what we have learned that is worth attending to, and we invite learners to express, clarify, and articulate their own vision of supervision. The aim is to develop learners' aesthetic of supervision, not to replicate ours in others. Sanders expresses it this way:

> The word *aesthetic* derives from the Greek root meaning sensitive, which derives in turn from a verb meaning to perceive. . . . For most of human history, that training has come from elders who taught the young how to pay attention. By paying attention, we learn to savor all sorts of patterns, from quantum mechanics to patchwork quilts. (pp. 152–153)

Although the notion of functioning as an elder may seem anathema to constructivism, we nonetheless seek the constructivist aesthetic in a relational context whereby we simultaneously transmit and advance what is known about supervision.

How can something beyond teaching, such as an aesthetic of supervision, be learned? Although the existing literature is sparse, a few gifted counselors have approached with great insight the question of how to teach supervision from both a constructivist (Gonzalez, 1997; Neufeldt, 1997; Schön, 1987) and an experiential perspective (e.g., Resnick & Estrup, 2000). The pedagogical model we use for teaching supervision is learner centered, experiential based, constructivist, and developmental.

We are heavily influenced by Kolb's (1984) mode of experiential learning in which concrete, personal experiences take center stage. Thus, we place the concrete experience of supervising counselor-trainees as the starting point. These experiences provide the structure and content for the supervision course. From this perspective, experiences teach us what we need to know about supervision and supervisees; moreover, experiences married with reflection, conceptualization, and experimentation teach us modes of understanding and ways to use what we know. Concrete experiences offer sensorimotor feedback to the learner about supervision (or teaching supervision) from which to assess outcomes and to extract what needs to be known. This is bread making of the most complex kind. Recipes take one only partway there: One must develop a feel for what the dough requires. If one persists honestly and long enough, an aesthetic emerges.

How do we as teachers of supervision nurture this aesthetic? If we see ourselves as guides rather than teachers in this process, then our task is to point out to supervision trainees aspects of their experiences that strike us as remarkable and draw them into more expansive conversations about the phenomenon. This model assumes that every learner in our group is responsible, ethical, capable, and organized. Ultimately, each of us is responsible for what we learn. In this model, we do not "give" knowledge; knowledge is something that we create together. In other words, we aim to structure learning environments and activities in which our collective wisdom may coalesce.

To begin this chapter, we introduce an overview of constructivist supervision education with assumptions to guide constructivist supervision instruction. Then we propose a structure for a constructivist course in

supervision using suggested constructivist objectives and activities to amplify learning points.

## ASSUMPTIONS FOR CREATING CONSTRUCTIVIST SUPERVISION COURSES

Our *teaching* of supervision is profoundly informed by and, in many ways, parallels many of the assumptions outlined in the literature regarding *practicing* constructivist supervision. Authors such as Neufeldt (1997, 2001) and Gonzalez (1997) were instrumental in adding constructivist supervision assumptions to the supervision lexicon. This makes intuitive sense to us: Constructivist supervision teachers must also be constructivist supervisors. Thus, we begin thinking about and designing courses in supervision from the following seven assumptions borrowed from the literature on constructivist supervision.

First, like all relationships, supervision, and by extension the teaching of supervision, changes in different social contexts. Just as the constructivist supervisor invites and values the previous work and personal experiences of the counselor, so too does the constructivist supervision teacher. However, in the classroom environment, the learner is the one who is encouraged to bring experiences into the learning environment. Those experiences are then embraced and discussed as valuable commodities to the learning market.

For example, based on work experience, a learner might have a unique understanding of a supervisee. This understanding is shared with others, who may then add to it. Knowledge for understanding supervision and supervisees has just been co-created. The supervision teacher, in this case, would be a guide in the co-creation of the knowledge, adding to it as she or he sees fit. We agree with the points in Chapters 1, 2, and 3 that our greatest challenge as supervision teachers is to add much *less* than we are perhaps inclined to add. We believe that by honoring the various social contexts of the learner, the relational climate is marked by mutuality and a readiness to validate the learner's experience.

The second assumption, a more specific extension of the first, is that the supervision teacher assumes that knowledge is co-constructed with learners. In this way, we collaborate in learning and teaching, rather than merely dispensing or receiving knowledge. Gonzalez (1997) suggests the notion of supervisors as partial learners, and we see constructivist supervision teachers in the same vein. Teachers have only partial understandings of what they are observing or teaching regarding supervision. Thus, the teacher should also remain open for feedback and conversations about the learner's view of what is being learned.

The third assumption that we borrow from the literature on constructivist supervision is the notion that supervisees should be encouraged to be knowledge creators, to hypothesize, to plan interventions, to be reflective, and to use the results of their own supervision and counseling experiences to create new hypotheses (Neufeldt, 2001). For constructivist supervision teachers, this becomes one of the more challenging tasks to accomplish. Often a learner enters graduate work with years of exposure to top-down or learner-silent classroom structures. When the new expectation of sharing their voice is presented, it can be awkward for learners. The challenge becomes a journey of moving learners to a place of confident expression in the classroom. We want a classroom filled with learner voices. The voices represent hypotheses, personal reflections, vulnerabilities to overcome, and a stronger sense of knowledge. Strengthening the supervisee's voice may be accomplished through reflection. Such reflection occurs during supervision discussions in which the actions, emotions, and thoughts of learners are examined (Zimmer & Dickerson, 1996).

The fourth assumption of constructivist supervision instruction that we use is the power of dialogue to influence people. Similarly to how a constructivist supervisor views dialogue, we attempt to hear not only the learner's voice and contextual experiences, but also the learner's voice related to the classroom process itself.

The fifth assumption involves what Schön (1987) describes as reflection in action, which begins with an analysis of the events within the given context. In a course dedicated to supervision, the given context could vary from a classroom discussion about the supervision literature to learners engaging in supervision. The context could also vary from live supervision to reflecting teams to the supervisor in the session. Regardless of the context, the teacher and learner gradually construct a picture of the focused topic (e.g., client cases, supervisory relationship issues, supervision models). The teacher's role is not only to observe and assess, but to engage the learner in dialogue, wondering aloud, and posing questions in order to promote learner reasoning. While constructivist supervisor teachers do not avoid giving directives when the need arises, they primarily encourage learners' solutions, instead of imposing their own. The idea is for learners, when possible, to figure things out for themselves.

The sixth assumption is attending to the isomorphism among teaching, supervision, and counseling contexts. As noted above, the process of teaching supervision parallels the process and model of supervision itself. The concept of parallel process is helpful for highlighting the ways in which interactions between supervision teachers and learners may parallel interactions between supervisors and counselors and those between the counselors and their clients. Similarly, just as supervisors can shift the supervision relationship into the type of relationship that would be more helpful in the counselor-client relationship, so too can the supervision teacher in the classroom shift the teacher-learner relationship into the type of relationship that would be more helpful in the supervisor-counselor relationship. The assumption is that the process in one relationship can be observed in the other relationships, and that changes created in one relationship can effect changes in the other relationships. This parallel process presents itself at an additional level in that, as students are learning to become supervisors, their understanding of supervision, in terms of both models and processes, grows through their experiences of being supervised by the teacher.

The last assumption comes from Kolb's (1984) Experiential Learning Theory, which was discussed in Chapter 2, and is the starting point of this chapter (see Figure 15.1). This model provides a framework for constructing and teaching the supervision course. Kolb theorizes that there are four modes for learning: concrete experiences, reflective experiences, abstract conceptualization, and active experimentation.

**FIGURE 15.1** Kolb's (1984) Experiential Learning Theory

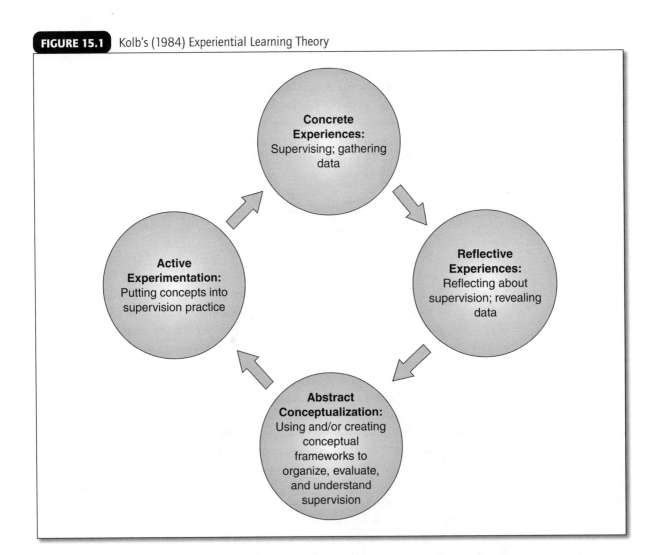

In the supervision course, Kolb's (1984) learning cycle would be implemented in the following ways. In terms of concrete experience, learners would be engaged in many of the following actions while practicing supervision: evaluating the counselor (e.g., grading counselor performance); trying out ways to teach counseling concepts to counselors; attempting to help counselors manage anxiety; attending to relationship dynamics; finding consultation opportunities for themselves, the counselor, and the client(s); and addressing interpersonal and intrapersonal issues with the counselor.

The second learning mode, reflective observation, would be promoted in a variety of ways. Learners would observe their supervision teacher conduct supervision and would reflect on that supervision during class. Learners would also watch and analyze their supervision recordings individually and then with their peers, their teacher, and the counselor's practicum teacher (if applicable). Learners would additionally reflect on how others—their teacher and their peers—conduct supervision.

Abstract conceptualization, the third of Kolb's learning modes, is the discovery or creation of overarching concepts or patterns that can be generalized across situations. During the supervision course, learners are encouraged to both use established supervision models and create their own personal models or theories to explain what they observe during their own supervision and during their peers' experience.

Lastly, active experimentation occurs when learners use their accumulated supervision knowledge to solve problems and make decisions in the real-life supervision of counselors.

By adopting the seven assumptions above as a framework, supervision teachers have a solid grounding for teaching supervision in a constructivist fashion. Constructivist supervision instruction emphasizes that learning is not an all-or-nothing process, but that learners learn new information by building upon knowledge that they already possess. It is therefore important that teachers constantly assess the knowledge that learners have gained to make sure that learners' perceptions of the new knowledge are what was intended.

## CONCEPTUAL DOMAINS FOR DESIGNING A CONSTRUCTIVIST SUPERVISION COURSE

Learning supervision best begins when a student has developed some experience and competency with a variety of counseling issues. The course in constructivist supervision usually occurs in doctoral training or advanced master's training after learners have engaged in their own counseling skill-building courses and field experience. Not only does the conceptual framework of supervision affect, therefore, the worldview and methods of teaching (process), but it is also the center of *what* is being taught (content). Since our model is experiential, what is learned depends on the teacher being at once both an effective teacher and an effective constructivist supervisor.

We consider three domains when organizing the supervision course: knowledge from supervision literature (supervision models and theories, supervision relationship dynamics, and supervisory structural items), supervision field experience (learners supervising less experienced counselors), and reflection on learning experiences (learners engaging in self-growth and self-assessment to strengthen their personal and professional development).

For the first domain, supervision texts offer a variety of information regarding theories, ethical considerations, and relationship dynamics. The supervision

teacher could assign reading that ranges from a general overview of these topics (e.g., Bernard & Goodyear, 2008) to more specific discussions of topics, such as a particular supervision model (e.g., Stoltenberg, McNeill, & Delworth, 1998). The supervision teacher would also want to consider including information about legal considerations and supervisory structural items as mentioned in the Falvey (2002) text *Managing Clinical Supervision: Ethical Practice and Legal Risk Management*. From a constructivist frame, these and other resources have validity and encourage more involvement from learners in constructing their own growth in the course.

For the second domain, supervision field experience, learners conduct individual supervision sessions with designated counselors. We suggest that the field experience occur concurrently with the conceptual learning in the supervision course. In this way, learners apply the knowledge developed from the first domain as they conduct the second domain. For example, before learners start their first supervision session, they might be given a First Session Checklist (see Appendix A on page 240), which compiles information from the Bernard and Goodyear (2008) and Falvey (2002) texts into a quick reference for the first supervision session. The checklist provides a bridge between supervision literature and the act of conducting supervision.

Third, learners engage in reflection regarding the knowledge they are gaining from both the supervision course content and the supervision experience itself. This third domain brings the supervision training experience full circle. Learners discuss their experiences as supervisors-in-training with the teacher of the supervision course and with their peers in the same course, and thus process the connections between the first and second domains.

Chapter 5 provides teaching methods that fit this domain of reflection. Specifically, activities for this domain might include the "Act As If" theory role-play, reflective loops, reflective theory development, discussion topics, process awareness through contrast highlight exercises, reciprocal learning, and counselor caricature. These activities are discussed in more detail later in this chapter. Another layer to add to this domain is to have learners receive individual supervision of their supervision work from either an appropriate practicum teacher or the supervision course teacher. This additional layer allows learners to amplify their learning experiences in private conversations and to bring that knowledge back to the group.

These domains occur not in sequential fashion such as stages, but more as intertwining actions. For example, during the first week of the supervision course, more emphasis would be given to supervisory structural items, such as expectations of the supervision experience, informed consent, assigning counselors to be supervised, and ethical considerations. Simultaneously, course conversations should include reflections from learners on personal understandings of the supervisory process and personal anxieties. Later in the course, the domains continue to overlap, with more or less emphasis, depending on the needs expressed by learners or on teacher observations. While we believe that the supervision teacher would be the primary guide in engaging the different domains, learners also benefit from initiating discussions relevant to any or all three domains.

# COURSE CONTENT

The weeks of the constructivist supervision course can be organized around several topics. These could include, but are not limited to, (a) supervision models and techniques used in counselor education and clinical practice, such as those that are extensions of counseling theories (i.e., psychodynamic supervision) and supervision-specific models such as the Integrated Developmental Model or Discrimination Model; (b) ethical issues in supervision; (c) constructing an effective working theory of supervision, which would include understanding and implementation of supervision administrative tasks; (d) managing supervisory relationships in ways that effectively improve reception of feedback, address counselors' anxiety, and encourage personal and professional growth; and (e) understanding how issues in a pluralistic society affect the supervision process, such as cultural influences on supervisory interactions. Table 15.1 outlines these five topics and connects them to suggested objectives of the course. It also summarizes the course activities and their related constructivist principles.

**TABLE 15.1** Course Objectives, Content, Activities, and Constructivist Principles

| Learning Objectives | Content | Suggested Activities | Constructivist Principles |
|---|---|---|---|
| Demonstrate ability to manage administrative tasks effectively in the supervisory relationship. | Constructing working theory of supervision<br><br>Ethical issues in supervision | Reflective loops (video feedback)<br>First session checklist<br>Video vignettes | The context influences the meaning of individual events.<br><br>Individuals are free to construct meaning and shape relationships through intentional ritual and discourse. |
| Demonstrate awareness of cultural influences on individuals that serve as foundations for the personal, therapeutic, and supervisory interactions. | Understanding cultural influences<br><br>Ethical issues in supervision | Reflective loops (video feedback)<br>Constructivist case staffing<br>Discussion topics | People construct their worldview from a context-based perspective.<br><br>Knowledge is inseparable from social and qualitative context. |
| Demonstrate ability to separate observations from projections. | Constructing working theory of supervision<br><br>Managing supervisory relationships | Reflective loops (video feedback)<br>Counselor caricatures<br>Reciprocal learning | Perception is a creative act. |

| Learning Objectives | Content | Suggested Activities | Constructivist Principles |
|---|---|---|---|
| Demonstrate awareness of various theoretical approaches to supervision. | Supervision models and theories<br><br>Constructing working theory of supervision | "Act As If" theory role play<br>Reflective theory development<br>Reciprocal learning<br>PATCH | Individuals interpret the present in terms of explicit and implicit epistemologies. |
| Demonstrate ability to manage conflict in a way that improves the supervisory relationship. Demonstrate ability to separate positions from issues. | Constructing working theory of supervision<br><br>Managing supervisory relationships<br><br>Understanding cultural influences | Reflective loops (video feedback)<br>Counselor caricatures<br>Discussion topics<br>Constructivist case staffing<br>PATCH<br>"Act As If" role play | Positions and discourse are inseparable from historical context. Deconstructing hegemonic discourse allows individuals to reconstruct what cannot be denied. |
| Be knowledgeable about professional roles, including ethical and legal obligations for related mental health fields. | Constructing working theory of supervision<br><br>Ethical issues in supervision | Reflective loops (video feedback)<br>Discussion topics<br>Constructivist case staffing<br>PATCH | Individuals exist in social structures with bidirectional influence. |
| Experience opportunities for enhancing self-awareness and personal growth. Be able to facilitate these same experiences with supervisees. | Constructing working theory of supervision<br><br>Managing supervisory relationships<br><br>Understanding cultural influences | Reflective loops (video feedback)<br>Counselor caricatures<br>Discussion topics<br>Constructivist case staffing<br>PATCH | Learn to manage various forms of socially constructed and individually experienced phenomenological data. |

## "Act As If" Theory Role Play

This activity encourages discussion of supervision models. It aims to provide learners with opportunities to develop personalized understandings of particular supervision models. It is structured in the following fashion: During any discussion regarding a particular supervision model, the teacher sets up the learning activity with the model at the center of the discussion. Learners take turns applying the particular model to one of their counselor's cases or to a fabricated case. As they apply the model, learners interpret and experiment with what they would do if they were following it.

This activity, in general, follows a two-part sequence. First, all learners come to class prepared to present a supervision session from the framework of a particular model (we suggest that the teacher choose the model ahead of time so that all learners prepare for the same model). Second, learners present their case utilizing the model. They take turns, but the learners that follow must also account for the material and ideas presented by the learners that came before them. Each learner, no matter her or his place in the rotation, is expected to add to the discussion of the model.

For example, each learner might prepare to present a case from the perspective of the discrimination model of supervision. Learner 1 presents her case, and the group members, including the teacher, provide feedback on the presentation. Learner 2 then presents his case, but is also asked to consider how he might add to his presentation given the discussion and presentation offered by Learner 1. This format would continue, with Learner 1 given a second opportunity to add to her presentation after the discussion and material presented by other learners.

## Reflective Loops (Video Feedback)

In this activity, learners first lead and record group supervision sessions with counselors. Then learners choose one or two recordings to showcase during class.

The learner who is presenting guides the conversations by asking lead questions of the group. For example, after presenting a recorded supervision session, the learner provides the class with guiding questions to focus the feedback loops. He could ask, "The counselor appears uninterested in my feedback. In what ways might my perception be accurate? Also, if I am accurate, what are some suggestions for addressing the apparent disinterest?" After viewing the recordings, all learners and the teacher make observations and address the guiding questions. The learner who has presented then comments on what feedback stood out for him and what he is likely to use in future supervision sessions. It is important to note that this activity can be very flexible regarding the focused intent. The teacher could add variations, such as having the learner who is presenting also offer his evolving supervision theory of choice, using the Process Awareness Through Contrast Highlight exercises (described in more detail later in the chapter), such as Shameless Projection or I Observe I Imagine, to structure the feedback.

## Reflective Theory Construction

In this activity, students articulate their supervision model and encourage discussion of that model during reflective loops or general course conversations. The purpose is to encourage critical thinking, as students are accountable for their actions through verbalizing their use of a model. For example, a learner might state that she is using the Discrimination Model in the supervision session. Before watching a video of that session, the learner describes how she has been using the three components of the model (teaching, counseling, consulting) during the session. For example, she might describe how she has been instructing the counselor on the use of immediacy in session. The learner might also note to the class that she is struggling with how to address choices made by the counselor during the session. Thus, she poses questions to the class about the counselor component of the model. As a result, the learner will gain more confidence in understanding and applying her chosen model. In addition, she might also begin constructing her own variation of an established model and subsequently begin to develop her own model of supervision.

## Constructivist Case Staffing

In this activity, learners take turns leading a case staffing meeting. The activity aims to give learners practice in facilitating supervision groups. The learner who is leading for the day decides how he would like to structure the discussion of a case. The other learners follow the chosen structure. After the case discussion has been completed, all participants provide feedback to the learner facilitator regarding what was useful and what could be improved. The learner facilitator then notes what stood out for him and what he will utilize in the future when structuring group supervision.

## Supervisor Caricature

Michael White (1991) describes the idea of externalizing as a dialogue that objectifies problems rather than persons. This dialogue opens space between the person and a problem. Often a "problem" in supervision is evaluation of the learner's performance, a process that can induce considerable anxiety for the learner. The level of anxiety can make feedback from supervision teachers to learners go unheard. The aim of the caricature is to improve the likelihood that feedback will be received and utilized by the learner (Chambers, 1992). Addressing the caricature allows space between the feedback and the learner. The learner is able to hear the feedback more clearly and address the issue through the caricature.

The specifics of this activity are as follows: Learners choose a fictional character from television, movies, books, or other media. They then complete the Caricature Supervising Style form (see Appendix B on page 242). The questions on the form ask learners to describe how the caricature would conduct supervision. Example questions focus on defining characteristics of the caricature (positive and negative), how the caricature would behave as a supervisor, and how the caricature would respond when a counselor does not do what is asked.

Supervision teachers utilize the caricature process at moments when learners might need to hear feedback that is likely to elicit a shame response or, more simply defined, feedback that may be tough to hear. Most people have trouble listening fully when they feel hurt by the words being said to them. For example, while watching a supervision tape, the teacher notices that the learner appears defensive when challenged by the counselor. The more the learner felt challenged, the more she pushed for the counselor to listen. In this brief example, a variety of items might be addressed, but any one of them could be difficult for the learner to hear. Thus, the caricature approach becomes a good option.

The teacher could simply start with "What is happening for (the caricature)?" and follow up with a conversation directed to the caricature, but with the learner responding for the caricature. A caricature represents a safer space in which to work with feedback. Consider the caricature to be a metaphorical workspace in which tough conversations can occur. We believe that caricatures provide an excellent means for reducing the threat associated with difficult supervision feedback.

In general, only feedback that might be viewed as negative or critical suggests use of the caricature (J. Chambers, personal communication, March 10, 2009). Positive feedback is best directed to the learner. The more detailed the caricature's development, the more uses a supervision teacher will find for the caricature. Users of this activity will find that it is very flexible and has relevance to almost any supervision issue.

## Discussion Topics

A variety of issues arise in the supervision context that can benefit from group discussion. This activity begins with reading from a textbook, for instance, *Clinical Supervision: A Handbook for Practitioners* (Fall & Sutton, 2004). Students then discuss questions related to the reading. For instance, Fall and Sutton ask learners what to do when a supervisee

- is overly dependent
- is not taking risks in learning
- feels anxious
- is not prepared for supervision
- says, "Let's hang out."

Learners might submit their responses to these questions in an online discussion forum as well as respond to other postings on the same question. This structure creates a community of responses and extends learners' thoughts about how they might respond to the issues when they occur in a real supervisory relationship.

## Video Vignettes

In this activity, learners think through how to handle common video supervision issues. We use Baltimore and Crutchfield's (2003) interactive CD-ROM, *Clinical Supervisor Training,* which offers short vignettes on a variety of different issues. Teachers and/or students can choose a vignette for discussion or presentation.

## Reciprocal Learning

In this activity, "each one teaches one." The aim is for learners to develop their instructional skill by teaching on a particular topic (e.g., resistance, ethics, feedback) to the others in the class. Each learner can choose or be assigned a particular class meeting, and then can present on an assigned or personally selected topic.

## Process Awareness Through Contrast Highlight (PATCH) Exercises

The purpose of PATCH exercises is to offer learners the opportunity to deepen their awareness of their own personal issues and processes and to become more aware of the areas in which they need to grow. By using specific pairs of contrasting concept prompts to structure their sharing, learners gain experience attending differentially to various aspects of the environment. Examples of contrasting prompts might be "I observe" versus "I imagine" or "I should" versus "I can." Of course, even these contrasts are not fixed opposites. One could just as easily contrast "I observe" with "I was told" or "I should" with "I must." With practice, learners take greater ownership of their experience, becoming able to interpret and report on their experience. By sharing with each other, learners have an opportunity to both discover their own processes and observe, reflect on, and respond (within the current PATCH framework) to perceptions of other learners.

First, learners are given an overview of the steps. After they have done one or two PATCH exercises, they are usually familiar enough with the process that the teacher only needs to give one or two examples before starting. Second, the supervision teacher picks a pair of contrasting concepts and provides some examples. The pair should be designed to highlight a difference between two ways of reporting on experience (phenomenological data), ways that are sometimes confused. The more powerfully the difference between the two statements is felt, the more effective the PATCH exercise will be in helping learners differentiate between their own experiences. It is not always necessary that the opposite be spoken aloud each time, but it is helpful to have a contrast in mind and to share that contrast with learners so that everyone is on the same page. The following are some examples that have been used with success in the past.

*I observe, I imagine.* Perhaps the most central of the PATCH exercises and a Gestalt Therapy classic (Perls, Hefferline, & Goodman, 1994; Van De Riet, Korb, & Gorrell, 1980), the "observe" versus "imagine" distinction is designed to increase experiential awareness of the fundamental constructivist principle: Perception is a creative act. The activity itself is simple; however, it may take some time before students become proficient. To begin, learners look at something and make two statements about it. The first statement, beginning with "I observe," should be as close as possible to an observation of immediately experienced data. While our core constructivist assumptions prevent us from labeling this data "objective," the observation should at least be generally amenable to easy consensus.

The second statement should begin with "I imagine" and may include whatever the person thinks as a result of the observation. This is the learner's interpretation of what was observed. Some common targets include asking learners to look at others' behavior in the room, the room itself, video demonstrations by professionals, or learner tapes. In the beginning, it is best to limit the exercise to things that can be seen by everyone in the room. However, later on, the same exercise can be used to explore observation-imagination pairs with respect to learners' friends, families, or supervisees.

*I should, I can.* Statements here begin with "I should" and "I can." These can be the same statements, and often experimenting with making them helps learners determine which group they want the object of the statement to be in. For instance, by pairing "I should read the chapter for this week" with "I can read the chapter for this week," or "I should eat healthy" with "I can eat

healthy," learners identify external expectations and increase their internal locus of control.

*I have to, I want to.* Pairing statements beginning with these two phrases helps learners separate internal desires from external obligations. Sometimes these things are discrepant, and sometimes they're not. For example, "I have to meet with my supervisee for 60 minutes a week" communicates a different experience than "I want to meet with my supervisee twice a week."

Finally, learners share their experiences with the contrasting concepts in round-robin fashion or in small groups. Supervision teachers gently correct learners if they do not appear to understand the contrast, and provide additional examples of statements or pairs. For example, if the class were practicing the "I observe, I imagine" distinction, in response to a learner who is being overly didactic, an instructor might say, "I observe you repeating information from the book, and I imagine that it's important to you to get the 'right' answer." Similarly, if a learner were to say, "I observed that my counselor-in-training was happy, and I imagined he was thinking of his family," the supervision teacher might ask, "Can you please say what you *observed* that led you to *imagine* he was happy?" To which the learner could reply "Ah . . . I *observed* my counselor-in-training smile."

## CONCLUDING REFLECTIONS

Taking our cue from Kolb's (1984) model, we begin the end of this chapter with our experience of writing this chapter. We were challenged to succinctly capture and express what we had been experiencing and learning about teaching supervision. Processes such as reflection in action (Schön, 1987) eluded our efforts to corral them at every turn. Nonetheless, we gathered our notions together in the hopes of providing an overview of our paradigm for constructivist supervision education, one centered on experiential learning. In other words, we believe that one can learn how to teach supervision from a constructivist perspective by doing supervision from the same vantage point. Therefore, we built much of our work upon seven assumptions drawn from the supervision literature regarding constructivist models. We also proposed a structure and objectives for a constructivist course in supervision and offered related activities.

Due to the scant outcome research on constructivist teaching practices and their effects upon learning, we did not offer much empirical evidence of the efficacy of the model. Much empirical work is needed. Thus, our ideas should be considered as a work in progress. Upon reflection, we also did not offer much, if any, guidance to current and future teachers of supervision on how to sustain themselves as they teach from a constructivist position. Teaching from the constructivist paradigm seems to require a goodly amount of what Palmer (1998) identifies as courage, the kind that fuels humility, vulnerability, connectedness, and perseverance. Perhaps the outcomes of such courage are simply enough.

# REFERENCES

Baltimore, M. L., & Crutchfield, L. B. (2003). *Clinical supervisor training: An interactive CD-ROM training program for the helping professions.* Boston: Pearson Education.

Bernard, J., & Goodyear, R. (2008). *Fundamentals of clinical supervision* (4th ed.). Boston: Allyn & Bacon.

Chambers, J. (1992). *Triad-training: A method for teaching basic counseling skills to chemical dependency counselors.* Unpublished doctoral dissertation, University of South Dakota, Vermillion.

Fall, M., & Sutton, J. (2004). *Clinical supervision: A handbook for practitioners.* Boston: Pearson Education.

Falvey, J. E. (2002). *Managing clinical supervision: Ethical practice and legal risk management.* Pacific Grove, CA: Brooks/Cole-Thomson Learning.

Gonzalez, R. (1997). Postmodern supervision: A multicultural perspective. In D. Pope-Davis & H. Coleman (Eds.), *Multicultural counseling competencies: Assessment, education and training and supervision* (pp. 350–386). Thousand Oaks, CA: Sage.

Kolb, D. (1984). *Experiential learning: Experience as the source of learning and development.* Englewood Cliffs, NJ: Prentice Hall.

Neufeldt, S. (1997). A social constructivist approach to counseling supervision. In T. Sexton & B. Griffin (Eds.), *Constructivist thinking in counseling practice, research, and training* (pp. 191–210). New York: Teachers College Press.

Neufeldt, S. (2001). Educating supervisors: A constructivist approach to the teaching of supervision. In K. Eriksen & G. J. McAuliffe (Eds.), *Teaching counselors and therapists: Constructivist and development course design* (pp. 169–184). Westport, CT: Bergin & Garvey.

Palmer, P. (1998). *The courage to teach: Exploring the inner landscape of a teacher's life.* San Francisco: Jossey-Bass.

Perls, F. S., Hefferline, R., & Goodman, P. (1994). *Gestalt therapy: Excitement and growth in the human personality.* Gouldsboro, ME: Gestalt Journal Press.

Resnick, R., & Estrup, L. (2000). Supervision: A collaborative endeavor. *Gestalt Review, 4,* 121–137.

Rogers, C. R. (1969). *Freedom to learn.* Columbus, OH: Charles E. Merrill.

Sanders, S. R. (1998). *Hunting for hope.* Boston: Beacon Press.

Schön, D. (1987). *The reflective practitioner: How professionals think in action.* New York: Basic Books.

Stoltenberg, C., McNeill, B., & Delworth, U. (1998). *IDM supervision: An integrated developmental model for supervising counselors and therapists.* San Francisco: Jossey-Bass.

Van De Riet, V., Korb, M. P., & Gorrell, J. J. (1980). *Gestalt therapy: An introduction.* New York: Pergamon Press.

White, M. (1991). Deconstruction and therapy. *Dulwich Centre Newsletter, 3,* 21–40.

Zimmer, J., & Dickerson, V. (1996). *If problems talked: A narrative therapy in action.* New York: Guilford Press.

## Expectations of the Supervisory Process

- [ ] The supervisee shall be encouraged to determine a theoretical orientation that can be used for conceptualizing and guiding work with clients.
- [ ] The supervisee has the right to work with a supervisor who is responsive to the supervisee's theoretical orientation, learning style, and developmental needs.
- [ ] Since it is probable that the supervisor's theory of counseling will influence the supervision process, the supervisee needs to be informed of the supervisor's counseling theory and how the supervisor's theoretical orientation may influence the supervision process.
- [ ] Supervisors must keep a file on their supervisees (examples available in Falvey, 2002). These files must include Supervisee Profile and all Supervision Records (there must be a note for each supervision session). In addition, there is a Supervision Packet that includes these forms as well as Emergency Contact, Log Sheet, and Termination Summary forms. All of these items must be filled out and be included in the supervisee file for the supervisor to receive a grade for the course.
- [ ] Supervisors will meet weekly for an hour with Practicum Teachers to review the development of supervisees. Missing meetings will reduce the final grade. Supervisors will honor all requests made by Practicum Teachers regarding the management of the supervisees.

## Expectations of Supervisory Sessions

- [ ] The weekly supervisory session shall include a review of cases, audiotapes and/or videotapes, and may include live supervision. The supervisee must be informed of this observation process.
- [ ] The supervisee is expected to meet with the supervisor face to face in a professional environment that ensures confidentiality. The supervisee must meet for a minimum of an hour per week during the training semester. Missed appointments will impact grading. Meeting more than an hour per week is possible if needed.
- [ ] The initial supervision session should be scheduled for two hours in order to get through all of the preliminary information and organization of supervision.
- [ ] The supervisee must come to each session prepared to discuss cases. At a minimum, these discussions must include case review of clients being seen by supervisee, video tapes cued by supervisee to show supervisor, questions by supervisee to direct session, and verbal notes of any high-risk situations any high-risk situations.

## Expectations of the Evaluation Process

- [ ] During the initial meeting, the supervisee shall be provided with a copy of the formal evaluation tool(s) that will be used by the supervisor.
- [ ] The supervisee shall receive verbal feedback and/or informal evaluation during each supervisory session.
- [ ] The supervisee shall receive written feedback or written evaluation on a regular basis during the beginning phases of counselor development. Written feedback may be requested by the supervisee during intermediate and advanced phases of counselor development.
- [ ] The supervisee should be recommended for remedial assistance in a timely manner if the

supervisor becomes aware of personal or professional limitations that may impede future professional performance.

☐ Beginning counselors receive written and verbal summative evaluation during the last supervisory meeting (as part of the final evaluation tool used). Intermediate and advanced counselors may receive a recommendation for licensure and/or certification.

## Suggested Conversation Topics During Initial Supervisory Session

List three therapeutic skills that you would like to further develop.

1.

2.

3.

List three general goals that you would like to attain during the supervisory process.

1.

2.

3.

List three specific counseling or professional development experiences that you would like to have during the next three months (e.g., attending a conference, facilitating a group, presentation).

1.

2.

3.

# Appendix B
## Caricature Supervising Style

(The more depth you can generate the better)

1. Focus on the way in which you would interact with the counselor. How would you describe yourself by choosing a TV, cartoon, movie, or book character (fictional)?

2. What are the significant defining positive characteristics of this character? Generate at least five.

3. What are the significant defining limitations of this character? Generate at least five.

4. Consider the character that you have chosen. What are some of the unique ways this character would look or behave in supervision? "How to be a _____ type supervisor?"

5. How would _____ go about getting clients/learners to do what she or he wants them to do?

6. How does _____ respond when clients/learners do not do what she or he wants them to do? Provide examples.

# Creating Constructivist Courses in Practicum and Internship

James S. Korcuska and Seth Olson

*Of those so close beside me, which are you? God bless the Ground! I shall walk softly there,*
*And learn by going where I have to go.*

Theodore Roethke (1953, p. 527)

On the first day of practicum, one of our colleagues takes her group rock climbing. This promotes a cohesive team and fosters a sense of accomplishment. We think it encapsulates the essence of teaching practicum and internship.[1] Teaching the art of professional counseling practice is not unlike teaching someone to climb a rock face. No one completes a climb by thinking like a climber; rather, one completes a climb by practicing as a climber. Professional practice such as counseling resists capture by models (Schön, 1987). The acts of climbing and counseling require learning by doing. In Roethke's (1953) words, we learn by going where we have to go and not by thinking about it. Schön suggests that one learns a practice such as counseling by (a) doing, (b) interactions with others, and (c) exposure and immersion. As practicum/internship supervisors,[2] we grasp the belay line, linking us to the climber (or counselor trainee). A belay line takes the load of a fall. When the risk is low for the counselor trainee and the client, we let out a longer belay line, liberating the counselor trainee to feel her own way up the rock face. When the risk is high, we cinch the line more tightly, allowing the counselor trainee to feel the gentle tug of our support.

Learning by doing highlights the importance of reflection in action (Schön, 1987). Doing without reflecting reduces the impact of learning. Questions invite reflection. The model we propose for teaching practicum and internship is fundamentally a question-based, or inquiry-oriented, practice. In this model, our focus shifts from teaching learners to impacting learning.

---

[1]For the purposes of this chapter, we do not go out of our way to separate *practicum* and *internship*. The terms are interchangeable.

[2]We use the term *practicum/internship supervisor* to describe teachers of such courses since they require faculty members to meld teaching and supervision roles.

The centrality of asking students essential questions is grounded in the constructivist-developmental framework, which we briefly describe in the first section below (see Chapter 1 for a more extensive discussion). In the first section of this chapter, we discuss how counselor trainee ways of knowing impact learning the practice of counseling. We also introduce the notion of tacit knowledge (Polanyi, 1962). This concept offers insight into how we may move counselor trainees from experiencing counseling to building knowledge of counseling practice. In the final section of the chapter, we translate these ideas into specific ways to promote critical thinking during practicum and internship.

# WHAT MAKES LEARNING BY DOING RISKY BUSINESS?

Between the knowledge acquired in the classroom and the world of professional practice lie practicum and internship. Arrival at this stage signals to novice counseling professionals that they have attained sufficient competency to practice professional counseling and that they are ready to function as beginning professionals with assistance from faculty and site supervisors. Rønnestad and Skovholt (2003; Skovholt & Rønnestad, 1995) call this the Advanced Student Phase (see Chapter 4 of this book). Although not every counselor trainee arrives at this phase with the same thinking and skill sets, all must make the shift in roles and expectations that accompany clinical practice. To emphasize the role shift required of students in practicum and internship, throughout this chapter we will use the term *counselor trainee* in place of the term *students.*

Additional pressures exist for counselor trainees as well, and, in turn, for counselor educators. In this vein, we agree with McAuliffe, who in Chapter 4 describes practicum and internship as "busy times." Not only are these times hectic for even the most facile multitasking and thinking trainees, they keep practicum/internship supervisors busy as well. If one question could possibly embrace the complexity of creating constructivist practica and internships, it might look like this: How do constructivist practica and internships get counselor trainees from here to there? *Here,* in this formulation, is living the graduate counseling academic life. *There* is living the professional counseling life. The task of ferrying counselor trainees across this transition is not, of course, the counselor educator's alone. Much learning has already occurred before counselor trainees enter clinical training. Nevertheless, practicum and internship intensify the risks.

# Ways of Knowing

Compounding the risks and rewards of counseling practice are the developmental challenges inherent in good counseling. Counseling practice requires a way of thinking that parallels the complexity of the counseling task; specifically, the nature of clinical training calls for relativistic ways of thinking (McAuliffe & Lovell, 2006). Counselor trainees whose thinking resembles the relativistic position enjoy the challenge of integrating personal and empirical ways of knowing (Knowles, Holton, & Swanson, 2005). For them, knowledge is contextual, never certain or complete. Moreover, for relativists, knowledge arises out of community-based conversations, not from a final authority. Relativism increases the chances that novel and ambiguous situations will engender more excitement than anxiety, more curiosity than automaticity. In our view, the outcome of the relativistic position is confident uncertainty.

However, the ambiguity inherent in the practice of professional counseling may challenge counselor trainees who view knowledge as something more concrete, which is where we find many counseling students (McAuliffe & Lovell, 2006). In some ways, they are trying to learn how to dance by looking at dance steps drawn on the floor. In contrast to the counselor trainee operating comfortably within the relativistic position, counselor trainees whose thinking resembles the dualistic position in Perry's (1970) scheme see the world of knowledge and themselves more simplistically. They tend to look outward toward external sources of knowledge, such as supervisors, even to the extent of diminishing their own voice (McAuliffe & Lovell, 2006). Ambiguity, which is embraced by the counselor trainee working from the relativistic position, may provoke in the more dualistic counselor trainee a dissonance that gets in the way of more relativistic ways of thinking. It is ideal, although unlikely, for counselor trainees to arrive at practicum and internship securely situated as relativistic thinkers. If they do not, one of the objectives of these courses is to challenge counselor trainees toward such a way of knowing.

The tasks of practicum and internship consist of ill-structured problems, which, by definition, have no ready or certain solutions. Sorting out how best to work with a client is complex. Instead of solutions drawn from a flowchart, actual counseling solutions are partial, temporary, and contextual. Under these conditions, the chance of a less-than-successful outcome becomes higher. By contrast, counselor trainees' desire for structure, guidance, and expert solutions is understandably high, especially for those who operate from a mostly dualistic mindset. The challenge for practicum/internship supervisors is to create environments where counselor trainees embrace the concept of productive failure (Kapur, 2008) and the state of not knowing (De Jong & Berg, 2008) as gateways to understanding. Those environments match the relativist's thinking and may over-challenge more dualistic thinkers. "Not knowing" how to be helpful to a client invites vulnerability into the room. Perhaps it is little wonder that counselor trainees resist practicing from a state of "not knowing."

The inherent riskiness of practicum and internship (Rønnestad & Skovholt, 2003), regardless of a person's way of knowing, is its personal nature. Counseling is simultaneously an intensely personal and public professional act. Counselors are the instruments of counseling (Woldt & Toman, 2005). Thus, who they are as people (the personal element) is who they are as professionals (the public element). This is risky business for the counselor trainee and the practicum/internship supervisor. Relative success or failure becomes a high-stakes proposition since a change in one element (e.g., the professional) stands a good chance of affecting the other (e.g., the personal). Reputations, personal and professional, are at stake.

In sum, the interactions between counselor trainee thinking (way of knowing) and the complexity of counseling practice impacts learning. In the learning-by-doing model, we find the notion of productive failure extremely helpful, one that we share repeatedly with counselor trainees. In doing so, we hope to create a culture with counselor trainees in which productive failure is embraced as a way to promote appropriate risk taking and creativity. Returning to our example of the belay line used at the start of the chapter, we extend our supervision belay line on behalf of productive failure to encourage exploration and draw it tighter to heighten the sense of security without stifling action. In addition to balancing challenge and support to promote cognitive development in counselor trainees, the next section addresses how we use Polanyi's (1962) idea of tacit knowledge to conceptualize how we might enhance the transfer from counselor trainees' experiences with counseling clients to their knowledge of professional counseling practice.

## Tacit Knowledge

Using a learning-by-doing model requires practicum/internship supervisors to move a counselor trainee *from* her or his experiences of counseling *to* using these experiences to build knowledge of counseling practice. Developing and articulating knowledge of counseling practice largely happens in the relationship between the supervisor and the supervisee (Tarule, 1998). This approach to working with counselor trainees draws from Polanyi's (1962) notion of tacit knowledge. Polanyi offers a window onto the delicate architecture of counselor trainees' nascent understanding of counseling practice. Through this window, practicum/internship supervisors can assist counselor trainees in transforming hunches into professional practice.

The central premise of tacit knowledge is that one knows more than one can tell. This idea is not a radical one for the counseling profession. We instinctively cast our eyes and ears to that which is just out of sight or earshot. However, tacit knowing is not the same thing as repression or even the unconscious. Tacit knowing is an active process whereby we use our bodies to *attend* to the world and *dwell* within it (Polanyi, 1962). Counselor trainees, fresh from experiences with clients, frequently arrive for supervision unable to easily express or understand what happened. They have been actively attending to the world of their clients. Experiences, however, can take time to form meaning. Thus, their silence or struggle for clear expression is due to the fact that "understanding precedes language" (Tarule, 1998, p. 277). This understanding without language may first express itself as a hunch. Hunches, properly attended to and nurtured by others such as the practicum/internship supervisor, may evolve into something meaningful and useful. Thus, counselor trainees often know more about the client and counseling practice than they can tell at any given moment.

How do counselor trainees begin to speak about what they only tacitly understand? The first step we take is to introduce the concept of tacit knowing. In this way, we set the stage for a continuing conversation about tacit and other ways of knowing. We ask counselor trainees for personal examples of their own tacit knowing, such as a hunch that one's parents were heading for divorce. We expand this discussion to include how tacit knowledge is a necessary building block to more expansive understanding, the kind gained only through social interaction such as supervision. We affirm the value of tacit knowledge and of its place in counseling practice. We stress that within this personal or tacit knowing lies the possibility of something novel (Gelwick, 1991). Our hope is that counselor trainees will not only see the importance of hunches, but also bring them into the supervisory conversation.

In the midst of this conversation about tacit knowledge, we use inquiry to draw counselor trainees from their internal personal knowing to more socially constructed ways. With telling comes the possibility for explanation, interpretation, application, perspective, empathy, and self-knowledge (Wiggins & McTighe, 1998). The first telling of the counselor trainee's hunch, however, may be gestural, a kind of finger pointing. Counselor trainees may lack words to describe what is happening within themselves, within the session, and within the client. With few words to describe an emerging construct, counselor trainees may resort to acts of figurative pointing, such as pointing to the video replay of a counseling segment. Wittgenstein (Baker & Hacker, 2005) called these *ostensive explanations* or *ostensive definitions*. To give an ostensive definition is to literally point one's finger at the object one lacks words to define. Ostensive explanations frequently need to be coaxed into language; they require care to flourish. When words elude counselor trainees' attempts to define or express a phenomenon, we often ask them to sit with the experience for a while to see if something surfaces. If video or audio is available, we simply ask counselor trainees to point at what they are trying to express. Alternatively, we remind them of the elusive nature of tacit knowing. We remind them that ostensive explanations are forms of tacit knowledge, which is a precursor to explicit knowledge (Polanyi, 1962).

# SUGGESTED ACTIVITIES

Constructivist practica and internship supervision engages in the complex task of promoting more relativistic thinking among counselor trainees. It also encourages movement from tacit knowledge of counseling experiences to explicit knowledge of counseling practice. The question remains: "How may we create practicum and internship experiences that simultaneously support and nudge counselor trainees (Kloss, 1994) toward more complex ways of knowing and to move tacit to explicit knowledge?" Put another way, "How can counselor educators compassionately usher students toward embracing *confident uncertainty* in counseling practice?" What follows is a discussion of activities whose aim is to achieve that goal.

## Essential Questions

As we stated earlier, ours is fundamentally a question-based, or inquiry-oriented, practice. We find that questions are one way to help counselor trainees realize the potential of tacit knowledge as something worth the effort to uncover (Wiggins & McTighe, 1998). We can help counselor trainees take these first steps toward explicit knowledge by helping them create questions that give shape and expression to what is known but cannot be told. Importantly, however, we seek not to ask questions ourselves; rather, we prompt counselor trainees to ask questions. Learning to ask meaningful and useful questions is foundational to initiating and maintaining a robust counseling practice knowledge base. For example, when counselor trainees struggle to make sense of an interaction with a client, we assist them in shaping their question, one inferred by the tacit knowledge of the counseling experience. Thus, we seat questions front and center as tools to use in exploring hunches and extending understanding. We help counselor trainees use what Goldberg (1998) calls "questions with heart" (p. ix), questions that speak to the multidimensional nature of experience. A question with heart can reverberate long after being asked. For instance, during one of our supervision sessions with a counselor trainee, he asked, "Will this [the doctorate] be enough to satisfy my father?"

We call the kind of inquiry used above *essential questioning* following Wiggins and McTighe (1998), as these interventions ask us to identify something worth knowing. *Essential* communicates their necessity for ushering into collective and personal conversations an "enduring evolutionary understanding" (p. 23). Such understanding endures beyond the counseling session or classroom and well into professional practice. It is also evolutionary in the sense that our individual and collective responses contribute to and transform the knowledge base of counseling practice. Essential questions, in part, fuel this evolution toward more adaptive understandings. Again, our primary task as practicum/internship supervisors is not to ask questions, but to assist counselor trainees in asking them. We use Bloom's (1956) Taxonomy to help students develop sophisticated questions as they are triggered during counseling experiences and from tacit knowledge.

## Applying Bloom's Taxonomy

We base essential questions, our own and those from counselor trainees, in Bloom's (1956) Taxonomy of educational objectives, a classification of thinking skills. Although the taxonomy has been a mainstay of curricular design for over 50 years, it was not until 2000 that Bloom's Taxonomy was adapted to promote the epistemological complexity of counselor trainees (Granello, 2000). Granello and Underfer-Babalis (2004) extended its use to supervising group counselors. Kindsvatter, Granello, and Duba (2008) further proposed its utility in assisting supervisees out of unhelpful patterns of thought.

As shown in Table 16.1, Bloom (1956) created six broad categories of educational objectives: knowledge, comprehension, application, analysis, synthesis, and evaluation. Specific activities in each category (e.g., "application") are represented as action verbs (e.g., "apply"). He envisioned the taxonomy moving with increasing complexity from left to right on the table. Thus, as can be seen in Table 16.1, thinking aimed at acquiring knowledge involves less complexity and yields less nuanced, less creative, and less sophisticated responses to questions and tasks than thinking that is directed at evaluation. The taxonomy builds on itself. Therefore, all levels can be important for learning. For example, evaluation is not possible without a sufficient knowledge base.

Basic counseling skills courses (which largely utilize knowledge through application thinking skills) focus on building knowledge that can later be used to solve the more sophisticated counseling problems found in practicum and internship (which largely utilize application through evaluation thinking skills). Practica and internships ask counselor trainees to access existing knowledge and skill bases and use them in novel ways. Counselor trainees also must develop new knowledge and skill bases. Furthermore, they are expected to apply and create knowledge and must perform competently. Doing the act of counseling is now needed to finish the task of teaching counselor trainees what they need to be able to do. In other words, the only

**TABLE 16.1** Bloom's Taxonomy of Thinking Skills

| Knowledge | Comprehension | Application | Analysis | Synthesis | Evaluation |
|---|---|---|---|---|---|
| List | Summarize | Solve | Analyze | Design | Evaluate |
| Name | Explain | Illustrate | Organize | Hypothesize | Choose |
| Identify | Interpret | Calculate | Deduce | Support | Estimate |
| Show | Describe | Use | Contrast | Schematize | Judge |
| Define | Compare | Interpret | Compare | Write | Defend |
| Recognize | Paraphrase | Relate | Distinguish | Report | Criticize |
| Recall | Differentiate | Manipulate | Discuss | Justify | |
| State | Demonstrate | Apply | Plan | | |
| Visualize | Classify | Modify | Devise | | |

*Source:* Bloom, 1956.

*Note:* During practica and internships, we aim toward questions related to the shaded areas in this chart).

way to finish the job of transforming prepracticum trainees into professional counselors is to practice counseling and, through such practice, to apply, analyze, synthesize, and evaluate counseling work.

We use Bloom's (1956) Taxonomy to frame essential questions in practicum/internship supervision. For instance, at the very start, many questions are at the knowledge level. Counseling intake forms and interviews yield knowledge about clients and their worlds. From the intake, a counselor may know that the client has two sisters (e.g., "How many siblings do you have?" is a knowledge-based question). Moving forward on the taxonomy to comprehension, the counselor may also learn that the client has less-than-satisfying relationships with the sisters, describing such sibling relationships as "not good" (e.g., "How would you describe your relationship with your sisters?" is a comprehension-based question). Although this information is interesting and important at one level, it is still relatively superficial, doing little to inform the counselor's understanding of what this information means to the client and how it influences current behaviors, emotions, and perceptions. It does not describe how these "not good" relationships play out in the client's life.

The more complex questions on Bloom's (1956) Taxonomy may offer the counselor trainee more substantial understandings of the client's experience. For instance, an analysis-based question would further the counselor's understanding. For instance, the counselor might ask, "How do you think your 'not good' relationships with your sisters play out in your relationships with your female coworkers?" Then, once the client analyzes this phenomenon, the counselor can use questions or reflections that utilize thinking skills across the taxonomy spectrum. For example, the counselor can use knowledge about the client (e.g., that she or he has "not good" relationships with sisters and female coworkers) to encourage deeper exploration. This may be accomplished by combining a comprehension-based counseling response (e.g., "So you seem to having trouble making friends with your female coworkers.") with an analysis-based counseling response (e.g., "But you have no trouble making friends with your male coworkers."). Moving deeper still, the counselor can ask the client an evaluation-based question (e.g., "How is that working out for you?"). This question puts the evaluation of lifestyle squarely onto the client's lap. Once answered by the client, the counselor's job is to promote solution building (analysis and synthesis) and then action (application).

Bloom's (1956) Taxonomy, if used in this way, increases supervisor intentionality (Granello, 2000). Moreover, as Granello suggests, the taxonomy gives supervisors a structured format for understanding a trainee's current way of knowing. And understanding a trainee's current development allows the supervisor to create essential questions within, but at the uppermost limits of, trainees' developmental capacities. The goal of working in this way, then, becomes increasing complexity of thinking in the counselor trainee by thoughtfully structuring essential questions that match current ways of knowing and challenge toward the next ways of knowing.

In this approach, counselor trainees not only create essential questions, they also categorize them according to Bloom's (1956) Taxonomy. The act of categorization (which is not always an easy thing to do) leads counselor trainees to evaluate the results of their thinking, another developmental accomplishment. Counselor trainees who create essential questions themselves become more independent and collaborative learners. To prompt this kind of development, we keep essential questions at the upper levels of Bloom's Taxonomy (e.g., the categories of application, analysis, synthesis, and evaluation; the shaded areas in Table 16.1). This guideline moves trainees toward more complex ways of knowing. To carry this reflection process a step further, practicum/internship supervisors can ask counselor trainees to post their essential questions to an online discussion board. That medium extends the supervision dialogue beyond the face-to-face encounters of a seminar or of face-to-face supervision. The online discussion board allows others to offer possible solutions or alternative views related to the question and to suggest new questions and edit existing ones.

The use of essential questions is wide-ranging in the practicum/internship course. These questions are used in individual and group supervision, on discussion boards, and in the counseling sessions themselves that counselor trainees have with clients.

# Overview of Objectives, Content, Learning Activities, and Principles

The following activities have utility in both practicum and internship settings. They acknowledge the idea that clinical knowledge is socially constructed, that is, it is formed in the context of a community of professional counselors. Bloom's (1956) Taxonomy is a tool to deepen and expand understanding. We carry a number of activities, such as case presentations, across time so that counselor trainees can see a progression in their knowledge and understanding. We emphasize writing so that counselor trainees may share and have record of their conversations. Table 16.2 summarizes the objectives, content, and various learning activities of this course and how they fit with constructivist principles. Some of the specific methods will be described next.

**TABLE 16.2** Course Objectives, Content, Activities and Processes, and Constructivist Principles

| Learning Objectives | Content | Activities and Processes | Constructivist Principles |
|---|---|---|---|
| Develop effective relationship, interviewing, and problem-conceptualization skills. | Therapeutic relationship | Peer interview<br>Practice sessions<br>Recorded reviews<br>Case presentations<br>Reflecting teams<br>Journals | Exploring multiple possibilities in the counseling context |
| Adequately implement theoretical models in the process of counseling. | Counseling theories and research outcomes | Workbook<br>Journals<br>Practice sessions<br>Recorded reviews<br>Case presentations | Constructing hypotheses and plans for interventions |
| Develop and implement effective counseling plans that demonstrate skills in assessment, management, and technology use and an awareness of and sensitivity for issues of diversity. | Treatment planning<br>Cultural understanding | Feedback loops<br>Reflecting teams<br>Peer interviews<br>Case presentations<br>Mock counseling sessions | Knowledge is co-constructed. Collaboration occurs in learning and teaching. |
| Perform counseling work functions within a structured setting, and assume the roles and responsibilities of a professional staff member. | Professional counselor roles and responsibilities | Field experience<br>Learning drops<br>Journals | Negotiating relationships over time through reciprocal understanding |
| Demonstrate behavior and attitudes consistent with the roles and ethical expectations of a professional counselor. | Ethical code discussions | Workbook<br>Case studies and review<br>Case presentations<br>Journals | Counseling takes place within social context with various viewpoints to consider. |
| Utilize supervision in a constructive manner for continued personal and professional growth. | Supervision requirements and evaluation methods | Reflecting teams<br>Supervision sessions in and outside of classroom<br>Journals | See Chapter 18 of this text for constructivist supervision assumptions. |

## Journals or Diaries

In this course, counselor trainees keep semistructured journals or diaries about their counseling work. Loose templates organize the writing tasks with the goal of steering responses toward the right side of Bloom's (1956) Taxonomy (i.e., application, analysis, synthesis, and evaluation). These templates also include a few major topic headings, such as Personal Responses. The templates create just enough structure to organize experience without imposing too much.

Trainees post these journals online so that others in the discussion group may respond. The template for the postings asks for a brief description (100 words or less) of an important event, realization, and/or relationship related to their counseling life. The word limit drives writers to make their points succinctly. Next, writers describe their reactions in emotional, cognitive, and behavioral terms. These two parts of the assignment require thinking tasks that Bloom (1956) would associate with knowledge and comprehension. Once counselor trainees have reflected on their knowledge and comprehension, they identify key themes that have emerged for them. Next, counselor trainees create one or two essential questions that summarize and draw together the key themes. Essential questions replace the more traditional summary. These tasks—identifying themes and abstracting essential questions from them—guide counselor trainees to move beyond comprehension toward synthesis. Finally, counselor trainees identify and discuss how they would apply what they have synthesized to clinical counseling practice. These applications should integrate personal dimensions with professional development needs.

The template offers structure to counselor trainees who are anxiously seeking it. Templates do not seem to hinder counselor trainees' creativity or expression of their unique voice. Below is a journal entry, unedited and used with the permission of the doctoral counselor trainee who created it (as part of an advanced practicum) using the template as described in the preceding paragraph.

> During supervision this week, the issue of feelings and drawing them out was a topic that I left the session thinking more about. Am I comfortable with the client experiencing strong feelings in session? Am I fearful that those feelings might get out of hand and interfere with the cognitive-behavioral process directed at solutions that I see myself engaged in on the recordings? Where in my theoretical orientation does expression of feelings come into play? I do know that I am comfortable when strong feelings are expressed, I "feel" them with my client, I stay "in the game" with them when they are expressed. The question I am coming to is a theoretical orientation issue: how does the expression of feelings help? I have a quote that I posted at one time to remind myself that to feel is to heal. I suppose it spoke to me so loudly when I saw it because it is an issue that I am finding myself struggling with.

Her journal entry is brief, to the point, and shows a progression of thinking from the personal (e.g., how comfortable am I with feelings) to the professional (i.e., thinking about researching the topic of feelings as they relate to counseling) and ultimately back toward herself.

## Reflecting Teams

In family therapy's reflecting teams, counselors share their hypotheses with the family in order to make therapy more transparent and less hierarchical (Anderson, 1995). Cox, Banez, Hawley, and Mostade (2003), in their research on reflecting teams, note that reflecting teams create a collaborative atmosphere between clients and counselors. While multiple methods may be used for reflecting teams (e.g., Friedman, 1995), they always allow a team to quietly observe an existing interpersonal dynamic or system. The team then shares its observations with the clients, and the clients offer reflections on the team's thoughts. The reflecting team concept initiates moderately unusual conversations about internal and external thoughts and emotions (Anderson, 1991) or tacit knowledge (Polanyi, 1962) from its members.

In practicum or internship courses, reflecting teams can be used in a similar fashion. The aim of reflecting teams is to engage conversations characterized by multiple perspectives. In practicum, for example, this activity might start with a student showing a video of a counseling session to the supervisor and/or supervision group. Then the counselor trainee and practicum/internship supervisor might hold a conversation about the session as the video is reviewed. Simultaneously, the other counselor trainees in the class serve as the reflecting team. They watch the counseling video and the supervision session from their unique vantage points. They think carefully about their observations, not only of the interactions between counselor trainee and client, but also the interactions between counselor trainee and practicum/internship supervisor. The reflecting team members then pose questions and discuss their observations with each other and *without* input from the counselor trainee and practicum/internship supervisor. Finally, the counselor trainee and the practicum/internship supervisor process the observations and plot a course for future counseling sessions.

## Follow-up Case Presentation

The case presentation follow-up extends traditional case presentation conversations beyond the initial sharing of a case conceptualization and suggested plans for action. Typically, counselor trainees present cases only once. We propose that counselor trainees benefit from engaging in conversations about the same case over time. Therefore, we ask counselor trainees to present the same case several times during the semester. Making case presentations an ongoing conversation changes the experience because the kinds of questions asked and discussed by the counselor trainee and the group typically shift upward along Bloom's (1956) Taxonomy in the ways they consider the case. We can prompt this progression by asking for questions relevant to tasks further to the right on Bloom's Taxonomy.

## Personal Career Development Portfolio

Counselor trainees in our practicum and internship classes develop a portfolio using PowerPoint or a personal website containing evidence of their competency in four areas. (More on portfolios is discussed in Chapter 26.) First, trainees articulate and briefly state how counseling works and how change occurs. Related to this, they develop a site-specific professional disclosure statement. This is an explicit statement of services they will deliver to clients at their training sites. Next, counselor trainees

produce an advertisement directed to clients at their site. There they must market themselves and the counseling profession to clients in a professional and ethical manner. Finally, they provide evidence for competency in specific areas of interest (e.g., papers written in other classes). Counselor trainees then submit a copy of the portfolio (on CD or via URL) for evaluation by instructors. Finally, they present the portfolio to the class.

## Field Experience Project and Presentation

Counselor trainees contribute, or "give back," to their placement site by collaborating with their internship site supervisor on a project. First, the counselor trainee suggests a project or consults with the site supervisor regarding a project that will enhance or improve the daily activities of the internship site. Project ideas must have the approval of the site and/or the site supervisor and the course instructor. The project should require a considerable amount of time to develop. Examples of projects might include organizing resource materials, creating a resource manual, organizing or creating clinical files for supervision, or developing a psychoeducational program or group experience. The main objective is for counselor trainees to leave their mark on the internship environment in a lasting and positive way. At the end of the internship experience, counselor trainees present to the class the nature of their project and its outcomes.

## Oral Case Presentations

Counselor trainees also present organized and relevant cases during their group supervision meetings. Case presentations resemble clinical "staffings" where the group provides help and/or support after the trainee has presented the case. During the presentation, the counselor trainee provides a brief overview of the client's background information, identified concerns, and defined goals for counseling. The presenter asks the group for insight into areas that they have identified as problems.

## Transcribed Recordings

We have found it valuable for counselor trainees to transcribe their work because much information can be missed by merely viewing recorded counseling sessions. Transcription is a labor-intensive exercise, so we typically ask for transcription of a 5- to 10-minute segment of a session, a segment about which the counselor trainee has questions. We ask them to characterize the interactions between themselves and the client using Bloom's (1956) Taxonomy. By characterizing interactions in this way, mismatched intervention and communication between client and counselor trainee become apparent. As noted earlier in the section on Bloom's Taxonomy, a counselor trainee who knows that the client has two sisters (e.g., after asking the knowledge-based question, "How many siblings do you have?") does not know much about the quality of the relationship with the sisters. This information gap may suggest to the counselor trainee a future direction along Bloom's Taxonomy.

Naturally, not all of the learning activities that we use in practicum and internship fit neatly into a model. The activities outlined here represent those that we link closely to the socially constructed, developmental framework we use. Our greatest challenge with this model is ourselves. We continue to explore ways to be more creative and adventuresome; our desire is to stretch and grow the model in ways that continue to surprise and delight us.

## CONCLUDING REMARKS

In introducing this chapter, we posed a question: How do constructivist practica and internships move students from a more restricted knowledge of counseling work to a fuller, more adaptive knowledge base? We have proposed that a question-centered approach to constructivist practica and internships is one such way. This approach, in our view, seems well suited to the tutorial, intimate, interpersonal nature of practicum and internship. Moreover, a question-centered approach brings the tacit knowledge of counselor trainees into the explicit conversations of professional counseling. We use essential questions coupled with a focus on the right side of Bloom's (1956) taxonomy to bring greater complexity into counselor trainees' ways of thinking. We aim to help counselor trainees learn how to ask questions with heart (Goldberg, 1998), questions that evolve enduring

understanding (Wiggins & McTighe, 1998). By doing so, we hope to promote more relativistic ways of knowing. We propose that by creating a learning and supervision culture in which questions fulminate, we liberate counselor trainees to move beyond what each one currently knows toward what collectively they may know together.

## REFERENCES

Anderson, T. (1991). *The reflecting team: Dialogues and dialogues about the dialogues.* New York: Norton.

Anderson, T. (1995). Reflecting process; acts of informing and forming: You can borrow my eyes, but you must not take them away from me! In S. Friedman (Ed.), *The reflecting team in action: Collaborative practice in family therapy* (pp. 11–37). New York: Gilford Press.

Baker, G. P., & Hacker, P. M. S. (2005). *Wittgenstein: Understanding and meaning: Volume 1 of an analytical commentary on the philosophical investigations, part 1: Essays* (2nd ed.). Cambridge, MA: Blackwell.

Bloom, B. S. (Ed.). (1956). *Taxonomy of educational objectives, Volume 1: The cognitive domain.* New York: McKay.

Cox, J. A., Banez, L., Hawley, L. D., & Mostade, J. (2003). Use of the reflecting team process in the training of group workers. *Journal for Specialists in Group Work, 28*(2), 89–105.

De Jong, P., & Berg, I. K. (2008). *Interviewing for solutions* (3rd ed.). Belmont, CA: Thomson Brooks/Cole.

Friedman, S. (1995). *The reflecting team in action: Collaborative practice in family therapy.* New York: Guilford Press.

Gelwick, R. (1991). Polanyi: An occasion of thanks. *Cross Currents: Religion and Secular Life, 41,* 380–381.

Goldberg, M. C. (1998). *The art of the question: A guide to short-term question-centered therapy.* New York: John Wiley & Sons.

Granello, D. (2000). Encouraging the cognitive development of supervisees: Using Bloom's taxonomy in supervision. *Counselor Education and Supervision, 40*(1), 31–47.

Granello, D. H., & Underfer-Babalis, J. (2004). Supervision of group work: A model to increase supervisee cognitive complexity. *Journal for Specialists in Group Work, 29*(2), 159–174.

Kapur, M. (2008). Productive failure. *Cognition and Instruction, 26,* 379–424.

Kindsvatter, A., Granello, D. H., & Duba, J. (2008). Cognitive techniques as a means for facilitating supervisee development. *Counselor Education and Supervision, 47*(3), 179–192.

Kloss, R. J. (1994). A nudge is best. *College Teaching, 41*(2), 60–65.

Knowles, M., Holton, E., & Swanson, R. A. (2005). *The adult learner* (6th ed.). New York: Butterworth-Heinemann.

McAuliffe, G. J., & Lovell, C. W. (2006). The influence of counselor epistemology on the helping interview: A qualitative study. *Journal of Counseling and Development, 8,* 308–317.

Perry, W. G., Jr. (1970). *Forms of intellectual and ethical development in the college years: A scheme.* New York: Holt, Rinehart & Winston.

Polanyi, M. (1962). Tacit knowing: Its bearing on some problems of philosophy. *Reviews of Modern Physics, 34,* 601–616.

Roethke, T. (1953). *The waking.* In N. Sullivan (Ed.), *The treasure of American poetry: A collection of the best loved poems by American poets* (p. 527). New York: Barnes & Noble Books.

Rønnestad, M. H., & Skovholt, T. M. (2003). Struggles of the novice counselor and therapist. *Journal of Career Development, 30*(1), 5–44.

Schön, D. A. (1987). *Educating the reflective practitioner.* San Francisco: Jossey-Bass.

Skovholt, T. M., & Rønnestad, M. H. (1995). *The evolving professional self: Stages and themes in therapist and counselor development.* New York: John Wiley & Sons.

Tarule, J. M. (1998). Voices in dialogue: Collaborative ways of knowing. In N. Goldberger, J. Tarule, B. Clinchy, & M. Belenky (Eds.), *Knowledge, difference, and power: Essays inspired by* Women's Ways of Knowing (pp. 274–299). New York: Basic Books.

Wiggins, G., & McTighe, J. (1998). *Understanding by design.* Alexandria, VA: Association for Supervision and Curriculum Development.

Woldt, A. L., & Toman, S. M. (2005). *Gestalt therapy: History, theory, and practice.* Thousand Oaks, CA: Sage.

# 17

# Teaching the Diagnosis and Treatment Planning Course

Victoria E. Kress and Karen P. Eriksen

Some irony exists in presenting a chapter on how to teach diagnosis and treatment to counselors. The counseling profession typically emphasizes growth and development, multiculturalism, and contextual thinking, all of which stand in apposition to the illness and remediation worldview traditionally implied in "doing" diagnosis and treatment planning (Eriksen & Kress, 2005, 2006; Zalaquett, Fuerth, Stein, Ivey, & Ivey, 2008).

However, counselors do need diagnostic capacities for a number of reasons. For one, were counselors to give up diagnosing, they would be disadvantaged financially. Third-party payers will most likely continue their requirements that counselors diagnose in order to be reimbursed for providing mental health services. Further, *Diagnostic and Statistic Manual of Mental Disorders* (DSM; APA, 2000) labels have some professional advantages. For instance, diagnoses may enable research on particular types of psychopathology. They provide a means of communicating with other mental health professionals. Particular diagnoses may also point to the need for referral to a different type of professional. For instance, after determining a bipolar diagnosis, a counselor would be clear about the need to refer the client to a psychiatrist for medication consult.

Or upon hearing that a child was suffering from attention deficit hyperactivity disorder, a school counselor might need to work with the child's teachers on some behavior modification procedures or medication monitoring.

Counselors are thus unlikely to give up their use of the DSM in the near future. How, then, can counselor educators retain their allegiance to a developmental, strengths-based, constructivist perspective of human experience while operating within the very well-established DSM diagnostic system that is currently essential to mental health care reimbursement? This chapter responds to that question by describing a diagnosis and treatment planning course that is guided by postmodern and constructivist principles.

## TRADITIONAL MODELS OF TEACHING DIAGNOSIS AND TREATMENT PLANNING

Before considering constructivist approaches to teaching the diagnosis and treatment planning course, we will review how the course has typically been taught. As readers will see, both the content and the course structure are tied to the objectivist paradigm.

## Content

Traditionally, the content of diagnosis and treatment planning courses has resembled the fields of clinical psychology and psychiatry more than professional counseling. The words *diagnosis* and *treatment* alone are part of the medical illness-and-cure tradition, in which clients are "diagnosed" with a "mental disorder" and subsequently "treated" to "cure" their "illness." The illness-and-cure tradition is further emphasized in the course's typical reliance on two texts, an abnormal psychology textbook and the DSM, as their primary information sources.

As typically taught, then, this course is grounded in an objectivist paradigm in at least two ways. First, it tries to pin down pathology as an entity. Second, it separates disease labels from understandings about how labels have been constructed and how social contexts might interact with illness experiences or difficult emotional experiences. From a social constructivist perspective, students learn historically contingent and socially situated moralities when they learn about "abnormal" behavior from a traditional DSM perspective (Maracek, 1993); and yet, these moralities are often not acknowledged.

## Structure

The typical structure of this course also follows objectivist principles. Instructors usually expect students to take exams in which they memorize and then apply diagnostic categories that have been established by experts. Memorizing categories is, in itself, not problematic if the categories are understood as situated within a cultural context and if they are not reified or universalized. Further, rejecting a diagnostic nomenclature is not required in order to learn the material in this course in a more inclusive, historically sensitive fashion. Even if students memorize diagnostic categories as a starting place, teachers and students can also analyze, contextualize, deconstruct, and reconstruct what are usually presented as "facts." Students might then discover that a more postmodern approach to diagnosis begins with a holistic understanding of their clients' histories and contexts, as well as an understanding of how these diagnoses intersect with the history and context of the diagnostic system.

## A POSTMODERN APPROACH

In this chapter, we aim to present a less traditional and hopefully more helpful approach to both the content and the structure of the diagnosis and treatment planning course. We aim to help students understand both clients' emotional struggles and the DSM in a less rigid, hierarchical, and pathologizing way. We begin by applying postmodern principles to the broad notions of diagnosis and treatment planning. Then, we specifically apply constructivist learning principles (see Chapters 2 and 3) to the teaching of the course.

Postmodern and constructivist philosophies propose at least two principles, one related to language and the other related to who makes meanings and how. Postmodern and constructivist thinkers assert that meanings are historically situated and are constructed and reconstructed through the medium of language (Gergen, 1985; Parker, Georgaca, Harper, McLaughlin, and Stowell-Smith, 1995; Rorty, 1979; Segal, 1986). Therefore, the language we use in this chapter and in teaching this course becomes very important. Further, a constructivist approach points toward an evolving co-construction of the counseling plan *with* clients, rather than a more structured, problem-saturated, predetermined plan that is applied *to* clients (Hoyt, 1994). Therefore, in the postmodern, constructivist spirit, we might, in the title of the course and in discussions thereafter, replace the traditional term *treatment planning* with the less pathologizing *collaborative counseling planning,* and the word *diagnosis* with *assessment* (Neimeyer, 1993).

## ASSESSMENT AND COLLABORATIVE COUNSELING PLANS

So-called postmodern thinkers actively challenge the objectivism of scientific and positivist assumptions; this has ramifications for counseling assessment and the development of collaborative counseling plans. As described in Chapter 1, postmodernists propose that knowledge is not a representation of facts existing in one static reality. Instead, they emphasize three concepts—social constructionism, contextualism, and deconstruction—that illustrate how meaning is *represented* rather than found. Postmodern scholars propose the social constructionist notion that what people consider knowledge is really a construction, or a hypothesis about reality, based on the sociocultural and historical contexts within which the scholars pursue that knowledge (Watzlawick, 1984). Determinations about the "reality" of people's behavior (i.e., psychological evaluations), from this skeptical, postmodern perspective should then also be considered to be historically situated constructions.

A review of social constructionism will be helpful before this course is described, as it is fundamental to its teaching (see Chapter 1 for basic definitions of social constructionism). Social constructionism emphasizes two primary ideas: (1) knowledge is constructed rather than discovered, and (2) knowledge is constructed within, and therefore affected by, its social context (Bohan, 1995). This means that knowledge cannot be separated from its contexts, such as ethnicity, social class, gender, or time in history.

Counselors are immersed in personal biases and experiences, as well as in a sociocultural milieu; these all impact what counselors know and how they come to know it (Bohan, 1995). The sociopolitical environment affects counselors' assessments and measures, the models used for searching, and the questions asked in seeking knowledge. All of these affect counselors' creation of knowledge, which includes decisions about assessment and counseling plans (Bohan, 1995). Therefore, knowledge gained during the assessment process is not equivalent to discovering "truth," but merely, in Bohan's words, a "best guess, based on selective vision, using limited tools, shaped by the contextual forces surrounding the search" (p. 8). Clearly, positivist and constructivist questions about assessment differ. While the positivist diagnostician asks, "What are the facts?" social constructionists ask, "What are the assumptions?" While the positivist asks, "What are the answers?" social constructionists ask, "What are the questions, and how were they decided?"

Three illustrations of positivist assessment may clarify the differences between positivist and social constructionist assessment. First, during the turn of the 20th century, mental health providers believed that women were incapable of engaging in serious intellectual endeavors and risked sterility if they pursued higher education (Bohan, 1995). The reader might imagine practitioners' recommendations to women and to their families and communities when a woman aspired to pursue higher education or something else that was different from what society at that time considered normative. In the current sociohistorical context, these turn-of-the-last-century beliefs seem ludicrous. At the time, the ideas made "sense." In response to this historical experience of women, a social constructionist might ask, "What socially constructed assumptions were guiding the mental health providers' inquiries about women and families, and why were particular questions being asked?"

Women who are victims of intimate partner abuse offer another example. These women often exhibit muscle tension, irritability, and sleep disturbance, symptoms that would seem to meet the *DSM-IV-TR* criteria for a generalized anxiety disorder. A positivist or mechanistic view might assert that counseling should focus on alleviating anxiety using traditional means for doing so: medication management, individual relaxation training, and refutation of cognitions. Essentially, the message would then be, "Here are ways to be less anxious and upset about being beaten." Or if clinicians were to label these women "dependent," a simplistic picture would be created in people's minds that failed to consider social factors, access to resources, or societal power dynamics occurring within the culture or within these women's partnerships.

Social constructionists, in contrast, would examine multiple sources of information, especially those related to social power. They would contend that the woman's individual and cultural contexts should be considered, that treatment ought to at least focus some attention on system change and on the woman's safety (i.e., eliminating the domestic violence; Eriksen & Kress, 2008). The following question would at least be raised within a social constructivist dialogue: "In a context in which women are encouraged to defer to, and depend on, males, should dependent behaviors (e.g., staying with an abuser) be pathologized?" They might also ask, "Where does one draw the line between 'normal' dependency and 'abnormal' dependency, particularly in a society that favors individualism and independence?"

The positivist perspective on eye contact offers a third example. A positivist would propose a unified evaluation of those who avoid eye contact, regardless of their cultural heritage or norms. Such avoidance of eye contact would be used as important evidence in some diagnoses. Yet, clearly, direct eye contact means different things within different cultures. For instance, within most Western cultures, direct eye contact communicates strength, self-confidence, and integrity, while avoidance of eye contact may indicate fear, insecurity, shyness, and, most likely, some degree of interpersonal difficulties. Within Asian cultures, on the other hand, direct eye contact may be considered rude or aggressive, and may only be engaged in by a superior toward a subordinate. Lowered eyes might, from an Asian perspective, instead be viewed as respectful. Social constructionists propose that without considering such sociocultural contexts, counselors cannot understand the meaning of such behaviors as avoiding eye contact, nor the degree to which they are normal or abnormal, acceptable or of concern (Kress, Eriksen, Dixon-Rayle, & Ford, 2005).

Social constructionists particularly ask questions about the use of power, for instance, "To what extent are diagnoses a means of social control, ensuring conformity to the interests of those in power and denying the connection between social inequities and psychological distress?" (Marecek & Hare-Mustin, 1991, p. 525). Maracek (1993) notes that key contextual questions, such as those involving ethnic differences, gender roles, domestic violence, and sexual abuse, are virtually unmentioned in the vast catalog of books that deal with diagnosis and treatment planning. Often individual behaviors or emotional or illness experiences are not considered within their socio-political-cultural milieu, but are labeled as and considered to be diseases, independent of the environments that may have caused them or that have at least affected them (Parker et al., 1995). Counseling students need to understand that many of the most debilitating diagnoses, such as schizophrenia, anorexia/bulimia, and alcoholism, have well-documented differences in expression and in explanation from one culture to another and from one historical time period to another.

In summary, by challenging traditional, mechanistic diagnostic and treatment ideas, social constructionists question commonly held assumptions. Because social constructionist questions and assumptions differ from traditional understandings, different realities and meanings of behavior also emerge within this perspective. Students benefit from considering these questions and examining the differing assumptions. They also benefit from accounting for context and exploring the consequences of diagnostic labeling.

## Why Teach the DSM at All?

Given the difficulties with DSM diagnosis, particularly as traditionally taught, the question arises: Why teach the DSM at all? A variety of answers might be offered. First, in the United States and a number of other countries, the DSM provides the diagnostic system used for communicating among professionals. It is applied as a way of organizing client behaviors. When used flexibly, it may provide clues for the counselor to explore further. Axes 4 and 5 of the DSM system may also assist counselors in identifying situations and life contexts that intersect with specific diagnoses (Eriksen & Kress, 2005). In addition, sometimes clients who feel immoral or weak because of their "symptoms" find it helpful to have a name for what was once a nameless set of experiences, such as anxiety or sadness.

It is also almost impossible for counselors to avoid using the DSM. All counseling settings where community, mental health, addictions, and family counselors work (e.g., hospitals; community mental health, private practice, and residential settings) require a *DSM–IV–TR* diagnosis in order for counselors' and other providers' services to be reimbursed by insurance companies. The particular DSM diagnosis may determine what services clients need or will be permitted to receive as a result of insurance companies' reimbursement limitations. Although from a postmodern perspective, DSM diagnosis can be thought of as merely one (potentially useful) way of making meaning about a client's presenting concerns, it is an inescapable reality of professional reimbursement in today's health care environment.

Within the context of a postmodern understanding of diagnosis and of how this course might be taught, the goals are (1) to help students understand clients' emotional and psychological distress or disturbance experiences, but to do so from multiple perspectives and in collaboration with the clients and their communities, and (2) to help students work together with clients and their communities to build meaningful counseling plans. Therefore, in the constructivist version of this course, students learn to use the DSM to develop multi-axial diagnoses. However, we particularly emphasize how Axis 4 psychosocial stressors interact with the other Axes. In this way, when students develop collaborative counseling plans, they address all of the levels of experience that clients or those who care about clients find troubling, or that keep clients from functioning well in their social contexts.

In summary, the postmodern movement has challenged traditional ways of knowing and standard ways of thinking about assessment and counseling plans. While single-minded diagnosis and overly structured treatment plans are antithetical to postmodern philosophies, necessity dictates that clinically oriented counselors be trained to use the DSM and have the skills necessary to develop structured, documented plans in working with clients. The best resolution to the discrepancy between a postmodern perspective and the demands and expectations of the mental health field is to help counselors find a balance between the assumptions and behaviors of traditional clinical ways of understanding and a postmodern skepticism.

# APPLYING CONSTRUCTIVISM TO TEACHING THE COURSE

As mentioned earlier, the postmodern perspective contributes to both the structure and the content of the assessment and collaborative counseling planning course. Counselor educators use reflexive, inclusive, context-sensitive classroom strategies as well as challenging traditional notions of diagnosis and treatment planning. Constructivist (which will here be used interchangeably with postmodern) classroom techniques parallel students' actual work with clients. The course, as we have designed it, is largely experiential and incorporates the constructivist educational principles outlined in the initial chapters of this book. Table 17.1 summarizes the course's learning objectives, activities, and social constructivist or constructivist-developmental aims. What follows the table are more specific applications to the course of some of Chapter 3's guidelines for constructivist-developmental education.

**TABLE 17.1** Course Objectives, Activities, and Constructivist Principles

| Learning Objectives | Learning Activities | Constructivist Principles |
|---|---|---|
| Know textbook material on diagnosing and treating. | • Read text<br>• Develop DSM-related role plays<br>• Develop questions for guest speakers<br>• Develop lists of behaviors to look for in role plays/videos/cases<br>• Classroom discussions of material before applying it to role plays/cases/videos | Providing structure to support interpersonal or dualistic knowers |
| Apply DSM and treatment concepts to people with various mental health issues and problems in living. | • Conduct counseling/assessment sessions using role plays<br>• Apply DSM/treatment information while viewing role plays, videos, or discussion cases and listening to guest speakers<br>• Observe, discuss, and reflect in personal reaction/response papers on the DSM/treatment material | Application of principles in action (breaking down ambiguous stimuli into manageable parts, asking for evidence of position, including diversity of perspectives) creates real-world ambiguity, requires deciding for oneself, standing back from own work to evaluate = challenge toward procedural knowing.<br><br>Structured grading rubrics and feedback sheets = support. |

*(Continued)*

**TABLE 17.1** (Continued)

| Learning Objectives | Learning Activities | Constructivist Principles |
|---|---|---|
| Apply DSM and treatment concepts to themselves or people they know. | • Paper and/or collaborative counseling plan in which they apply the information learned to themselves or another person, with a special emphasis on cultural context and development | Applications in action (personalizing the learning) reflects real-world ambiguity, requires deciding for oneself, standing back from own work and from self to evaluate = challenge toward procedural knowing.<br><br>Structured grading rubrics and feedback sheets = support. |
| Demonstrate ability to reflect on progress, evaluate own skill development, make plans for improvement. | • Reflection papers | Standing back from own work and from self to evaluate = challenge toward procedural knowing.<br><br>Exemplars, grading rubrics, and feedback sheets = support. |
| Demonstrate developmental and culturally appropriate diagnosis and treatment-related counseling skills. | • Instructor modeling of behaviors in role plays in class<br>• Students conduct role plays with each other<br>• Practicing deconstructing language | Application of principles in action (breaking down ambiguous stimuli into manageable parts, asking for evidence of position, including diversity of perspectives) creates real-world ambiguity, requires deciding for oneself = challenge toward procedural knowing. |
| Advance developmentally. | • Dialectical discourse, e.g., debates/controversial topics<br>• Consider client cases from multiple perspectives<br>• Final paper—multiple perspectives emphasized<br>• Presentations—multiple perspectives emphasized; active learning<br>• Hearing other students' voices<br>• Applying theory/critical thinking<br>• Personalized learning<br>• Process questions<br>• Abdicating authority role<br>• Modeling incompleteness | |

# Varying Course Structure and Content

To communicate the value of diverse learning styles and personalities, as well as the existence of multiple perspectives, constructivist instructors vary the ways in which they present or introduce students to material and present a range of material (e.g., various theoretical perspectives for addressing client needs).

## Diversity in Materials and Methods

The constructivist perspective advocates the use of a diversity of materials and methods (see Chapter 3) for teaching, in recognition of the fact that students differ in their learning preferences, styles, and needs. Varying the structure and teaching styles aims to both match a variety of student learning styles and challenge students to consider new styles of learning. Additionally, variety in learning experiences may better hold students' attention and may reach and challenge students at different levels of constructive development (Kegan, 1998; McNamara, Scott, & Bess, 2000). Therefore, we combine minilectures with experiential activities, such as group discussions, role plays, small-group activities, writing assignments, group presentations, watching popular movies or videos, and interacting with guest speakers.

In addition, we use articles and books beyond those that are typically used in order to offer students alternative views of diagnoses and their contexts. These alternative materials provide students with a broader understanding of assessment and counseling planning, thus breaking the "textbook and DSM" routine. Materials that express contradictory views also introduce students to the controversies surrounding diagnosis and challenge students to think more independently. For instance, Eriksen and Kress's (2005) *Beyond the DSM Story* reviews many authors' perspectives on challenges to the DSM. Also, Parker et al. (1995), in *Deconstructing Psychopathology,* dispute the categorization and individualization of mental disorders and contend that diagnoses are not descriptive of "reality out there" but actually constitute the reality. That is, the authors claim that the existence of diagnostic categories actually creates diagnoses. The classic research by Broverman, Broverman, Clarkson, Rosenkrantz, and Vogel (1970)—in which mental health professionals evaluated "normal" feminine characteristics more negatively and pathologically and "usual" masculine characteristics more positively—may also challenge students to think about the dilemmas that exist in labeling clients. Articles that discuss DSM diagnoses as normal developmental reactions to stress may provide further alternative viewpoints.

In addition, readings that describe the individual variations in expression of diagnoses help students take a nuanced perspective on diagnostic labels. In that vein, we choose articles that tell the stories of clients who have received various DSM diagnoses, and find that these more holistic stories encourage students to complement the traditional individualized medical model with an understanding of the client's context. For example, instructors might choose an article about a trauma survivor, in which the author considers multiple factors before choosing to diagnose posttraumatic stress disorder (PTSD) over borderline personality or dissociative identity disorder. It is worth explaining to students during discussions about such an article that PTSD is a less stigmatizing diagnosis. One particularly rich resource for understanding potential problems in diagnosis is *Counseling and Psychotherapy Transcripts, Client Narratives, and Reference Works: A Resource for Mental Health Educators and Practitioners* (McAuliffe, 2008).

In addition to diagnosis, the course also addresses so-called treatment plans, which we have renamed *collaborative counseling plans.* In assisting students to determine helpful approaches to client problems, instructors might use at least two different types of texts: a traditional treatment planning book that addresses both concrete cognitive-behavioral and insight-oriented interventions (e.g., Jongsman & Peterson, 1999), and various articles or books that describe narrative or solution-oriented interventions and that focus on client strengths (e.g., Hoyt, 1994). Using a variety of materials communicates to students that many approaches exist for working with clients, and that counselors have many factors to consider in deciding what would be best to use with a particular client. This particular combination of approaches introduces students to both traditional approaches and less pathology-laden conceptualizations of client experiences.

## Encouraging Students to Actively Construct Their Educational Experience

As described in Chapter 1, students enter this course with varying cognitive developmental capacities (Kegan, 1998; Perry, 1981), ranging from more dualistic or conformist epistemologies to relativistic, self-authorized thinking. Students' capacities relate to their need for structure and direction. While teaching with this range of readiness in mind, we consider it a course goal to promote students' development toward self-authorized thinking. Toward that end, instructors provide more structure early in the course, and as students develop cohesion as a class and comfort with the course material, instructors become less structured.

To assist students in owning the course as adult learners, instructors might introduce the course with a "card sort" activity that allows students to contribute to the design of the course. In this activity, students, first individually and then in groups of increasing size, brainstorm a list of needs and desires for the course (see Eriksen, Uellendahl, Blacher, & McAuliffe 2002, for specifics on this activity). This flexible, relatively open activity challenges students to rely on their own judgment and to determine what matters to them in the learning and meaning-making process. It sets the tone for the rest of the course by requiring dialogue and negotiation as part of the learning and deciding process. Instructors can additionally encourage students to actively assist in constructing the course by asking them questions such as "Which topic or issues would you like to focus on today?" and "How would you like to go about processing this topic?" With the realization that they are active creators of knowledge, students develop the ability to better reflect on others' knowledge (e.g., in textbooks, in the DSM itself) and to recognize knowledge as created, rather than only available from authorities.

Students continue to take an active role in creating the class by inviting friends, family members, and others who have been diagnosed with various disorders into class to share their experiences. These visitors are, in a sense, cultural informants. Students help construct the classroom experience by inviting people whom they know. They develop questions to ask the visitors, questions that will help students better understand the visitors' "disorders." After the guest visits, students openly share their responses and questions and thoughts, and they suggest important counseling strategies or other considerations to remember with people who struggle with particular issues.

Engagement with live people who have struggled or are struggling with diagnosable problems helps students discover that people are not entirely defined by the labels that they have been given. Instead, these visitors possess many admirable characteristics and life situations with which students can identify. The distance between client and counselor may thus become diminished. The dichotomous thinking—sick or well, crazy or normal, good or bad—also decreases as a result.

## Personalizing Teaching

Counselors place a premium on developing and maintaining the counseling relationship. Although the teacher-student relationship is less intimate than the counselor-client relationship (e.g., the former has an evaluative component), constructivist educators still strongly emphasize building relationships with students, that is, they apply the constructivist learning principle of personalizing their teaching. In that vein, instructors can try to remember names, know what students' personal goals are for the class, and know about students' identities and professional experiences outside of class. For instance, at the beginning of the class, students might answer a list of questions about their class goals, professional goals, experiences and interests, and how they enjoy learning (e.g., visual, auditory, experiential). Students might then share this information with class members. Instructors can make a point of learning these preferences so that they can pull class members' experiences and interests into the course when relevant. Personalizing the teaching-learning experience in this way builds a sense of connectedness among students and between students and the teacher, and creates an environment in which students feel safe to do the work of socially creating meaning.

Additionally, a community (see Chapter 3) emerges from the twofold actions of the instructor (1) encouraging and engaging difference and (2) emphasizing dialogue and interaction. To assist in building such a community, instructors might set up the room so that students sit in a circle facing each other. In addition, instructors can encourage students to exchange ideas and concerns among themselves, rather than only with the teacher. Instructors can display openness to and genuine interest in all comments, even if they diverge from their own. They can encourage expression of different opinions and thoughts, considering the differences to be ripe opportunities for challenging their own and students' ways of knowing. To assist in awareness and exploration of different ideas, instructors might encourage and reinforce the risk taking involved in expressing different opinions.

Also, consistent with personalized teaching and with building relationships, educators can disclose experiences from their personal lives and from their own work in various counseling settings. They can share what different clients have taught them and the ambiguities and practical problems associated with various diagnoses and treatments. Instructors might also reveal their continuing struggles with many of the issues and concerns, particularly those presented in class by students.

Further, instructors can ask students to personalize their learning by applying class experiences to themselves (Schutz, Drogosz, White, & Distefano, 1999). Many students or their friends or family members have received diagnoses or have been in counseling. Class members can share what these encounters were like for them, if they feel comfortable doing so. For example, in the first author's class, a student discussed her experience of being diagnosed with anorexia as a teenager and how that diagnosis and subsequent treatment, in her opinion, had further exacerbated her struggles. The class found her disclosure to be very interesting and reported many resulting shifts in their thinking. Other students have reported what it was like growing up with a sibling or parent or grandparent who bore a diagnosis.

# Valuing and Promoting Experience

A third constructivist teaching strategy is valuing and promoting experience. Constructivist educators place a high premium on experiential learning, believing that the more active students are with the material, the more they will learn and remember, the more they will be challenged to think critically about the material and learning experiences, and the more they will progress developmentally. Experiential learning has been described as grounding concepts in personal life experience, illustrations, and experiments (see Chapter 3). In other words, experiential learning focuses on both *saying* and *doing* (Dale, 1969). It engages students actively in meaning-making and contrasts with treating students as passive recipients of the teacher's wisdom. In addition to the activities already discussed, the following practices offer energizing experiences during the course: interactive interviews and guest speakers, role plays, watching videos and/or popular movies that depict a mentally ill character, writing counseling plans, and creating presentations.

## Interviews and Guest Speakers

As indicated above, students benefit from meeting people who are currently in some type of counseling (e.g., a person diagnosed with PTSD who is participating in counseling at a rape crisis center). Instructors and students may have access to friends and former clients who would be able and willing to speak with the class. Instructors can ask local mental health providers to recommend client speakers—those who, in their professional assessment, are functioning well enough to do so.

We have found that clients often feel empowered by this experience. They also are very committed to ensuring that future counselors are well informed because frequently they have approached many practitioners before finally finding help for themselves. Students also find it fascinating to have the opportunity to hear people talk about their counseling experiences. Afterwards, they see clients in more holistic ways than would be possible from merely reading a text. They cease seeing clients as their diagnostic label.

There are some challenges in having guest visitors of this kind, however. One is ethical, the other is logistical. Logistically, instructors have to make many phone calls in order to find visitors who are both competent psychologically and available on the necessary date. Should a guest fail to appear (although this hasn't ever happened in our experience), instructors need to have backup plans. It is sometimes difficult to strike a balance between perseverance and reminder calls, and protecting the visitor's well-being and boundaries.

In addition, at least three ethical proscriptions may disincline some educators from having clients speak with their classes: the professional mandates (1) for confidentiality, (2) to do no harm, and (3) not to use clients for our own personal benefit. To mitigate these perils, instructors can rely on the referring mental health providers to ensure that the clients are up to the task. Instructors might also send ideas to the client visitors about the specific questions that they might want to address in their presentations. Instructors should inform visitors that it is completely up to them as to what they would like to share and how much, and that, if they become uncomfortable, they may end the presentation at any time. A signal between the visitor and the instructor can be arranged, by which the visitor can indicate that she or he wants to end the presentation, and the instructor can then end it and escort the visitor out. Taking a class break at this time allows the instructor to debrief the visitor if necessary.

A variety of people have visited our classrooms. People have shared their experiences with depression, anxiety, and PTSD. Parents have come in with their autistic children and have told the stories of the autism, including the worries that the parents have about the future. Parents who have brought their autistic children have also illustrated the children's limitations by asking them questions while the class looks on. A man with Asperger syndrome, who had spent his life in and out of psychiatric hospitals, usually enduring high doses of medications, was able, as a result of a groundbreaking placement in a mental health provider's home, to come and share his experiences. His caretaker came with him to describe the program that they were a part of that had made such a difference in his life. A man with a "spanking" fetish came in and described spanking parties. A transsexual woman, who was now a Catholic priest, told her life's story, a story that included many life-threatening experiences both before and after her surgery. A parent of a transsexual man also came in to share her family's experiences.

One story is particularly illustrative. A woman who struggled with generalized anxiety disorder responded to my (Eriksen's) request for class visitors. She had presented in my human development class in a rather strident and defensive way and, as a result, had not been well received by the students. Needless to say, I was a bit worried about having her speak again, particularly given that many of the same students would be hearing her presentation. But when she shared in the diagnosis class, quite vulnerably and tearfully at times, her story about experiences with anxiety and difficulties with finding help softened the students' hearts. Their perceptions of her changed to caring and understanding, in contrast to the irritation that they had previously expressed. The shift in their experiences of her provided a great deal of food for thought and discussion about preconceptions and assumptions, about how psychological problems might be expressed, and about the interpersonal difficulties that might be experienced by those with even mild "disorders."

Some counselor educators may have reservations about bringing vulnerable clients into such a challenging situation. However, it is our belief that clients have many strengths; they are not just their illness. By forbidding this sort of experience, we communicate to students and clients that clients have nothing to offer us or teach us, or that clients have no ability to set limits for themselves. If we so communicate, we model a truth that we don't want our students to adopt. We also betray our counseling identity by defining clients solely in terms of their illness (Eriksen & Kress, 2006). Don't we believe that people are empowered by offering of themselves to others, by actualizing their strengths? Clients and their mental health providers can determine whether the clients have the capacity to share in this way. And all of the clients who have come to our classes have spoken of wanting to make sure that counselors know about people like them. Sometimes their sense of urgency comes from their own experiences of visiting many therapists before finding someone who understood their situation and could help them.

However, should this sort of learning experience feel daunting, it may be more feasible to instead invite counselors from various mental health agencies. Agencies that might be selected include an adolescent residential facility, a community mental health agency, a rape crisis center, or a private practice. I (Kress) ask counselors and guest speakers to talk about their work with clients who meet the criteria for one particular DSM diagnostic category or one presenting issue (e.g., diagnoses and interventions with trauma survivors). Speakers discuss practical and logistical issues associated with diagnoses and treatment planning—perspectives that are not typically presented in textbooks and must otherwise be learned on the job.

## Role Plays

Role plays provide other opportunities for active, experiential learning related to assessment and collaborative counseling plan development. Instructors can ask students to role play a presenting problem with class members. Those playing the role of "counselor" can then try to identify the DSM category that is being portrayed. In addition, "counselors" can be asked to develop a collaborative counseling plan with the "client." During plan development, "counselors" would practice their listening skills and other counseling techniques and actively include the "clients" in the process of planning future counseling.

During the role plays, instructors might also ask students to be alert to their own pathologizing or, conversely, normalizing of client issues and to deconstruct their underlying assumptions. When students choose to role play someone they know, they often make rich and surprising contributions to the deconstruction process. For instance, one student in our class played her alcoholic and frequently suicidal sister. At certain stopping points in the counseling process, the class processed their thoughts about the "client." Because the "client" knew the situation much more holistically and personally, she was able to help the class recognize how judgmental and demeaning some of their assumptions were. This experience encouraged students to be less judgmental in assessing future clients and helped them question what personal issues might be leading to the judgments. Finally, following the role plays, students process what it was like to be the counselor or the client, and they discuss the challenges of applying diagnoses and of working within the client's reality.

## Videos and Movies, With Counseling Plans

Another experiential opportunity asks students to watch videos or movies and then write counseling plans—including five axis diagnoses—for various characters. Instructors who teach the diagnosis and treatment planning course generally have access to videos which portray clients who have received various diagnoses are portrayed. The videos bring the textbook material to life; words on the page simply do not convey what it is like to sit with a person who is struggling emotionally or behaviorally. Instructors might sometimes *not* tell students what they will be watching, and afterward ask students to apply a DSM diagnosis. The exercise tunes students in to the subtlety with which symptoms sometimes present themselves. The videos of actual psychotic patients further persuade students of the difficulties that these people have in navigating the usual demands of life.

Instructors might also collect a list of movies that portray characters with emotional or other psychological troubles. Several times during a semester, students may be asked to schedule a movie night to watch one of these movies. One value of this assignment lies in the fact that movie characters "live" life in many different situations. Therefore, students gain through the movies a good sense of the characters' difficulties in living. Students also see examples of clients' strengths, their impact on the people around them, the challenges faced by family members and friends, the contextual contributors to their difficulties, and the impact of various "treatment" strategies, whether by professionals or well-meaning friends and relations. Again, through well-made and referenced movies, students can see, feel, and experience the whole person rather than a mere list of symptoms on a page. They also get a sense of how they might feel in the presence of the client, and what counselor or family member responses might be helpful or unhelpful.

To engage students more fully in the learning goals during movie watching, instructors can ask students, after watching the movie, to complete a formal counseling assessment and plan on the "client" or person with emotional or relational problems. Their watching becomes more active and involved as they take notes in preparation for writing the plan. This formal assessment and plan parallels a real-life activity, one that will be required of them during practicum and internship experiences and, later, in their lives as counselors. Repeated efforts at completing the plan, with class reviews, suggestions, and discussions, help students think holistically about clients and develop expertise in a necessary skill. (A sample counseling assessment and collaborative plan is included in the Appendix to this chapter.)

## Presentations

In the next section readers will find a description of an end-of-semester writing activity or final paper. An experiential alternative to the final paper engages small groups of students more actively in creating presentations for the end of class. Instead of the traditional approach of asking students to present material from papers they have written, or to present on a particular diagnostic group, each small group might present on one chapter in our book *Beyond the DSM Story* (Eriksen & Kress, 2005) or from another book or chapter that challenges the traditional diagnostic system. The chapters in our book include extensive literature reviews on ethical concerns related to diagnosis, the conflicts between diagnosis and counseling's identity, feminist challenges to diagnosis, and multicultural concerns with diagnosis. Students consult with the instructor to ensure that their presentation includes active learning experiences and multiple learning formats.

In planning the presentation, students become very active with the material. But perhaps the most important benefit of this assignment is that, because students begin their presentation planning when the course begins, they bring material from their chapter into classroom discussions throughout the semester. This adds richness to class discussions, role plays, and debates without requiring another textbook in an already textbook-rich class. And students become active creators of the learning experience in their weekly contributions to class.

# Emphasizing Multiple Perspectives

Another constructivist guideline for teaching asks instructors to emphasize multiple perspectives. This can be done through presenting cases that illustrate the need to consider multiple perspectives, offering historic illustrations, considering multiple approaches to treatment, engaging in debates, and deconstructing language.

As instructors engage students in these activities, they can help students hear and respect differing experiences during course assignments so as to encourage a level of tolerance and openness to other views. Instructors can also model openness to varied viewpoints and experiences. They can demonstrate comfort with ambiguity and take a "not knowing" stance on various issues. Instructors can also use their counseling skills to encourage students to pay attention to changes in their ways of thinking and being in the world that may emerge as a result of discussing such perspectives.

Considering multiple perspectives will be quite challenging for more dualistic or interpersonal students. As a result, instructors need to provide appropriate supports to hold such students in the midst of the challenges. For instance, instructors need to support more concrete thinkers by offering clear guidelines for assignments and discussions (e.g., rubrics, specific questions). Such structure "holds" the students while they consider more complex issues and real-life examples.

## Illustrative Cases

Cases from an instructor's practice offer opportunities to consider multiple perspectives. For example, I (Kress)

have presented a female Puerto Rican client who initially reports characteristics of depression and anxiety, and who has been subject to violence within her marriage for many years. Students who are more concrete, authority-reliant thinkers (Lovell & McAuliffe, 1997) tend to contend that the client "is" dysthymic and "has" generalized anxiety, and that the goal of counseling should be to decrease these symptoms through counselor-generated "treatment." Students who think from a more constructivist position consider broader, more contextual, and less rigid possibilities, for instance, "Maybe the client has PTSD secondary to the sustained violence. Perhaps the client should be encouraged to leave or radically change her relationship with her husband." A constructivist thinker can consider a variety of contextual issues simultaneously (e.g., maybe the client doesn't want to leave her husband, maybe she is safer staying with her husband, maybe she has PTSD along with another primary diagnosis, maybe there are cultural issues contributing to the family violence). As indicated above, instructors encourage exploration of multiple perspectives while providing supports for more concrete students.

## Historic Illustrations

Historic illustrations present perspectives that may be foreign to students, but illustrate the situatedness of people's perspectives in a particular time and place. Specific, historical practices in diagnosis and treatment reveal much that abstractions cannot. For instance, in the late 19th century, Dr. S. Weir Mitchell garnered praise for his treatment of female neurasthenia patients (i.e., those with fatigue, loss of energy and memory, and feelings of inadequacy), treatment that involved overfeeding the women and depriving them of intellectual and social stimulation. At a similar time in history, Dr. Isaac Baker Brown advocated and practiced clitoridectomy as a cure for female masturbation. He contended that the fragile women of the upper class could not survive masturbation and would succumb to idiocy and eventually death if they practiced it. Interestingly, the women for whom he recommended clitoridectomies were usually considering divorce (Maracek, 1993). Providing such examples to students encourages rich discussion about how values, society, and historical context affect our assumptions about how best to counsel clients.

Another lively class discussion emerges when instructors share the following information and ask the following questions:

At one point, the DSM labeled gays and lesbians as "mentally ill." However, this designation was eventually dropped from the DSM-III. More recently, diagnoses such as paraphilic rapism, self-defeating personality disorder, and premenstrual syndrome were proposed for inclusion in the DSM-IV. Much debate ensued and these proposed "disorders" did not win a place in the DSM-IV (Marecek & Hare-Mustin, 1991). What do you think about how experts decide what is and isn't labeled as "abnormal" behavior? How do individuals' perspectives change when it is decided that some characteristic or issue is "disordered"? What legal or educational implications ensue from these decisions?

Inviting discussion about controversial diagnoses and treatments encourages questioning, exploration of abuses of power and victimization of those who were different, and dialogue about socially situated reasons for diagnostic or treatment choices.

## Multiple Perspectives on Treatment

In acknowledging the historically or contextually situated nature of diagnosis and treatment, educators bring to the foreground questions about who ought to be "treated" and what strategies ought to be used in "treatment." The person who seeks help has traditionally been considered the only one open to or available to treatment. If those who seek help are worried about their relationships or their children, the boundaries of counseling may be extended to include other members of the family. However, the question about who is to be included in counseling creates larger questions for the profession: In what system(s) ought counselors to intervene? Should they broaden their interventions to include *all* of the factors in problems?

The field of family counseling, of course, always considers individual problems to exist in the context of a family (or a culture or a neighborhood or some other system) and so aims its interventions at the larger systems, and some counselors who specialize in family work may do the same. Perhaps all mental health professionals should ask whether an individual complaint is ever really an individual problem. For instance, if a counselor believes that a woman's depression emerges from being victimized by the discrimination in her rather traditional small town, discrimination that supports her husband's rather demeaning sexual demands on her, should the counselor intervene in the very town itself? Or if the counselor believes that an African American man's drug addiction results in part from the despondency he feels from experiencing discrimination—a discrimination that keeps him in jail for having hurt a White man who was trying to tie him up in a tree—should the counselor focus individually on his addiction; or on the social inequities in his town; or on the broader society that makes his addiction, or blocking the pain of his experience in his society, quite understandable?

Counselors for social justice might ask, "If counselors know that these social conditions lead directly to mental health problems, how can they *not* work just as tirelessly to change society as they do in the counseling office?" Posing these questions, along with multiple perspectives on possible answers, may trigger the internal struggle necessary for students to think more systemically and contextually, and to consider how advocacy at the political, community, or school level might augment the individual, family, and group work done in the counseling room.

## Debates

Debates may also encourage consideration of multiple perspectives. Debates direct students, particularly students who are more *multiplistic* (Perry, 1981) or *subjectivist* (Belenky, Clinchy, Goldberger, & Tarule, 1986), that is, in between dualistic and constructivist (McAuliffe & Lovell, 2000), to carefully evaluate the usefulness of particular methods in different situations. If handled and processed thoroughly and productively, debates can reduce dualistic thinking. Debate topics might include the following controversies:

- Mental disorders are located within the individual vs. mental disorders are located within society.
- Abnormal behavior *can* be differentiated from normal behavior vs. abnormal behavior *cannot* be distinguished from normal behavior (see Parker et al., 1995, for a more thorough review of additional polar

oppositions, and Eriksen et al., 2002, for specifics about conducting debates).

- Diagnostic labels hinder the effective treatment of persons with mental disorders vs. diagnostic labels enable effective treatment.
- Women experience higher rates of psychopathology (Slife, 2000) vs. society is structured in a way that disadvantages women, making more of them look as though they are disturbed.
- Counselors overdiagnose certain disorders, such as attention deficit hyperactivity disorder, when they aren't really present vs. diagnosis is an objective and accurate process.

## Deconstructing Language

Deconstruction refers to the process of examining the foundations of meanings by exploring their context (Combs & Freedman, 1994; White & Epston, 1990). Deconstructive listening requires counselors to believe that people's stories can have many possible meanings and that the meaning the listener makes may not be what the speaker intended. In listening deconstructively, instructors and students develop a "not knowing" attitude in order to encourage the discussion of multiple possible interpretations of client verbalizations and symptoms. Deconstructive listening, by definition, requires openness to multiple perspectives.

Instructors can ask students to consciously practice deconstruction in diagnostic interviews and in creating counseling plans. For instance, clients frequently come to counseling saying that they are "depressed," "obsessive," or "codependent." A constructivist counselor helps such clients deconstruct these labels by asking, in response, "What does that mean to you?" or "How does that label help you?" rather than imposing the counselor's own meanings onto their words.

## Encouraging Intrapersonal Process Awareness

A final constructivist guideline that might inform the teaching of the assessment and counseling planning course is encouraging intrapersonal process awareness. Thinking about thinking, or metacognition, is critical to developing reflective constructivist thinkers. The use of videos and case studies provides opportunities for metacognitive thought.

## Videos

In response to the videos mentioned above, instructors can encourage metacognition by asking students to use Interpersonal Process Recall (IPR; Kagan, 1980) to discuss what they are thinking at various points in the video. They might, for example, ask such IPR questions as "Why were you thinking that?" "Where does such thinking come from?" and "What does such thinking tell you about yourself?"

Similarly, students may make recordings of role-played counseling sessions and then share what they were thinking during particular sections of the recording and why. To ensure that students don't forget what they were thinking or that they don't change their responses from their immediate reactions, students can stop the recording during the session to jot down their thoughts. This technique of quickly having students write down their thoughts helps them be more aware of their automatic thoughts, hence increasing reflectivity and awareness of biases. Students then process their automatic thoughts with the class. They benefit from hearing other students' thought processes in response to the same information and situation. They also become aware of automatic thoughts that may not be accurate or helpful to the client. They can be asked to think carefully about where those thoughts came from and whether they fit with their personal story in any way. Thinking about their thoughts helps them get their own issues out in the open, reduces judgmentalism, and reduces the automaticity of concrete or inherited beliefs.

## Case Studies

Interpersonal process awareness (as well as multiple perspective taking and experiential learning) may also be encouraged by discussing cases interactively (see Eriksen et al., 2002, for specifics). Students may develop their own case studies, or the instructor can provide case studies. Some instructors use case examples from their own work with clients and incorporate what their clients have taught them. In response to these cases, students construct a diagnosis and possible collaborative counseling plan goals and process their thoughts on the case with regard to various diagnoses and counseling strategies. During this process, instructors encourage students to brainstorm freely, without monitoring their thoughts, in an attempt to help them become more aware of what their immediate impressions might be.

After initial work on the cases, instructors can add a contextual factor that they had not initially mentioned in order to trigger new thinking and different discussion directions. Instructors again ask students to think about their thinking: for instance, what it means that they changed their diagnosis when different contextual information was added. This activity helps students solidify the importance of context and challenges students to consider the course material in new ways.

## Writing Assignments

Instructors may also apply the constructivist principles so far mentioned in writing assignments. Writing assignments give students the opportunity to grow and change during the process of demonstrating their learning (Neimeyer, 1993). As we have designed them, the writing assignments for this course help students personalize their learning, provide an opportunity for active knowledge creation and student reflectivity between class sessions, act as catalysts for class discussions, and encourage co-creation of meaning in the social setting.

For instance, in the effort to illustrate for students how diagnoses are invented and not discovered (Parker et al., 1995), instructors might give students a series of writing assignments in which they respond to articles (or to a book such as the aforementioned *Beyond the DSM Story,* Eriksen & Kress, 2005) that propose particular perspectives. For instance, students can consider the myriad of changes in the DSM over the years and the fads and fashions that have affected diagnosing. Or they might consider Maracek's (1993) perspective that diagnoses such as hysteria, nymphomania, erotomania, and machoism have served to enforce culturally sanctioned ideas of female subordination to men's sexual desires and have, over the years, changed in response to societal pressure. Students might then consider such questions as "How is the boundary drawn between disorder, on one

hand, and eccentricity and/or crime, on the other?" "What kinds of circumstances surround the death of some diagnoses and the birth of others?" "What social contexts correlate with different diagnoses?" "Where does one draw the line between normal adaptation to stress and pathology?" (adapted from Parker et al., 1995).

Students may also be asked to think critically about the counseling *process* in a series of writing assignments. For instance, they might respond to the following: "What is your theory about how people change, and what role do you believe you play in this change process?" "List five beliefs you have about the counseling and client change process." "How can it be helpful and/or harmful to share client diagnoses with clients?" "How can you use diagnoses with clients in ways that are empowering, rather than reinforcing the client's beliefs that *they* are pathological?" "What are five ways you can actively involve clients in the development of a collaborative counseling plan?"

Another writing assignment might ask students to research the relationship between a particular diagnosis and the current socio-political-cultural milieu. For example, in the United States, anorexia nervosa was most commonly diagnosed in young European American females during the late 20th century. However, the demographics of this diagnosis appear to be changing, and a discussion of these changes and contexts helps to expand students' ways of knowing beyond the typical perception that only certain people "get" certain diseases or diagnoses.

In other writing assignments, instructors might ask students to name five ideas in their assigned readings that were confusing, surprising, or interesting or that generated cognitive dissonance or emotions. Students might be asked to make a list of five differences and similarities between particular diagnoses or treatments. They might also be asked to indicate how they will improve their strategies for collaborative assessment and counseling planning. These writing assignments encourage reflective thinking and integration of the course material. To integrate the writing assignments into class meetings, each week the instructor might call upon a different student to share his list with the class. The students' lists provide a rich source of discussion and meaning-making within the class and encourage further development of cohesion among students. Calling on one person each week also provides enough external structure to motivate students to reflect on the material during the week.

Processing writing assignments in class also presents students with perspectives that differ from their own. When students encounter different perspectives among their classmates and have to think critically about the different responses, they begin to progress developmentally. As instructors respond to and encourage dialogue about students' differing responses in class, a microcosm of society is formed within the classroom. Students begin to see that the line between normal and abnormal behavior is not as easily drawn as they had previously thought.

## The Final Paper

Throughout the semester, instructors might ask students to keep in mind their final paper, in which they will consolidate their thoughts and assumptions about diagnosis, collaborative assessment, and developing collaborative counseling plans. For that paper, students draw from experiences (e.g., panel discussions, interviews) that they have had during the class and incorporate what they have learned in previous writing assignments. The assignment for the paper is as follows:

> Write a paper about a pseudo-client (e.g., a character from a movie or book, someone you know). In the paper, apply a *DSM–IV–TR* diagnosis and develop a collaborative counseling plan. The paper should be no more than 20 pages in length and should be written in APA style. Please consider the following questions in writing your paper:
>
> 1. In what ways does your client conform with specified DSM criteria? What is your client's assessment of the presenting concerns?
>
> 2. In what ways does your client differ from the DSM criteria?
>
> 3. How might the client's cultural background/sexual orientation affect her or his diagnosis and collaborative counseling plan?
>
> 4. What historical/social/political/cultural issues do you need to consider before applying this diagnosis?

> 5. How does the client's gender affect her or his diagnosis and collaborative counseling plan?
>
> 6. What strengths does the client have that can be integrated into the collaborative counseling plan?
>
> 7. What specific needs does the client perceive that she or he has, and what specific goals would the client want to have incorporated into the collaborative counseling plan?
>
> 8. How would you integrate the client's goals with your goals as the counselor?
>
> 9. What theory or approach will help the client reach her or his goals and objectives?
>
> 10. What is your theory of change, and how would you assist your client to change?
>
> 11. How would you regularly evaluate, with the client, whether the collaborative counseling plan goals were being achieved and whether the means of achieving the goals were satisfactory to the client?

This final paper helps students pull together the varieties of new meanings they have developed during the class and gives structure to their emerging thoughts. Students share their experiences in writing the paper during the final class meeting.

# CONCLUSION

A former student of one of the authors stated, while reflecting on her counselor training, that through this course she had developed a respect for her clients, their life situations, and their strengths. She discussed how, in her clinical practice, a context and strengths perspective differentiated her from colleagues in other professions. She felt proud to be a counselor and to have a clear professional identity. Clearly, a postmodern perspective contributes to students achieving a professional identity that emphasizes normal growth and development and strength-based approaches just at the time in their educational and professional lives when they are struggling to figure out what counseling is about.

In addition, when taught this way, the diagnosis course is active and fun. It is often the first time that students engage with clients—live and on video—and the needs of clients were what drew them to the field in the first place. Finally, postmodern perspectives and techniques encourage students' constructivist-developmental growth, which research has demonstrated is related to better counseling (Eriksen & McAuliffe, 2006; McAuliffe & Lovell, 2000).

However, instructors face a number of challenges when teaching diagnosis and treatment planning from a postmodern perspective. For one, instructors need comfort with ambiguity and the ability to tolerate a non-expert role. In addition, they need skills in reflecting on the process of the class and the ability to be attentive to student needs. Finally, instructors need to be able to challenge the status quo. It is clear that instructors need to have achieved a relativistic (Perry, 1981) or institutional (Kegan, 1982, 1998) level of development themselves in order to tackle these challenges, and research seems to indicate that many have not.

But given the benefits to clients, to students, and to the profession of a course taught in this way, in a course that develops students' contextual, social constructionist, and deconstructive capacities, while concurrently helping them develop their professional identities and grow and develop personally, it seems well worth it to urge counselor educators to both design courses in this way and to pursue the developmental capacities necessary for success.

# RESOURCES

## Movies Illustrating Various Diagnoses

Agoraphobia with panic attack and PTSD

*Copycat*

Posttraumatic Stress Disorder

*Fearless*
*Behind the Lines*

Bipolar Disorder

*Mr. Jones* (mania)

Depression/suicide

*Ordinary People*
*Prince of Tides*
*Night Mother*

Obsessive Compulsive Disorder and Obsessive Compulsive Personality Disorder

*As Good As It Gets*

Delusional Disorder and Bipolar Disorder/mania

*12 Monkeys*

Fugue State

*Random Harvest*

Multiple Personality Disorder

*Three Faces of Eve*
*Sybil*

Dissociative Disorder (faked)

*Primal Scream*

Schizophrenia

*Fisher King*
*A Brother's Promise*
*A Beautiful Mind*

Personality Disorder

*Good Will Hunting* (sociopath)
*Dead Man Walking* (sociopath)
*Fatal Attraction* (borderline)
*Blue Skies* (borderline)
*What About Bob?*

Alcohol Dependence

*Ironweed*
*Leaving Las Vegas*
*When a Man Loves a Woman*
*The Morning After*
*Verdict*
*Days of Wine and Roses*
*Lost Weekend*
*Postcards From the Edge*

Substance Dependence

*Trainspotting*
*Drugstore Cowboy*
*The Basketball Diaries*

## Sources for Videos

Most psychopathology or diagnoses books come with video examples of people with difficulties. As instructors teach the class regularly, they receive these books from publishers, along with the videos. Instructors might also ask other faculty who have taught the course for the videos they have been sent. In addition, videos are available for purchase from Microtraining (www.emicrotraining.com) and from the American Psychological Association (www.apa.org/videos).

# REFERENCES

American Psychiatric Association. (2000). *Diagnostic and statistical manual of mental disorders IV-TR*. Washington, DC: Author.

Belenky, M. F., Clinchy, B. M., Goldberger, N. R., & Tarule, J. M. (1986). *Women's ways of knowing*. New York: Basic Books.

Bohan, J. S. (1995). *Re-placing women in psychology: Readings toward a more inclusive history* (2nd ed.). Dubuque, IA: Kendall/Hunt.

Broverman, I. K., Broverman, D. M., Clarkson, F. E., Rosenkrantz, P. S., & Vogel, S. R. (1970). Sex-role stereotypes and clinical judgements of mental health. *Journal of Consulting and Clinical Psychology, 34*, 1–7.

Combs, G., & Freedman, J. (1994). Narrative intentions. In M. F. Hoyt (Ed.), *Constructive therapies* (pp. 67–91). New York: Guilford Press.

Dale, E. (1969). *Audio-visual methods in teaching*. New York: Holt, Rinehart & Winston.

Eriksen, K., & Kress, V. E. (2005). *Beyond the DSM story: Ethical quandaries, challenges, and best practices*. Thousand Oaks, CA: Sage.

Eriksen, K., & Kress, V. E. (2006). The DSM and professional counseling identity: Bridging the gap. *Journal of Mental Health Counseling, 28*, 202–217.

Eriksen, K., & Kress, V. E. (2008). Gender and diagnosis: Struggles and suggestions for counselors. *Journal of Counseling & Development, 86*, 152–162.

Eriksen, K. P., & McAuliffe, G. J. (2006). Constructive development and counselor competence. *Counselor Education and Supervision, 45*, 180–192.

Eriksen, K., Uellendahl, G., & Blacher, J., & McAuliffe, G. (2002). In class group activities. In G. McAuliffe & K. Eriksen (Eds.), Teaching strategies for constructivist and developmental counselor education (pp. 139–163). Westport, CT: Bergin & Garvey.

Gergen, K. J. (1985). The social constructionist movement in psychology. *American Psychologist, 40*, 266–275.

Hoyt, M. F. (Ed.). (1994). *Constructive therapies*. New York: Guilford Press.

Jongsman, A. E., & Peterson, L. M. (1999). *The complete adult psychotherapy treatment planner*. New York: John Wiley & Sons.

Kagan, N. (1980). *Interpersonal process recall*. East Lansing, MI: Author.

Kegan, R. (1982). *The evolving self: Problem and process in human development*. Cambridge, MA: Harvard University Press.

Kegan, R. (1998). *In over our heads: The mental demands of modern life*. Cambridge, MA: Harvard University Press.

Kress, V. E., Eriksen, K., Dixon-Rayle, A., & Ford, S. (2005). The *DSM–IV–TR* and culture: Considerations for counselors. *Journal of Counseling & Development, 83*, 97–105.

Lovell, C., & McAuliffe, G. (1997). Principles of constructivist training and education. In T. L. Sexton & B. L. Griffin (Eds.), *Constructivist thinking in counseling practice, research and training* (pp. 211–227). New York: College Teachers Press.

Maracek, J. (1993). Disappearances, silences, and anxious rhetoric: Gender in abnormal psychology textbooks. *Journal of Theoretical and Philosophical Psychology, 13*, 115–123.

Marecek, J., & Hare-Mustin, R. T. (1991). A short history of the future: Feminism and clinical psychology. *Psychology of Women Quarterly, 15*, 521–536.

McAuliffe, G. J. (2008). *Counseling and psychotherapy transcripts, client narratives, and reference works: A resource for mental health educators and practitioners*. Thousand Oaks, CA: Sage.

McAuliffe, G., & Lovell, C. (2000). Encouraging transformation: Guidelines for constructivist and developmental instruction. In G. McAuliffe & K. Eriksen (Eds.), *Preparing counselors and therapists: Creating constructivist and developmental programs* (pp. 14–41). Alexandria, VA: Association for Counselor Education and Supervision.

McNamara, D. S., Scott, J., & Bess, T. (2000). Building blocks of knowledge: Cognitive foundations for constructivist counselor education. In G. McAuliffe & K. Eriksen (Eds.), *Preparing counselors and therapists: Creating constructivist and developmental programs* (pp. 62–76). Alexandria, VA: Association for Counselor Education and Supervision.

Neimeyer, G. J. (Ed.). (1993). *Constructivist assessment: A casebook.* Newbury Park, CA: Sage.

Parker, I., Georgaca, E., Harper, D., McLaughlin, T., & Stowell-Smith, M. (1995). *Deconstructing psychopathology.* London: Sage.

Perry, W. G., Jr. (1981). *Forms of intellectual and ethical development in the college years: A scheme.* San Francisco: Jossey-Bass. (Original work published 1970)

Rorty, R. (1979). *Philosophy and the mirror of nature.* Princeton, NJ: Princeton University Press.

Schutz, P. A., Drogosz, L. M., White, V. E., & Distefano, C. (1999). Prior knowledge, attitude, and strategy use in an introduction to statistics course. *Learning and Individual Differences, 10,* 291–308.

Segal, L. (1986). *The dream of reality: Heinz von Foerster's constructivism.* New York: Norton.

Slife, B. (Ed.). (2000). *Taking sides: Clashing views on controversial psychological issues.* New York: McGraw-Hill Higher Education.

Watzlawick, P. (Ed.). (1984). *The invented reality: Contributions to constructivism.* New York: W. W. Norton.

White, M., & Epston, D. (1990). *Narrative means to a therapeutic ends.* New York: W. W. Norton.

Zalaquett, C. P., Fuerth, K. M., Stein, C., Ivey, A. E., & Ivey, M. B. (2008). Reframing the *DSM–IV–TR* from a multicultural/social justice perspective. *Journal of Counseling and Development, 86,* 364–371.

# Appendix
## Clinical Case Presentation Report

Date: _____

Family/Client Name: _____

Identified Client: _____
Date of Birth: _____
School: _____

Others in home (name, age, sex, relationship):

_____

## Identifying Information

GARREACS (gender, age, religion, race, ethnicity, ability, class, sexual orientation); current employment and educational situation of client/family members; current family constellation and living arrangements; current marital situation.

## Present Problems and Condition

Reason for referral; who referred; client/family's subjective perceptions of problems; response to and progress made in counseling; other professionals involved with client/family. What precipitated counseling at this time? Include symptomatology needing attention.

## Mental Status

Appearance, orientation, affect, mood, thought processes, motor functions, judgment, insight, intellectual functioning, presence of psychotic processes or thought disorders, suicidality/homocidality, overall nonverbal/process presentation.

## Social History

Chronological history of: Family constellation and description of family relationships—current family and family of origin; custody arrangements; adaptive level of other family members; number of marriages and divorces; outstanding events or abnormal situations in family; client/family level of cooperation with helping agencies; relationship with peers and community supports; level of social skills; relationship with authority figures; leisure activities such as hobbies or sports.

## Educational/Employment History

If identified patient (IP) is child, client's current grade and school placement, level of performance academically, extracurricular activities. If IP is adult, current employment, types of jobs held, highest grade completed, degrees or certifications. Also indicate any problems with performance, attendance, tardiness.

## Medical History

Date of last physical; present state of health; any medical conditions, including neurological and physical; major illnesses; hospitalizations, surgeries, injuries, allergies; current medications. Include sexual history, if applicable. Any special diets, eating or sleeping problems.

## Psychological/Counseling History

Include reasons for past treatment, type, outcomes, suicide attempts, hospitalizations, medications, and diagnoses. Is anyone in home currently under the care of a mental health professional or on psychotropic medications?

## Chemical Use History

Include drugs used, significant life experiences related to beginning, ending, or changes in addiction, any periods of sobriety, drug treatment received.

## Legal History

Include any encounters with police, charges pending, court dates pending, convictions, jail terms served, probation, or parole.

## Financial History

Include current stresses experienced due to finances, bankruptcy, borrowing or stealing money, selling/pawning of items.

## Religious/Spiritual Practices

Indicate religious preference, if any, and describe client's/family's involvement with group or individual spiritual practices.

## Family's/Client's Strengths

(Include processes observed in session that may assist in resolving presenting problems.)

## Family's/Client's Deficits/Needs

(Do not include factors related to the presenting problems here.)

## Dynamic Formulation

Family work—Please answer the following questions: Describe the structure of the family, including who is in charge, what is the nature of the boundaries between people and subsystems, where do family members lie on the continuum of engaged versus disengaged? How do the family's patterns of interaction maintain the presenting problem? How are the presenting problems helpful to the family? What is your systemic hypothesis?

Individual work—Using theoretical language, answer the question: Why does the client(s) have this problem at this time?

## *DSM–IV–TR* Diagnostic Impressions

Axis I _____

Axis II _____

Axis III _____

Axis IV _____

Axis V _____

## Cultural Factors

Hypothesized and observed impact of gender, age, ability/disability, race, religion, ethnicity, socioeconomic class, sexual orientation on the counseling process. How might these factors impact client's perceptions of counselor and counselor's perception of client? How might these perceptions interact to impact the counseling relationship?

## Treatment Plan

A. Goals

B. Objectives (steps client/family will take to reach goals)

C. Approach (strategies counselor will use to achieve goals and objectives)

D. Modality, frequency, estimated length of treatment

E. Staff responsible

## Progress Made Thus Far

Please indicate the progress made thus far on treatment goals and objectives and any new goals and objectives that you have established that have not yet been achieved.

# Teaching Counseling Children and Adolescents

Toni R. Tollerud and Ann Vernon

*Atticus says to Scout, "If you learn a simple trick, Scout, you'll get along a lot better with all kinds of folks. You never really understand a person until you consider things from his point of view . . . until you climb into his skin and walk around in it."*

*To Kill a Mockingbird,* Harper Lee (1962, p. 113)

As counselor educators whose primary responsibility is to help students learn about counseling children and adolescents, we often use this quotation on the first day of class as a way of reminding future counselors that they have to step into the world of children and adolescents. They need to see things from a different perspective if they are to have any hope of being successful with this age group. We then proceed to structure class sessions in a variety of creative ways that enable students to climb "inside the skin" of children and adolescents.

This chapter identifies teaching strategies that prepare prospective counselors to work with children and adolescents. The ideas we present correspond with the principles of constructivist teaching, which in turn mirror many of the concepts proposed by Carl Rogers (1969) in his pioneering work, *Freedom to Learn.* We wonder if we would need this discussion about transforming teaching and learning if Rogers' conditions for facilitating learning—"prizing the learner, prizing his [*sic*] feelings, his opinions,

his person" (p. 109); stressing the importance of the learner taking responsibility for what she or he wants to achieve; valuing experiential learning; and encouraging inquiry—which all seemed revolutionary at the time, had been taken more seriously. Perhaps these ideas didn't take hold because they were (and still are, to some extent) such a radical departure from more traditional ways of teaching, in which the teacher is clearly in control of the learning environment and the focus is exclusively on content.

Currently, however, there seems to be renewed interest in more student-centered learning. As presented today, constructivist teaching principles are more empirically grounded and developmentally targeted than Rogers' ideas, and hopefully they will succeed in transforming the way that counselor educators teach.

Educational psychology offers many examples of how constructivist principles might be used to facilitate effective learning. Building upon the theories of Piaget and Vygotsky, research suggests that the social construction of meaning occurs when the teacher provides relevant experiences for the student and then helps the student make sense of the experiences through processing them. The teacher thus mediates the learning experience (Omrod, 2006). These methods, according to Woolfolk (2005), put the student at the center of learning, as reflected in cooperative learning and problem-based learning.

In problem-based learning, for example, students confront a realistic problem that has meaning for them but may not necessarily have a "right" answer (Woolfolk, 2005). This approach aligns well with the field of counseling children and adolescents, in which there are generally few "right" ways to work with clients. Consistent with the "few right answers" notion, McAuliffe contends in Chapter 1 that effective counselors refrain from entering the learning or counseling environment with preconceived ideas. He suggests that counselors enter a situation or a counseling session open to the experience, ready to reexamine what is already known, with the possibility of challenging that information and seeing the world from a different perspective.

The role of the counselor educator might seem to contrast with the client-centered spontaneity of a counseling session. After all, counselor educators, as teachers, are thought to impart knowledge and skills to students who aim to become counselors, some of whom will work with children and adolescents. The constructivist notion of the teacher role recognizes the expertise of the counselor educator, but also encourages counselor educators to move beyond being mere "imparters of knowledge" to becoming facilitators. As facilitators, educators instigate meaningful experiences to help students *discover* what they need to know.

With Rogerian and constructivist aims in mind, we make specific suggestions in this chapter for enhancing learning through five of the constructivist teaching themes described in Chapter 3: (1) personalizing teaching through building a sense of community, (2) stimulating learning by varying the structure of the class, (3) emphasizing experiential learning, (4) encouraging exploration of multiple perspectives, and (5) encouraging intrapersonal process awareness and reflection. Each will be discussed in turn and applied to teaching the course on counseling children and adolescents. Table 18.1 describes the course objectives, content, processes, learning activities, and related constructivist principles as detailed in this chapter.

**TABLE 18.1** Course Objectives, Content, Processes, Activities, and Constructivist Principles

| Learning Objectives | Content | Processes | Learning Activities | Constructivist Principles |
|---|---|---|---|---|
| Understand childhood development stages and issues. | Developmental characteristics of each stage of childhood<br><br>"Baggage" that affects working as counselors with children<br><br>Insight into a client's experience | Dyads<br><br>Small- and large-group work<br><br>Journaling<br><br>Debriefing<br><br>Listservs, web board sharing | Do you remember when?<br><br>When I was that age<br><br>Four directions<br><br>Pair and share<br><br>Mingle and huddle | Personalized teaching through building a sense of community |
| Gain skills in counseling children on their issues. | Illustrate strategies that work with children and adolescents<br><br>Demonstrate different learning styles and individual differences<br><br>Develop flexibility, confidence, and competence in working with children<br><br>Increase knowledge about issues affecting childhood and adolescence | Use of props<br><br>Dyads<br><br>Small-group work<br><br>Reflective writing and sharing—webpage, podcast, video, YouTube, PowerPoint, video streaming<br><br>Interviewing<br><br>Role plays | Setting the stage for individual differences<br><br>Dear Professor letter<br><br>Oral exam<br><br>Paper bag activity<br>Allowing choice following an interview<br><br>Diverse interventions— bibliotherapy, play therapy, art, music, creative writing | Stimulating learning by varying the structure of the class |

| Learning Objectives | Content | Processes | Learning Activities | Constructivist Principles |
| --- | --- | --- | --- | --- |
| | Explore a variety of interventions with children and adolescents | Skits<br>Game show/talk show | Internet searches<br>Creative presentation<br>Simulated conference presentations | |
| Apply theory to counseling children and adolescents. | Engagement leads to higher-order, creative thinking skills<br>Self-esteem theory<br>Process of counseling children and adolescents<br>Non-talk strategies and interventions<br>Model use of content and personalization questions | Peer presentations on researched topic<br>Debriefing<br>Role play with feedback<br>Case presentations<br>Round robin<br>Fish bowl<br>Small-group work<br>Dyads | Self-esteem fair<br>Simulated counseling young clients<br>Learning-by-doing activities<br>Unfinished sentences<br>Relaxation exercises<br>Age-appropriate games<br>Bibliotherapy<br>Music and art | Emphasizing experiential learning<br>Learning by doing |
| Understand diversity issues as they apply to work with children and adolescents. | No "one right way"<br>Exploring multiple perspectives to the same scenario<br>Extend multiple perspectives to include race, gender, ethnic background, social class, sexual orientation, and the impact this has on counseling youth | Movie clips<br>Role play—perspective taking<br>Discussion<br>Case studies<br>Debriefing | What if<br>From this perspective<br>In their shoes | Encouraging exploration of multiple perceptions |
| Gain self-awareness and process awareness related to becoming a counselor of children and adolescents. | Student moves from content to process<br>Who a counselor is is as important as what she or he does<br>Develop a counselor identity<br>Awareness of blind spots | Journaling<br>Reflective processing and sharing<br>Web board interactions<br>Role play<br>Small- and large-group discussions | Multicultural guest speakers<br>Portfolio presentations—combined with final class reflective paper | Encouraging intrapersonal process awareness and reflection |

# PERSONALIZING TEACHING

One of the most fundamental ways of personalizing teaching is to create a climate of connectedness, or a sense of community in the classroom. We see this as a critical first step in establishing a classroom atmosphere that is conducive to learning, sharing, and reflecting. By involving students in an environment where they are encouraged to share ideas, where diverse opinions are valued, and where learning can occur in a nonthreatening atmosphere, instructors may notice both in- and out-of-class results. Such results include reduced absenteeism, because students feel more involved and connected with other students; increased participation in class discussions and activities, because students feel more comfortable sharing their ideas and opinions when they trust their classmates; increased commitment to this community of learners; and more interaction outside of class (Franken, Wells, & Vernon, 1983).

The following activities are designed to encourage reflection and critical thinking as well as to develop greater awareness of the developmental process. We have used these activities successfully in the introductory class meetings to encourage student interest in the course. We also encourage students' own personal reflections, use an activity-based format, and stress community-building activities. We continually promote the notion that there is no "one right answer," which reflects the constructivist philosophy.

## Do You Remember When?

We begin building community by inviting counseling students to reflect on their own childhood and adolescence. This also begins their understanding of what their future child and adolescent clients might experience. The activity reflects the constructivist goal of experiential learning, actively engaging learners in making sense of their own experiences.

To begin, the instructor asks each student to imagine that the room represents a map of the United States. (The U.S. map can be extended to the world if the makeup of the class warrants this.) Students move to a spot on the map that corresponds with where they spent their early childhood (ages 4–5). Students then pair up with someone standing "geographically" close to them and share a significant memory of what growing up was like in that location. After several minutes of dyad sharing, the facilitator invites reflections back to the total group by asking such questions as "What was it like for you to share a significant memory from this period of your development?" "What feelings did this memory evoke?" "What else, if anything, was triggered for you as you shared your memory or heard others share theirs?"

Next, students move to a spot corresponding with where they lived (primarily) during middle childhood (ages 6–11). This time, they form a triad with the two people standing closest to them and share a significant memory from that period of development. Again, they are invited to share with the total group for a few minutes. They continue these procedures for the place where they spent their early adolescence (ages 12–14) and their

mid-adolescence (ages 15–18). With each new period of development, the facilitator asks what it was like for them to recall or share this memory, what feelings this evoked, and what else might have been triggered for them through this sharing.

Finally, the facilitator debriefs this activity by asking students to share how they selected these particular memories, whether they were good or bad memories, and whether it was easier to think of memories for a particular period of development than for others. In addition, the facilitator asks students to think about how their own personal reflections might impact their work with young clients. For example, the facilitator might ask if any of their memories trigger "issues" that might make it difficult for them to work with young clients with similar problems or how they might incorporate the use of memories into their future counseling sessions.

## When I Was That Age

In another activity designed to stimulate interest, we engage students in an experientially based strategy, develop student insight into what their future clients might be experiencing, and encourage students to reflect on their own experiences at different developmental stages. Students focus on memories that are more specifically related to feelings and developmental issues. They consider how experiences at similar developmental stages might differ from person to person. And they draw conclusions about implications for their future work with clients.

For this activity, the instructor divides students into four groups: early childhood, middle childhood, early adolescence, and mid-adolescence (subdivide if necessary to keep each group at approximately six students). The instructor then asks students to individually think about the following for their assigned developmental period and to privately record their responses on paper: something they remember learning or mastering at this age; something they recall being anxious or afraid of; something they remember about their interactions with parents, teachers, or friends; and something they recall that was associated with feeling happy, excited, or proud. Next, the instructor invites them to share their responses within their small group. Finally, the activity is debriefed with the total group. The instructor encourages discussion about the specific items, asks what it was like to think about these issues, and inquires about which issues were the most difficult to remember or discuss. Instructors then engage students in a brief discussion about characteristics of particular developmental stages, clarifying the range of similarities and differences that might exist for future counselees.

## Other Community-Building Activities

Community building is an ongoing goal throughout the semester. Emphasizing dialogue and interaction through small-group work enhances community building and personalization in the classroom. For instance, as an icebreaker during the first class meeting, to introduce students to one another, we often use the "four directions" activity. It not only builds community, but punctuates the types of activities necessary for working with children. The instructor stands in the middle of the room to represent the campus on which the class is being held. The instructor then asks students to move to one of the four sides of the classroom, based on the directions they live from campus. Thus, if they live north of campus they move in front of the teacher, if they live east they move to the right, and so forth. The instructor next asks students to pair up with one other student and talk about why they are in this class or why they want to counsel children and adolescents. Then the twos join with two others, and next the fours join with four others, until the whole class has been introduced to one another. An added benefit of this exercise is that it helps students consider options for carpooling to class and for working on class projects.

Another community-building activity is to have students work in dyads at the beginning of class for a five-minute "pair and share" session with a different partner each week. The topics can be generated by the class members and may relate to questions, concerns, observations, and thoughts that they have about counseling children and adolescents.

Listservs, web boards, and email also offer opportunities for community building, if they are used to encourage informal dialogue among students and with the instructor. Students might be required to post on the web board weekly, or if the focus of the class session was intense, students can be required to post a response within 24 hours of the class. Both the instructor and the students can suggest specific topics and invite conversation.

Still another exercise that builds community and personalizes the learning is an activity that we call "mingle and huddle." First, the instructor hands out index cards to everyone and gives students three to five minutes to write answers to specific questions that relate to the topic of the week. For example, in a class session that focuses on the learning standards across grade levels for children's social and emotional development, students might think about something in their lives that happened that week that relates to one of the three learning goals or 10 standards posted on the overhead. Students privately write down their response and then consider from whom they learned any skills related to the week's event. Finally, they identify how the skills contribute to who they are today. After writing, the group members stand up and mingle with two or three others in the class whom they do not know and share their answers. After three to four minutes, they mingle again with a different group of three or four students. In a variation on this activity, the instructor might introduce a question for discussion after the groups have formed.

## VARYING THE STRUCTURE

The following anecdote illustrates the power of introducing variety into the classroom. During one of my (Vernon) first years as a middle school counselor, a science teacher asked for help with some students who were inattentive, disruptive, and failing. It appeared that their problems resulted from confusion and boredom. I am sure that the teacher wanted me to "fix" these problem students. However, I took a different approach. I asked for permission to observe in the classroom to get a better understanding of what was occurring. He reluctantly agreed, even though I am convinced that he was suspicious about my motives. Luckily for me, he was desperate for help, even if that help didn't come in the form he was expecting.

After I had observed his class several times, there was no doubt in my mind that if I were a young adolescent in that environment, I might be as disruptive and uninvolved as these students were because every class session was the same: Students listened to a long lecture by a teacher who had very little ability to engage his students, and then they either discussed the chapter or worked on experiments. There was no variety in assignments, no small-group work, and nothing to stimulate interest in the subject matter. Classroom rules, even though they weren't followed, were rigid. No personal relationship existed between the teacher and the individual students.

As I look back, I have to admire this teacher's willingness to invite me to share some observations that were no doubt hard for him to hear. However, he agreed to participate with me in an experiment designed to increase participation in learning through varying the class structure. Over the year, I saw a "turned off" teacher develop energy and enthusiasm as we worked together to develop a sense of community among the students. We established teams and involved students in setting goals and designing their own methods of learning the content. The biggest transformation resulted from varying the structure of the class: No longer were students bored, because, from assignments to class activities, variety prevailed. Lectures were interspersed with small-group activities and experiential lessons. Gradually students began to show enthusiasm, take responsibility for their own learning, and work cooperatively with other students in achieving their goals. Discipline problems decreased dramatically, and communication among the teacher and students improved. Science was no longer a class that students dreaded.

As Chapter 3 of this book discussed, varying the structure is an important cornerstone of the constructivist philosophy. Variety in assignments, classroom activities, and evaluation procedures may contribute to this goal. Students may increase their engagement when allowed to suggest assignments that would be meaningful for them, to give feedback about class activities designed by the instructor, or to decide how they would like to learn a particular concept.

Since many college professors never received training to teach at any level, they may not be aware that some of the same methods used by elementary and secondary teachers to stimulate interest in learning also work at the college level. In a college classroom, variety is also key.

Learners of all ages get bored if the weekly routine never varies and, thus, doesn't stimulate them, particularly because most graduate classes include three to four hours of instruction per class period. The following specific ideas have been used successfully to enhance learning by varying the in-class structure.

## Setting the Stage for Individual Differences

To help graduate students understand the importance of looking at children and adolescents as individuals with differences in talents, preferences, and abilities; to encourage students to develop their own style of counseling young clients; and to illustrate the type of strategy that works with children and adolescents, we use props such as the following: a bottle of window cleaner, paper towels, and a rag; a roll of toilet paper; and a sheet of paper and a tape recorder. First, the instructor holds up the window cleaner, paper towel, and rag and asks how many of the students prefer to wash windows using paper towels and how many prefer to use rags. Then the instructor displays the toilet paper and asks how many students put the toilet paper on the holder so that the paper rolls off the top and how many do it so the paper rolls off the bottom. Next, the teacher holds up the sheet of paper and a DVD, asking how many learn best by writing things down and how many learn best by listening or watching. After students respond, the instructor points to the purpose of the illustration: that everyone is an individual and that, just as the students differ from one another, they need to consider individual differences when counseling children and adolescents. Children and adolescents will respond differently to interventions, will have different ways of interacting with the counselor, and will demonstrate varying levels of commitment to the counseling process, for example.

Classroom instructors also need to accommodate differing learning styles and developmental stages when structuring learning experiences for graduate students, and regular input from students assists instructors in succeeding at this. For instance, the instructor might give each student an index card and ask for input on the following: "How do you learn best?" "How would you like the class to be structured?" "What kinds of learning experiences are most meaningful to you?" "What do you think you can contribute to the class?" Students might then share this information in small groups and with the instructor. Also, instructors might invite periodic feedback by asking students (anonymously) to write a short "Dear Professor" letter at the end of class that describes what they have learned, what they are becoming aware of, what they might be struggling with, what they appreciated about the class activities, and what changes might optimize their learning. Students often appreciate the opportunity to be heard in this way, particularly with guarantees of anonymity, and when instructors adapt their teaching to what they have heard from students.

## Oral Exams

An activity that has been very successful in terms of varying structure is to give an oral final exam instead of the traditional paper-and-pen exam. This approach not only challenges students to experience a different structure for examination, but it parallels the role of the professional counselor or the school counselor. When I (Tollerud) conduct these oral exams in my classes, I hand out a list of topics ahead of time that may be on the exam. Students have two weeks to review these questions and can even write them out and bring them to the exam. They may use their books and notes, but the key is that it is a timed test. While this can cause anxiety, it requires students to organize the class material so that they can find it easily and quickly; only then will they be able to give correct answers to their group.

During the exam, students are randomly placed in groups of four. Each group remains intact for the entire test. Students then take turns answering questions in their small group. The instructor moves from small group to small group, listening to student responses and evaluating their participation. Each question consists of several parts so that each student in the group has a chance to answer orally. For example, one question might ask students to consider different issues that young clients bring into counseling and what nonverbal interventions might best address their concerns. In turn, each student selects one of four or five situations listed in the question. The student then has three minutes to discuss nonverbal interventions that they could use to address that problem; they must support their choices. Only the student who is answering the question can talk. After the time is up, the other three group members have one minute to give feedback to the speaker. Then, in turn, another person in the group selects a different topic and shares her or his response, and the feedback process is repeated.

The exam emulates "real life" counseling, in which counselors only have a few minutes to review a topic before having to work with a child or a parent, and in which quick consulting with other counselors may make the difference between success and failure with a counselee. This approach builds confidence and competence on important issues that emerge when counseling children and adolescents. In the end, if students have reviewed and organized their material well, they realize that they know more than they thought they did about counseling young clients and, more important, that they have a lot to share with their peers and instructors.

## Films

Films help to vary the structure by providing vivid and concrete examples from which abstractions might be generated. For example, to introduce a lesson on the developmental characteristics of adolescents, the instructor can show segments from several movies reflecting issues such as poverty (*The Pursuit of Happiness*, 2008), childhood death (*Bridge to Terabithia*, 2007), intimate relationships (*Before and After*, 1996), and individuation and pressure from parents (*Dead Poets Society*, 1989; *The Secret Life of Bees*, 2008). Films not only help to illustrate concepts in a very concrete way, but they also stimulate student interest. Counselor educators can find relevant film ideas on a website called *Teach With Movies* (http://teachwithmovies.org). The site charges a yearly fee, but it can assist teachers in identifying movies that have an educational theme. It allows the user to download the movies for use in the classroom. Music may be used in a similar way. For instance, students might listen to the song "Father and Son" by Cat Stevens to identify developmental issues portrayed in the lyrics.

# The Paper Bag Activity

Another activity that helps to stimulate interest in developmental issues, while providing vivid and concrete examples and the opportunity for active, experiential learning, is the "paper bag" activity. On the class period preceding the activity, the instructor divides students into four groups: early childhood, middle childhood, early adolescence, and mid-adolescence. Each class member brings two items that she or he feels represent some developmental aspect of that age period. Examples of adolescent items might include, for instance, car keys, a graduation announcement, or a college catalog to represent freedom, transition, and the future. Early adolescent items might include a mirror, a pack of cigarettes, or a cell phone to represent preoccupation with appearance, experimentation, and connecting with peers. Middle childhood items could include a book, a scout badge, a board game, or a video game to represent mastery, group participation, and the importance of play. Early childhood items might include a night light, a shoelace, or dress-up clothes to represent fears, learning, and imaginary play.

During class, the instructor collects the items and puts them into four bags, each of which corresponds with one of the developmental periods. The teacher then redistributes the bags so that each group has a bag of items different from those that they contributed. Students discuss how the items in the bag relate to the stated stage of development. They list their responses on poster paper and present them to the rest of the class. This activity is followed by a lecture on characteristics at each stage of development.

# Choosing From Alternatives

One-size-fits-all teaching strategies don't work well with the diverse graduate students that we encounter in counseling programs. For example, some students learn best by doing, whereas others learn best by listening to a lecture or reading the material. Therefore, instructors can offer students some opportunities to choose among learning activities and instructional methods. Similarly, instructors can offer a variety of ways for students to demonstrate what they have learned. Teachers can even allow students to design a unique approach for presenting what they have learned, as long as it meets with the approval of the instructor. The following learning options offer students in the Counseling Children and Adolescents course the opportunity to make choices that fit their interests and learning styles:

## Interviewing Counselors in the Field

- Students interview two counselors who work with children and adolescents. Prior to the meeting, they identify at least 10 things they would like to ask the counselors about their work. After they conduct the interviews, students present their information in one of the following ways: writing a report that summarizes the material, developing a board game that incorporates the learning, or composing a song or a short story that conveys the concepts.
- Students could also utilize current technology in developing a web page related to their interview, creating a podcast presentation, or filming a video and setting it up on YouTube.

## Diverse Interventions

- Students select two of the following counseling strategies: bibliotherapy; play therapy; or the use of art, music, or writing as a counseling intervention. They then find out more about the topics by reading at least three journal articles or book chapters. They present what they learned about each type of intervention, demonstrating how the technique could be used, writing a short paper describing the selected approaches, or developing a PowerPoint presentation. Video streaming could also be set up within PowerPoint.
- Students, alternatively, might select a counseling theory and identify four interventions based on this theory that could be used effectively with children or adolescents. They present their learning in one of the following ways: doing a short demonstration of the interventions in class, illustrating the concepts in a skit or role play, or setting up a group on Facebook to discuss the concepts.
- Because of their relevance for work with children and adolescents, students should be encouraged to use technical variations in presentations, for instance, video clips, sound clips, clip art, animation, fade in and out, or virtual reality with programs such as Second Life or Avitar.

## Internet Searches

Students can also search the Internet to find current resources on topics in counseling. For instance, they might access podcasts at www.counseloraudiosource .net. At this site, visitors can find 20- to 30-minute interviews with practicing counselors or counselor educators on topics relevant to the support and growth of counselors. Topics vary; a recent podcast dealt with working with children in poverty.

## Creative Presentations

Students can select a topic or area of interest that was addressed during the course pertaining to counseling children and adolescents. Then, in small groups, they develop a creative way to present information on this topic to the class. Presentation strategies might include skits, game shows, mock interviews, or talk shows. Sometimes it helps to assign projects that do not allow technology components. Presentations should be 20–30 minutes long.

## Simulated Conference Presentation

As a final project for the course, students select and research a topic that is relevant to counseling children and adolescents. Then, they imagine that the class members are participants at a conference. They present their findings in a poster session, a formal presentation, or an experiential workshop.

# EXPERIENTIAL LEARNING

As described in Chapter 2, the concept of experiential learning, or learning by doing, was introduced by John Dewey and others and was advocated by the educational reformers of the late 1960s and early 1970s. Experiential learning "produces significant behavior change" (Stanford & Roark, 1974, p. 4), promotes retention of concepts, stimulates interest in a topic, and involves students in the learning process.

Experiential learning is particularly significant in light of what is necessary to support the 21st-century learner. For instance, Daggett (2008) emphasizes the importance of learner engagement. Engagement includes a sense of belonging, motivation, healthy relationships with peers and teachers, and coexisting in a safe environment, which includes both physical and emotional safety. Daggett states, "Students need to be engaged before they can apply higher order, creative thinking skills. They learn most effectively when the teacher and the material being taught make sense. . . . [T]hat encourages students to meet challenges and apply high-rigor skills to real-world, unpredictable situations inside and outside of school" (p. 50).

We wonder why college educators don't embrace this concept and why so much of higher education is still dominated by traditional teaching methods. McAuliffe and Eriksen (2000) explore some of the possible reasons for this condition and conclude that it might be because lecturing is easier; being creative, varying class structure, and designing alternative assignments can take a lot more time; and poorly paid adjuncts and untenured instructors who are required to teach too many classes may be disinclined to spend the time necessary for more creative classroom experiences.

Another reason instructors default to lecture-only is their reluctance to give up the role of the "expert"; some college professors may find giving up their expert role to be too threatening. Students also might conspire to encourage lecturing because of their developmental desires to be told answers, along with their past experiences with the "right answers" being dictated. Giving students some of the responsibility for creating the learning environment sometimes generates anxiety in those who are used to a traditional structure where all knowledge is "deposited" into them. However, based on our personal experiences, we find experiential learning to be much more engaging for students and much more rewarding for instructors. The following experiential learning ideas have been used in teaching graduate students about counseling children and adolescents.

# Self-Esteem Fair

For this experience, students research and present on how to promote self-esteem in children and adolescents. Students select a game, a book, or an activity that they think would enhance self-esteem and prepare a two-page handout describing the specific objectives of the book, game, or activity; the intended age level; the procedure; and the publication source. If they wish, students may do the same with an activity that they have created. In addition, each student decorates a space in the classroom with a poster illustrating the activity, book, or game. Students should also bring props and activities that help demonstrate what they have described in the handout. Having balloons, music, and refreshments makes this a much more festive event.

During one class period, half of the class sets up to present their self-esteem idea, and the other half of the class participates as attendees of the "self-esteem fair." The attendees mill around the room, going from table to table to hear about the activities and to receive handouts. After attendees have visited each table (usually takes about an hour, depending on class size), the presenters become the attendees and vice versa.

Following the fair, it is important to debrief the experience, with the instructor asking questions such as these: "What did you learn about . . .?" "How can you use this information?" "Which ideas were the most helpful?" "How do you think these ideas will help children and adolescents increase their self-esteem?" "How did it feel to share your activity?" "How is learning in this way (the self-esteem fair) relevant to your future as a counselor?"

This same format might be used for topics such as decision making, emotional expression, and interpersonal relationships. Students in the class not only gain experience in researching and presenting ideas, but they also discover a variety of new content and process ideas to apply to their work with future counselees.

## Counseling Young Clients

It is one thing to talk to students about how to counsel; it is a different story entirely for them to actually do the counseling (Ivey, Ivey, & Zalaquett, 2010). In counseling courses, one common way to involve students who are learning to counsel young clients is to have them role play a counseling session, with one student acting as a young client and another as the counselor. The rest of the class members observe. The instructor can distribute typical presenting problems for various age groups, such as friendship problems, difficulty getting along with parents, issues about school performance, or anxiety about new experiences. (Sample role play vignettes are included in the Appendix to this chapter.) After 15 minutes of the role play, the instructor stops the process

and asks the client and the counselor to discuss what the experience was like for them. The instructor invites the observers to write both positive statements and constructive suggestions for improvement, and to give these to the student counselors.

A variation on this experience is to divide the class into triads, with a client, a counselor, and an observer in each group. This arrangement may decrease the anxiety that is often associated with counseling in front of an entire class. Another alternative is to do a round-robin counseling experience, where half of the class members sit in an inner circle and the other half sit in an outer circle. In the inner circle, one person is designated as the young client, and she or he sits in the middle of the circle. The first person in the inner circle begins counseling the young client and, after several minutes, passes this responsibility to the next counselor in the circle. The session proceeds in this fashion, with each member of the inner circle taking a turn counseling the client. Meanwhile, members in the outer circle take notes on what occurs as each person takes a turn counseling the client, noting differences in approaches, effective responses and techniques, and suggestions for enhancing the process. After asking the counselors in the inner circle to reflect on the process, the client and observers also share their impressions.

Once students have had a significant amount of laboratory/role-playing experience in the classroom, they can further develop their skills by working with actual young clients. If there is no counseling clinic in the college, the instructor can develop a partnership with local school counselors who will agree to supervise a university student as she or he practices counseling a child or an adolescent. The course instructor can write a letter to parents explaining the purpose of this activity and can include a form asking for permission for their child to be counseled by a counselor-in-training and for permission for the sessions to be video recorded. Students typically see their young clients for six sessions. After each weekly session they present their cases in class, either in small groups or to the whole class, reporting on what they did, how the client responded, how they felt about the experience, and what feedback and suggestions they would like from other students and the instructor for future sessions. Three times during the semester, small groups of students might play their recordings and receive feedback from the instructor or from the school-based counselors who have volunteered to be the students' supervisors. By actually counseling young clients, students learn by doing, following the philosophy of John Dewey. They are able to improve their skills on the basis of feedback from their peers, practitioners, and the instructor.

# Other Learning-by-Doing Activities

To continue the spirit of students learning by experiencing, we offer here a number of activities that help students experience important concepts, get firsthand experiences with strategies that may be helpful with their future counselees, and practice counseling strategies that may be helpful to their future.

## Unfinished Sentences

Using unfinished sentences with young clients is a helpful assessment as well as intervention strategy. To teach this concept, we discuss the strategy, give several examples, and demonstrate how counselors might develop an unfinished sentences assessment. Then we ask students to select a typical child or adolescent problem—such as failing in school, relationships with parents, or feelings about friends—and write four sentences that correspond to the topic they selected. For example, if the topic selected was relationships with parents, the following unfinished sentences might be developed:

> When I am with my mom, I feel . . .
>
> When I am with my dad, I feel . . .
>
> My favorite thing to do with my parents is . . .
>
> If my parents and I disagree, it is about . . .

After they have constructed their sentences, students choose a partner and take turns finishing each other's sentences as if they were a young client, using the procedure that was demonstrated by the instructor. An adolescence-related variation on this activity might be to have the counseling students develop sentence stems related to being a teenager to use with teenage clients. Examples might include the following:

> My favorite kind of music is . . .
>
> My best feature is . . .
>
> My favorite TV or radio DJ is . . .
>
> My worst class is . . .
>
> I could tell my secrets to . . .
>
> My most embarrassing moment is . . .

## Relaxation Exercises

After a short discussion about the purpose and procedures involved in relaxation training, students work with a partner to develop a script for a relaxation exercise for a high school student who is experiencing stress. When they have finished writing the script, they join another pair and take turns walking this small group through the relaxation process. Group members offer them feedback and suggestions for improvement. In this way, students learn experientially how to use relaxation interventions with future clients who may benefit from this type of approach. Group members also take responsibility for co-creating learning with their peers.

## Games

The instructor shares with the counseling students several examples of commercial or self-developed board games, video games, and interactive games that can be used therapeutically with children and adolescents for a variety of different issues, such as awareness of feelings, self-esteem, behavior management, or situational-specific issues like loss, divorce, or attention deficit hyperactivity disorder. Then the instructor directs students to get into small groups. There they select an age level and a topic, and develop a board game that focuses on this issue. After they have completed the game, the instructor asks groups to exchange games and to play them. Again, students co-construct the learning process by offering one another feedback and suggestions for improving the games. Further, in processing the experience after the activity, we ask students to stand back from their experience to reflect on it, which is crucial to their learning and development.

## Bibliotherapy

Bibliotherapy very effectively addresses a variety of problems presented by children and adolescents. It can invite catharsis, identification, and insight in clients. We want students to learn bibliotherapy experientially, in keeping with constructivist goals. Therefore, the instructor discusses the concept of bibliotherapy and then demonstrates it by reading a story that addresses a concern that a young client might present (e.g., parents getting a divorce).

Both during and after the story, the instructor models the use of *content* and *personalization* questions. Examples of the two types of questions should be clear enough that counseling students understand the differences between them: Content questions encourage the client to reflect on the content of the story (e.g., "What did the boy in the story do when his parents told him they were getting a divorce?"), while personalization questions help clients apply the learning to their own lives (e.g., "How did you feel when your parents told you they were getting a divorce?"). This demonstration illustrates vividly to graduate students how to use a process that they will ultimately use with young clients.

After demonstrating the strategy and asking counseling students to identify examples of content and personalization questions, the instructor asks counseling students to practice bibliotherapy. They choose an age group and identify a topic that would be relevant for this age group. They then select a book that addresses that topic and prepare content and personalization questions. Next, in small groups, students read their books to each other and debrief the story by asking their fellow students to respond to their content and personalization questions. By becoming actively involved in learning and carrying out bibliotherapy, students' mastery of the content and process is much greater.

After counselors practice bibliotherapy, instructors process the experience, asking students what they learned and how they might use this procedure in their work with children and adolescents. Sample processing inquiries might include the following: "How did you feel when you read your book to the other students in your group?" "What did you learn about bibliotherapy and how to use it?" "How do you think you will use this approach in your future work as a school counselor?"

## Music

Music can also contribute to counseling goals with children and adolescents. Therefore, instructors can teach counseling students how to use music and how to develop their own songs by adapting typical nursery rhymes. For example, the instructor might share this song about procrastination, to the tune of "Mary Had a Little Lamb":

> *(Insert name) had some chores to do, chores to do, chores to do*
>
> *(Insert name) had some chores to do that (he or she) just did not do.*
>
> *So her mother chewed her out, chewed her out, chewed her out*
>
> *So her father chewed her out and said he'd give her two*
>
> *So (insert child's name) knew she had to work, had to work, had to work*
>
> *(Insert name) knew she had to work or miss out on all the fun.*
>
> *So (insert name) turned the tv off, tv off, tv off*
>
> *(Insert name) put her book away and decided not to play*
>
> *Before (insert name) knew it, the chores were done, chores were done, chores were done*
>
> *Before (insert name) knew it, the chores were done and then (he or she) had some fun.*
> (Vernon, 2009, p.185)

After demonstrating a song like this, the instructor breaks the class into small groups, asking them to select a topic relevant to child or adolescent development; to write a song based on nursery rhymes, contemporary music, rap, or other types of music; and to perform it for other class members. After their presentations, instructors and students process the experience, asking what it was like to write the song, how they felt presenting it, and how they might use this intervention with their future clients.

# ENCOURAGING EXPLORATION OF MULTIPLE PERSPECTIVES

Exploring multiple perspectives plays a central role in constructivist teaching. In the counseling field, where there are few if any absolutes, educators particularly need to allow space for discussions of alternate perspectives and viewpoints. Unfortunately, counselor educators sometimes find themselves stuck in proposing "one right way" to counsel.

For example, most counseling textbooks stress the importance of an open body posture. However, such a posture often looks and feels very unnatural and may be less relevant to playing therapeutically with children or adolescents. Yet when students read these textbooks, they may assume that an open body position and other proposed strategies are the only ways to counsel *all* clients. Therefore, adapting textbook materials to the varied cultural situations presented by children and adolescents is particularly important (Ivey, Ivey, & Zalaquett, 2010).

Another area in which multiple perspectives need to be discussed is counselors' self-disclosure. In one situation, our students had read about self-disclosure by counselors and had interviewed practitioners on their viewpoints on the topic. Several students reported that their interviewees were adamantly opposed to self-disclosure, going so far as to say that when they had experienced this as a client, they were extremely uncomfortable. Our students, who were new to the counseling field, were nodding their heads in agreement that self-disclosure would always be a negative.

In pursuit of exploring multiple perspectives, we encouraged the students to think about times that counselor self-disclosure might be facilitative. Then we showed parts of the movie *Good Will Hunting,* encouraging students to consider an alternative perspective by watching how Robin Williams's character, as the counselor, used self-disclosure and his own personal journey in his role as therapist. Certainly Williams's character defies many traditional notions about "good counseling," but what he does in the film nevertheless

has a positive effect on the client. Therefore, in the course on counseling children and adolescents, we invite students to consider multiple perspectives on a number of different issues. The following illustrations offer possible ways to do so.

## What If

Multiple perspectives can be explored in the classroom by building on some of the experiential learning activities previously described. For example, in the counseling role plays, after one student assumes the role of counselor, another the role of the client, and others roles as observers, the instructor might invite the observers to give feedback to the counselor by saying, for example, "What do you suppose would have happened if you had pursued this adolescent's anger with her teacher instead of focusing on her school performance?" or "What do you think would have happened if you had used role-playing in the session?" These "what if" suggestions are offered within a context of inquiry; they are not intended to be a judgment about what was or wasn't done. This activity has been very effective in helping students broaden their perspectives.

## From This Perspective

A humorous and entertaining version of exploring multiple perspectives asks students to act out different viewpoints, approaching a difficult situation from the point of view of "cheerfulness and hope" and alternatively from the point of view of "doom and gloom." The instructor uses a pair of glasses, a sheet of yellow construction paper, and a sheet of gray construction paper. The teacher cuts two lenses out of each sheet of construction paper and then tapes the yellow lenses to the glasses. She or he then holds up these glasses and tells students that they represent cheerfulness and hope, and that when they have on the yellow-lensed glasses, they will experience any problem from the perspective of cheerfulness and hope. Then the instructor informs the students that a 15-page paper is due next week and will constitute 70% of their grade. She or he asks students to put on the yellow-lensed glasses and share from the cheerfulness and hope perspective.

Next, the instructor tapes the grey lenses to the glasses and indicates that these are the "doom and gloom" lenses; everything seems bad when people look through these lenses. The instructor invites students to look at the assignment through the grey lenses and to share their doom-and-gloom perspectives about the paper.

Finally, the teacher and students discuss the concept of acknowledging multiple perspectives. The instructor asks students to discuss how race, gender, ethnic background, values, social class, and sexual orientation might affect work with children and adolescents. After that discussion, the instructor distributes several short case scenarios to small groups of students (see the Appendix) and invites group members to discuss how counseling would change relative to factors such as race, gender, ethnicity, values, or social class.

## In Their Shoes

Another way to encourage consideration of other perspectives is to assign different roles to participants when considering various counseling situations. First, the instructor divides the class into four groups, asking one group to take on the role of the counselor and giving each of the other groups a large pair of shoes. These groups will represent different roles, such as the student, the parent, or the teacher. Then the instructor reads one of the following scenarios:

- An eighth grader is getting bad grades in her or his classes. Dad lost his job several months ago, and there is talk that the family may lose their car soon.
- A high school senior wants to go on senior skip day. The teacher has assigned a presentation that day and warned students that they will get a zero if they are not present for the assignment.
- A fourth grader isn't getting along with her peers. The teacher has tried several classroom interventions to draw her into activities with her peers, but they have been unsuccessful.
- A seventh grader has been bullied at school. He is afraid to tell his parents about the incident.

After reading a scenario, the instructor asks students to briefly indicate how they might respond to

the situation. Then, the instructor asks one member from each group to "step into the shoes" of another (e.g., student, teacher, parent) and talk about the problem from that perspective. Several "shoes" positions are explored. This process continues for several different scenarios. After each scenario, the instructor debriefs by focusing on the different perspectives and how important it is to consider varied viewpoints when counseling children and adolescents. The instructor also asks students to consider how the counselor's feelings, thoughts, or behaviors might have changed as a result of hearing the varied perspectives.

## ENCOURAGING INTRAPERSONAL AWARENESS

Patterson (1973), a pioneer in the field of humanistic education, strongly maintains that teaching focuses too much on "the teacher rather than the learner, on content rather than process" (p. 147). Educators who adopt a constructivist philosophy realize that they need to help students move from content to process in order to encourage intrapersonal process awareness. This is particularly critical in counselor education because who a counselor is is as important as what she or he does.

As was noted in Chapter 3, monitoring one's thought processes is central to constructivist ideas. This intrapersonal awareness goes beyond simply reflecting about content or processing what occurred in an activity or role play scenario. It requires students to be aware of how they experience a counseling session, a role play, or a simulation exercise *as they experience it*. For example, a counselor may become aware of how intimidated she felt when counseling a belligerent adolescent and may step back internally to reflect on what she was reacting to. As she thinks about herself, instead of focusing on the techniques she used or why the client was behaving in this manner, she increases her self-awareness about issues or behaviors that trigger her. She can then decide whether her response is her own countertransference or a reaction that may regularly be triggered by this adolescent.

We use immediate journaling as one way to help counseling students develop awareness of what they have experienced internally during various activities. Right after they have engaged in role plays or in actual counseling with young clients, we ask them to write about what was going on with them as they were engaged in the activity. For example, we ask, "Were you bored? Stimulated? Too enmeshed in the client's problem? Did the problem tap into your own issues?" We also suggest that students think about what the client might have been doing or saying that triggered their reaction, or what else might have been going on with them at the time. We allow time in class for counseling students to share their reflections, and we encourage discussion about their growing awareness of self–other issues in the counseling process. We also encourage weekly journaling following both in-class and out-of-class activities.

Contemporary technology offers opportunities for students to share their thoughts and ideas with each other electronically immediately after a class. For example, we had a guest speaker come to class to talk about diversity. She was an African American counselor who challenged most of the students in the class to think about race and their own racial identities. She involved students in several activities that expanded their ways of thinking and caused some to feel uncomfortable. Some processing occurred in the classroom. However, just as important, following the class students were required to go to the web board and share their thoughts about the impact that this speaker had on them as developing counselors.

The online dialogue was very powerful. Some students were willing to share deep feelings. They showed an increased awareness of their own blind spots regarding race and culture. For example, several suddenly realized how little they knew about other races even though the topics of race and ethnicity had been discussed in their classes many times. In the electronic forum, everyone had to participate, so those students who tended to sit back and not raise their hands in class became active voices in the online discussion.

Intrapersonal awareness is essential for counselors; therefore, instructors must intentionally engage students' intrapersonal awareness. Students can use a variety of means to increase intrapersonal awareness. They might reflect on their learning by recording their thoughts, by journaling, or by writing reflective papers.

In many counseling programs, a culminating class activity asks students to reflect on what they have learned about themselves during the class and how that will be influential in their development as a counselor. Reflecting more personally encourages students to examine their attributes, their shortcomings, their culture, their strengths and experiences, their attitudes, and how they will advocate for the profession and their clients. An ultimate reflective activity often occurs in the final internship class, when each student must offer a 15- to 20-minute presentation to the instructor and classmates called the Portfolio (see Chapter 25 for more on this topic). The expectation is that students will reflect on the impact of all of their classes, experiences, and insights in the development of their professional identity as a counselor.

## CONCLUSION

The specialty of counseling children and adolescents has changed as children face a more complex world that leaves them feeling vulnerable and fearful (Vernon, 2009). If educators are to adequately prepare today's counselors to meet this challenge, counselor educators must also change. Counselor educators need to practice what they preach: learning through doing. We believe that learning happens best if there is a sense of community in the classroom, characterized by a sense of trust and authentic interaction among students themselves and between students and the instructor. We believe that the teacher is fundamentally a facilitator, not an imparter, of learning; it is the teacher's job to co-create a stimulating environment, an environment that students want to be in because they are excited about what happens there. We believe that significant learning takes place when students feel that the content is relevant and that they have had some voice in determining what they want to learn and how they want to learn it. We believe that students learn best when they self-evaluate, reflect on their own processes, and set their own goals.

These ideas are not new. The educational reformers of the 1920s and '30s, as well as the '60s and '70s, introduced ideas that ran parallel to many of the concepts presented in this book on constructivist teaching. It is our hope that this time around we can more effectively transform teaching and learning so that counselors are fully prepared to be reflective practitioners.

# REFERENCES

Daggett, W. R. (2008). *Rigor and relevance: From concept to reality.* New York: International Center for Leadership in Education.

Franken, M., Wells, J., & Vernon, A. (1983). *Creating community: Transforming a college classroom.* Unpublished manuscript.

Ivy, A. E., Ivey, M. B., & Zalaquett, C. P. (2010). *Intentional interviewing and counseling* (7th ed.). Belmont, CA: Brooks/Cole.

Lee, H. (1962). *To kill a mockingbird.* New York: Fawatt Popular Library.

McAuliffe, G. J., & Eriksen, K. P. (2000). Implementing constructivist counselor education: Pushing the zone of proximal development. In G. McAuliffe & K. Eriksen (Eds.), *Preparing counselors and therapists: Creating constructivist and developmental programs,* (pp. 196–217). Alexandria, VA: Association for Counselor Education and Supervision.

Omrod, J. E. (2006). *Educational psychology: Developing learners* (5th ed.). Upper Saddle River, NJ: Pearson, Merrill Prentice Hall.

Patterson, C. H. (1973). *Humanistic education.* Englewood Cliffs, NJ: Prentice Hall.

Rogers, C. R. (1969). *Freedom to learn.* Columbus, OH: Charles E. Merrill.

Stanford, G., & Roark, A. E. (1974). *Human interaction in education.* Boston: Allyn & Bacon.

Vernon, A. (2009). *Counseling children and adolescents* (4th ed.). Denver, CO: Love Publishing.

Woolfolk, A. (2005). *Educational psychology* (9th ed.). Boston: Pearson, Allyn & Bacon.

# Appendix
## Cases and Vignettes

## Role Play Vignettes

1. Danielle is a sophomore who doesn't get along with her parents. One minute she is affectionate, and the next minute she is hostile and defiant. She claims they "never" let her do anything.

2. Damien is a fifth grader who gets into fights on the playground when he doesn't get his way or when others refuse to play with him.

3. Kayla is a kindergartener who is having trouble getting to sleep at night because she is afraid there are monsters in her room.

4. Carmen is an eighth grader who is constantly upset because her friends don't include her in their activities.

5. Javier is a junior who is very social and outgoing. Today he was sent to the office for using his cell phone in class.

## Case Scenarios

1. Anna is a 16-year-old Latina who has just discovered she is pregnant. What perspectives do you need to consider in working with her on this issue?

2. Antonio's mother is coming in to discuss a resource room placement. What perspectives do you need to consider in meeting with her about this issue?

3. Sonja doesn't know what she wants to do next year after she graduates. She is a very bright student from a working-class family. What perspectives do you need to consider in working with her on this issue?

4. Thad got picked up for stealing. His father, a fundamentalist minister, is coming in with Thad to talk with you. What perspectives do you need to consider when working with them?

5. Cassandra is a seventh grader who is rather shy and comes from a single-parent home. Her mom works most of the time. Cassandra lacks social skills and is awkward around her peers. She was given a laptop computer to use at home through the school's technology program. Yesterday she received three emails from peers calling her names, putting her down, and threatening to take her lunch the next day. She is frightened and angry. She has not talked to her mother but has come to see you, her counselor.

# Teaching Family Counseling

Montserrat Casado-Kehoe, Angela R. Holman, and Charles R. McAdams

*Our knowledge of the world comes from gathering around great things in a complex and interactive community of truth. But good teachers do more than deliver the news from that community to their students. Good teachers replicate the process of knowing by engaging students in the dynamics of the community of truth.*

Parker Palmer (1998, p. 115)

Facilitating an "interactive community of truth" is a challenging but necessary goal in the family counseling course. Certainly the "truth" about family counselors' roles in developing healthy families is steeped in complexity and conflict. Families, in their own right, are culturally embedded, diverse, and complex, and so too are the practices that counselors employ when working with families. Therefore, in seeking a way through the maze, counselor educators seek to engage students in activities that promote dialogue, guided reflection, and lived experience. Rather than merely "delivering the news" about best practices in the field of family counseling, counselor educators create opportunities for students to *interact* with best practices in family counseling, trying on new behaviors and discarding old myths about families as they challenge their former positions with the new evidence that they construct in class.

Students bring to an introductory course in family counseling a variety of understandings about how families *should* be. In fact, quite often they bring to the course a dualistic vision of families, believing that there are "normal families" and then "all the rest." For example, at the beginning of one semester, a nervous student remarked that she was not sure how to be a family counselor because she did not know what a normal family was. She revealed with some regret that she was not part of a so-called normal family and felt that this limited her capacity to assist other families toward functionality. Interestingly, she had significant personal and professional experiences as a mother, daughter, partner, and social worker; and yet, she felt intimidated by the idea of assuming the role of a family counselor. She believed that she would be ineffectual. The "truths" she told herself about her limited understandings of families threatened to inhibit her capacity to grow into her future role.

Helping students move beyond entrenched perspectives about families requires more than instruction in the techniques of family therapy. It also requires that students encounter family norms and values that genuinely challenge their own ways of knowing about family life. Such

295

encounters help them begin to recognize that their understandings of families and of how best to provide family counseling are never "true" or final, but rather that they are contextual and shaped substantially by social class, gender, history, ethnicity, and culture. At the same time, there must be adequate support provided to students as they are faced with challenges to their established systems of thought and action. Without adequate support during the instructional process, the fear and discomfort of relinquishing narrow but comfortable views of family functioning may override students' willingness and abilities to consider new views that might more fully and accurately encompass the experience of the client families that they intend to serve.

The 21st century brings a paradigm shift that requires marriage and family counselors to examine societal issues with a different lens. Social interactions and economic factors have affected the definition, structure, and functioning of the family; how the life cycle of the family may progress; and issues that may bring families to counseling (Casado, Young, & Rasmus, 2002). As a result, the work of marriage and family counselors has changed to address the needs of the many different kinds of families that may come to family counseling, and part of the family counselors' task is to make themselves more available to meet the varied needs of families. Perhaps an entire family will not visit the office, but only a couple of members; perhaps a mother and daughter after a divorce; a couple who recently married and for whom this is a second marriage; an elderly healthy couple who is dealing with grief and trying to redefine the definition of marriage and end-of-life issues; a father and his son who is struggling with hyperactivity issues in school; or a lesbian couple who has just adopted a child and is struggling with extended family issues. With this awareness, paying attention to the diversity that the family brings and helping them identify their unique resources may help counterbalance the challenges that bring them to family counseling and provide them with a sense of hope (Gehart, 2010). Therefore, the task of the counselor educator is to not only expose students to the traditional and postmodern models of family counseling, but also to address the diverse range of family forms that students will likely encounter in their professional practices.

To achieve the necessary qualities of challenge and support in family counseling instruction, this chapter proposes a pedagogical approach that is grounded in constructivist, multicultural, and cognitive developmental principles. It begins with a look at the principles of constructivist teaching and learning that call for an abandonment of socially stereotyped definitions of family health and dysfunction in favor of definitions shaped by each family's unique social history and context. Next, it considers the construct of multiculturalism, emphasizing a need for attentiveness to diversity in all aspects of family understanding, assessment, and intervention. Finally, it proposes a cognitive developmental teaching and learning framework aimed at promoting students' abilities to conceptualize family process and formulate counseling intervention in accordance with the unique socially and culturally shaped meanings that client families give to their lives.

# CONSTRUCTIVIST TEACHING AND LEARNING

In today's world, the concept of constructivism means entering the classroom with the idea that knowledge, understanding, and meaning emerge within a social and interactional context (Goolishian & Anderson, 1992; Hanna, 2007; Russo, 2001). This notion informs us that students create meaning in a cultural context and in relationship with others. From a pedagogical perspective, old beliefs are replaced with new beliefs as we invite multiple realities and multiple solutions (Russo, 2001). One size does not fit all anymore, and hierarchy is being replaced by democracy. In the classroom, each student brings a story that is informed by her or his context, culture, and personal experience. With this in mind, the constructivist educator implements teaching strategies that bring students together to openly discuss ideas in the service of constructing new knowledge and critically questioning family practices and personal values that color their world and define their present reality (McAuliffe & Lovell, 2006). It is in this spirit of permissiveness and collaboration that new meanings are created.

In a constructivist classroom, students learn that reality is constructed and knowledge is co-created (McAuliffe & Lovell, 2006). Further, reality is constructed through language, since words affect our relationships and define the meaning that we give to life experiences (Gehart, 2010). The instructor attends to the words that she or he chooses or that students use as they become a community of learners, knowing that quality relationships strengthen the learning experience. Throughout this process, shared meanings and differences are respected in order to create a community that celebrates diversity and multiple perspectives. In this atmosphere of learning, the instructor shares power and also learns with and from the students.

# MULTICULTURALISM AND FAMILY COUNSELING

The growing cultural diversity of client populations brings forth new opportunities for the education and training of future family counselors who need to be prepared to accommodate the increasing complexity of family diversity. Contemporary families reflect broader societal diversity and may include gay, lesbian, and multiracial families, for example (Mio, Trimble, Arredondo, Cheatham, & Sue, 1999). In addition, family members will be embedded within their own cultures (Sanchez, 2001).

The evolution of marriage and family therapy is seen in the postmodern approaches, such as collaborative, solution-focused and solution-oriented, and narrative therapies. In these approaches, the therapist moves from being an expert, coach, or director (modern/structuralist) to being a collaborator, participant, and observer who engages the client/family in deconstructing the story of their lives (Becvar & Becvar, 2003). Theorists such as Tom Andersen, Steve de Shazer and Insoo Kim Berg, Bill O'Hanlon and Michele Weiner-Davis, Michael White and David Epston, and Harlene Anderson and Harry Goolishian have shifted the way family therapy was previously understood to include more modern perspectives (Becvar & Becvar, 2003; Gehart, 2010). These models have evolved as a result of a culture that recognizes that there are multiple realities and that the social issues that clients bring to therapy matter and define their individual experiences. For instance, these models recognize that the therapist does not have a solution to the presenting problem but gives the client an opportunity to define what would be helpful, what solution to seek, and how to co-create solutions in therapy. They give therapists a chance to focus on strengths rather than considering the diagnosis of pathology as the only way to fix the problem.

Furthermore, these models look at social issues that define the meaning people give to problems, how they experience them, and how society defines them (Gehart, 2010).

The response to increasing diversity among client populations has been a push for the infusion of multiculturalism into the theory and practice of family counseling and, as we address in this chapter, into the education and training of future family counselors. Consequently, counselor educators are called upon to find ways to encourage the development of multicultural counseling competence among students. To do so, they promote students' awareness of personal biases and assumptions that may inhibit their work, guide students to seek knowledge about families' unique cultural compositions, and provide students with the skills needed to flexibly integrate the various models of family counseling so as to increase the cultural relevance of counseling for the clients.

To accomplish these aims, this course emphasizes dialogue among students, among students and their family members, and among students and the instructor. For example, culturally focused reflective journaling assignments provide pathways for one-on-one dialogue between students and the instructor. The creation of personal family history genograms, with specific instructions to investigate the cultural contexts of their own families of origin, provide opportunities for students to speak with their family members about cultural values. Presenting their completed genograms to the class creates opportunities for students to dialogue with one another about the unique cultural compositions of their own families of origin. In addition to learning about different cultures during the genogram presentation, students also acquire specific cultural knowledge through the reading and discussion of texts that expose them to the influence of ethnic values on family life (e.g., McGoldrick, Giordano, & Pearce, 1996). Classroom dialogue provides an opportunity to critically examine each of the traditional models of family counseling, such as structural or strategic family counseling, through a multicultural lens. Rather than relying on a singular approach to family counseling practice, students consider the cultural relevance of each model, ultimately arriving at a flexible and contextual, theoretically grounded approach to practice.

In sum, multicultural counseling competency development is a critical task that counselor educators are encouraged to consider when preparing family counselors. Exploration of personal biases and acknowledgment of cultural relativity can be challenging. Therefore, the instructor meets students' efforts toward cultural competence with supportive guidance, affirmation, and individualized feedback. Specific guidelines for the activities suggested here are addressed later in this chapter.

# A COGNITIVE-DEVELOPMENTAL TEACHING-LEARNING FRAMEWORK

The complexity of engaging families from within their own socially and culturally shaped realities requires a corresponding mental complexity on the part of the counselor. If students are unable to sit comfortably with that complexity and work effectively with circular (as opposed to linear) dynamics, the experience of couples and family counseling may become overwhelming and miseducative. It seems that a positive relationship exists between a counselor's level of cognitive development and her or his ability to comprehend and respond accurately to complex family dynamics (Brendel, Kolbert, & Foster, 2002; Hayes, 1994; Kaiser & Ancelotti, 2003; McAuliffe & Lovell, 2006). In particular, counselors at higher levels of cognitive development have shown correspondingly greater ability to "read and flex" in response to variable client situations, that is, they are able to more accurately assess client needs in a given situation and choose appropriate interventions to address those needs (Foster & McAdams, 1998). For these reasons, family counselor training that promotes cognitive development as well as skills development may be preferable to training that offers instruction in skills alone.

Educational interventions that promote cognitive development share several underlying assumptions. Generally, they assume that growth in cognitive complexity occurs when learners encounter experiences that challenge their current levels of meaning-making (Manners, Durkin, & Nesdale, 2004; Wadsworth, 1989) concurrently with adequate supports for accommodating the greater complexity. Such psychological growth occurs through a sequence of cognitive processes.

Three assumptions drive development-oriented education. They relate to the process of accommodation and assimilation, the notion of hierarchy, and the idea of mismatch. The first assumption is that, when attempting to make meaning of a new experience, a learner initially attempts to fit or assimilate the experience into existing cognitive structures. However, when those structures prove insufficient, the learner creates new meaning-making structures that accommodate for the new experience. The disparity between a learner's environment and her or his ability to comprehend it results in anxiety or disequilibrium that provides the drive for cognitive growth.

A second general assumption is that cognitive development occurs in hierarchical and sequential stages that reflect qualitative advances in the learner's capacity for processing and making meaning of complex experiences (Sprinthall, Peace, & Kennington, 2001). Higher-stage learners are assumed to have a more sophisticated capacity for meaning-making than are those at lower stages. For that reason, higher stages of cognitive development are assumed to be preferable to lower stages in providing a functional organizing structure for a person's experiences in increasingly complex and abstract social environments.

A third general assumption is that, for cognitive development to occur, there must be a "constructive mismatch" established between a learner's current stage of cognitive development and an educational intervention with developmental intentions (Hoare, 2006). Developmentally focused interventions must specifically challenge learners to function within one stage above their current developmental level so as to create growth-promoting disequilibrium without overwhelming learners.

## Deliberate Psychological Education

One set of strategies for promoting development lies in Deliberate Psychological Education (DPE; Mosher & Sprinthall, 1971). DPE provides five necessary learning conditions to trigger development (Reiman & Peace, 2002). First, learners encounter *a qualitatively significant new role-taking, or perspective-taking, experience*. Such an experience is defined as one that requires more sophisticated systems of meaning-making than learners have thus far acquired. By challenging their old and insufficient systems of meaning-making, the significant new role creates the necessary cognitive disequilibrium to drive the assimilative and accommodative growth processes. At the same time, the level of challenge must be carefully monitored to ensure that it is not so substantial that it becomes incomprehensible and overwhelming. As noted previously, a challenge that falls within one stage above a learner's current developmental stage is considered to be optimal.

The second necessary condition in DPE is *guided reflection*. New experience alone is insufficient to promote cognitive development (Schmidt, McAdams, & Foster, 2009). Experience must be accompanied by instructor-guided exercises that facilitate reflection on the meanings of the new experience, whereby new ways of knowing can be constructed to replace current ways that are no longer adequate or functional for the learner.

The third condition suggests that, at minimum, a *balance between experience and the opportunity for reflection* on that experience is necessary to promote developmental growth. Experience without equal opportunity for meaning making may remain unprocessed by the learner. Conversely, reflection that is not balanced with experience that is pertinent for the learner may encourage little growth (Schmidt et al., 2009). Therefore, for developmental change to occur, learners must be provided with both a relevant reason and a forum for the task of new perspective taking.

The fourth developmental learning condition in DPE calls for a combination of instructor *challenge and support*. There is a certain degree of comfort in the familiarity of existing systems of thought and action, no matter how obsolete or inadequate those systems may have become (Reiman & Peace, 2002). To move beyond stasis, learners may need to be challenged by the instructor to give up their comfortable patterns of thinking and acting in favor of more functional ones. At the same time they must be supported by the instructor, who uses developmentally appropriate levels of structure and direction during the learning process, encouragement to persist in the challenge, and reassurance that any discomfort is a normal and necessary part of the learning process, one that will abate as new perspectives become more familiar.

An assurance of *continuity* is the final classroom learning condition in DPE. Developmental interventions must be of a duration that is sufficient for the processes of assimilation and accommodation to effectively occur. Research has suggested that weekly interventions delivered over a period of six months to a year may be optimal; however, positive outcomes from interventions of shorter duration have been reported (Reiman & Peace, 2002).

Family counselor training seems to lend itself readily to the application of a developmental instruction model. Specifically, a graduate course in couples and family counseling can be structured so as to satisfy all of the five learning conditions considered to be necessary for promoting cognitive complexity. The five conditions and examples of corresponding elements in the marriage and family course structure are outlined in Table 19.1 and described below. Specific instructions for each of the activities will be described in greater detail later in this chapter.

| TABLE 19.1 | Necessary Conditions for Cognitive Development and Corresponding Couples and Family Course Activities |
|---|---|
| *Necessary Conditions* | *Corresponding Course Activities* |
| Qualitatively significant role-taking experience | • Introduction to the interpersonal counseling paradigm<br>• Family counseling role play<br>• Family genogram development<br>• Case study exercises |
| Guided reflection | • In-class discussion<br>• Weekly journal feedback<br>• Role play supervision<br>• Case study feedback |

*(Continued)*

| TABLE 19.1 (Continued) | |
|---|---|
| *Necessary Conditions* | *Corresponding Course Activities* |
| Balance of experience and reflection | • Balance of didactic and experiential course components<br>• Regular journal feedback<br>• Personalized examination feedback<br>• Regular role play debriefing |
| Challenge and support | • Challenge<br>• Alternatives vs. answers<br>• Comfort with disequilibrium<br>• Expectation of student engagement<br>• Support<br>• Provision of developmental stage-specific structure and direction<br>• Emphasis on student engagement vs. competency<br>• Attention to signs of miseducative impact<br>• Acknowledgment of disequilibrium as normal and necessary |
| Continuity | • Weekly classes<br>• Semester-long courses<br>• Regular homework assignments |

## Qualitatively Significant Role-Taking Experience

For many students, an introduction to family systems theories alone requires significantly new perspective taking. The systems theories of family counseling challenge the linear notions of individual (intrapsychic) theories, which students have typically been introduced to in their initial theories and techniques courses. Systems theories often require learners to reconsider their initial assumptions about mental health, psychopathology, and the counselor's role in addressing both.

Another challenge toward perspective-taking lies in the family role plays that we enact during this course. Such role plays promote revised student perspectives by requiring students to assume and articulate the often unfamiliar roles of dysfunctional family member, family counselor, cotherapist, and clinical team member.

Still another way of challenging students' perspectives is having them construct genograms. In so doing, students face the challenge of examining their own families from an unfamiliar metaperspective. That view may trigger the exploration of new and sometimes disturbing aspects of their family history.

Finally, the course can include case study exercises, that is, exercises requiring students to apply theoretical concepts introduced in the classroom to developing clinical approaches for unique family situations and contexts. Case study exercises assess student understanding of course content in ways that objective evaluations cannot. By focusing less on the correctness or incorrectness of clinical concepts and more on their functionality for the given counselor, client, and context, case study exercises are more likely than objective tests of memory to challenge students' personal positions and perspectives.

## Guided Reflection

Instructors help students reflect on their experience through classroom discussions, role play debriefings, feedback and comments on case study exercises, and journaling. Each of these activities can include interactive dialogue between the instructor and the students. Such dialogue can afford instructors the opportunity for stimulating new student perspectives through the previously introduced process of constructive mismatching in which students are challenged to function slightly beyond their current developmental stage in order to produce disequilibrium. In the classroom, instructors can expand student perspectives through emphasizing multiple approaches to understanding and problem solving. Instructor assessments of the aforementioned case study exercises can similarly promote new ways of knowing by suggesting alternative perspectives that students had not previously considered. Additionally, in debriefings immediately following role play sessions, instructors can assist students in developing more complex understandings of the clinical and personal challenges that have just been illustrated. In addition, through written responses to weekly student journal reflections, educators can challenge entrenched perspectives. Finally, they can offer guidance in the change process, guidance that is personalized to each student's particular context and needs. Instructors should provide consistent and deliberate feedback on all reflective activities.

## The Experience–Reflection Balance

As noted previously, neither new experience nor guided reflection alone stimulates cognitive development. Rather, growth requires that there be an appropriate balance of each. Such a balance occurs readily when a family counseling course includes a combination of didactic and experiential components. By design, students in such a course encounter challenging new concepts in the classroom, apply those concepts in family counseling role plays, and then reflect on the application of concepts during instructor-guided debriefings. The course instructor takes on the responsibility for achieving and maintaining the required experience-reflection balance. The instructor must ensure that role plays do not encroach into reflection time or vice versa, thus upsetting the balance. Additionally, the instructor must see to it that students receive thoughtfully mismatched feedback on all assignments that require student reflection. Without

instructor input as part of a dialogue, students might settle into preconceived notions in their reflections.

## Challenge and Support

The overall notions of challenge and support guide good teaching, as well as good parenting, coaching, and counseling (Sanford, 1962). Developmental growth occurs most readily when learners are challenged to change old and ineffective ways but, at the same time, receive adequate support in their current ways. Such support helps learners overcome the anxiety that accompanies all change. As with the experience-reflection balance, the developmentally oriented course instructor takes on the responsibility for ensuring that students are both challenged and supported.

Challenge in the classroom occurs when course activities intentionally stretch students beyond their current, comfortable ways of knowing to create cognitive disequilibrium. However, instructors must facilitate active student engagement in those activities if their intrinsic challenges are to be fully realized. For example, emphasizing engagement rather than competency as the goal of the role play experiences can encourage student participation by reducing performance anxiety. To maintain challenge in the classroom, instructors must become comfortable with disequilibrium as engaged students struggle to make meaning of new experiences, and they must avoid the temptation to rescue students from the discomfort that accompanies developmental growth. By offering alternatives rather than answers in problem solving, instructors can challenge students to consider multiple perspectives and make informed commitments to new ways of knowing.

As in nearly any learning experience, the instructor of a family counseling course that has developmental objectives is advised to support learners through encouragement and by reassuring them that discomfort in the learning process is normal, expected, and temporary. However, the instructor's most important source of developmental support may come through her or his careful provision of structure and direction in course activities (i.e., constructively mismatched), structure that is relevant to students' respective developmental stages. This ensures that activities are challenging enough to keep students engaged, yet not so challenging that they become overwhelmed. Developmental support often requires an abandonment of standardized rubrics for assessing student performance in favor of more subjective oral and written feedback that attends to each student's experience as a unique one. The case study exercises described previously are an example of an activity in which instructor assessment and feedback cannot be standardized and must consider each student's understanding of family counseling theory as it is uniquely applied to her or his role play family.

## Continuity

There are a number of ways that the developmental learning condition of continuity can be met in a semester-long family counseling course. They include (but are not limited to) class scheduling, course assignments, journaling, and take-home exams. The once-per-week schedule of typical graduate courses provides a satisfactory interval for students to assimilate and accommodate the new perspectives introduced in the classroom. However, the semester-long duration of a typical couples and family counseling course falls short of the six-month-to-one-year recommendations for a developmental education intervention. As a result, every possible effort must be made to maximize the impact of the learning experiences during the limited time in which students engage in them.

Homework assignments provide one way of keeping students actively engaged in the learning process between classroom sessions. The genogram assignment, for instance, requires students to identify themselves as part of a larger system. In addition, the weekly journal requirement keeps students thinking about in-class experiences. Take-home case study exercises likewise require students to apply developmental learning principles (e.g., choosing among alternatives, matching clinical approach to client need) outside of the classroom. Through carefully selected homework assignments, the continuous challenge needed for developmental growth can be extended beyond the bounds of the classroom.

In concluding the discussion of the DPE framework, it is important to note that its application to a course in family counseling has shown to be "cost-efficient."

As shown in Table 19.1, numerous activities and attributes of this course can readily satisfy all of the learning conditions necessary for moving students forward developmentally. Therefore, there is no added cost in terms of class time, personnel, or instructional resources in considering cognitive development as a goal for couples and family counseling instruction, yet there may be much to gain.

## COURSE OVERVIEW

An introductory family counseling course can be organized in a variety of ways. The topics can include, but are not limited to, the study of family definitions, individual life cycle developmental models versus family developmental models, family counseling issues, multicultural issues in family counseling, family counseling specialties, ethical and legal issues in family counseling, counseling skills in family counseling, healthy family patterns, family life stressors, family health, first-order and second-order changes within the family, family resources, family dynamics, family problems in context, history of family counseling, family practice, and competency-based family counseling. A major goal is to help students shift from an individual paradigm to a family systems conception. The learning objectives and activities presented in this chapter provide guidelines for teaching an introductory course in family counseling. Table 19.2 summarizes the objectives, content, processes, activities, and constructivist principles for the course.

As an initial foundation in teaching students how to work with families, we begin the course by presenting different views of what constitutes a family to increase awareness and explore various definitions. While presenting a family framework, we compare different developmental models: individual life cycle, Erickson's developmental model, Carol Gilligan's developmental model, and Betty Carter and Monica McGoldrick's family life developmental model (Gladding, 2007). In learning how to work with families, it is important for students to understand how both individual and family life cycles influence the course of an individual's life (Casado et al., 2002). At the same time, we present concepts that describe healthy and dysfunctional characteristics of families, knowing that as society changes, definitions of family health will vary.

| Learning Objectives | Content | Processes | Learning Activities | Constructivist Principles |
|---|---|---|---|---|
| Demonstrate awareness of different views of what makes up a family, exploring various definitions and models of development. | Family theories as they relate to family definitions<br><br>Individual life cycle development—Erickson's developmental model<br><br>Carol Gilligan's developmental model<br><br>Betty Carter and Monica McGoldrick's family life developmental model | Individual reflection workbook<br><br>Dyads<br><br>Small and large groups<br><br>Case study activities | Focused discussions<br><br>Define your family and draw who is in it<br><br>Time line of your own family's development<br><br>Culture and development discussion<br><br>Learning Checkpoint 1 | People construct their definition of family based on their personal experience, marked by culture, ethnicity, and the social system.<br><br>The context in which they live marks their way of understanding the world and families.<br><br>Development is marked by the context of culture. |
| Develop an understanding of healthy and dysfunctional characteristics of families. | Healthy-functioning systems thinking<br><br>Family life stressors: Carter and McGoldrick's family life stressor model<br><br>Beaver's concept of family health<br><br>First-order and second-order changes<br><br>Family resources | Individual reflection workbook<br><br>Dyads<br><br>Small and large groups<br><br>Case study activities<br><br>Family role plays<br><br>Reflection exercises<br><br>Reaction to and analysis of a video clip—family vignette | Drawing your family stressors<br><br>Wheel of strengths<br><br>A family approach to a case study: Identifying healthy and dysfunctional patterns<br><br>Learning Checkpoint 2 | Reality is defined by one's context.<br><br>As societal changes occur, our definition of health varies.<br><br>Context is crucial to functioning and family development. |
| Demonstrate an understanding of systemic theories and how they compare and contrast with theories that emphasize individual functioning. | Basic systems thinking<br><br>Common problems in doing family counseling<br><br>Understanding the problem: Family problems require family counseling | Classroom lecture<br><br>Dyads<br><br>Small and large group discussion<br><br>Reaction to case study scenarios<br><br>Family role plays<br><br>Reflection exercises | Eco-map<br><br>Whose problem is it?<br><br>Wheel of influence | The prism we look through defines reality.<br><br>The model we use defines our interpretation of reality and the meaning we make.<br><br>Systems frameworks organize our thoughts and feelings about the family structure. |
| Understand the tenets of general systems theory. | Rationale and history of family counseling<br><br>The process of family counseling | Classroom lecture<br><br>Individual reflection workbook<br><br>Dyads<br><br>Family role plays<br><br>Reflection exercises<br><br>Self-assessment quiz | Learning Checkpoint 3<br><br>Processing session exercise<br><br>A family at play | Constructing a worldview<br><br>Ways of knowing and understanding the world of families |

*(Continued)*

**TABLE 19.2** (Continued)

| Learning Objectives | Content | Processes | Learning Activities | Constructivist Principles |
|---|---|---|---|---|
| Develop an understanding of ethical and legal issues in family counseling. | American Association for Marriage and Family Therapy and International Association of Marriage and Family Counseling codes of ethics<br><br>Professional competence issues | Case study activities<br><br>Small- and large-group discussion | Learning Checkpoint 4<br><br>Dyad discussion of case study<br><br>Informed consent | Family counseling practice exists in a social structure with norms that govern it.<br><br>The legal context influences the practice of family counseling. |
| Identify known couples and family theories, and be able to discuss the primary constructs and methods associated with each of these theories. | Family counseling theories<br><br>Specific populations in family counseling<br><br>Family counseling specialties | Classroom lecture<br><br>Dyads<br><br>Small and large groups<br><br>Personal reflection workbook<br><br>Family role plays<br><br>Reflection exercises<br><br>Reactions to family counseling videos<br><br>Self-assessment quizzes | Learning Checkpoint 5<br><br>Evaluation of family theories: Premises and concepts<br><br>What is this family's structure? | Our beliefs inform our understanding of reality.<br><br>A premise in family counseling work is that problems originate in the family and can be solved within the family.<br><br>Individuals understand the world and make meaning based on their cultural experience.<br><br>Context is relevant.<br><br>A constructivist learner takes initiative in her or his own learning, making the experience personal and meaningful. |
| Experience opportunities that increase self-awareness and understanding of one's family functioning. | Basic counseling skills used in family counseling<br><br>Understanding self and the influence of others<br><br>Identify family patterns: Functional and dysfunctional<br><br>Integration of a variety of family theories: Concepts and practice<br><br>Competency-based family counseling | Individual reflection<br><br>Dyads<br><br>Family role plays<br><br>Demonstration of theories<br><br>Reflection exercises | Learning Checkpoint 6<br><br>Family genogram<br><br>Genogram—family story paper<br><br>Experiential case study group presentation<br><br>Termination activity | Meaning making results from experiencing.<br><br>Individuals learn best when experiencing concepts.<br><br>Reality is relative and contextual. |

One of the major components of an introduction to family counseling course is developing an understanding of the evolution of thought in the field of family counseling, beginning with a basic understanding of systems theory, then leading to an understanding of various systems models of family counseling (e.g., Bowenian, structural, or strategic), and concluding with the constructivist and social constructivist models of family counseling. In addition, students develop an understanding of ethical and legal issues to be considered in family counseling. Attention to multicultural and sociopolitical concerns is infused throughout the course content.

In the classroom, students participate in a variety of ways: by critically examining topics and ideas raised in assigned readings, by applying knowledge to case studies and in family role plays, by examining their own family dynamics, and by debating multiple perspectives in the classroom. Perhaps the most important element in the course is facilitating discussion and reflection of the meanings that students make out of the information presented. As we present the specific content for this family counseling course, we are aware that people construct their definition of family based on their personal experiences, marked by culture, ethnicity, and the social system. The context in which each individual lives marks her or his ways of understanding the world and families. Thus, not all cultures or eras define health and dysfunction in the same manner. So reality is relative and contextual. Consequently, in learning about family theories, students also learn that the meaning they make is indeed connected to the framework they use when working with families. The prism they look through defines their reality.

In class, a systems framework helps students organize their thoughts and feelings about the family structure and its functioning. Through the use of experiential activities, the instructor presents a variety of family scenarios to help students develop clinical skills and make meaning of these cases. These types of activities encourage students to personalize experience, engage in self-reflection, and make meaning of what helps families function better and how to use themselves as family counselors in that process.

# ROLE OF THE INSTRUCTOR

The instructor serves as a guide through the learning process, encouraging students to share their own ideas and construct new knowledge. The instructor provides opportunities for experience, knowing that those activities will help students develop clinical skills and apply the concepts presented in the classroom. The instructor models a collaborative relationship, recognizing that knowledge is created in relationship and that dialogue is essential for learning. Students become more invested in learning when they find that the instructor is invested in understanding their point of view. In this sense, teachers and students become conversation partners in the classroom. The instructor acts as a facilitator in this dialogue process to assist students in constructing knowledge and making meaning of their learning experiences. The instructor also seeks feedback from the students, feedback that guides the learning process and helps the instructor tailor teaching to each student's unique needs.

In the family counseling course that we propose, the instructor promotes the multicultural competence and cognitive development of the students. To that end, the instructor is responsible for maintaining an appropriate balance of support and challenge, a balance that can be varied through use of feedback and structuring of course activities. Initially, the amount of structure and specific instruction is high, and the feedback is predominantly supportive. As the course progresses, the instructor can vary the feedback and specific instructions, creating room for the unfolding growth of the students and for the emergence of their increasing tolerance for complexity and ambiguity.

# IN-CLASS STRUCTURE

The constructivist educator recognizes the importance of including a variety of perspectives and learning experiences as new knowledge is constructed. Students might discuss ideas, apply knowledge presented to cases, look at their own family dynamics, identify functional and dysfunctional patterns of behavior, and comment on subjects that raise an element of conflict.

As instructors do so, they create connections and relationships in the classroom, bringing themselves and encouraging students to bring themselves fully into the classroom. Instructors might share personal experiences and encourage students to do the same. Students are encouraged to bring their existing knowledge into the learning experience as well. As we try to create a community of learners, we remember that students learn best by doing and that their full engagement allows them to make the information personally meaningful.

In teaching family counseling using constructivist, cognitive-developmental, and experiential-reflective approaches, instructors select assignments that encourage students to look within, gain understanding of their own family lives, and construct new knowledge about families. For instance, students reflect on the family values that they themselves hold and how those values may have resulted from their personal upbringing or other life experiences. They also apply family theories and family concepts to clinical cases. In particular, role-playing facilitates the application of theoretical concepts and clinical skills.

## KEY COURSE ACTIVITIES

As we have discussed, key course activities used within this family course are intended to promote the cognitive-development and multicultural competence of students. Below we describe the assignments recommended for the course: a genogram and family story paper, a family role play, and a case study paper.

## Genogram and Family Story Paper

Students complete genograms of their own families and present the completed diagrams to the class. Prior to the independent assignment, the instructor provides didactic guidance about how to construct genograms and how to use genograms as assessment tools in family counseling. Drawing from tenets of Murray Bowen's family counseling model, the genogram assignment should include at least three generations of the students' family histories. A written reflection paper that describes relationship patterns, trends, alliances, cut-offs, separations, and cultural elements accompanies the genogram.

This assignment also draws on tenets of narrative family counseling, allowing students to tell the stories of their own families of origin and creation. Students describe their lives, how their families got started, who is in the family, where these people live, how the parents met, what children they had, and what family members do currently. Students identify who is a significant family member, who is tied to whom, and who is isolated or cut off. Students also identify functional and dysfunctional behavior and communication patterns, career and health patterns, and so on—anything that might have impacted the family members' relationships and choices. The reflective paper includes each student's personal reaction to the genogram experience and an integration of relevant course material into the personal reaction. The reflection should provide evidence of an understanding of the text and readings as applicable to trends represented in the genogram.

The genogram assignment serves a number of purposes. When students reflect on their family by writing the paper and constructing the genogram, they gain greater understandings about the family patterns that influence their own behavior. By drawing attention to the cultural history within each student's family, the genogram assignment provides a way for the instructor to promote multicultural counseling competence (Hardy & Laszloffy, 1995). In constructing their own genograms with a cultural perspective, students gain greater self-awareness. By listening to classmates present their own culturally infused genograms, students are challenged to increase their own cultural sensitivity, a much-needed skill for a family counselor.

## Family Counseling Role Play

Consistent with the DPE condition of optimizing growth through experiencing qualitatively significant role-taking experiences, students in the family counseling course participate as both family counselors and family counseling clients during in-class role plays. In fact, the mock family role plays can be structured so as to meet all five of the DPE conditions. Role plays provide students with the opportunity to practice and receive feedback on their family counseling skills and techniques. Appropriate delivery of feedback to peers is essential and provides practice for career-long peer supervision.

For this course activity, students divide into mock client families that last for the duration of the course. These mock family groups also serve as treatment teams.

Each mock family/treatment team group consists of four to five students, and students rotate within their roles as family counselors, treatment team members, family members, and observers. For example, if there are four family groups in a class, then these four family groups are also the four treatment teams. When one student group is playing a family, another group becomes that family's treatment team. One student in the treatment team becomes the family counselor and joins the mock family during the session, and is supported by treatment team members who simulate live supervision. The two family groups that are not participating as treatment team or family members observe the mock family counseling session and live supervision. The sessions last approximately 20 minutes, but the time length can vary as needed.

By the third class meeting, each mock family establishes its general characteristics and presenting problems. The mock client families can be constructed of students role-playing parent, child, and extended family member roles. For example, a group of four students could role play a single-parent family with a grandfather living in the household and two school-age children, one of whom has been having behavioral problems at school; as a result, the entire family is seeking treatment. The instructor meets with each mock family group to assess the appropriateness of their selected presenting problems and characteristics. In general, presenting problems should be low-level concerns that allow the focus to remain on the student counselor's development of intervention and case conceptualization skills.

Prior to beginning the mock family counseling session, the instructor also meets with the treatment team student group and discusses their plans for the session. The instructor and treatment team members can practice conceptualizing the family's presenting concerns and might create a plan for the session. Once the session is over, the instructor processes the experience with all involved, beginning with the family counselor. The counselor, for instance, might reflect on the experience and evaluate the efficacy of the techniques she or he used. The treatment team members provide feedback to the student counselor and brainstorm conceptual issues about the family. This dialogue promotes cognitive development through balancing experience with the opportunity for reflection. The DPE condition of continuity is met through the consistency of the role play experience, given that students observe "progress" within the mock family over the course of the semester.

## Reflection Exercises

Students engage in an additional DPE condition through guided reflection. At assigned points over the course of the semester, students journal about their experiences with the mock family role plays. The guided reflections are an opportunity for reflective conversations between student and instructor about the learning experiences. In these reflections, students clarify their thinking, create knowledge, develop self-awareness, keep track of their learning, and make meaning. Instructor responses can be individualized to meet each student's unique developmental needs. Further, students can journal on whatever topic is most relevant to their development. Examples of possible guided reflection prompts are offered below, but instructors can vary the reflection prompts to meet the needs of students:

1. Write a journal entry related to your thoughts and feelings about getting started in family counseling. Consider your experiences working with families in a professional role, your experiences with your own family (real and mock), and any preexisting ideas about family counseling. How do you feel about participating in mock family role plays as a family member and as a family counselor? What do you believe are the qualities that an effective family counselor must have? How would you like to grow with regard to these qualities this semester? What will be helpful to you as you grow in your understanding of family counseling?

2. In this journal entry, describe your thoughts about the family that your treatment team is providing with family counseling services. How do you conceptualize this family's concerns, at this stage, from a systems or interpersonal perspective (considering the family as a whole)? How do you conceptualize this family's concerns from an intrapsychic or individual perspective (considering each of the family members only as individuals)?

3. In this journal entry, describe your thoughts, ideas, and feelings about this week's role play session. For

instance, if you were one of the family members, what did you notice the family counselor doing? How did you feel during the session? How did the rest of the family interact with you? If you had been the family counselor, what would you have done? If you were the family counselor, what was your intent during the session? What techniques did you use to demonstrate a specific theory? How did you feel during the session as you interacted with the family?

## Case Studies

Case studies afford students with an initial opportunity to integrate family counseling theory with individual client needs. They provide a safe venue for such practice in advance of application to actual clients during practicum and internship. Two variations of case study activities are described below.

In one variation, students choose a theory that appeals to their own way of understanding people and decide on ways that they will apply that theoretical model. The case study paper, then, invites students to deconstruct the meaning of the case presented and to create possible clinical observations and interventions that fit with their personal style. For many students, thinking within a particular theoretical perspective is difficult. Yet it is important to learn to do if one is to become an effective family counselor. In this variation, students receive a case vignette and are asked to apply one of the following models of family therapy: (1) intergenerational family therapy, (2) object relations therapy, (3) structural family therapy, (4) Mental Research Institute brief strategic therapy, (5) strategic family therapy; (6) Milan systemic family therapy, (7) experiential/creative approaches to family therapy, (8) solution-focused therapy, (9) narrative family therapy, and (10) cognitive-behavioral family therapy. In the paper, they introduce the model of family therapy and its primary protagonists. They describe key theoretical concepts. They then apply the chosen theory to a case vignette, including a problem definition, the goals of family counseling, and the particular interventions (two major techniques minimum) that they would use if they were the family counselor.

In another variation, students can apply one of the above theories to their role-play client families. However, in this variation, their assessment is based on their actual interaction with their role play client family, rather than on merely the factual content of a case study. If this second variation is used early in the course (e.g., at midterm), the requirement that a single theory be applied to the case is recommended for the reasons cited in the first variation. However, if used later in the course, when students are more familiar with theoretical concepts and with the role play family, they might be permitted to integrate concepts from multiple theories into their treatment design in order to optimize its potential responsiveness to the family's unique context and needs.

## CONCLUSION

A cognitive-developmental, experiential, and reflective model of counselor education is essential to developing higher thinking skills, promoting the learning of future counselors, and grounding students in the clinical skills of family counseling. In this chapter, we have shared some ideas on how to integrate constructivist teaching into the teaching of family counseling. Such a pedagogy takes into account the idea that students learn in a social context and that the social activities in which they engage facilitate the meaning-making of new knowledge. As demonstrated in the activities presented in this chapter, we see experience as a vital part of learning. We value the knowledge that students bring into the classroom and encourage them to share their voices as part of the learning. We believe that creating a community of learners and providing opportunities for reflection are critical elements of learning. Thus, the activities presented in this chapter offer opportunities to engage students in thinking critically and clinically about how to work with families. It is our hope that the information and activities presented here encourage others to create new knowledge and construct their personal view of family counseling from a variety of realities.

## RESOURCES

American Association for Marriage and Family Therapy (AAMFT): www.aamft.org/

AAMFT Code of Ethics: www.aamft.org/resources/lrm_plan/Ethics/ethicscode2001.asp

International Association of Marriage and Family Counseling (IAMFC): www.iamfconline.com/

IAMFC Ethical Codes: www.iamfconline.com/PDFs/Ethical%20Codes.pdf

Tip Sheet for Genogram/Family Tree: http://manuals.chfs.ky.gov/dcbs_manuals/dpp/docs/Tip%20Sheet%20for%20Genogram%20-%20Family%20Tree.doc

Family Diagrammatic Assessment—Genogram: http://family.jrank.org/pages/526/Family-Diagrammatic-Assessment-GENOGRAM.html

More About Genograms, by Monica McGoldrick: www.multiculturalfamily.org/genograms/

# REFERENCES

Becvar, D. S., & Becvar, R. J. (2003). *Family therapy: A systematic integration* (5th ed.). Boston: Allyn & Bacon.

Brendel, J. M., Kolbert, J. B., & Foster, V. A. (2002). Promoting student cognitive development. *Journal of Adult Development, 9*, 217–227.

Casado, M., Young, M. E., & Rasmus, S. D. (2002). *Exercises in family therapy.* Upper Saddle River, NJ: Prentice Hall.

Foster, V. A., & McAdams, C. R. (1998). Supervising the child care counselor: A cognitive developmental model. *Child and Youth Care Forum, 27*, 5–19.

Gehart, D. (2010). *Mastering competencies in family therapy: A practical approach to theories and clinical case documentation.* Belmont, CA: Brooks/Cole.

Gladding, S. T. (2007). *Family therapy: History, theory and practice* (4th ed.). Upper Saddle River, NJ: Prentice Hall.

Goolishian, H. A., & Anderson, H. (1992). Strategy and intervention versus nonintervention: A matter of theory? *Journal of Marital and Family Therapy, 18*(1), 5–15.

Hanna, S. M. (2007). *The practice of family therapy* (2nd ed.). Belmont, CA: Thomson Brooks/Cole.

Hardy, K., & Laszloffy, T. (1995). The cultural genogram: Key to training culturally competent family therapists. *Journal of Marital and Family Therapy, 21*, 227–237.

Hayes, R. L. (1994). The legacy of Lawrence Kohlberg: Implications for counseling and human development. *Journal of Counseling and Development, 72*, 261–267.

Hoare, C. H. (Ed.). (2006). *The handbook of adult development.* New York: Oxford University Press.

Kaiser, D., & Ancelotti, T. (2003). A family counselor practicum based on a deliberate psychological education model. *Counselor Education and Supervision, 42*, 286–301.

Manners, H., Durkin, K., & Nesdale, A. (2004). Promoting advanced ego development among adults. *Journal of Adult Development, 11*, 19–27.

McAuliffe, G., & Lovell, C. (2006). The influence of counselor epistemology on the helping interview: A qualitative study. *Journal of Counseling and Development, 84,* 308–317.

McGoldrick, M., Giordano, J., & Pearce, J. (Eds.). (1996). *Ethnicity and family therapy* (2nd ed.). New York: Guilford.

Mio, J. S., Trimble, J. E., Arredondo, P., Cheatham, H. E., & Sue, D. W. (1999). *Key words in multicultural interventions: A dictionary.* Westport, CT: Greenwood Press.

Mosher, R., & Sprinthall, N. (1971). Psychological education: A means to promote personal developmental during adolescence. *The Counseling Psychologist, 2*(4), 3–82.

Palmer, P. J. (1998). *The courage to teach: Exploring the inner landscape of a teacher's life.* San Francisco: Jossey-Bass.

Reiman, A. J., & Peace, S. D. (2002). Promoting teachers' moral reasoning and collaborative inquiry performance: A developmental role-taking and guided inquiry study. *Journal of Moral Education, 31*, 51–66.

Russo, T. (2001). Family counseling training and the constructivist classroom. In K. Eriksen & G. McAuliffe (Eds.), *Teaching counselors and therapists: Constructivist and developmental course designs* (pp. 235–254). Westport, CT: Bergin & Garvey.

Sanchez, A. R. (2001). Multicultural family counseling: Toward cultural sensibility. In J. G. Ponterotto, J. M. Casas, L. A. Suzuki, & C. M. Alexander (Eds.), *Handbook of multicultural counseling* (2nd ed., pp. 672–700). Thousand Oaks, CA: Sage.

Sanford, N. (1962). *The American college.* New York: John Wiley & Sons.

Schmidt, C. D., McAdams, C. R., & Foster, V. A. (2009). Promoting the moral reasoning of undergraduate business students through a deliberate psychological education-based classroom intervention. *Journal of Moral Education, 38*, 315–334.

Sprinthall, N. A., Peace, S. D., & Kennington, P. (2001). *Cognitive developmental stage theories for counseling.* Alexandria, VA: American Counseling Association.

Wadsworth, B. J. (1989). *Piaget's theory of cognitive and affective development* (4th ed.). New York: Longman.

# School Counselor Preparation Within a Constructivist Framework

Tim Grothaus, James Devlin, Christopher Sink, and Cher Edwards

*The kind of expectations the teacher creates in a classroom play a large role in fostering either superficial . . . or deep understanding. . . . [T]he goal of instruction is to make knowledge building possible.*

Kintsch (2009, p. 225)

Constructivist approaches to learning and instruction remain controversial, despite recent empirical support and increasing inroads in the popular lexicon and professional literature (Fosnot, 2005; Kintsch, 2009). Evidence indicating the efficacy and efficiency of techniques anchored in more didactic, content-centered approaches to learning, especially for more concrete learning tasks (such as memorization of formulas and terms), has fueled a vigorous discourse among proponents of both positivist and constructivist approaches (Fosnot & Perry, 2005; Rosenshine, 2009; Tobias & Duffy, 2009). This chapter focuses predominantly on the preparation of reflexive school counseling practitioners and the constructivist principles that appear to most optimally invite this development (Fletcher, 2009). However, we acknowledge that this deep understanding sought by constructivistically oriented instructors can be enhanced, some might say predicted, by the learner having some basic topic knowledge (Fletcher, 2009; Kintsch, 2009). As Sternberg (2009) assents, asserting that "content in the

absence of thinking is inert and meaningless; but thinking in the absence of content is vacuous" (p. x).

In this chapter, we hope to share both paradigmatic and practical ideas for facilitating the development of school counseling professionals. We present a balance of both content conveyance and critical discourse analysis. The orientation espoused here is constructivism, which, as described in Chapter 1, blends elements of developmental constructivism and social constructionism in an "attempt to respect both *individual* (self-generative) agency and dynamic *social* embeddedness" (Mahoney, 1996, p. 132).

An assumption of ours is that instructors of a school counseling course can intentionally instigate enhanced cognitive development. Research indicates that higher levels of cognitive development are "positively related to several essential counseling behaviors, including greater empathic communication, greater autonomy, valuing cultural diversity, decision-making in accord with democratic principles of equity and fairness, and greater self-knowledge and awareness" (Brendel, Kolbert, &

Foster, 2002, p. 220). Therefore, techniques and contexts associated with promoting this development permeate the chapter. In particular, we describe having students take on a qualitatively new role (i.e., that of school counselor), intermingle reflection and action (e.g., incorporate field experience, projects, and presentations with reflective journals and discussions), and blend support with challenge (e.g., creating a safe atmosphere in which learners are encouraged to question their own assumptions, class content, the instructor, each other, and currently touted school counseling knowledge; Grothaus, 2007).

The learning experiences shared here fulfill the Council for the Accreditation of Counseling and Related Educational Programs (CACREP; 2009) standards for school counseling. This is not intended as an endorsement of unquestioned adherence to the CACREP paradigm, however. We invite readers to always engage in critical discourse analysis with these *taken-as-shared* (Fosnot, 2005) best practice standards and all chapter content. The chapter begins with considerations for creating a classroom context that invites deep learning; followed by a discussion of class process possibilities and suggestions for learning units, potential resources, suggested activities and projects; and concludes with ideas about assessment of learning and teaching.

## Classroom Context

"Constructing . . . ideas is not only a cognitive activity; it is also a social one. . . . The classroom becomes a workshop. . . . Learners share perceptions with each other . . . and their ideas become modified, selected, or deselected, as common meanings develop" (Fosnot, 2005, pp. 285–286). In that vein, using instructional practices that are responsive to the culture, background, and learning styles of students can encourage inquiry, investigation, and introspection, while promoting active engagement in learning. Social constructionist teaching also encourages the creation of a respectful learning community, as described in Chapters 1 and 3 (DeVries & Zan, 2005; Erford, Moore-Thomas, & Mazzuca, 2004; Falk, 2009; Kintsch, 2009).

We suggest the creation of a classroom context where all are acknowledged to be on a learning journey together. Ideally, participants will feel safe and encouraged to engage in critical analysis, questioning, and

discourse about their own ideas, the concepts held by others (including the text and the professor), and the assumptions of best practice in the school counseling field (Dykstra, 2005; Falk, 2009; Fosnot & Perry, 2005). The instructor can actively encourage collaboration and also share authority and responsibility as a learner among learners (Stanton, 1996). Arranging seats in a circular fashion can also promote an egalitarian learning atmosphere (Goodnough, Perusse, & Erford, 2011).

## Class Process

A number of topics and processes characterize the constructivist school counseling class. Primary among these is culture. Culturally alert engagement of learners is essential for deep understanding as "knowledge objects do not stand alone but are grounded on a shared cultural knowledge base. . . . [C]ultural knowledge is necessary for understanding objects in a culture" (Kintsch, 2009, p. 225).

Next, we recommend particular processes for creating or encouraging an engaged classroom, many of which parallel ideas from Chapter 3. Inviting learner input about class goals and processes as well as using problem- and project-based learning can enhance a sense of salience for students, which often increases their interest and motivation (DeVries & Zan, 2005; Kintsch, 2009). Activating students' previous knowledge on the topic being addressed may also contribute to the goal of increased learner engagement (e.g., when discussing educational philosophy, initiating inquiry by asking learners to complete a sentence stem, such as "When it comes to the goals and purposes of education, I believe . . ."). In addition, we find that offering content that represents alternative views on the topic of the day can provide fodder for critical discourse analysis. Encouragement of student discussions in small or large groups also appears essential. Debates, presentations, research, role plays, interviews, guest speakers, creation of representative art or symbols, and journaling can also supplement the processes named above and assist in fostering the disequilibrium that may lead to "structural shifts in cognition" (Fosnot, 2005, p. 279).

Instructors can also invite reflection and critical analysis via statements or questions intended to encourage learners to react, respond, and "question the unspoken assumptions that underlie current practice" and perspectives (Dykstra, 2005, p. 243). Sample statements/questions that students are asked to respond to include the following:

- "Competent counselors have to be described as those with the ability to see the social and political implications of their actions; and to use their skills to promote greater equality, justice, and humane conditions inside and beyond their work" (Sprinthall, Peace, & Kennington, 2000, p. 24).
- School counselors are called to "address the needs of every student, particularly students of culturally diverse, low social-economic status and other underserved or underperforming populations" (American School Counselor Association, 2005, p. 77)
- "To devalue . . . language or to presume Standard English is a better system is to devalue the child and her/his culture and to reveal a naiveté concerning language" (Gollnick & Chinn, 2006, p. 268).
- "I believed the myth that if students didn't succeed in school, it was because of their unwillingness to achieve. . . . I learned that . . . in many cases, schools fail students by implementing biased policies and tolerating culturally incompetent educators" (Holcomb-McCoy, 2007, p. viii).
- "How can we ensure that schools are equitable—that they support and are responsive to children from diverse backgrounds who possess different strengths and learning styles?" (Falk, 2009, p. 4).
- Supporters of standardized testing are, knowingly or unintentionally, endorsing a system that essentially promotes racism and socioeconomic oppression (Garrison, 2009).
- "The first step for counselors . . . is to work through their own ethnocentrism" (Ponterotto, Utsey, & Pedersen, 2006, p. 151).
- If we're not engaged in advocacy, we're part of the problem.
- What are the beliefs, assumptions, and values behind a particular policy, structure, action, or orientation? If we act according to the identified beliefs, who prospers? Who is disempowered or dehumanized? Who is included in the decision-making process? How can we encourage a diversity of views and alternatives? (McAuliffe, Grothaus, Pare, & Wininger, 2008).
- What do the disaggregated data show us in terms of patterns of inclusiveness and/or oppression? How can we make a given situation more equitable and democratic? (McAuliffe et al., 2008).

- Describe the role of the school counselor as a leader in the school. Is it viable for school counselors to be in a leadership role? What particular gifts/strengths/talents/skills do you have that will assist you in becoming a leader, if you choose to do so?
- Name one topic or issue affecting students that calls for professional school counselor (PSC) advocacy and school-family-community collaboration. Explain why you believe it merits action, and describe how a PSC can advocate and collaborate with families and community stakeholders regarding this issue.
- Your neighbor is on the local school district school board. She asks you, "Why are PSCs so important? In an era of tight budgets, do we really need them?" Construct a convincing and concise response.
- Presently, a student's zip code and/or race/ethnicity are powerful predictors of their achievement test scores (Falk, 2009; Gordon, 2006; Holcomb-McCoy, 2007).
- What does a culturally competent school counseling program look like? (If you were to spend time observing or working in an MC-competent program, what would you see/hear/do?)
- Choose a noncounseling duty that PSCs might be expected to perform. Construct a persuasive and concise argument to justify that PSCs should be relieved of this duty and possible steps that can be used to transfer this duty to someone more appropriate.
- You've just selected the fortunate school that will gain your services as a new PSC. Please share the process, step by step, that you'll follow to implement a school counseling program in your new school.
- You get a call from a parent/guardian of one of your middle school students. She or he claims that the child has been the subject of bullying and name calling (slurs about perceived sexual orientation) especially in science class. When the student approached the science teacher, the teacher allegedly told the student to "start acting like a man" and people would stop bothering him. Share your ideas for use of consultation with

  ○ the parties directly involved (student, parent/guardian, and teacher) and
  ○ dealing with this issue on a schoolwide basis (data informs you that this is not an isolated incident).
  ○ Include strategies for dealing with different views on the topic/incident.

- Name and explain at least five strategies you might choose to use to enhance your success as an ethical and effective first-year PSC.

- Share ways that you can serve students with exceptional learning needs. Please include at least one systemic change example and at least one example that also serves or involves community stakeholders. Show that you consider cultural factors.
- Describe an educational and career planning program you could coordinate as a PSC. Include the following:
  - ensuring equity for historically oppressed groups
  - involving stakeholders in planning the program
  - assisting in transitions from school to school and high school to postsecondary options (with examples of adaptations for at least one specific population, e.g., students with autism)

# Learning Experiences

The resources, activities, and projects in Table 20.1 and the appendices at the end of the chapter are samples drawn from two school counseling courses facilitated by the first author. They could inform school counseling courses that incorporate all of the CACREP (2009) standards for school counselor preparation while utilizing constructivist learning strategies. Soliciting learner input regarding activities and strategies employed during class may augment active engagement in the process and increase the potential for accessing preferred learning styles.

**TABLE 20.1**   Standards (Course Objectives), Content, Resources, and Activities and Processes

| CACREP (2009) School Counseling Standards (Course Objectives) | Content | Sample Resources | Activities and Processes |
|---|---|---|---|
| A. 1, 2, 3, 4; B. 2 | History, status quo, and transformation of school counseling  Evolving identity for school counselors | Baker & Gerler, 2008 (Chapters 1 & 2); Cobia & Henderson, 2007 (Chapter 1); Dollarhide & Saginak, 2008 (Chapter 1); Herr & Erford, 2011; Holcomb-McCoy, 2007 (Chapter 2); Lambie & Williamson, 2004; Martin & Robinson, 2011; Schmidt, 2008 (Chapter 1); Sink, 2005 (Chapter 1); Stone & Dahir, 2006 (Chapter 1); Stone & Dahir, 2011 (Chapter 1); Studer, 2005 (Chapter 1) | Class discussion of hopes and expectations for the course (including constructivist view of learning process)  Self-exploration questionnaire followed by discussion (e.g., previous experience with school counselors [SCs]; desire to be an SC; view of the current strengths and concerns of the SC profession; identifying the strengths they bring and their "growing edges"; their cultural identity; their current understanding of the role and identity of school counselors; their fears/concerns and hopes/desires for themselves, the class, the profession); can be revisited later to assess and reflect on evolving views/constructions  Introduction of web-based, interactive, reflective journal to be used before, possibly during, and after class for processing reaction to readings and class activities and discussion, answer (and question or comment on) guided reflection questions  Group discussion about epochs/eras and movements that constitute SC history, with small-group presentations (can involve visual or performance products, e.g., a living timeline) about selected periods, people, or movements  Bringing in and discussing news items relating to youth and families, including relevance to SC  Imagining that the entire educational world was temporarily asleep (those present are exceptions). The class has the power to change any aspect of education before everyone wakes up. Discussing how, what, and why they would change the educational world and what they can do as SCs to make this happen. |

| CACREP (2009) School Counseling Standards (Course Objectives | Content | Sample Resources | Activities and Processes |
|---|---|---|---|
| A. 5; E. 1, 2, 3, 4; K. 1, 2 | School counselors and the context of K–12 systems—school culture, climate, and colleagues<br><br>Student learning styles and processes | Bennett, 2007 (Chapters 6 & 7); D. Brown & Trusty, 2005 (Chapter 2); Children's Defense Fund, 2009; Education Trust, 2006, 2008; Erford, Moore-Thomas, & Mazzuca, 2004; Gordon, 2006; Grant & Gillette, 2006 (Chapter 7); Hines & Fields, 2004; Holcomb-McCoy, 2007 (Chapter 1); Lindwall & Coleman, 2008; Manning & Baruth, 2004 (Chapter 13); Marshall & Young, 2006; National Center for Education Statistics, 2010; Nieto, 2005; Robles de Melendez & Beck, 2010 (Chapter 4); Schellenberg, 2008; Simcox, Nuijens, & Lee, 2006 | Reflecting on and sharing each student's philosophy of education (e.g., "When it comes to education, I believe . . . " "The purpose and goals of schools are . . .")<br><br>Discussion about assumptions, movements, and choices in education, including benefits and concerns about alternative movements (e.g., centric schools, charters)<br><br>Discussion of interview project (Appendix A page 329)<br><br>Inviting educational stakeholders (possibly selected by students) as guest speakers engage in Q&A and share their views, hopes, and concerns about education, equity, the achievement gap, high-stakes testing, tracking, their view of and collaboration with SCs.<br><br>Discussion/debate about current events involving stakeholder concerns and/or influence on educational process (items from news, e.g., inequity in funding across districts, effects of poverty on learning, tenure, local vs. state or federal control)<br><br>Learning styles inventory and group presentation about and featuring identified learning styles |
| D. 1, 3; E. 1, 2, 3, 4; F. 1, 2, 3; H. 1 | School counselor multicultural competence<br><br>School counselors promoting social justice and equity | American School Counselor Association (ASCA), 2009a; Brown & Trusty, 2005 (Chapter 3); Cartwright, Daniels, & Zhang, 2008; Cholewa & West-Olatunji, 2008; Cokley, 2006; Day-Vines & Day-Hairston, 2005; Day-Vines et al., 2007; Gay, Lesbian and Straight Education Network, 2008; Holcomb-McCoy, 2007 (Chapter 9); Holcomb-McCoy & Chen-Hayes, 2011; McAuliffe, Danner, Grothaus, & Doyle, 2008; McAuliffe, Grothaus, Pare, & Wininger, 2008; Ponterotto, Utsey, & Pedersen, 2006; Portman, 2009; Smith & Chen-Hayes, 2004; Sue, 2006; Vera, Buhin, & Shin, 2006; Vilallba, 2007 | Asking individuals who are right-handed and left-handed to separately make a list of privileges for the right-handed in PreK–12 schools. Discussing. Brainstorming other privileged and oppressed statuses in schools, including those they enjoyed/suffered.<br><br>Examining disaggregated data indicating differences in achievement, discipline, placement in special education, access to resources, etc. Discussing the SC's role (e.g., maintaining status quo, social justice advocate).<br><br>Exploring the benefits and concerns about accessing cultural informants. Discussing encouraging students and stakeholders to use and value code switching.<br><br>Analyzing case studies, having groups develop and present culturally destructive, culturally blind/ignorant, and culturally competent responses.<br><br>Reading varying views on topics with equity implications (e.g., high-stakes testing, academic tracking, disparities in resources and teacher quality/experience across schools and districts, desire for equality and/or equity); discussing views and possible SC roles and responses. Developing a class position statement on a chosen issue. |

*(Continued)*

**TABLE 20.1** (Continued)

| CACREP (2009) School Counseling Standards (Course Objectives | Content | Sample Resources | Activities and Processes |
|---|---|---|---|
| | | | Discussing and analyzing Holcomb-McCoy's (2007) Assessing School Equity and Multicultural Competence Checklist (pp. 123–131) and the Virginia School Counselor Association's (2008) suggestions for culturally competent SC programs (pp. 104–106). |
| E. 1, 2, 3; F. 2, 3; K. 2; O. 1, 2, 4, 5 | School counselors as leaders, advocates, and systems change agents | Amatea & West-Olatunji, 2007; Bemak & Chung, 2008; Brown & Trusty, 2005 (Chapters 8 & 10); Chen-Hayes, Miller, Bailey, Getch, & Erford, 2011; Crethar, 2010; DeVoss & Andrews, 2006; Education Trust, 2008; Friere, 1994; Grothaus, Crum, & James, 2010; Hipolito & Lee, 2007; Holcomb-McCoy, 2007 (Chapter 7); Lindsey, Roberts, & CampbellJones, 2005; Parsons & Kahn, 2005 (Chapters, 3–5); Ratts, DeKruyf, & Chen-Hayes, 2007; Singh, Urbano, Haston, & McMahon, 2010; Steele, 2008; Stone & Dahir, 2011 | Discussion of effective leaders they admire—their qualities? strategies? cultural relevance? Which of these attributes might SCs have and use? How or why are SCs leaders?<br><br>Each person taking a leadership style or characteristics questionnaire. Discussing strengths and areas of growth associated with their style and their comfort level with leadership.<br><br>Discussion of how and why SCs are (or are not) advocates, which issues merit advocacy, advocating for or advocating with (empowerment), and their strengths/areas of growth as an advocate.<br><br>Dissecting examples of systems/organizational change, and discussing applicability to SC.<br><br>Evaluating ingredients/priorities of schools with no achievement gap; discussing the merits of various practices and policies used to eliminate the achievement and access gaps.<br><br>Small-group research to discover an inequitable systemic concern (at the school, district, or state/federal level) and engaging in action to address the concern (e.g., visit to a legislator's office, MEASURE project [see Stone & Dahir, 2011], consultation with administrators or other stakeholders). |
| B. 2; C. 2; L. 1; O. 3; P. 1 | Designing and implementing a comprehensive school counseling program | ASCA, 2005; Brown & Trusty, 2005 (Chapters 4 & 5); Dollarhide & Saginak, 2008 (Chapter 6); Galassi & Akos, 2007; Gysbers & Henderson, 2006; Lee & Goodnough, 2011; Virginia School Counselor Association, 2008 | Discussing stakeholder views about of SC programs (Appendix A and/or research articles).<br><br>Analyzing and evaluating various models for constructing SC programs.<br><br>Critical discourse analysis of the assumptions and biases of the ASCA (2005) National Model<br><br>Via class discussion, constructing consensus about which elements are desired in an SC program<br><br>Having small groups lead learning on each aspect of the SC program<br><br>Noting the ASCA (2005) National Model's assertion that it is not meant to be "a cookie cutter" approach for constructing SC programs (p. 10), develop elements of an SC program (Appendix C, page 331) and discuss choices made and assumptions used. |

| CACREP (2009) School Counseling Standards (Course Objectives | Content | Sample Resources | Activities and Processes |
|---|---|---|---|
| C. 1, 3, 5; D. 2; M. 6; N. 4 | Individual, group, and family counseling<br><br>Peer helping programs | Bosworth & Walz, 2005; Brown & Trusty, 2005 (Chapter 11); Bruce, Getch, & Ziomek-Daigle, 2009; Holcomb-McCoy, 2007 (Chapter 3); Jacobs & Schimmel, 2005; Karcher, 2009; Murphy, 2008; Sklare, 2005; Ungar, 2006; Whiston & Bouwkamp, 2005; Winslade & Monk, 2007 | Critical discourse analysis regarding views and assumptions concerning the place and type of counseling in schools, including whether it needs to be a part of the SC's role, how or whether it's different from counseling in other settings, how prominent it "should" be in terms of time and SC identity (e.g., Are we counselors in a school setting or educators with counseling skills? Both? Neither?)<br><br>Reflection and discussion on what *family* means and assumptions and biases learners hold about criteria for "healthy family functioning/parenting"<br><br>Discussion about learners' theoretical orientations for counseling (e.g., cultural responsiveness; appropriateness for use in PreK–12 schools; using case scenarios, discuss and critique how different theoretical orientations would approach the case, view concerns and successful addressing of concerns)<br><br>Small groups leading discussion about extant research and personal views of various peer helping programs' efficacy and means of implementation. |
| A. 6; D. 4; G. 1, 2; K. 2 | School counselor response to student issues and concerns (e.g., homelessness, LGBTQ students, grief, self-injury, fears, bullying, dropout prevention, substance abuse children of alcoholics, English language learners, child abuse and neglect, mental health concerns, suicide assessment and prevention) | ASCA, 2009b; Auger, 2005; Baggerly & Borkowski, 2004; Bardick et al., 2004; Burnham, 2009; Erford, Lee, Newsome, & Rock, 2011; Gibbons & Studer, 2008; Gollnick & Chinn, 2006 (Chapter 7); Huss, 2004; Kaffenberger, 2011; Kress, Gibson, & Reynolds, 2004; Lambie, 2005; Lee, 2004; Ovando, 2005; Schwiebert, Sealander, & Dennison, 2002; Smink & Reimer, 2005; Walley, Grothaus, & Craigen, 2009; Watkins, Ellickson, Vaiana, & Hiromoto, 2006 | Student facilitation of learning on current student concerns (Appendix B, page 330)<br><br>Discussion of different views, current policies, and desired roles, priorities (e.g., amount of time spent with this type of issue), and collaborative relationships desired in addressing the concerns covered (and other student and stakeholder issues and needs learners identify)<br><br>Instructor or guest speaker beginning class by speaking in a non-English language (or show clip of foreign film with subtitles off). Processing the exercise for parallels to what English language learners might experience.<br><br>Role playing suicide risk assessment and management.<br><br>Constructing professional development plans to enhance competencies in addressing student issues and concerns.<br><br>Developing resource and referral list for a chosen school (Appendix C), and discussing and constructing guidelines for when, where, how, and what to refer. |

*(Continued)*

**TABLE 20.1** (Continued)

| CACREP (2009) School Counseling Standards (Course Objectives) | Content | Sample Resources | Activities and Processes |
|---|---|---|---|
| F. 2; G. 1; L. 3 | Students with exceptional learning needs (special education services, 504 plans, and/or gifted)<br><br>Response to intervention (RTI) | Ford, 2005; Geltner & Leibforth, 2008; Gibbons & Goins, 2008; Gollnick & Chinn, 2006 (Chapter 5); Jenkins, 2007; Milsom, 2006; Quigney, 2005; Rock & Leff, 2011; Taub, 2006 | Reflection/discussion about personal experiences as well as biases and assumptions concerning students and families receiving services for exceptional learners<br><br>Discussion of language use (e.g., merits of person-first language as opposed to use of terms such as *handicapped*)<br><br>Critical examination of societal attitudes and policies regarding exceptional students, using moral (result of sin) to medical (broken) to minority/civil rights paradigms<br><br>Inviting guest speaker stakeholders (e.g., school psychologist, special education teacher, parent/guardian, older student) with Q&A about aspects of RTI, diagnosis, services, inclusion, resources, and SC roles<br><br>Field observation of and reflection on RTI, Individualized Education Plans, 504 committees in diverse PreK–12 schools |
| D. 2; K. 3; L. 3; P. 2 | Creating and delivering the school counseling curriculum<br><br>Classroom management and teaching techniques | Bennett, 2007 (Chapters 8 & 9); Brown & Trusty, 2005 (Chapter 13); Dollarhide & Saginak, 2008 (Chapter 8); Falk, 2009; Gollnick & Chinn, 2006 (Chapter 9); Goodnough, Perusse, & Erford, 2011; Grant & Gillette, 2006 (Chapters 3–5); Hennington & Doggett, 2004; Rosenshine, 2009; Stanton, 1996; Vernon, 2004; Weinstein, Tomlinson-Clarke, & Curran, 2004 | Observation (live or recorded) of teachers and discussion about instructional methods and classroom management strategies used<br><br>Discussion/critique of theories and models of learning and teaching (e.g., constructivist, positivist) and strategies associated with each philosophy<br><br>Presentation of one lesson from Lesson Plan project (Appendix D, page 332) to small group. Group constructs feedback format or rubric and then shares critiques using this. All lessons are then presented in the field and discussed with a classroom teacher and practicing SC. |
| B. 1 | Legal and ethical issues | ASCA, 2004; Cobia & Henderson, 2007 (Chapter 12); Houser, Wilczenski, & Ham, 2006; Linde, 2011; Remley & Huey, 2002; Stone & Dahir, 2006 (Chapter 11); Stone & Zirkel, 2010 | Discussion of assumptions, biases, and cultural sensitivity of American Counseling Association and ASCA ethical standards<br><br>Interviewing practicing SCs about legal and ethical concerns and steps taken to resolve these.<br><br>Learner-led discussions using case scenarios and/or Grothaus and Neukrug (2010) Ethics Questionnaire (Appendix E, page 333), including consideration of how scenario might be viewed using different ethical paradigms and cultural lenses (e.g., Houser et al., 2006)<br><br>Construction of an ethical problem-solving model or steps by small groups; whole class then analyzes each group's model |

| CACREP (2009) School Counseling Standards (Course Objectives | Content | Sample Resources | Activities and Processes |
|---|---|---|---|
| C. 4; L. 2 | Career and college counseling<br><br>Individual student planning and academic counseling | Akos, Niles, Miller, & Erford, 2011; Baum & Ma, 2007; Bryan, Holcomb-McCoy, Moore-Thomas, & Day-Vines, 2009; College Board, 2007; Gibbons & Shoffner, 2004; Gysbers & Lapan, 2009; Hughey, 2005; Jackson & Grant, 2004; Milsom & Dietz, 2009 | Examining our own received messages, assumptions, and biases about careers and life roles. Discussing career constructs and messages about gender, race/ethnicity, socioeconomic status. Promoting critical discourse analysis of messages students receive (e.g., in media, via career programs used in schools, family preferences).<br><br>Small groups researching and developing priority list of skills, attitudes, and knowledge students need for career or college success. Constructing a plan to promote these.<br><br>Examining data given the inequity in graduation and college attendance, discussing possible SC responses (possibly using SC roles: leader, advocate, collaborator, systemic change agent).<br><br>Small groups constructing culturally responsive, individual planning system for PreK–12 students. Discussing assumptions behind plan and possible alternative views. |
| E. 3; F 4; H. 4; M. 1, 2, 3, 4, 5, 7; N. 1, 2, 3, 5; P. 2 | Consultation<br><br>School-family-community collaboration | Amatea, Daniels, Bringman, & Vandiver, 2004; Baker, Robichaud, Westforth Dietrich, Wells, & Schreck, 2009; Bemak, Murphy, & Kaffenberger, 2005; Brigman, Mullis, Webb, & White, 2005; Brown, Dahlbeck, & Sparkman-Barnes, 2006; Bryan & Henry, 2008; Dougherty, 2005; Erford, 2011b; Giles, 2005; Hoffman et al., 2006; Holcomb-McCoy, 2007 (Chapters 4, 5, & 8); Kampwirth, 2006; Parsons & Kahn, 2005; Search Institute, 2007; Van Velsor & Orozco, 2007 | Role playing different models and SC roles in consultation; discussing benefits and drawbacks of each one for various situations.<br><br>Interviewing SC stakeholders about school-family-community collaboration; analyze results (Appendix A).<br><br>Analyzing different school policies and plans to promote school-family-community collaboration (e.g., Are they culturally inclusive?).<br><br>Procuring disaggregated data (e.g., by socioeconomic status, race/ethnicity) profiling levels of school-family-community collaboration and also salient school policies and practices. Collaborating with school stakeholders to construct a plan to enhance meaningful family and community involvement in schools (including removal or transformation of barriers that discourage involvement, e.g., faculty or administrator attitudes).<br><br>Collaborating on school improvement project with educational leadership graduate students, preservice teaching students (including special education), and other stakeholders at the university (e.g., school psychology or social work students).<br><br>Creating parent/guardian or faculty/staff training module(s) on relevant educational or counseling issues. |

(Continued)

**TABLE 20.1** (Continued)

| CACREP (2009) School Counseling Standards (Course Objectives | Content | Sample Resources | Activities and Processes |
|---|---|---|---|
| A. 7; C. 6; H. 4; M. 7 | Prevention programming<br><br>School climate<br><br>Crisis management planning and crisis response | Allen et al., 2002; Baker & Gerler, 2008 (Chapter 8); Devine & Cohen, 2007; Echterling, Presbury, & McKee 2005; Kerr, 2008; Pransky, 2001; Search Institute, 2007; Studer, 2005 (Chapter 10) | Discussion of philosophies and strategies regarding prevention programming (established efficacy; prioritizing concerns; SC roles in constructing, executing, and evaluating school- or community-wide plans).<br><br>Discussion of: What are we preventing? How do we prevent it? What is our target population or system? How might we tell if our prevention efforts are successful?<br><br>Discussion of resiliency and developmental assets. Constructing school and community action plans to enhance acquisition of desirable assets or qualities.<br><br>Examination and critical analysis of various models and actual crisis response plans<br><br>Class construction of a crisis management plan and crisis response enactment for an identified scenario |
| G. 3; H. 1, 2, 3, 5; I. 1, 2, 3, 4, 5; J. 1, 2, 3 | Assessment<br><br>Evaluation<br><br>Accountability | Brigman & Campbell, 2003; Brown & Trusty, 2005 (Chapter 7); Dimmitt, 2009; Dimmitt, Carey, & Hatch, 2007; Erford, 2011a; Garrison, 2009; Gronlund & Waugh, 2009; Holcomb-McCoy, 2007 (Chapter 6); Kaffenberger & Young, 2007; Lapan, Gysbers, & Kayson, 2007; Paniagua, 2005; Spinelli, 2008; Stone & Dahir, 2011; Whiston & Quinby, 2011; Wood & D'Agostino, 2010 | Given data from a student assessment, discussing inferences that might be made and questions to ask (e.g., cultural sensitivity of assessment instrument). Discussing uses of assessment data: What purposes are served? What are the goals? What, who, and how do we assess? Why use assessment?<br><br>Analyzing data from a school report card, identifying school strengths and areas of concern/inequity.<br><br>Reading ASCA position statement on high-stakes testing and statements from other sources, pro and con. Constructing individual and group position statements on evaluation and assessment in education. Engaging in debate with multiple perspectives represented.<br><br>Designing an evaluation tool for a specific SC intervention and/or the SC program as a whole. |
| C. 4; D. 5 | Helping students with transitions<br><br>Use of technology<br><br>Professional development | Akos, 2004; Barna & Stone, 2008; Brown & Trusty, 2005 (Chapter 14); Cobia & Henderson, 2007 (Chapter 6); Dollarhide & Saginak, 2008 (Chapter 16); Lambie & Sias, 2009; Lassiter, Napolitano, Culbreth, & Ng, 2008; Luke & Bernard, 2006; Milsom, 2007; Milsom & Bryant, 2006; Ober, Haag Granello, & Henfield, 2009; Ohrt, | Small-group development of a needs assessment leading to creation of a model for a specific transition (e.g., grade to grade, elementary to middle) and a representative group of students (e.g., students with an Individualized Education Plan, new students, students who are English language learners). Having groups discuss and get feedback on plans from current SCs and other educational stakeholders. Discussing common and contrasting elements of various models.<br><br>Discussion of digital divide and SC responses to inequitable access to technology |

| CACREP (2009) School Counseling Standards (Course Objectives | Content | Sample Resources | Activities and Processes |
|---|---|---|---|
| | | Lambie, & Ieva, 2009; Thomas, 2005; Wilkerson, 2006; Wood & Rayle, 2006 | Class project: small-group creation of SC program web site, including interactive components and two-way communication elements. |
| | | | Discussion of merits and types of supervision. Critique of various supervision models and construction and modeling/use of peer supervision model by learners. |
| | | | Sharing and discussion of portfolios (Appendix F, page 336), highlighting plans for continued professional development. |

## Evaluation of Student Learning

In addition to having curricular plans and instructional activities promote development, assessment of learning can serve such a function (Gronlund & Waugh, 2009). Given the biases inherent in most assessment measures (Paniagua, 2005), acknowledging and honoring the multiple ways of learning may be best achieved by collecting evaluative data from multiple sources over time (Falk, 2009). Project-based, performance, and portfolio assessments can be beneficial methods for achieving this purpose (Gronlund & Waugh, 2009).

If learners' input about their goals and desired outcomes has been solicited (DeVries & Zan, 2005), facilitating periodic dialogues about progress toward those results can be fruitful. This may involve both self-assessment and instructor feedback. In addition, student self-assessment can be employed as an aspect of measuring performance and progress with both the projects and also participation in the class discussions and activities. Another option could be the use of mutual charting of student strengths and growth/progress as part of both formative and summative evaluations (Falk, 2009). Soliciting learner input about the efficacy of class instruction and proceedings is also recommended. A final suggestion for self-assessment and/or instructor assessment would be to have a classroom or web-based conversation with students about accomplishments of the class objectives or some endorsed standards for content coverage or performance (e.g., ASCA, 2008; CACREP, 2009).

I (Grothaus) also choose to measure content comprehension, application, analysis, evaluation, and synthesis by means of either essay exams or weekly web-based essay questions on the topic covered in the previous class. The results of these procedures usually only count for one-quarter to one-third of the final grade. Responsibility for constructing questions for these assessments is shared with the learners. Only content assigned in the syllabus is covered by the exams or weekly questions. It is hoped that this reduces the likelihood that learners will be distracted by worry about "whether this will be on the test" during class discussions, presentations, activities, or projects—freeing them to be more fully engaged.

## CONCLUSION

We hope that the concepts, suggestions, and resources shared here may enhance school counselor educators' efforts to design, implement, and evaluate courses that promote development in learners' content knowledge, skills, self-awareness, and deep comprehension (Kintsch, 2009). Promoting learners' cognitive development and their ability to engage in reflective learning and practice may enhance the likelihood that these future school counselors will continue on their path of self-authorized learning and professional development. All of these efforts may help instructors of school counseling classes answer an adaptation of ASCA's (2005) question: How are school counseling learners different because of their school counseling preparation?

# REFERENCES

Akos, P. (2004). Transition programming for professional school counselors. In B. T. Erford (Ed.), *Professional school counseling: A handbook of theories, programs, and practices* (pp. 881–888). Austin, TX: Pro-Ed.

Akos, P., Niles, S. G., Miller, E. M., & Erford, B. T. (2011). Promoting educational and career planning in schools. In B. T. Erford (Ed.), *Transforming the school counseling profession* (3rd ed., pp. 202–221). Upper Saddle River, NJ: Pearson.

Allen, M., Burt, K., Bryan, E., Carter, D., Orsi, R., & Durkan, L. (2002). School counselors' training for and participation in crisis intervention. *Professional School Counseling, 6*, 96–102.

Amatea, E. S., Daniels, H., Bringman, N., & Vandiver, F. M. (2004). Strengthening counselor-teacher-family connections: The family-school collaborative consultation project. *Professional School Counseling, 8*, 47–55.

Amatea, E., & West-Olatunji, C. (2007). Joining the conversation about educating our poorest children: Emerging leadership roles for school counselors in high-poverty schools. *Professional School Counseling, 11*, 81–89.

American School Counselor Association. (2004). *Ethical standards for school counselors.* Alexandria, VA: Author.

American School Counselor Association. (2005). *The ASCA national model: A framework for school counseling programs* (2nd ed.). Alexandria, VA: Author.

American School Counselor Association. (2008). *School counselor competencies.* Alexandria, VA: Author.

American School Counselor Association, (2009a). *The professional school counselor and cultural diversity.* Retrieved August 31, 2010, from http://asca2.timberlakepublishing.com//files/CulturalDiversity.pdf

American School Counselor Association, (2009b). *The professional school counselor and student mental health.* Retrieved August 31, 2010, from http://asca2.timberlake publishing.com//files/StudentMentalHealth.pdf

Auger, R. (2005). School-based interventions for students with depressive disorders. *Professional School Counseling, 8*, 344–352.

Baggerly, J., & Borkowski, T. (2004). Applying the ASCA national model to elementary school students who are homeless: A case study. *Professional School Counseling, 8*, 116–123.

Baker, S. B., & Gerler, E. R., Jr. (2008). *School counseling for the twenty-first century* (5th ed.). Upper Saddle River, NJ: Pearson.

Baker, S. B., Robichaud, T. A., Westforth Dietrich, V. C., Wells, S. C., & Schreck, R. E. (2009). School counselor consultation: A pathway to advocacy, collaboration, and leadership. *Professional School Counseling, 12*, 200–206.

Bardick, A. D., Bernes, K. B., McCulloch, A. R. M., Witko, K. D., Spriddle, J. W., & Roest, A. R. (2004). Eating disorder intervention, prevention, and treatment: Recommendations for school counselors. *Professional School Counseling, 8*, 168–174.

Barna, J., & Stone, V. (2008). The savvy school counselor's guide to surviving the first years. *Virginia Counselors Journal, 30*, 59–65.

Baum, S., & Ma, J. (2007). *Education pays: The benefits of higher education for individuals and society.* Washington, DC: College Board.

Bemak, F., & Chung, R. C. (2008). New professional roles and advocacy strategies for school counselors: A multicultural/social justice perspective to move beyond the nice counselor syndrome. *Journal of Counseling & Development, 86*, 372–381.

Bemak, F., Murphy, S., & Kaffenberger, C. (2005). Community-focused consultation: New directions and practice. In C. Sink (Ed.), *Contemporary school counseling: Theory, research and practice* (pp. 327–357). Boston: Houghton Mifflin.

Bennett, C. I. (2007). *Comprehensive multicultural education: Theory and practice* (6th ed.). Boston: Pearson.

Bosworth, K., & Walz, G. R. (2005). *Promoting student resiliency.* Alexandria, VA: American Counseling Association.

Brendel, J. M., Kolbert, J. B., & Foster, V. A. (2002). Promoting student cognitive development. *Journal of Adult Development, 9*, 217–227.

Brigman, G., & Campbell, C. (2003). Helping students improve academic achievement and school success behavior. *Professional School Counseling, 7*, 68–77.

Brigman, G., Mullis, F., Webb, L., & White, J. (2005). *School counselor consultation: Skills for working effectively with parents, teachers, and other school personnel.* Hoboken, NJ: John Wiley & Sons.

Brown, C., Dahlbeck, D. T., & Sparkman-Barnes, L. (2006). Collaborative relationships: School counselors and non-school mental health practitioners working together to improve the mental health needs of students. *Professional School Counseling, 9*, 332–335.

Brown, D., & Trusty, J. (2005). *Developing and leading comprehensive school counseling programs: Promoting student competence and meeting student needs.* Belmont, CA: Brooks/Cole.

Bruce, A. M., Getch, Y. Q., & Ziomek-Daigle, J. (2009). Closing the gap: A group counseling approach to improve test performance of African-American students. *Professional School Counseling, 12,* 450–457.

Bryan, J., & Henry, L. (2008). Strengths-based partnerships: A school-family-community partnership approach to empowering students. *Professional School Counseling, 12,* 149–156.

Bryan, J., Holcomb-McCoy, C., Moore-Thomas, C., & Day-Vines, N. L. (2009). Who sees the school counselor for college information? A national study. *Professional School Counseling, 12,* 280–291.

Burnham, J. (2009). Contemporary fears of children and adolescents: Coping and resiliency in the 21st century. *Journal of Counseling & Development, 87,* 28–35.

Cartwright, B. Y., Daniels, J., & Zhang, S. (2008). Assessing multicultural competence: Perceived versus demonstrated performance. *Journal of Counseling & Development, 86,* 318–322.

Chen-Hayes, S. F., Miller, E. M., Bailey, D. F., Getch, Y. Q., & Erford, B. T. (2011). Leadership and achievement advocacy for every student. In B. T. Erford (Ed.), *Transforming the school counseling profession* (3rd ed., pp. 110–128). Upper Saddle River, NJ: Pearson.

Children's Defense Fund. (2009). *Cradle to prison pipeline factsheet: Virginia.* Retrieved August 1, 2010, from http://www.childrensdefense.org/child-research-data-publications/data/state-data-repository/cradle-to-prison-pipeline/cradle-prison-pipeline-virginia-2009-fact-sheet.pdf

Cholewa, B., & West-Olatunji, C. (2008). Exploring the relationship among cultural discontinuity, psychological distress, and academic outcomes with low-income, culturally diverse students. *Professional School Counseling, 12,* 54–61.

Cobia, D. C., & Henderson, D. A. (2007). *Developing an effective and accountable school counseling program* (2nd ed.). Upper Saddle River, NJ: Pearson.

Cokley, K. (2006). The impact of racialized schools and racist (mis)education on African American students' academic identity. In M. G. Constantine & D. W. Sue (Eds.), *Addressing racism: Facilitating cultural competence in mental health and educational settings* (pp. 127–144). Hoboken, NJ: John Wiley & Sons.

College Board. (2007). *The college keys compact.* Washington, DC: Author.

Council for the Accreditation of Counseling and Related Educational Programs. (2009). *School counseling standards.* Retrieved August 1, 2010, from http://www.cacrep.org/doc/2009%20Standards%20with%20cover.pdf

Crethar, H. C. (2010). ACA advocacy competencies in school counseling. In M. J. Ratts, R. L. Toporek, & J. A. Lewis (Eds.), *ACA advocacy competencies: A social justice framework for counselors* (pp. 107–117). Alexandria, VA: American Counseling Association.

Day-Vines, N. L., & Day-Hairston, B. O. (2005). Culturally congruent strategies for addressing the behavioral needs of urban African-American male adolescents. *Professional School Counseling, 8,* 236–242.

Day-Vines, N. L., Woods, S., Grothaus, T., Craigen, L., Holman, A., Dotson-Blake, K., et al. (2007). Broaching the subjects of race, ethnicity, and culture during the counseling process. *Journal of Counseling & Development, 85,* 401–409.

Devine, J., & Cohen, J. (2007). *Making your school safe: Strategies to protect children and promote learning.* New York: Teachers College Press.

DeVoss, J. A., & Andrews, M. F. (2006). *School counselors as educational leaders.* Boston: Houghton Mifflin.

DeVries, R., & Zan, B. (2005). A constructivist perspective on the role of the sociomoral atmosphere in promoting children's development. In C. T. Fosnot (Ed.), *Constructivism: Theory, perspectives, and practice* (2nd ed., pp. 132–149). New York: Teachers College Press.

Dimmitt, C. (2009). Why evaluation matters: Determining effective school counseling practice. *Professional School Counseling, 12,* 395–399.

Dimmitt, C., Carey, J., & Hatch, T. (2007). *Evidence-based school counseling: Making a difference with data-driven practices.* Thousand Oaks, CA: Corwin.

Dollarhide, C. T., & Saginak, K. A. (2008). *Comprehensive school counseling programs: K–12 delivery systems in action.* Boston: Pearson.

Dougherty, A. M. (2005). *Psychological consultation and collaboration in the school and community settings: A casebook* (4th ed.). Belmont, CA: Brooks/Cole.

Dykstra, D. I., Jr. (2005). Teaching introductory physics to college students. In C. T. Fosnot (Ed.), *Constructivism: Theory, perspectives, and practice* (2nd ed., pp. 222–245). New York: Teachers College Press.

Echterling, L. G., Presbury, J., & McKee, J. E. (2005). *Crisis intervention: Promoting resilience and resolution in troubled times.* Upper Saddle River, NJ: Pearson.

Education Trust. (2006). *Yes we can: Telling truths and dispelling myths about race and education in America.* Washington, DC: Author.

Education Trust. (2008). *Dispelling the myth. It's being done: Graham road elementary school, Falls Church, Va.* Retrieved August 1, 2010, from http://www.edtrust.org/sites/edtrust.org/files/publications/files/DTM08_Graham Rd.pdf

Erford, B. T. (2011a). Accountability: Evaluating programs, assessing needs, and determining outcomes. In B. T. Erford (Ed.), *Transforming the school counseling profession* (3rd ed., pp. 245–287). Upper Saddle River, NJ: Pearson.

Erford, B. T. (2011b). Consultation, collaboration, and parent involvement. In B. T. Erford (Ed.), *Transforming the school counseling profession* (3rd ed., pp. 222–244). Upper Saddle River, NJ: Pearson.

Erford, B. T., Lee, V. V., Newsome, D. W., & Rock, E. (2011). Systematic approaches to counseling students experiencing complex and specialized problems. In B. T. Erford (Ed.), *Transforming the school counseling profession* (3rd ed., pp. 288–313). Upper Saddle River, NJ: Pearson.

Erford, B. T., Moore-Thomas, C., & Mazzuca, S. A. (2004). Improving academic achievement through an understanding of learning styles. In R. Perusse, & G. E. Goodnough (Eds.). *Leadership, advocacy and direct service strategies for professional school counselors* (pp. 34–70). Belmont, CA: Brooks/Cole.

Falk, B. (2009). *Teaching the way children learn.* New York: Teachers College Press.

Fletcher, J. D. (2009). From behaviorism to constructivism: A philosophical journey from drill and practice to situated learning. In S. Tobias & T. M. Duffy (Eds.), *Constructivist instruction: Success or failure?* (pp. 242–263). New York: Routledge.

Ford, D. Y. (2005). Recruiting and retaining gifted students from diverse ethnic, cultural, and language groups. In J. A. Banks & C. A. McGee Banks (Eds.), *Multicultural education: Issues and perspectives* (5th ed., pp. 379–397). Hoboken, NJ: John Wiley & Sons.

Fosnot, C. T. (2005). Constructivism revisited: Implications and reflections. In C. T. Fosnot (Ed.), *Constructivism: Theory, perspectives, and practice* (2nd ed., pp. 276–291). New York: Teachers College Press.

Fosnot, C. T., & Perry, R. S. (2005). Constructivism: A psychological theory of learning. In C. T. Fosnot (Ed.), *Constructivism: Theory, perspectives, and practice* (2nd ed., pp. 8–38). New York: Teachers College Press.

Friere, P. (1994). *Pedagogy of the oppressed.* New York: Continuum.

Galassi, J. P., & Akos, P. (Eds.). (2007). *Strengths-based school counseling: Promoting student development and achievement.* Mahwah, NJ: Lawrence Erlbaum.

Garrison, M. J. (2009). *A measure of failure: The political origins of standardized testing.* New York: State University of New York Press.

Gay, Lesbian and Straight Education Network. (2008). *2007 National School Climate Survey.* Retrieved August 1, 2010, from http://www.glsen.org/cgi-bin/iowa/all/library/record/2340.html?state=research&type=research

Geltner, J. A., & Leibforth, T. N. (2008). Advocacy in the IEP process: Strengths-based school counseling in action. *Professional School Counseling, 12,* 162–165.

Gibbons, M. M., & Goins, S. (2008). Getting to know the child with Asperger Syndrome. *Professional School Counseling, 11,* 347–352.

Gibbons, M. M., & Shoffner, M. F. (2004). Prospective first-generation college students: Meeting their needs through social cognitive career theory. *Professional School Counseling, 8,* 91–97.

Gibbons, M. M., & Studer, J. R. (2008). Suicide awareness training for faculty and staff: A training model for school counselors. *Professional School Counseling, 11,* 272–276.

Giles, H. C. (2005). Three narratives of parent-educator relationships: Toward counselor repertoires for bridging the urban parent-school divide. *Professional School Counseling, 8,* 228–235.

Gollnick, D. M., & Chinn, P. C. (2006). *Multicultural education in a pluralistic society* (7th ed.). Boston: Pearson.

Goodnough, G. E., Perusse, R., & Erford, B. T. (2011). Developmental classroom guidance. In B. T. Erford (Ed.), *Transforming the school counseling profession* (3rd ed., pp. 154–177). Upper Saddle River, NJ: Pearson.

Gordon, E. W. (2006). Establishing a system of public education in which all children achieve at high levels and reach their full potential. In T. Smiley (Ed.), *The covenant with Black America* (pp. 23–45). Chicago: Third World Press.

Grant, C., & Gillette, M. (2006). *Learning to teach everyone's children: Equity, empowerment, and education that is multicultural.* Belmont, CA: Thompson.

Gronlund, N. E., & Waugh, K. E. (2009). *Assessment of student achievement* (9th ed.). Upper Saddle River, NJ: Pearson.

Grothaus, T., (2007). Integrating cognitive developmental theory into the clinical supervision of school counselors. *Virginia Counselors Journal, 29,* 40–47.

Grothaus, T., Crum, K. S., & James, A. B. (2010). Effective leadership in a culturally diverse learning environment. *International Journal of Urban Educational Leadership, 4*(1), 111–125.

Grothaus, T., & Neukrug, E. (2010). *Perceptions of ethical behavior for school counselors.* Manuscript in preparation.

Gysbers, N. C., & Henderson, P. (2006). *Developing and managing your school guidance and counseling program.* Alexandria, VA: American Counseling Association.

Gysbers, N. C., & Lapan, R. T. (2009). *Strengths-based career development for school guidance and counseling programs.* Chelsea, MI: Counseling Outfitters.

Hennington, C., & Doggett, R. A. (2004). Setting up and managing a classroom. In B. T. Erford (Ed.), *Professional school counseling: A handbook of theories, programs, and practices* (pp. 287–301). Austin, TX: Pro-Ed.

Herr, E. L., & Erford, B. T. (2011). Historical roots and future issues. In B. T. Erford (Ed.), *Transforming the school counseling profession* (3rd ed., pp. 19–43). Upper Saddle River, NJ: Pearson.

Hines, P. L., & Fields, T. H. (2004). School counseling and academic achievement. In R. Perusse & G. E. Goodnough (Eds.), *Leadership, advocacy and direct service strategies for professional school counselors* (pp. 3–33). Belmont, CA: Brooks/Cole.

Hipolito, C. P., & Lee, C. C. (2007). Empowerment theory for the professional school counselor: A manifesto for what really matters. *Professional School Counseling, 10,* 327–332.

Hoffman, M. A., Phillips, E. L., Noumair, D. A., Shullman, S., Geisler, C., Gray, J., et al. (2006). Toward a feminist and multicultural model of consultation and advocacy. *Journal of Multicultural Counseling and Development, 34,* 116–128.

Holcomb-McCoy, C. (2007). *School counseling to close the achievement gap: A social justice framework for success.* Thousand Oaks, CA: Corwin.

Holcomb-McCoy, C. & Chen-Hayes, S. F. (2011). Culturally competent school counselors: Affirming diversity by challenging oppression. In B. T. Erford (Ed.), *Transforming the school counseling profession* (3rd ed., pp. 90–109). Upper Saddle River, NJ: Pearson.

Houser, R., Wilczenski, F. L., Ham, M. A. (2006). *Culturally relevant ethical decision-making in counseling.* Thousand Oaks, CA: Sage.

Hughey, K. F. (2005). Preparing students for the future: Career and educational planning. In C. Sink (Ed.), *Contemporary school counseling: Theory, research and practice* (pp. 214–256). Boston: Houghton Mifflin.

Huss, S. N. (2004). Loss and grief in the school setting. In R. Perusse & G. E. Goodnough (Eds.), *Leadership, advocacy and direct service strategies for professional school counselors* (pp. 262–282) Belmont, CA: Brooks/Cole.

Jackson, M., & Grant, G. (2004). Equity, access, and career development: Contextual conflicts. In R. Perusse & G. E. Goodnough (Eds.), *Leadership, advocacy and direct service strategies for professional school counselors* (pp. 125–153). Belmont, CA: Brooks/Cole.

Jacobs, E., & Schimmel, C. (2005). Small group counseling. In C. Sink (Ed.), *Contemporary school counseling: Theory, research and practice* (pp. 82–115). Boston: Houghton Mifflin.

Jenkins, T. (2007). *When a child struggles in school.* Charleston, SC: Advantage.

Kaffenberger, C. (2011). Helping students with mental and emotional disorders. In B. T. Erford (Ed.), *Transforming the school counseling profession* (3rd ed., pp. 342–370). Upper Saddle River, NJ: Pearson.

Kaffenberger, C., & Young, A. (2007). *Making data work.* Alexandria, VA: American School Counselor Association.

Kampwirth, T. J. (2006). *Collaborative consultation in the schools: Effective practices for students with learning and behavior problems.* Upper Saddle River, NJ: Pearson.

Karcher, M. (2009). Increases in academic connectedness and self-esteem among high school students who serve as cross-age peer mentors. *Professional School Counseling, 12,* 292–299.

Kerr, M. M. (2008). *School crisis prevention and intervention.* Upper Saddle River, NJ: Prentice Hall.

Kintsch, W. (2009). Learning and constructivism. In S. Tobias & T. M. Duffy (Eds.), *Constructivist instruction: Success or failure?* (pp. 223–241). New York: Routledge.

Kress, V. E. W., Gibson, D. M., & Reynolds, C. A. (2004). Adolescents who self-injure: Implications and strategies for school counselors. *Professional School Counseling, 7,* 195–201.

Lambie, G. W. (2005). Child abuse and neglect: A practical guide for professional school counselors. *Professional School Counseling, 8,* 249–258.

Lambie, G. W., & Sias, S. M. (2009). An integrative psychological developmental model of supervision for professional school counselors in training. *Journal of Counseling & Development, 87,* 349–356.

Lambie, G. W., & Williamson, L. L. (2004). The challenge to change from guidance counseling to professional school counseling: A historical proposition. *Professional School Counseling, 8,* 124–131.

Lapan, R. T., Gysbers, N. C., & Kayson, M. (2007). *Missouri school counselors benefit all students.* Jefferson City: Missouri Department of Elementary and Secondary Education.

Lassiter, P. S., Napolitano, L., Culbreth, J. R., & Ng, K.-M. (2008). Developing multicultural competence using the structured peer group supervision model. *Counselor Education and Supervision, 47,* 164–178.

Lee, V. V. (2004). Violence prevention and conflict resolution education in the schools. In R. Perusse & G. E. Goodnough (Eds.), *Leadership, advocacy and direct service strategies for professional school counselors* (pp. 222–261). Belmont, CA: Brooks/Cole.

Lee, V. V., & Goodnough, G. E. (2011). Systemic, data-driven school counseling practice and programming for equity. In B. T. Erford (Ed.), *Transforming the school counseling profession* (3rd ed., pp. 129–153). Upper Saddle River, NJ: Pearson.

Linde, L. (2011). Ethical, legal, and professional issues in school counseling. In B. T. Erford (Ed.), *Transforming the school counseling profession* (3rd ed., pp. 70–89). Upper Saddle River, NJ: Pearson.

Lindsey, R. B., Roberts, L. M., & CampbellJones, F. (2005). *The culturally proficient school: An implementation guide for school leaders.* Thousand Oaks, CA: Corwin Press.

Lindwall, J. J., & Coleman, H. L. K. (2008). The elementary school counselor's role in fostering caring school communities. *Professional School Counseling, 12,* 144–148.

Luke, M., & Bernard, J. M. (2006). The school counseling supervision model: An extension of the Discrimination Model. *Counselor Education & Supervision, 45,* 282–295.

Mahoney, M. J. (1996). Connected knowing in constructive psychotherapy. In N. R. Goldberger, J. M. Tarule, B. M. Clinchy, & M. F. Belenky (Eds.), *Knowledge, difference, and power: Essays inspired by women's ways of knowing* (pp. 126–147). New York: HarperCollins.

Manning, M. L., & Baruth, L. G. (2004). *Multicultural education of children and adolescents* (4th ed.). Boston: Pearson.

Marshall, C. & Young, M. (2006). The wider societal challenge: An afterword. In C. Marshall & M. Oliva (Eds.), *Leadership for social justice: Making revolutions in education* (pp. 307–317). Boston: Pearson.

Martin, P. J., & Robinson, S. G. (2011). Transforming the school counseling profession. In B. T. Erford (Ed.), *Transforming the school counseling profession* (3rd ed., pp. 1–18). Upper Saddle River, NJ: Pearson.

McAuliffe, G., Danner, M., Grothaus, T., & Doyle, L. (2008). Social diversity and social justice. In G. McAuliffe (Ed.), *Culturally alert counseling: A comprehensive introduction* (pp. 45–83). Thousand Oaks, CA: Sage.

McAuliffe, G., Grothaus, T., Pare, D., Wininger, A. (2008). The practice of culturally alert counseling. In G. McAuliffe (Ed.), *Culturally alert counseling: A comprehensive introduction* (pp. 570–631). Thousand Oaks, CA: Sage.

Milsom, A. (2006). Creating positive experiences for students with disabilities. *Professional School Counseling, 10,* 66–72.

Milsom, A. (2007). Interventions to assist students with disabilities through school transitions. *Professional School Counseling, 10,* 273–278.

Milsom, A., & Bryant, J. (2006). School counseling departmental web sites: What message do we send? *Professional School Counselor, 10,* 210–216.

Milsom, A., & Dietz, L. (2009). Defining college readiness for students with learning disabilities: A delphi study. *Professional School Counseling, 12,* 315–323.

Murphy, J. J. (2008). *Solution-focused counseling in schools* (2nd ed.). Alexandria, VA: American Counseling Association.

National Center for Education Statistics. (2010). *The nation's report card.* Retrieved August 1, 2010, from http://nces.ed.gov/NATIONSREPORTCARD/

Nieto, S. (2005). School reform and student learning: A multicultural perspective. In J. A. Banks & C. A. McGee Banks (Eds.), *Multicultural education: Issues and perspectives* (5th ed., pp. 401–420). Hoboken, NJ: John Wiley & Sons.

Ober, A. M., Haag Granello, D., & Henfield, M. S. (2009). A synergistic model to enhance multicultural competence in supervision. *Counselor Education & Supervision, 48,* 204–221.

Ohrt, J. H., Lambie, G. W., & Ieva, K. P. (2009). Supporting Latino and African-American students in Advanced Placement courses: A school counseling program's approach. *Professional School Counseling, 13,* 59–63.

Ovando, C. J. (2005). Language diversity and education. In J. A. Banks & C. A. McGee Banks (Eds.), *Multicultural education: Issues and perspectives* (5th ed., pp. 289–313). Hoboken, NJ: John Wiley & Sons.

Paniagua, F. A. (2005). *Assessing and treating culturally diverse clients: A practical guide* (3rd ed.). Thousand Oaks, CA: Sage.

Parsons, R. D., & Kahn, W. J. (2005). *The school counselor as consultant: An integrated model for school-based consultation.* Belmont, CA: Brooks/Cole.

Ponterotto, J. G., Utsey, S. O., & Pedersen, P. B. (2006). *Preventing prejudice: A guide for counselors, educators, and parents* (2nd ed.). Thousand Oaks, CA: Sage.

Portman, T. A. A. (2009). Faces of the future: School counselors as cultural mediators. *Journal of Counseling & Development, 87,* 21–27.

Pransky, J. (2001). *Prevention: The critical need* (2nd ed.). Springfield, MO: Burrell Foundation.

Quigney, T. A. (2005). Students with special needs. In J. R. Studer (Ed.), *The professional school counselor: An advocate for students* (pp. 82–106). Belmont, CA: Brooks/Cole.

Ratts, M., DeKruyf, L., & Chen-Hayes, S. (2007). The ACA advocacy competencies: A social justice advocacy framework for professional school counselors. *Professional School Counseling, 11,* 90–97.

Remley, T. P., & Huey, W. C. (2002). An ethics quiz for school counselors. *Professional School Counseling, 6,* 3–11.

Robles de Melendez, W., & Beck, V. (2010). *Teaching young children in multicultural classrooms: Issues, concepts, and strategies* (3rd ed.). Belmont, CA: Wadsworth.

Rock, E., & Leff, E. H. (2011). The professional school counselor and students with disabilities. In B. T. Erford (Ed.), *Transforming the school counseling profession* (3rd ed., pp. 314–341). Upper Saddle River, NJ: Pearson.

Rosenshine B. (2009). The empirical support for direct instruction. In S. Tobias & T. M. Duffy (Eds.), *Constructivist instruction: Success or failure?* (pp. 201–220). New York: Routledge.

Schellenberg, R. (2008). *The new school counselor: Strategies for universal academic achievement.* Lanham, MD: Rowman & Littlefield.

Schmidt, J. J. (2008). *Counseling in schools: Comprehensive programs of responsive services for all students* (5th ed.). Boston: Pearson.

Schwiebert, V. L., Sealander, K. A., & Dennison, J. L. (2002). Strategies for counselors working with high school students with attention-deficit/hyperactivity disorder. *Journal of Counseling & Development, 80,* 3–10.

Search Institute. (2007). *The 40 developmental assets for adolescents.* Minneapolis, MN: Author.

Simcox, A. G., Nuijens, K. L., & Lee, C. C. (2006). School counselors and school psychologists: Collaborative partners in promoting culturally competent schools. *Professional School Counseling, 9,* 272–277.

Singh, A. A., Urbano, A., Haston, M., & McMahon, E. (2010). School counselors' strategies for social justice change: A grounded theory of what works in the real world. *Professional School Counseling, 13,* 135–145.

Sink, C. A. (2005). *Contemporary school counseling: Theory, research, and practice.* Boston: Houghton Mifflin.

Sklare, G. B. (2005). *Brief counseling that works: A solution-focused approach for school counselors and administrators.* Thousand Oaks, CA: Corwin.

Smink, J., & Reimer, M. S. (2005). *Fifteen effective strategies for improving student attendance and truancy prevention.* Clemson, SC: National Dropout Prevention Center.

Smith, S. D., & Chen-Hayes, S. F. (2004). Leadership and advocacy for lesbian, bisexual, gay, transgendered, and questioning (LBGTQ) students: Academic, career, and interpersonal success stories. In R. Perusse & G. E. Goodnough (Eds.), *Leadership, advocacy and direct service strategies for professional school counselors* (pp. 187–221). Belmont, CA: Brooks/Cole.

Spinelli, C. G., (2008). Assessing the issue of cultural and linguistic diversity and assessment: Informal evaluation measures for English language learners. *Reading & Writing Quarterly, 24,* 101–118.

Sprinthall, N. A., Peace, S. D., & Kennington, P. A. D. (2000). *Cognitive developmental stage theories for counseling.* Alexandria, VA: American Counseling Association.

Stanton, A. (1996). Reconfiguring teaching and knowing in the college classroom. In N. R. Goldberger, J. M. Tarule, B. M. Clinchy, & M. F. Belenky (Eds.), *Knowledge, difference, and power: Essays inspired by women's ways of knowing* (pp. 25–56). New York: HarperCollins.

Steele, J. M. (2008). Preparing counselors to advocate for social justice: A liberation model. *Counselor Education & Supervision, 48,* 74–85.

Sternberg, R. J. (2009). Foreword. In S. Tobias & T. M. Duffy (Eds.), *Constructivist instruction: Success or failure?* (pp. x–xi). New York: Routledge.

Stone, C. B., & Dahir, C. A. (2006). *The transformed school counselor.* Boston: Houghton Mifflin.

Stone, C. B., & Dahir, C. A. (2011). *School counselor accountability: A MEASURE of student success* (3rd ed.). Upper Saddle River, NJ: Pearson Education.

Stone, C. B., & Zirkel, P. A. (2010). School counselor advocacy: When law and ethics may collide. *Professional School Counseling, 13,* 244–247.

Studer, J. R. (2005). *The professional school counselor: An advocate for students.* Belmont, CA: Brooks/Cole.

Sue, D. W. (2006). The invisible Whiteness of being: Whiteness, White supremacy, White privilege, and racism. In M. G. Constantine & D. W. Sue (Eds.), *Addressing racism: Facilitating cultural competence in mental health and educational settings* (pp. 15–30). Hoboken, NJ: John Wiley & Sons.

Taub, D. J. (2006). Understanding the concerns of parents of students with disabilities: Challenges and roles for school counselors. *Professional School Counseling, 10,* 52–57.

Thomas, S. T. (2005). The school counselor alumni peer consultation group. *Counselor Education & Supervision, 45,* 16–27.

Tobias, S., & Duffy, T. M. (2009). The success or failure of constructivist instruction: An introduction. In S. Tobias & T. M. Duffy (Eds.), *Constructivist instruction: Success or failure?* (pp. 3–10). New York: Routledge.

Ungar, M. (2006). *Strengths-based counseling with at-risk youth.* Thousand Oaks, CA: Corwin.

Van Velsor, P., & Orozco, G. L. (2007). Involving low-income parents in the schools: Communitycentric strategies for school counselors. *Professional School Counseling, 11,* 17–24.

Vera, E. M., Buhin, L., & Shin, R. Q. (2006). The pursuit of social justice and the elimination of racism. In M. G. Constantine & D. W. Sue (Eds.), *Addressing racism: Facilitating cultural competence in mental health and educational settings* (pp. 87–103). Hoboken, NJ: John Wiley & Sons.

Vernon, A. (2004). Designing developmental guidance lessons. In B. T. Erford (Ed.), *Professional school counseling: A handbook of theories, programs, and practices* (pp. 279–286). Austin, TX: Pro-Ed.

Vilallba, J. A., Jr. (2007). Culture-specific assets to consider when counseling Latina/o children and adolescents. *Journal of Multicultural Counseling and Development, 35,* 15–25.

Virginia School Counselor Association. (2008). *Virginia professional school counseling program manual.* Yorktown, VA: Author.

Walley, C., Grothaus, T., & Craigen, L. (2009). Confusion, crisis, and opportunity: Professional school counselors' role in responding to student mental health issues. *Journal of School Counseling, 7*(36). Retrieved August 1, 2010, from http://www.jsc.montana.edu/articles/v7n36.pdf

Watkins, K. E., Ellickson, P. L., Vaiana, M. E., & Hiromoto, S. (2006). An update on adolescent drug use: What school counselors need to know. *Professional School Counseling, 10,* 131–138.

Weinstein, C. S., Tomlinson-Clarke, S., & Curran, M. (2004). Toward a conception of culturally responsive classroom management. *Journal of Teacher Education, 55,* 25–38.

Whiston, S. C., & Bouwkamp, J. C. (2005). Peer programs and family counseling. In C. Sink (Ed.), *Contemporary school counseling: Theory, research and practice* (pp. 116–147). Boston: Houghton Mifflin.

Whiston, S. C., & Quinby, R. F. (2011). Outcomes research on school counseling interventions and programs. In B. T. Erford (Ed.), *Transforming the school counseling profession* (3rd ed., pp. 58–69). Upper Saddle River, NJ: Pearson.

Wilkerson, K. (2006). Peer supervision for the professional development of school counselors: Toward an understanding of terms and findings. *Counselor Education & Supervision, 46,* 59–67.

Winslade, J. M., & Monk, G. D. (2007). *Narrative counseling in schools* (2nd ed.). Thousand Oaks, CA: Corwin.

Wood, C., & D'Agostino, J. V. (2010). Assessment in counseling: A tool for social justice work. In M. J. Ratts, R. L. Toporek, & J. A. Lewis (Eds.), *ACA advocacy competencies: A social justice framework for counselors* (pp. 51–59). Alexandria, VA: American Counseling Association.

Wood, C., & Rayle, A. D. (2006). A model of school counseling supervision: The goals, functions, roles, and systems model. *Counselor Education & Supervision, 45,* 253–266.

# Appendix A
## Rubric for Interview Project

**Interviews with five school counseling program stakeholders.** (Each interviewee must be a separate person. Participants can be from your observation sites.) Include:

- A certified, practicing, professional school counselor (PSC) *and* four of the following five choices:
  - an administrator (e.g., principal, assistant principal, dean, central office supervisor)
  - a community stakeholder (e.g., local business owner, agency counselor, school board member, Child Protective Services worker)
  - a teacher
  - a parent
  - a K–12 student (adapt questions as needed for comprehension)

**Interview questions** (co-constructed via class dialogue, samples below):

1. What is the current role of the PSC(s) in the school or district?

2. What would be the ideal role for the PSC(s) in the school or district?

3. What is their opinion of the American School Counselor Association National Model?

4. To what degree is a comprehensive school counseling program being implemented in the school or district?

5. How are the students different because of the school counseling program?

6. What is the PSC's role in creating a positive multicultural school and community climate?

7. How and to what degree is school-family-community collaboration implemented?

8, 9, & 10. Three of your own questions (can vary with each interviewee).

**Incorporate the elements below into a final report.** Format choices include writing a paper, posting it on your school counseling website, or reporting the results on a DVD or social media site.

\*\*Please safeguard participant confidentiality by removing any identifying information.\*\*

I. **Interview Summaries.** Summarize each interviewee's answers to the questions asked.

II. **"State of School Counseling" Assessment.** Based only on the evidence gathered in your interviews, write an assessment of the state of school counseling (don't make claims that your data can't support). Be sure to address evident patterns in stakeholder answers, including, from your perspective, the positives that can be celebrated and the areas of concern that need to be addressed.

III. **Reflection**—Share:
- your reactions to each interviewee's responses (e.g., areas/topics of agreement or disagreement, challenges to your perceptions and/or to our profession)
- cultural considerations that may influence your reactions to or perceptions of the interviews
- how you might collaborate with these stakeholders to address their concerns and incorporate their assistance and input to strengthen your school counseling program

# Appendix B
## Facilitate Class Learning on a Current School Counseling Topic

**Example Topics**: Students experiencing homelessness; grief; self-injury; dropout prevention; substance abuse and children of alcoholic concerns; LGBTQ issues; English language learners; eating disorders; child abuse and neglect; and suicide prevention.

**Assignment:** Lead a class segment on your chosen/assigned topic. The class will have read one assigned article or chapter on your topic. Challenge and support your peers in their construction of additional knowledge and questions regarding the topic. Sharing general information on the subject should be brief; focus more on this issue's relevance for PreK–12 students and their families and on possible implications for school counselors. Incorporate information from your peer-reviewed professional sources and your interviews with at least two people familiar with the topic as it exists in PreK–12 schools. During your presentation, fulfill the following:

- Class facilitation/learning about your topic should last 30–40 minutes.
- Use at least one tech/media device.
- Engage the class in at least one activity related to the topic that encourages higher-order thinking or deep processing (e.g., discussion, role play, case study, dilemma discussion).
- Share and discuss potential cultural considerations.
- Lead the class in learning about potential roles for a school counselor to play in preventing or intervening in this area (include leadership and advocacy roles/actions).
- Expose what you consider to be misunderstanding(s) and/or seemingly unhelpful school personnel or institutional responses to this issue, and justify your stance.

- Discuss how school counselors can facilitate alternative, more helpful intervention or prevention strategies than those you shared above, and give your reasons for favoring these alternative strategies.
- Include discussion about ways school counselors can collaborate with school and community stakeholders to address concerns in this area.
- Share at least one example of how your perception, knowledge, awareness, attitude, or skills have changed as a result of your involvement in preparing this class facilitation.
- Provide a handout with the key content (and a reference and resource list) for everyone.
- Prepare a reference and resource list to all in our class with the following components:
  o Include at least four references from professionally recognized, peer-reviewed sources.
  o Identify and share at least three sources of additional information (e.g., websites, support groups, agencies specializing in this area).
  o Provide background information about your interviewees (at least two people familiar with the topic as it exists in PreK–12 schools), data that will inform us about your sources without revealing their identity (e.g., role/position: community agency counselor, parent/guardian, student, administrator, etc.; relevant cultural information; source or reason for familiarity with the topic).

- Information gained from the sources and the interviews listed above should be evident in your presentation.
- Presentation should engage our class in active learning and discussion.
- Provide at least four items/questions (and answers) to the instructor for possible use on the final exam (e.g., multiple choice, short answer, case study).

# Appendix C
## Construct Elements of a School Counseling Program

While elements II–X below need to be your own created work, researching and adapting ideas from actual schools and the professional literature (cite and list these sources) is encouraged.

I. Create the following data (or retrieve it from the website of a PreK–12 school of your choice):

o School counselor-to-student ratio, enrollment disaggregated by ethnicity, Annual Yearly Progress rating, pass rates by identified populations, percentage free/reduced price lunch, percentage of courses taught by highly qualified teachers, attendance, number in gifted program and number receiving special education services (preferably disaggregated by race/ethnicity), school safety data (number of incidents). Also, describe the community setting for the school, and create a resource list of at least 10 sources of assistance and/or advocacy for/with youth/ families in the area, with brief descriptions of services provided and contact information.

II. Your School Counseling Program Philosophy and School Counseling Mission Statement

III. Needs Assessment, Evaluation, and Accountability

o Sample Needs Assessment: Include assessment, and answer the following: Who will be assessed? How will you gain the data needed? How will the data be used?

o Program Evaluation: How, when, and by whom will the school counseling program *and* the school counselor(s) be evaluated?

o How (and to whom) will the school counseling program evaluation results be disseminated?

IV. Design an advocacy intervention for an equity issue based on data from your school, district, or community. Create a MEASURE and Report Card showing how you addressed the concern (do it as if you completed the collaborative intervention).

V. Theoretical Orientation of the Program

o Which counseling theory(ies) form the theoretical orientation for the counseling services?

o Justify this(these) choice(s) given the particular level and needs of the school.

o Give an example of how the theory(ies) chosen would influence your interventions.

VI. Share a completed School Counselor-Administrator Management Agreement.

VII. Program Calendars: One sample weekly calendar (time distribution should match management agreement) and an annual calendar of major school counseling events and interventions.

VIII. Crosswalk 1 Domain for your school (e.g., Career, 6–8): Share interventions and programming planned to achieve your designated set of standards or competencies.

IX. Pamphlet/Brochure and PowerPoint Presentation Slides

o Describe the purpose and targeted stakeholder audience of each.

o One needs to be a general overview of the school counseling program, and the other needs to focus on a specific aspect of your school counseling program.

X. Your Plan for Professional Development (include multicultural competency enhancement)

XI. List of References (and citations used when appropriate) in APA style

# Appendix D
## Create Developmental Guidance Lesson Plans

Construct three sequential classroom guidance lessons. You are welcome to get ideas from established lesson plans, but the final plans should be substantially your own creation. Your set of three consecutive lessons on the same topic for an identified grade or group should be designed to promote learning that includes application, synthesis, analysis, and evaluation.

1. Present an accurate reference list. (Use of references should be evident in lessons: minimum of five references, including at least one from a refereed professional counseling journal and one from an educational journal or text.)

2. Justify the developmental appropriateness of topic *and* share relevant cultural considerations.

3. Create an informational letter for a specified audience (your choice) containing an overview of the content of your lessons and the logistics (e.g., length and location of lessons).

4. For each lesson, list the standards and competencies that you hope to have the students accomplish, from either the ASCA (2005) National Model or your state's school counseling standards and competencies (list these at the beginning of each individual lesson; they should be clearly related to the lesson that follows). For **at least one lesson**, list at least one subject area (e.g., math, language, social studies) state standard or competency you will cover.

5. Develop and name specific learning objective(s) for each individual lesson. Each learning objective will specify the intended audience, expected measurable behavior(s) by the audience, and level of acceptable performance of the behavior(s).

6. Create an evaluation instrument measuring achievement of one or more of your learning objectives. It can be a written, oral, portfolio, or performance-based assessment instrument.

7. Identify other data to be assessed (e.g., attendance, grades, test scores, number of discipline referrals) that could be correlated to your lessons. Explain which data you'll analyze and with whom you'll share the results of your assessment.

8. Describe follow-up activities (e.g., for students needing additional assistance after the lesson).

9. For each separate lesson (in addition to the list above) please share the following:
   o a list of supplies/equipment and coleaders
   o your detailed lesson plans, including an introduction, how you plan to activate your audience's previous knowledge, a description of the learning activities geared to construct new knowledge (specific enough in explanation so that a substitute could teach in your place if necessary), evaluate achievement of learning objective(s), and conclusion/summary
   o at least one accommodation for an audience member with an exceptional learning need (e.g., as might be specified on an Individualized Education Plan or 504 plan)

# Appendix E
## Ethics Scenarios for Discussion

## PERCEPTIONS OF ETHICAL BEHAVIOR FOR SCHOOL COUNSELORS

(GROTHAUS & NEUKRUG, 2010)

The following statements describe a variety of school counselor behaviors. After examining each statement, rank each item from **1 to 10** in the column to the left of the item using the following scale.

**1 = Clearly *Unethical* Behavior**—--—-—--—-—-—-—-—-—-—-—-—-—--— **10 = Clearly *Ethical* Behavior**

Example response:

| 1–10 | ITEM |
|---|---|
| 1 | Taking money from a student in exchange for not reporting an illegal behavior |

*This respondent believed that the statement described a clearly unethical behavior by a school counselor (as indicated by the score of 1 in the column to the left of the item).

## PLEASE COMPLETE THE FOLLOWING ITEMS USING THE SCALE BELOW

**1 = Clearly *Unethical* Behavior**—--—-—--—-—-—-—-—-—-—-—-—-—--— **10 = Clearly *Ethical* Behavior**

| 1–10 | ITEM |
|---|---|
| | 1. Accepting a 17-year-old student's decision to commit suicide and not reporting it |
| | 2. Viewing your student's personal web page (e.g., MySpace, Facebook, blog) without informing your student |
| | 3. Choosing not to report suspected child abuse because you don't have confidence in the Child Protective Service workers due to past mistakes on their part |
| | 4. Not informing parents/guardians about their 10-year-old child engaging in "cutting" because the child says he or she has only done it a few times and won't do it again |
| | 5. Withholding information when a parent/guardian of a 7-year-old repeatedly insists on knowing about the specific content of counseling sessions with his or her child |
| | 6. Not allowing the noncustodial parent of a student to view his or her child's educational records if the custodial parent requests that you not share any information |
| | 7. Refusing to voluntarily appear in court to support a responsible mother who is fighting with a neglectful father so he'll provide financial support for their children |
| | 8. Counseling the child of a friend who's also a faculty member at your school |
| | 9. Guaranteeing confidentiality for members of a group |

*(Continued)*

| 1–10 | ITEM |
|---|---|
| | 10. Keeping student records on your office computer |
| | 11. Counseling students from a culture different from your own without having much knowledge about that student's culture |
| | 12. Choosing to work only with students from specific cultural groups (e.g., race/ethnicity, gender, sexual orientation) |
| | 13. Breaking confidentiality to inform parents that their 13-year-old child is involved in a gay or lesbian sexual relationship |
| | 14. Sharing confidential student information about a high school student's drug use when your administrative supervisor requests the information |
| | 15. Sharing confidential student information about a student's family concerns with a student's teacher without the student's permission |
| | 16. Breaking confidentiality to inform parents that their 13-year-old child is involved in a heterosexual sexual relationship |
| | 17. Being an advocate by promoting school policy changes to make access to resources and educational opportunities more equitable for students |
| | 18. Trying to persuade your student to not have an abortion even though she wants to |
| | 19. Not using a theory or identifiable blend of theories when providing counseling |
| | 20. Publicly advocating on school grounds for a political candidate |
| | 21. Giving or accepting a gift from a student or his or her family worth more than $25 |
| | 22. Counseling a 15-year-old pregnant student without informing the parent/guardian about the pregnancy |
| | 23. Making a *DSM–IV–TR* diagnosis of attention deficit hyperactivity disorder for a student |
| | 24. Reporting a student to a school administrator after the student tells you that he or she cheated on a standardized test |
| | 25. Using a student to act as the interpreter in a meeting with his or her parent/guardian when the parent/guardian's primary language is different from yours |
| | 26. Despite a 14-year-old student's request for confidentiality, reporting to a parent/guardian that the student has plans to run away from home |
| | 27. Confronting a school counseling colleague about his or her unethical behavior that you've witnessed |
| | 28. Keeping student records in an area that cannot be secured with a lock |
| | 29. Attempting to console an eighth-grade student by hugging him or her |
| | 30. Counseling a student who is your neighbor and your child's friend |
| | 31. Informing the sexual partners of an HIV-positive student when the student refuses to reveal this condition to his or her partners |
| | 32. Encouraging a student to join your church, mosque, or synagogue |
| | 33. Becoming sexually involved with a parent/guardian of one of your students |

| 1–10 | ITEM |
|---|---|
| | 34. Not screening prospective members for appropriateness for a counseling group |
| | 35. Not informing students of their rights (e.g., confidentiality and its limits) when providing counseling |
| | 36. Attending a formal ceremony or party for a student at his or her request |
| | 37. Counseling a 10-year-old student at his or her request even though a parent/guardian has specifically asked you not to work with the student |
| | 38. Fearing deportation of the student and his or her family, not reporting that a 15-year-old honor student is an illegal immigrant despite legal obligation to do so |
| | 39. Developing academic and career goals only for the students who request them |
| | 40. Sharing confidential student information with your spouse/significant other |
| | 41. Telling a student on your caseload that you are attracted to him or her |
| | 42. Charging a fee to see students from your school in your private practice after school |
| | 43. Not evaluating your school counseling program for its effectiveness in helping to close the achievement gap |
| | 44. Collaborating with community organizations to assist students (e.g., provision of mental health services, helping secure financial assistance for the student's family) |
| | 45. Providing counseling to your students over the Internet |
| | 46. Reporting to a parent/guardian that his or her 15-year-old is having a sexual relationship with a 21-year-old (even though the student asked you not to tell the parent/guardian) |
| | 47. Engaging in counseling with a student while the student is in another helping relationship (e.g., family counseling) without trying to contact the other counselor |
| | 48. Not participating in continuing professional development after obtaining your degree |
| | 49. Counseling a student when you've not had training about his or her presenting problem (e.g., eating disorder) |
| | 50. Not being a member of a professional counseling association |
| | 51. Selling a product to your student related to the counseling relationship (e.g., book) |
| | 52. Due to your family's financial need, taking a job with an evening shift that leaves you very tired and absentminded in your school counseling job performance |
| | 53. Reporting a student to police who tells you that he or she stole items from a local store |
| | 54. Telling a parent/guardian when an 11-year-old reveals that he or she smokes cigarettes |
| | 55. Reporting a student who reveals that he or she vandalized school property |
| | 56. Choosing to inform the parent/guardian about his or her 16-year-old child's substance abuse despite the student's request to receive substance abuse treatment without parent/guardian consent or knowledge |

## I. Introduction

The portfolio is a collection of experience-based and reflective materials that demonstrate dimensions of your work, philosophy, abilities, attitudes, and goals. The goal of the portfolio is to articulate how diverse activities and insights contributed to your identity development as a professional school counselor.

## II. Purposes

There are two primary purposes for the portfolio: to facilitate your intentional shaping and synthesis of learning and to provide a format for presentation of professional qualifications.

## III. Content

A guiding principle in deciding what to include in the entries is to ask, "How will this entry demonstrate my knowledge, awareness, skills, and developing professional identity?" Other questions to consider in creating the reflective portions include the following: How did it help your professional growth? In retrospect, how might you do things differently? What did you learn? What attitudes, values, and beliefs were validated and/or reexamined as a result of the experience? How does this help in the attainment of your professional goals?

## IV. School Counseling Portfolio Guidelines—Please include the following:

- professional resume and two letters of recommendation
- narrative explaining how your experiences (including both your participation in the graduate program and life experiences outside of the program) have helped prepare you to be a Professional School Counselor
- theoretical orientation (with explanation/justification for its use in schools)
- philosophy of education
- self-assessment of strengths, needs, and "growing edges" or challenges (these areas of growth should be addressed in your goals and professional development plan)
- statement of professional goals, including multicultural competence goal(s), which includes advocacy
- plan for your professional development (including enhanced multicultural competence)
- list of professional development activities (with a brief reflection on each)
- evidence of specific area of interest/focus/expertise in the school counseling field
- analysis of professional interpersonal relationships during field experiences (include reference to culture)
- statement about your identity as a school counselor (especially as a leader, advocate, collaborator, and change agent)
- examples of your problem solving, using actual problems from your field experiences
- representative work and reflection on what you have gained from coursework and field experiences

# Teaching Community Agency/Mental Health Counseling and Crisis Intervention

Sarah E. Peterson and Rick A. Myer

*The project method . . . may work a complete transformation in school life, and a correspondingly profound transformation in the attitudes, standards, and methods of thinking and of acting in the coming generations. It represents something more than a method of teaching in the narrower sense of this term. It means a new point of view toward the whole problem of education.*

William C. Bagley (1921, p. 288)

One of the often-dreaded teaching assignments in counselor education is content courses not directly tied to the learning and development of counseling skills. One such course deals with administration and management of community agencies. Students enter counselor education programs to learn how to do counseling or therapy, not to ponder seemingly mundane information such as administration, finance, and accountability. How can counselor educators best facilitate their students' understanding of this important content? How can educators do so in a way that helps students appreciate the relevance of the content even though it is not directly tied to counseling skills? A constructivist approach can be a guide for answering both questions. As McAuliffe (Chapter 1, this volume) has suggested, this approach calls for counseling students to generate solutions to complex, real-life problems rather than

rely on answers from teachers. In addition, counselor educators must be willing to accept the challenge of reflecting on their own teaching practices in order to help students construct their understandings of community agency counseling. In Dewey's (1933) terms, a constructivist approach requires counselor educators to be creative in developing courses that challenge students to learn experientially so that they can use professionally what they have learned in their courses (McAuliffe, Chapter 2, this volume).

In this chapter we describe how a foundational course on community agencies can be taught using project-based learning, an approach that actively engages students in inquiry into authentic problems (Mergendoller, Markham, Ravitz, & Larmer, 2006; Polman, 2004; Tal, Krajcik, & Blumenfeld, 2006). Such projects require that instructors generate an important question or problem whose solution challenges students to use a variety of investigative methods. Students then produce some type of culminating product that answers the targeted question or problem (Blumenfeld et al., 1991). Project-based learning helps students become more motivated to learn important concepts because those ideas are studied within the context of an important question or problem. In addition, projects allow classrooms to simulate realistic settings with real-life problems. They also require use of knowledge from a variety of sources and disciplines, resulting in expanded perspectives on the chosen subject (Blumenfeld et al., 1991). Thus, project-based learning begins early to engage future counselors in the substantive questions, problems, and solutions of their future professional work in community agencies (Schön, 1991).

This chapter is divided into three sections. In the first section, we offer a contextual framework for the community agency course that includes three components: (a) the social constructivist theoretical foundations in which project-based learning is situated, (b) the professional context dictated by the standards of the Council for Accreditation of Counseling and Related Educational Programs (CACREP; 2009) for the foundations course in community agencies, and (c) a programmatic context into which the course typically fits. In the second section, we describe the community agency course, specifically addressing (a) content and learning objectives, (b) in-class structure and objectives, and (c) course assignments. Finally, in the third section, we offer reflections based on my (Myer's) experience using project-based learning when teaching the course.

## CONTEXTUAL FRAMEWORK FOR THE COURSE ON FOUNDATIONS OF COMMUNITY AGENCY AND MENTAL HEALTH COUNSELING

In this section, we describe three components that provide a contextual framework for the course. The first includes three theoretical foundations of social constructivism, the second includes CACREP standards that serve as guidelines for course content, and the third describes the programmatic context within which the course resides.

# Theoretical Foundations

As mentioned previously, counselors-in-training often do not immediately recognize the relevance of courses that do not focus on skills needed for direct service to clients. In my (Myer's) experience, teaching "non-skills" courses using a traditional lecture format generally results in students being even more convinced that they do not need the material. They memorize information for the test and then forget it within a few weeks. The problem with this type of didactic teaching style is that the learning is decontextualized, separated from the realities of community agencies as professional workplaces. Given that counselor educators consider the community agency course to be necessary to students' success as professional counselors, such a problematic learning experience is unacceptable.

Project-based learning, in contrast, is a teaching method rooted in several theoretical traditions, all of which reflect social constructivist approaches: situated cognition, cooperative learning, and Vygotsky's sociohistorical theory of development.

## Situated Cognition

In her seminal work on situated cognition, Resnick (1987) identified three typical differences between learning in school and outside of school, such as in work settings. The first distinction is between individual and shared cognition. Most school learning occurs individually, whereas most activities outside of school occur with colleagues. Even though activities within the classroom may involve group discussion, performance is usually judged on an individual basis, using scores from tests and papers. In contrast, performance in work settings is often at least partially based on the successful completion of a project by a team. The second distinction is between pure thinking and use of cognitive tools. Students in traditional courses usually perform tasks without the aid of external tools, such as reference material, computers, and expert help. In actual work settings, however, it is expected that counselors will use all of the tools available to best serve their clients. The third distinction is between general and situation-specific competencies. School learning focuses on general, widely transferable theoretical principles and skills, whereas in the workplace, individuals develop situation-specific competencies. Project-based learning engages students in collaborative, relevant learning tasks that simulate tasks found in professional settings, tasks in which they use authentic tools and develop professional quality competencies.

## Cooperative Learning

A second theoretical tradition that informs project-based learning is cooperative learning. Based on a rich tradition of theory and research on cooperative goal structures, cooperative learning is characterized by having small groups of students experience positive interdependence; that is, students perceive that they can achieve their own goals only when others in the group also achieve their goals (Johnson & Johnson, 1994). Proponents of this perspective argue that collaboration, rather than competition, more often characterizes real-life work settings and that competition in classroom settings demotivates many students, to their detriment (Johnson & Johnson, 1994).

A substantial body of research points to the benefits of cooperative learning on student achievement, interracial relations, acceptance of students with disabilities, improved self-esteem, motivation, time on-task, cooperative behavior, and altruism (Slavin, 1995). In particular, research on cooperative learning with college students has demonstrated positive effects on student engagement and motivation when compared with large-group instruction, especially when tasks are structured so that individuals contribute appropriate effort to the group outcomes (Johnson & Johnson, 1994; Peterson, 1992, 1993; Peterson & Miller, 2004a, 2004b). In addition, students believe that group projects contribute to developing the skills needed for actual work settings (Peterson & Myer, 1995).

## Vygotsky's Sociohistorical Theory of Development

A third guiding perspective for the foundations of community agency course lies in Vygotsky's (1978) assertion that human beings are largely products of their cultural and social environments. He argued that people develop complex mental functions by moving from social interaction to internalized knowledge. An important condition for such development is that instruction must take place within a learner's zone of proximal development (ZPD), or at a level of complexity or difficulty at which the learner can accomplish tasks with guidance.

An important implication of these two basic concepts is that instruction should provide for social interaction and negotiation. Although Vygotsky's (1978) original notion of the ZPD implied a more capable adult teacher providing instruction within a developing child's ZPD (Wlodkowski, 1999), researchers who have applied Vygotskian perspectives to adults have determined that the basic process of learning is similar whether applied to adults or children. That is, learning involves constructing meaning through interacting with others and building on their prior experiences (Rogoff & Lave, 1984; Wlodkowski, 1999). Vygotsky's theory emphasizes several key factors in meaningful learning among adults: the role of instructor as guide or coach, consideration of adults' experiences, social interactions within their cultural context, and authentic applications to work settings. These factors influence our choices in constructing the community agency course.

# CACREP Guidelines for Education in Community Agency Counseling

In addition to the teaching *process* articulated in the previous section, instructors must think carefully about the *content* of the course. The CACREP (2009) guidelines provide an important outline of what should be taught in the foundations course. The guidelines describe relevant competencies under both the Professional Identity and Professional Practice sections. These are described in general here, although specific competencies are also cross-referenced below in the more specific description of the community agency course (see Table 21.1 on page 342).

## Professional Identity

The first theme articulated in the CACREP (2009) standards relates to the history and philosophy of the mental health movement, particularly referencing counseling's unique identity in comparison with other mental health professions. This theme creates a context for students as they learn about issues related to managing community counseling agencies. As a result, students see the influence of history on the current practice of counseling and acquire a foundation for anticipating mental health needs in the future. In addition, they discover their profession's roots in social justice.

A second CACREP theme related to Professional Identity addresses the role of counselors operating within and between community counseling agencies, particularly as they serve diverse populations. During the course focus on this theme, students begin to understand the unique contributions that counselors make in multidisciplinary teams and in advocating for clients with diverse needs. In addition, through learning about their professional roles and responsibilities, counselors-in-training begin to recognize the need for securing appropriate credentials and participating in lifelong learning.

A third theme related to Professional Identity requires that counselors develop assessment and evaluation skills. They need to be able to assess client and community needs, evaluate the effectiveness of community agency programs, and use evaluation findings to improve agency offerings. Counseling students need to receive ongoing supervision to ensure that they provide quality and ethical therapy to all clients.

## Professional Practice

The second section of the CACREP (2009) standards that is relevant to the community agency counseling course stresses the essential role of effective management in community agencies. CACREP recognizes that while mastery of counseling skills is necessary, full professional competence requires skills that enable counselors to take leadership roles within community agencies. In that vein, effective professional practice requires knowledge of program development, needs assessment, and program evaluation. Further, history challenges students to carefully reflect on how to systematically and ethically establish and assess programs.

Other Professional Practice themes address (1) organizational matters, including types of community agencies—public and private; (2) networking among these agencies; (3) details associated with daily management; and (4) fiscal management, including topics such as budgeting and reimbursement. Again, presenting such information in the community agency course helps students understand the organizational complexity of community agencies.

The CACREP (2009) standards include additional competencies in crisis intervention and prevention. The intention of this standard is not to focus just on provision of crisis intervention for individuals, but also on program development that allows intervention early in a crisis situation so as to prevent mental and emotional problems. This addition to the standards recognizes the growing trend to acknowledge crisis intervention and prevention as a unique specialty in the field (Myer & Moore, 2006).

# Context of the Course in the Program of Study

The third component of the contextual framework for the course in community agency counseling is its placement within students' overall program of study. Students should be encouraged to enroll in this course early in their programs, particularly before practicum and internship, because it helps them understand the professional context in which they will practice as counselors. Through experiential learning in which students solve real-world problems by creating agencies, they can better understand the importance to their future clients of effective administration and management of community agencies. In addition, they can come to appreciate the political issues affecting community agencies and how to create political changes that benefit their clients. This political perspective helps students realize that they will be working in a community with others who may or may not share their views. Because these insights are integral to developing a professional identity, the course should be taken early in their programs.

## DESCRIPTION OF THE COMMUNITY AGENCY COURSE USING PROJECT-BASED LEARNING

Our course on community agencies introduces students to practical aspects of administration and management of community agencies, including needs assessment, program development, funding, and evaluation. The course as presented here is based largely on my (Myer's) previous experiences in teaching this course, but has also been updated to reflect current CACREP (2009) standards as well as recent theory and research on the use of social constructivist teaching methods.

The course uses two sets of constructivist teaching guidelines. The first, developed by Driscoll (2005), begins with an analysis of instructional design principles and results in a description of five constructivist conditions for learning. The second, developed by McAuliffe (Chapter 3, this volume), relates more specifically to teaching counseling and is generated from a variety of perspectives.

Driscoll (2005) proposed that constructivists focus on higher-level learning goals such as problem solving, reasoning, critical thinking, and personal reflection. The learning goals in the community agency course described here incorporate these higher-level thinking skills (see Table 21.1). To achieve these goals, Driscoll argued that constructivist classrooms should incorporate five learning conditions:

1. Embed learning in complex, realistic, and relevant environments.

2. Provide for social negotiation as an integral part of learning.

3. Support multiple perspectives and the use of multiple models of representation.

4. Encourage ownership in learning.

5. Nurture self-awareness of the knowledge construction process. (pp. 393–394)

Several constructivist teaching guidelines articulated by McAuliffe (Chapter 3, this volume) are also reflected in this project-based learning course. Guidelines most relevant to the course include value and promote experience, vary the structure and methods, personalize teaching, emphasize multiple perspectives (which overlaps with Driscoll's third characteristic), and encourage intrapersonal process awareness or metacognition (which overlaps with Driscoll's fifth condition).

## Course Content and Learning Objectives

The components of the course structure are summarized in Table 21.1. The learning objectives not only help students achieve the professional competencies called for in the CACREP (2009) standards, but also reflect a constructivist emphasis on higher-level learning (Driscoll, 2005). The learning objectives primarily reflect conceptual, procedural, and metacognitive knowledge, three of the four knowledge dimensions in the revised Bloom's taxonomy of educational objectives (Anderson & Krathwohl, 2001). Conceptual knowledge refers to complex knowledge of interrelationships among elements of a larger structure, as opposed to memorization of isolated facts. Procedural knowledge refers to knowledge of processes—knowing how and when to do something. Metacognitive knowledge refers to knowledge and awareness about one's cognition. Taken together, these levels of knowledge encourage counselors to engage in reflection, defined by Schön (1991) as necessary to professional work, in this case the professional work of community agency management and administration.

In addition to learning objectives related to professional skills, the course also includes a learning objective related to self-awareness. More specifically, this objective asks students to be aware of themselves in the roles of administrator and manager and as members of a professional team. Taken together, the goals remind instructors that the lessons extend far beyond covering content; they aim at developing constructivist counselors (McAuliffe, Chapter 1, this volume) and reflective practitioners.

**TABLE 21.1**  Course Objectives, Content, Activities, and Constructivist Principles

| Learning Objectives* | Content | Activities and Processes | Constructivist Principles |
|---|---|---|---|
| Understand how history and philosophy of the profession affects current trends in community agency counseling. (Standards 1, 10) | Major advancements in field of community agency counseling from 1900 to present | Focused discussion<br><br>Small-group work during class time<br><br>"Invent a Disease" activity based on current societal trends | Social negotiation<br><br>Multiple perspectives<br><br>Self-awareness<br><br>Promote experience<br><br>Vary structure and methods |
| Apply and adhere to ethical and legal standards in community agency counseling. (Standards 6, 11) | American Counseling Association Ethical Code<br><br>American Mental Health Counseling Association Ethical Code | Focused discussion of case studies related to ethics<br><br>Small-group work during and outside of class time | Relevant learning environments<br><br>Social negotiation<br><br>Multiple perspectives<br><br>Student ownership<br><br>Promote experience<br><br>Vary structure and methods |
| Develop strategies for conducting a needs assessment. (Standards 9, 24, 26) | Needs assessment models | Focused discussion<br><br>Brainstorming<br><br>Small-group work, during and outside of class time, on purpose and rationale for program | Complex, realistic, and relevant learning environments<br><br>Social negotiation<br><br>Multiple perspectives<br><br>Student ownership<br><br>Self-awareness<br><br>Promote experience<br><br>Vary structure and methods |
| Outline program using needs assessment and current research. (Standards 9, 13, 15, 16, 17) | Various programs to meet counseling needs | Focused discussion<br><br>Small-group work, during and outside of class time, on purpose and rationale for program | Complex, realistic, and relevant learning environments<br><br>Social negotiation<br><br>Multiple perspectives<br><br>Student ownership<br><br>Promote experience<br><br>Vary structure and methods |
| Identify resources to secure financial support for programming and service delivery. (Standards 5, 13, 15, 21) | Grant writing resources for private foundations and public agencies<br><br>Fiscal management concepts | Focused discussion<br><br>Find resources for funding online<br><br>Small-group work, during and outside of class time, on plan for funding | Complex, realistic, and relevant learning environments<br><br>Social negotiation<br><br>Multiple perspectives<br><br>Student ownership<br><br>Promote experience<br><br>Vary structure and methods |

| Learning Objectives* | Content | Activities and Processes | Constructivist Principles |
|---|---|---|---|
| Develop plans for an agency-wide response to disasters and crises. (Standards 3, 14) | Crisis intervention and prevention theory<br><br>Disaster mental health planning | Focused discussion<br><br>Small-group work, during and outside of class time, on organizational structure and procedures | Complex, realistic, and relevant learning environments<br><br>Social negotiation<br><br>Multiple perspectives<br><br>Student ownership<br><br>Promote experience<br><br>Vary structure and methods |
| Identify consultation issues related to multidisciplinary teams and treatment planning. (Standards 2, 3, 12, 17, 18, 19) | Descriptions of human service professionals and groups | Focused discussion<br><br>Role play<br><br>Small-group work, during class time, on organizational structure and procedures | Complex, realistic, and relevant learning environments<br><br>Social negotiation<br><br>Multiple perspectives<br><br>Student ownership<br><br>Promote experience<br><br>Vary structure and methods |
| Demonstrate sensitivity to cultural issues in program development and service delivery. (Standards 5, 7, 8, 16, 20, 22, 23) | Theories of multicultural counseling | Focused discussion<br><br>Role play<br><br>Dyads<br><br>Small-group work, during and outside of class time, on organizational structure and procedures | Complex, realistic, and relevant learning environments<br><br>Social negotiation<br><br>Multiple perspectives<br><br>Student ownership<br><br>Promote experience<br><br>Vary structure and methods<br><br>Self-awareness |
| Design program evaluation plan to determine effectiveness. (Standards 9, 24, 25, 26) | Program evaluation models | Focused discussion<br><br>Small-group work, during and outside of class time, on program evaluation plan | Complex, realistic, and relevant learning environments<br><br>Social negotiation<br><br>Multiple perspectives<br><br>Student ownership<br><br>Promote experience<br><br>Vary structure and methods<br><br>Self-awareness |
| Develop awareness of self in the role of collaborative administration and management of community agencies. (Standards 2, 3, 27) | Professional roles | Focused discussion<br><br>Self-reflection | Student ownership<br><br>Promote experience<br><br>Vary structure and methods<br><br>Self-awareness |

*See corresponding CACREP (2009) standards at end of chapter.

# In-Class Structure and Activities

The proposed course structure and activities aim to help students achieve the aforementioned learning objectives. A course using project-based learning requires a novel structure. Unlike traditional university courses in which instructors are experts engaging in one-way transmission of knowledge to students, this type of course is more interactive, with knowledge flowing back and forth among instructors and students. The different sense of the flow begins in the initial class. It continues in the "Invent a Disease" activity, case studies, brainstorming, role-playing, focused discussions, use of class time, and other active learning roles, as described below.

## The Initial Class

The tone of the course should be set in the first class meeting. During this meeting, students receive a syllabus describing the rationale for the course structure and for activities and assignments. Since many students may not have taken a course that uses project-based learning as a primary teaching strategy, instructors should take time to explain and respond to questions regarding this method of course delivery. For instance, instructors might offer examples about how effective teamwork has solved problems, making reference to projects in the world outside of the classroom. They might ask students to reflect on their work in their own places of employment, to recall the times that they were asked to work totally alone on a project and had one chance to get it right. Generally, few students report individual work situations like this, and most students cannot remember any. This realization serves as a springboard for discussing the purpose and strategies of a course using project-based learning. Instructors need to be familiar with the rationale and research supporting this method of teaching and learning in order to be able to defend it as an approach.

## "Invent a Disease" Activity

The purpose of this activity is to help students understand the importance of historical context and trends in the counseling profession. Specifically, the activity helps students understand that needs for counseling services have evolved within a historical context. As the profession responds to these needs, it expands and shifts its emphases. To begin the activity, the instructor leads a discussion to get students actively involved in creating a historical timeline, starting with 1900 and continuing to the present, that pairs historical events and trends with major developments in the field of counseling. For example, the year 1900 is selected as a starting point because of the move from an agrarian to a more industrial society, and also because of the increased influx of immigrants into the United States. It was also during this first decade that Frank Parsons, who is considered by many as the parent of modern-day counseling, first developed his ideas about career counseling in response to the shift in occupations. Another example of an important date that directly influenced counseling is the 1957 launching of Sputnik. In reaction to the perceived need to keep up with the Russians, Congress passed the National Defense Education Act, providing grants to train counselors. Many similar examples that pair history with developments in the field of counseling can be found in the 20th century.

After creating the timeline as a class, students work in small groups and discuss current issues facing society. We use Zilbergeld's (1983) ideas from his seminal work, *The Shrinking of America: Myths of Psychological Change*, as a springboard for their discussions. Zilbergeld demonstrated how mental health professionals can be successful when a society or a group of experts "invent" a disease and spread the alarm. Eventually the disease becomes acceptable and the counseling profession can fashion a cure. A familiar example is the rapid growth of codependency as a disorder in the 1980s (Myer, Peterson, & Stoffel-Rosales, 1991). Students work through this activity by inventing a disease, such as *technology associative disorder*, then speculating on ways to inform the public about it, and finally hypothesizing about ways to help people overcome it. This activity should be approached with an air of humor as students work in groups. Ultimately, students begin to internalize what it means to be a professional as they make the connection between current events and the practice of counseling.

## Case Studies

Case studies offer opportunities to actively involve students in discussions about ethical and legal quandaries that counselors face in community agencies. We use case studies developed by Welfel (2006) that are related to each of the five basic ethical guidelines (i.e., nonmaleficence, beneficence, justice, fidelity, and respect for autonomy). The cases include issues related to working with clients as well as issues related to interacting with other professionals. Students break into groups of no more than four. They discuss the case for approximately 15 minutes. The time varies depending on the case and the issue. The groups report to the class their thoughts and actions, if any are needed in response to the case. The instructor reinforces as well as plays the devil's advocate during the discussions.

## Brainstorming

Brainstorming also offers opportunities to promote student engagement in the learning process (Johnson & Johnson, 1994). According to Johnson and Johnson, brainstorming encourages divergent thinking, increases participation and problem solving, and reduces the possibility of negative subgrouping. The instructor uses a brainstorming activity at the beginning of the project by asking students to freely name any community agencies in which counseling takes place. Usually a class will name 40 to 50 community agencies. Next, students classify the agencies by category, such as those that provide long-term or short-term counseling, serve particular population groups, provide prevention or remediation, are classified as for-profit or nonprofit, or provide inpatient or outpatient care. At the completion of a brainstorming activity, students reflect on the process of brainstorming itself. The instructor helps students focus their discussion on the amount of information that they generated and on their ability to think critically. Students feel empowered by this activity because it gives them a glimpse of what it is like to guide their own learning.

## Role-Playing

Before students spend time in groups to design their projects, it is helpful to have them engage in role-playing. Role-playing aims to help students understand issues related to working in multidisciplinary teams. Role plays are enhanced by providing students with clinically oriented cases that involve complex and challenging problems. We believe that the best source for cases is the instructor's professional counseling experiences because the instructor can add personal perspective, but case studies can also be found in sources listed in the Appendix. Students take on the roles of professional and possibly nonprofessional participants who might be included in a community agency meeting to review the case study. Professionals might include psychiatrists, psychologists, social workers, psychiatric nurses, rehabilitation counselors, occupational therapists, recreation therapists, case managers, family therapists, and counselors. Nonprofessionals who might be included in such meetings, depending on the agency, might be the client, family members, or other people who could advocate for the rights of the client. If instructors choose, each participant could also adopt an approach such as being argumentative, neutral, supportive, apathetic, and so on.

Students break into groups of two or three, with each group taking on one role. They then discuss and plan how that professional or nonprofessional might interact during the case review. The groups select one member to participate in the case review meeting, and the meeting convenes as a "fish bowl" activity. One person from each group acts out the role during a simulated case meeting, while the remainder of the class observes. The instructor interferes little and does so only to encourage students to play the assigned roles during the case review meeting, which lasts between 15 and 45 minutes. Following the case review meeting simulation, the instructor leads a discussion on the issue of the professionalism of counselors and their roles in multidisciplinary teams.

## Focused Discussions

In addition to the previously described activities, the remainder of time in any class meetings may be devoted to a more traditional lecture-and-discussion format. We refer to this time as focused discussion rather than lecture because instructors share information while also structuring the time to encourage student interaction. For example, Socratic questioning might be used to engage students more fully in the learning process.

The success of focused discussions depends on how well instructors know the material and how flexible they are in presenting it. If instructors have only a passing familiarity with the material, they may have difficulty building on students' input. The more comprehensive the instructors' knowledge, the more flexible they can be in emphasizing critical elements over inconsequential details. Because discussions also benefit from students' prior knowledge of the topic, instructors should ask students to complete reading assignments in preparation for class discussions (Ormrod, 2008).

## Active Learning Roles

Constructivist classrooms require that both teachers and students take an active role in the learning process. Regardless of the type of learning activity, the key to encouraging students to take responsibility for their learning is the nature of the communication in the class (McCown, Driscoll, & Roop, 1996). Instructors' interactions with students either facilitate or discourage students from becoming active participants in the learning process. Students either learn to take risks in classroom discussions and in creatively completing assignments, or they learn that only one way is "correct." The instructor's role, therefore, is different in the constructivist classroom from that in the traditional classroom, in which lecture is the primary teaching method.

According to McCown et al. (1996), a central issue for teachers is that of power and control: How much power should be exercised for what amount of control? For project-based learning courses, instructors exercise less power in controlling the learning process, thereby requiring students to be active rather than passive participants. One way to depict the instructor's role is to describe it as that of a consultant who serves as a facilitator, a model, and a coach for students (Tinzmann et al., 1990). As *facilitators*, instructors encourage students to guide their own learning through self-regulation (see Schunk & Zimmerman, 2008, for a full discussion of motivating self-regulated learning). Instructors also *model* beneficial strategies that help students understand both the content and the process of collaborative learning (Tinzmann et al., 1990). As *coaches*, instructors encourage students' efforts through helping them set and clarify goals, formulate plans to meet the goals, and monitor their own progress. Instructors also give constructive feedback on student projects (McCown et al., 1996).

The students' roles in project-based learning courses are also atypical. Unlike courses employing a standard lecture format in which instructors impart information and require students to simply receive knowledge, in the project-based learning course, instructors encourage students to become active in creating the learning environment (McCown et al., 1996). In a sense, as instructors utilize project-based learning, students must take more active roles. Students become active through setting personal goals, being motivated to accomplish those goals, and becoming creative in discovering means to achieve the goals.

A key element in the success of project-based learning is students' curiosity about finding answers to questions generated during course assignments. This approach builds on students' curiosity, causing them to become excited about the learning process. We have found that the more excited students are about the learning process, the more active they are.

## Use of Class Time

In order to create a sense of expectancy, class meeting times must be structured to encourage students to interact with and question not only themselves, but the instructor (Slavin, 1995). Instructors should also set aside time during each class meeting for small groups to work on the project-based cooperative learning tasks, such as brainstorming, locating funding sources, or designing a program evaluation. Instructors communicate the importance of the project and the way of learning by setting aside class meeting times. We usually allow half to two-thirds of each class meeting for teams to work on their projects. Instructors should also remain active during project work periods by circulating among teams, providing reinforcement and constructive feedback, and responding to specific requests for advice.

Instructors should be careful, however, to maintain their role as coaches or guides, providing scaffolding to support student learning rather than slipping into the role of experts who are dictating what should be done. In other words, instructors "should provide the guidance required for learners to bridge the gap between their current skill levels and a desired skill level" (Driscoll, 2005, p. 258). Scaffolding requires a careful balance between using expertise to pull students' learning to higher levels and avoiding the temptation to quickly solve a problem or overcome an obstacle. Instead, instructors need to sustain the role of constructivist educators in order for students to sustain their sense of responsibility in the learning process.

# Assignments

Course assignments evolve directly out of the educational objectives. For instance, given that overall the course aims to help students develop an identity as community counselors, instructors structure course assignments to promote that process. Assignments also promote students' regulation of the learning process.

## Guiding Elements for Course Assignments

Specifically, we structure assignments so that students take responsibility for monitoring, adjusting, self-questioning, and questioning others (Tinzmann et al., 1990). The first, monitoring, means that students check their individual and group progress in completing the assignments. The second, adjusting, refers to altering the content and/or direction of their efforts based on such monitoring. Finally, in project-based learning assignments, students share ideas and provide constructive feedback through self-questioning and questioning of others. Assignments that incorporate these four elements challenge students not only to learn content, but also to develop skills in locating resources and in working as a team. Students use these elements as they create a community agency and reflect on their team experience in creating that agency.

## Creating a Community Agency Project

In this central course assignment, students work in teams of three or four to create a community agency of their choice. The agencies can be for-profit or nonprofit. Instructors may assign groups, as recommended by Ormrod (2008), or students may choose their own. Choosing their own groups gives students a greater sense of ownership and requires that they take more responsibility for themselves (Driscoll, 2005). Either way, students or instructors need to consider factors such as compatibility of schedules, physical proximity

for meeting outside of class, and interest in developing a specific type of agency.

The Creating a Community Agency Project includes four components, each addressing a different aspect of working in a community agency. In Part I, teams propose a *purpose and rationale* for their community agency. They include a brief description of the agency's mission and its programs, a preliminary needs assessment, goals and objectives for the agency, an outline of basic program components, and a plan for selecting a board of directors.

Part II of the project requires students to develop a two-part *plan to fund* the agency. Section 1 of planning funding asks teams to describe two possible funding sources. Teams that create a nonprofit agency briefly describe two funding sources that have previously provided grant monies for their type of agency. Teams developing a for-profit agency describe expected client-generated monies, possible business loans, and buy-in or startup arrangements for investors and partners. Section 2 of planning funding requires teams to develop a budget for the agency. Teams generate a budget that includes ongoing costs for one year, as well as startup costs. These budgets include commodities (such as paper, postage, stationery) and contractual costs (including building rent, utilities, phone, maintenance, travel, professional development). Budgets also include detailed descriptions of one-time startup purchases, such as office furniture and equipment.

In Part III, teams describe the *organizational structure and procedures* of the proposed agency. The organizational section addresses management, supervisory roles, and job descriptions of all professional and staff persons. The procedures section discusses client confidentiality, billing procedures, staff meetings, operating hours, office assignments, vacation and sick leave, crisis intervention and guidelines, and relationships with other agencies. Teams may develop flow charts to illustrate their decisions.

In Part IV teams establish *program evaluation procedures*. Students set the boundaries for evaluation and describe at least two types of evaluation procedures to be used. They also describe the types of data to be collected and explain two methods that could be used to collect these data. Teams then describe how and to whom the information from the evaluation will be disseminated.

In Part V students complete an individual *self-reflection paper* after completing the community agency project. To increase intrapersonal awareness, students reflect on their individual roles as learners during the project. In addition, they reflect on their role as members of the team and the interpersonal dynamics of the team, thus addressing the interpersonal awareness guideline. Finally, they reflect on the benefits and challenges of collaboration in authentic counseling settings. An instructor who wishes to place an even greater emphasis on self-reflection could ask that students maintain a journal throughout the entire semester, writing reflections as they engage in each step of the project.

## Evaluation Rubrics

Because all of the course assignments are authentic activities, it is appropriate to evaluate students using carefully developed performance rubrics. We believe that the most appropriate type of rubric for a complex project is an analytic one, in which detailed descriptions reflect varying degrees of quality for each criterion (Brookhart, 2009). For example, if one of the criteria for Part I (purpose and rationale) is content, then the following descriptions might be used for grades in that portion of the rubric:

A = In addition to clearly describing the agency's mission and programs, preliminary needs assessment, goals and objectives for the agency, basic program components, and plan for selecting a board of directors, the paper shows clearly how these components are aligned to effectively serve the needs of future clients.

B = The agency's mission and programs, preliminary needs assessment, goals and objectives for the agency, basic program components, and plan for selecting a board of directors are clearly described.

C = A general description of the agency is provided, but lacks one or more of the following: mission and programs, preliminary needs assessment, goals and objectives for the agency, basic program components, and plan for selecting a board of directors.

D = The paper does not highlight the agency's mission and programs, preliminary needs assessment, goals and objectives for the agency, basic program components, and/or plan for selecting a board of directors.

Rubrics scaffold students' thinking and writing by describing clear achievement targets. They provide a means by which students can monitor and evaluate their progress, and they clearly communicate to students how their work will be evaluated. Finally, rubrics provide a means by which to provide students with constructive feedback.

In summary, this community agency project promotes students' learning on three levels. First, students learn the content required by CACREP (2009). However, rather than simply memorizing the material, students apply the material to an authentic situation. This learning promotes students' sense of professionalism, fosters a sense of accomplishment, and increases attention and retention of knowledge. The second level of learning occurs as students improve their abilities to locate resources. Students are invited to be creative in gathering information and are encouraged to share strategies with other teams. Finally, students engage in important self-reflection, a crucial component in becoming a constructivist counselor (McAuliffe, Chapter 1, this volume).

# CONCLUDING REFLECTIONS

Although project-based learning is thoroughly grounded in theory and supported by research, integrating these concepts and translating them into teaching requires creativity and good problem-solving abilities on the part of the instructor. As McAuliffe (this volume) has argued, instructors must move beyond the traditional postsecondary classroom experience and become learners themselves. They need to be willing to confront students who are in a "velvet rut"—that is, those who do not like the traditional lecture-format class, but who also are reluctant to entertain other formats, especially formats that challenge and require greater responsibility on their part. We have found that although many students do not like the traditional lecture format, they are comfortable with it and are often willing to maintain the status quo rather than change to an unknown. Because constructivist approaches can be threatening for students, it can be challenging to implement project-based learning.

Another challenge arises from the dominance of group work in the community agency course that we have described. Many students experience increased anxiety when their grades depend on the productivity of others in their group. Concerns also emerge when teams do not work well together. Instructors need to anticipate these concerns and be prepared to respond when asked. Instructors also need to consider very carefully how much of a student's grade will depend on a group project grade. Although few clear-cut answers exist to address these concerns, instructors should always have a plan for which they can provide a professional and reasonable rationale.

In conclusion, project-based learning promotes mastery through authentic learning experiences and helps to assure agencies that students are equipped with the skills needed for entry-level positions. Since the goal of counselor education is to prepare students for positions as professional counselors, and since research supports the use of learning experiences that mirror authentic work situations, project-based cooperative learning more likely prepares professionals who know what they need to know when they enter the workforce.

# RESOURCES
## Books

Listed below are several books that can be used as a text for this course. However, instructors may decide to develop their own text. Many publishers allow instructors to select specific chapters from several books and compile these as a text for a specific course. Authors of the chapters selected to be included for the specialized text receive royalties based on the contract they have with the publisher.

Cohen, R., & Cohen, J. (2000). *Chiseled in sand: Perspectives on change in human service organizations.* Florence, KY: Cengage.

Gerig, M. S. (2007). *Foundations for mental health and community counseling: An introduction to the profession.* Upper Saddle River, NJ: Merrill.

Gladding, S. T. (2009). *Counseling: A comprehensive profession* (6th ed.). Upper Saddle River, NJ: Merrill.

Gladding, S. T., & Newsome, D. W. (2010). *Clinical mental health counseling in community and agency settings* (3rd ed.). Upper Saddle River, NJ: Merrill.

Hull, G. H., & Kirst-Ashman, K. K. (2004). *The generalist model of human services practice.* Florence, KY: Cengage.

Lewis, J. A., Lewis, M. D., Daniels, J. A., & D'Andrea, M. J. (2003). *Community counseling: Empowerment strategies for a diverse society.* Pacific Grove, CA: Brooks/Cole.

MacCluskie, K. C., & Ingersoll, R. E. (2001). *Becoming a 21st century agency counselor: Personal and professional explorations.* Florence, KY: Cengage.

Peterson, J. V., & Nisenholz, B. (1998). *Orientation to counseling* (4th ed.). Upper Saddle River, NJ: Merrill.

## Websites Related to Community Agency Counseling

The American Counseling Association and related professional organizations have websites that students can use to find information for this course. However, websites that might prove more useful are those that give information regarding grants and grant writing. A few of these are listed below. A Google search is also an excellent way to locate resources for possible funding sources. Finally, we encourage instructors to use the resources that are often available on their campus. These are unique for each campus and are usually housed in the office assigned for working with faculty on sponsored research.

www.samhsa.gov/

http://foundationcenter.org/pnd/rfp/cat_intl_affairs.jhtml

http://web.archive.org/web/20041018133314/http://www.abanet.org/crimjust/juvjus/linkprofit.html

## Websites for Project-Based Learning

http://pblchecklist.4teachers.org/

www.edutopia.org/project-learning

http://pbl-online.org/

www.bie.org/index.php/site/PBL/overview_pbl/

## Sources for Case Studies

Golden, L. B., & Norwood, M. L. (1993). *Case studies in child counseling.* Upper Saddle River, NJ: Merrill.

Herlihy, B., & Corey, G. (2006). *ACA ethical standards casebook* (6th ed.). Alexandria, VA: American Counseling Association.

Keith-Spiegel, P., & Koocher, G. P. (1985). *Ethics in psychology: Professional standards and cases.* New York: McGraw-Hill.

Spitzer, R. L., Gibbon, M., Skodol, A. E., Williams, J. B. W., & First, M. B. (1994). *DSM-IV casebook: A learning companion to the* Diagnostic and Statistical Manual of Mental Disorders (4th ed.). Washington, DC: American Psychiatric Press.

Welfel, E. R. (2006). *Ethics in counseling and psychotherapy: Standards, research, and emerging issues* (3rd ed.). Florence, KY: Cengage.

## CACREP Standards
## From Table 21.1

1. Knowledge of history and philosophy of the counseling profession

2. Knowledge of professional roles, functions, and relationships with other human service providers, including strategies for interagency/inter-organization collaboration and communications

3. Knowledge of counselors' roles and responsibilities as members of an interdisciplinary emergency management response team during a local, regional, or national crisis, disaster, or other trauma-causing event

4. Knowledge of the role and process of the professional counselor advocating on behalf of the profession

5. Knowledge of advocacy processes needed to address institutional and social barriers that impede access, equity, and success for clients

6. Knowledge of ethical standards of professional organizations and credentialing bodies, and applications of ethical and legal considerations in professional counseling

7. Knowledge of multicultural and pluralistic trends, including characteristics and concerns within and among diverse groups nationally and internationally

8. Knowledge of counselors' roles in eliminating biases, prejudices, and processes of intentional and unintentional oppression and discrimination

9. Knowledge of principles, models, and applications of needs assessment, program evaluation, and the use of findings to effect program modifications

10. Understands history, philosophy, and trends in clinical mental health counseling

11. Understands ethical and legal considerations specifically related to the practice of clinical mental health counseling

12. Understands the roles and functions of clinical mental health counselors in various practice settings and the importance of relationships between counselors and other professionals, including interdisciplinary treatment teams

13. Understands the management of mental health services and programs, including areas such as administration, finance, and accountability

14. Understands the operation of an emergency management system within clinical mental health agencies and in the community

15. Applies knowledge of public mental health policy, financing, and regulatory processes to improve service delivery opportunities in clinical mental health counseling

16. Describes the principles of mental health, including prevention, intervention, consultation, education, and advocacy, as well as the operation of programs and networks that promote mental health in a multicultural society

17. Knows the models, methods, and principles of program development and service delivery (e.g., support groups, peer facilitation training, parent education, self-help)

18. Understands the range of mental health service delivery—such as inpatient, outpatient, partial treatment, and aftercare—and the clinical mental counseling services network

19. Recognizes the importance of family, social networks, and community systems in the treatment of mental and emotional disorders

20. Understands how living in a multicultural society affects clients who are seeking clinical mental health counseling services

21. Understands effective strategies to support client advocacy and influence public policy and government relations on local, state, and national levels to enhance equity, increase funding, and promote

programs that affect the practice of clinical mental health counseling

22. Knows public policies on the local, state, and national levels that affect the quality and accessibility of mental health services

23. Advocates for policies, programs, and services that are equitable and responsive to the unique needs of clients

24. Knows models of program evaluation for clinical mental health programs

25. Develops measurable outcomes for clinical mental health counseling programs, interventions, and treatments

26. Analyzes and uses data to increase the effectiveness of clinical mental health counseling interventions and programs

27. Actively identifies with the counseling profession by participating in professional organizations and by participating in seminars, workshops, or other activities that contribute to personal and professional growth

# REFERENCES

Anderson, L. W., & Krathwohl, D. R. (Eds.). (2001). *A taxonomy for learning, teaching, and assessing.* New York: Longman.

Bagley, W. C. (1921). Dangers and difficulties of the project method and how to overcome them: II. Projects and purposes in teaching and in learning. *Teachers College Record, 22,* 288–296.

Blumenfeld, P. C., Soloway, E., Marx, R. W., Krajcik, J. S., Guzdial, M., & Palincsar, A. (1991). Motivating project-based learning: Sustaining the doing, supporting the learning. *Educational Psychologist, 26,* 369–398.

Brookhart, S. M. (2009). *Grading* (2nd ed.). New York: Merrill.

Council for Accreditation of Counseling and Related Educational Programs. (2009). *CACREP accreditation standards and procedures manual.* Alexandria, VA: Author.

Dewey, J. (1933). *How we think: A restatement of the relation of reflective thinking to the educative process.* Boston: D. C. Heath.

Driscoll, M. P. (2005). *Psychology of learning for instruction.* Boston: Allyn & Bacon.

Johnson, D. W., & Johnson, F. P. (1994). *Joining together: Group theory and group skills* (5th ed.). Boston: Allyn & Bacon.

McCown, R., Driscoll, M., & Roop, P. G. (1996). *Educational psychology* (2nd ed.). Boston: Allyn & Bacon.

Mergendoller, J. R., Markham, T., Ravitz, J., & Larmer, J. (2006). Pervasive management of project based learning: Teachers as guides and facilitators. In C. M. Evertson & C. S. Weinstein (Eds.), *Handbook of classroom management: Research, practice, and contemporary issues* (pp. 582–615). Mahwah, NJ: Lawrence Erlbaum.

Myer, R. A., & Moore, H. (2006). Crisis in context: An ecological model. *Journal of Counseling and Development, 84,* 139–147.

Myer, R. A., Peterson, S. E., & Stoffel-Rosales, M. (1991). Co-dependency: An examination of underlying assumptions. *Journal of Mental Health Counseling, 13,* 449–458.

Ormrod, J. E. (2008). *Human learning* (5th ed.). Upper Saddle River NJ: Pearson Merrill Prentice Hall.

Peterson, S. E. (1992). A comparison of causal attributions and their dimensions for individual and cooperative group tasks. *Journal of Research and Development in Education, 25*(2), 35–44.

Peterson, S. E. (1993). The effects of prior achievement and group outcome on attributions and affect in cooperative tasks. *Contemporary Educational Psychology, 18,* 479–485.

Peterson, S. E., & Miller, J. A. (2004a). Comparing the quality of college students' experiences during cooperative learning and large-group instruction. *Journal of Educational Research, 97*(3), 123–133.

Peterson, S. E., & Miller, J. A. (2004b). Quality of college students' experiences during cooperative learning. *Social Psychology of Education, 7*(2), 161–183.

Peterson, S. E., & Myer, R. A. (1995). The use of collaborative project-based learning in counselor education. *Counselor Education and Supervision, 35*(2), 150–158.

Polman, J. L. (2004). Dialogic activity structures for project-based learning environments. *Cognition & Instruction, 22,* 431–466.

Resnick, L. B. (1987). Learning in school and out. *Educational Researcher, 16*(9), 13–20.

Rogoff, B., & Lave, J. (1984). *Everyday cognition: Its development in social context.* Cambridge, MA: Harvard University Press.

Schön, D. A. (1991). *The reflective practitioner: How professionals think in action.* Aldershot, UK: Avebury.

Schunk, D. H., & Zimmerman, B. J. (2008). *Motivation and self-regulated learning: Theory, research, and applications.* New York: Lawrence Erlbaum.

Slavin, R. E. (1995). *Cooperative learning* (2nd ed.). Boston: Allyn & Bacon.

Tal, T., Krajcik, J. S., & Blumenfeld, P., C. (2006). Urban schools' teachers enacting project-based science. *Journal of Research in Science Teaching, 43,* 722–745.

Tinzmann, M. B., Jones, B. F., Fennimore, T. F., Bakker, J., Fine, C., & Pierce, J. (1990). The collaborative classroom: Reconnecting teachers and learners. In M. B. Tinzmann (Ed.), *Restructuring education to promote learning in America's schools* (pp. 86–99). Elmhart, IL: North Central Regional Education Laboratory.

Vygotsky, L. S. (1978). *Mind in society: The development of higher psychological processes.* Cambridge, MA: Harvard University Press. (Original work published 1934)

Welfel, E. R. (2006). *Ethics in counseling and psychotherapy: Standards, research, and emerging issues* (3rd ed.). Florence, KY: Cengage.

Wlodkowski, R. J. (1999). *Enhancing adult motivation to learn: A comprehensive guide for teaching all adults.* San Francisco: Jossey-Bass.

Zilbergeld, B. (1983). *The shrinking of America: Myths of psychological change.* Boston: Little, Brown.

# 22

# Teaching Substance Abuse/Addictions Counseling

Brigid M. Noonan and Scott A. Wykes

"What is the first word or picture that comes to your mind when you hear the word *addict*? How about *addiction*? *substance use*? *substance dependence*? Think about it . . . really think about it . . . carefully." When teaching an introductory course on addictions counseling, the teacher who asks these questions challenges students, during the first class meeting, to think about their biases regarding this particular client population. The teacher might follow such questions by asking, "When clients seek help with an *addiction* how will you help them in the process of *recovery*? If clients tell you that they want to moderately drink, or recreationally use substances, will you be able to offer them counseling services?" And, in a slight variation of the question, she or he asks, "What approach will you choose in order to assist a parent who is concerned about the addictive behavior of her or his teen?"

We ask these questions right at the beginning of the addictions course because clients do not fit any one pattern when it comes to the issues that they bring to counseling. How a counselor works with a client with a heroin addiction takes on a different meaning depending on the particular heroin addict. How each client experiences addiction is just that, her or his individual experience. This chapter introduces the teaching of substance abuse/addiction counseling from the perspective of helping counselors-in-training become more self-aware and self-transformed as they encounter clients who struggle with the challenge of addiction.

This chapter uses the constructivist paradigm to explain both the teaching of an addictions counseling course and a perspective on addictions counseling itself. First, we discuss addiction from a constructivist approach, then three constructivist theories that can be used when working with this population (solution-focused brief therapy, motivational interviewing, and narrative therapy), and finally, how a counselor educator might structure an addictions course.

## ADDICTIONS COUNSELING ITSELF AS A CONSTRUCTIVIST ENDEAVOR

Clients come to counseling with their experiential knowledge of addictions and perhaps with a history of attempts to "fix" the problem or "fix" someone they care about who is displaying addictive behavior. In spite of any attempts at healing that they might have made, at this point the problem stills exists for them. This current status, however, does not mean that these clients don't also have solutions that could bring relief and preferred living. This is the hope that constructivist addictions counseling offers—that is, much of constructivist addictions work acknowledges or creates the language of change, particularly as it relates to solutions.

The process begins with the deconstruction of the client's definition of the problem. Deconstruction is a process of inquiry that identifies the details of the problem. It breaks addiction down into its component parts, or the *who, what, where, when,* and *how* of the contributing circumstances that keep the addiction going. Counselors-in-training may feel overwhelmed by this process because of their difficulties with avoiding attempts to fix a problem, prescribe a solution, or affix a label—as they may already have been trained. However, for clients, the deconstruction process may be a first; it may be the first time that they have described the addiction in detail, seen its parts, and understood that, broken down into its component parts, addiction may not be quite so overwhelming.

The constructivist methodology for addictions counseling shares some common elements with other therapeutic models, for instance, the need for relationship building or reframing. However, the process that heals in constructivist counseling is collaborative conversation rather than finding answers to questions.

Three constructivist counseling approaches will next be described, as they apply to addictions.

## Solution-Focused Brief Therapy

Solution-Focused Brief Therapy (SFBT) was developed by Steve de Shazer, Insoo Kim Berg, and associates at the Brief Family Therapy Center, in Milwaukee, in the late 1970s (de Shazer, 1988). Additional key contributors to this approach include Eve Lipchik (1988), Michele Weiner-Davis and Bill O'Hanlon (1989), and Scott Miller (Berg & Miller, 1992).

Constructivist epistemology posits that reality is co-created by the therapist and client in therapeutic conversation (Walsh & McGraw, 1996), and, when applied to treating addictions, the counselor and client co-construct effective solutions to bring about preferred living. Two main tenets center the work: (a) Clients are experts on themselves, and (b) the awareness of exceptions to the problem, or times when the addictive behavior is not

happening, assists clients in moving beyond being captured by the problem (de Shazer, 1988).

Solution-focused counseling offers many techniques to assist counselors in the collaboration of building solutions with clients. In many of the techniques, counselors highlight subtle yet sustainable change based on the belief that change is constant and inevitable. Some examples include, but are not limited to, scaling, rating, and the miracle question. The structure that allows SFBT to be successful is the change in language from "problem talking" to "solution building." This shift is accomplished as the collaborative therapeutic relationship builds—the counselor is not the expert per se, but is rather a sojourner with the client.

## Motivational Interviewing

A collaborative stance can also be found in Motivational Interviewing (MI). MI was developed by William Miller and Stephen Rollnick and provides a semidirective approach to dealing with substance abuse issues. Much like SFBT, MI is nonjudgmental, nonconfrontational, and nonadversarial. With an emphasis on an awareness of the stages of change, the main goals of MI are to establish rapport, elicit change talk, and establish commitment from the person with addictive behaviors. In some respects, MI seems to borrow from the best of many therapeutic interventions and based upon five general principles: express empathy, develop discrepancy, roll with resistance, support self-efficacy, and avoid argumentation (and direct confrontation). In comparative studies of confrontational interviewing and cognitive behavioral interventions, MI shows significant differences in better treatment effects over the long term (McCambridge & Strang, 2005).

## Narrative Therapy

Another constructivist approach for addressing addictive behaviors is Narrative Therapy, which was developed by Michael White and David Epston. Their approach became known in North America with the publication of their book *Narrative Means to Therapeutic Ends* (White & Epston, 1990). Narrative therapy begins with respectful, nonblaming conversations in which clients can safely explore the stories of their lives. To understand addictive behaviors and the impact of such behavior on family, friends, employment, and other areas, counselors and clients explore the stories, or narratives, that have led to those issues. Narratives are accounts or portrayals of subjective experiences that reveal the reasoning used to negotiate the "understood world" in a particular way (Nelson-Becker, 2004; White & Epston, 1990).

In "deconstructive questioning," similar to SFBT, counselors and clients investigate the influence of the problem on the life and relationships of the addicted. A counselor may ask questions that are contrary to problem focused approaches, for instance, "When was the problem nonexistent?" or "In what instances did this problem not defeat you?" Through "real talk," destructive beliefs become changeable interpretations. As the problem is externalized, clients discover their own personal influence over the life of the problem. Externalizing the problem helps to revise the relationship with the problem and immobilize its restraint on their lives (Koerner & Fitzpatrick, 2006; Pembroke, 2005; White & Epston, 1990). In other words, the problem is the problem; the client is not the problem (White & Epston, 1990). Another example of a narrative therapy question might be "How were you able to trust your own thoughts about no longer drinking?" A more problem-centered approach would be more concerned about powerlessness over drinking. Once deconstructed, then, the "landscape" of preferred living can be co-constructed. Techniques that flow out of this therapeutic model include deconstructive listening, questioning, externalizing, identifying coping abilities and support systems, and seeking unique outcomes (Goldenberg & Goldenberg, 2008).

In this narrative process, positive and constructive explanations emerge out of negative and destructive ones. Focusing directly on addictive behaviors can produce powerful thoughts of hopelessness. However, narrative therapists believe that liberation from these same destructive beliefs and stories begins by constructing alternative beliefs that will offer new options and possibilities for a landscape of preferred living (Goldenberg & Goldenberg, 2008).

Constructivist approaches to teaching addictions courses do not have to rely solely upon the previously mentioned theories, as there are many approaches that add value to the process. In fact, having a theoretical orientation constitutes only a partial consideration in the construction of the content of the course.

# TEACHING FOR THE CONSTRUCTIVIST ADDICTIONS COURSE

The following sections outline the reasons that addictions training is necessary, the learning objectives and content for the addictions course, definitions, and historical and multicultural perspectives. Following those components, readers will find some "how to's" for teaching addictions counseling.

## The Case for the Course in Addictions Counseling

To understand the importance of an addictions counseling course or program within counselor education programs, the teacher may want to start with a snapshot of illicit and licit drug use. The Substance Abuse and Mental Health Administration conducts an annual survey of illicit alcohol and tobacco use in Americans. In 2007, an estimated 19.9 million or 8% of Americans 12 and older were current illicit drug users, meaning they had used an illicit drug during the month prior to the survey interview. Illicit drugs include marijuana/hashish, cocaine (including crack), heroin, hallucinogens, inhalants, and prescription-type psychotherapeutics used nonmedically. This rate was similar to reported rates in 2006 (8.3%).

As a result of statistics such as these, the Council for the Accreditation of Counseling and Related Education Programs (CACREP) proposed that both a *course* and a *program* in addiction counseling are necessary. As a result, beginning with the adoption of the CACREP 2009 standards, addiction counseling has been added as an accredited program area. In their article on the inclusion of substance abuse training in CACREP-accredited programs, Salyers, Ritchie, Cochrane, and Roseman (2006) specifically state that "developing a substance abuse program area would ensure that the most comprehensive and consistent standards of practice are being taught to counseling students" (p. 55).

An issue that arises when offering only one course in substance abuse counseling is that not all students enrolled in the program actually take the course. Morgan and Toloczko (1997) and Whittinghill, Carroll, and Morgan (2004) surveyed CACREP-accredited programs and, in both cases, found that, of the programs that offer a substance abuse course, only 30% *required* coursework in substance abuse training. In the study by Salyers et al. (2006), "27% of the respondents reported that 91% to 100% of students included substance abuse course work in their program of study, but this included students who took a separate course on substance abuse and students who took other courses that included this topic" (p. 54). Furthermore, Salyers et al. indicate that many programs include the topic in other courses, and a listing of more than 25 different courses shows that little agreement exists as to how and when substance abuse issues should be addressed in a counselor education program.

Our belief is that all students, regardless of their course of study in counselor education, benefit by taking at least one course in addiction counseling. Studies have clearly indicated the need for a more systematic and comprehensive coverage of substance abuse issues in counselor education programs (Morgan & Toloczko, 1997; Salyers et al., 2006; Whittinghill et al., 2004).

## Course Context

The course in addictions counseling commonly fits within the first or second year of the counselor education program. Mental health counselors, marriage and family counselors, school counselors, and those training to work with the college student population all benefit by taking an introductory addictions counseling course. The course is an introduction to the basic tenets of addiction and substance abuse as well as an introduction to practicing counseling skills with a variety of clients. For some students, the introductory course will be followed by more in-depth learning experiences related to addictions, as well as a yearlong counseling internship in an addictions treatment setting(s).

## Course Content

Table 22.1 summarizes the learning objectives, content, processes, and learning activities of a proposed course in addictions. Constructivist principles illustrated by these strategies are also indicated.

**TABLE 22.1** Course Objectives, Content, Activities, and Constructivist Principles

| Learning Objectives | Content | Activities and Processes | Constructivist Principles |
|---|---|---|---|
| Demonstrate an awareness and understanding of the impact of addiction and the impediments it may pose on the system (e.g., individuals, groups, families, school, career) and its culture. | Models of chemical dependency<br><br>Counseling theories<br><br>Cultural development theory | *Lectures*<br>*Individual reflection*<br>**Exercise:** Historical/cultural meaning attached to addiction<br>**Exercise**: Multicultural role plays of personal narratives and diversity issues<br>*Individual reflection*<br>**Assignment:** Abstinence project/journal<br>*Case study evaluation*<br>**Exercise:** Discussion of case studies presented by instructor examining different stages of addiction/recovery<br>*Individual reflection*<br>**Assignment:** 12-step program immersion<br>*Treatment center interview*<br>*Guest speaker* (e.g., current treatment providers, law enforcement personnel, individuals in recovery) | Individuals are engaged in the construction of knowledge and accept responsibility for continually evaluating their assumptions about addictions and the effects on their clients. |

| Learning Objectives | Content | Activities and Processes | Constructivist Principles |
|---|---|---|---|
| Demonstrate an understanding of the theories and etiology of addictions and addictive behaviors, including strategies for assessment, prevention, intervention, and treatment. | Models of chemical dependency<br><br>Counseling theories | *Lectures*<br>*Treatment center interview*<br>*Movie analysis/discussion*<br>**Assignment:** Write three reaction papers and engage in online dialogue with other students regarding media presentation with addiction themes<br>*Case study evaluation*<br>**Exercise:** Discussion of case studies presented by instructor examining different stages of addiction and recovery<br>*Guest speaker* (e.g., current treatment providers, law enforcement personnel, individuals in recovery)<br>*Final exam* | Stories of reality come from language and experience. |
| Recognize the potential for substance use disorders to mimic and coexist with a variety of medical and psychological disorders. | *Diagnostic and Statistic Manual of Mental Disorders* diagnostic criteria | *Lectures*<br>*Case study evaluation*<br>**Exercise:** Discussion of case studies presented by instructor examining different stages of addiction and recovery<br>*Individual reflection*<br>**Assignment:** 12-step program immersion<br>*Treatment center interview*<br>*Guest speaker*<br>*Final exam* | Development in cognitive capacity requires support and challenge. |

## Learning Objectives

From a constructivist perspective, the following learning objectives might be considered helpful in preparing students for addictions work:

*Students will learn assessment* according to the *Diagnostic and Statistical Manual of Mental Disorders* (DSM; American Psychiatric Association, 2000) as well as in terms of the Patient Placement Criteria established by American Society of Addiction Medicine (ASAM). Those assessment tools will be considered from a constructivist perspective. Students will understand how treatment agencies and the assessments used in client intakes sometimes place clients into predesigned programs that may or may not match their goals or needs. Students will distinguish between the efficacy of traditional programs and programs that espouse constructivist, developmental, and experiential philosophies.

*Students will understand* that the term *treatment* is usually associated with court-ordered clients, while the term *counseling* is reserved for those who volunteer to make changes in their substance use. Students will instead understand the conceptualization of the client from a consultant perspective.

*Students will understand constructivism* and the challenge of integrating constructivist theory with traditional addictions treatment programs. They will increase their tendency, in Hayes and Paisley's (2002) words, "to be flexible, tolerant of ambiguity, comfortable with a wide range of emotions, open-minded, self-directed yet collaborative and enthusiastic learners [who] embrace diversity and can be critical and creative thinkers" (p. 170).

*Students will discover the contemporary view of substance abuse treatment* and how it involves an acceptance of the concept of denial. Additionally, students will learn that clients struggle with how professionals, who have never struggled with an addiction, can be considered the experts. Through a constructivist approach, students will take into account the learned addictions culture, how it is shared and symbolically transmitted, and how it influences all aspects of a person's life, which strongly challenges the claim that there are universal addictions principles to understand (Lee, 1996). As students will begin to ascertain, these concepts can collide and create space for dialogue and learning for both client and counselor.

## Addiction Defined

The first step in learning about addictions is helping students struggle with how to define addiction. It should be noted that, from substance use to substance abuse to substance dependence to addiction, theorists and counselors have yet to agree on one universal definition of this phenomenon. The following exercise helps instructors glimpse students' knowledge, values, and biases as they work at defining addictions.

First, the instructor points to the various attempts at defining addiction. For instance, the class might consider the DSM definitions, ASAM's definition, and the National Institute on Drug Abuse's (2010) definition. The instructor can discuss with students the different meanings of these definitions as students engage in the process of generating their own definitions. The DSM divides substance-related disorders into *substance dependence disorders* and *substance abuse disorders*. Instructors can use these distinctions as part of this dialogue.

## Historical Perspective

As part of examining definitions of addictions, the instructor can explore historical and multicultural perspectives on substance use. A brief examination of addiction from a historical perspective informs students that the use of substances has been around since ancient times. When students look at different countries and cultures (e.g., Chinese, Ancient Greek, Ancient Roman, Hebrew, Middle Eastern, South American indigenous,

Caribbean Indian) and the use of alcoholic beverages, binging and purging of food, as well as heroin, cocaine, marijuana, and nicotine use, they note that not all use and abuse turns into addiction (van Wormer & Davis, 2003). Many times, these substances were used for ceremonial and celebratory purposes and did not develop into what we now know as addiction.

When looking at addiction in the United States, one critical point for future counselors to understand is the impact of the introduction of alcohol into British America. Instead of being a reason to celebrate, alcohol became both culturally and economically destructive to Native American people who were not given the opportunity to understand its power and ways to resist it. The devastating consequences of alcohol on Native American tribes continues today; they have one of the highest rates of alcoholism, suicide, and unemployment in the United States (Galliher, Evans, & Weiser, 2007).

Even a brief historical perspective can help students realize that there is meaning attached to substances. Whether those substances are food, sex, the Internet, or legal or illegal drugs, individuals make their own discoveries and mistakes with substances. While it can be seen that all individuals have a susceptibility toward substance abuse or dependence, it is the meanings that people attach to their own personal and social realities that play a key role in whether or not an addictive behavior develops.

The following activity can engage students in the discovery of addiction's meaning to them. The instructor distributes cards containing the terms *drunk, drug addict, sex addict, junkie, compulsive overeater,* and *shopping addict.* Working in pairs, students define what each word or phrase means to them, whether as a result of their own experiences or other ways of knowing. From these discussions, the class discovers differences in how individuals look at people with addictions. In a second part of the exercise, instructors ask students how they might work with a client with one of the addictions listed. Discussions such as this shed further light on possible values and biases regarding this population.

## Multicultural Perspectives

Implicit in the teaching of addictions counseling is the acknowledgment that clients come from varying cultural experiences and backgrounds. These experiences bring with them their own meanings about addiction, which are critical for students to hear. For instance, as students listen to why clients might be coming for counseling, instructors urge them to use both constructivist and multicultural perspectives to resist imposing 20th-century theories about counseling and addictions onto the client. Specifically, students are urged to resist conceptualizing addictions only in terms of irrational beliefs, behavioral contingencies, and unconscious conflicts. Instead, students might participate in counseling role plays in which they encourage clients to re-create and articulate their own personal narratives about their lives. This sort of role-playing allows students to see how collaboratively co-constructing new understandings of the client's life, so as to co-create new solutions to the problems (e.g., addiction), can contribute to the therapeutic process (Guterman, 1996; Hayes & Oppenheim, 1997).

Further, during the role plays, students can be urged to attend to the racial, ethnic, cultural, gender, socioeconomic, disability status, religious, and political aspects of the client; to their own values and biases regarding the client; and to the meaning of these cultural factors in understanding the client's experience of addictions. Some questions to pose to students include the following: "Have you thought about working with an addicted client? If so, do you believe that 'cure' happens as the result of an individual merely stopping the behavior? Do you believe that stopping is always a choice? Or that by continuing addictive behaviors, the client is making her or his intentions known? Or might you work with the client to help her or him make meaning of the addictive behavior and then assist her or him in the co-creation of a different (and hopefully more positive) meaning for the role of addiction in her or his life?"

## COURSE STRUCTURE

This section outlines more specifically how the addictions course might be designed. Class structure might include lectures, group discussions, role plays (using dyads or triads), and guest speakers. Assignments and projects can include online discussions, an immersion project at a treatment facility, outside reflection projects, and a final examination.

## Lectures and Role Plays

Lectures in this course might take the form of didactic instruction with large- or small-group discussions and guest speakers. Speakers might include law enforcement officers, directors of treatment facilities, or individuals in various stages of recovery. In response to lecturers who present cases or political issues (e.g., why more money is spent on prisons than on prevention and treatment), instructors or speakers might lead group discussions. Following lectures and discussions, depending on the size of the class, students might role play the scenarios discussed in dyads or triads. Case scenarios can include clients in need of addictions counseling, such as an adolescent caught smoking and drinking for the third time, a mother arrested for drunk driving, or a college student who binge drinks.

## Assignments and Projects

Activities that draw students to a place of "participant observer" encourage students to assimilate learning beyond what is possible by merely reading a text. Direct observation of media or unobtrusive observation of recovery activities also enhance learning. Following are samples of assignments and projects that aim to help students in learning about the impact that addiction has on clients and on the subsystems in which clients live.

### Immersion Project and Guided Reflection Activity

This assignment requires students to choose an addictions-related group outside of their comfort level in which to immerse themselves. Examples include Alcoholics Anonymous, Al-Anon, and Rational Recovery. Students attend at least six meetings throughout the semester to expand their knowledge and create understanding of and connections with course material. They then reflect in writing at the end of the semester in a short paper, based on the following questions:

- What were your initial thoughts, feelings, and reactions to this immersion experience?
- Why do you think that you reacted in this manner?

- How has this immersion experience influenced your thoughts, feelings, and reactions about this type of group/person?
- If you could change something about this experience to expand your current knowledge, what would it be and why?
- How might this experience benefit you in your future work as a counselor, counselor educator, or supervisor?
- How do you plan to integrate this immersion experience into your real-life practice?

## Media Observation and Discussion

This assignment asks students to write reaction papers to at least three movies or documentaries that have addictions themes. Access to media that portrays the life of a person with addictive behaviors can begin the process of understanding what such a life is like. Media portrayals offer a visceral experience of people's lives and provide an emotional depth that merely reading about addictions fails to do. Furthermore, such portrayals give students the opportunity to "see themselves," perhaps not as the addicted characters, but in other roles surrounding the addicted characters (e.g., spouse/partner, parent, child, caregiver, treatment provider).

During the first two weeks of class, students form groups of three or four to view any of the media suggested as options and to discuss both affective and cognitive reactions to the presentations. Students or instructors can pick the movie. Dialogue about the movies then takes place in small groups through asynchronous online discussion boards, online class forums, or live classroom breakout sessions. Appendix A offers a partial list of possible media offerings. Questions that students might react to in their discussions are included in Appendix B.

## The Abstinence Project and Journal

During this project, students refrain from a substance or behavior that brings them a lot of joy (e.g., coffee, sex, certain foods, using a cell phone, texting). They remain abstinent for the duration of the course. Students reflect regularly on the meaning of the behavior for them, addressing what thoughts and behaviors take place when the behavior is halted, how they cope when they stop the behavior, and what happens when they relapse. Students record their thoughts and feelings in a journal (typed or handwritten), which is turned in at the completion of the semester.

## Case Studies

Students discuss cases of individuals from different cultures who are in varying stages of addiction or recovery (e.g., addictions work with women, individuals with disabilities, individuals with a psychiatric disability, adolescents, older adults, individuals from visibly different racial ethnic groups who may perceive addictions differently). Instructors and students may present and discuss real-life case studies (with identifying information changed) of addictions. Case studies can be explored online through discussion boards, Skype, or other means that provide flexibility in "meeting" outside the classroom. It is important for students to discuss not only the presenting issues, but how they will proceed with a treatment plan.

## Treatment Facility Visit/Interview

Students identify and visit a facility in their area that treats people with addictions, and they write up their experience. They also reflect on why it is important to have information about available facilities. They might visit an inpatient facility, intensive outpatient facility, or combination of both. The questions in Appendix C might aid students in gathering information at the facility. Students are free to include other information in their write-ups as well.

## Final Examination

The final is an in-class examination consisting of multiple-choice items, true/false questions, short answer questions, and one or two case studies in which students explain how to appropriately assess and treat the individual, couple, or family presented in the case.

# CONCLUDING REFLECTIONS

In a course on addiction counseling, counselors-in-training need prompting to keep in mind how their values, biases, and "lenses" might interact with their definitions of addiction and treatment. As students complete the course assignments, it becomes clearer that addiction holds different meanings for each individual client. It also becomes clear that, during the journey toward sobriety, effective communication between counselor and client is essential and clients must remain the experts on their own addiction. Indeed, clients hold the key to their own sobriety. Counselors, then, treat different addicted clients differently. Seasoned and beginning counselors may draw on the wisdom of a wide range of addictions interventions. The counselor's training and experience will direct how she or he utilizes those treatments with her or his clients in order to make it an empowering experience for both. Taking the clients' experiences into account, meeting them where they are, and helping them re-create different and healthier lifestyles, whatever that means for each client, is the goal of counseling. Students' understanding of the client's addiction experience is paramount to becoming an effective addictions counselor. All of this becomes the content for teaching the addictions course.

# REFERENCES

American Psychiatric Association (2000). *Diagnostic and statistical manual of mental disorders* (4th ed., text rev.). Washington, DC: Author.

Berg, I. K., & Miller, S. (1992). *Working with the problem drinker: A solution-focused approach.* New York: W. W. Norton.

Council for Accreditation of Counseling and Related Educational Programs. (2009). *CACREP accreditation standards and procedures manual.* Alexandria, VA: Author.

de Shazer, S. (1988). *Clues: Investigating solutions in brief therapy.* New York: W. W. Norton.

Galliher, R. V., Evans, C. M., & Weiser, D. (2007). Social and individual predictors of substance abuse for Native American youth. *Journal of Child and Adolescent Substance Abuse, 16*(3), 1–16.

Goldenberg, H., & Goldenberg, I. (2008). *Family therapy: An overview* (7th ed.). Belmont, CA: Thomson Brooks/Cole.

Guterman, J. T. (1996). Doing mental health counseling. *Journal of Mental Health Counseling, 18,* 228–252.

Hayes, R. L., & Oppenheim, R. (1997). Constructivism: Reality is what you make it. In T. L. Sexton & B. L. Griffin (Eds.), *Constructivist thinking in counseling practice, research, and training* (pp. 19–40). New York: Teachers College Press.

Hayes, R. L., & Paisley, P. O. (2002). Transforming school counselor preparation programs. *Theory Into Practice, 41*(3), 169–176.

Koerner, A., & Fitzpatrick, M. (2006). Family communications patterns theory: A social cognitive approach. In D. O. Braithwaite & L. A. Baxter (Eds.), *Engaging theories in family communication: Multiple perspectives* (pp. 50–65). Thousand Oaks, CA: Sage.

Lee, M. Y. (1996). A constructivist approach to the help-seeking process of clients: A response to cultural diversity. *Clinical Social Work Journal, 24,* 187–202.

Lipchik, E. (1988). Purposeful sequences for beginning the solution-focused interview. In E. Lipchik (Ed.). *Interviewing* (pp. 105–116). Rockville, MD: Aspen.

McCambridge, J., & Strang, J. (2005). Deterioration over time in effect of motivational interviewing in reducing drug consumption and related risk among young people. *Addiction, 100,* 470–478.

Morgan, O. J., & Toloczko, A. M. (1997). Graduate training of counselors in the addictions: A study of CACREP-approved programs. *Journal of Addictions & Offender Counseling, 17,* 66–77.

National Institute on Drug Abuse & U.S. Department of Health and Human Services. (2010). *Drugs, brains, and behavior: The science of addiction* (NIH Publication 07-5605). Rockville, MD: National Institutes of Health.

Nelson-Becker, H. (2004). Spiritual, religious, non-spiritual, and nonreligious narratives in marginalized older adults: A typology of coping styles. *Journal of Religion, Spirituality & Aging, 17,* 21–38.

Pembroke, N. (2005). A Trinitarian perspective on the counseling alliance in narrative therapy. *Journal of Psychology and Christianity, 24,* 13–20.

Salyers, K. M., Ritchie, M. H., Cochrane, W. S., & Roseman, C. P. (2006). Inclusion of substance abuse training in CACREP-accredited programs. *Journal of Addictions & Offender Counseling, 27,* 47–58.

van Wormer, K., & Davis, D. R. (2003). *Addiction treatment: A strengths perspective.* Pacific Grove, CA: Brooks/Cole.

Walsh, W. M., & McGraw, J. A. (1996). *Essentials of family therapy: A therapist's guide to eight approaches.* Denver, CO: Love.

Weiner-Davis, M., & O'Hanlon, W. (1989). *In search of solutions: A new direction in psychotherapy.* New York: W. W. Norton.

White, M., & Epston, D. (1990). *Narrative means to therapeutic ends.* New York: W. W. Norton.

Whittinghill, D. W., Carroll, J. J., & Morgan, O. (2004). Curriculum standards for the education of professional substance abuse counselors. *Journal of Teaching in the Addictions, 3*(2), 63–76.

# Appendix A
## Movies Depicting Addiction

**Affliction:** Family dynamics

*Barfly:* Two individuals meet in a bar where they establish a relationship

*Basketball Diaries:* An adolescent struggles with addiction

*Clean and Sober:* One man's story of addiction/recovery

*Days of Wine and Roses:* A couple struggles with alcohol

**Drunks:** Good depiction of a 12-step meeting

*Leaving Las Vegas:* A man arrives in Las Vegas with the intention of drinking himself to death

*The Lost Weekend:* An excellent depiction of alcoholism during the 1950s

*Mrs. Parker and the Vicious Circle:* A woman writer during the 1920s uses/abuses alcohol

*Once Were Warriors:* A multicultural examination of alcohol abuse in New Zealand

*Thirteen:* Multi drug abuse, family dynamics and issues

*Traffic:* Four stories about addiction

*Trees Lounge:* The devastating effects alcohol plays in the life of one man

*Trainspotting:* A good representation of living a life of heroin addiction

*When a Man Loves a Woman* Good depiction of family dynamics in alcoholism

*Who's Afraid of Virginia Woolf?* Based on the Edward Albee play

### Other programming that involves TV series formats:

*Intervention* (A&E series): Series about individuals who confront their addictions with possible treatment and the support of family and friends through alcohol and drug intervention

*Addiction* (HBO series): A feature-length documentary with nine different segments from the world of addiction

# Appendix B
## Online Discussion Questions for Student Groups

1. About the issue (e.g., what kind of an addiction)
   a. How was it depicted?
   b. Were there any stereotypes that you saw that perpetuated or refuted the addiction?
   c. What might viewers learn about addiction from this film? About any consequences to using?

2. Main character(s)
   a. How was the main character(s) with the addiction portrayed?
   b. How did this character deal with her or his addiction?
   c. Was there a counselor to help? If so, how did the main character interact with the counselor? Were there other characters who also struggled with addictions? If so, what was their role?
   d. How did the main character's culture, race, gender, and/or sexual orientation play a part in the addiction?

3. If a counselor was portrayed . . .
   a. What was this person's level of competency? How do you know?
   b. Did the counselor act ethically or not? Legally?
   c. What does the counselor's personality as depicted in the film say about mental health counseling? What is the message to nonprofessionals?
   d. What is at least one struggle, either intrapersonal or interpersonal, that the counselor must resolve? How does she or he do it?
   e. What important lesson does the counselor learn?
   f. How might the counselor be impeded in effectively practicing mental health counseling?

4. Other
   a. What other lessons learned about substance abuse/addictions counseling can you discuss as it relates to working with individuals who struggle with this issue?
   b. What type of emotional (visceral) reaction did you experience as you watched the movie?

# Appendix C
## Questions for Treatment Facility Visit

1. What is the center's treatment philosophy?

2. What is the center's accreditation?

3. What are the admission procedures? Accept anyone? Court-remanded versus non-court-remanded?

4. What types of payment do they accept? Insurance? Payment plans?

5. If a residential facility . . .
   a. How long is the stay?
   b. For whom? Everyone? Ages? Gender?
   c. Is there separate treatment for women (and their children), men, adolescents, older folks?
   d. How about for parents?

6. What are the detoxification procedures?
   a. Do they specialize in any type of detox?
   b. Is detox treated similarly for all substances (e.g., heroin, opiates, alcohol, stimulants)?

7. Is there a day treatment center option? If so, what does it consist of? For whom?

8. Are outpatient services available? If so, what do they consist of? For whom?

9. What is available for family and friends? What kinds of education are available for them?

10. How is relapse management addressed?

11. How is aftercare addressed?

# PART III

## Innovative Program Practices

# 23

# What Do Students Know and What Can They Do?

## Assessing Competence in Counselor Education

Debra C. Cobia, Jamie S. Carney, and David M. Shannon

The public demand that educational systems assume greater responsibility for what students know and are able to do when they graduate from college has increased steadily since the release of several landmark reports on education in the 1980s (e.g., Ewell, 2001; National Commission on Excellence in Education, 1983; National Governors Association, 1986). These reports questioned the efficacy of educational systems in the United States and called for greater accountability for student learning. In response, higher education and related accrediting bodies called for more systematic assessment of goals at institutional, program, and individual student levels. Accrediting bodies, such as the Council for Accreditation of Counseling and Related Educational Programs (CACREP, 2009), now require academic programs to develop and implement assessment systems and procedures that provide concrete, direct evidence of student learning and to report the assessment outcomes to the public in a manner that is readily understandable (Council for Higher Education Accreditation, 2006; Ewell, 2001).

With respect to counselor education program accreditation, CACREP (2009) specifies that program faculty engage in "continuous systematic program evaluation indicating how the mission, objectives, and student learning outcomes are measured and met" (p. 7). The most recent set of standards adopted by CACREP are a clear departure from the past. They have moved from simply describing what students are taught to instead emphasizing what students know and are able to do. This paradigm shift, from teacher-centered assessment to learner-centered models, signals a move away from traditional assessment approaches that rely on student grades, satisfaction surveys, and other indirect measures of student learning. Assessment data in the emerging, learner-centered model aims to improve curricula, pedagogies, and decision making (Suskie, 2009). Programs that previously relied on indirect methods of evaluation to assess program quality (e.g., satisfaction surveys) are now being challenged to provide more direct evidence that both program goals and related expectations for student learning have been achieved. To support efforts by programs to meet these new demands, in this chapter we describe an approach to developing an effective assessment plan, including specific strategies for evaluating student learning (knowledge) and performance (skill). The examples provided are linked to the CACREP (2009) standards.

## PLANNING FOR ASSESSMENT

Planning to create effective systems for program evaluation requires a number of factors. First, the planning must account for the systematic collection of assessment information, to be done over time (Office of Academic Planning and Assessment [OAPA], 2001b). In particular, in the planning stage, the purposes of the evaluation should be clear to all. They should be focused on program improvement. And evaluators must include a variety of assessment strategies. Finally, the plan must include how faculty will implement strategies.

Planning begins with the understanding that assessment is characterized by four elements: continuousness, focus, variety, and ownership by the faculty. First, assessment of learning is an ongoing effort. Effective systems for program evaluation are those that collect assessment information systematically and over time, not episodically (OAPA, 2001b). The ongoing, cumulative collection of assessment data results in a body of information about programs.

Second, the purposes of the evaluation should be clear and focused on program improvement. For example, assessments may be summative or formative. The purpose of summative evaluations is to determine whether students have acquired the appropriate knowledge or have demonstrated the needed skill, to assign a grade, or to determine whether students are making adequate academic progress. The purpose of formative assessments is to engage faculty in an ongoing process to determine what students have learned throughout a course or program and to identify areas that require additional attention.

Third, effective systems are multifaceted and include a variety of assessment strategies. That is, demonstrations of student knowledge and skill are assessed at multiple points during enrollment, observations of learning occur in more than one situation or context, and assessment strategies used are matched to the expected outcome (e.g., tests to assess knowledge).

And fourth, the effective assessment system is designed and implemented by faculty, rather than being imposed on programs from above by administrators. Faculty need to be actively engaged in discussions about what and how they teach, about their expectations of students, about how courses in programs link together, and about where resources need to be shifted to align with priorities (Suskie, 2009).

## A Model Learning Assessment Plan

A planning process that may be used by programs to develop assessment plans is that of California State University, Chico (1998; cited in OAPA, 2001a). The process includes four phases for planning assessments: (1) determining learning goals (outcomes), (2) naming learning processes and assessment measures, (3) determining assessment processes, and (4) making decisions and recommendations.

### Determining Learning Outcomes

The following fundamental question guides assessment plan development: What will our graduates know, be able to do, and believe as a result of their enrollment in our degree programs? Answers to this question take the form of learning outcomes.

Initially, program faculties should discuss and reach agreement on goals at both program and individual course levels (OAPA, 2001a). Program goals are different from individual learner outcomes. Program goals are broad statements about student learning (e.g., "Graduates will be culturally competent counselors"). Individual student learning outcomes are more specific statements of what students achieve in a particular degree program (Ewell, 2001; OAPA, 2001a). For example, a student learning outcome related to the broad goal stated previously might be "Demonstrates the ability to modify counseling systems, theories, techniques, and interventions to make them culturally appropriate for diverse populations" (CACREP, 2009, p. 33).

Specifically, student learning outcomes include the levels of knowledge, skills, attitudes, and abilities that students attain as a result of participating in a particular degree program (Ewell, 2001; OAPA, 2001a). The first, knowledge outcomes, refers to disciplinary or professional content that students recall and deploy (e.g., "Understand and use research for decision making."). Skills outcomes refer to what students have learned to do (e.g., "Conduct mental status exam"). Attitudinal outcomes involve changes in, or the development of, certain values (e.g., "Demonstrate empathy, warmth, and positive regard"). Abilities refer to the integration of knowledge, skills, and attitudes in ways that are applicable to different situations (e.g., "Engage in reflective practice and decision making").

Some student learning outcomes for programs seeking CACREP accreditation are predetermined. For example, the CACREP (2009) program area standards for community mental health counseling specify three knowledge outcomes (what students know) and three skills and practices outcomes (what students will be able to do) in research and evaluation. Other learning goals may be unique to individual programs and relate directly to the institutional and program missions.

## Naming Learning Processes and Assessment Measures

Following the articulation of student learning outcomes, programs specify the learning processes in the curriculum that will enable students to attain the goals. Learning processes consist of curricular and co-curricular strategies used to teach the content and/or skills that students need in order to demonstrate the outcome. For example, for a learning goal such as "Students will demonstrate consistency of theoretical identity," an integrative paper assigned in the counseling theories course might be one of the learning processes used to help students achieve the learning outcome.

Once learning outcomes are established, program faculty identify the information that is needed to assess student learning. Guiding questions at this stage of planning include "What information is needed to assess this outcome?" "Where might the most reliable/valid information be found?" and "How will the information be collected?" (Fitzpatrick, Sanders, & Worthen, 2004).

Assessment strategies might consist of the following: Assessments in prerequisite courses (e.g., skills may be assessed in a course that is prerequisite to counseling practicum, competency may be assessed in practicum prior to internship) may be used to assess learner outcomes at a variety of points across the degree program.

Pre-post measures at the beginning and ending of the program, as well as self-assessment or self-reflection, may be used to identify growth and development over time. Interviews and surveys may be used as exit strategies to identify student perceptions of their own strengths and weaknesses, as well as those of the program. Standardized tests and faculty-developed comprehensive examinations measure knowledge and generate outcome data that are easily comparable across cohorts. Portfolio ratings by multiple faculty and supervisors who work with students under a variety of conditions are useful for looking at how knowledge is applied in multiple contexts (see American Psychological Association, 2009).

The following is an example of how program goals, learner outcomes, learning processes, and assessment evidence might be linked to CACREP (2009) standards in learning environment (Section I.P) and professional identity (Section II.G.1.d) in the area of counselor wellness.

Program Goal: Graduates will actively engage in self-care strategies that sustain counselor wellness.

Learner Outcome: Students will monitor their wellness status and respond to signs of burnout with effective self-care strategies.

Learning Processes: (1) Students will create a plan of self-care in response to a self-assessment of wellness practices to be administered during the first term of enrollment (embedded course assignment); (2) Students will evaluate the effectiveness of their plans in maintaining wellness as part of their annual student evaluation and ongoing portfolio development.

Assessment Evidence: (a) Faculty-developed rubric to evaluate the adequacy of student's wellness plan (e.g., goals and measurable objectives clearly linked to individual wellness assessment, strategies consistent with wellness literature), (b) self-assessment (pre-post scores on wellness measure), (c) reflection (portfolio component for annual review and summative evaluation), and (d) observation (annual review checklist, site supervisor evaluation of items related to observable self-care practices).

## Determining Assessment Processes

In addition to deciding on the measures used, assessment processes (e.g., at what points during enrollment, how, and by whom will data be collected) must be determined.

For example, program faculty, students' advisory committees, and others may view student portfolios at intervals such as 12, 24, 36, and 48 credits. Or every student enrolled in the counseling skills course, pre-practicum, practicum, and internship might be assessed using a standard performance measure (see, e.g., Eriksen & McAuliffe, 2003, *Counseling Skills Scale*) to show progression toward an acceptable level of skills competency.

## Making Decisions and Recommendations

Assessment findings logically lead to the final phase of the comprehensive plan: decision making and recommendations. Based on findings about student attainment of learning outcomes and program goals, faculty need to decide which instructional and assessment strategies will be continued and which will be revised or replaced. During the initial assessment planning period, plans need to be made about time lines for decisions and recommendations as well as for disseminating report information to various stakeholders.

Data that are collected (e.g., ratings based on rubrics for all students completing the wellness plan) are aggregated and analyzed to determine the extent to which learner outcomes have been attained. Based on the results, an action plan can be developed for learner outcomes that have not been achieved by the majority of students. Finally, findings are used to develop action plans aimed at improving identified areas of weakness. These reports and action plans are made available to interested publics.

# ASSESSMENT OF LEARNING OUTCOMES

Now that a model assessment plan has been described, the particular issue of assessing learning outcomes will be discussed in some detail. There is broad, professional consensus among educators that "knowing" is a precursor to "doing." The CACREP (2009) standards help counselors identify the knowledge base that is necessary for all counselors, which includes knowledge in eight curricular areas (professional orientation and ethical practice, social and cultural diversity, human growth and development, career development, helping relationships, group work, assessment, and research and program evaluation). In the program area specialization sections of the

CACREP standards, knowledge required of those who will practice in particular work settings provides further direction about what students need to know and be able to do. Some of the likely expected outcomes derived from these standards require student recall of basic knowledge. Others require demonstrations of students' ability to apply what they've learned from coursework and other program experiences, analyze and synthesize a variety of information and experiences, and evaluate their abilities as professionals. After planning has taken place in each of these areas, the assessment process can be implemented. The following sections, therefore, address how counselor educators might best use the various assessment possibilities to their maximum effectiveness.

# Knowledge Outcomes Assessment

Those objectives that pertain to student knowledge acquisition will vary in their degree of difficulty or level of expectation for student learning. A taxonomy widely used to classify objectives is the one developed by Benjamin Bloom (Bloom, Englehart, Furst, Hill, & Krathwohl, 1956). Bloom's taxonomy (discussed in Chapter 16 of this book) offers a six-level hierarchy of student cognitive outcomes: knowledge, comprehension, application, analysis, synthesis, and evaluation. The revised taxonomy includes the following: remember, understand, apply, analyze, evaluate, and create (Anderson & Krathwohl, 2001).

In some instances, educators are interested in lower-level outcomes for students, represented by the terms *knowledge* and *remember*. Examples of such lower-level outcomes include recognizing examples of appropriate practice and understanding foundational knowledge of counseling theories.

On the other hand, objectives may focus on higher-level learner outcomes, such as *application, synthesis*, and *evaluation*. These can be translated into how students apply theories to practice, compare and contrast different theories, or evaluate the appropriateness of a specific theory in different situations. Selecting the most appropriate method for assessing knowledge depends on what one expects students to know or be able to do.

Once objectives have been established, valid assessment depends on the extent to which assessment methods match the objectives established for students. For example, the objective "Students will know the major theories of racial identity development" might be fairly easy to assess with objective tests. However, "Students will be able to compare and contrast theories of racial identity development" would not generally be assessable through the same method. Several methods of assessing knowledge outcomes along Bloom's continuum will be presented next, namely, selective-response assessment, constructed-response assessment, and informal assessment approaches.

## Selective-Response Assessment

The most common traditional method used to assess student knowledge is the objective test. Objective tests are those in which students select the correct answer (e.g., true/false, multiple-choice, matching). These tests may be used quite effectively to measure student knowledge, particularly for the targets of remember, understand, and apply (Anderson & Krathwohl, 2001). Many selective-response test items can be completed within a reasonable period of time, and scoring these objective tests is relatively easy.

The objective test format is widely used in the field of counseling to assess knowledge. For instance, the National Counselor Examination consists of multiple-choice questions (www.nbcc.org/certifications/ncc/NCE.aspx), as does the Counselor Preparation Comprehensive Examination (CPCE; www.cce-global.org/cpce). Both assess counseling students' knowledge of the content that is believed to be important to the field of counseling. One advantage of such tests is the ability to compare results against those of students at other colleges and universities (peer benchmarking). Suskie (2009) suggests using such objective tests or surveys as part of an assessment plan when learning goals clearly match those covered by the instruments and results are readily and easily used to improve teaching, learning, and programs.

While objective items have many advantages, they require skill and practice to construct so that they are understandable and so that the correct answer is clear. Without a clear "best response" or a set of "acceptable responses," the objectivity of this approach becomes compromised, weakening its reliability and validity as an assessment method.

Objective tests may be used to assess different levels of learning objectives. However, it is much more difficult to construct items that measure knowledge at the upper levels of Bloom's taxonomy. The challenge is that these types of items require more divergent responses. For more information about developing selective-response items, see Haladyna (1999), Popham (2002), and Stiggins (2008).

## Constructed-Response Assessment

Constructed-response assessments ask students for short-answer responses and essays. They are very useful for measuring higher-level student outcomes because they require students to think about what they know. In particular, they are useful for assessing students' abilities to analyze, create, and evaluate. Under these conditions, students have an opportunity to describe what they know in their own words, compare and contrast concepts or theories, and create something new using their knowledge.

Although short answers and essays are useful for measuring higher-level student outcomes, scoring student responses might lead to frustration unless students have been provided with clear guidelines for responding to such items or tasks. Directions provided to students should be clear regarding length. More important, the task should be clearly described for students, using prompts that focus them on the target. For example, students enrolled in a career counseling course may be provided with a case describing a college student who is soon to graduate. Let's assume that the client pursues counseling to obtain help with making some decisions about what she will do following graduation. Through a series of prompts, counseling students apply their knowledge of career development theory to identify possible counseling goals. Responses are scored based on the extent to which they meet the demands of rubrics established for each prompt (more on rubrics to follow). Constructed-response assessments might, thus, be used to assess students' attainment of learning goals related to CACREP (2009) Standards II.G. 4.a. and 4.g, which specify students' knowledge of career development theories and models and their abilities to use career counseling approaches. Other methods used by faculty to assess knowledge are ratings on oral presentations in a specified course (formative), oral exams conducted at or near the end of a program of study, poster presentations, locally developed exams, graded online discussions about specified topics, and classroom response systems (clickers) that allow students to respond from their seats to questions posed by the teacher.

## Informal Assessment Approaches

Some assessment approaches used by faculty are intended to gauge what students are learning in order to modify instructional methods during a class meeting or periodically throughout the semester. The most common form of informal assessment is questioning (see Gall, 1970; Redfield & Rousseau, 1981; Rowe, 1974; Tobin, 1987; Wilen, 1987), which can be a very effective assessment tool. As discussed in Chapter 5, convergent questions may be used to gather a desired response and may be very useful when reviewing foundational knowledge and concepts. On the other hand, more open-ended, divergent questions may be useful in helping students think about numerous ways to respond and in generating discussions.

Angelo and Cross (1993) discuss other informal classroom assessment strategies that faculty may find helpful. Two simple-to-use techniques are the "one-minute paper" and the "muddiest point." As described in Chapter 5, the one-minute-paper technique consists of instructors handing out a piece of paper at the end of class and asking students to describe the most important thing they learned during that class. The muddiest point uses the same approach, but asks students to write about what they did not understand and what they think might help them. These strategies may be used anonymously, thus relieving the pressure that some students feel during formal assessments.

## Skills Outcomes Assessment

In contrast to knowledge outcomes, skills outcomes generally refer to the learned capacity to do something (Ewell, 2001). Many such outcomes are identified in the latest CACREP (2009) standards. Skills outcomes are easily identifiable because they focus on what students will do (i.e., demonstrate, apply, model, advocate, provide, design and implement, assess, select, conduct; CACREP, 2009). Skills assessments might also evaluate the ability to think critically, communicate effectively, collaborate, or perform a particular operation (Ewell, 2001). The assessment of skills usually involves demonstrations of

student competence through a performance (e.g., a video-taped counseling session) or the development of a product (e.g., a treatment plan).

This section of the chapter contains general information about performance assessment, including how to develop and use rubrics (faculty-developed and standardized) and portfolios to assess performance.

## Performance Assessment

Performance assessment is linked to the curriculum and assesses skills that are demonstrated in real examples of student work (OAPA, 2001b). Examples of activities assessed include, but are not limited to, course assignments (e.g., advocacy skills might be assessed following students' development and implementation of the advocacy plan required in a professional issues course), demonstrations (e.g., counseling skills and tasks presented in a video of a counseling session might be assessed during practicum or internship), presentations, and other activities. Performance assessments that ask students to demonstrate skill outcomes through a real-life task (e.g., demonstrate counseling skills with clients during internship) are also called authentic assessments.

Performance assessments involve two parts: a prompt that conveys to students what is expected of them and a scoring guide or rubric to evaluate their response to the prompt (Suskie, 2009). Scoring guides might include checklists to identify which elements of the skills or practices a counselor demonstrates. Rating scales that include a range of scores for items may also be used to provide information about the degree of competence demonstrated (see Eriksen & McAuliffe, 2003). Both checklists and rating scales are variations of rubrics. Although time-consuming to create, rubrics offer several advantages over other methods. They speed up grading and, once written, may be used by more than one rater for accurate, consistent, unbiased, and reliable ratings of a performance or assignment (Suskie, 2009).

Rubrics specify different levels of quality (e.g., beginning, developing, proficient, advanced) and include descriptions of what represents each level of quality so that the rubric can be applied reliably.

Two degrees of specificity are possible: holistic and analytic. *Holistic* rubrics are created and applied to an overall performance or product. Holistic rubrics include specific descriptors at each designated performance level, detailing performance indicators for exemplary to poor or unsatisfactory work. *Analytic* rubrics are designed to assess each dimension or specific criterion related to the performance or product (Mertler, 2001). Analytic rubrics may also be used as a learning tool, providing students with specific information about performance expectations at each performance level.

Rubrics can be developed according to the following guidelines provided by Mertler (2001). First, instructors clearly identify the learning objectives being assessed. Second, instructors specify the observable attributes (evidence) that they want to see demonstrated (and possibly those that they do not). Third, instructors identify the specific characteristics that would describe these attributes (see Marchel, 2004). In other words, the rubrics are created first to include what program leaders want students to know and do. Then, the assignments/performances to be rated are created. Rubrics may be used to score many different types of student activities, including products, performances, and reflective essays. The example below shows a skill-based learning outcome rubric for school and clinical mental health counseling students who complete a common class assignment. The assignment is scored using a 4-point descriptive rubric.

Program Goal: Program graduates will use evidence to inform practice.

Learner Outcome: (1) The student applies relevant research findings to inform the practice of clinical mental health counseling (CACREP, 2009, p. 33); (2) The student applies relevant research findings to inform the practice of school counseling (CACREP, 2009, p. 42).

Learning Experiences: All students enrolled in Counseling Skills 101 will develop a treatment/counseling plan for a specific clinical mental health or school counseling case provided by the instructor. As part of the planning process, students will develop an integrated review of the literature regarding empirically supported practices with like cases and will describe how they used these references to develop the counseling plan.

Assessment Method: A departmentally developed holistic rubric (see Table 23.1) will be used to measure goal attainment, scored as 1: Unsatisfactory, 2: Developing, 3: Competent, 4: Exemplary.

Assessment Process: Every spring, students enrolled in 101 will complete the treatment planning assignment. The course instructor, the individual student, and the peer supervisor will complete scoring rubrics for the assignment. Results will be entered into the electronic departmental portfolio where assessment data are collected and maintained. As well, students will include the assignment and evaluations in individual portfolios.

Outcome: Measured by number of students achieving each level of mastery included on the rubric.

Plan: When the number of students attaining competent to exemplary ratings is fewer than 75%, the plans will be reviewed by faculty in an effort to determine what prerequisite skills or knowledge are required for students to achieve mastery.

**TABLE 23.1**  Sample Treatment Plan Rubric: Counseling Skills 101

**Learner Outcome:** The student *applies* relevant research findings to inform the practice of clinical mental health or school counseling

| Unsatisfactory (1) | Developing (2) | Competent (3) | Exemplary (4) |
|---|---|---|---|
| The student selects interventions based on her or his comfort and perceived competence without regard to the appropriateness of these interventions for the client. | The student applies knowledge of counseling theory to client needs. | The student analyzes information found in the professional literature regarding treatments that have been demonstrated through research to be effective in similar circumstances and uses this information to guide development of goals and selection of interventions. | The student synthesizes information about empirically supported treatments and the unique, personal contexts and systems within which the individual client resides in order to create a treatment plan that is both evidence based and personally relevant. |

For some learner outcomes assessments, existing valid and reliable assessment tools may be available. One such measure of performance is the Counseling Skills Scale (CSS; Eriksen & McAuliffe, 2003) discussed in Chapter 7 of this book. Learner outcomes related to CACREP Standard II.G. 5.c, essential interviewing and counseling skills, can be assessed using this scale, as it identifies specific interviewing and counseling skills (e.g., "encourages exploration"). The CSS is a significant improvement over dichotomous scales that assess the presence or absence of a particular skill. Five rating categories with specific descriptions allow for finer distinctions about the level of skill attainment, which make the CSS useful for course and curricular planning and improvement.

## Portfolio Assessment

Portfolios are included in the skills outcomes section because assessment of performance is one of the primary purposes of this particular assessment strategy.

**The Value of Portfolios.** Portfolio assessment is also appropriately used to assess knowledge, abilities (integration of skills and knowledge), as well as growth and development. Portfolio assessment is an authentic evaluation method that also allows for the demonstration of learning over time in relation to program requirements (Cobia et al., 2005; James & Greenwalt, 2001). Perhaps more important, portfolio assessment actively engages students and professionals in the development, demonstration, and evaluation of their own competence (Taylor, Thomas, & Sage, 1999).

For these reasons, portfolios are used as both a learning tool and an assessment strategy. Several researchers have discussed and outlined models of portfolios for counselor education (see Carney, Cobia, & Shannon, 1996; Cobia et al., 2005; James & Greenwalt, 2001). The knowledge, skill, and practice outcomes specified in the CACREP (2009) standards, along with program-specific learner outcomes, form the framework of the portfolio.

Learner outcomes may be related to skills: "Demonstrate the ability to develop and evaluate a treatment plan for clients from diverse backgrounds." Outcomes may also be related to the deployment of knowledge: "Demonstrate understanding of assessment measures and their use with children and adolescents of diverse backgrounds." In addition, outcomes may focus on growth, development, and awareness: "Discuss results of the hidden bias inventories you took during your first and second years of enrollment in the program and the professional improvement plan you created and implemented in response to your initial results. Reflect on the outcomes of this plan (evaluation) and how it may have influenced your personal and professional growth during the program."

Portfolios may also be viewed as systems for collecting, analyzing, and interpreting all types of assessment results used in a comprehensive, systematic plan of assessment. For example, students may be asked to include in their portfolios specific course-embedded assignments that faculty have designated as learning opportunities to develop and demonstrate competence (e.g., an excerpt from a video demonstration of empathy), scores from objective examinations (e.g., CPCE results), milestones (e.g., a skills demonstration checklist), or capstone projects (e.g., an advocacy plan). Scoring rubrics, particularly those used by multiple assessors, allow for the aggregation of student data for the various portfolio components so that evidence of learning is demonstrated at both individual student and program outcomes levels.

**The Content of Portfolios.** Portfolio assessment typically involves student selection of some components that they believe demonstrate their attainment of required outcomes. Examples of demonstrations of competence may be found in materials from class experiences, professional development experiences, practicum and internship experiences, and personal development activities (Collins, 1990). Students may include artifacts and reproductions, including materials developed in courses, student-selected items, student-developed items, required artifacts, and materials developed in response to specific portfolio requirements. In addition to the materials to be included in the portfolio, whether student selected or required, reflection is a key component of portfolio assessment. Students consider what and how they have learned by writing reflections on the significance of the items that they have chosen to include (Suskie, 2009). Portfolios are particularly useful in programs such as counseling that emphasize the development of thinking skills and metacognition skills (i.e., learning how to manage one's own learning). Portfolios are updated frequently and scored with rubrics that include student learning outcomes and the criteria for acceptable performance.

## The Value of Performance Assessment

Many performance assessments, including demonstrations, products, and portfolios, are popular with faculty because they combine learning and assessment (Suskie, 2009). Such "authentic" assessments also provide students with learning opportunities that require them to solve complex, multidimensional problems in a real-world context, rather than focusing on fabricated examples that have a single best response (i.e., objective assessments). In performance assessments, students actually demonstrate the skills of effective counseling through performance rather than writing about effective counseling.

## CONCLUSION

To summarize, for an assessment plan to be effective, faculty and students alike will have an understanding of the process of assessment and will demonstrate an understanding of the value of assessment in both program planning and improvement (Urofsky, 2009). A clear link between assessment and student learning will also be evident. As was suggested early in this chapter, one hallmark of a systematic, comprehensive plan of assessment is that the plan is developed by program faculty, based on the clearly articulated expectations for what graduates will know and be able to do as a result of their enrollment in the degree program(s). Once the expectations have been identified, program faculty develop specific learner outcomes (i.e., knowledge, skills, and practices) that students will demonstrate to meet expectations. Then, program faculty do what they do best and plan instructional experiences (learning opportunities) that they believe will lead to the development of the designated learner outcomes. Finally, faculty determine the processes that will be used to assess student learning, review the assessment data, and use data to make improvements in programs, courses, and, when necessary, in individual student's development.

A culture of assessment in counselor education programs will be characterized by faculty and students who have a clear understanding of the purpose(s) of assessment and the relationships between assessment and both instruction and learning outcomes. Goal setting, curriculum design, and teaching methods are all parts of an integrated system that includes a plan for assessing how well the methods used lead to desired outcomes. A successful plan will lead to evidence-based program planning, improved teaching and learning, and the sense of accomplishment that results from knowing that specified program and learner goals have been achieved.

## ADDITIONAL RESOURCES

Internet Resources for Higher Education Outcomes Assessment: http://www2.acs.ncsu.edu/UPA/assmt/resource.htm

Authentic Assessment Toolbox: http://jonathan.mueller.faculty.noctrl.edu/toolbox/whatisit.htm

Rubistar Rubric Generator: http://rubistar.4teachers.org/index.php

## REFERENCES

American Psychological Association. (2009). *The assessment cyberguide for learning goals and outcomes.* Retrieved August 2, 2010, from http://www.apa.org/ed/governance/bea/assessment-cyberguide-v2.pdf

Anderson, L. W., & Krathwohl, D. R. (Eds.). (2001). *A taxonomy for learning, teaching and assessing: A revision of Bloom's taxonomy of educational objectives: Complete edition.* New York: Longman.

Angelo, T. A., & Cross, K. P. (1993). *Classroom assessment techniques: A handbook for college teachers* (2nd ed.). San Francisco: Jossey-Bass.

Bloom, B. S., Englehart, M. D., Furst, E. J., Hill, W. H., & Krathwohl, D. R. (Eds.). (1956). *Taxonomy of educational objectives: Handbook 1, Cognitive domain.* New York: McKay.

Carney, J. S., Cobia, D. C., & Shannon, D. M. (1996). The use of portfolios in the clinical and comprehensive evaluation of counselors-in-training. *Counselor Education & Supervision, 36,* 122–132.

Cobia, D. C., Carney, J. S., Buckhalt, J. A., Middleton, R. A., Shannon, D. M., Trippany, R., et al. (2005). The doctoral portfolio: Centerpiece of a comprehensive system of evaluation. *Counselor Education & Supervision, 44,* 242–254.

Collins, A. (1990, April). *Novices, experts, veterans, and masters: The role of content and pedagogical knowledge in evaluating teaching.* Paper presented at the annual meeting of the American Educational Research Association, Boston.

Council for the Accreditation of Counseling and Related Educational Programs. (2009). *2009 CACREP standards.* Retrieved August 2, 2010, from http://www.cacrep.org/doc/2009%20Standards%20with%20cover.pdf

Council for Higher Education Accreditation. (2006). *Accreditation and accountability: A CHEA special report.* Retrieved August 2, 2010, from http://www.chea.org/pdf/Accreditation_and_Accountability.pdf

Eriksen, K. P., & McAuliffe, G. J. (2003). A measure of counselor competency. *Counselor Education and Supervision, 43,* 120–133.

Ewell, P. T. (2001). *Accreditation and student learning outcomes: A proposed point of departure.* Retrieved August 2, 2010, from http://www.chea.org/pdf/EwellSLO_Sept2001.pdf

Fitzpatrick, J. L., Sanders, J. R., & Worthen, B. R. (2004). *Program evaluation: Alternative approaches and practical guidelines* (3rd ed.). Boston: Allyn & Bacon.

Gall, M. (1970). The use of questions in teaching. *Review of Educational Research, 40,* 707–721.

Haladyna, T. M. (1999). *Developing and validating multiple-choice test items* (2nd ed.). Mahwah, NJ: Lawrence Erlbaum.

James, S. H., & Greenwalt, B. C. (2001). Documenting success and achievement: Presentation and working portfolios for counselors. *Journal of Counseling & Development, 79,* 161–165.

Marchel, C. A. (2004). Evaluating reflection and sociocultural awareness in service learning classes. *Teaching Psychology, 31*(2), 120–123.

Mertler, C. (2001). Designing scoring rubrics for your classroom. *Practical Assessment, Research, and Evaluation, 7*(25). Retrieved August 2, 2010, from http://pareonline.net/getvn.asp?v=7&n=25

National Commission on Excellence in Education. (1983). *A nation at risk: The imperative for educational reform.* Washington, DC: U.S. Government Printing Office.

National Governors Association. (1986). Time for results: The governors' 1991 report on education. Washington, DC: National Governors Association.

Office of Academic Planning and Assessment. (2001a). *Course-based review and assessment: Methods for understanding student learning.* University of Massachusetts Amherst. Retrieved August 2, 2010, from http://www.umass.edu/oapa/oapa/publications/online_handbooks/course_based.pdf

Office of Academic Planning and Assessment. (2001b). *Program-based review and assessment: Tools and techniques for program improvement.* University of Massachusetts Amherst. Retrieved August 2, 2010, from http://www.umass.edu/oapa/oapa/publications/online_handbooks/program_based.pdf

Popham, J. (2002). *Classroom assessment: What teachers need to know* (3rd ed.). Boston: Allyn & Bacon.

Redfield, D. L., & Rousseau, E. W. (1981). A meta-analysis of experimental research on teacher questioning behavior. *Review of Educational Research, 51,* 237–245.

Rowe, M. B. (1974). Wait-time and rewards as instructional variables, their influence on language, logic, and fate control: Part 1. Wait time. *Journal of Research in Science Teaching, 11,* 81–94.

Stiggins, R. (2008). *An introduction to student-involved assessment for learning* (5th ed.). Columbus, OH: Pearson/Merrill.

Suskie, L. (2009). *Assessing student learning: A common sense guide* (2nd ed.). San Francisco: Jossey-Bass.

Taylor, I., Thomas, J., & Sage, H. (1999). Portfolios for learning and assessment: Laying the foundations for continuing professional development. *Social Work Education, 18*(2), 147–160.

Tobin, K. G. (1987). The role of wait time in higher-cognitive-level thinking. *Review of Educational Research, 57,* 69–95.

Urofsky, R. (2009, March). *CACREP team chair renewal.* Presentation at the meeting of the American Counseling Association, Charlotte, NC.

Wilen, W. W. (Ed.). (1987). *Questions, questioning techniques, and effective teaching.* Washington, DC: National Education Association. (ERIC Document Reproduction Service No. ED310102)

# The Use of Technology in Counselor Education and Supervision

Lisa L. Buono, Gail E. Uellendahl, Lorraine J. Guth, and Claire J. Dandeneau

A counselor educator, Professor Smith, checks her email while drinking her morning coffee. There is a message from a counseling student who is currently interning as a school counselor. He has concerns about his emotional reaction during a recent counseling session with one of his middle school students. Professor Smith provides a few prompts in her return message that require reflection and introspection on the part of the counseling student. She also suggests that he post an entry on the weekly blog that is part of the student's practicum class. This blog enables other students in the class to respond to his dilemma, thus providing multiple perspectives that enhance his understanding about the experience. Later that day, Professor Smith observes another counseling student doing a session. She uses digital analysis software to tailor a visual playback of the session to highlight specific skills that the student is using. After the session, Professor Smith and the student discuss the student's thoughts about the session; then they watch the cued clips of the session, giving the student immediate visual cues to reflect upon.

These are just a few examples of how counselor educators and supervisors are using technology to support student learning and professional development. This chapter discusses an array of technology tools, some commonplace and some novel, that might be used in a constructivist manner in counselor education, supervision, and counseling practice.

The risk of writing a chapter on the use of technology in counselor education is that, by the time the text is published, the information may be outdated. We will take that risk in order to highlight possible uses of technology in our field and to frame those uses within the context of constructivist practice. This discussion includes specific technology tools that can support classroom instruction and clinical supervision.

The use of technology for enhancing students' development may, at first glance, seem counterintuitive. When counselors think of technology, many conjure up cold, dispassionate barriers to human connection. Our experience with technology has led to a different conclusion. We believe that certain technology applications can actually support and extend students' knowledge of self and encourage the dialogue, or the *negotiated understanding* (Gergen, 1985), that is called for in constructivist models of education.

The use of instructional technology has become fairly commonplace in college classrooms in general (Parker, Bianchi, & Cheah, 2008). However, the literature suggests that counselor educators are not uniformly comfortable with or competent in using technology (Berry, Srebalus, Cromer, & Takacs, 2003; Karper, Robinson, & Casado, 2005; Lewis, Coursol, Kahn, & Wilson, 2000). Myers and Gibson (1999), for instance, found that "counselor educators and counseling students lack a uniformly high level of technology competence" (p. 4). It is our position that increased competence in the use of technology is still needed.

When most counselor educators *do* use technology, most often they choose simple technologies, such as email and PowerPoint (Quinn, Hohenshil, & Fortune, 2002). Fewer report the use of more sophisticated technologies, such as course management systems (CMSs) or the emerging applications to be discussed in this chapter. While progress toward the use of technology is ongoing, there is likely to still be some hesitance, discomfort, or even technophobia remaining among counselor educators, supervisors, and counselors.

The failure by counselor educators and supervisors to be fully current with technology has implications for their students' future success as counselors. For example, their graduates are increasingly being required to use technology by managed care companies; technology is now pervasive in schools, where email is used to connect with students and their parents; and online career assessment and scoring are the norm. Without counselor educators' competence, their students may find themselves less able to meet the technology demands in their jobs.

Despite some confusion and disinclination, counselor educators, supervisors, and counselors are clearly moving in the direction of greater use of technology (Hayes, 2008; Layne & Hohenshil, 2005). The emergence of the *Journal of Technology in Counseling* and the adoption of ethical guidelines for the use of technology in counseling by professional associations (American Counseling Association [ACA], 2005; National Board for Certified Counselors [NBCC], 2005) are evidence of this trend. While much of the research on technology in counselor education still focuses on traditional applications for instruction and supervision, such as PowerPoint, video, and email (Clingerman & Bernard, 2004; Hayes, Taub, Robinson, & Sivo, 2003), additional, emerging technologies have more recently drawn attention in the literature (Anson & Miller-Cochran, 2009). How broadly these newer technologies are used still remains unclear, however.

What is clear is that technology tools can enhance student development. As with any sort of development, educators must understand what their students know with respect to technology, what they do not know, and what they are ready to know. Educators need to proceed with caution when their students experience disequilibrium in response to technology during learning experiences (Brooks & Brooks, 1993). The selection of particular technology applications should always be based on students' readiness (Hayes, 2008) as well as the technological competence of both instructors/supervisors and students/clients (Karper et al., 2005; Vaccaro & Lambie, 2007). We refer the reader to Wang, Teo, and Woo (2009) as well as Anson and Miller-Cochran (2009) for recently outlined design models for web-based constructivist learning environments.

Our experience is that well-selected technology applications can support the instruction and supervision of students, especially when used within a constructivist framework. This chapter focuses on the identification and selection of various technology tools that might enhance constructivist approaches to both instruction and supervision in counselor education. The chapter will be organized in two major sections: an overview of technologies that enhance classroom instruction and applications of technology for supervision.

# TECHNOLOGY-ENHANCED CONSTRUCTIVIST COUNSELING INSTRUCTION

The use of technology can enhance constructivist learning environments, as recommended by Ernest (1995), Honebein (1996), Jonassen (1991), Wilson and Cole (1991), and the constructivist teaching guidelines outlined in Chapter 3 of this text, particularly by varying structure and methods and emphasizing dialogue and interaction. For instance, technology can enhance case studies, real-world learning situations, reflective practice, the inclusion and appreciation of multiple perspectives, and instructors-as-coaches and supervisors-as-guides.

In particular, technology can help instructors and supervisors instigate students' ongoing reflections about their learning (Vygotsky, 1978) through the use of such tools as electronic discussion boards and blogs. These tools, as well as some of the others described in this chapter, provide a means for helping students reflect on their learning and include one another and the instructor in their reflections during both counselor education and supervision. Technology-enhanced learning environments can promote students' readiness to discover new knowledge and experiences, particularly when those experiences are outside of, or incongruent with the lens through which they have typically observed and understood the world. In such cases, technology may help students identify their biases and open up discussions about diversity. The anonymity offered by technology can provide a certain degree of safety for the exploration of diversity issues. Later in this chapter, we discuss the student response systems that allow for such anonymity. We also describe other technology applications that can facilitate learning and provide students with opportunities to "interact and negotiate with others" (Wang et al., 2009, p. 83) in constructivist fashion.

As Lovell and McAuliffe (1997) suggest, much of what happens in the counseling office already adheres to a constructivist model, with its discovery and experiential emphasis. However, the same is not always true in the classroom training environment, which often lacks the experiential and dialogical dimension necessary for the mutual knowledge construction discussed in Chapter 1. It is time to bring pedagogy in counselor education and supervision up to speed with teacher training pedagogy—where, for many years, teachers have been prepared using a constructivist instructional model. The following sections survey the use of technology, under a constructivist model, for instructional and supervisory aims.

## TECHNOLOGY IN CONSTRUCTIVIST COUNSELING INSTRUCTION

During the past decade or so, technological applications to instruction have increased exponentially. The most common applications include PowerPoint, email, email lists, electronic journals, web resources, and CMSs. However, in the last several years, further technological advances, such as blogs, podcasts, wikis, and student response systems (among others), have increased the number of tools available to counselor educators to enhance instruction. Below, we describe how these tools might be applied to counselor education, along with pointing out their potential advantages and, sometimes, disadvantages.

## PowerPoint

PowerPoint is a useful, albeit familiar, aid for delivering lectures to students. Slides can be developed and projected during class to deliver subject material. Slides of a well-developed PowerPoint presentation contain talking points (an outline) for each topic or major concept presented. Such an outline keeps lectures structured and keeps students focused and engaged (Clark, 2008). Artfully and thoughtfully inserting pictures, clip art, graphics, web content, hyperlinks, videos, and narration can visually or aurally reinforce talking points as well as break the monotony of a PowerPoint presentation.

However, effective PowerPoint presentations are not simply vehicles for delivering a lecture. According to Clark (2008), PowerPoint presentations, if done well, "can encourage students to make their own connections and construct their own understanding of the visual and aural stimuli" (p. 43). Thus, PowerPoint presentations provide opportunities to generate insightful discussions and serve as a jumping-off point for students to take concepts, talk about them, and begin to make them their own (Vygotsky, 1978).

For example, in a skills-based counselor education course, part of a lesson might call for examining client reluctance. One PowerPoint slide might therefore give a brief definition of reluctance, the next slide might list a few reasons for reluctance in bullet-point fashion (e.g., lack of trust, fear of intensity), and the following slide might have a link to a clip of a counselor-client session, followed by a prompt. The professor first asks students to look at the definition of reluctance and asks them to describe the concept in their own words. With the second slide, the professor elaborates on the listed reasons for reluctance, giving some examples. The professor then asks the students to get into small groups and discuss when they have experienced these types of reluctance as well as to generate other reasons for reluctance.

The professor brings the class back for a larger class discussion, followed by their watching the counseling clip on the third slide. The prompt following the link to the session asks students to analyze the clip, identify the reasons for reluctance, and discuss how they might work with the client. In this scenario, the visual cues from the PowerPoint presentation provide a visual aid to help students reflect on their experiences with reluctance, hear others' perspectives, and construct a new understanding of the concept.

The strength of a PowerPoint presentation does not simply lie with the instructor. Students can be given opportunities to create their own PowerPoint presentations. The process of researching a topic, digesting the information, and organizing and delivering a PowerPoint presentation to classmates empowers students to do their own knowledge construction.

PowerPoint can, of course, also be done poorly. Putting all of the content on each slide and simply reading this content to students defeats the purpose of a constructivist education. This use of PowerPoint perpetuates the "sage on the stage" type of instruction whereby students receive information but have no opportunity to explore concepts *with* the instructor, thereby co-constructing meaning.

# Email

Email has been used for some time as a way to communicate electronically. Quite often, counselor educators use email for instructional purposes as well as for advising or informally counseling their students. Used in a give-and-take fashion, email correspondence can provide opportunities for scaffolding (Vygotsky, 1978). Scaffolding involves strongly supporting students as they learn and then slowly removing this support as students independently organize concepts, construct their knowledge, and make it their own. In this vein, instructors give feedback to help students learn or achieve beyond what they might have without educator guidance (Clingerman & Bernard, 2004). Through such instructor-initiated experiences, students can undergo states of disequilibrium (Piaget, 1954) in which they are challenged to rethink an assignment, assumption, or course of action.

The following example illustrates how an email assignment might be used to stimulate knowledge construction about counseling diverse populations in a school counselor education course. First, students might be asked to reflect on the following scenario, to think about how they might work with this young woman, and to email their reflections to the course instructor:

*A 16-year-old female high school student is dating a male classmate behind her parents' backs. The reason for this is that she is a first-generation student from India and her parents forbid her to date; she has already been promised in marriage. The young woman's friends help her hide the relationship from her parents, as they believe her parents are horrible for not letting her date and for arranging her marriage. However, the young woman's parents find out and threaten that if she does not end the relationship, she will be sent back to India. With her friends' encouragement, the young woman decides to continue the relationship but tries harder to hide it. Once again her parents find out and follow through on their threat. The young woman finishes her junior year of high school in India. She is allowed to return for her senior year, but she is escorted to and from school, and she is not allowed to spend time with her former friends. The young woman is unhappy and seeks guidance from the school counselor.*

Many of the student reflections look similar to the following:

*I find this very challenging. I would sever my relationship with my parents before I would allow something like this to happen. I think the parents are being unrealistic. How can they expect their child to remain true to their traditional culture when they rear her in a different country? It is unfair to their daughter. She should be true to herself. Arranged marriages are archaic. If she wants to date her current boyfriend, she should do so. That is what I would do. I would have a conversation with my parents and tell them that I love them, but I do not share their belief system. They would have to learn how to deal with that. I would support this young woman and encourage her to be true to herself. If she was open to it, I would be willing to meet with both the young woman and her parents and to educate her parents if necessary.*

The instructor might respond to the student via email with the following:

*Clearly this scenario has touched a nerve for you. Can you think about what caused such a strong reaction? How do your values differ from those of this young woman and her parents? How did your values develop? Does reflecting on your values give you any new insights into this scenario?*

The student might email the following response:

*In thinking about my values, I realize that many of them were influenced by my family and how I was reared. My traditions are so different from this young woman's and her parents. I was taught to stand up for myself and for what I believe in, even if it means going against authority (including my parents). That may not be the case for this student. If she embraces the traditional values of her parents, it probably would not be okay for her to go against her parents. So she is probably very confused and quite torn. I was reacting from my values and I wanted her to react like I would. I need to think more about her values and culture. This also makes me think about our class discussion on empathy. I think I need to think about how she is experiencing this situation given her upbringing and experience.*

Instructor prompts during such email interactions can encourage students' self-reflection, appreciation of multiple perspectives, and construction of new knowledge and meaning. While such email assignments/exchanges may be time consuming for the instructor, they provide an opportunity for continued knowledge construction outside the classroom. Using them two to three times during a semester can provide meaningful reflective opportunities.

## Blogs and Discussion Boards

As technology quickly morphs and advances, opportunities arise for counselor educators to think creatively about how to appropriately use newer applications in their instruction. Several tools—for instance, blogs, wikis, and student response systems—naturally lend themselves to constructivist instruction. Blogs (also known as weblogs and edublogs) are more and more frequently being used in instruction. Blogs are essentially public online journals. In blogs, individuals reflect on such matters as their lives or their daily happenings, literature they love, music that inspires them, or activities they pursue. Blogs can be created so that others can only view them, or they can be created to stimulate interaction and dialogue, for instance, in the form of comments (feedback) from whoever reads the blog. Many CMSs include blog capabilities. For educators who are not using a CMS, free shareware exists to create blogs (e.g., Google's Blogger, www.blogger.com). One cautionary note is in order. To protect students' and clients' privacy, counselor educators must be careful when using public blogging technology. To meet ethical guidelines (ACA, 2005; NBCC, 2005), it is important that instructors choose public technology that is only accessible to those invited to participate in the blog.

At this point it should be noted that blogs and discussion boards are very similar in nature. Both provide places to share thoughts on a topic as well as space for comments. However, easy-to-navigate public blogging software is more prevalent than software for discussion boards. For faculty who lack access to a CMS, blogging software may prove more user-friendly. Therefore, we will focus on blogs, with the understanding that discussion boards can be used in a similar fashion.

In using blogs in counselor education programs, instructors can provide prompts to stimulate online discussions, create an electronic space where students can generate their own probes and discussions, or offer some combination of the two options. The types of problems, probes, and questions that counselor educators pose will dictate the depth of students' inquiries (Brooks & Brooks, 1993). It is therefore important to choose prompts intentionally.

Instructors should decide on how to use a blog based on the nature of the course being taught. For skills-oriented courses, the instructor might use probes that promote connections among classmates and reflections about personal skill development. In theory-based courses, the teacher can provide prompts that lead to personal reflection about and application of key concepts.

In the following paragraph is an example of a blog prompt used to stimulate reflection and co-construction of meaning about diversity in a counselor education course. In responding to such a prompt, students first write about their own perspectives. Then, as they read their classmates' responses, many make new connections with their classmates and often rethink what they have written. At that point they either write about this co-construction of knowledge in the blog or discuss it in class.

For instance, the instructor might ask students to respond to the prompt, "What is your ethnicity?" A student might respond, "Although I am American and my ancestors were Italian, German, Norwegian, and English, I identify as White." The instructor would ask in the next prompt, "How do you define your culture?" Students might in turn respond with "Culture may mean many things. I identify with many cultures that make me who I am. They combine to create the lens through which I process information and respond to others: I am White, female, heterosexual, Catholic, an educator, Gen X." Finally, the instructor might offer the following prompt: "How are you privileged? Think about privilege along many different lines including but not limited to race/ethnicity, socioeconomic status, and gender." And/or "Are you, or have you ever been oppressed? If so, how?" And students would respond. As with the guided email activities previously discussed, such an assignment may be time intensive for the instructor, but it provides a valuable constructivist learning environment for the student. It is important to note that, as with a classroom-based discussion, students are responding to *each other* in the blog, thereby co-constructing meaning. It is important for the instructor to check in and add additional perspectives when needed, but the instructor does not need to respond to every student in detail. Furthermore, a blog assignment can be used intermittently throughout a semester to reinforce and supplement class activities and assignments.

## Course Management Systems

CMSs (e.g., at the time of this writing, Blackboard, Moodle) are used to support learning and to deliver courses online. Many systems offer tools such as vehicles for email, asynchronous and synchronous (real-time) discussion boards, electronic journals (diaries), chat rooms, and blogs. In addition, CMSs provide places for educators to deliver content (e.g., assignments, lectures), places for students to upload assignments, and the means for instructors to post grades and for departments to collect and assess student outcome data.

CMSs serve as the link between traditional and nontraditional instructional tools. The educational advantage for both synchronous (information transmitted in real time) and asynchronous (delay in transmission) courses is described by Almala (2006). In his words, the interactive dimensions of CMSs afford students the opportunity to "use their prior knowledge and the knowledge of their peers and instructor to enrich the class discourse and negotiation process and, therefore, find the appropriate solutions to the problem on hand" (p. 35). CMSs provide vast opportunities for collaborative and cooperative interaction, consistent with constructivist teaching practices (Brooks & Brooks, 1993). In addition to providing a place for organizing course materials online, most CMSs allow for uploading articles and PowerPoint presentations and house a plethora of other tools, including email, blogs, discussion boards, and journals all in one place. See our previous discussion of such tools for examples of how they may be used to aid students in constructing their learning.

## Wikis

A wiki is a website that allows anyone who visits the site to edit or contribute input or comments. (Wikipedia is an example of a wiki.) A wiki is a collaborative knowledge-building tool, one that facilitates the social construction of knowledge in the classroom (Anson & Miller-Cochran, 2009). Caverly and Ward (2008) further explain that "wikis allow a group to collaboratively construct a document online by subscribing and then editing multimedia using simple text editors" (p. 26). They emphasize that wikis encourage community knowledge construction, as many individuals are actively involved in the process of reading and editing text. Thus, a wiki can be seen as a collaborative learning environment where knowledge is socially constructed (Vygotsky, 1978). Students can create a wiki by going to any number of host sites (e.g., PBworks, http://pbworks.com;

Wetpaint, www.wetpaint.com). Once they sign up for their wiki, they can work to write papers collectively, to research topics, to develop presentations, or even to study for exams.

Counselor educators can also create a course wiki. For example, a counseling case study may be housed in a wiki. Students may then discuss and analyze the case, ultimately co-constructing a counseling plan. The instructor can provide feedback while the students are engaged in the process of negotiating their counseling plan, which illustrates the opportunities that wikis provide for scaffolding and further co-construction of knowledge (Vygotsky, 1978).

## Student Response Systems

Student response systems (also referred to as classroom response systems or "clickers") allow faculty to gather immediate data from students participating in a class. In such a process, all students in the course are given a handheld keypad (like a remote control). The instructor poses a multiple-choice or true/false question, and students touch the appropriate response on the keypad. Students and instructor receive immediate statistical data (usually in a projected chart), which can then be used to generate a discussion (Herreid, 2006; Skinner, 2009). Responses are anonymous, which reduces peer influence and increases the likelihood of collecting accurate responses (Herreid, 2006). Responses can be saved so that the data can be used in future discussions.

Student response systems have many uses. They particularly help instructors find out what students know prior to a discussion or course reading, to gauge where students are in terms of their learning, and to discover whether students have actually done the reading or assignments. All of this data provides clues for the type of scaffolding (Vygotsky, 1978) that students need for constructing new learning. Student response systems can also be used to test assumptions (Herreid, 2006), making such systems ideal aids for exploring controversial or delicate topics. For example, we (Buono and Uellendahl) have used a response system to poll a group of school counseling students on their estimations about equal access to honors and Advanced Placement classes for high school students by race and ethnicity. Once polled, we share the actual data about enrollment by race and ethnicity. Because responses are anonymous, students

are more likely to be forthright and honest about their answers, which can lead to more meaningful and fruitful discussions, which would certainly be advantageous in the co-construction of knowledge.

# TECHNOLOGY IN CONSTRUCTIVIST SUPERVISION

Supervision also can benefit from technology. In fact, in many cases, supervisors have used various forms of technology since the 1940s. The discussion that follows suggests ways to use technology while supervising, for skill building, and for teaching supervision.

The same technology that is used for supervising counselors can be used to augment the *teaching* of supervision (discussed more fully in Chapter 15). This is especially true for doctoral programs, in which the emphasis is on advanced training in supervision. The focal points of the technology, then, are the supervisor-in-training, to provide remote supervision-of-supervision, and to influence the process of the supervision-of-supervision.

For the purposes of this chapter, we organize the use of technology in supervision practice into three types:

- Face-to-face supervision using technology
- Remote supervision (cyber-supervision or e-supervision)
- Live supervision

## Face-to-Face Supervision

Face-to-face supervision is perhaps the most common form of clinical supervision. It can be augmented with technology that gleans clinical data from audio or video recordings of actual counseling sessions. Using the methods described next, the supervisor and the supervisee analyze, quantify, and/or qualify this recorded data while in face-to-face supervision in order to help supervisees make meaning of their experiences with clients and decide how to proceed with counseling clients.

### Audio Recordings

In the 1940s, audiotape was first used to record clinical sessions so that the supervisee could review the recordings at a later time with the supervisor (Bernard & Goodyear, 2009). Such recording devices allowed both the student and the supervisor to gain insight into session choices with minimal effects on the counseling process. This method was an advance over traditional self-report supervision, but was limited by its consisting of only sound, which was sometimes of poor quality.

## Video Recordings

Beginning in the 1960s, with the invention of video recording devices (Huhra, Yamokoski-Maynhart, & Prieto, 2008), the supervision process was enhanced by the addition of visual images of the counselor and client(s). Soon after the development of the videotape, research began comparing the differences between supervision using audio versus video recording devices. A few programs still utilize analog technology (VCRs), but that technology is rapidly becoming obsolete and being replaced by digital technology (DVDs). However, both DVD and VCR technology have the limitation of not allowing for easy cueing of specific segments.

## Digital Analysis Software

Digital analysis software overcomes the limitation of not being able to easily access and cue specific segments that one might want to watch during supervision. Products such as the Landro Play Analyzer as well as Noldus Observer and Theme software offer ways to easily access and cue specific segments of counseling sessions.

The Landro Play Analyzer (LPA; www.landro.com) was initially intended to analyze football plays. When programmed for clinical training, supervisees can break down their recorded sessions by inserting "clipmarks" at particular points in the recording, allowing them to identify the type of response they have made, the theoretical basis for the response, and their thoughts about response effectiveness. The instructor can enter categories into a database that are directly related to course learning objectives (e.g., eye contact, paraphrasing, reflecting feelings, skills related to particular theories). After reviewing the session, the student then uses the categories to code the specific skill or theory being demonstrated in

a segment of the recorded session. Once the responses are coded, they may be easily searched and retrieved with the touch of a button. Supervisors thus have easy and immediate access to any coded clipmarks and can tailor individual and group supervision sessions to a specific supervisee's goals and needs. This technology can complement, or replace, a typed, annotated transcript.

Here is an example of using the Landro technology for supervising a male supervisee who worked with a female client. During the counseling session, the client discussed her thoughts about feeling inadequate as a mother and employee. The supervisee attempted to reflect the client's feelings, but was having difficulty articulating what these feelings might be. The supervisee gave responses such as "You feel that you are not doing a good job as a mother and worker."

Later, in face-to-face supervision, before showing the Landro video clips, the supervisor asked the supervisee to describe what he understood about the client's history and what some of his clinical hypotheses might be about the client (Neufeldt, 1997). The supervisee said to the supervisor, "I want to know if what I was doing in the session was right. I also want to know how I can get the client to express her feelings more. I feel that the sessions are just going OK. I feel as if I can be doing better." In response, the supervisor then skillfully inquired about the counselor's intentions or feelings as they jointly viewed and processed the Landro video clips. For example, the supervisor asked, "What were you feeling and thinking in this part of the session?" Such inquiries led to understandings of parallel process (Friedlander, Siegel, & Brenock, 1989), in this case, the dynamics of the counseling session (inadequacy and difficulty expressing feelings) that were played out in the supervision session.

Inquiries like the supervisor's in response to the Landro video clips may lead to the type of reflection necessary to enhance both a counselor's personal and professional development. In this example, the supervisee learned to better express his own feelings in the moment and, later, to more accurately reflect the feelings that his client was experiencing during the session. The supervisee then used his insight to more clearly articulate the hypotheses he had about the client. He also thoughtfully reflected on his discovery experience during the supervision session and, as a result, increased his understanding of his own interpersonal and counseling capacities.

A second type of digital analysis software is Noldus technology (www.noldus.com). Noldus has been designed to study a wide range of human behavior. First, behavior is recorded on video, and afterward it is analyzed with the company's Observer and Theme software. This software allows for the collection, analysis, and presentation of observational data and has been used by some programs for clinical training and supervision.

# Remote Supervision

A second type of supervision that may be augmented by technology is remote supervision. Technology allows for enhanced communication across time and distance. Remote supervision can be used as either the means of supervision itself or to supplement supervision. It can occur in two ways. One strategy uses the synchronous communication of real-time chats, with or without video connections via webcams (e.g., Skype, live chats in online course management software). The other strategy uses asynchronous communication, or interactions that are delayed in time, such as bulletin board discussions or email. Chapman (2008) provides an overview of the literature for the effective use of these technologies in supervision and found some support for using these modalities to enhance supervision. Three specific means of remote supervision, namely email, CMSs, and Skype, are discussed below.

## Email

Email is asynchronous. It is a modality that can be used to supplement traditional face-to-face supervision. Supervisors and supervisees email their thoughts and questions between the regularly scheduled face-to-face supervision sessions. Supervisees have reported positively on the increased level of support that they have felt from such communications (Graf & Stebnicki, 2002; Stebnicki & Glover, 2001).

A modification of the Interpersonal Process Recall (IPR; Kagan, 1983) supervision activity offers an example of how reflectivity can be encouraged using email in supervision. What follows are supervisor leads that can be used during the IPR process and sent to supervisees via email.

*Tom –*

*I appreciate the work that you have been doing to be more aware of internal processes that are influencing your work with clients. I'd like you to review a segment of your last session. Watch the session until you come to a segment that you feel represents a critical or important area that was not addressed in the session. Stop the tape. Now briefly describe this moment in a paragraph and then respond to the following prompts:*

1. *What would you have liked to have said to your client at this moment?*

2. *What feelings or thoughts were present related to your role as a counselor?*

3. *What personal agenda may be influencing your response to this client in the moment?*

*Please send me your responses, and I will react with additional prompts to get you to try to go deeper with your understanding of yourself and explore how you might use this awareness to create meaning and enhance your therapeutic plans for this client.*

This modified IPR is an excellent way for supervisees to construct their own meaning from self-reflection. The email then becomes an interactive reflective journal where knowledge is co-constructed with the supervisee and can result in clinical wisdom. These insights can be further discussed at the next face-to-face supervision session.

## Course Management Systems

A second vehicle for conducting remote supervision lies in the CMSs that were mentioned earlier. Trolley and Silliker (2005) discuss how WebCT (now merged with Blackboard) can be incorporated into the supervision of counseling interns. Features of CMSs that can enhance the supervision process include postings to bulletin boards, live chats, suggested supervision topics and relevant readings, and postings of supervision journals.

There are both strengths and some limitations to this technology. For example, some strengths lie in the organization of supervisees' journals and the stimulation of more open group discussions. A limitation of CMSs is that the interaction is one-dimensional, where the supervisor is not aware of the supervisee's feelings and/or nonverbal behaviors.

## Skype (Voice over Internet Protocol)

Finally, remote supervision can actually be provided using Skype (www.skype.com), a freeware tool that provides visual and aural communication between two computers (Woo, 2006). With this program, users can talk, instant message, or make video calls for free. The unique feature of Skype is the ability to utilize webcams to provide remote supervision that is closely akin to face-to-face supervision. Users go to the Skype website, sign up for an account, and download the software to their computer. Using this computer program, a webcam, and the users' computers, the supervisor can video call one supervisee for individual supervision or set up a contact list to have a video conference call with a group of supervisees for group supervision. Preliminary results from a study of graduate students taking an online class suggest that this program is an "effective tool to build synchronous interaction and to provide just-in-time clarification and information" (Pan & Sullivan, 2005, Major Results and Discussion, para. 1).

# Live Supervision

The third form of supervision, live supervision, consists of the supervisor viewing and/or interacting with the supervisee while the session is actually occurring. Its intent is to bring the here-and-now into the counselor's experience and to help her or him take such in-the-moment awareness and apply it to counseling.

It should be noted that technology doesn't automatically solve the problem of supervisors overly directing the session in a positivistic, authoritarian way. Such supervisors are likely to give advice and make interpretations for the supervisee. The supervisee becomes "the puppet" who

gives voice to these clinical pseudo-commands. However, when live supervision is done in a constructivist fashion, the supervisor provides gentle and purposeful probes for counselors to be aware of their own covert thoughts and feelings, as well as to be aware of the clients' thoughts and feelings (Cashwell, 1994). So regardless of the technology, the supervisor must engage the supervisee in discovery, as Chapters 15 and 16 iterate.

Technology for live supervision can be less intrusive than having the supervisor in the room with the counselor and client. Technology such as a telephone, an in-room computer, or an earbud allows the supervisee counselor to hear the supervisor's instructions while the supervisor is watching the session through a window with sound enhancement or via live-feed video. In each of these live modalities, the supervisor can inject immediate feedback and instruction that the supervisee can also use immediately to improve her or his thought processes, clinical behavior, and clinical awareness. The three modalities will be touched on next.

## Telephone

The telephone has been used in several ways for live clinical supervision (Bernard & Goodyear, 2009; Wetchler, Trepper, McCollum, & Nelson, 1993). When using the telephone for live supervision, the supervisor phones in to a session in order to provide supervisees with feedback in the moment.

## Bug in the Ear

This technology offers supervisors the opportunity to provide live nonintrusive feedback to a supervisee who is wearing a small headphone in her or his ear, called an earbud (Goodman, Brady, Duffy, Scott, & Pollard, 2008). Supervisors can, as a result, offer positive and constructive feedback to supervisees with minimal disruption to the counseling session (Bernard & Goodyear, 2009).

## In-Room Computers—Bug in the Eye

The "bug in the eye" strategy uses a computer system through which supervisors deliver immediate feedback. Counselors read the feedback from a computer screen that is over the shoulder of the client (Klitzke & Lombardo, 1991). Miller, Miller, and Evans (2002) found that this technology improved counseling effectiveness due to students receiving immediate feedback from supervisors and being able to correct mistakes.

## Illustration of Technology-Enhanced Live Supervision

An example may help to illustrate the benefits of technology-enhanced live supervision. Imagine a group counseling practicum where the student supervisee, Ann, wants some assistance. She feels very skilled at listening to and managing the content of the group practicum sessions. However, she finds it very difficult to move the group to deeper levels of sharing and disclosure. In supervision, she reports feeling happy that the group is interacting and yet, at the same time, is frustrated by the superficial nature of their interactions. She has difficulty surfacing her feelings in the moment. Thus she has not been able to express these feelings to the group. Together, Ann and her supervisor agree that they will utilize a "bug" to raise her awareness of her feelings during the next session. The supervisor agrees to help prompt Ann to attend and give voice to her feelings. In fact, Ann even rehearses in supervision what she might say to the group in response to this awareness, such as, "In this moment, I am aware that I feel happy with your interactions, but at the same time I am aware that I am feeling somewhat frustrated by the lack of depth in your sharing. Let's stop and talk about what prevents you all from going deeper with each other."

During the next group counseling session, Ann puts the earbud in her ear. In the first few minutes of the session, the supervisor waits for a quiet group moment and then says, "Ann, remember to slow down and be aware of your feelings." As the group progresses, the supervisor notes the pattern in the group's interactions. The supervisor turns on the microphone and says softly, "Feelings." With that gentle prompt, Ann is reminded to utilize her feelings in the moment. Given that heightened awareness, Ann says to the group, "I am aware that your conversations always seem to stay at surface level, I feel concerned that your level of trust has not risen to a point where you all feel safe with each other." Ann's comments succeed in

stimulating the group's discussion about their level of trust. Further, without prompting from the supervisor, Ann recognizes that her current feelings and the group's feelings seem to be parallel. She says, "We seem to feel energized by this discussion, and I sense that there are feelings of relief that we have gotten some things out in the open." Seeing this growth, the supervisor says to Ann, "Take a moment to attend to your growth."

As a result of her success, Ann is eager for supervision. She acknowledges that she succeeded in attending to feelings during the group counseling session. Her growth was facilitated by the supervisor's three interventions: (1) a pre-group reminder, (2) a here-and-now prompt, and (3) an acknowledgment of growth. It is easy to see how the live supervision facilitated by the "bug" technology served as a vehicle to enhance the constructivist supervision experience and thus counselor growth.

## Advantages of Applying Technology to Supervision

Now that the different technology types have been introduced, the main question to be further addressed is: How can this technology be used to enhance the supervision process? It can do so in terms of the principles that Neufeldt (1997) describes for constructivist supervision: "[1] Supervision changes in each context; . . . [2] knowledge is co-constructed with the supervisee; . . . [3] knowledge is based on personal and professional experience; . . . [4] the test of knowledge is pragmatic, and the result is clinical wisdom" (p. 196–200). Using Neufeldt's terms, technology can now be considered part of the context of supervision. Technology can facilitate the "knowing" of the experience. In particular, it can enhance the ability of supervisor and supervisee to co-construct meaning.

Technology especially allows the clinical experience to be brought into the supervisory session. For example, video recordings are commonly reviewed during individual and group supervision sessions. Video recordings allow moment-by-moment analysis, clinical hypothesis building, intervention planning, and counselor self-reflection and self-evaluation to emerge from the actual events of the session's clinical data. Supervisor and supervisee then make sense of the data as the joint personal and professional experiences are shared in the moment. Thus, technology, when used appropriately, can substantially enhance the supervision process.

Figure 24.1 highlights the constructivist supervisory experience and its interface with technology. The center of the figure represents the core of the constructivist supervisory experience that is guided by Neufeldt's (1997) key principles. The supervisor and supervisee choose the appropriate method of supervision (e.g., live, face-to-face, remote) and the type of technology to enhance the constructivist supervisory experience. It is important to note that this influence is bidirectional: Technology enhances supervision, and supervision goals dictate the technology that is used.

Technology can help counselor educators be the *midwife teachers* that Belenky, Clinchy, Goldberger, and Tarule (1986) describe. Extending that idea, midwife supervisors facilitate the birth of ideas and support the counselor's growth and development throughout the learning process. Counselor educators and supervisors then become partners in the experience and, together with the supervisee, use technology to facilitate this collaborative birthing process.

**FIGURE 24.1**  Constructivist Supervision and the Technology Interface

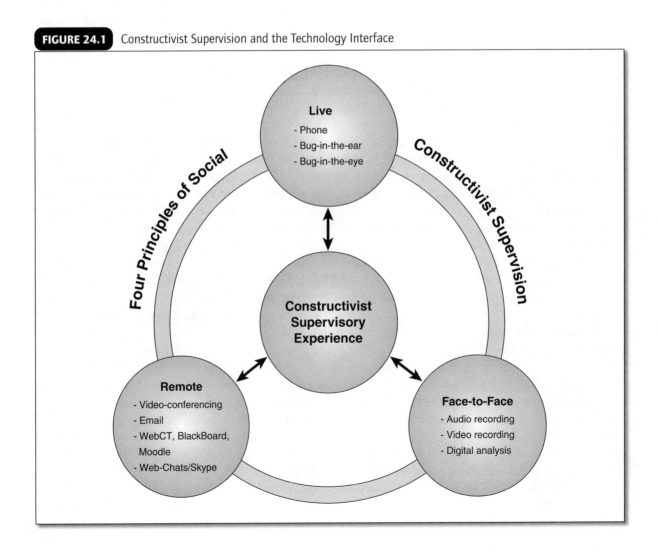

# FURTHER THOUGHTS ON APPLYING TECHNOLOGY TO COUNSELOR EDUCATION AND SUPERVISION

A number of access and ethical considerations need to be considered when applying technology to counselor education and supervision.

## Including All Students

When deciding whether to use technology to enhance learning (be it for instructional or supervision purposes), counselor educators and supervisors must keep in mind their students' access to technology and abilities with different forms of technology. While technology may provide greater inclusion of those students who are generally more introverted, there are others who may be negatively impacted without careful attention. In particular, economically disadvantaged students and students with disabilities may have greater difficulties in terms of access and abilities. Even at the graduate level, some disadvantaged students do not have access to home computers or Internet providers; it is imperative that counselor educators ensure that all students have access to technology prior to requiring its use (Lewis et al., 2000). Technology can be made available, if necessary, in the institution's library or via departmental computers. Further, at times technology poses challenges for students with disabilities. Educators have a legal obligation to do their best to accommodate students with disabilities in their classrooms and on their campuses. Questions about how to best accommodate students with disabilities should be directed to a campus's office for students with disabilities.

## Ethical Considerations

According to Vaccaro and Lambie (2007), there are currently no specific guidelines for computer-based supervision or instruction, despite there being guidelines for computer-based counseling itself (ACA, 2005; NBCC, 2005). Vaccaro and Lambie encourage counselor education programs to establish their own guidelines for the use of technology by instructors and supervisors. The ethical guidelines provided by ACA and NBCC regarding technology and counseling could conceivably be generalized to instruction and supervision. In particular, those guidelines could direct informed consent and legal decisions with regard to the use of technology in supervision and instruction (Watson, 2003).

For instance, confidentiality is a major concern in informed consent guidelines (ACA, 2005; NBCC, 2005). In that regard, one of the challenges with Internet-based instruction and supervision is that, even with encryption software, confidentiality cannot be guaranteed (Wilczenski & Coomey, 2006). When using many of the web-based technologies previously described, students (and in supervision cases, their counselees) must be informed about the requirement to maintain confidentiality. They must especially make clients aware of anyone who may have authorized or unauthorized access to electronic transmissions (e.g., technicians). And then they must give clients the option to refuse technology-enhanced supervision.

## Underlying Framework

It is also important that counselor educators not get so distracted by technological widgets that they fail to implement an underlying model of clinical supervision, a model that provides a framework for the supervision process and interactions. The same caveat holds true for classroom instruction. A theoretical orientation toward teaching and supervision must guide the decisions on the appropriate use of technology. The supervision and instruction processes and goals need to drive the technology that is used, rather than the technology dictating the supervision or teaching process. Also, to be effective, the technology used for clinical training, supervision, and instruction needs to be easy to use and manage (Salandro, personal communication, October 14, 2002) and not be intrusive to the supervision process. Care should also be given to training incoming counseling students about the various technologies that will be used during the course of their education and beyond. This support can serve to reduce their anxiety at a time when such feelings may already be heightened.

# CONCLUSION

Technology can enhance constructivist teaching and supervision, providing for greater immediacy and dialogue. The technology revolution is only limited by current methods and by their proper use. But this is not a static enterprise. As was mentioned in the beginning of this chapter, the risk of writing a chapter on current technologies is that, by the time the text is published, the information may be outdated. Because of the rapid changes in technology, readers would be best served by remaining open to emerging technologies and their possibilities for enhancing student learning, rather than seeing the list of technologies mentioned here as exhaustive or static (Brooks & Brooks, 1993).

# REFERENCES

Almala, A. H. (2006). Applying the principles of constructivism to a quality e-learning environment. *Distance Learning, 3*(1), 33–40.

American Counseling Association. (2005). *ACA code of ethics.* Alexandria, VA: Author. Retrieved May 4, 2009, from http://www.counseling.org/Resources/CodeOfEthics/TP/Home/CT2.aspx

Anson, C. M., & Miller-Cochran, S. K. (2009). Contrails of learning: Using new technologies for vertical knowledge-building. *Computers and Composition, 26,* 38–48.

Belenky, M. F., Clinchy, B. M., Goldberger, N. R., & Tarule, J. M. (1986). *Women's ways of knowing: The development of self, voice, and mind.* New York: Basic Books.

Bernard, J. M., & Goodyear, R. K. (2009). *Fundamentals of clinical supervision.* Upper Saddle River, NJ: Pearson Education.

Berry, T., Srebalus, D. J., Cromer, P. W., & Takacs, J. (2003). Counselor trainee technology use skills, learning styles, and preferred modes of instruction. *Journal of Technology in Counseling, 3*(1). Retrieved August 3, 2010, from http://jtc.colstate.edu/vol3_1/Takacs/Takacs.htm

Brooks, J. G., & Brooks, M. G. (1993). *In search of understanding: A case for constructivist classrooms.* Alexandria, VA: Association for Supervision and Curriculum Development.

Cashwell, C. S. (1994). Interpersonal process recall. Greensboro, NC: ERIC Clearinghouse on Counseling and Student Services. (ERIC Document Reproduction Service No. 372342)

Caverly, D. C., & Ward, A. (2008). Techtalk: Wikis and collaborative knowledge construction. *Journal of Developmental Education, 32*(2), 36–37.

Chapman, R. A. (2008). Cybersupervision of entry level practicum supervisees: The effect on acquisition of counselor competence and confidence. *Journal of Technology in Counseling, 5*(1). Retrieved August 3, 2010, from http://jtc.colstate.edu/Vol5_1/Chapman.htm

Clark, J. (2008). PowerPoint and pedagogy: Maintaining student interest in university lectures. *College Teaching, 56*(1), 39–45.

Clingerman, T. L., & Bernard, J. M. (2004). An investigation of the use of e-mail as a supplemental modality for clinical supervision. *Counselor Education & Supervision, 44,* 82–95.

Ernest, P. (1995). The one and the many. In L. P. Steffe & J. Gale (Eds.), *Constructivism in education* (pp. 459–486). Hillsdale, NJ: Lawrence Erlbaum.

Friedlander, M. L., Siegel, S. M., & Brenock, K. (1989). Parallel process in counseling and supervision: A case study. *Journal of Counseling Psychology, 36,* 148–157.

Gergen, K. J. (1985). The social constructionist movement in modern psychology. *American Psychologist, 40,* 266–275.

Goodman, J. I., Brady, M. P., Duffy, M. L., Scott, J., & Pollard, N. E. (2008). The effects of "bug-in-ear" supervision on special education teachers' delivery of learn units. *Focus on Autism and Other Developmental Disabilities, 23,* 207–216.

Graf, N. M., & Stebnicki, M. A. (2002). Using email for clinical supervision in practicum: A qualitative analysis. *Journal of Rehabilitation, 68,* 41–49.

Hayes, B. G. (2008). Counselor education: Integration of teaching strategies. *Journal of Technology in Counseling, 5*(1). Retrieved August 3, 2010, from http://jtc.colstate.edu/Vol5_1/Hayes.htm

Hayes, B. G., Taub, G. E., Robinson, E. H., III, & Sivo, S. A. (2003). An empirical investigation of the efficacy of multimedia instruction in counseling skill development. *Counselor Education and Supervision, 42,* 177–188.

Herreid, C. F. (2006). "Clicker" cases: Introducing case study teaching into large classrooms. *Journal of College Science and Teaching, 36*(2), 43–47.

Honebein, P. C. (1996). Seven goals for the design of constructivist learning environments. In B. G. Wilson (Ed.), *Constructivist learning environments* (pp. 11–24). Englewood Cliffs, NJ: Educational Technology Publications.

Huhra, R. L., Yamokoski-Maynhart, C. A., & Prieto, L. R. (2008). Reviewing videotape in supervision: A developmental approach. *Journal of Counseling and Development, 86,* 412–418.

Jonassen, D. (1991). Objectivism versus constructivism. Do we need a new paradigm? *Educational Technology Research and Development, 39*(3), 5–14.

Kagan, N. (1983). Classroom to client: Issues in supervision. *The Counseling Psychologist, 11,* 69–72.

Karper, C. M., Robinson, E. H., III, & Casado, M. (2005). Computer assisted instruction and academic achievement in counselor education. *Journal of Technology in Counseling, 4*(1). Retrieved August 3, 2010, from http://jtc.colstate.edu/Vol4_1/Karper/Karper.htm

Klitzke, M. J., & Lombardo, T. W. (1991). A "bug-in-the-eye" can be better than a "bug-in-the-ear": A teleprompter technique for on-line therapy skills training. *Behavior Modification, 15,* 113–117.

Layne, C. M., & Hohenshil, T. H. (2005). High tech counseling: Revisited. *Journal of Counseling and Development, 83,* 222–226.

Lewis, J., Coursol, D., Khan, L., & Wilson, A. (2000). *Life in a dot.com world: Preparing counselors to work with technology.* (ERIC Documentation Reproduction Service No. ED449410)

Lovell, C., & McAuliffe, G. J. (1997). Principles of constructivist training and education. In T. L. Sexton & B. L. Griffin (Eds.), *Constructivist thinking in counseling practice, research and training* (pp. 211–227). New York: Teachers College Press.

Miller, K. L., Miller, S. M., & Evans, W. J. (2002). Computer-assisted live supervision in college counseling centers. *Journal of College Counseling, 5,* 187–192.

Myers, J. E., & Gibson, D. M. (1999). *Technology competence of counselor educators.* Greensboro, NC: ERIC Clearinghouse on Counseling and Student Services. (ERIC Documentation Reproduction Service No. ED435947)

National Board for Certified Counselors. (2005). *Code of ethics.* Retrieved August 3, 2010, from http://www.nbcc.org/AssetManagerFiles/ethics/nbcc-codeofethics.pdf

Neufeldt, S. A. (1997). A social constructivist approach to counseling supervision. In T. L. Sexton and B. L. Griffin (Eds.), *Constructivist thinking in counseling practice, research, and training* (pp. 191–210). New York: Teachers College Press.

Pan, C., & Sullivan, M. (2005). Promoting synchronous interaction in an elearning environment. *T.H.E Journal, 33*(2). Retrieved August 3, 2010, from http://thejournal.com/articles/2005/09/01/promoting-synchronous-interaction-in-an—elearning-environment.aspx

Parker, R. E., Bianchi, A., & Cheah, T. Y. (2008). Perceptions of instructional technology: Factors of influence and anticipated consequences. *Educational Technology and Society, 11,* 274–293.

Piaget, J. (1954). *The construction of reality in the child.* New York: Basic Books.

Quinn, A. C., Hohenshil, T., & Fortune, J. (2002). Utilization of technology in CACREP approved counselor education programs. *Journal of Technology in Counseling, 2*(2). Retrieved August 3, 2010, from http://jtc.colstate.edu/Vol2_2/Quinn/Quinn.htm

Skinner, S. (2009). On clickers, questions, and learning. *Journal of College and Science Teaching, 38*(4), 20–23.

Stebnicki, M. A., & Glover, N. M. (2001). E-supervision as a complementary approach to traditional face to face clinical supervision in rehabilitation counseling: Problems and solutions. *Rehabilitation Education, 15,* 295–304.

Trolley, B., & Silliker, A. (2005). The use of WebCT in the supervision of counseling interns. *Journal of Technology in Counseling, 4*(1). Retrieved August 3, 2010, from http://jtc.colstate.edu/Vol4_1/Trolley/Trolley.htm

Vaccaro, N., & Lambie, G. W. (2007). Counselor-based counselor-in-training supervision: Ethical and practical implications for counselor educators and supervisors. *Counselor Education and Supervision, 47*(1), 46–57.

Vygotsky, L. S. (1978). *Mind in society: The development of higher psychological processes.* Cambridge, MA: Harvard University Press.

Wang, Q., Teo, T., & Woo, H. L. (2009). An integrated framework for designing web-based constructivist learning environments. *International Journal of Instructional Media, 36*(1), 81–91.

Watson, J. (2003). Computer-based supervision: Implementing computer technology into the delivery of counseling supervision. *Journal of Technology in Counseling, 3*(1). Retrieved August 3, 2010, from http://jtc.colstate.edu/Vol3_1/Watson/Watson.htm

Wetchler, J. L., Trepper, T. S., McCollum, E. E., & Nelson, T. S. (1993). Videotape supervision via long-distance telephone. *American Journal of Family Therapy, 21,* 242–247.

Wilczenski, F. L., & Coomey, S. M. (2006). Cyber-communication: Finding its place in school counseling practice, education, and professional development. *Professional School Counseling, 9,* 327–331.

Wilson, B., & Cole, P. (1991). A review of cognitive teaching models. *Educational Technology and Research Development, 39*(4), 47–64.

Woo, S. (2006, December 8). Professors and students ask colleges not to hang up on Skype. *The Chronicle of Higher Education.*

# 25

# Narrative/Postmodern Perspectives on Counselor Education

Kathie Crocket and Elmarie Kotzé

*The narrative metaphor proposes that persons live their lives by stories—that these stories are shaping of life, and that they have real, not imagined, effects—and that these stories provide the structure of life.*

White (1991, p. 28)

The metaphor of story, the central organizing idea in narrative counseling, has much to offer counselor education. This chapter describes an approach to counselor education that emphasizes the storying of professional identity as a central practice. While at first glance the metaphor of story is both everyday and accessible, the practices we describe here may take readers into unfamiliar theoretical and philosophical landscapes beyond the humanistic and structuralist understandings of personhood that tend to be taken for granted in the fields of counseling and counselor education. Therefore, we invite you, as a reader, to turn for a moment to the professional identity stories that you have available to you. For example, can you call to mind a previous experience when you traversed what may have been unfamiliar theoretical landscapes? What resources did you employ as you found your way? How might these past experiences be useful to you as, while reading this chapter, you meet with what this book's editors suggest is a paradigm-shifting approach to counselor education?

We ask these questions for both practical and theoretical reasons. We hope that your responses will support you in stitching together the fabric of your personal and professional experiences and the storylines of counselor education that we offer in this paradigm-shifting account. We also hope that, as you move between your experience and ours, you will generate new possibilities in the storying of your own practice as a counselor educator.

Story is at the heart of our particular narrative approach to counselor education at the University of Waikato. We will use our program as an illustration of the narrative practice of counselor education. At each phase of such a program, we work to make visible and to engage with the narratives or storylines into which and with which students have already woven their lives, storylines of personal identity, learning identity, and professional identity. We offer learning experiences that support students in stitching between and thus drawing together[1] two dimensions: (1) the storylines of their own lives and (2) the counseling practices that they learn, which emphasize narrative counseling practices (see Monk, Winslade, Crocket, & Epston, 1997; White, 2007), social constructionist notions, and poststructuralist ideas (see Burr, 2003). As a result of these experiences, we intend that students will graduate with richly textured professional identity stories. Those consist of stories of themselves as counselors, including accounts of what they value and how they enact these values. There is thus an ethical and epistemological resonance between the narrative counseling practice that we teach and the pedagogy that we employ in our teaching, that is, between the content and the process.

Our approach to counselor education calls on two traditions in particular: (1) poststructuralist/social constructionist theory, and (2) narrative counseling practice. In this chapter, we illustrate these ideas in action by drawing closely on our own teaching practices and situating them in theory. To repeat: Ours is a local and situated account. We hope that readers might stitch between the social constructionist account we offer and the storylines of their own local practice in counselor education.

## Social Constructionism and Discourse

To reiterate the discussion in Chapter 1 of this book, social constructionism suggests that people's lives—and thus the tasks of counselor education—are shaped by a range of cultural stories or discourses. Counselor education is shaped by such discourses as professionalism, individualism, competition, gender, consumerism, race, and class, to name a few. As working systems of knowledge, these discourses have effects on teachers' and students' lives and relationships. As Davies (1993) explains it, "Each person takes up the discourses through which they and others speak/write the world into existence *as if they were their own*" (p. 13, italics in original). People both shape and are shaped by discourses. This shaping happens through what Burr (2003) refers to as micro and macro versions of social constructionism. At the micro level, counselor educators offer in their teaching many opportunities for students to focus on everyday speaking/listening and writing/reading as colleagues, family members, counselors, and students. This everyday speaking and writing produces and reproduces macro discourses—gender, culture, class, education, economics, and so on. The teaching examples we offer in this chapter illustrate these complex ideas in action.

## Overview of the Chapter

Our illustrations of narrative approaches in counselor education begin with admission to our program. Through a small example we show how words about admissions in a letter (micro-constructionism) enact or disturb the power relations produced by and within discourses of education (macro-constructionism). Our next two examples (a group selection approach and group introductions) illustrate our emphasis on learning as a social and relational process. We go on to describe practices that invite students to engage in thoughtful storying of their learning identities, an experience that offers students meaningful skills toward storying their professional identities.

The chapter then returns to an emphasis on learning as a social activity, showing the scaffolded steps of teaching the particular reflecting responses known as *outsider witnessing* (White, 2007) and *compassionate witnessing* (Weingarten, 2003). The development of these reflecting responses enhances both practice skills and the storying of professional identity.

The chapter then connects again directly with the theories in which these practices are grounded, describing one aspect of how we take a storying approach to teaching "complex theory" for counseling. This complex theory also underpins our approaches to exploring cultural narratives and commitments to social justice, which is the next focus of this chapter.

Finally, we turn to supervision. We show some of the inquiry practices we use to prepare students to engage in supervision as a collaborative partnership. Before ending, we offer some cautions, noting the spirit of generosity that we believe these approaches to counselor education invoke. Readers should note that the narrative approaches to counselor education that we write about here include examples from both face-to-face and online teaching.

## Admission as a Two-Way Process

A small example from our early contact with applicants for our counselor education program illustrates how we attend to power relations shaped by educational discourses. As noted above, this example shows both micro- and macro-constructionism at work.

First, we send a letter with the following message to all prospective students, inviting them to participate in a day of group selection activities:

> The selection day offers an opportunity for you to meet some of the staff who teach in the counselor education program, to hear from some students who have been part of the program in recent years, and to meet other students who are applying for the program. We hope that the events of this day give you a chance to decide whether you will choose to work with us.

Taking a micro-constructionist orientation in the words we use—that is, saying "the events of this day give you a chance to decide whether you will choose . . ."—draws attention to a major discourse that shapes the admission process: By naming the possibility of a two-way, reciprocal process of selection, declare a position on use of power. Those at the center of institutions are powerfully positioned to determine who speaks and what they may say (Davies, 2000). Our step of suggesting a two-way selection makes overt, and disturbs, the power relation of the selection process within an academic institution.

This purposeful attention to language in the letter to applicants opens alternative positions within the discourses of education, competition, and selection. These discourses carry stories of privilege, access, success, and failure. Through our making overt the power relation of our selection processes, even in this nuanced way, applicants may experience themselves as also positioned to select, rather than to merely be selected. Through reflexively considering our positioning in the discourses of education and in the pedagogical practices it produces, we take care that the admissions process offers students possibilities for agentic responses.

A further example of relational practice in the student admission process is the following question on our application form: "What abilities would you most like us to appreciate about you in relation to your present helping or counseling knowledge?" With this question, we invite applicants to position themselves in dialogue with us, and to consider us as an audience for the account they tell of themselves on their application. This practice is based in the social constructionist idea that identity is not the property of an individual. Rather, people actively construct identities in the social realm as they tell stories about themselves and others respond to those stories. This question on the application form signals something of our understanding that learning is a social and relational practice, an emphasis of contemporary learning theory (see, e.g., Rogoff, 2003).

## COURSES AND CURRICULUM: LEARNING AS A SOCIAL AND RELATIONAL ACTIVITY

The group format of our admissions process begins the first steps of building a learning community. Social constructionism conceptualizes such learning in a community. In other words, it is rooted in discursive, rather than individualistic, psychology. A discursive psychology suggests that the storylines that shape people's lives are themselves shaped by the stories of the wider culture, people's own lived experiences, and their families and communities. Thus, personhood is always relational: The stories that others tell about us and we tell about ourselves produce our lives and identities. Narrative counseling has used this relational idea to help clients recruit audiences who can contribute to the rich storying of clients' lives (White, 2007). So too in our teaching we develop learning communities. There students build collegial student-to-student relationships and act as audiences to each other.

On the first meeting of the first course, we start with experiential learning that enacts the idea that identity is relational. In a New Zealand context, openings and beginnings of meetings or classes often echo with formal Maori[2] greeting processes (see Anderson & Winslade, 1998), which also attend to relationship. As we begin the class, we ask students to stand and introduce themselves:

> Please introduce us to someone who has contributed to your being here today and becoming part of this course. For example, the person may be someone who is taking

care of things at home or at work so that you are free to be here; or the person may be someone who many years ago encouraged you to learn, in ways that have a further significance for you now; or it may be someone who offered you a crucial invitation, or acknowledged some particular skills you had shown, and thus contributed to your being here today.

In response, students tell stories of relationship. Our classroom becomes alive with connectedness to others and with moving stories. These stories center relationship and also relate something of the students' own lives and values.

We may hear, for example, stories of the caring words of an undergraduate teacher many years ago, words that were held onto by the student even in the context of academic challenges. We also hear stories of the struggle, even today, for women to have adequate access to childcare so that they can pursue their studies. We hear stories of grandparents who cherished education for their families even when they had not had access to education themselves.

Thus, the students experience the effects of storying relational identity, before we formally teach the counseling skills of *re-membering* conversations (White, 2007), which is a narrative approach to maintaining connection to lost loved ones, an approach on which this class introduction is loosely based. In re-membering conversations, narrative counselors invite a client to consider and select those people whom they wish to include as members of the "club" of their life (White, 2007, p. 138). People are included in the club of life on the basis of their contributions to the hopes the client has for her or his life. This re-membering practice is grounded in the idea that identity is a social and relational process: "Re-membering conversations are shaped by the conception that identity is founded upon 'association of life' rather than a core self" (White, 2007, p.129).

From the first words, teaching activities are multilayered. This particular introduction process has many effects, including sidestepping an individualistic competitiveness that can arise in new groups. An emphasis on learning as a social and relational activity destabilizes traditional educational psychology's construction of the person as an individual learner, engaged primarily in internal processes. In social constructionist terms, social

psychologist Ken Gergen (1985) suggests that "knowledge is not something people possess, somewhere in their heads, but rather something that people do together" (p. 270). From the outset, our students experience doing knowledge and doing identity together. While we embed this way of doing introductions in a social constructionist program of counselor education, this practice is also transferable to other contexts.

## STORYING LEARNING IDENTITY

An emphasis on relational identity and learning communities does not absolve individual students from the responsibilities of positioning themselves to learn. But it does focus on our responsibilities as teachers to take care in how our speaking and actions position students. Once again, this is micro- and macro-constructionism at work.

In helping students develop their own learning identities, we provide opportunities for students to consider the multiple learning positions available to them. For example, as preparation for the first class, we ask students to read a brief paragraph from Manthei (1997) about student responsibilities in counselor education. Manthei's advice includes the following: "You owe it to yourself to be motivated, well-prepared, accepting of feedback, open to new ideas and honest with yourself" (p. 47). After they have attended the initial class, each student reflects on the following questions before sharing her or his reflection with the group in an online group discussion:

- How did your experiences of the on-campus course enact the ideas Manthei (1997) proposes about "being an effective trainee" (pp. 47–48)?
- What have you learned, in terms of what counselor education might ask of you, that may be helpful for your preparation for the next steps in the program?
- As you prepare to step into the next counseling skills course, are there any practices that you might want to add to your repertoire of responses in order to enhance your positioning for effective engagement in counselor education?

These small, focused opportunities for students to story their learning contribute to possibilities for them to take up positions as active authors of their ongoing professional learning.

# STORYING LEARNING IDENTITY IN ASSESSMENT

Academic assignments provide further opportunities for counselor educators to consider how they contribute to shaping the learning positions available to students, and thus contribute to students' stories of themselves as learners of counseling practice. The next example involves students' first video assignment of a counseling conversation with a client in their practicum setting. It demonstrates the steps of (1) preparing students to engage with our feedback, (2) providing feedback on the video itself, and (3) structuring students' reflections on our feedback about their counseling practice.

In our assessment of their assignments we include acknowledgments, comments on our concerns, and questions for further reflection and development of practice. We offer summative assessment by providing a grade and clear evaluative comments. Alongside that, we offer formative assessment, with the intention of shaping students' ongoing skill development for future practice.

Recognizing that students might be most strongly positioned to engage with only the summative aspect of assessment, we provide a receiving context that invites students to read the formative aspect of our assessment (K. Crocket, Kotzé, & Flintoff, 2007). Before students submit their assignments, we begin to set a receiving context by requesting that they write a brief summary of their personal histories with assessment. We also ask them to think about the limitations and opportunities of the discourses of assessment. Such discourses of assessment might invite self-doubt, a sense of personal failure, judgment, or competition with other students. To help students negotiate other positions within assessment discourses, we take a second step in producing a receiving context. We invite them to consider how they might be positioned by our assessment. We ask them to imagine the following scenarios:

> At the time you read the feedback, you hear convincing critical voices suggesting that our assessment speaks a singular truth of your work. Positioned in this option, how will you read the assessment? What responses might you find yourself invited into? How will the responses shape the next step you might take?

> At the time you read the feedback, you take up a position as a person who can face difficult patches in your life. You hold onto the ideas of self that this position offers you while you read the feedback. Positioned in this option, how will you read the assessment? What responses might you find yourself invited into? How will these responses shape the next step you might take?

> Earlier in the program, you began a course by speaking about someone who cared for and supported you in your study. At the time you read the assessment, you are positioned by their knowledges and hopes for you. Positioned in this way, how will you read the assessment? What responses might you find yourself invited into? How will these responses shape the next step you might take?

Through these questions and reflections, as students prepare to submit their first video assignment, we acknowledge the reciprocal producing and reproducing of discourses of evaluation, measuring, and assessing. We invite students into actively storying their experiences of assessment. We think of these practices in terms of preparing a receiving context for ongoing assessment feedback in order to grow and shape experiences of reflexive practice.

It is in assessment that the power that we are assigned as educators is perhaps most keenly experienced by students (Davies, 2000), and we find it helpful to make the effects of the power relations transparent. We do this, in part, by providing small spaces for first and subsequent words about the assignment to be spoken by students themselves through the pedagogical practices we describe next.

Counselor educators generally require transcripts as part of the assessment of counseling skills and reflexivity in practice. Along with the familiar commentaries that teachers make on students' skills, and alternative practice suggestions, we also require students to respond to the following terms that are intended to enhance relational reflexivity:

1. *Making Inner Dialogue Visible.* In annotating the transcript, students first make visible their inner dialogue (Andersen, 1995) from when the counseling session was underway. They theorize this dialogue in terms of the witnessing positions of Weingarten's (2000) schema. The schema distinguishes, on one plane,

between being available to engage with both another's experiences and one's own, or being more caught up with one's own experience to the extent that there is only minimal engagement with the other's experience. On the second plane, Weingarten's schema distinguishes whether one has access to ethical and agentic action.

2. *Identifying the Discourses.* The assignment also asks that students identify the discourses shaping the conversational moves in which the client and counselor are engaged. This task illuminates discourse at work at a micro level, including the discourses from which they are listening as counselors. For example, a student with a practicum in a community counseling agency meets with a mother whose adolescent son is in trouble with the law. The student identifies mother-blaming discourse at work when the woman client says that everyone is telling her that her son got into trouble because she returned to her work on the night shift. Without access to feminist discourse, the counselor/student could have also reproduced mother-blaming discourse. In these video assignment tasks, students move between storying learning identity and storying professional identity: In this particular aspect of the task, they are storying themselves as purposeful users of discourse (Davies, 1998).

Professional identity is further shaped in other aspects of the assignment that focus on counseling skills. We offer assessment comments on this assignment in written format, accompanied by an audio recording. The recording is one way of making our voices as educators known and accountable to students[3] in order to support them to story their learning. On the recording we engage in four actions: We (1) acknowledge the development of the practice, (2) comment on skills that need attention, (3) reference relevant literature to enhance development, and (4) extend invitations to discuss the ideas with the student's supervisor.

We then ask students to engage in reading and responding to our assessment, and in dialogue through writing their own reflection on the assessment. We grade this reflection. By summatively assessing the reflection, we demonstrate the significance of this recursive, reflexive learning process. Each step of this process offers students opportunities to reposition themselves in relation to their practice and learning. This is constructionism at micro and macro levels. In these relational practices of learning and teaching, students and teachers collaborate in the storying of students' counselor identities and practices.

# OUTSIDER WITNESSING PRACTICES TO COUNSELOR PREPARATION

When identity is understood as socially produced, it follows that how people respond to each other has effects on people's lives. Among the counseling skills we teach are outsider witnessing practices (White, 2007). This set of skills is a particular form of structured response developed in part from reflecting team practices of family therapy (Andersen, 1995).

In counseling practice, outsider witness practices are divided into three distinct phases (White, 2007, p. 185). In the first phase, a person tells aspects of a life story. In the second phase, an invited audience retells the story while the person at the center listens. In the third phase, the person at the center of the interview then retells the meanings she or he made of the retelling. The structure of these phases is similar to reflecting team practice. However the retelling practices in the second phase of outsider witnessing has a particular focus, particular categories of inquiry (p. 190) that we outline shortly.

We introduce students to the practices of outsider witnessing for two purposes. First, they practice these skills in class and use them in witnessing to one another as they each story their own learning and professional identity. The second purpose is to take outsider witnessing skills into client practice.

Outsider witness processes are complex. Therefore, we carefully scaffold students' learning by taking small steps. Before we name the practice as outsider witnessing, we introduce students to the audience position of the second phase in the following assignment that requires them to respond to a reading about social justice and culture in counseling practice (Waldegrave, 2003). We provide guidelines for the assignment, based on White's (2007, pp. 190–196) discussion of the categories of inquiry in the second phase of outsider witness practice.

Read Waldegrave (2003), pages 3–56. Then please respond using these guidelines, in this order:

1. *Expression:* Quote the words of a particular phrase, sentence, or sequence that stands out for you.

2. *Image:* What values do you speculate might be important to either the people who wrote these words or the person about whom the words are written? What image, or metaphor, does this phrase/sentence/sequence evoke for you?

3. *Resonance:* What are the connections with your own life? What experiences in your own life might account for your connection to those particular words or their sentiment? In what ways do these words offer resonance with your own life?

4. *Transport:* Where has responding to this writing taken you, in terms of your hopes or thoughts or ideas about your future practice or your life? What is becoming clearer, about what you value or about what is important to you, as you reflect? (about 500 words)

We invite students to respond both personally and professionally to this reading about culture and counseling, in the belief that taking up this particular kind of witnessing position will help them extend the range of their responsiveness to the stories that people tell in counseling. We want to foster responsiveness, both for counseling in general and for outsider witness practices in particular. The fourth guideline, referred to as acknowledging *transport*, draws students' attention to the ways in which counseling shapes counselors as well as clients.

This assignment sets the scene as we scaffold the learning of outsider witness practices and the particular form of listening required to provide acknowledgment of a person's preferences for her or his life (White, 1999). Further preparation is done in the following online discussion, which requires students to respond to a series of questions.

Please read White (2007) on outsider witnessing (pages 165–218, Chapter 4, Definitional Ceremonies), and discuss the following:

1. If you were in the position of a person who is telling an aspect of her or his life story, what values would you hope that the outsider witnesses would embrace as they listened to you and as they prepared to speak to witness your story?

2. Having read this chapter, what hopes would you hold for your contribution as a member of the outsider witness group?

3. As a member of the outsider witness group, what responses would you want to avoid or restrain?

4. What key words will you take forward with you to support the development of your skills in attending to each of the four categories of inquiry that make up outsider witness responses (White, 2007, pp. 190–196)?

These questions contribute to reflexivity as students learn to shape outsider witnessing responses in the second-phase audience position.

Witnessing practices contribute to teaching students a discursive empathy (Sinclair & Monk, 2005) that is responsive to people's circumstances as they are shaped by discourse. Students go on to use outsider witnessing skills both in response to each other's professional identity stories and in interviews with clients.

Following Weingarten (2003), we have found benefit in interweaving the teaching of practices of witnessing others and witnessing self for preparing students for counseling practice. In Weingarten's words,

to practice compassion one has to have an open heart, but not an overwhelmed one. This is absolutely essential for aware and active witnessing. If we are going to witness others' suffering, we don't want to be shattered the first time out. Knowing our own limits is part of living a compassionate life. It helps us to use our resources optimally. In my experience, compassion arises when we allow ourselves to have rich and complex understanding of the material out of which people forge their lives. (p. 170)

Preparing students to appreciate the richness and complexities out of which they and others have forged their lives, we offer the following online discussion that requires students to engage with Weingarten's (2003) ideas of compassionate witnessing.

---

**Online Discussion Questions for Compassionate Witnessing**

Please read the articles by Kaethe Weingarten (2000, 2003). Discuss how you understand the different witnessing positions that she describes and possible effects of these positions.

1. As you think about the practice of compassionate witnessing of self, what do you imagine this will contribute to your counseling practice?
2. As you think about using the practice of compassionate witnessing of others in your counseling practice, what do you hope this will contribute to a client's experience?
3. Please think of one incident in your life that in retrospect you will view differently as a result of inviting the practice of compassionate witnessing of others into your life.
4. Please think of one incident in your own life in which you would like to compassionately witness yourself. As you do this, what do you notice shifting, or what becomes available to your understanding, that previously was unavailable?

---

Further preparation for students to understand, with compassion, the complexity of the discursive materials out of which people forge their lives comes from an assignment that requires students to engage in and reflect on a conversation with someone from their own networks of friends or family. They each interview someone with insider (Epston, 1999) knowledge of discursive practice with which the student is unfamiliar.[4] For example, a student might interview a person with a full-body tattoo; a student from a pro-life position might interview someone from a pro-choice position; a mother might interview a man who has experienced infertility. The following are examples of the questions we use for students' postinterview reflections:

- What new understandings have you come to about the particular insider knowledges?

- What discourses shaped your previous and current understanding of this aspect of life?
- What have you come to appreciate about how the person navigates her or his life?

Through witnessing both self and other, and storying this witnessing, students extend their capacities for discursive empathy and their repertoire of responses for counseling practice.

# TEACHING COMPLEX THEORY THROUGH STORYING

We noted at the beginning of this chapter that the editors of this volume suggest that social constructionist ideas and narrative approaches offer paradigm-shifting approaches to counselor education. How, then, do we go about teaching our students the paradigm-shifting, complex poststructuralist theory that produces a discursive, storying approach to counseling? We find that some students have had some previous introduction to social constructionism and poststructuralist theory during their undergraduate study, but many have not. In this context, we approach the teaching of theory in many ways, including traditional didactic approaches, and through assigning readings for discussion. We list here selected authors for readers wishing to follow up this theory, discussion of which is precluded by chapter size.

- discourse theory (Burr, 2003; Parker, 1999)
- positioning theory (Davies, 1991, 1998; Davies & Harré, 1999)
- agency and relational subjectivity (Drewery, 2005; Winslade, 2005)
- deconstruction (Davies, 2000; Sampson, 1989)
- poststructuralist feminism (Davies, Flemmen, Gannon, Laws, & Watson, 2002; Davies et al., 2006)
- relational power and power/knowledge relations (Chambon, 1999; Foucault, 1980; Madigan, 1998; Markula & Pringle, 2006)

We enhance the accessibility of these complex ideas through a carefully structured assignment in which students apply the ideas in their own lives. This assignment follows the guideline to personalize learning that is discussed in Chapter 3. We find that students are particularly moved by alternative understandings of themselves that they derive from applying these ideas to their own lives. For example, students often take understandings of gender power relations into their own lives and make visible the shaping effect of gender discourse in the trajectories that their lives have taken. Over the years, in class presentations, we have heard repeated many times versions of the dominant story that fathers need sons to carry on the family name or to continue the family business. We have heard how this patrilineal discourse has shaped—both widening and limiting—the possibilities of the lives of both women and men students.

As students situate their experiences in discursive terms—such as discourses of gender power relations—they engage concurrently with theory and with expanding their understandings of aspects of their own lives.

A step into the complexity of the theory thus also becomes a step into the witnessing of self in new ways. But it is not only a witnessing of self. This assignment requires each student to present to the class, and each presentation is responded to by two other students. These learning experiences serve at least three purposes: (1) enhancing students' understanding of theory, (2) furthering their development of discursive empathy, and (3) building skills of responding to others' stories of their lives. Important for the learning of narrative practice, students come to understand how discourse works to shape lives and how counselor responses might contribute to the stories available for clients to tell and live their lives. There is a direct relationship, we believe, between understanding the philosophy of practice, and crafting the skills of counseling conversations.

## SOCIAL JUSTICE AND STORYING ETHNOCULTURAL IDENTITY

Our program's emphasis on the storying metaphor continues as we focus on cultural identity. As Laird (2000), writing in the United States, suggests, "Our own cultural narratives help us to organize our thinking and anchor our lives, but they can also blind us to the unfamiliar and unrecognizable, and they can foster injustice" (p. 101). Teaching in New Zealand, we center consideration of cultural narratives in a number of ways, in order to find ways to see differently what might be familiar as well as to work for justice. Throughout the program, we ask students to consider stories of culture in their own lives in the context of the challenges, responsibilities, possibilities, and potential richness of this country's colonial history. In New Zealand, cultural identities are shaped by the Treaty of Waitangi, the founding document of our nation, signed by iwi[5] and the British Crown in 1840 (The Royal Commission on Social Policy, 1988; Te Puni Kokiri, 2001). Although effectively repudiated by settlers and government for more than a hundred years, the Treaty, through Maori activism and advocacy, has become central to contemporary New Zealand, as government and people work out its far-reaching implications for life in Aotearoa New Zealand.[6] Parallel explorations can be done in any country in which people have been colonized and oppressed.

Three principles are widely cited (The Royal Commission on Social Policy, 1988): (1) protection (the Crown's responsibility to honor the Treaty's promises to Maori), (2) participation (the Crown's responsibility to ensure that Maori have access to full participation), and (3) partnership (between the Crown and iwi). Through these principles, the Treaty shapes daily lives and practices. The New Zealand Association of Counsellors (2002) has responded to the principle of partnership by listing partnership in its Code of Ethics as one of a number of Core Values of Counselling. Use of the term *partnership* invokes the Treaty-based partnership between iwi and the Crown. Thus, the association calls members of the counseling profession to consider how lives and identities are shaped by the relationships between the peoples of this land.

When we teach and enact social justice in our counselor education program, our responsibilities are shaped by the historical and contemporary context of the Treaty and by our country's colonial history (A. Crocket, 2009). For those in other parts of the world, social justice and cultural identities are storied in terms of local and national histories and political relationships. Thus, we offer here some examples from our teaching practice that might be translated into other national and local contexts.

The first set text that students read (Waldegrave, 2003) elaborates Just Therapy, a groundbreaking and internationally recognized[7] approach to social service practice that emphasizes social justice. Most particularly, this approach involves a partnership whereby members of the dominant group, Pakeha,[8] are accountable to other cultural groups, Maori and Pasifika. By introducing students to this reading first, we center social justice, culture, and cultural identity from the outset of our program. From this beginning, we then continue to structure students' engagements with their own cultural narratives and with considerations of socially just practice.

Of central significance in our counselor education program is that we have the privilege of ongoing invitations for learning opportunities on the marae.[9] These invitations have been possible through the generosity of a number of cultural advisors and consultants, whose contributions we acknowledge.[10] Our experience is that noho marae[11] offer opportunities for weaving cultural and intercultural knowledges and for deepening understanding of privilege and its effects.

In preparation for the noho marae, we assign a number of readings. For example, a reading by Raheim et al. (n.d.) invites students to reflect on privilege and dominance. The following questions, which might be adapted to other contexts, focus students on cultural narratives in this reading:

- Please name one of your ancestors who came to New Zealand.
- Please think of the values that they might have brought to this land and name these.
- What were they looking for in this land? What were their hopes?

Reflection on these questions, and on the stories that they invoke, helps students engage with Aotearoa New Zealand's narrative of colonization and its complex and painful effects. Not all students bring a settler ancestry, but *partnership* responsibility also extends to more recent migrants as they bring their hopes to this country. For Maori students, the teaching week spent at Maniaroa marae, under the mantle of the leadership of Whaea Hinekahukura (Tuti) Aranui, offers a significant opportunity to story cultural identities and knowledges.

Through bringing history into counselor education, we work toward honoring the Maori proverb and practice: "Hoki whakamuri kia anga whakamua" ("Look to the past in order to go forward"). As we go forward into counseling practice, we acknowledge how history has shaped our lives and the lives of those we meet as clients. From these histories we can acknowledge the shaping of culture in everyday life. In New Zealand, counselor identity is inevitably shaped by Maori knowledge (Te Wiata, 2006). We suggest that counseling in any land cannot be separated from its people's cultural narratives.

We offer these examples from a New Zealand context, where the tangata whenua, First Nations, status of Maori is acknowledged through an emphasis on biculturalism. The complexities of cultural identities and relationships play uniquely in each cultural landscape. In the United States and Canada, the emphasis is on multiculturalism. We believe that social constructionist ideas and storying practices have significant implications for understandings of cultural identity and the practice of intercultural counseling relationships in the context of biculturalism and multiculturalism. We hope that through exploring cultural narratives, our own and our students', we can stitch our counselor education practice into the hopeful story line of hospitality toward difference suggested by Monk, Winslade, and Sinclair (2008):

> A critical piece in the necessary dialogues about and across difference is a sharpened awareness of how power operates in sometimes subtle ways in interactions between people. . . . A multicultural vision of what counseling might offer to the world is therefore an effort to promote social justice. It must be a dialogic vision rather than a one-size-fits-all vision. It must be more than tolerant of difference. It must welcome people and offer them hospitality on the very basis of their difference. (p. 461)

We acknowledge the hospitality of Maori in producing the possibilities of dialogic vision that shapes our approaches to narrative practice in counselor education.

## SUPERVISION AS NARRATIVE PRACTICE

Supervision offers a further domain for using the storying metaphor as practice. (Discussion of constructionist-oriented supervision has occurred in previous chapters of this book.) We see a central task of supervision as storying of professional identity (K. Crocket, 2004). Thinking that supervision best positions students when it is conceptualized as a two-way process, we work to shape students' understandings of their contributions to collaboration in supervision. For instance, because a discourse of supervisor responsibility may limit the positions available to students as active knowledge producers, I (K. Crocket; 2002) drew attention to possible effects of some of the familiar language of supervision—such as *receiving supervision* as a *supervisee*—in order to produce subtle shifts in the discursive practice of supervision for students. Since social constructionism emphasizes that language is constitutive, that is, the language we use shapes reality, how we speak about supervision produces its practice.

Students' introduction to supervision begins with a reading of selected material (K. Crocket, 2002, 2004) and

online discussions. Starting points for discussions include the following questions:

- What can you expect of supervision? (Consistent with Crocket's questioning of a supervisor-centered version of supervision, this first question focuses on the students' expectations of the relational professional practice of supervision rather than on the students' expectations of the supervisor.)
- How would you prefer to position yourself as you begin to negotiate the supervision relationship? (This question is an invitation for students to position themselves agentically, to produce the possibility that the discourse of supervision might call them into collaborative partnership. Although students are relatively new to social constructionist ideas at this time, our experience is that the social constructionist language of this "position" question is quite accessible to them. They stitch between the reflective inquiries we have already offered in other contexts and this inquiry.)
- How would you prefer to position yourself in your regular meetings with your supervisor for supervision? (Just by asking this question, we disturb the taken-for-granted unilateral construction of supervision.)
- What ideas about preparing for a supervision session are you mulling over? (This question opens possibilities for student agency and implies the need for reflexivity in the constructing of knowledge and practice.)

The kind of working supervision relationship that we hope to make available for students to take up is reflected in the questions we invite the supervisors to comment on in the final practicum supervision report:

- What has been most satisfying to you in supervision with this particular student/counselor?
- What particular developments in her or his work have you addressed together in supervision?
- What particular strengths and attributes would you be likely to recommend if called upon to refer a client to this person?
- Please comment on the style and processes of supervision.
- What has been your experience, over the course of the year, of sharing tapes of this student's counseling work?
- Are there any gaps in this student's learning or experiences that you would recommend that she or he

address in the next year? Please note if you consider any of these particularly significant.

- From your experience of the student in supervision, what experiences in supervision might you expect her or him to seek next year? (See Winslade, Crocket, Monk, & Drewery, 2000.)

We ask supervisors and students to discuss this report together before submitting it to us as faculty. In responding to these questions and engaging in this discussion, supervisors have the opportunity to further participate in the storying of students' professional identities.

## CAUTIONS

Our account of selected narrative practices in counselor education carries what Morss and Nichterlein (1999) refer to as "the high ideals of the [narrative] paradigm" (p. 167), ideals that may not be easily accomplished by us or by our students. Thus, alongside the ethic of risk (Welch, 1990), these practices call for an ethic of care, which includes care in times of difficulty or struggle (K. Crocket et al., 2007). This work depends upon a spirit of generosity toward ourselves and others, for the practices we describe here do not "protect us from mistakes, from producing disturbances in relationship, or from failing to notice the effects for others of our speaking positions" (K. Crocket et al., 2007, p. 31). As a wider team, we work for a relational and dialogic ethos to see us through inevitable interdiscursive moments and times of challenge. In Shotter's (1996) words, "in joint action . . . we have between us to 'dance' or to 'navigate' toward the common point of our dialogue and toward our 'positions' in relation to it and to each other" (p. 8).

## CONCLUSION

We have found that the careful scaffolding of learning, in the context of a learning community, helps students richly story their narrative practice over the course of a master's program. The scaffolding supports them in weaving backward and forward among their own lived experiences, previous academic study, complex poststructuralist theories, narrative counseling skills and knowledge, and

practicum experiences with clients. As they weave these threads, they story professional counseling identities. Thus, in the *process* of teaching, we enact the philosophies, theories, and practices (that is, the *content* of narrative counseling) that we are teaching. The practices that we describe here have emerged from our teaching community, as together we stretch our understandings of poststructuralist and social constructionist ideas and narrative practice, and their implications for our pedagogy. Through this stretching, new possibilities for our teaching open up, and new stories of counselor education become available to tell. We acknowledge current and former colleagues who have contributed to the stories that we tell here. Just as in learning community students perform their professional identity stories, so too in teaching and learning communities we have come to perform the identities that we tell here in this story of counselor education. While Gergen (1992) suggests that the challenge for a postmodern psychologist is not to tell it like it is, but rather to "tell it as it may become" (p. 27), we suggest that for counseling students and their teachers, the storying of practice through telling it like it is opens richer possibilities for how it may become.

## REFERENCES

American Family Therapy Academy. (2007, March). Distinguished contribution to social justice. *Update*, p. 8.

Andersen, T. (1995). Reflecting processes; Acts of informing and forming: You can borrow my eyes but you must not take them away from me! In S. Friedman (Ed.), *The reflecting team in action: Collaborative practice in family therapy* (pp. 11–37). New York: Guilford.

Anderson, B., & Winslade, J. (1998). Powhiri (welcome). *Western Association for Counsellor Education and Supervision Journal, 36*(3), 6–7.

Burr, V. (2003). *Social constructionism* (2nd ed.). London: Routledge.

Chambon, A. S. (1999). Foucault's approach: Making the familiar visible. In A. Chambon, A. Irving, & L. Epstein (Eds.), *Reading Foucault for social work* (pp. 51–82). New York: Columbia University Press.

Crocket, A. (2009). Interpreting the "partnership" value in the NZAC Code of Ethics. *New Zealand Journal of Counselling, 29*(2), 61.

Crocket, K. (2002). Introducing counsellors to collaborative supervision. *International Journal of Narrative Therapy and Community Work, 4,* 19–24.

Crocket, K. (2004). Storying counselors: Producing professional selves in supervision. In D. Paré & G. Larner (Eds.), *Collaborative practice in psychology and therapy* (pp. 171–181). New York: Haworth Press.

Crocket, K., Kotzé, E., & Flintoff, V. (2007). Reflections on shaping the ethics of our teaching practice. *Journal of Systemic Therapies, 26*(3), 29–42.

Davies, B. (1991). The concept of agency. *Postmodern Critical Theorising, 30,* 42–53.

Davies, B. (1993). *Shards of glass: Children reading and writing beyond gendered identities.* Cresskill, NJ: Hampton Press.

Davies, B. (1998). Psychology's subject: A commentary on the relativism/realism debate. In I. Parker (Ed.), *Social constructionism, discourse, and realism* (pp. 133–147). London: Sage.

Davies, B. (2000). *(In)scribing body/landscape relations.* Walnut Creek, CA: AltaMira Press.

Davies, B., Brown, J., Gannon, S., Hopkins, L., McCann, H., & Wihlborg, M. (2006). Constituting the feminist subject in poststructuralist discourse. *Feminism & Psychology, 16*(1), 87–103.

Davies, B., Flemmen, A., Gannon, S., Laws, C., & Watson, B. (2002). Working on the ground. A collective biography of feminine subjectivities: Mapping the traces of power and knowledge. *Social Semiotics, 12*(3), 159–181.

Davies, B., & Harré, R. (1999). Positioning and personhood. In R. Harré & L. van Langenhove (Eds.), *Positioning theory: Moral contexts of intentional action* (pp. 32–52). Oxford, UK: Blackwell.

Drewery, W. (2005). Why we should watch what we say: Position calls, everyday speech and the production of relational subjectivity. *Theory & Psychology, 15,* 305–324.

Epston, D. E. (1999). Co-research: The making of an alternative knowledge in narrative therapy and community work. In *Narrative therapy and community work: A conference collection* (pp. 137–157). Adelaide, Australia: Dulwich Centre.

Foucault, M. (1980). *Power/knowledge: Selected interviews and other writings 1972–1977* (C. Gordon, Ed.; C. Gordon, L. Marshall, J. Mepham, & K. Soper, Trans.). New York: Pantheon.

Gergen, K. (1985). The social constructionist movement in modern psychology. *American Psychologist, 40,* 266–275.

Gergen, K. (1992). Toward a postmodern psychology. In S. Kvale (Ed.), *Psychology and postmodernism* (pp. 17–30). London: Sage.

Laird, J. (2000). Theorizing culture. *Journal of Feminist Family Therapy, 11*(4), 99–114.

Madigan, S. (1998). Practice interpretations of Michel Foucault. In S. Madigan & I. Law (Eds.), *Praxis: Situating discourse, feminism, and politics in narrative therapy* (pp. 15–34). Vancouver, British Columbia, Canada: Yaletown Family Therapy.

Manthei, R. J. (1997). *Counselling: The skills of finding solutions to problems.* Auckland, New Zealand: Longman.

Markula, P., & Pringle, R. (2006). *Foucault, sport and exercise: Power, knowledge and transforming the self.* London: Routledge.

Monk, G., Winslade, J., Crocket, K., & Epston, D. (Eds.). (1997). Narrative therapy in practice: The archaeology of hope. San Francisco: Jossey-Bass.

Monk, G., Winslade, J., & Sinclair, S. (2008). *New horizons in multicultural counseling: New directions for working with diversity.* Thousand Oaks, CA: Sage.

Morss, J., & Nichterlein, M. (1999). The therapist as client as expert: Externalizing narrative therapy. In I. Parker (Ed.), *Deconstructing psychotherapy* (pp. 164–174). London: Sage.

New Zealand Association of Counsellors. (2002). *Code of ethics.* Hamilton, New Zealand: Author.

Parker, I. (Ed.). (1999). *Deconstructing psychotherapy.* London, UK: Sage.

Raheim, S., Carey, M., Waldegrave, C., Tamasese, K., Tuhaka, F., Fox, H., et al. (n.d.). *An invitation to narrative practitioners to address privilege and dominance.* Available from http://www.narrativetherapylibrary.com/catalog_details.asp?ID=9

Rogoff, B. (2003). *The cultural nature of human development.* New York: Oxford University Press.

The Royal Commission on Social Policy. (1988). *The April report (Vol. 2).* Wellington, New Zealand: Author.

Sampson, E. E. (1989). The deconstruction of the self. In J. Shotter & K. Gergen (Eds.), *Texts of identity* (pp. 1–19). London: Sage.

Shotter, J. (1996). Wittgenstein in practice: From the way of theory to a social poetics. In C. Tolman, F. Cherry, &

R. van Hezewijk (Eds.), *Problems of theoretical psychology* (pp. 3–12). North York, Ontario, Canada: Captus University Press.

Sinclair, S., & Monk, G. (2005). Discursive empathy: A new foundation for therapeutic practice. *British Journal of Guidance & Counselling, 33,* 333–349.

Te Puni Kokiri. (2001). *He tirohanga o kawa ki te Tiriti o Waitangi* [A guide to the principles of the Treaty of Waitangi as expressed by the courts and the Waitangi Tribunal]. Wellington, New Zealand: Author.

Te Wiata, J. (2006). *A local Aotearoa New Zealand investigation of the contribution of Maori cultural knowledges to Pakeha identity and counselling practices.* Unpublished master's thesis, University of Waikato, Hamilton, New Zealand.

Waldegrave, C. (2003). *Just therapy: A journey—A collection of papers from the Just Therapy Team, New Zealand.* Adelaide, Australia: Dulwich Centre.

Weingarten, K. (2000). Witnessing, wonder, and hope. *Family Process, 39,* 389–402.

Weingarten, K. (2003). *Common shock: Witnessing violence every day: How we are harmed, how we can heal.* New York: Dutton.

Welch, S. D. (1990). *A feminist ethic of risk.* Minneapolis, MN: Fortress.

White, M. (1991). Deconstruction and therapy. *Dulwich Centre Newsletter, 3,* 21–40.

White, M. (1999). Reflecting team work as definitional ceremony revisited. *Gecko, 2,* 55–82.

White, M. (2007). *Maps of narrative practice.* New York: Norton.

Winslade, J. (2005). Utilising discursive positioning in counselling. *British Journal of Guidance & Counselling, 33,* 351–364.

Winslade, J., Crocket, K., Monk, G., & Drewery, W. (2000). The storying of professional development. In G. McAuliffe & K. Erikson (Eds.), *Preparing counselors and therapists: Creating constructivist and developmental programs* (pp. 99–113). Alexandria, VA: Association for Counselor Education and Supervision.

## NOTES

1. See Te Wiata (2006, pp. 9–10) for a description of the significance of the stitching metaphor, from an indigenous New Zealand perspective. The metaphor also invokes the careful handcrafting familiar in many cultures to produce fabric with qualities such as aesthetics, warmth, or utility.

2. Maori are tangata whenua, the indigenous people of New Zealand.

3. We acknowledge our colleague Dr. Kay O'Connor, who introduced us to this practice.

4. We acknowledge our colleague Wally McKenzie, whose teaching emphasizes the value of insider knowledge.

5. Iwi: tribe. The treaty was signed by the British Crown and tribal chiefs representing their people in different parts of the country.

6. Within New Zealand, this Maori-English naming of the country is frequently used.

7. See American Family Therapy Academy (2007) for details of the award by AFTA to the Just Therapy Team for Distinguished Contribution to Social Justice.

8. The descendants of European settlers.

9. The marae is the "traditional meeting ground." See O'Connor and Macfarlane (2002) for details.

10. Cultural advisors and consultants whom we acknowledge include Hinekahukura (Tuti) Aranui, Angus Macfarlane, Ray Gage, Tina Williams, Bill Anderson, and Ted Glynn.

11. Noho marae: learning events where staff and students live as guests for several days at a marae.

# PART IV

## Conclusions and Implications

**Chapter 26**
Implementing Constructivist Counselor
Education: Pushing the Zone of Proximal
Development

# 26

# Implementing Constructivist Counselor Education

## Pushing the Zone of Proximal Development

### Garrett J. McAuliffe and Karen P. Eriksen

*At once it struck me what quality went to form [an individual] of achievement. . . . I mean "negative capability," that is, when [she or he] is capable of being in uncertainties, mysteries, doubts, without any irritable reaching after fact and reason.*

John Keats (2002)

*The growth of any craft depends on honest dialogue among the people who do it.*

Parker Palmer (1998, p. 144)

*Research into cognitive complexity suggests that counselors with lower levels of complexity are three times more likely to be influenced by social stereotypes and experience added difficulty when integrating information across a range of domains. Furthermore, counselors who possess a high degree of cognitive complexity investigate a broader range of client-related dimensions, formulate hypotheses with increased accuracy, and confront ambiguous environmental situations with greater confidence and skill.*

Sean Hall (2010, p. 13)

The preceding chapters might by now have stirred enthusiasm for the constructivist inclination in some readers. You have been urged, ever so gently, to pay attention to both the teacher's and learner's experiences, to honor both instructional process and content, to share and reinvent methods in dialogue with students, to strive for equity between teacher and learner, to favor induction, and to embrace uncertainty and contradiction. These proposals resonate with those who gather together under the constructivist umbrella, who acknowledge that learning occurs in a zone among the teacher, the subject matter, and the learners. In order to move toward a constructivist counselor education, we might heed both Keats's appreciation of uncertainty and

Palmer's call for dialogue. The result is likely to be the difference in the types of counselors we produce, as described by Sean Hall in the third epigraph above.

Perhaps we now agree that constructivist education is more than any one method. Above all, it is the practice of having teacher and learner become mutual knowledge creators in a continuing cycle of input and feedback, construction, and deconstruction. It includes much of what Dewey (1938) has already said about the necessity of experience, the meeting of student and curriculum, and the value of inductive exploration (cf. Freiberg & Driscoll, 1996). Many of us also embrace the implications of social constructionism—valuing diversity, being multiculturally competent, and helping students think from a "socially critical" perspective. Thirty years of educational research seem to support many of the programmatic and teaching strategies delineated thus far (Freiberg & Driscoll, 1996).

These seemingly compelling findings bring us to a disturbing question: Why aren't these ideas implemented more extensively in counselor education, let alone in undergraduate education? Why does 80% of teaching in most disciplines continue to be of the traditional, lecture, read, and test style?

We offer in this chapter a litany of the possible obstacles to a constructivist counselor education. We hope that naming these obstacles will not be daunting to instructors. At the same time, we offer correctives here, or conditions that might enhance constructivist education. These include both internal and external factors that might make a consistent, reflexive educational practice possible. We particularly describe those habits of mind that might serve as a roadmap for faculty training and development.

## SOME OBSTACLES AND POSSIBLE SOLUTIONS

The constructivist educational endeavor is not for the faint of heart, nor for the developmentally overchallenged. My (McAuliffe) own experience of opening up my pedagogy to more constructivist dimensions was accompanied by the following "disconcerting" consequences: It was "epistemologically irritating" to co-create understandings with other learners. It was harder work and it was less predictable. It required interpersonal and intrapersonal

skill, comfort with dissonance, and vigilance about my own tacit assumptions. I had to be willing to self-disclose and to behave in an egalitarian manner. These dimensions are, in many ways, countercultural to the norms of the academy. They challenge the prevailing super-rationality, the pursuit of certainty, the aim for objectivity, the norm of hyperautonomy, and the established hierarchies. Luckily, counselor educators are perhaps already inclined to question the "normal science" of college education. Not only are they grounded in a developmental perspective, but constructivist education has striking parallels to the act of helping itself.

## Internal Obstacles

In this section we name seven so-called conditions that might constitute internal obstacles to enacting a more constructivist counselor education: (1) epistemological irritation, (2) comfort with the hegemony of intellect and reason in the academy, (3) discomfort with dissonance, (4) disinclination to examine our tacit assumptions, (5) squeamishness about personal disclosure, (6) the threat of egalitarianism, and (7) the necessity of harder work.

### Obstacle 1: Epistemological Irritation

Constructivist-developmental counselor education might be said to aim at creating constructivist, self-authorizing professionals (Kegan, 1994). Such helpers would be reflective, dialogical, socially critical, and humble. They would have the "negative capability," using Keats's phrase, to dwell in uncertainty, to consult, to hear, to shift direction, and, ultimately, to recognize that the story they are telling is one among many, contingent on historical, temporal, personal, and cultural contexts.

We would include under such negative capability Parker Palmer's (1998) notion of *holding paradoxes*. Palmer proposes that "good" teaching incorporates such paradoxes as keeping structure (e.g., through the information supplied by a text) while being open to student ideas; being supportive and hospitable, but making the environment "charged" (read "challenging"); valuing individuality, but encouraging group consensus; and honoring both personal ("little") stories, and abstract ("big") generalizations. Such is the negative capability of simultaneously focusing on one method while leaving room for its seeming opposite. Tensions would be held between action and reflection, intellect and affect, closure and divergence—but they would each be entertained.

With the negative capability of holding such tensions, the tacit would be exposed, whether in teacher allegiance to a method or student adherence to a cultural moré Accepted norms would not be so accepted. Worldviews underlying "normal science" (Kuhn, 1970) would be exposed.

And there is the rub. Setting a goal of negative capability may stretch us as counselor educators beyond our current capacities. For constructivist education requires a corresponding epistemology, a capacity to recognize that all human beings, including social scientists, live and tell stories; they do not "find" ultimate realities about human behavior. How many of us are willing to deconstruct our stories, to recognize the intertextuality that is masked when we declare "our" opinion, "our" chosen theory, "our" worldview?

Negative capability is a rare achievement, given our current educational modes. Research shows that fewer than 20% of counselors (Kegan, 1994; Neukrug & McAuliffe, 1993) seem to be consistently able to engage in dialogue, entertain uncertainty, and let experience unfold in a social context. Many practitioners, perhaps up to 50% (Kegan, 1998; Neukrug & McAuliffe, 1993), are prone to either an individualistic hyperautonomy or a convention-embedded dependency. Either of these tendencies can be dangerous for clients, as they may be accompanied by cultural encapsulation, adherence to a single technique, and/or maintenance of the status quo when more inclusive and socially critical interventions are needed.

If so few counselors achieve an interdependent, reflective state of mind, what can we say about counselor educators? How ready are we, as counselor educators, to face this mental challenge? Many of us are "ready," but not consistently "there," if the current research on postformal (or nonabsolute/relativistic) thinking in college faculty is to be believed (cf. Yan & Arlin, 1995). We might define postformal thinking as having a full constructivist (Lovell & McAuliffe, 1997) bent, that is, an interest in and ability to think outside of systems, to consistently embrace fluidity and change, and to recognize the socially constructed nature of one's perspectives. Commons (M. L. Commons, personal communication,

June 19, 1999) found that only 25% of faculty at a regional state university were able to think postformally. The vast majority of the others tended toward a more convention-reliant, nondialogical orientation.

I (McAuliffe), for instance, certainly find myself declaring allegiance to my favorite, and always limited stories. Mine often favor practices such as encouraging affect in the classroom, promoting use of words over numbers, and preferring cultural explanations for human behavior over individualistic ones. Derrida (1978), as I understand him, indicates that we constantly practice *erasure* when we make declarations. That is, we erase other unsaid but possible declarations each time we speak or think. I should know better, however. I should instead relativize my current story, turn it into a verb, recognize that a phenomenon is more complex than words (and numbers) can ever express, and try to include other, even seemingly contradictory stories in my attempts at understanding the world. Trying this is both humbling and liberating, and perhaps exemplifies a practice of negative capability.

But there is hope. According to the developmental literature (e.g., Kohlberg, 1969), individuals can understand reasoning that is slightly beyond their current capacities (called *one-up* reasoning by Kohlberg, 1969). Therefore, nonabsolute/relativistic thinking is within faculty members' reach, or their zone of proximal development (Vygotsky, 1934/1986). With the help of inservice faculty development activities, many of us might be able to periodically enter the constructivist zone.

How might the development of negative capability occur? We must have opportunities to safely lose composure. Constructivism asks that we recognize that we are already composed, by individual others and by culture, as much as we compose. And, in Kegan's (1982) usage, we can lose our composure when we expose our tacit assumptions as "mere" constructions. The constructivist epistemology asks us to lose composure in favor of an ongoing composing. We would have to incorporate the following assumptions into our composing: recognition of the pervasiveness of power in all relationships (cf. Foucault, 1972), the ultimacy of dialogue as "reality" creator (Derrida, 1978; Habermas, 1984), and subjectivity as the only certainty (Nietzche, 1974). Can we as counselor educators be ever so humble as to embrace the finality that there is no final, objective truth in human affairs? And can we give up the sinecure of the professor who is the arbiter of counseling truths, in favor of a context-sensitive storying? Most of us are ill prepared for such an amorphous condition. Yet we propose here that this understanding is within our grasp; it is one up epistemologically for most of us; it is in our zone of proximal development.

## Obstacle 2: Comfort With the Hegemony of Intellect and Reason in the Academy

Another obstacle to constructivist education lies in many educators' exclusive comfort with reason and intellect and corresponding lack of attunement to the emotional domain. "Above the shoulders" (i.e., intellectual only) education (Belenky, Clinchy, Goldberger, & Tarule, 1986) is the model academics have inherited in our one-size-fits-all university culture. For many good reasons, the Enlightenment's emphasis on rational deliberation was seen as a major advance over the traditional dominance of emotion, intuition, and, worst of all, superstition in public discourse. Thus rationalism became the hallmark of the university.

Yet such is the sway of a once-good idea that it can exclude other, complementary, and more inclusive ways of knowing. This is seen in the problematizing of emotion in education. The reigning knowledge-transfer model of education allows information and skills to crowd out emotional experience (hooks, 1994). Here is how bell hooks, an English professor, describes the tension: "Few professors talk about the place of emotions in the classroom. . . . [Yet] if we are all emotionally shut down, how can there be any excitement about ideas? . . . The restrictive, repressive classroom ritual insists that emotional responses have no place . . . [yet] the emotions . . . keep us aware or alert . . . they enhance classrooms" (pp. 154–155). Her views on the value of emotion or arousal in learning are confirmed in the literature cited in Chapter 2 of this book.

In that vein, two dimensions of emotion seem important in education: (1) affective excitement, which enhances memory, and (2) personal attention and support. Each has been overlooked as a factor in learning in the academy. We as faculty must rediscover and use our interpersonal and intrapersonal intelligence to increase our comfort and interest in affectively loaded encounters and to be sensitive to students' emotional messages. When we wear our emotional intelligence "hat," we would perhaps show the constructivist characteristics of feeling connected with others in spite of seeming differences and showing attentive caring for the lives of others.

In the interpersonal domain, an instructor must have the sensitivity to read student cues—from indifference to discomfort to involvement—whether in the advising moment or during a class discussion. The instructor must then follow up her or his sensitivity to cues with listening in a manner that encourages students to further disclose and explore. Only then can the instructor judge the optimal mix of challenge and support that might be needed for particular students at particular times. This alertness to the interpersonal domain contrasts with the monological single-mindedness that characterizes much traditional college teaching.

We must also practice internal reflexivity if we are to include affect in education. Such reflexivity might, for instance, include the intrapersonal affective attunement that allows the instructor to bracket her or his immediate responses of dislike and discomfort or attraction, and to instead choose the response that is most helpful in meeting student needs. The struggle to know and integrate personal feelings toward a student is captured in the words of Jane Vella (1994): "This [teacher-student] relationship must transcend personal likes and dislikes. If a teacher feels a strong dislike for an adult learner, she knows she must be even more careful about showing respect, affirming, and listening carefully. When the teacher fails to show respect or fails to affirm a learner in a group . . . the whole group begins to doubt the learning relationship and often manifests anger, fear, and disappointment" (p. 9). Emotional intelligence thus requires both the interpersonal ability to judiciously blend support with challenge (e.g., "Although I think your directness can be very challenging for the client, that tone of voice could make the client feel ashamed. Try this. . . .") and the intrapersonal ability to access personal responses (e.g., "I'm feeling defensive," "I'm prejudging this student").

## Obstacle 3: Discomfort With Dissonance

A further obstacle to constructivist education is discomfort with dissonance. Most of us, in the traditional autonomous mode of the academy, aim for closure, convergence, and "finishedness." We quake at challenges to our clean-cut arguments. We prepare our lectures so that our logic is unassailable. Belenky et al. (1986) describe the predicament of an English professor whose students sit silently after he has delivered a well-formed, tightly constructed argument for a literary interpretation. He had hoped that they would "rip into it" after he was finished:

> He has probably toiled much of the previous night over his interpretation [of a novel]. They treat his words as sacrosanct. He cannot understand why they will not risk a response. But the teacher himself takes few risks. . . . He invites the students to find holes in his argument, but he has taken pains to make it airtight. He would regard as scandalous a suggestion that he make the argument more permeable. . . . So long as teachers hide the imperfect processes of their thinking, allowing students to glimpse only the polished products, students will remain convinced that only . . . a professor . . . could think up a theory. (pp. 214–215)

Belenky et al. (1986) remind us that "the problem is especially acute with respect to science" (p. 215). However, we would also include the social science and counseling fields as problematic. For instance, many adherents of behaviorism, psychodynamic thinking, reality therapy, and humanism present their theories as final and as available for wholesale adoption by students, rather than as one way to story their experiences of clients or students.

In contrast, constructivist educators must be willing to tolerate the dissonance that arises from co-constructing both the class content and the teaching process with their students and colleagues. The constructivist instructor must be able to entertain and manage her or his own irritation in the face of contradiction and uncertainty.

Dialogue and attention to the process of the class might mean that we do not feel the satisfaction of proving a point at times and that we are not fully in control of the classroom process. Dialogue inevitably invites difference and newness. I (McAuliffe) think of a recent student whose rabid opposition to affirmative action was initially daunting to me. When I was able to entertain her perspective and ask her to consider multiple dimensions of the issue, we both learned and she felt both heard and challenged. When members of the class ask me to rethink an assignment or to emphasize a particular topic, I inevitably experience an initial discomfort, for I have been knocked off of my pedagogical track. And while

some educators might pray for patience, I repeat the mantra of dialectical thinking (learned from Michael Basseches, 1991): "Contradiction is my friend." Similarly, I remind myself of Paolo Freire's (1994) position that education might be viewed as an event in which a teacher-learner is among learner-teachers and that knowledge is created by the community (Olson, 1989).

## Obstacle 4: Disinclination to Examine Our Tacit Assumptions

Still another obstacle to constructivist education is many educators' ignorance about their tacit assumptions and standpoints. Stepping back from and evaluating one's constructions requires constant vigilance and courage. We often hold unquestioned loyalties to counseling theories, teaching methods, and moral positions. We also may be "subject to" (Kegan, 1982) our inherited cultural norms, religious allegiances, and gender-based values. These tacit allegiances may drive much of our sense-making. When we don't take responsibility for the sense we make, we are likely to impose culturally derived personal constructions on others, in the name of "objectivity," "reality," or "truth" (Kegan, 1994).

To counter the potential obstacle of educators imposing such an objectivist (Palmer, 1998) worldview on students, constructivist education asks instructors to develop *standpoint awareness*, which in the feminist literature refers largely to the ability to step back from gender, race, and class-based assumptions and to evaluate the impact these assumptions might have on our current perspectives. We must have faith that what is tacitly constructed can also be deconstructed, that is, examined for the implicit stories embedded in all human discourse (Derrida, 1978). Constructivist educators are asked to relativize all of their stories by remembering that, but for the (mis)fortune of being thrown into a particular cultural context, they might be different. The poet Walt Whitman asks for such deconstruction in a line from *Leaves of Grass*: "Question everything you have been taught in church, at home, or in school."

An example of a story that we might deconstruct is that of a male colleague's certainty that a competitive debate-style class discussion format is the only way to get students to challenge ideas and analyze evidence. And yet that type of academic discourse, which depends upon point-counterpoint competition, fails to extend others' ideas in favor of looking for holes in their arguments. It also precludes the expression of emotion (cf. Belenky et al., 1986; hooks, 1994). The debate style of academic discourse is founded on the possibility of there being a Kantian "pure reason" that will emerge from tightly argued analyses.

Our objectivist colleague might instead have asked himself a variation on philosopher Richard Rorty's questions: "Have I been 'fooled' into thinking that the predominantly male, European-based academic traditions are somehow a final, objective way to teach and learn?" and "Perhaps I have been inducted into a 'tribe' that has socialized me to favor this perspective." By exercising standpoint awareness or critical consciousness (Freire, 1994) about the origins and effects of our historically and culturally based constructions, we can take responsibility for the sense we make, and thus we are more likely to make choices from among options. We are more likely, in turn, to allow others to make such choices. Open-minded inquiry, or "leaning into" challenges to our comfortable assumptions (McGoldrick, 1994), would replace the insular privileging of theories, disciplines, and cultures. We might be heard to say, "How might my understanding of the optimal counseling training program be limited by my current standpoints, and how might I inquire about alternative views on admissions, curricula, and field work?"

## Obstacle 5: Discomfort With Personal Disclosure

Discomfort with sharing personal stories can be another barrier to constructivist education. Traditional education often expunges personal stories from the classroom. The only way of knowing that is considered valid is the supposedly depersonalized, scientific method. Further, some educators—hopefully not counselors—may echo the cliché that "familiarity breeds contempt," that is, they fear that sharing vulnerable aspects of their personal lives makes them less respectable to students and thus makes what they teach less credible or authoritative. However, students might be empowered by our personal stories. They might identify themselves as part of the same universe as we are. They might see themselves in us.

Constructivist education can be a big tent. hooks (1994), for instance, suggests that the general and the personal, and the intellectual and the emotional can share the stage in education. In parallel fashion, Palmer (1998) asks us to welcome the tension between the "big" stories (e.g., theories) and "small" stories (e.g., concrete individual experiences).

How might the personal be brought into education? Instructors might share their doubts and their enthusiasms, and relate anecdotes. We might include our struggles for intimacy, gratification, and success. Remembering the humanness of the supposed fools in Shakespeare's plays, we could risk looking foolish in some eyes. We could demonstrate that we too are unfinished learners-in-process. Through this self-disclosure, we as educators will be known in our act of making sense, and others will be heartened to see knowledge creation in action. Knowledge creation will then no longer be the province of, in one student's words, "experts who are different from us." Students may in fact join the "club of knowledge creators," which would now have an open admissions policy.

## Obstacle 6: The Threat of Egalitarianism

Many educators are uncomfortable with the notion of egalitarianism in the classroom. This automatic allegiance to hierarchy might further hinder the movement toward constructivist education. Constructivist and postmodern thinkers have proposed that the role of power needs to be considered when evaluating all human relationships (Burbules & Rice, 1991), from teacher-to-student encounters to colleague-to-colleague relationships. Misuse of power or allegiance to hierarchies might show itself in considering oneself superior because of title, age, height, strength, gender, rank, and ability, to name just a few reference points in the social environment. How might we counter such misuse? Perhaps by being alert to its role and defusing its strength, when it seems appropriate.

Constructivist educators would recognize the fundamental equality in all relationships while noticing and distinguishing their use of both official authority and informal influence that is due to their power. Authority might then be explicitly used in context, as in the case of the instructor who says, "Yes, this paper is required, and I do want you to work in groups." However, even when such power is exercised, instructors can still maintain an open ear to student input on possible modifications of topic, instructional format, and grading methods.

Counselor educators can also encourage themselves to find greater comfort with the instability that egalitarianism brings. They can encourage emergent ideas to grow in conversation with colleagues and students (and themselves) through "exploration, talking and listening, speculation, sharing, and questions" (Belenky et al., 1986, p. 144). Such power-sharing might generate discomfort as instructors create more self-revealing, spontaneous human relationships, and more genuine encounters with students. The alternative, however, is to hide behind the illusory sinecure of authority.

### Obstacle 7: The Necessity of Harder Work

Constructing education in the ways described in this book is harder to do than traditional, autonomous teaching. It is easier to merely read material, line out a lecture, and deliver it verbatim, leaving room for a few questions. Constructivism, as does counseling, demands instead that educators explicitly attend to the experience of the "other." Attention to the other requires the willingness and ability to match and mismatch instruction to the students' learning needs.

The constructivist-developmental teacher in me (McAuliffe) follows this progression in class preparation: Read the material (after assigning it in a sequence that might work), jot down notes on the content (so far, all responsible college teachers are with me), and then *begin* to plan the teaching process. I must ponder ways to instigate mental activity on the part of the learners. And that way lies the labyrinth. If I "go inductive," I will set up a problem to begin the session, perhaps an illustrative role play or anecdote. Or I might trigger student reflections on their own experiences in order to elicit generalizations. The results of such induction are somewhat unpredictable; I cannot fully control the direction of the discoveries. So I live with ongoing concerns about focusing the direction of the learning, and I worry about whether I have covered the objectives sufficiently. And thus I labor—wheeling through Kolb's (1984) learning cycle—from experience to reflection to abstraction and back again to new experience.

Education does not begin and end at the classroom door, of course. The hard work of constructivist teaching may also be understood more broadly to include attending to the learner's experience during advising, graduate assistant mentoring, admissions interviewing,

and cohort group facilitation. In each case, I pay attention to the process—the intersection among teacher, learner, and curriculum—that results in epistemological growth. That is hard work.

## External Constraints

Constructivist education, then, clearly places demands on the person of the educator. However, educators also function as members of the larger educational system, and this system exerts pressures that may also work against the practice of constructivist education. These constraints include the traditional reward system in academia, the related subordination of teaching to scholarship, the absence of pedagogical training for college faculty, and possible student opposition to an inclusive pedagogy.

Teaching has not historically been given the highest priority by tenure and promotion committees at many universities. In turn, faculty members, in order to survive professionally, reduce the time spent preparing for teaching. The faculty member might justifiably fear that time taken to think about changing course structures, assess student development, and engage in dialogue with colleagues about creative ideas for stimulating critical thinking would take away from investing in the scholarly activities that are a priority for tenure and promotion. Some would say that the tenure and promotion process weighs success in promoting a profession through research and scholarly writing more heavily than educating students. Those of us who are interested in constructivist education might thus feel threatened by a diminishment in reward if we "steal" the time necessary for constructivist teaching from time that could have been invested in writing and research.

Worries about achieving tenure in such university systems may drive junior faculty to overcontrol the classroom environment. For instance, if some of the main goals of constructivist-developmental education relate to helping students think critically, challenge the status quo, reflect on the ways things have always been done, become self-authoring systemic thinkers, become activists, and develop a "voice," we cannot expect that students will only apply such new learning to settings outside the university. It also means that students will question and challenge us. Faculty will have to prepare themselves to hear divergent views on methods and procedures that they may have invested a great deal of time in developing.

Some university systems and tenured professors may not want to have their content-driven, directive ways examined during such student challenges. Some constructivism-inclined junior faculty may not want to encourage students to question the system that is "owned" by the tenured faculty, for fear that their own prospective tenure may be threatened. Some personal anecdotes may illuminate faculty and program inability or unwillingness to deal with empowered students. I (Eriksen) remember one dean telling me that this university's students rarely complained. I wondered if that was really the indicator of success that she seemed to think it was. In yet another situation, I remember my own anxious experience of wondering whether I should really teach my students about advocacy, because if they were unhappy with my teaching, I might be giving them the tools to advocate for my removal. I have also felt quite intimidated by being handed the past syllabus for a course and discovering that for the past five years the course I was to teach had not included assessment by project-based or experiential learning, but had included only multiple-choice exams. I remember asking myself if I should continue that tradition in the interests of fitting in, even though I was pretty sure that the students would learn skills and information more relevant to their future work from a more participatory learning experience.

The emphasis on scholarship over teaching also results in universities hiring faculty members who have minimal interest in teaching. I (Eriksen) made a midcareer shift to counselor education precisely because I wanted to teach. However, I have seen evidence that not all educators share my enthusiasms. For example, it is now a truism to note that university professors usually teach without themselves having received pedagogical training. In contrast, kindergarten through 12th-grade teachers are required to take methods courses in which they learn to design curricula and promote students' intellectual development. In such courses, they encounter research on teaching strategies and ideas about creative ways to help students learn. University professors seldom have such opportunities (or requirements). We are hired largely on the basis of our scholarly potential. We might expect our students to complain. However, they often don't protest, for, fortunately or unfortunately, many of them have received 16 years or more of traditional education and may not know the alternative.

A final external threat to constructivist innovation lies in the reaction by students themselves to participatory education. In one new teaching situation, I (Eriksen) wondered how my students would handle the obvious disparities between the way my class was taught and the way the rest of their courses were taught. I worried that students, particularly those whom developmentalists might describe as operating out of a received or conventional knowing framework, might be unwilling to participate so fully in creating their own learning experiences, might be uncomfortable with the ambiguity of co-constructed learning, and might complain about inductive and experiential teaching strategies.

And such has been the case, in our experience. One group of my (Eriksen's) students in an undergraduate Human Service Agencies course expressed many fears as they faced experiential learning assignments. In that course, they were required to visit an agency, interview a counselor, and then demonstrate, in class, some form of human service work in a staged simulation. When I inquired further about why they had so many questions, I discovered that in four years of education at a teaching institution, they had never encountered a teacher who hadn't largely lectured. Needless to say, I wondered whether, with such a contrast, I would survive to teach there again. As Perry (1970) has noted, our own teaching evaluations may reflect the developmental variations among students' own as much as our pedagogical proficiency or lack thereof.

# Possible Responses to Obstacles

Happily, colleges and universities have begun to focus on teaching and learning. We can certainly encourage or actively advocate for our institutions to implement such measures. This section suggests changes in organizational culture, in the academy in general, and in professional association practices that might serve to support a shift toward constructivist education.

## Organizational Culture

Our efforts to rethink teaching and learning will be enhanced if our organizations themselves move toward a more constructivist culture (Cunningham & Gresso, 1993; Torbert, 1987). Such a culture would honor the twin themes of egalitarianism and multiple perspective-taking. It would provide a "counter-cultural" challenge to the hierarchy and autonomy that is characteristic of the academy (hooks, 1994; Kegan, 1998; Palmer, 1998).

The inclusive egalitarianism that is implicit in constructivism favors co-construction in organizational decision making. It favors dialogue among equals over "auto-construction" (Lovell & McAuliffe, 1997), manipulation, and so-called political uses of power in the organization. This is consistent with the social constructionist paradigm, where it is recognized that the community creates knowledge. Social constructionism recognizes the illusion of complete autonomy, as any seemingly autonomous act is inextricably influenced by the historical, social, and political environments that swirl around the decision maker. It asserts that organizational decision making can ultimately benefit, in the form of new perspectives, from recognizing those influences.

In contrast, auto-naming (autonomy) or auto-governing (autocratic) impulses rely exclusively on the wisdom of the individual, rational decision maker. An autonomy-oriented organization suffers from an absence of diverse perspectives. A constructivist egalitarianism does not discount the use of selective autonomy or hierarchy, but instead relativizes their use. For instance, an instructor might use her authority to choose a text after she has filtered the voices of others.

An organizational emphasis on egalitarianism also implies a fundamental equality between student and teacher and among faculty members. Such equality replaces the privileges of title, rank, age, gender, and expertise with more open, authentic encounters. Equality might manifest itself in such practices as student participation in position searches and program meetings, and full inclusion of new, nontenured faculty in deliberations. Instructors would exhibit inclusion by regularly checking in on the student learning process, asking, "How am I doing? How are you doing?" An air of openness and humility would characterize the halls of the counselor education program, perhaps symbolized by the at-least-occasional use of first names and circular seating arrangements in the classroom.

Inclusive egalitarianism links easily with the constructivist theme of valuing multiple perspectives. The domain of ethnic culture provides a ready example. A constructivist organization would be characterized by affirmative, proactive attempts to ensure that cultural standpoints are not tacitly assumed and represented. The multicultural organization is one that zealously seeks out potentially hidden or underrepresented perspectives. It embraces "otherness," making the other part of its (multi)culture. It consistently and vigilantly opposes the deadening, hegemonic dominance of any one perspective, whether in classroom décor or admissions and hiring policies. In the "multiperspectival" organization, staff would consistently look under every metaphorical rock for new life in the form of additional gender, ethnic, religious, and class perspectives. And where there is life, there is movement—for better and worse—as, for instance, in a family, when the quiet of a coupleship is forever changed by the arrival of a new child. Similarly, the noise of multiple perspectives in an organization vitalizes any moribund patterns. These are the prices and the gains of having a diverse learning community.

An anecdote might illustrate: I (McAuliffe) noticed at one point a few years ago that very few African American students were attending graduate student social gatherings in our counseling program. When I made inquiries, I discovered that student gatherings were being held in predominantly White neighborhoods and in settings to which African Americans rarely went. When we varied the location to a place more oriented to African Americans, attendance was more diverse. Black students attended in greater numbers. My lesson was that actively challenging hegemonic assumptions, even about the location and style of a restaurant, had to be engaged if we weren't to commit the sin of omission, or erasure (Derrida, 1978), that is, taking our perspective as universal.

Multiple perspective-taking is not, however, limited to the ethnic cultural domain. Inductive teaching and qualitative research, with their focus on discovery, also invite multiple narratives. Within and without the classroom, we can invite alternate views. For example, I recently commented on my own liberal political bias in teaching of social and cultural issues in counseling (McAuliffe, 1999). I then invited and nurtured, I hope, the expression of alternative, perhaps more conservative, views on culture. Thus, an ethic of equality breeds a welcoming organization, one in which many voices are heeded. In the service of such an ethic, our stories must be constructed, deconstructed, and reconstructed constantly.

## Changes in the Academy

Many practices of the academy have been under scrutiny in recent years. Among them, a tenure system that values research over teaching and the failure to produce educational outcomes that are clearly relevant to social problems and practice expectations have increasingly been criticized. Perhaps such scrutiny foreshadows changes in the academy along the lines that we have been suggesting.

There has, in fact, been a slow movement over the past 10 years to recognize good teaching in the academy. Some universities already require teaching experience and demonstrations of teaching competence in their new faculty. Programs might go further and require prospective professors to take a course on teaching prior to graduation from their doctoral programs. In such a course, students would learn about adult and student development and might have their own epistemologies challenged. Programs could require demonstrations of teaching during faculty hiring interviews (rather than the more typical presentation, which often ends up being a formal presentation of the candidate's doctoral research).

Some universities have also instituted teaching projects—offering incentives for participating—in which faculty discuss how to teach, observe one another's teaching, receive feedback on their teaching strategies, and attempt to incorporate strategies more in line with the principles in this book. Perhaps teaching specialists, who are educated in such strategies and may be outside of our own departments, could be recruited to evaluate faculty so that student evaluations alone would not be the measure of a faculty member's successful performance. In this way, creative teachers could be rewarded, rather than being punished for failing to conform to longstanding and habitual departmental teaching methods. An additional incentive might include making merit pay for tenured faculty contingent on improvements in their teaching. Such an approach might motivate them to seek and accept feedback on their teaching. Such faculty evaluation strategies offer an alternative to the common current system that is almost exclusively reliant on the "customer's" (in this case, student's) feedback. And customer-driven practices may be partially responsible for the "dumbing down" of education,

as students may not know what they need to know or be willing to become active creators of knowledge.

Other options that would require collegial departmental environments include the following. Faculty might agree to observe each other's teaching, to team teach, and to collaborate in creating more active teaching styles and strategies. They could be encouraged to pursue such collaborations by the dissemination of research that supports active, experiential teaching. They might engage in new research in which experiential methods are compared with traditional lecture in terms of long-term retention of knowledge and skills.

Multiple tracks for faculty have been considered, but are not yet common. Institutions would recognize "gifts differing" in setting up teaching and research tracks. In the counseling field, we are already familiar with the benefits of matching people and environments (e.g., Holland, 1985). Organizations have found that, for example, in promoting researchers into management positions, they often mismatch "investigative" personality types with "enterprising" tasks. It seemed that the skills necessary to be a strong researcher are not the skills necessary to be an effective manager. So some organizations have changed the system, creating two tracks—manager and researcher—and rewarding them with equal status and pay. Employees are then promoted within their track and not required to perform in a track for which their skills are not well matched.

Some colleges and universities might follow this example by creating research and teaching tracks with equal status, recognition, and pay. Teachers could focus on teaching. Researchers could focus on knowledge creation. Researchers could then serve as resources to teachers, and vice versa, to ensure that both stay current.

## Professional Association Shifts

Professional associations might highlight the training dimension as well. For example, the Association for Counselor Education and Supervision (ACES) might dedicate a section of its journal to innovative and constructivist teaching methods. ACES might also develop a special interest group on teaching. The American Psychological Association already has such a division. Further, significant portions of the ACES national and regional conferences might be dedicated to forums on creative teaching ideas.

# CONCLUSION

The work of reconstructing counselor education will require us to challenge the way of knowing that is marked by finality and autonomy. In their place would be a commitment to fluidity, reflexivity, and inclusion. Constructivist counselor education would be marked by thoughtful choices, rather than assumed and tacit allegiances to any metanarratives—for instance, rationalism, humanism, and traditionalism. Such counselor education would particularly require that we pass thorough the Scylla and Charybdis of tradition and fear. No longer would college pedagogy be only content driven, teacher centered, and predominantly directive. Two of our education colleagues have reported such a confrontation with tradition and fear when they tried to introduce inclusive, experiential methods to a training setting.

In the first case, Jane Vella (1994) describes the shock she engendered when she was training Bangladeshi physician educators to teach. Preventable deaths of patients had created a crisis, and this crisis had led the physicians to recruit her expertise. She asked the medical educators to be open to being critiqued, and she proposed that they try more inclusive, experiential teaching methods. In doing so, she met much shock and resistance, for she had challenged ancient hierarchical relationships. The physicians were not used to receiving personal feedback. Vella's experience bespeaks both the difficulty and urgency of opening up the conversation. Like the patients who were dying as a result of faulty medical training, are our students mismanaging their work with clients because they have not achieved a self-authorizing consciousness, one that seeks alternate assessments and methods and identifies social structures that maintain disabling conditions for their clients?

In the second case, Jean Peterson (personal communication, 1999), the author of a chapter in this volume, had a similar experience when teaching principals-in-training about school counseling. She wanted them to tune in to the affective concerns of teachers, parents, students, and other staff. Soon after she introduced inductive and participatory learning methods, she faced a class rebellion. Many of the administrator-students cried, "This isn't relevant," "It isn't clear," and "I don't like gray areas." They had lost their epistemological and pedagogical bearings. They wanted "content" and to be given clear solutions. They themselves used exclusively directive methods in dealing with student discipline and faculty performance. They were used to being in charge. They expected a parallel method from Peterson. As she describes it,

> by the middle of the second week I might have feared mutiny, except that I have faith in my approach, and I could see that some of the most assertively negative students were beginning to become more receptive. . . . I used my own counseling skills as I listened to their frustrations and anxiety. I carefully self-monitored my internal responses and outward reactions in order to model counselor behaviors and not take their challenges personally. I taught them about "processing." I de-emphasized "product." . . . I made sure we continually came back to basic counseling tenets, ethical standards, and principled decision making.

Peterson persisted in her experiential method, which included leading dilemma discussions and requiring students to interview practicing counselors. By the three-quarter mark of the course, as she reports, "There was a palpable difference in atmosphere." Students were able to consider multiple factors when confronting problem behaviors. They honored ethical principles. They had energy and enthusiasm for group work and in-process thinking. Peterson's students swam through the fear, buoyed by her supportive manner and her empathic hearing of their concerns, until they reached a different shore. They had begun to explore the territory of social construction.

What made the difference for Vella, Peterson, and their students? Peterson's response is instructive for both adult learners and adult teachers: "The opportunity to process the experiences and to promote parallel processing [of the course itself by the students], recognition and affirmation of varying learning styles, individual and group nurturance, patience, and application of my own counseling skills in response to their . . . distress. I think these factors were key." Peterson personified the characteristics of the constructivist knower herself in her willingness to stay with the dialogical process, to pay attention to others' experiences, and to dedicate herself to a larger moral vision of the work. In any faculty development program, these factors need to be accounted for so that fear and tradition might not overwhelm dialogue and risk taking.

So we must tread gently, but with faith in our colleagues' and students' capacities to let go of the fixities of over-structure, hyperautonomy, super-rationality, and ultimate hierarchy. In their place, while we might

honor fear and recognize tradition, we would ultimately, in Parker Palmer's (1998) words, "teach from
curiosity or hope or empathy or honesty . . . [and] have
fear, but . . . not be fear" (p. 57). We might then participate with the whole community of designer-
builders who would construct a more inclusive, and
therefore more humane, counselor education.

# REFERENCES

Basseches, M. (1991, June). *Dialectical thinking*. Paper presented at the Clinical-Developmental Institute, Harvard
University, Cambridge, MA.

Belenky, M. F., Clinchy, B. M., Goldberger, N. R., &
Tarule, J. M. (1986). *Women's ways of knowing: The development of self, voice, and mind*. New York: Basic Books.

Burbules, N. C., & Rice, S. (1991). Dialogue across differences.
*Harvard Educational Review, 61*, 393–416.

Cunningham, W. G., & Gresso, D. W. (1993). *Cultural leadership:
The culture of excellence in education*. Boston: Allyn & Bacon.

Derrida, J. (1978). *Writing and difference* (A. Bass, Trans.).
Chicago: University of Chicago Press.

Dewey, J. (1938). *Logic: The theory of inquiry*. New York: Holt.

Foucault, M. (1972). Truth and power (C. Gordon, Trans.). In
C. Gordon (Ed.), *Power/knowledge: Selected interviews
and other writings, 1972–1977* (pp. 131–133). New York:
Pantheon.

Freiberg, H. J., & Driscoll, A. (1996). *Universal teaching strategies*. Boston: Allyn & Bacon.

Freire, P. (1994). *Pedagogy of the oppressed*. New York: Continuum.

Habermas, J. (1984). *Theory of communicative action*
(T. McCarthy, Trans.). Boston: Beacon.

Hall, S. B. (2010). *Facilitating student cognitive development:
A teaching philosophy for counselor educators*.
Unpublished manuscript, Old Dominion University,
Norfolk, VA.

Holland, J. L. (1985). *Making vocational choices*. Englewood
Cliffs, NJ: Prentice Hall.

hooks, b. (1994). *Teaching to transgress: Education as the practice of freedom*. New York: Routledge.

Keats, J. (2002). Letter to George and Thomas Keats December
22, 1817. In G. F. Scott (Ed.). *Selected letters of John Keats*.
Cambridge, MA: Harvard University Press.

Kegan, R. (1982). *The evolving self: Problem and process in human
development*. Cambridge, MA: Harvard University Press.

Kegan, R. (1998). *In over our heads: The mental demands of
modern life*. Cambridge, MA: Harvard University Press.

Kohlberg, L. (1969). Stage and sequence: The cognitive-
developmental approach to socialization. In D. Goslin
(Ed.), *Handbook of socialization theory and research*
(pp. 347–480). Chicago: Rand McNally.

Kolb, D. (1984). *Experiential learning*. Englewood Cliffs, NJ:
Prentice Hall.

Kuhn, T. S. (1970). *The structure of scientific revolutions*.
Chicago: University of Chicago Press.

Lovell, C. W., & McAuliffe, G. J. (1997). Principles of constructivist training and education. In T. L. Sexton &
B. L. Griffin (Eds.), *Constructivist thinking in counseling practice, research, and training* (pp. 211–227).
New York: Teachers College Press.

McAuliffe, G. J. (1999, Summer). Is there a liberal bias in multicultural counselor education? Becoming a "multicultural liberal." *ACES Spectrum, 9–12*.

McGoldrick, M. (1994). The ache for home. *Family Therapy
Networker, 18*, 38–45.

Neukrug, E. S., & McAuliffe, G. J. (1993). Cognitive development and human service education. *Human Service
Education, 13*, 13–26.

Nietzche, F. (1974). *The gay science* (W. Kaufmann, Trans.).
New York: Random House.

Olson, G. A. (1989). Social construction and composition
theory: A conversation with Richard Rorty. *Journal of
Advanced Composition, 9*, 1–9.

Palmer, P. J. (1998). *The courage to teach: Exploring the inner
landscape of a teacher's life*. San Francisco: Jossey-Bass.

Perry, W. (1970). *Forms of intellectual and ethical development
in the college years*. New York: Holt, Rinehart & Winston.

Torbert, W. (1987). *Managing the corporate dream*. Homewood,
IL: Dow-Jones Irwin.

Vella, J. (1994). *Learning to listen, learning to teach*. San
Francisco: Jossey-Bass.

Vygotsky, L. S. (1986). *Thought and language* (A. Kozulin,
Trans.). Cambridge, MA: MIT Press. (Original work published 1934)

Yan, B., & Arlin, P. K. (1995). Nonabsolute/relativistic thinking: A common factor underlying models of postformal
reasoning? *Journal of Adult Development, 2*, 223–240.

# Author Index

421

Galassi, J. P., 316 (table)
Gall, M., 372
Galliher, R. V., 358
Gannon, S., 401
Garrison, M. J., 313, 320 (table)
Gay, Lesbian and Straight Education Network., 315 (table)
Gehart, D., 296, 297
Geisler, C., 319 (table)
Geltner, J. A., 318 (table)
Gelwick, R., 246
Georgaca, E., 256, 258, 261, 267, 269
Gergen, K. J., 4, 5, 6, 41, 125, 126, 154, 256, 377, 396, 404
Gerler, E. R., Jr., 314 (table), 320 (table)
Geroski, A., 126
Getch, Y. Q., 316 (table), 317 (table)
Gibbons, M. M., 317 (table), 318 (table), 319 (table)
Gibson, D. M., 155, 317 (table), 378
Gibson, R. L., 86
Giles, H. C., 319 (table)
Gillette, M., 315 (table), 318 (table)
Gilligan, C., 24
Giordano, J., 297
Giroux, H., 203
Giroux, H. A., viii, ix, 170, 171
Gladding, S. T., 82, 86, 302
Glover, N. M., 385
Goins, S., 318 (table)
Goldberg, M. C., 246, 252
Goldberger, N. R., ix, 7, 8, 10, 20, 23, 33, 34, 36, 38, 39, 41, 50, 51, 53, 61, 63, 68, 69, 92, 97, 99, 193, 200, 267, 389, 412, 413, 414, 415
Goldenberg, H., 355
Goldenberg, I., 169–170, 171, 355
Goldfried, M. R., 24
Gollnick, D. M., 313, 317 (table), 318 (table)
Gomez, E., 172, 173
Gonzalez, R., 230, 231
Goodman, J. I., 387
Goodman, P., 238
Goodman, R., 7
Goodnough, G. E., 312, 316 (table), 318 (table)
Goodyear, R., 233, 384, 386, 387
Goolishian, H. A., 296
Gordon, E. W., 313, 315 (table)
Gorrell, J. J., 238
Graf, N. M., 385
Granello, D., 148, 247, 248
Grant, C., 315 (table), 318 (table)
Grant, G., 319 (table)
Gray, J., 319 (table)
Greenwalt, B. C., 374
Gresso, D. W., 416
Gronlund, N. E., 320 (table), 321
Gross, D. R., 86

Grothaus, T., 9, 10, 171, 172, 173, 177, 312, 313, 315 (table), 316 (table), 317 (table), 333
Gruber, H. E., 20
Guterman, J. T., 359
Guzdial,M., 338
Gysbers, N. C., 316 (table), 319 (table), 320 (table)

Haag Granello, D., 320 (table)
Habermas, J., 10, 411
Hacker, P. M. S., 246
Haladyna, T. M., 371
Hall, S. B., 409
Ham, M. A., 318 (table)
Hanna, F. J., 9
Hanna, S. M., 296
Hansen, J. C., 216
Hansen, J. T., 113
Hansen, L. S., 209
Hanson, G. R., 194
Hardy, K., 306
Hare-Mustin, R. T., 258, 267
Harkins, A. M., 213
Harper, D., 256, 258, 261, 267, 269
Harré, R., 401
Harris, I. B., 3
Haston, M., 316 (table)
Hatch, T., 320 (table)
Hawley, L. D., 250
Hayes, B. G., 113, 378
Hayes, R. L., 298, 357, 359
Healy, C. C., 214, 216
Healy, P., 38, 39
Hefferline, R., 238
Helms, J. E., 86, 193
Henderson, D. A., 314 (table), 318 (table), 320 (table)
Henderson, J. G., 44
Henderson, P., 316 (table)
Henfield, M. S., 320 (table)
Hennington, C., 318 (table)
Henry, L., 319 (table)
Heppner, P. P., 153
Herr, E. L., 314 (table)
Herreid, C. F., 383
Higgins, A., 20, 23
Highlen, P. S., 165
Hill, W. H., 370
Hines, P. L., 315 (table)
Hipolito, C. P., 316 (table)
Hipolito-Delgado, C. P., 169
Hiromoto, S., 317 (table)
Hoare, C. H., 298
Hofer, B. K., 32, 34, 39, 60, 63, 71
Hoffman, L., 111
Hoffman, M. A., 319 (table)

National Institute of Drug Abuse U.S. Department of Health and Human Services, 358
Neimeyer, G., 215, 216, 256, 269
Neiwert, P., 5
Nelson, T. S., 386
Nelson-Becker, H., 355
Nesdale, A., 298
Neufeldt, S., 230, 231, 384, 387–388
Neukrug, E., 91, 93, 99, 111, 113, 122, 141, 333, 411
Newsome, D. W., 317 (table)
Ng, K.-M., 320 (table)
Nichterlein, M., 404
Nieto, S., 315 (table)
Nietzche, F., 411
Niles, S. G., 319 (table)
Noumair, D. A., 319 (table)
Nugent, F. A., 86
Nuijens, K. L., 315 (table)

O'Connor, M., 406 (note) 9
O'Donnell, K., 184
O'Hanlon, W., 354
Ober, A. M., 320 (table)
Ocampo, C., 169
Ohrt, J. H., 320 (table)–321 (table)
Olson, G. A., 413
Omrod, J. E., 278
Oppenheim, R., 359
Orlinsky, D. E., 56
Ormrod, J. E., 346, 347
Orozco, G. L., 319 (table)
Orsi, R., 320 (table)
Ottens, A. J., 9
Ovando, C. J., 317 (table)

Paisley, P. O., 357
Palincsar, A., 338
Palmer, P., 239
Palmer, P. J., 295, 409, 410, 413, 414, 417, 420
Pan, C., 386
Paniagua, F. A., 320 (table), 321
Pare, D., 177, 313, 315 (table)
Parker, C. A., 95, 195, 203
Parker, I., 256, 258, 261, 267, 269, 401–402
Parker, R. E., 377
Parker, W. M., 171
Parsons, F., 209
Parsons, R. D., 316 (table), 319 (table)
Patterson, C. H., 112, 290
Peace, S. D., 298, 299, 313
Pearce, J., 297
Peavy, R. V., 209, 210, 212, 214, 215, 219–220
Pedersen, P., 73 (box), 165, 313, 315 (table)
Pembroke, N., 355

Perez, M., 5
Perls, F. S., 238
Perry, R. S., 311, 312
Perry, W., 220, 416
Perry, W. G., 34, 36, 41, 44, 193, 194, 197, 206
Perry, W. G., Jr., 7, 8, 10, 20, 63, 68, 244, 261, 267, 271
Perusse, R., 312, 318 (table)
Peterson, J. S., 201, 204
Peterson, L. M., 261
Peterson, S. E., 339, 344
Phillips, E. L., 319 (table)
Piaget, J., ix, 6–7, 20, 198, 380
Pierce, J., 346, 347
Polanyi, M., 244, 245, 246, 250
Pollard, N. E., 387
Polman, J. L., 337
Ponterotto, J. G., 313, 315 (table)
Popham, J., 371
Portman, T. A. A., 315 (table)
Power, F. C., 20, 23
Pransky, J., 320 (table)
Presbury, J., 320 (table)
Prieto, L. R., 384
Prilleltensky, I., 170
Pringle, R., 401

Quenk, N. L., 41
Quigney, T. A., 318 (table)
Quinby, R. F., 320 (table)
Quinn, A. C., 378

Raheim, S., 402
Rasmus, S. D., 296, 302
Ratts, M., 86, 87, 316 (table)
Ravitz, J., 337
Rayle, A. D., 321 (table)
Redfield, D. L., 372
Reiman, A. J., 298, 299
Reimer, M. S., 317 (table)
Reisser, L., 35, 40
Remley, T. P., 318 (table)
Resnick, L. B., 338
Resnick, R., 230
Rest, J., 44, 197
Reynolds, C. A., 317 (table)
Rice, F. P., 204
Rice, S., 5–6, 158, 414
Riddle, D., 180
Riegel, K., 197
Ritchie, M. H., 355, 356
Roark, A. E., 285
Roberts, L. M., 316 (table)
Robichaud, T. A., 319 (table)
Robinson, E. H., 125, 378

# Subject Index

Absolutes, rejection of, 5–6
Abstinence project and journal, 360
Abstract conceptualization, 25–26, 232
Abstract-concrete learning style, 27
Abstract experimenters, 27
Abstract reflectors, 28
Accommodators (concrete experimenters), 28
"Act As If" theory role play, 235
Active experimentation, 26, 233
Active-reflective learning style, 27–28
Addiction. *See* Substance abuse/addictions counseling course
Adolescents. *See* Child and adolescent counseling course
Adult education principles, 31–34
 engagement, 32
 equity, 33
 needs assessments/accountability, 32–33
 opportunities for immediate application, 33
 respect for learners as agents, 32
 safety, 31–32
 sequence and reinforcement, 33
 sound relationships, 32
 teamwork, 33–34
Advanced Student phase, 53–56
Advocacy Competency Domains, 86, 87
Affect, role in counselor development, 50–51
Analogy illustration, 62
Analytic rubrics, 373
Approximation, valuing over precision, 41–42, 205
Assessment, of competence, 367–376
 constructed-response, 371–372
 decisions and recommendations, 370
 informal approaches, 372
 knowledge outcomes, 370–372
 learning outcomes, 368–369, 370–375
 model learning assessment plan, 368–370
 performance assessment, 372–374
 portfolio assessment, 374–375
 processes and measures, naming, 369

processes for, 369–370
 rubrics for, 372–373 (table)
 selective-response, 371
 skills outcomes, 372–375
 value of, 375
 video-recording for, 96–97, 217
Assessment and testing course, 125–135
 basic concepts, 129–131
 case study, 135
 Conducting Standardized Assessment, 132–133
 Conducting Unstructured Interviews and Mental Health Assessments, 131–132
 course content/process, 127–133
 Historical Perspectives and Types of Assessments, 129
 mastering concepts in client need context, 130–131
 outline of course, 127 (table)–128 (table)
 philosophical applications, 126–127
 self-narrative assignment, 131–132
 social constructionism on, 126
 writing assessment report, 133
Assimilators (abstract reflectors), 28
Association for Counselor Education and Supervision (ACES), 418
Association for Specialists in Group Work (ASGW), 138, 139
Audio recordings, 383
Audiovisuals, 61
Authority-reliant thinkers, 7
Auto-governing, 417
Auto-naming, 417

Banking deposit style of teaching, 15
Beginning Student phase, 52–53
Bias management assignment, 159
Bibliotherapy concept, 288
Bifurcated thinking, 43–44
Blackboard, 382, 386
Blogs, 381–382
Bloom's taxonomy, 247 (table)–248, 251, 370, 371

# About the Editors

**Garrett J. McAuliffe** is University Professor of Counselor Education at Old Dominion University, in Norfolk, Virginia. His work focuses on culture, constructivism, counselor education, and career decision making. He received his doctorate in counseling from the University of Massachusetts at Amherst, for which he received the national Outstanding Dissertation Award; his master's degree from the University of Albany; and his bachelor's degree in literature from Queens College in New York City. He has written or cowritten six books and over 75 articles on topics ranging from working with troubled youth to culturally alert counseling. He was co-recipient of the ACES National Publication Award in 2001 and the CSJ Social Justice Award in 2009. He has created models for cultural de-centering and health-oriented client assessment. He spent 13 years as a community college and university counselor. Prior to that, he was a public school teacher in New York.

**Karen P. Eriksen** is the founder and CEO of the Eriksen Institute for Ethics, which promotes Conscious and Reflective Leadership—an approach to reflecting and becoming intentional about developing character and grounding one's organization in ethics, building the personal and interpersonal capacities of one's employees or members, and pursuing optimal development. Dr. Eriksen earned a doctorate in education from George Mason University and a master's in psychology from California State University, Fullerton. She spent 15 years as a nationally known presenter, trainer, and counseling profession leader; 25 years training counselors privately and as a university professor, researcher, and author; and 18 years as a marriage and family therapist.

Dr. Eriksen regularly inspires groups, organizations, universities, and businesses in their character and ethics aspirations, interpersonal relations and communication, conflict resolution, and development. She has authored eight books on related topics.

**The Association for Counselor Education and Supervision (ACES)** emphasizes the need for quality education and supervision of counselors in all work settings. Through its accreditation process and professional development activities, ACES strives to continue to improve the education, credentialing, and supervision of counselors. The association strives to encourage publications on current issues, relevant research, proven practices, ethical standards, and conversations on related problems. Persons who are engaged in the professional preparation of counselors will find leadership through ACES. The ultimate purpose of the association is to advance counselor education and supervision in order to improve the provision of counseling services in all settings of society.

# About the Contributors

**Linda L. Black** is Professor of Counselor Education and Chair of the Department of Counselor Education at the University of Northern Colorado, in Greeley. Her scholarship is focused on social privilege, mentoring, leadership, and counselor training. She received her doctorate in Counselor Education and Supervision from the University of Northern Colorado. She is the current coeditor of *Counselor Education and Supervision* and has numerous professional publications and presentations in the field of counselor education and supervision.

**Bill Bruck** has been the lead solutions architect for Q2Learning, of which he is a founding partner, since 2001. He designed the eCampus technology and end-to-end methodology that has been used in deploying over a hundred blended learning solutions for Fortune 500 corporations, and as general manager has grown the company by 40% in each of its first three years. Prior to joining Q2, Bill served as chief knowledge officer and professional services team lead at Caucus Systems, where he designed the virtual workplace technologies featured in *HR Executive* that were adopted by Fortune 500 customers to support distributed project teams and communities of practice. Bill comes from academia, where he was a tenured full professor of psychology and director of institutional research at Marymount University. There he designed a system for assessing institutional effectiveness that was cited as an exemplar during reaccreditation by the Southeastern Association of Schools and Colleges. Bill has written over a dozen books on the effective use of technology, which have been translated into five languages. Microsoft Press published his latest book, *Taming the Information Tsunami*. He serves as a luminary for media and industry relations and provides keynotes internationally on collaboration technologies and their impact on organizations. Bill earned his bachelor's degree in Human Studies from Brown University, his master's degree in Clinical Psychology from Duquesne University, and his doctorate in Counseling Psychology from the University of Florida.

**Lisa L. Buono** is an Instructor and Field Work Coordinator for the Department of Counseling and Guidance at California Lutheran University (CLU), in Thousand Oaks, where she also coordinates field experiences for both school counseling and college student personnel candidates. She is currently a doctoral candidate in the School of Education at CLU. Her scholarship focuses on technology in higher education in general and counselor education in particular.

**Yvonne L. Callaway** is a Professor in the Department of Leadership and Counseling at Eastern Michigan University, in Ypsilanti. Her publications have included work in multicultural influences on counseling processes, self-efficacy, positive psychology, and constructivism as an approach to counseling training and development. She received her master's and doctorate in Counseling from Wayne State University, in Detroit, Michigan, and her bachelor's degree from the University of Michigan, in Ann Arbor.

**Jamie S. Carney** is a Professor in the Counselor Education Program at Auburn University. Her work has focused on assessment and attitudinal development as it relates to pedagogy in counselor education. She received her doctorate in Counselor Education from Ohio

University and her master's in Community Counseling from Youngstown State University. She has published several articles on issues related to assessment and evaluation in counselor education with a focus on portfolios. She is currently working on initiatives in the College of Education at Auburn University to promote leadership and advocacy skills among counselors and educators in training involving at-risk schools. She has been a faculty member in counselor education for almost 20 years.

**Montserrat Casado-Kehoe** is an Associate Professor of Counseling Psychology and Internship Coordinator at Palm Beach Atlantic University, in Orlando, Florida. Montse is a Licensed Marriage and Family Therapist and Registered Play Therapist, and currently has a small private practice serving children and families in Clermont, Florida. Her work has focused on marriage and family therapy, play therapy, supervision, and counselor education. She has written or cowritten on topics such as family therapy, couples therapy, clinical cases, multicultural issues related to working with Hispanic families, and use of creative arts in supervision. She received her EdS in School Counseling with an emphasis in marriage and family therapy and her doctorate in Counselor Education from the University of South Carolina.

**Debra C. Cobia** is Professor and Doctoral Program Director, Professional Counseling and Supervision, at the University of West Georgia, in Carrollton. She earned a doctorate in Counselor Education and Supervision at the University of Alabama in 1990 and spent 19 years at Auburn University where she is Professor Emeritus. Dr. Cobia's area of specialization is school counseling, and she has coauthored a textbook for the graduate-level preparation of school counselors. She has authored numerous articles related to supervision, assessment, and evaluation in counselor education and school counseling.

**Kathie Crocket** is Director of Counsellor Education at the University of Waikato, in Hamilton, New Zealand. This program is distinctive in its emphasis on narrative and social constructionist approaches in counseling, family therapy, supervision, and research at the master's and doctoral levels. Kathie's publications focus on narrative approaches in counseling, supervision, teaching, and research. She received her doctorate in Counseling Supervision from the University of Waikato.

**Claire J. Dandeneau** is a Professor and Department Chair in the Department of Counseling at Indiana University of Pennsylvania. She received her doctorate in Counselor Education, her master's in Community Counseling from Purdue University, and her bachelor's degree in Biology and Statistics from Purdue University. Her work interests are quite varied. She has published two school counseling books: one on elementary school counseling and one on working with students with disabilities. Claire is also involved with a federal grant that focuses on correctional education. She has worked collaboratively with Dr. Lorraine Guth to develop a prototype digital counselor training facility. She is a former Therapeutic Wilderness Counselor and Supervisor for the Texas Youth Commission, and she served as Director of Residential Treatment services for the John de la Howe children's home in South Carolina.

**James Devlin** is an Assistant Professor of Counselor Education at Seattle Pacific University. He currently serves on the executive board of the International Association of Marriage and Family Counselors. His research interests include research training environments, best practices in family and couples counseling, supervision model development, and counselor education wellness.

**Cher Edwards** is an Associate Professor of Counselor Education at Seattle Pacific University (SPU), in Seattle, Washington, where she teaches courses on multicultural counseling, counseling theory and practice, and special education. Cher also supervises school counseling interns. She is the founding president of Washington Counselors for Social Justice and is currently the Vice President of Postsecondary Education for the Washington School Counselor Association.

**Judy Emmett** is retired from the Department of Counseling and School Psychology at the University of Wisconsin—River Falls, where she was a Professor from 1991 to 2004. She received her doctorate at Northern Illinois University and focused her graduate teaching and publication in the fields of constructivist career counseling and school counselor preparation.

**Varunee Faii Sangganjanavanich** is an Assistant Professor of Counselor Education in the Department of

Counseling at the University of Akron, in Akron, Ohio. Her work focuses on multicultural competencies in clinical counseling and supervision, career counseling and development, and counselor education. She received her doctorate in Counselor Education and Supervision from the University of Northern Colorado. She has authored and coauthored a number of publications and presentations in the field of counseling and counselor education.

**Tim Grothaus** is an Associate Professor and Coordinator of the school counseling specialty area in the Counseling and Human Services Department at Old Dominion University. He received a doctorate in Counselor Education from the College of William and Mary in 2004, after serving for over 20 years as a school counselor, teacher, therapist, coordinator of a youth leadership development program, and youth minister. He currently serves as the Social Justice/Human Rights Cochair for the Virginia School Counselor Association and is on the American School Counselors Association Positions Statement Committee. His primary research interests include professional development of school counselors, multicultural competence (including advocacy and social justice), and supervision.

**Lorraine J. Guth** is a Professor of Counselor Education at Indiana University of Pennsylvania. Her work focuses on diversity, sexuality, group work, and technology in counselor education. She received her doctorate in Counseling Psychology from Indiana University, her master's degree in Counseling from the University of Memphis, and her bachelor's degree in Marketing and Psychology from Pennsylvania State University. She has written or cowritten numerous articles and book chapters and has presented at international, national, and regional professional conferences. She has also worked in a variety of community counseling settings.

**Angela R. Holman** is an Assistant Professor of Counseling at the University of North Carolina, Pembroke, and maintains a private practice in Laurinburg, North Carolina. Her academic and clinical work focuses on family counseling, relationships, and sexuality. She has presented and published on topics such as families, feminism, culture, and identity. Her master's degree in Community Counseling and bachelor's degree in Human Services are both from Old Dominion

University, in Norfolk, Virginia. She has practiced counseling in a substance abuse–focused community agency, a family counseling clinic, and a college counseling center.

**Michael G. Ignelzi** is Associate Professor of Counseling and Development at Slippery Rock University, in Slippery Rock, Pennsylvania. He serves as Program Coordinator for the Student Affairs in Higher Education master's program. His work focuses on professional development and supervision of student affairs staff; professional ethics; and moral/ethical reasoning, development, and education of college students. He received his doctorate in Human Development and Psychology from Harvard University, his master's degree in College Student Personnel from the Ohio State University, and his bachelor's degree in Psychology from the University of California, Riverside.

**James S. Korcuska** is an Associate Professor of Counseling at the University of South Dakota, in Vermillion. His teaching and research interests are in counseling research methodology, counselor education, men's studies, and ethical/clinical/critical reasoning-to-action phenomenon. He has published 11 articles in peer-reviewed journals. His doctorate is in counselor education from Kent State University, in Kent, Ohio, and his master's degree is in counseling from Walsh University, in Canton, Ohio. A Licensed Professional Counselor, he directed a university counseling center for eight years. Previously, he was a university director of academic advising, developmental counseling, and tutoring.

**Elmarie Kotzé** is Senior Lecturer of Counselor Education at the University of Waikato, in Hamilton, New Zealand. Her publications focus on narrative approaches in counseling, community, teaching, and research. For her doctorate in psychology, Elmarie researched a social constructionist approach to teaching family therapy to educational, counselling, and clinical psychology students in South Africa.

**Victoria E. Kress** is a Professor in the counseling program at Youngstown State University. She also serves as Director of the program's Community Counseling Clinic. She is a Licensed Professional Clinical Counselor and has over 17 years of clinical experience working in various settings, such as community mental health centers, hospitals, residential treatment facilities, private practice, and college counseling centers. She cowrote a book on ethics and diagnosis and over 40 other publications, and has given 80 presentations. Her primary areas of interest with regard to research and clinical work are self-injurious behavior, counselors' use of the DSM, sexual assault and child sexual abuse, developmental trauma, and strength-based and creative counseling approaches.

**Aretha Marbley** is an Associate Professor and Director of Community Counseling in Counselor Education at Texas Tech University. She received her doctorate in Counselor Education and Supervision from the University of Arkansas. She is a critical social justice womanist activist scholar with a research focus on global multicultural-social justice counseling and education; womanist activism; human, social, and cultural rights; and oppressive social institutions. This includes the stories and counternarratives of silenced voices, specifically those of women, people of color, and communities of color in oppressive social structures (philanthropy, business, education, academia, athletics, mental health, health, criminal justices, and faith-based organizations).

**Charles R. McAdams** is a Professor of Counselor Education and Codirector of the New Horizons Family Counseling Center at the College of William and Mary, in Williamsburg, Virginia. For 30 years, his professional service and research have centered on understanding and intervening with aggressive youth and their families. His counseling intervention and counselor training models have been featured in numerous professional journals and book chapters. He received his master's degree and doctorate in Counselor Education from North Carolina State University.

**Brian Mistler** is a psychologist at Hobart and William Smith Colleges, in Geneva, New York. He completed five years of advanced training at the Gestalt Center of Gainesville and is an active member of the Association for the Advancement of Gestalt Therapy. He received his doctorate in Counseling Psychology from the University of Florida, his master's degree in Conflict Resolution from the University of Bradford, in the United Kingdom, and was named an Academic Ambassadorial Scholar in 2001 by Rotary International. In addition to providing

supervision and psychotherapy, Mistler has been recognized for excellence in teaching and has developed and taught a range of courses in areas such as community psychology, practicum supervision, gestalt therapy, humor, minority experiences, and conflict resolution.

**Rick A. Myer** is a Professor in the Department of Counseling, Psychology, and Special Education at Duquesne University, in Pittsburgh, Pennsylvania. He earned his doctorate in Counseling Psychology at Memphis State University in 1987. Rick is a Licensed Psychologist in the state of Illinois and the commonwealth of Pennsylvania. He has been working in crisis intervention and management for over 25 years and is in his 24th year of teaching. His primary area of interest and research is crisis intervention.

**Brigid M. Noonan** is an Associate Professor and Chair of the Department of Counselor Education at Stetson University. She has over 18 years of clinical experience working with individuals, couples, and families while working for employee assistance programs, working in private practice, and consulting for companies. Her areas of clinical interest include addictive disorders; eating disorders; gay, lesbian, bisexual, and transgendered clients; working with women; chronic illness; and disability. She has over 12 years of experience as a counselor educator. Her areas of counselor education interest include curricular development, advocacy within the counselor education field, career development, multicultural development, and mentoring.

**Seth Olson** is an Associate Professor in the Counselor Education Program at the University of South Dakota. His counselor education career has focused on supervision, clinical practice, brief approaches to substance abuse, couples counseling, and counseling theories. He received his doctorate in Counselor Education from Kent State University and his master's degree in Counseling from the University of South Dakota. He has written five articles in the area of counselor education and an article describing how to apply narrative leagues to the school setting. He is currently active in a clinical mental health practice providing primarily Gottman-centered marital and couples counseling.

**Jean Sunde Peterson** is Professor and Director of School Counselor preparation at Purdue University. A former longtime secondary-level teacher and counselor, she is currently a Licensed Mental Health Counselor with a small clinical practice. She has authored more than 80 publications, focused largely on the social and emotional development of high-ability adolescents and on the asset-burden paradox of giftedness, often using longitudinal and qualitative methods to explore the subjective experience of various phenomena. The most recent of her seven books are *Gifted at Risk: Poetic Profiles*; *The Essential Guide to Talking with Teens*; *Models of Counseling Gifted Children, Adolescents, and Young Adults*; and *Portrait and Model of a School Counselor*.

**Sarah E. Peterson** is an Associate Professor of Educational Psychology in the Department of Educational Foundations and Leadership at Duquesne University, in Pittsburgh, Pennsylvania. Previously, she held faculty positions at Northern Illinois University and Indiana-Purdue University at Ft. Wayne. She received her bachelor's degree in Music Education at the University of Iowa, her master's degree in Counselor Education at the University of Wyoming, and her doctorate in Educational Psychology at Arizona State University. Her research interests are centered around motivation and collaborative learning and teachers' beliefs about motivational teaching practices.

**Sheri Pickover** is an Assistant Professor in the Department of Counseling and Addiction Studies at the University of Detroit, Mercy, in Detroit, Michigan. She received her bachelor's degree from the University of Michigan, her master's degree from the University of Pennsylvania, and her doctorate from Oakland University, in Rochester, Michigan. Her research and publications focus on the application of attachment theory to clinical work with children and adults, including the development of a group-based treatment plan to develop empathy skills. Sheri has 18 years of clinical experience working in the child welfare system as a counselor, case manager, clinical supervisor, and trainer.

**Yegan Pillay** is an Assistant Professor in the Department of Counseling and Higher Education at Ohio University. Prior to his faculty appointment, he held positions as the Head of Academic Development in the Department of Military Science at Stellenbosch University in South Africa, Clinical Director at a domestic violence shelter in Ohio, and Director of Disability Services at Ohio University. His research interests include racial and cultural identity, psychological health, clinical assessment, counselor education and supervision, and non-Western approaches to psychotherapy. Yegan is from South Africa, where he completed his formative education, culminating in a doctorate in the United States.

**David M. Shannon** has a doctorate in Research Methodology and Statistics from the University of Virginia and is currently the Humana-Sherman-Germany Distinguished Professor at Auburn University. He teaches classes in research methods and statistics. His research has focused on teaching and student assessment, evaluation, and methodological issues. He has published two books pertaining to assessment and statistical analysis and over 50 articles in refereed journals. He has served as an evaluation coordinator for projects funded for over $125 million, managing evaluation budgets for these projects totaling approximately $5 million, and the principal investigator for projects funded for approximately $1 million. He is Past-President of the Eastern Educational Research Association, serves on the editorial board for three journals, and is coeditor of an international journal.

**Christopher Sink** has been a Professor of Counselor Education at Seattle Pacific University for more than 16 years and has been actively involved with the counseling profession for nearly 30 years. Concurrently, he is a Visiting Professor of Education and Theology at York St. John University, in York, England. Prior to serving as a counselor educator, Chris worked as a secondary and postsecondary counselor. He has published extensively in the areas of school counseling and educational psychology. Chris is an advocate for systemic and strengths-based, school-based counseling. Currently, his research agenda includes the exploration of spirituality as an important feature of adolescent resiliency. He has significant experience as a journal editor.

**Janeé Steele** is a Limited Licensed Professional Counselor and a Licensed School Guidance Counselor in the state of Michigan. She is a doctoral candidate in the Counselor Education and Supervision Program at Western Michigan University, in Kalamazoo. Her research interests include counselor education, multiculturalism, and social justice advocacy. She is the creator of the Liberation Model, a constructivist approach to social justice advocacy training. Janeé received bachelor's degrees in Elementary Education and Psychology and a master's degree in School Counseling from Southern Illinois University, in Carbondale. She currently works as a parent educator and advocate for early childhood education.

**Sue A. Stickel** is a Professor in the Department of Leadership and Counseling at Eastern Michigan University, in Ypsilanti. Her publications have included work in school counseling, positive psychology, leadership, and constructivism in counselor training. She received her doctorate in Counselor Education at the University of Wyoming and her bachelor's and master's degrees at Miami University of Ohio.

**Donald A. Strano** is an Associate Professor in the Department of Counseling and Development at Slippery Rock University, in Slippery Rock, Pennsylvania. He earned his doctorate and master's degree in Counseling and Educational Psychology from Texas Tech University and his bachelor's degree in Individual and Family Studies at the Pennsylvania State University. His work has focused on the Adlerian construct of inferiority feelings, alcohol and other drug prevention in higher education, and narrative and constructivist approaches to counseling. He has numerous works published on these and other related topics. He spent 11 years as a college counselor at Indiana University of Pennsylvania, Washington University in St. Louis, and the University of New Orleans, and four years as the Assistant Dean of Students at Washington University, creating programs for AOD prevention and disability services.

**Toni R. Tollerud** is a Presidential Teaching Professor at Northern Illinois University, in DeKalb. Her areas of research interest and service focus on developmental school counseling; career development; lesbian, gay, bisexual, and transgender issues; social and emotional learning; and supervision. She is a consultant to many school districts on career development and social-emotional learning, sits on several key state boards, and conducts supervision training throughout Illinois. She has spent over 40 years in education, beginning as a public school teacher in grades 6–12. Her teaching spans elementary through doctoral students and includes working as a school counselor and in private practice. She is a graduate of the University of Iowa and loves music, traveling, and Italian food.

**Gail E. Uellendahl** is a Professor and Chair of the Counseling and Guidance Department at California Lutheran University, in Thousand Oaks. She received her doctorate in Counseling Psychology from New York University and is a Licensed Psychologist in New York and California. She also holds the California Pupil Personnel Services Credential in School Counseling. She earned her bachelor's degree in Education from Queens College in New York and her master's degree in Special Education from Hofstra University, and she worked for 17 years directing college counseling services for students with disabilities at Queens College. Her current scholarship focuses on counselor education and counseling practice.

**Ann Vernon** is Professor Emerita at the University of Northern Iowa, where she served as Professor and Coordinator of Counseling for many years. She is recognized as a leading expert on applications of rational emotive behavior therapy with children and adolescents, and several of the 18 books she has published, in addition to chapters and articles, address this topic. Dr. Vernon is the Vice President of the Albert Ellis Board of Trustees and Visiting Professor at the University of Oradea, in Romania. She conducts training programs throughout the world on effective counseling with children and adolescents.

**Scott A. Wykes** is an Assistant Professor for the Counselor Education and Supervision doctoral program at Regent University, in Virginia Beach, Virginia. His work focuses on counselor education and supervision as it relates to individual, group, marriage and family therapy, and substance misuse issues. Teaching in an online doctoral program, he specializes in online and distance teaching formats. He received his doctorate from the University of Northern Colorado and his master's degree from Ashland Theological Seminary.

# SAGE Research Methods Online

## The essential tool for researchers

**Sign up now at www.sagepub.com/srmo for more information.**

### An expert research tool

- An **expertly designed taxonomy** with more than 1,400 unique terms for social and behavioral science research methods
- **Visual and hierarchical search tools** to help you discover material and link to related methods

- Easy-to-use navigation tools
- Content organized by complexity
- Tools for citing, printing, and downloading content with ease
- Regularly updated content and features

### A wealth of essential content

- The most comprehensive picture of quantitative, qualitative, and mixed methods available today
- More than **100,000 pages of SAGE book and reference material** on research methods as well as editorially selected material from SAGE journals
- More than **600 books** available in their entirety online

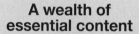

**Launching 2011!**

**$SAGE** research methods online